ETHNIC
POLITICS
IN
EASTERN
EUROPE

EASTERN EUROPE

Key:
STATES
Regions
Ethnic Minorities

0   100   200

MILES

BALTIC SEA

Gdańsk
Kaliningrad
(RUSSIA)

LITHUANIA

Pomerania

Szczecin

Mazuria

Kaszuby

Berlin

Poznań

Warsaw

GERMANY

POLAND

Wrocław

Lublin

Silesia

Sudetenland

Prague

Plzeň

Bohemia

Katowice

Kraków

Kyiv

CZECH REPUBLIC

Moravia

Brno

Galicia

Lviv

UKRAINE

Vienna

SLOVAKIA

Košice

Bratislava

Carpathian
Ruthenia

Komárno

Hungarians

Miskolc

Mukachevo

Chernivtsy

AUSTRIA

Budapest

Bukovina

MOLDOVA

Trans-Dniestra

HUNGARY

Cluj

Hungarians

Bessarabia

Iaşi

Chişinău

SLOVENIA

Ljubljana

Pécs

Tirgu Mureş

Trieste

Zagreb

Hungarians

Transylvania

Trans-Dniestra

Rijeka

Istria

CROATIA

Slavonia

Timişoara

Banat

ROMANIA

Muslims

Banja Luka

Novi Sad

Krajina

Serbs

Vojvodina

BOSNIA
HERCEGOVINA

Muslims

Belgrade

Bucharest

Dalmatia

Split

Croats

Sarajevo

Mostar

SERBIA

Wallachia

Dobrudja

BLACK

Serbs

Novi Pazar

Turks

SEA

ADRIATIC SEA

Sandžak

MONTENEGRO

Podgorica

Kosovo

Prištna

Sofia

Burgas

ITALY

Balkans

Skopje

Blagoevgrad

BULGARIA

Albanians

Tirana

MACEDONIA

Pomaks

Turks

TURKEY

Greeks

Thessaloniki

Thrace

Istanbul

Gjirokastër

GREECE

AEGEAN SEA

TURKEY

ETHNIC POLITICS IN EASTERN EUROPE

A Guide to Nationality Policies, Organizations, and Parties

Janusz Bugajski

The Center for Strategic and International Studies

M. E. Sharpe

Armonk, New York ▪ London, England

947
BUG

Library of Congress Cataloging-in-Publication Data

Bugajski, Janusz, 1954–
Ethnic politics in Eastern Europe:
a guide to nationality policies, organizations, and parties / Janusz Bugajski.
p. cm.
Includes bibliographical references and index.
ISBN 1-56324-282-6
1. Europe, Eastern—Ethnic relations.
2. Nationalism—Europe.
3. Minorities—Europe, Eastern.
4. Europe, Eastern—politics and government—1989-
I. Title.
DJK26.B935   1993
305.8′00947--dc20
93-37732
CIP

Printed in the United States of America

The paper used in this publication meets the minimum requirements of
American National Standard for Information Sciences—
Permanence of Paper for Printed Library Materials,
ANSI Z39.48–1984.

∞

BM   10   9   8   7   6   5   4   3   2   1

CONTENTS

PART II. The Balkans: Nationalism Released

PART III. Central Europe: Ethnicity Reborn

ACKNOWLEDGMENTS

───────────

This book marks the completion of a long and meandering journey that began during the collapse of Communist rule in Eastern Europe. Prior to 1990, my chief focus in the region was on the burgeoning democratic dissident movements that challenged the illegitimate one-party states. The suddenness and peacefulness of the Communist downfall dramatically and surprisingly exposed the fragility of the old system. But it did not usher in the prophesied millennium of pluralism, peace, and prosperity. On the contrary, in many states it exposed much deeper fissures and tensions, often based on ethnic, religious, regional, cultural, and national differences and divisions. To a large extent, the future of Eastern Europe remains dependent on the reduction and defusion of such conflicts, which we first need to define, dissect, and understand. This volume is intended to advance the process of understanding.

My involvement in questions of ethnicity and nationalism during the past few years has been fueled by the richness and diversity of the region's societies and cultures. Such phenomena were invariably stifled by Marxist-Leninist orthodoxy but rapidly released with the new outburst of political and organizational pluralism. Post-revolutionary Eastern Europe has become a new frontier of exploration and adventure; I have spent the last three years traveling to its many corners and flashpoints, gathering material, and talking to hundreds of activists. Some colleagues have remarked that I have probably met every demagogue and loony between the Baltic and the Aegean, as well as countless numbers of rational, intelligent, and courageous personalities. In sum, I have visited Poland (May 1990, April 1991, November 1992), the Czech Republic (January 1990, June 1990, July 1991), Slovakia (June 1990, July 1991), Hungary (June 1990, November 1992), Romania (February 1992, September 1992), Slovenia (May 1992, April 1993), Croatia (August 1991, August 1992, April 1993), Bosnia-Herzegovina (November 1990, August 1992), Serbia (December 1990, May 1992, November 1992, December 1992, February 1993), Montenegro (May 1992, November 1992, February 1993), Macedonia (November 1990, May 1992), Bulgaria (January 1991), and Albania (March 1991, March 1992, July 1992, February 1993).

During these sojourns, in addition to my work for the Center for Strategic and International Studies (CSIS) in Washington, DC, I completed survey missions or political assessments for the U.S. Agency for International Development, the Department of Defense, the International Republican Institute, the Free

Trade Union Institute (AFL-CIO), and the Twenty-First Century Foundation. In particular, I would like to thank my two favorite traveling companions, Mary Catherine Andrews (World Bank) and Stacey Heath (FTUI), for making my adventures even more unforgettable. It would take another chapter to list all my friends and colleagues throughout Eastern Europe, but I simply cannot omit Mjuša Sever and Aimee Breslow, my soul mates and friends. Among the interns at CSIS who were closely involved at various stages of the project, and without whom the book could not have been completed, I have to mention: Anne Horvath, Sarah Despres, Kim Brinck-Johnsen, Anne Nisenson, Marianne Oglo, Nancy Oglo, Dimitri Osipov, Marek Michalewski, John Kenny, Karen Orsic, Viden Nedialkov, Augustine Arthur, Marion LeBlanc, Julie Mazur, Marisa Toso, Stoyan Radov, Sabina Neumann, Ellen Troy, Anna Sheinberg, Sarah Lang, Karl Laskas, Zarmineh Rab, Philip Johnston, Kathleen Avvakumovits, and, of course, Jan Tisnado. In particular, my warmest gratitude must go to Anne Truslow and David Augustyn, my irreplaceable research assistants at CSIS who kept the home fires burning while I wandered along the Eastern Front.

INTRODUCTION

Nationalism and Ethnic Politics

> The strength of a primordial attachment is that emotional cohesion derives not only from some minor "consciousness of kind," but from some external definition of an adversary as well. . . . It was once hoped that the politics of ideology might be replaced by the politics of civility, in which men would learn to live in negotiated peace. To replace the politics of ideology with the politics of ethnicity might only be the continuation of war by other means.
>
> —Daniel Bell[1]

The 1990s will long be remembered as the "springtime of ethnicity" in Eastern Europe. After four decades of Marxist-Leninist uniformity, statist centralism, and enforced "socialist internationalism," a dramatic ethnic, cultural, and political reawakening accompanied the disintegration of Soviet domination and Communist rule at the close of the 1980s. Moreover, a number of new states emerged from the defunct multi-national federations of Yugoslavia and Czechoslovakia, with several confronting further territorial and sub-regional divisions. An upsurge of ethnically based politics has been evident alongside the burgeoning of political pluralism and the erosion of central state controls. After nearly half a century of dormant or disguised nationalism, virtually all the East European states have been profoundly racked by ethnic, regionalist, and autonomist movements demanding some degree of political self-determination, a stake in national decision making, and more equitable economic redistribution. Both majority and minority populations have been affected by this rebirth of ethnicity, and in some cases the programs and goals of different national communities have clashed, resulting in manifestations of conflict that threatened to derail the further progress of democratic reform.

To understand the breadth and scope of ethnic politics in post-Communist Eastern Europe, it is clearly insufficient simply to rummage through history and to apply uncritically the experiences of the nineteenth century or the pre–World War Two period of independence. Communist rule not only froze or disfigured many of the unresolved nationality questions, but it also created additional grievances and new sources of friction in various parts of the region. Any analysis of the post-Communist ethnic reawakening must therefore begin with an over-arching assessment of the renewed significance of ethnicity and nationalism throughout the region. This will provide a useful basis for a country-by-country survey of the numerous ethnically based political organizations that have mush-roomed in Eastern Europe since the disintegration of the monolithic one-party regimes.

Ethnic groups can be beneficially defined as ascriptive collectivities that rec-ognize themselves as being distinct on the basis of a common history, a specific homeland, and shared social and cultural characteristics such as language, relig-ion, customs, residence, and intermarriage.[2] Members of an ethnic group possess some fundamental cultural values and common myths that may be expressed in ideological forms and can become prime foci for mass mobilization. In this context, an ethnic reawakening may be either a positive or a negative phenome-non: it can be aggressive or defensive, future oriented or backward looking; it contains both rational and emotional elements; it may be consistent or unpre-dictable; it has moments of intensity and periods of relative passivity; and it is often contradictory.[3]

On the positive side, ethnically based nationalism, focusing on primary group loyalties, may be a binding, cohesive, and motivating force in asserting a group's cultural identity and regaining autonomy, sovereignty, or statehood during peri-ods of occupation and subordination, while limiting the influence of unwelcome outside powers in domestic affairs.[4] It may instill a sense of patriotism, commu-nity loyalty, pride in one's ethnic history and recorded cultural achievements, and develop a sense of common purpose. Ethnicity is not simply an outmoded traditionalism but an embodiment of a rational calculation of individual and group interests. During particularly traumatic and revolutionary periods, shared ethnicity with all its mythic, ritualistic, symbolic, cultural, and social attributes may provide an important anchor of continuity, predictability, and stability. At such times, a sense of community and mutual identity compensates for profound feelings of uncertainty and confusion in a rapidly changing environment.[5]

In Eastern Europe, several ethnic groups possessed or were dominant in dis-tinct state structures before the advent and expansion of multi-national empires such as the Ottoman, Austrian, Russian, and Prussian. However, some ethnicities were more easily integrated or assimilated in the imperial states because their national identities were embryonic or ill-defined and lacked a sovereign or dura-ble state structure. In several borderline areas, such as the Carpathians and in parts of the Balkans, local populations did not readily identify themselves with a specific nationality or language group, and indeed local dialects and cultures were often mixed, uncodified, and ambiguous. In a number of cases, ethnic distinctiveness and national identity were actually formed or strengthened during the closing stages of the imperial era. Under the leadership of nationalist-minded intellectuals, several ethnic groups gained a more concrete and coherent self-identity under foreign occupation, particularly during and after the revolutionary "age of nationalism" in the mid-nineteenth century.

Although nationhood and statehood remained separated and submerged within Europe's multi-national empires, various forms of group identity were preserved through distinct languages, cultures, and value systems, alternative educational programs, independent religious denominations, separate social organizations, and membership of specific economic strata. East European nationalism grew partly in response to foreign domination and thus became a movement of protest, particularly among ethnic or national groups that had lost their political sovereignty to occupying forces.[6] The nationalist upsurge in the late nineteenth century and after the collapse of the imperial conglomerates in the wake of World War One heralded the re-creation of statehood among several East European nations. In many cases, the pre-imperial past and the struggle for liberation were both mythified and the degree of foreign oppression was purposely exaggerated in order to gain legitimacy for the new independent governments and to solidify sentiments of ethnic cohesiveness.

East European nationalisms have often been closely intertwined with religious faiths and in some instances with religious hierarchies and church leaders.[7] National churches played an important role in transforming ethnic groups into national communities by, for example, codifying language scripts, elaborating ethnic histories, and providing national leadership in the absence of a coherent intelligentsia or a viable political elite. In some areas, the church became a primary source of ethnic identity and cultural preservation, and a virtual surrogate quasi-governmental authority vis-à-vis the occupying powers. Vivid examples included the Orthodox churches in Bulgaria and Serbia under Ottoman domination, the Catholic church in Russian (Orthodox) and Prussian (Protestant) occupied Poland, and the Hussite church in Czech Bohemia during the period of Catholic Habsburg expansionism.

After the separation between the Roman and Byzantine churches in the eleventh century, the East European region was divided between a Catholic north and west and an Orthodox east and south. In addition, sizable Protestant and Islamic communities took shape during the Protestant Reformation and the Ottoman Turkish occupation, respectively. Religious affiliation served as both an integrative and a divisive factor in the region; it buttressed national unity and spurred inter-national conflicts. Religion endowed nationalism and ethnic peculiarity with additional sources of legitimacy, especially where a specific church became associated with a particular nation in contradistinction to various non-confessional neighbors. National churches strengthened the position of national governments, but they also undermined the stability of multi-national empires by supporting the rights of ethnic minorities to political emancipation and self-determination.[8] Churches could also help transcend national peculiarities by emphasizing an international community of co-religionists. While this may have fostered cooperative efforts between some nations, it also contributed to polarizing international alliances and exacerbating inter-alliance rivalries on the basis of religious denomination.

Religious affiliations may significantly aggravate ethnic conflicts where they sanction ethnocentric perceptions and intolerant behavior against other religious communities or against atheists. Such "fundamentalist" impulses have been evident not only among some Muslim societies but also among both Orthodox and Catholic nations in Eastern Europe. Churches may contribute to raising ethnic identity to an exalted and almost divine concept in contrast to other nations and minorities. This may stimulate a puritanical religious messianism, where a particular nation is believed to possess a divinely sanctioned mission to proselytize and expand its influence, sometimes coercively, or to expel heathens and non-religionists. A close identification between church and state may also result in clerical interference in government policy and discrimination against non-believers. Religious beliefs, institutions, and rituals may be consolidating forces in ethnically and religiously homogeneous states, but in multi-ethnic and multi-religious countries the favoring of one denomination over others can seriously aggravate both domestic and inter-state conflicts.

Ethnic nationalism is a collectivist ideology employed in the pursuit of group interests, but it is not necessarily xenophobic or reactionary. Indeed, during the nineteenth century nationalism based on ethnic identity became an international revolutionary creed aimed at destroying the power of ossified autocratic empires and liberating the subject peoples. It was advocated by leading intellectuals in both Western and Eastern Europe and was closely linked with political and economic liberalism. Nationalists from one country sometimes fought for the national independence of other national groups. Nationalism, often defined as "patriotism," was also used to transcend class differences and to act as a collective unifying bond between rulers and ruled and among diverse economic groups. It was based on a loose ideological foundation that could mobilize populations for goals that a foreign government was simply unable to accomplish. It could thereby often ensure prolonged public sacrifices for some common national causes.

Nationalism may become a negative force where, by strictly defining the boundaries of a community, it generates a pronounced anti-liberal and ethnocentric bias, asserting the superiority of one group's culture, language, religion, and folkways, while denigrating outsiders as contemptible, immoral, and inferior.[9] In forging a single political unit, nationalist leaders may deliberately exclude various categories of non-members, defined as alien elements, in order to strengthen the sense of ethnic identity vis-à-vis outsiders. They thereby operate on the axiom that a perceived foreign or domestic threat helps to unite a "people."[10] This can lead to discrimination against other nationalities and minorities and engender hostility toward neighboring states. The persecution of minorities by newly independent nations may be a form of aggressive compensation for their own prior subjugation and oppression, whether at the hands of leaders of current domestic minorities or foreign elites. It can also be an indication of political immaturity and exaggerated defensiveness based on inflated fears of domination, absorption, or extinction.[11]

The growth of national consciousness among one group, particularly where it assumes pronounced ethnocentric proportions, tends to stimulate nationalism and a search for a distinct identity among neighboring groups often for purposes of self-protection. Recently revived nationalism can be vibrant and confident without necessarily being chauvinistic, or it may prove insecure and destabilizing by breeding paranoia and fostering the growth of ethnic or religious differentiation and communal conflicts. Xenophobic nationalism is more likely to be manifested among groups with larger and potentially more threatening minorities, especially where there is competition over scarce resources and where there are deep-rooted historical grievances and seemingly irreconcilable cultural or religious differences. In such circumstances, numerous issues can provoke hostility and confrontation, including questions of land ownership, immigrant versus native status, language policy, religion, the disparate allocation of power and resources, and instigations by local provocateurs or outsiders.[12]

Nationalism can be manipulated by governments and political movements for defensive or offensive purposes, and it can hold up progress toward international integration by fostering isolationism and preventing the surrender of any element of national sovereignty. Moreover, if political life is organized according to strictly ethnic criteria, with distinct and exclusive ethnic parties, then power may become polarized with little opportunity for compromise or the alteration of political elites and with a restricted input of minority parties in decision making. Ideally, ethnically based parties in a well-balanced democracy, depending on their size and the country's electoral laws, may receive sufficient representation in national parliaments and local administrations to influence government decisions and even help to resolve pending nationality conflicts.

In the international arena, exclusivist and short-sighted nationalism may prevent the formation of valuable alliances between neighboring states. This was evident during the inter-war period; when Nazi Germany and Soviet Russia renewed their military strength, Eastern Europe lacked dependable regional alliances and found itself fragmented and vulnerable to outside pressures. The region failed to achieve any degree of solidarity or mutual assistance and was racked by multiple rivalries. For example, the Balkan Entente between Romania, Yugoslavia, Turkey, and Greece, or the Little Entente between Czechoslovakia, Romania, and Yugoslavia did not engender meaningful mutual cooperation or long-term commitments and did little to contribute to East European unity. Each state therefore became susceptible to German economic pressure, political influence, and eventual military domination in the late 1930s and early 1940s.[13]

Some nationalist groups in Eastern Europe have attempted to transcend ethnic, cultural, or linguistic borders and claimed leadership or membership in pan-Slavic international movements, either because they felt too weak to act alone or needed an international justification for their political ambitions.[14] Several nations upheld claims to a "historic mission," whether as bastions of Christianity versus Islam, or Catholicism versus Orthodoxy (or vice versa), or as the ramparts of Western civilization versus "barbarian" domination (Turk, Mongol), or as the "chosen" or "martyred" nation, in order to stir national passions and elicit international sympathy. Nationalism and international pan-movements are also susceptible to manipulation by outside powers seeking to gain influence and advantage over a country or some of its minorities or territories. Indeed, several governments have deliberately fanned ethnic and religious conflicts to gain political or economic benefits and to justify their political or military intervention in a neighboring state.

The defeat of the imperial states at the close of World War One liberated numerous national groups in Eastern Europe and profoundly altered national boundaries and inter-ethnic relations throughout the region. As new states were established, in some instances there were large-scale population transfers and border adjustments; while some countries became largely ethnically homogenous, others remained ethnically extremely mixed, particularly as some nationalities had failed to obtain full political recognition through independent statehood.[15] Many former minority groups in the old empires assumed majority status, while large segments of some groups were separated and transformed into sizable minorities within the new states. In fact, of the approximately 115 million "liberated peoples," about 24 million became national minorities within the newly established countries.

The post-war frontier settlements placed several large minorities, including Hungarians, Albanians, Ukrainians, and Turks, under foreign rule. Even with the most honorable Wilsonian intentions, it was virtually impossible to establish ethnically uniform states that would be simultaneously economically viable and strategically defendable. Some areas were so demographically complex that a policy of massive and costly population rearrangements would have been necessary to unscramble the ethnic mix. However, such measures would have severely disrupted economic ties, territorial attachments, administrative networks, and cultural links and may have provoked new conflicts. These problems were compounded by the fact that in many territories two or more groups possessed equally valid historical claims to indigenous status or residential longevity.

Not surprisingly, Eastern Europe developed a pattern of autonomist, secessionist, and irredentist movements. Such movements could be fomented by rival states to promote instability among neighbors on route to possible annexation. The danger also existed that almost every manifestation of essentially non-separatist ethnic aspiration among minorities, especially when backed by outside powers or through international pressures, could be interpreted by a government and the local majority population as proof of deliberate subversion. If left unchecked, pressures for expanding minority rights could avowedly bring about the curtailment of central controls over a minority region or even the disintegration of the state. Moreover, governments feared that granting autonomy to one minority or to one region could have proved contagious elsewhere in the country.

The existence of ethnic or cultural minorities resisting assimilationist trends can become a serious obstacle to "nation building" or state integration, especially if they persistently claim cultural, political, and territorial autonomy that the government is pressured to permit. This can in turn fuel inter-communal conflicts and raise majority protests against government policies.[16] On the other hand, persistent government opposition may generate increasing repression against the minority population through forced assimilation, subjugation, or even expulsion. This in turn can transform moderate autonomists into radical separatists. Southeastern Europe in particular possesses a poor record in protecting the position of various minorities. These deficiencies have often been exploited by outside powers to press for territorial revisions and annexations based on some historical claims and precedents. This is largely where the term "balkanization" originated, as a negative description of persistent inter-ethnic clashes and territorial competition resulting in a spiral of international instability.[17]

Minorities may also have a positive role to play, as bridges between neighboring states that can help foster cooperation and mutual understanding. Unfortunately, such possibilities have often been negated and submerged in wider domestic and regional disputes. In fact, demands for minority rights can be divided into two kinds, and they may be irreconcilable. First is the right to fully equal opportunities regarding access to education, economic resources, cultural facilities, and political institutions, as well as non-discrimination based on ethnicity, race, culture, or religion. Second is the right to special protection, affirmative action, preferential access to certain resources, and positive discrimination by way of government funding to preserve and promote minority cultures. The application of the latter principle could seriously aggravate resentments among segments of the majority population that are fearful of reverse discrimination, or among other minorities not favored by government policy.

Nationalism manifested within a minority ethnic group may be a valuable lever for community mobilization and for gaining political influence in the state.[18] Conversely, the withholding of political inputs and economic resources from minority leaders by the administration could actually exacerbate anti-centralist feelings, strengthen the cohesion of ethnic minorities against the adversarial state, undermine the legitimacy of the government, and lead to more radical demands for autonomy or even secession.[19] In such instances, pressures for ethnic autonomy may evolve into more than just a means for protecting the cultural identity and territorial integrity of distinct population groups; they may indeed accelerate demands for outright separation. Aggrieved groups may even opt to secede regardless of purely material calculations and the prospect of economic decline in a separated region.

Autonomism itself may be divided into two general types: cultural and political. Cultural autonomy implies control by ethnic leaders and opinion makers over all aspects of their group's education, mass media, and a plethora of social and cultural activities. Political and territorial autonomy is more far-reaching and may cover most aspects of social, economic, and administrative life, short of national defense and foreign affairs.[20] In practice, autonomism covers a spectrum of demands for "self-determination," ranging from modest campaigns for linguistic rights to calls for outright self-rule within a federal or a loose confederal structure, or even as a separate political-territorial entity. Campaigns for secession are more likely to develop when previously acquired privileges are under threat or when underprivileged groups seize an appropriate opportunity to redress their grievances against the center by pushing for separate statehood.[21]

Eastern Europe's post–World War Two Communist regimes operated on the premise that social classes and not nationalities or ethnicities were the principal actors in socioeconomic development and foreign affairs. National borders were redrawn after the war largely to coincide with Soviet and Communist geopolitical interests and to placate some local national yearnings. Once again, some nations lost territories while others gained new regions, but nationality disputes were rarely satisfactorily resolved. Under the Stalinist tyranny and the Brezhnevite *status quo*, national demands were depicted as "bourgeois relics" that would disappear as the proletarianized citizenry gradually merged into a transnational "socialist" culture. Repressive police and bureaucratic measures were used to eliminate political dissent and to stymie calls for ethnic self-determination. Communist idealogues may have genuinely believed that the root causes of national and religious animosity could be extinguished through administrative measures and the formation of "proletarian" national units cutting across ethnic divisions. However, their coercive methods simply stifled nationalist yearnings without forging durable multi-national bonds. In some respects, by repressing competing political ideologies, Communism may have inadvertently encouraged nationalist impulses as people clung to familiar group loyalties as a form of resistance to the ruling system.[22]

Under the post-Stalinist Communist systems, various social and cultural organizations were established for recognized minority nationalities. But their leaders were either co-opted and directly served the interests of the party-state among the minority population, or remained neutral and focused on innocuous cultural, social, educational, and folkloristic activities that were deemed "national in form and socialist in content." Nonetheless, some minority leaders were able to gain a measure of autonomy and successfully pressed for various concessions from the state to help preserve or strengthen ethnic identity within the minority group. In most cases, however, there were clear limits to the development of ethnic rights, while manifestations of national distinctiveness were periodically under direct attack from the party-state apparatus. Severe prohibitions were placed against organizing separate political parties or independent organizations based on ethnic principles. Likewise, restrictions were placed on any campaigns for meaningful territorial autonomy and self-administration in minority areas.

During the forty-five years of Soviet rule in Eastern Europe, outside of Albania and Yugoslavia, Moscow became the final arbiter in any international disputes. The Kremlin sought to prevent any regional conflicts among its satellites from upsetting its hegemonistic "internationalist" goals and unraveling its imperial structures. But although nationalism was relegated by Communist ideology to a secondary phenomenon, it was nevertheless recognized in practice as a powerful mobilizer of public opinion. It was therefore often manipulated by local Communist leaders as a legitimizing device in their post-Stalinist "national roads to socialism" and in order to divert public hostility toward the capitalist Western states. More fervent nationalist positions were adopted by Communist regimes that obtained some degree of political independence from the Soviet Union, particularly in Albania, Yugoslavia, and Romania.

The dissolution of the Soviet bloc and the unraveling of the multi-national Yugoslav and Czechoslovak federations during the last few years released previously submerged national ambitions and stimulated the formulation of new foreign policies among all the East European states. Emerging nationalisms in the post-Communist period are unlikely to repeat all the destructive nineteenth-century and inter-war disputes. Nonetheless, a number of domestic and international enmities may have the potential of escalating into political crises, military threats, and even low-intensity armed conflicts.

Political leaders searching for popular support in the midst of often severe social and economic disruption may seek to capitalize on nationalist feelings and exploit the presence of minority scapegoats. Extremist groups will also attempt to take advantage of widespread public disorientation during the destabilizing reform process to deflect mass antagonism toward vulnerable minorities. If wrenching economic reforms fail to bring visible and rapid benefits to sizable segments of the populace, radical forces may exploit popular frustrations and apply pressure on the fragile government whether through parliamentary or extra-institutional means. In order to gain public influence, assorted populists and militant nationalists, sometimes in league with the remnants of the former Communist apparatus, may thereby launch attacks on various domestic minorities and historical foreign adversaries. Unfortunately, Leninism distorted political intercourse by prescribing simplistic solutions to often complex problems and depicting stark black-and-white contrasts between correct and incorrect policies. This legacy has persisted and impregnated the political debate, in which former class enemies can now be presented as irreconcilable ethnic foes. In such instances, social relationships and political interaction can easily become ethnicized and polarized.

Perceived internal and external threats may in turn act as a catalyst for the emergence of authoritarian regimes and autocratic political forces demanding "national unity" and displaying intolerance toward domestic criticism and political diversity. This could seriously jeopardize progress toward the institutionalization of political democracy and the emergence of thriving market economies. Nationalist-populist parties tend to blur the political spectrum and may veer between left-wing statism and free-market protectionism, while in essence they are intolerant of ethnic diversity, especially where this is manifested in unbridled political pluralism and recurrent demands for minority rights.

A central problem in Eastern Europe has revolved around the distinction between individual civil rights and collective national or group rights within any single state structure. Not all administrations that may guarantee the former will necessarily recognize the latter. Government officials may fear that bestowing special privileges or implementing "affirmative action" programs for national minorities may actually aggravate inter-ethnic relations. Such policies could breed resentment among the majority population, while arousing unacceptable ambitions for territorial autonomy and separatism among the minority group. Ethnic conflicts tend to intensify in states that either fail to ensure the protection of minorities or inhibit the emergence of a common non-ethnic civil society based on transparency, social mobility, occupational opportunity, and non-discrimination. In the latter instance, national identity, constitutional guarantees of sovereignty, and full citizenship rights may become the exclusive province of a single ethnic group, whether this is a majority or a minority population, thus raising the grievances and opposition of excluded communities.[23]

After the popular revolutions of 1989 and the evaporation of the Communist one-party states, the floodgates were opened for the revival of ethnic consciousness and a resurgence of national self-assertion. A plethora of ethnically based organizations quickly sprang to life in each country, representing both the majority and minority populations. While some organizations remained concerned principally with cultural, linguistic, educational, and religious rejuvenation, others pressed for more wide-ranging political and economic concessions. While some groups possessed a moderate political agenda, others adopted more militant or even chauvinistic positions toward autonomy and self-determination. While some minority organizations were more easily accommodated in the emerging system of political pluralism, others were viewed with suspicion and distrust by elements of the majority population and by the incumbent governments.

As Communist rule disintegrated in the multi-national federations of Yugoslavia and Czechoslovakia, cultural, linguistic, religious, and regional differences regenerated ethnic frictions. Political decentralization evidently failed to satisfy the leaders of the constituent republics, while the danger of recentralization also loomed over Yugoslavia. Romania and Bulgaria were defined as uni-national states, even though both contained large and vibrant minorities aspiring toward cultural and political self-determination. Increasing minority demands were also evident in the more ethnically homogeneous states of Albania, Hungary, and Poland. These potential antagonisms, coupled with the possibility of state repression and inter-communal disputes, have sparked controversies and ignited conflicts even as democracy and capitalism began to develop in the region. In the midst of a destabilizing and uncertain period of capitalist restoration and widening pluralism, ethnic politics began to occupy an important role not only for minority groupings seeking greater self-determination but also for some majority

populations fearful of losing influence, power, or their access to important resources.

Nationalist organizations of various hues sprang up among the majority nations. Some were suspected of being front groups or proxy parties for the disem-
powered ex-Communist apparatus, while others were created by former
anti-Communist nationalist dissidents. With the collapse of Communism and
Soviet rule and the renewed focus on "national interests" as opposed to East–
West politics, various competing political formations took aboard nationalist
issues principally to garner popular support. The emergence of a traditional
democratic left-to-right political-ideological spectrum was thereby obstructed or
impregnated by nationalist, ethnic, and regionalist politics. Indeed, a nationalist-
civic spectrum intersected with the traditional left-right continuum, often confusing the ideological identity of specific parties. For instance, both the non-ethnic
civic orientation and the collectivist ethnically based option were adopted by parties
espousing either right-wing, centrist, or left-wing economic programs. Moreover,
the focus on national and ethnic questions often delayed the gestation of clear
socioeconomic programs advanced by easily definable political organizations.

Theoretically, ethnically based parties in a balanced democracy may be able
to represent and defend the interests of distinct minority communities. Invariably, however, when political life is organized exclusively according to the
principle of group membership, permanent majorities and minorities are created.
In such conditions, there may be little opportunity for compromise, for the rotation of political elites, or for any substantive minority influence over policy
decisions. Analysts note that ethnic parties undermine the mediation of group
interests so that a political system built exclusively around ethnic parties is often
conflict prone. Ethnic parties act as special interest groups, focusing on single
issues, with little possibility of party competition across ethnic lines. Furthermore, an ethnic party system is vulnerable to transformation into an ethnically
centered authoritarian regime.[24] Political homogenization under Communist rule
obviously failed to deliver on its promise of a common proletarian culture or a
bonding transnational identity. Conversely, after the collapse of Communism,
slow progress was achieved in parts of the region in civic acculturation within a
democratic polity in which ethnic identity did not fully determine citizenship
rights. In some instances, assimilationist pressures or anti-minority programs
actually increased with the rise to power of authoritarian and nationalist forces.
This has been particularly evident in some of the former Yugoslav republics.

An additional process has also been visible in the post-Communist states:
both the revival of community life among recognized ethnic groups as well as
the reconstruction or "ethnogenesis" of cultural, religious, or regional groupings
whose distinctiveness had not been fully acknowledged by previous governments.[25] Such developments have been discernible among the Silesians, Kaszubians, Moravians, Dalmatians, Istrians, Ruthenians, Vlachs, Macedonians, Slavic
Muslims, Montenegrins, and Roma (Gypsies). In several cases, the latter

process has spurred hostility from the "historic nations" who had long since achieved statehood and whose leaders dismissed such ethnic redefinition as artificial and potentially destructive of the existing state. Nonetheless, new ethnic or regional identities may continue to develop in a liberalized or fractured political climate, especially where they can convey material or political rewards or where they can enhance community self-defense against unwelcome outside interests or foreign threats.

Ethnic politics in post-Communist Eastern Europe has revolved around one of five major variants. The precise form it takes in any state depends partially on historical traditions, on the policies and objectives of ethnic organizations, and on the comparative position of ethnic communities in the existing state structures. It is useful to outline some notable ingredients and distinctions between the five configurations:

- *Cultural Revivalism:* This phenomenon is particularly noticeable among small or dispersed ethnic, religious, or regional minorities with limited experiences of sovereignty or statehood but whose leaders demand the freedom and resources to rebuild their social, cultural, religious, and educational institutions, to redefine their history, to reinforce their identity, and to revive their dialect or language. These objectives may be framed in the context of increasing minority participation in regional and national politics, rather than as a challenge to the territorial integrity of the state. Such goals have been visible, for example, among Germans in Poland and the Czech Republic, Ruthenians in Poland and Slovakia, Slovaks and Romanians in Hungary, Italians and Hungarians in Slovenia, Vlachs (Arumuns) in Albania and Macedonia, Pomaks (Slav Muslims) in Bulgaria, and among Roma (Gypsies) throughout Eastern Europe.

- *Political Autonomism:* This is characterized by a more pronounced form of self-organization among minority populations that have either constituted majorities in previously existing states, that possess a history of organized political involvement in a multi-ethnic state, or whose co-nationals currently constitute a majority in a neighboring country. Examples of such movements are found among Hungarians in Slovakia, Transylvania (Romania), and Vojvodina (Serbia), among Greeks in Albania, and among Turks in Bulgaria. Calls for political autonomy rather than territorial self-government ment are also more likely in ethnically mixed regions in which no single group predominates and where the state system allows for the active participation of minorities in the country's political life.

- *Territorial Self-determinism:* Such goals are visible among reasonably large, well-organized, and territorially compact ethnic groups or sub groups in regions of a state where they form a relative or absolute majority of the population. These include the Moravians in the Czech Republic, the Montenegrins in Yugoslavia (who have a long history of independent statehood), and the Albanians in western Macedonia. Ethnic leaders may seek to reorganize the administration of the state from a unitary to a federal or confederal structure in which specific regions gain some degree of provincial autonomy or full republican status. Territorial self-determination may also be demanded jointly by several ethnic groups in mixed population areas with a distinct regional history and a tradition of autonomy and resistance to a centralizing state, as evident in the province of Vojvodina in Serbia (Yugoslavia).

- *Separatism:* This phenomenon is characteristic among ethnically and territorially compact populations, usually with some history of statehood, who openly oppose continuing inclusion in the existing federal or unitary state, or are fearful of increasing centralization and campaign to create their own independent state structures. In recent years, such movements have included the Slovenes, Croats, Bosnian Muslims, and Macedonians (in the former Yugoslavia), the Slovaks (in the former Czechoslovakia), and the Kosovo Albanians (in Serbia, in the present Yugoslavia).

- *Irredentism:* Separatist movements in one state may seek to join their territories and populations with a nearby state structure, either as an autonomous region or as an integral administrative unit. In some instances, such movements may be directly sponsored and assisted by a neighboring state seeking to expand its own borders. Pertinent current examples of separatist-irredentists include the Serbs in Croatia and Bosnia-Herzegovina and the Croats in Bosnia-Herzegovina.

These five variants of ethnic politics may not be mutually exclusive or permanent even among a single nationality that is represented by several competing political formations. They can be envisaged as potential stages of development, particularly in instances where an ethnically based organization, due to internal or external pressures, escalates its demands from cultural revivalism to full-scale territorial self-determination or even toward secession. Of course, the programs and achievements of distinct ethnic communities depend on several inter-related factors, including the response of the government and other in-state communities to minority and majority demands and the policies of foreign governments in sponsoring or discouraging various autonomist movements.

In exploring the significance of ethnic politics in the early post-Communist period, this guidebook seeks to identify and assesses the most significant, recently formed, nationalist and ethnically based, politically oriented organizations in all thirteen East European states. Each country study discusses official government policies toward different ethnic groups, outlines the origins, leadership, composition, program, and impact of nationalist and ethnically based organizations on domestic politics and foreign relations, and provides a condensed chronology of key developments in inter-ethnic relations since the fall of Communist rule. Associations and parties have been selected for inclusion according to two major criteria. First are the majority nationalists with explicit and often militant positions on ethnic questions or with a prime focus on "national interests" rather than on economic and social programs. While most of these organizations supported parliamentary democracy, several veered toward revolutionary, vanguardist-type parties often based on the leadership principle. In some cases, it was sectors of larger parties that propounded such an agenda. Second are the minority ethnic organizations that either possessed an overt political focus or that concentrated their efforts on community mobilization, development, and representation: in some cases, these could also be defined as nationalist or ultra-nationalist groupings.

Most of the sources used to compile this directory are studiously listed in the references, other than newspaper and news-agency coverage of major events. However, in many cases information or confirmation was obtained during one of the author's visits to the region: rather than footnoting each instance, the absence of a specific reference simply signals that the data were obtained personally and verbally by the author. Although the guidebook is intended to be as complete as possible, due to practical considerations it simply cannot be fully exhaustive. Undoubtedly, a number of nationalist and ethnic organizations have not been included or have been only briefly mentioned, because the sources either remained sketchy, incomplete, contradictory, questionable, or were not readily available. Moreover, in a highly fluid political climate, new associations and parties continue to be formed, while existing organizations often fracture, merge, or even disappear altogether. I apologize in advance to any significant groupings that may have been inadvertently overlooked in this survey. Despite such shortcomings, this volume aims to provide the most comprehensive, representative, and documented assessment to date of ethnic politics in post-Communist Eastern Europe. It is designed to serve as a source of reference in the years ahead to the emergence of multi-party and poly-ethnic systems in a volatile and rapidly changing region.

Notes

1. Daniel Bell, "Ethnicity and Social Change," in Nathan Glazer and Daniel P. Moynihan, eds., *Ethnicity: Theory and Experience* (Cambridge: Harvard University Press, 1975), p. 174.

2. For an insightful anthropological discussion of ethnicity, see the "Introduction" by Frederik Barth in Frederik Barth, ed., *Ethnic Groups and Boundaries: The Social Organization of Culture Difference* (Boston: Little, Brown & Co., 1969), pp. 9–38. Enlightening comments can also be found in Talcott Parsons, "Some Theoretical Considerations on the Nature and Trends of Change of Ethnicity," in *Ethnicity: Theory and Experience*, pp. 53–83.

3. See Woodrow J. Kuhns, "Political Nationalism in Contemporary Eastern Europe," in Jeffrey Simon and Trond Gilberg, eds., *Security Implications of Nationalism in Eastern Europe* (Boulder: Westview Press, 1986), pp. 81–107. Useful critiques of ethnic nationalism and the principles of the nation-state can be found in Orlando Patterson, *Ethnic Chauvinism: The Reactionary Impulse* (New York: Stein and Day, 1977); and Sanjay Seth, "Political Theory in the Age of Nationalism," *Ethics and International Affairs*, vol. 7, 1993, pp. 75–96.

4. For an analysis of nation formation see Anthony D. Smith, "The Origin of Nations," *Ethnic and Racial Studies*, vol. 12, no. 3, July 1989, pp. 340–67.

5. For an evaluation of the significance of ethnicity in the modern world, see Cynthia H. Enloe, *Ethnic Conflict and Political Development* (Lanham, NY: University Press of America, 1986).

6. See Peter F. Sugar, "External and Domestic Roots of Eastern European Nationalism," in Peter F. Sugar and Ivo J. Lederer, eds., *Nationalism in Eastern Europe* (Seattle: University of Washington Press, 1969), pp. 3–54.

7. Consult Michael B. Petrovich, "Religion and Ethnicity in Eastern Europe," in Peter F. Sugar, ed., *Ethnic Diversity and Conflict in Eastern Europe* (Santa Barbara, CA: ABC-CLIO, 1980), pp. 373–417.

8. Pedro Ramet, "The Interplay of Religious Policy and Nationalities Policy in the Soviet Union and Eastern Europe," in Pedro Ramet, ed., *Religion and Nationalism in Soviet and East European Politics* (Durham: Duke University Press, 1989), p. 6.

9. A pertinent analysis of nationalism can be found in Robert A. LeVine and Donald T. Campbell, eds., *Ethnocentrism: Theories of Conflict, Ethnic Attitudes, and Group Behavior* (New York: John Wiley and Sons, 1972).

10. Gregory Gleason, "Nationalism in Our Time," *Current World Leaders*, International Academy at Santa Barbara, California, vol. 34, no. 2, April 1991.

11. Some psychological explanations for ethnic conflict are contained in Vamik D. Volkan, *The Need to Have Enemies and Allies: From Clinical Practice to International Relationships* (Northvale, NJ: Jason Aronson Inc., 1988).

12. For a review of these issues, see Dan Landis and Jerry Boucher, "Themes and Models of Conflict," in Jerry Boucher, Dan Landis, and Karen Arnold Clark, eds., *Ethnic Conflict: International Perspectives* (Newbury Park, CA: Sage Publications, 1987), pp. 18–31.

13. For an analysis of inter-war Eastern Europe, consult Hugh Seton-Watson, *Eastern Europe Between the Wars*, 1918–1941 (New York: Harper Torchbooks, 1967), and Joseph Rothschild, *East Central Europe Between the Two World Wars* (Seattle: University of Washington Press, 1974).

14. A classic analysis of European pan-movements can be found in Hannah Arendt, *The Origins of Totalitarianism* (New York: Harcourt Brace Jovanovich, 1973), pp. 222–66.

15. For an assessment of minority and nationality problems, check Trond Gilberg, "State Policy, Ethnic Persistence and Nationality Formation in Eastern Europe," in *Ethnic Diversity and Conflict in Eastern Europe*, pp. 185–235.

16. Consult Anthony M. Birch, *Nationalism and National Integration* (London: Unwin Hyman, 1989).

17. See Paul R. Brass, "Ethnic Groups and Nationalities," in *Ethnic Diversity and Conflict in Eastern Europe*, p. 61.

18. See John Breuilly, *Nationalism and the State* (New York: St. Martin's Press, 1982).

19. For an analysis of autonomist and separatist movements, see Colin H. Williams, ed., *National Separatism* (Vancouver: University of British Columbia Press, 1982).

20. See Anthony D. Smith, *The Ethnic Revival* (Cambridge: Cambridge University Press, 1981), pp. 8–25.

21. A comprehensive assessment of separatism can be found in Alexis Heraclides, *The Self Determination of Minorities in International Politics* (London: Frank Cass and Co., 1991).

22. George Schöpflin, "National Identity in the Soviet Union and East-Central Europe," in *Ethnic and Racial Studies*, vol. 14, no. 1, January 1991, p. 11.

23. A valuable analysis of constitutional issues can be found in Robert M. Hayden, "Constitutional Nationalism in the Former Yugoslav Republics," in *Slavic Review*, vol. 51, no. 4, Winter 1992, pp. 654–73.

24. Consult Donald L. Horowitz, *Ethnic Groups in Conflict* (Berkeley: University of California Press, 1985), pp. 298, 363.

25. An incisive analysis of this phenomenon in the modern world can be found in Eugeen E. Roosens, *Creating Ethnicity: The Process of Ethnogenesis*, Frontiers of Anthropology, vol. 5 (London: Sage, 1989). See also Hugh Seton-Watson, "Unsatisfied Nationalisms," *Journal of Contemporary History*, vol. 6, no. 1, 1971, pp. 3–14.

PART I

Post-Yugoslavia

Ethnicity Multiplied

1

Bosnia-Herzegovina

POPULATION

Bosnia-Herzegovina was in a unique position among the former Yugoslav republics, in that no single nation or nationality formed an absolute majority of the population.[1] According to the 1991 Yugoslav census, the Muslims, defined as a nation in post-war Yugoslavia, had a relative majority of 43.6 percent with 1,902,954 inhabitants; the Serbs formed 31.4 percent with 1,370,476 people; and the Croats 17.3 percent with 755,071 people. The category of "Yugoslav" had declined over the years, particularly after each republic held its first multi-party elections during 1990; in Bosnia-Herzegovina it stood at 5.5 percent or 240,052 people in 1991. The remainder, 2.2 percent of the population, included Czechs, Slovaks, Ruthenians, Hungarians, and Albanians. The Muslim figure had grown in the previous decade, partly as a result of Serbian emigration, the decline of Yugoslav consciousness, the immigration of Muslims from Serbia, and the rise of Muslim identity. In 1981, out of a population of 4,125,000, 39.5 percent declared themselves as Muslim, 32 percent as Serbs, 18.4 percent as Croats, 7.9 percent as Yugoslavs, and 2.2 percent included several smaller nationalities.

Bosnia-Herzegovina's ethnic balance was compounded by a complex territorial mix among the three major communities. In the 99 municipalities outside the capital Sarajevo, Muslims formed absolute majorities in only 32, and few of these were territorially contiguous: the biggest concentrations were in northwestern, eastern, and central Bosnia. Serbs constituted absolute majorities in 30 municipalities, most of these in western, northeastern, and southeastern Bosnia. Croats formed absolute majorities in only 14 municipalities, the majority in the western Herzegovina region. In 23 municipalities, no ethnic group possessed a clear majority, and even in districts where one ethnic group predominated there were large minorities of one of the other two nationalities. Sarajevo, with a population of 525,980, included 49.3 percent Muslims, 29.9 percent Serbs, 6.6 percent Croats, 10.7 percent Yugoslavs, and 3.5 percent other groups.

Bosnia-Herzegovina: Population (1991)

Ethnic Groups	Number	Percent of Population
Muslims	1,902,954	43.60
Serbs	1,370,476	31.40
Croats	755,071	17.30
Yugoslavs	240,052	5.50
Others	96,021	2.20
Total Minorities	4,364,574	100.00
Total Population	4,364,574	100.00

To add to the complexity, the larger towns of Bosnia-Herzegovina were extremely diversified, although in general Muslims tended to be city dwellers and Serbs were concentrated in the countryside. As a result, even in many municipalities where Muslims formed an absolute majority, Serbs tended to predominate outside the district capitals. Serbs and Muslims shared the largest number of municipalities: in 37 Croats were barely visible, and in 27 more they formed less than 20 percent of the population. Muslims and Croats predominantly shared 6 municipalities: in 14 Serbs were barely visible, and in 29 more they totaled under 20 percent of the population. Muslims were only absent in 7 municipalities, and in a further 19 they formed less than 20 percent of the population. Serbs and Croats jointly predominated in only 6 municipalities.

Following the outbreak of armed hostilities in April 1992, there were massive movements of population within and out of the country. Indeed, one of the purposes of a war launched by Serb guerrillas with the assistance of Yugoslav army forces was to unscramble the ethnic mix and to create large contiguous tracts of "ethnically pure" territory. As a result, Muslim and to a lesser extent Croat populations were killed, imprisoned, brutalized, or expelled from areas Serb gunmen intended to dominate. By the spring of 1993, as Serbian successes became evident and the likelihood of U.N. military intervention to stop the aggression receded, both Croats and Muslims also proceeded to carve out ethnically pure areas, slaughtering or expelling rival ethnic groups. Although precise figures have proved extremely difficult to obtain, as the war continued to rage into the summer of 1993, over two million people were reportedly displaced within the country, more than 150,000 had either been killed or were simply unaccounted for, and over 500,000 sought refuge in neighboring states. The overwhelming majority in each category were Muslims.

Homogenous Serbian areas were established on nearly 70 percent of Bosnian territory, linking up western, northern, and eastern Bosnia. Croats sought to expand their "ethnically pure" areas in western Herzegovina northward and claimed to control nearly 20 percent of Bosnian territory. Muslims were left with two major zones, in central and northwestern Bosnia, in addition to a handful of enclaves surrounded by Serb forces in eastern Bosnia. Some Muslim forces also engaged in "ethnic cleansing" campaigns during the course of the war. The capital Sarajevo remained an ethnically mixed city under Bosnian government control, although the number of residents had declined by the summer of 1993 to some 350,000 people. Bosnia-Herzegovina was approaching partition; the only question remaining was whether any viable Bosnian or Muslim state would be preserved once the hostilities subsided. Serb- and Croat-controlled areas seemed slated for eventual incorporation into Serbia and Croatia, respectively, while the outgunned Muslims would be left with small pockets of territory to which the majority of Muslim refugees had already fled.

HISTORICAL OVERVIEW

Since the early Middle Ages, the territory of Bosnia-Herzegovina occupied the dividing line between Byzantine Orthodoxy and Roman Catholicism.[2] The majority of Bosnian Slavs, who were not affiliated to either major denomination, upheld their own cohesive regional identity and a separate Bogomil Christian Church as a means of preserving their independence and guarding their distinctiveness. During the fourteenth century, Bosnia emerged as an independent medieval principality. However, from the end of the fifteenth century until the close of the nineteenth century, the fledgling state was occupied by the Ottoman Turks. The majority of Bosnians, particularly the Bogomils, as well as large numbers of Catholics (Croats) and Orthodox (Serbs), converted *en masse* to the Sunni Islamic faith, often without coercion. By converting to Islam, local nobles were able to retain their feudal privileges, while peasants received land and were freed from feudal obligations. However, Bosnians were not generally turkified and maintained their own language, culture, and customs. As a result, a Bosnian Muslim ethnos was consolidated, built around religious, regional, and cultural foundations, although sharing the same language with neighboring Croats and Serbs who did not convert to Islam.

During the nineteenth century, Christian peasants, mostly Serbs, staged a series of revolts against Turkish overlordship and the local Islamic nobility. The Turks tried to establish a more centralized administration but their control over the western Balkans was increasingly weakened by domestic unrest, administrative decay, and conflicts with the European imperial powers. In the latter part of the nineteenth century, the revived Serbian Kingdom and the Austrian Habsburg Empire stepped up their rivalries over the region. Orthodox Serbian groups sought autonomy for Bosnia and eventual incorporation into an enlarged Serbia. The Catholic Croats wanted to reorganize Austria-Hungary on a tripartite basis as a prelude to the absorption of Bosnia-Herzegovina by an autonomous Croatian state.

In 1876, Serbia and Montenegro declared war on Turkey in support of a Bosnian insurrection against Ottoman rule, primarily involving Christian peasants and intellectuals. As Turkish rule receded, Muslim Slavs were exposed to repression, forcible conversions, and even extermination primarily perpetrated by radical Orthodox Serbs. Following the defeat of Turkish armies, the Treaty of

San Stefano in 1878 provided for the recognition of an autonomous Bosnian government. However, Vienna refused to recognize the legitimacy of the treaty, demonstrating concern about growing Russian influence in the region and the spread of Slavic nationalism within the empire. As a result, in 1878 the Congress of Berlin placed Bosnia under a provisional Austro-Hungarian administration despite substantial local resistance. In 1908, Austria formally annexed Bosnia-Herzegovina and eliminated all remaining vestiges of self-government. International tensions were thereby heightened, and, following the assassination of Austrian Crown Prince Archduke Franz Ferdinand by a Serbian terrorist in June 1914 in the Bosnian capital of Sarajevo, World War One broke out. During the conflict, Muslim Slavs continued to suffer from persecution as they were perceived to have benefited from centuries of Turkish occupation. Thousands of Muslims were also forced to depopulate several regions of Serbia and Montenegro that they had inhabited for centuries.

With the creation of the Kingdom of Serbs, Croats, and Slovenes in 1918, later renamed Yugoslavia, Bosnia-Herzegovina initially obtained a degree of provincial autonomy. But after the royalist Serbian coup in 1929, Yugoslavia was reorganized into new administrative regions. Bosnia-Herzegovina was partitioned among four such regions, and the Muslim population was slated to become a minority in each region. Serbs were given the dominant position in the central Bosnian areas, while Croats predominated in the southern Herzegovina region. Despite these measures, Muslim leaders tended to support the unified Yugoslav state as it offered some degree of protection from Serb and Croat pressures for outright partition.

During World War Two, the Nazi protectorate of Croatia was given possession of virtually the whole of Bosnia-Herzegovina. Some Muslim radicals collaborated with Croatia's *Ustaša* fascist regime, although the bulk of the population remained passive while refusing to surrender their distinct identity or convert to Catholicism. The *Ustaša* murdered hundreds of thousands of Serbs in Croatia and Bosnia and attempted forcibly to convert or expel the rest. Meanwhile, Serbian nationalist *Četnik* forces launched a guerrilla war against the Germans and the *Ustaša* and massacred tens of thousands of Muslims in eastern Bosnia during their campaigns. About 100,000 Muslims were believed to have perished during the course of World War Two—the highest percentage of deaths in relation to total population among all the Yugoslav nations. Thousands of Muslims fled their homes and sought shelter in the larger cities or emigrated altogether from the country. Meanwhile, the *Partizan* Communist forces under the leadership of Marshal Josef Broz Tito based their anti-Nazi guerrilla resistance movement in the mountains of Bosnia. The *partizani* managed to attract members of all three major ethnoreligious communities into their ranks, particularly people who were fleeing repression at the hands of rival extremist forces. German troops proved unable to subdue the guerrilla movement, although thousands of suspected resistance fighters were exterminated. Tito's forces were increasingly successful against the Nazis, particularly as the Germans began to retreat from the Balkans and the *Partizans* obtained weapons and supplies from the Allied powers.

Following the Communist takeover at the close of World War Two, Tito's security forces massacred thousands of nationalist, fascist, monarchist, and democratic activists from all three ethnic groups in order to ensure a Communist monopoly of power. The 1946 Yugoslav constitution established six constituent republics within a federal state, including that of Bosnia-Herzegovina, which was formed as an ethnically mixed unit. One of Tito's objectives was to prevent either Serbia or Croatia from dominating the federation and reviving claims to Bosnian territory; hence the political and economic infrastructure of the republic was substantially expanded. Tito sought to balance Yugoslavia's various national units and promote the growth of an overarching "Yugoslav" identity as well as a multi-ethnic "Bosnian" consciousness within Bosnia-Herzegovina. He also endeavored to strengthen Muslim identity to counteract Serb and Croat ambitions and helped to forge a distinct Muslim power base in the republic. In the 1961 census, the Communist authorities allowed citizens to register for the first time as "Muslims in the ethnic sense" rather than "Muslims ethnically undeclared." In the 1971 census, Slavic Muslims were finally elevated to the status of a distinct nation (and not only in Bosnia), equal to that of Serbs, Croats, Slovenes, Montenegrins, and Macedonians. Further constitutional reforms strengthened the *de facto* autonomy of each republic. During the 1970s, the government adopted a more tolerant approach toward organized religion, including Islam, and Bosnia's Muslims experienced a cultural, educational, and religious revival.

Under the 1974 Yugoslav constitution, Communist controls were further decentralized to the republics, and various economic reforms were instituted without eliminating one-party rule. In the late 1970s, Belgrade expressed fears about a potential Islamic resurgence in Bosnia, and periodic crackdowns were undertaken against political dissenters professing some form of either Islamic or democratic rule. Muslim leaders dismissed charges of a fundamentalist resurgence and calculated that Belgrade was concerned over closer Muslim-Croatian cooperation following the rise of Croatian nationalism earlier in the decade. Tito's death in 1980 removed the key bonding agent in the Yugoslav federation. The complex system of presidential and governmental succession did not allow for effective central rule while the republican administrations sought an accelerating devolution of powers. During the 1980s, the disintegration of the ruling League of Communists of Yugoslavia and growing national and ethnic polarization aggravated the position of Bosnia-Herzegovina as a key contested region between Yugoslavia's two largest nations—Serbs and Croats. Serious economic problems also fueled inter-republican competition for scarce funds and resources and increased social and ethnic tensions throughout the federation.

Political and economic liberalization was evident in the late 1980s under the government of federal prime minister Ante Marković. But the unraveling of

Communist rule also sparked demands for republican autonomy among all recognized nations and for ethnic self-determination among the smaller nationalities. The situation in Bosnia-Herzegovina remained especially complicated as no national group (Muslim, Serb, Croat) had an absolute demographic majority in the republic. In February 1990, the Bosnian Assembly passed an important law allowing for political parties to be freely formed and eliminating the monopolistic position of the Communist Party. In August 1990, the assembly declared the republic's sovereignty and drew up constitutional amendments legalizing the first post-war multi-party elections.

The republican elections in November 1990 were deliberately designed to balance the representation of the three constituent nations in the Bosnian presidency, in the government, and in parliament. Each ethnic group formed its own party to stand in the ballot: the Muslim-based Party of Democratic Action, the Serbian Democratic Party, and the Croatian Democratic Union. The pro-Yugoslav and reformist groupings performed poorly in the elections, and the three major parties formed a coalition government under the presidency of Alija Izetbegović, a long-time anti-Communist Muslim activist. As Slovenia and Croatia pressed for full independence from Yugoslavia, after the collapse of talks on a looser confederation, Bosnia-Herzegovina found itself caught in the middle of a tightening vise. Leaders of the republic's chief ethnic groups were increasingly pressured to side with either Serbia or Croatia. Serb leaders voiced concern about an emerging Muslim-Croat alliance that would exclude Serbs from key posts in the government. Serb activists also calculated that Croats and Muslims would seek closer political and military ties with Croatia if Slovenia and Croatia seceded from Yugoslavia. Meanwhile, Bosnian Muslim and Croat leaders grew anxious that local Serbian activists in league with the Socialist regime in Belgrade were planning to engineer a crisis in the republic in order to detach large areas of Bosnia and attach them to a "Greater Serbia."

Hostilities among leaders of the three national communities escalated throughout 1991, following the outbreak of armed warfare in neighboring Croatia and the seizure of large stretches of Croat territory by the Yugoslav People's Army and Serbian guerrillas. Muslim and Croat Bosnians feared that with the separation of Slovenia and Croatia, the republic would be prone to Serbian domination. The administration in Sarajevo, together with the newly elected Macedonian government, proposed a new confederal arrangement within Yugoslavia, a position that was opposed by Serbia, Montenegro, and the Bosnian Serb leadership, who were preparing for a more centralized system, and by Slovenia and Croatia, which sought full independence. Throughout late 1991 and early 1992, Serb leaders carved out their own jurisdictions in Bosnian municipalities where Serbs formed absolute or relative majorities and threatened civil war if Sarajevo moved toward independent statehood. Croat leaders in Herzegovina also began to make preparations for territorial autonomy in the event that Bosnia were to remain in a truncated Yugoslavia. Meanwhile, the Belgrade government accused the Bosnian Muslim leadership of planning to transform the republic into a separate Islamic state, with pretensions to other Muslim-inhabited areas of Serbia and Montenegro. The charge was vehemently denied by President Izetbegović, who considered it a propaganda ploy designed to mobilize both Serbs and Croats against Bosnian independence.

As tensions mounted, Muslim and Croat deputies in Bosnia's National Assembly declared the republic's full sovereignty and neutrality. Serb leaders boycotted the session, declared the vote illegal and unconstitutional, and announced that they would not recognize Bosnian laws. Fearing an assault by the Yugoslav army similar to the one in neighboring Croatia, Muslim and Croat leaders decided to hold a referendum on independence. The ballot in February 1992 was boycotted by the majority of Serbian residents, but over 64 percent of the electorate turned out and voted overwhelmingly for Bosnian independence and secession. Sarajevo promptly declared an independent state and gained comprehensive international recognition. The move proved unacceptable to local Serb leaders, who promptly launched an armed offensive within the republic with the active support of the Yugoslav army, charging that Sarajevo's policies threatened their national rights and even their physical existence.

With overwhelming firepower and material support from Belgrade, Serbian forces overran nearly two-thirds of Bosnian territory by the close of 1992, including municipalities where Serbs constituted a relative minority of the population. Bosnia's Muslim forces were caught unprepared and defenseless and suffered severe casualties across the republic. Serbian "ethnic cleansing" operations were comprehensively applied to terrorize and push out Muslim communities and create pure contiguous Serbian territories across western, northern, and eastern Bosnia. By the close of 1992, well over a million people were displaced from their homes or sought refuge in neighboring republics. As the conflict escalated, Croatian leaders in western Herzegovina formed their own army and government structures even while nominally pledging allegiance to the government in Sarajevo. Suspicions persisted that if Bosnia-Herzegovina were allowed to fracture, then Croatia would claim its share of about one-fifth of the republic, particularly those municipalities in Herzegovina where Croats formed absolute majorities. As Serb forces consolidated their hold over captured territories, a separate Serbian Republic was declared with the avowed aim of linking up with Serb-captured territories in Croatia and eventually joining the rump Yugoslavia. But although Serb forces controlled the major towns in about 70 percent of Bosnia's territory, Sarajevo remained under siege and the countryside became a battleground between competing guerrilla forces often outside of any central control. Muslim units attempted to regroup and rearm, with a clear danger that relatively moderate Muslim leaders would be superseded by radicals intent on retribution while determined to regain their lost territories.

Given the chaos and destruction, with over 150,000 presumed dead or missing by the spring of 1993 and nearly two million refugees, it was difficult to foresee any workable political solution to the conflict. What began as a rebellion against Bosnian statehood by radical elements of one of the major nationalities had turned into an ethnic war among the three communities seeking outright territorial control. Bosnia's Muslim and Serb leaders continued to uphold diametrically opposed positions on the republic's future. While Serb spokesmen sought a far-ranging "cantonization" tantamount to partition, the Muslim leadership endeavored to maintain a unitary state with extensive territorial and political decentralization but not based on ethnic criteria. The Croats occupied a mid-way position but increasingly veered toward a partition as the Bosnian government proved unable to control the republic or to regain territories from the well-armed Serbs. With the collapse of UN-sponsored peace plans and the receding probability of Western military intervention, by the summer of 1993 Bosnia-Herzegovina stood on the verge of partition. Fighting continued to rage in various parts of the republic, as the refusal of the Bosnian government to accept the *fait accompli* simply encouraged Serb and Croat forces to carve out more extensive territories and to push the outgunned Muslims into shrinking territorial pockets.

OFFICIAL POLICIES

The Yugoslav federal arrangement thwarted the potential chauvinism of the two largest nations, the Serbs and Croats, and provided a modicum of protection and recognition for the smaller nations: Muslims, Macedonians, Montenegrins, and Slovenes. While it did not offer them statehood or internal democracy, the system guaranteed their territorial integrity, defense against Serbian centralism and Croatian annexation, and a sustained period of economic development through industrialization, urbanization, and the provision of a large slice of the state budget. In this federal arrangement, Bosnia-Herzegovina became the only republic without a predominant nation; indeed, all three groups (Muslims, Serbs, Croats) were considered equal political and constitutional entities, even though both Croats and Serbs had their own "home" republics. The 1974 constitution underscored the equality of Bosnia's "constituent nations," an arrangement designed not only to prevent the dominance of one ethnic group but to avoid any compacts between two nations that would "minoritize" the third. The Muslims were formally defined as a nation, and thousands who had previously declared themselves as Serbs, Croats, or Yugoslavs assumed this definition in the new censuses.

Under the 1974 federal constitution, and particularly following Tito's death in 1980, political power continued to devolve to the six republics in a manner, at least in theory, that ensured that none of the federal units would be in a position to dominate the others. Nonetheless, widespread mistrust and frustration, accompanied by a parallel resurgence of nationalism, ethnic strife, and separatist sentiments, crept to the political foreground. This trend was further heightened by

Yugoslavia's poor economic performance during the 1980s and what was increasingly perceived as the unequal distribution of economic resources among the republics. Indeed, Croatian and Slovenian authorities loudly complained that their republics were subsidizing the poorer southern regions without any commensurate material benefits. Pressures mounted for the further decentralization of federal powers as republican leaders sought to benefit from a new mandate based on ethnic identity rather than ideological loyalty. Slovenia and Croatia held their first multi-party elections in April 1990, followed by Macedonia and Bosnia-Herzegovina in November 1990 and Serbia and Montenegro in December 1990. The ruling League of Communists of Yugoslavia was by now in an advanced state of decay, while the reformist federalists who emerged from the party proved unable to garner any significant public support.

As political liberalization gathered pace in all six republics, in February 1990 the Bosnian Assembly passed a law allowing for political parties to be formed freely in preparation for the first post-war multi-party elections.[3] In July 1990, the assembly declared the republic a "democratic and sovereign state with full and equal rights for all its citizens," signaling the first step toward a looser federal arrangement but avoiding any explicit moves toward separation from Yugoslavia. Constitutional amendments were simultaneously passed to legalize the holding of multi-party elections. Beginning in early 1989, Bosnian politics were driven by the same nationalist fervor that dismembered Yugoslavia. Thus, the result of the November 1990 elections read like a census of the republic's population, with nationalist parties of the three major groups taking 80 percent of the vote in proportions accurately reflecting their percentages of the population. Residents elected deputies to the 240-seat bicameral legislature, divided between a Chamber of Citizens (130 seats) and a Chamber of Municipalities (110 seats) as well as members of the collective presidency. Ethnic parity was to be maintained in all three institutions.

Concern over balancing the republic's three major nationalities complicated the election process. The election law itself reflected this fact, by apportioning seats according to national identification in the collective presidency to include two Muslims, two Serbs, two Croats, and one from the remaining ethnic groups. A total of 1,551 candidates representing 18 political parties ran for the National Assembly. Although 41 parties and associations were registered for the ballot, only a handful expected to win seats. Aside from the three largest ethnically based parties, the Party of Democratic Action (PDA), the Serbian Democratic Party (SDP), and the Croatian Democratic Union (CDU), the most credible contenders included the Socialist Democratic Party (SDP), formerly the League of Communists, and the Alliance of Reform Forces (ARF), led by Yugoslav prime minister Ante Marković. A Party of Yugoslavs also contested for seats, as well as several smaller ethnically based organizations including the Muslim Bosnian Organization (MBO), the Serbian Renewal Movement (SRM), and the Herzegovinian Democratic Community (HDC). The Serbian and Croatian nationalist parties were reportedly sponsored and financed by their sister parties in Belgrade and Zagreb, respectively.

The election law stipulated that in order to maintain an ethnic balance in the Assembly, each ethnic group had to receive a proportion of seats that matched, within 15 percent, their proportion of the Bosnian population according to the 1981 census. Although the purpose of this ruling was to maintain ethnic balance, leaders of non-ethnic parties expressed reservations about the quota system as it would encourage voting according to ethnic identification rather than political or economic program. The law specified that if the correct proportions were not achieved, the elections could be annulled and new ones staged until the required balance was attained. Of the 1,077 candidates who ran for the Chamber of Citizens, 416 were Muslims, 333 Serbs, 225 Croats, 85 Yugoslavs, and 18 represented other nationalities. Out of the 474 candidates running for the Chamber of Municipalities, 179 were Muslim, 167 were Serbian, 90 were Croatian, 34 were Yugoslav, and 4 represented other nationalities. Leaders of the main parties recognized the elections as legitimate, even though they had voiced fears that the ex-Communists would manipulate the balloting. Because of irregularities and inconclusive results, elections were repeated in 55 municipalities. In the final tally, the PDA gained 86 seats in the Assembly, the SDP 72, and the CDU 44; the 38 remaining mandates were shared among 8 political groups.

The list of 28 candidates for members of the presidency consisted of four parts, each alphabetized according to the candidate's ethnic identity and party affiliation. The three ethnic lists obtained two seats each, and the fourth one seat. The victory of the three ethnically based parties both reflected and encouraged national identification among the citizens. The key government positions were awarded to the three ethnic groups. Alija Izetbegović, a former political prisoner and head of the primarily Muslim PDA was chosen as president of the nine-member presidency, a post that was envisioned on a rotational basis among the three ethnic components. Juro Pelivan of the CDU was chosen as prime minister to head the republic's government, and Momčilo Krajisnik of the SDP became speaker of the assembly. Bosnia's ethnopolitical divisions were clearly displayed in the final election tally. The PDA received 37.8 percent of the popular vote; the SDP gained 26.5 percent; the CDU scored 14.7 percent. Only 21 percent of the electorate voted for the smaller ethnic parties, for the Yugoslav organizations, or for the non-ethnic political associations. Although the results preserved a tri-ethnic balance in the legislature and the presidency, they also served to polarize both the electorate and their political representatives along lines of ethnoreligious allegiance.

Since no party won a clear majority in the National Assembly, leaders of the three national parties formed a coalition government. Muslims obtained ten ministries, Serbs seven, and Croats five. While the three ethno-parties agreed to share power at the national level, in various municipalities (*opštinas*) the victorious parties proceeded to assume absolute control in the local governments. Moreover, the Serb *opštinas* increasingly refused to recognize Sarajevo's authority. Beneath the facade of cooperation at the republican level, an intense power struggle was brewing. This became evident when parliament attempted to enact new legislation in response to the accelerating disintegration of the federal system. It proved impossible to pass a new constitution as the agreement of all three major parties was required. In particular, the Serbian side refused to countenance any constitutional changes that would have propelled Bosnia toward independent statehood. Conversely, both the Muslim and the Croat sides voiced fears that the secession of Slovenia and Croatia would leave the republic in a precarious position and strengthen Serbia's position in the shrunken federation.

Throughout the early part of 1991, the Bosnian authorities were involved in intensive negotiations within the federal government on restructuring inter-republican elections. They supported something approaching "confederation," although the term was often short on specifics and Serbs viewed it as a smokescreen for independence. Sarajevo's position was made even more complex by differences within the republican presidency and government on the future of Yugoslavia. While the Muslim side favored a loose alliance rather than outright secession, having little experience of independent statehood, the Serbian side sought to preserve a unified Yugoslav state with some measure of republican autonomy. The Croat side veered toward Bosnian sovereignty and independence, particularly after the disassociation of Croatia and Slovenia in the summer of 1991. Caught between demands for Bosnian separatism and Yugoslav federalism, Bosnia's Muslim leaders simply could not afford to take a neutral position: either option would have led to confrontation with either the Serbs or the Croats. As war raged in neighboring Croatia and the prospect of international recognition appeared as a distinct possibility, the majority of the Muslim leadership leaned toward secession from Yugoslavia and the preservation of a unitary Bosnian state. While this move largely satisfied Croatian aspirations, the Serb leadership was dismayed and warned that they would not accept Bosnian independence as this would allegedly leave 1.5 million Serbs stranded in the new state. The slide into all-out conflict and a savage civil war had begun in earnest.

The Bosnian Assembly remained deadlocked over the issue of sovereignty, even though the three ethnic parties appeared to agree on maintaining the republic's territorial integrity. In February 1991, the SDP rejected a joint PDA–CDU proposal on declaring sovereignty and giving Bosnian laws precedence over federal legislation. Serb leaders contended that such moves would institutionalize the "minority status" of Serbs in Bosnia-Herzegovina. In April 1991, the PDA and CDU rejected SDP proposals for the "economic regionalization" of Bosnia, whereby each ethnic group would ensure the control of its own economic interests. Muslim and Croat leaders calculated that this would constitute the first step toward Serbian partition and the creation of a "Greater Serbia." Through the summer of 1991, conflicts continued to rage over a draft proposal for Bosnian sovereignty. SDP leaders appeared to be stalling over an agreement, evidently seeking to prolong the political deadlock until the military situation in Croatia became clarified.[4]

In October 1991, the Bosnian Assembly under the sponsorship of the PDA and CDU finally adopted a memorandum on sovereignty and neutrality, stopping just short of declaring the republic's independence. Refusing to accept this decision, Assembly president Krajisnik adjourned the legislature without approval prior to the vote. The adoption of the memorandum on sovereignty was declared illegal by the SDP, on the grounds that it broke an agreement reached in December 1990 among the three ruling parties, underscoring that a consensus was necessary in order to pass legislation or enact any constitutional amendments. The PDA and CDU countered that their initiative was in line with Bosnia's existing constitution and reflected growing popular concern over the disintegration of Yugoslavia. SDP representatives stormed out of the Bosnian parliament in protest over the sovereignty decision. In many respects, Bosnia-Herzegovina found itself in a similar political and constitutional position as the Yugoslav federation once Slovenia and Croatia withdrew from the federal government. It was marked by virtually unbridgeable polarization between the leaders of the component nations.[5] In November 1991, in a clear challenge to the declaration on sovereignty, the SDP organized its own referendum among Bosnian Serbs. According to Serb sources, the overwhelming majority participated in the ballot and voted for maintaining the federation with Yugoslavia, regardless of agreements between Muslims and Croats. Serb leaders asserted that they would not accept minority status in an independent Bosnia, as this would leave them susceptible to official persecution, as had been evident in Croatia. Conversely, Croat leaders charged that Serb activists in league with the Milošević regime were preparing a crisis in the republic similar to the one engineered in Croatia earlier in the year.

In fact, a series of pre-planned steps were undertaken during 1991 to solidify exclusive Serb control over the bulk of Bosnian territory, evidently as a prelude to secession. Indeed, as far back as October 1990, the SDP had set up a Serbian national council in the town of Banja Luka and demanded the creation of three national chambers in the republican parliament. The establishment of parallel organs of power was condemned by the government for violating Bosnia's sovereignty.[6] In April 1991, a Serb Community of Municipalities of Bosnian Krajina was declared, consisting of 14 Serb majority municipalities in western Bosnia that bordered the Serb-held territories in Croatian Krajina. Municipal governments in heavily Serb-populated areas of eastern, northern, and southeastern Bosnia also prepared to form autonomous communities avowedly to protect Serb interests against Muslim-Croatian separatism. Sarajevo charged that the self-proclaimed communities negated the rights of local minorities and undermined the Bosnian administration. They were viewed as the first steps toward establishing autonomous regions that would presage the fracturing of the republic into contested ethnic zones. At a joint session in June 1991, deputies of the assemblies

of Bosnian Krajina municipalities and the Serbian Autonomous Region of Krajina (in Croatia) adopted a "treaty on cooperation" and promulgated a "declaration of unification" of the two regions. These measures served to confirm that
Serb leaders in both republics were intent on linking up their territories and
creating an enlarged Serbian state that would remain in or rejoin a smaller
Yugoslavia.

In September 1991, Serb leaders announced the formation of a Serbian
Autonomous Region of Eastern and Old Herzegovina; it covered eight municipalities in southeastern Bosnia inhabited primarily by Serbs. Meanwhile, the
Bosnian Krajina region was declared the Serbian Autonomous Region of Krajina. Even more ominously, local Serb police forces and party radicals proceeded
to establish armed "volunteer units" and steadily eliminated Sarajevo's jurisdiction in these areas. The Bosnian presidency and legislature and all Muslim and
Croatian organizations condemned these initiatives as illegal and provocative.
Serb leaders claimed that they were simply protective measures designed to
ensure "self-determination" for Yugoslavia's largest nation. During the fall of
1991, three more autonomous Serbian regions were proclaimed in northeastern
Bosnia, northern Bosnia, and the Mount Romanija region east of Sarajevo. Recognizing the authority of the self-proclaimed Assembly of the Serbian People in
Bosnia-Herzegovina, leaders of the new territorial units threatened to establish a
unified Serbian republic, secede from Bosnia, and remain in a federal Yugoslavia. They asserted that a declaration of Bosnian independence and the non-recog-
nition of Serbian territorial autonomy would provoke even more radical steps
toward separation and could precipitate bloodshed. Muslim and Croat leaders
declared that no autonomous regions could be formed on the republic's territory
and dismissed as null and void any planned referendums on autonomy. The
Serbian leadership responded that Bosnia-Herzegovina would need to be divided
into three distinct ethnic territories if civil war was to be avoided. They proceeded to consolidate Serbian political control and in February 1992 adopted a
Constitution of the Serbian Republic of Bosnia-Herzegovina.

Although the CDU leadership criticized Serbian steps toward secession, local
leaders in Croatian-majority municipalities, evidently in close liaison with the
authorities in Zagreb, proceeded to form their own quasi-autonomous regions.[7]
They claimed that they did not want to live outside of Croatia if a large wedge of
Serbian-controlled territory were to separate them from other republics. In November 1991, a Croatian Community of Herzeg-Bosnia was established to include 30 municipalities containing a large Croatian population in western
Herzegovina and central Bosnia. The community was declared a distinct political
and economic entity that would recognize the government in Sarajevo only as
long as the republic upheld its sovereignty vis-à-vis Yugoslavia. During the same
month, a Croatian Community of the Bosnian Sava Valley was established to
incorporate eight municipalities in northern Bosnia. In January 1992, a third
Croatian Community of Central Bosnia was formed, comprised of four munici-

palities. Various local Croat leaders declared themselves in favor of union with Croatia.

Serbian moves toward secession were accompanied by a propaganda barrage emanating from Belgrade alleging that Muslim extremists led by President Izetbegović were intent on transforming Bosnia-Herzegovina into a militant Islamic state in which Serbs would be subject to persecution and genocide.[8] They cited passages from Izetbegović's previously banned *Islamic Declaration* as proof of his fundamentalist aims—passages that were invariably taken out of context and presented as a manifesto for the restructuring of Bosnia-Herzegovina into a Muslim state. Serb charges were strenuously denied by the PDA, which asserted that it supported a tolerant, secular, multi-ethnic, and democratic state. Indeed, on the eve of the outbreak of hostilities there was no perceptible threat from either the Muslim or Croat side to the safety of Serbian residents. However, Belgrade's propaganda evidently elicited enormous resonance among segments of the rural Serb population and provided ammunition to radicals intent on carving out a pure Serbian state. Muslim leaders and their followers were denounced as "Turks" and "fundamentalists." Indeed, the conflict was depicted as a primarily religious war in which the Serbian side was merely seeking to defend itself against an internationally sponsored Islamic *jihad* (holy war). As the war in Croatia began to wind down at the close of 1991 and both Croatia and Slovenia stood on the verge of international recognition as independent states, Serb leaders in Bosnia pushed ahead toward open confrontation with Sarajevo. In January 1992, the self-styled Serb Assembly claimed it was entitled to control 60 percent of the republic's territory and disclosed plans to establish its own security forces and governmental institutions.

Almost as soon as the Yugoslav crisis turned into a full-fledged "civil war" during the summer of 1991, calls were made to recognize Slovenia and Croatia as independent states. EC peace efforts failed to stem the conflict in Croatia, while the Yugoslav military and the Serbian government were considered primarily responsible for the continuation of the war. In December 1991, EC foreign ministers decided to recognize the independence of all Yugoslav republics fulfilling four fundamental conditions, including commitments to various human rights accords, guaranteeing rights to national groups and minorities, respect for the inviolability of frontiers, and agreement to settle state succession and regional disputes through agreement. Bosnia-Herzegovina, Croatia, Macedonia, and Slovenia submitted applications for international recognition, whereas Serbia and Montenegro claimed that they already represented Yugoslavia. The EC Arbitration Commission, chaired by French jurist Robert Badinter, concluded that only Macedonia and Slovenia had fully met the EC conditions. But in January 1992, under German pressure, Slovenia and Croatia were duly recognized while Macedonian recognition was blocked by Greece. Bosnia-Herzegovina evidently met most of the EC requirements, but it was not granted recognition because "the expression of the will of the inhabitants" for constituting an independent state had not been ascertained. This decision could be changed if the government organized a referendum in which "all citizens would participate and which would be conducted under international supervision."

In response to the EC decision, the Bosnian presidency, with the approval of the National Assembly, authorized that all necessary measures be taken to organize a referendum. With the exception of the SDP deputies, who left the session in protest, the Assembly slated the referendum on independence for the last week of February and the first week of March 1992.[9] Eligible voters were asked if they supported a sovereign and independent "state of equal citizens, the peoples of Bosnia-Herzegovina—Muslims, Serbs, Croats, and members of other nations living in it." The SDP, led by its chairman Radovan Karadžić, declared the referendum illegal because it was not approved by the full Assembly and did not have the support of all three constituent nations. Although Serbian leaders did not comprehensively disrupt the plebiscite, local officials in Serb-dominated areas who were charged with referendum-related responsibilities often refused to cooperate. In some locations, Serb radicals staged protests against the vote and distributed inflammatory propaganda. Observers contended that SDP leaders feared that without an active boycott, a substantial percentage of Serbs may have opted for independence and derailed the efforts of militants such as Karadžić who endeavored to prove that Serbs remained united against Bosnian statehood. In all, 63.4 percent of eligible voters participated in the referendum, and 99.7 percent of these cast their ballots for sovereignty and independence. The constitutionally required two-thirds majority was thereby attained. The figures indicated that the overwhelming majority of Muslims, Croats, Yugoslavs, and other minorities favored Bosnian statehood, while the Serb boycott was comprehensive. Immediately after the balloting, a shooting incident in Sarajevo suddenly raised tensions in the republic and Serb militias began to set up barricades in and around various cities, evidently in preparation for armed confrontation. Although the initial incidents led to only a handful of deaths, they were to prove an ominous indicator of the violence to come.

Bosnia-Herzegovina was recognized as an independent state in early April 1992. The day after recognition, the Serbian Republic of Bosnia-Herzegovina was formally proclaimed and SDP representatives withdrew from all governmental institutions and openly recognized the authority of their own separate administrative organs. Krajisnik, the former president of the Bosnian Assembly, assumed the presidency of the Serbian Assembly and Karadžić the presidency of the Serbian Republic. Meanwhile, three moderate Serbs outside the SDP entered Bosnia's collective presidency, which under war-time conditions assumed the powers of the republican Assembly. Although the multi-ethnic coalition was obviously collapsing, all factions continued to participate in a series of EC-sponsored negotiations for the decentralization or "cantonization" of the republic. As far back as February 1992, the three sides had reportedly agreed on an ethnic division into seven regions: two each for Muslims and Croats, and three for

Serbs. While the regions would not have been contiguous for any group, three ethnically based provinces within an integral Bosnia would have been established. According to a document on the Basic Principles for a New Constitutional Structure for Bosnia-Herzegovina, the central government would have retained minimal powers while regional units assumed jurisdiction over the police, financial institutions, and the media. The rights of minorities were to be protected through the rotation of government functions and the activities of special organs such as ombudsmen and a human rights court.

Despite indications that the three sides were prepared to reach a compromise and avoid all-out confrontation, under the facade of negotiations to placate the international community, preparations were under way for violent conflict. The EC-sponsored talks on a new constitutional order remained deadlocked over the question of maps: it proved impossible to devise any territorial delineations that would be acceptable to all three sides simultaneously. Muslim leaders remained wary of any regional divisions based on ethnic criteria, arguing that the populations were so intermingled that any form of cantonization needed to take account of existing administrative and economic criteria. A division based primarily on ethnic grounds would inevitably lead to discriminatory measures against minority groups in each canton and an eventual division of the embryonic state.

Stilted debates over cantonization also brought into focus persistent rumors of a secret deal between Zagreb and Belgrade to partition the republic. They were fueled by high-level statements and meetings between Serbian and Croatian leaders that served to heighten anxieties among Muslim officials. During the summer of 1991, presidents Milošević and Tudjman allegedly held two secret meetings to divide the republic even though no firm agreements were reached.[10] In June 1991, Croatian prime minister Josip Manolić indicated that a division of Bosnia-Herzegovina was possible, whereby municipalities inhabited predominantly by Serbs could join Serbia, Croatian areas would revert to Croatia, while Muslim majority zones could form a separate republic. While the Croatian side publicly denied that it was involved in any deals with Belgrade, it clearly suited the Serbs to publicize such negotiations and thereby share the blame for undermining Bosnian integrity. Meetings between the two protagonists continued to take place after the outbreak of armed hostilities: for instance, in a much-publicized meeting in Austria in May 1992, a plan was evidently formulated to divide Bosnia into three distinct regions.

In April 1992, the political impasse in Bosnia was transformed into outright armed conflict.[11] The war was launched by Bosnia's Serb leaders who calculated that the political and military situation was propitious to begin their assault. Politically, the truncated government had already lost administrative control in most of the Serbian autonomous regions and was unable to restore its powers. Militarily, Sarajevo was incapable of either neutralizing the Serb forces or protecting Muslim residents. As the war in Croatia died down in early 1992, the

Yugoslav army transferred much of its heavy equipment and troops into Bosnia; under instructions from Belgrade, military stocks were made readily available to local Serb forces. Militia detachments had already been formed in the five Serbian "autonomous regions," and a military command was already functioning parallel to the Serb Assembly. In June 1991, the Serb-dominated Yugoslav Army General Staff had ordered that all weapons belonging to Bosnia's Territorial Defense Forces be placed under the federal army's control. Much of this weaponry was apportioned to Bosnian Serb commanders, and additional war materiel began to flow in from Serbia and Montenegro. Between March and May 1992, the bulk of the Yugoslav army stationed in Bosnia was simply transformed into a new Serb army commanded by a former Yugoslav army general, Ratko Mladić.

The Bosnian government was clearly caught unprepared for armed conflict. It calculated that under the umbrella of international recognition, the Serbs would desist from open warfare and a political compromise would be reached under an EC mandate. Although Sarajevo had established special security units to suppress civil disorder, it had not bargained for the kind of sustained offensives organized by Serbian militants. Bosnia's military structure remained poorly organized, undermanned, and underarmed.[12] Sarajevo seriously underestimated the escalating threat and was slow in organizing an appropriate defense. At most, some local Muslim leaders on their own initiative began to form paramilitary groups, including a force known as the Green Berets. The presidency formally established an Army of Bosnia and Herzegovina in May 1992 and only declared a state of war in June 1992, by which time Serb forces had already overrun much of the republic. According to fairly reliable estimates, by the close of 1992 the Bosnian army consisted of about 80,000 combatants, although only half that number were adequately armed. By contrast, the Serbian side was able to field about 60,000 well-armed troops and about 10,000 paramilitaries. Moreover, the Serbs had an enormous advantage in all armament categories: from tanks and helicopters to artillery pieces of all calibers. The Croatian side quickly mustered nearly 40,000 soldiers, with direct assistance from Zagreb, and deployed a respectable number of tanks and artillery. Bosnian army inferiority was compounded by the absence of a strong central command and the operation of various local forces pledging only nominal allegiance to Sarajevo.

Serbian military objectives were twofold: to link up and expand the territories they controlled in western and eastern Bosnia, thus creating a contiguous Serb republic between Croatian Krajina and Serbia proper; and to eliminate the non-Serb populations in this new political entity, whether through threat, eviction, or outright murder. A campaign of terror was unleashed against non-Serb civilians; atrocities committed by irregular forces were loudly publicized to intimidate remaining residents and escalate the war psychosis. The anti-civilian offensive, euphemistically described by Serb leaders as "ethnic cleansing," had already been set in motion in Croatia the previous year.[13] In Bosnia-Herzegovina, the practice became more widespread and brutal, and it was largely defenseless Muslim civilians who fell victim to this centrally planned "civil war." With overwhelming firepower, Serb militias and irregular paramilitaries, some operating from Serbia itself, targeted Muslim villages or neighborhoods by rounding up residents and executing or imprisoning males of military age. Older people, women, and children were ordered to flee or they would suffer the same fate. In many cases, however, virtually all residents were slaughtered and reports of rape, torture, and mutilation became widespread. As word of Serb atrocities spread through Muslim towns and villages, local resistance was organized. In such cases, Serb artillery would first be deployed to destroy or weaken the defenders before the location was captured and its residents murdered or expelled. As the conflict expanded, thousands of civilian prisoners were ensconced in concentration camps; while many died of starvation, execution, or torture, others were used in prisoner exchanges with Muslim and Croat forces.

The systematic and purposeful nature of the "ethnic cleansing" campaign indicated that the policy had been planned and approved at the highest political levels in the SDP leadership and in Belgrade itself. It served several purposes simultaneously: to eliminate the non-Serb population as a potential source of future resistance; to create problems for Muslim-majority areas outside the regions designated for the "Serb Republic" by flooding them with refugees; to provide war booty for local guerrillas and gunmen recruited in Serbia; to gain the loyalty of Serbs evacuated from other locations by allowing them to occupy captured houses and land; and to entrap non-combatant Serbs in a permanent conflict with Muslims in which the militias could pose as defenders protecting ordinary Serbs from Muslim revenge attacks. In this way, an "ethnic conflict" was engineered across Bosnia, buttressed by an incessant propaganda barrage claiming that Serbs simply could not live with Muslims, that the Muslim leadership was intent on creating an Islamic state, and that Serbs primarily wanted "self-determination" to protect them from the tide of fundamentalism.

The rapid success of Serb forces in gaining absolute control over more than 60 percent of Bosnian territory galvanized Bosnia's Croat leadership and strengthened the position of those who favored partition. The moderate CDU leader, Stjepan Kljujić, who had strongly favored an integral Bosnia, was replaced, and the more radical Herzegovinian Mate Boban, under the patronage of Zagreb, took charge of political and military operations in the Croatian-majority regions. Initially, Croat forces did not engage in "ethnic cleansing" operations, particularly as they largely confined their operations to Croatian-majority municipalities and entered into a loose alliance with the Bosnian armed forces as protection against the Serbian onslaught. However, Boban and his cohorts criticized the Bosnian leadership for its lack of preparedness and military incompetence while establishing a separate military structure in western Herzegovina, central Bosnia, and the Posavina region, along the Sava River border with Croatia, styled as the Croatian Defense Council (CDC). The CDC also recruited thousands of local Muslims to fight in its ranks, while claiming that only Croats were able to offer a proper defense of their "national space." Although the CDC pledged nominal allegiance to the government in Sarajevo, under the chairmanship of Jadranko Prlić, it also made preparations to establish a separate Croatian republic with the option of joining Croatia at some future date.

Bosnia's Croat forces received military supplies and logistical assistance from Zagreb, as the border with Croatia virtually ceased to exist and thousands of soldiers from Croatia were reportedly active in Herzegovina. Boban dismissed accusations that he was intent on partitioning Bosnia, claiming that Croat forces were simply organizing the most effective resistance against Serbian aggression and actually protecting the integrity of Bosnia-Herzegovina. Conversely, to justify their control of approximately 20 percent of Bosnian territory, Croatian leaders occasionally imitated Belgrade's propaganda line that the Izetbegović-led PDA was intent on establishing an Islamic state in which non-Muslims would figure as second-class citizens. Such charges appeared to lay the groundwork for future claims to divide the republic.

Suspicions continued to surface that Boban and Karadžić had forged a secret deal to partition Bosnia under the sponsorship of Zagreb and Belgrade. These were reinforced in July 1992 when Boban declared the autonomy of "Herzeg-Bosnia" with its capital in Mostar and proceeded to consolidate a separate administrative structure. Croat spokesmen contended that this was merely a temporary arrangement designed to ensure political stability and the security of Croat municipalities in war-time conditions, something the government in Sarajevo was clearly unable to do. President Tudjman regularly signaled his support for Bosnian independence and territorial integrity and offered a closer Croat-Bosnian military alliance. Sarajevo's response remained lukewarm as the Bosnian presidency was wary of committing itself to an unstable accord with Zagreb. Observers believed that Tudjman's statements were designed to placate international opinion and to single out the Serbs as the prime aggressors, leaving Croats with the option of remaining in Bosnia or forging their own political entity depending on both internal and international developments.

The Croat side retained its membership in the Bosnian presidency and continued to provide some measure of military assistance to the beleaguered Muslim forces. However, on several occasions Croat forces appeared to avoid all-out confrontations with the Serb army. In some instances, they reportedly abandoned Muslim positions as Bosnian forces proceeded to lose their foothold in several key locations in the republic. Nonetheless, in Sarajevo, Tuzla, and other large towns, a marked degree of political and military cooperation remained visible. The Bosnian leadership claimed that members of all three ethnic groups were integrated in the security forces and recognized the authority of the central government. Indeed, many urban Serbs and Croats in Bosnian-controlled territory refused to recognize either the Karadžić or the Boban leadership and upheld their allegiance to the principles of a single multi-ethnic state. Nevertheless, the process of ethnic polarization and segregation was proceeding apace. Even at the highest political levels, the Croatian Bosnian prime minister Mile Akmadžić criticized Izetbegović for failing to abide by the principles of presidential rotation and claimed that he did not fully represent all three national communities. Izetbegović countered that under emergency conditions the presidency could not function normally. The situation on the ground was even more discouraging. By the close of 1992, not only did Serb forces control nearly 70 percent of the republic, but approximately one million non-Serbs had been expelled or fled from the Serbian advance. For all intents and purposes, a separate Serbian state was already functioning. In August 1992, a Serb Assembly meeting in Banja Luka renamed the new entity the Serb Republic.

In June 1992, the United Nations mounted a humanitarian operation in Bosnia and approximately 7,000 troops were dispatched to the republic. Their mission was largely confined to providing relief supplies to the capital of Sarajevo and other besieged towns and cities. Food and medical aid also became a weapon in the siege of Bosnian cities. Serb and Croat militias periodically blocked UN convoys and severed essential water, electricity, and gas supplies in order to demoralize and starve out Muslim defenders. In August 1992, under the direction of Cyrus Vance, the personal representative of the UN secretary general, and David Owen, an EC-appointed mediator, the London Conference on Yugoslavia intensified its efforts to find a political solution to the Bosnian war and to enforce an agreement on all three sides. Following several rounds of negotiations, in October 1992, a document was formulated that became known as the Vance–Owen plan.[14] It advocated the creation of a decentralized state consisting of nine largely autonomous provinces, three for each nationality, and a central region around the capital Sarajevo. In each province one of the three ethnonational groups would predominate, thus opening up the possibility of population transfers under international supervision. The central government would have only minimal responsibilities, including foreign affairs, international commerce, taxation, and national defense. The nine provinces would control all other governmental functions such as education, media, energy, finance, and local police. However, even national defense would remain highly decentralized and the demilitarization of the republic was envisioned under close international supervision. By January 1993, the authority of the central government had been further diluted in the Vance–Owen plan, and some observers noted that the effect would have been to turn Bosnia-Herzegovina into a UN protectorate.

While the constitutional and political arrangements appeared to be largely acceptable to all three sides, since Serb and Croat leaders viewed it as a means toward cantonization and eventual partition and the Muslims calculated that under international protection an integral Bosnia would be maintained, the delineation of provincial borders proved highly contentious. The map devised under the Vance–Owen plan was only acceptable to the Croats, who stood to gain pockets of territory outside the regions they already controlled, particularly in northern and central Bosnia. The Muslims would lose land in the north and the center but would regain some territories in eastern Bosnia that had been captured by Serb forces. The Serbs were outraged by the proposed maps: acceptance would have meant the surrender of nearly a quarter of the occupied territories, with extensive territorial fragmentation in eastern Bosnia and the loss of their northern corridor. The Croatian side promptly accepted the plan while the Muslims held out until March 1993, when they realized that continuing opposition would simply prolong the war and ensure further Serbian conquests. By accepting the plan, Sarajevo estimated that significant international pressure would be exerted on the Serbs, particularly as calls for UN military intervention escalated.

Fearful of international military involvement, Serb leaders adopted a dual-track approach. They continued to negotiate and procrastinated in giving a final decision on the plan, while they launched new offensives in eastern Bosnia during March and April 1993 to eradicate the remaining Muslim pockets. Karadžić initialed the Vance–Owen plan, under evident pressure from Milošević, who estimated that the combined effect of tightening UN sanctions against Yugoslavia and the possibility of bombing assaults on Serb supply lines, communications, and armaments factories would have precipitated a major crisis inside Serbia itself. However, the validation of Karadžić's signature was made contingent upon the acceptance of the plan by the self-styled Serbian parliament. In April 1993, the Serbian Assembly further delayed a decision by calling for a referendum among the Serb population: the ballot took place in May 1993 and the Vance–Owen plan was overwhelmingly rejected by voters. The long-drawn-out decision, coupled with the deteriorating military situation and a public dispute between the United States and its European allies, forestalled and eventually precluded any meaningful UN military response. A consensus could not be reached in the UN Security Council on whether to bomb Serbian targets and ease the arms embargo on the outgunned Bosnian forces.

The relationship between Karadžić, the Bosnian Serb military, and their patron, Milošević, gave rise to intensive speculation. Milošević's acceptance of the Vance–Owen plan and his public criticisms of the Bosnian Serb Assembly could have been taken at face value as a split over strategy and programs. Conversely, it may have been a tactical ploy intended for foreign consumption, whereby Belgrade could avoid further economic sanctions and any military retaliation for the rejection of the UN plan by the Bosnian side. Even though the rump Yugoslavia continued to supply fuel and military provisions to the Bosnian Serbs and both sides agreed on the establishment of a Greater Serbia, there were indications that Milošević did not fully control his former proxies. Strong ideological differences also materialized between an essentially neo-Communist leadership in Belgrade and a monarchist and religion-oriented Serb leadership in Bosnia supported by the ultra-nationalist Radical Party in Serbia. Milošević may have gauged that a swift unification of Serbian territories may have strengthened the position of nationalist rivals in Serbia, Bosnia, and Krajina—a coalition that could conceivably dislodge him from power.

Western indecision was quickly exploited by Bosnia's Serb leaders who pressed on with their military offensives in eastern and northern Bosnia. By the end of May 1993, the Vance–Owen plan was practically dead and the republic descended into an all-out land-grabbing operation by all three sides. Croatian forces launched offensives against their erstwhile Muslim allies in central Bosnia and proceeded to expel the remaining Muslim population from western Herzegovina. Serbs intensified their assaults on the surviving Muslim enclaves in eastern Bosnia, reducing them to barely defendable pockets that the United Nations technically declared as "safe havens" but failed to protect. In sheer desperation, Bosnian government forces launched offensives in central Bosnia to regain territory lost to the Croats, but they simply did not possess the firepower to dislodge Serbian forces from the occupied territories.

In June 1993, Serb and Croat leaders finalized a new plan for the division of Bosnia-Herzegovina into three ethnic provinces or mini-states with only a nominal central government. According to the proposals, Serbs would give back a small portion of their territory while the Muslim quasi state would be contained in central Bosnia with Sarajevo as the capital, in addition to a small enclave in the northwestern Bihać pocket. Croatia would avowedly guarantee Muslim access to the sea at the Adriatic port of Ploče.[15] The plan was deemed unacceptable by the Bosnian government, which continued to favor a multi-ethnic federal arrangement. However, rifts began to appear in the collective presidency between the majority of Muslim leaders who vehemently opposed the proposal and more pragmatic Croat members together with Fikret Abdić, the Muslim leader representing the Bihać-Cazinska Krajina area, who felt that without a speedy accord the state would be completely dismembered and the Bosnian side would be left with a fragmented "homeland" overflowing with refugees. President Izetbegović came under increasing criticism for his intransigence, and by July 1993 the Bosnian government seemed on the verge of collapse. The situation on the ground continued to deteriorate: Serb forces, occasionally in collaboration with Croats, launched offensives to open up a new corridor across north-central Bosnia and tightened their stranglehold around Sarajevo, while Croat troops prepared to reverse recent Muslim gains in south-central Bosnia and western Herzegovina. The country, which had already disintegrated politically, now stood close to formal partition. Even with agreement on a three-way division under a nominal confederal arrangement, armed clashes were likely to persist, especially along the designated border regions. Moreover, a new surge of refugees among the three para-states could be expected as Muslims, Serbs, and Croats would invariably seek shelter in their ethnic cantons to avoid persecution. In such a scenario, the fragile multi-ethnic rump Bosnia-Herzegovina looked set for transformation into a purely Muslim entity.

MUSLIM ORGANIZATIONS

Party of Democratic Action (PDA)
Stranka Demokratske Akcije (SDA)

The PDA was founded in May 1990 under the leadership of Alija Izetbegović and in the presence of 1,500 supporters. The PDA not only claimed to rally Bosnia's Muslims but sought a political alliance of all Yugoslav citizens with an affinity to Muslim cultural, historical, and religious traditions. Hence, the party established branches or affiliates in other republics including Serbia, Montenegro, and Macedonia; however, their links with the Bosnian party became increasingly tenuous as Yugoslavia dissolved and Bosnia approached open conflict. The PDA's founding assembly was attended by representatives from 73 locations in Bosnia-Herzegovina who anticipated a rapid growth in its power base. Party members predicted that 70 initiative councils would be quickly registered in the republic, including the larger towns of Mostar, Banja Luka, Tesanj, Zenica, Velika Kladuša, and Kladanj, and even in the Croatian capital of Zagreb where the PDA claimed more than 10,000 supporters.

In the 1990 elections, 37.8 percent of the electorate voted for the PDA, and the party won 86 of the 240 seats in the Bosnian Assembly. As envisaged in election stipulations, soon after the ballot Izetbegović, who was elected to the nine-man Bosnian presidency, moved to form a coalition government with the major Serb and Croat parties. Consequently, Izetbegović was nominated as the first president in the rotating Bosnian presidency. In its program, the PDA, considered the largest party in the republic, called for economic reform with an emphasis on the denationalization of government-owned enterprises and the privatization of property. For example, it called for the return of land confiscated by the Communist state after 1945. Furthermore, the party advocated that restrictions on land-holdings by private citizens should be removed. As part of its economic liberalization program, the party stressed modern market production in agriculture as well as a reduction in budgets and personnel with respect to government offices, the police force, and the military. At its inaugural meeting, the PDA declared its principles to include freedom and equality of all citizens, without any distinction in regard to religion, nationality, race, sex, language, social status, or political beliefs. The party proposed legislation guaranteeing the national, cultural, and religious rights of Bosnian Muslims and the free activity of all religious communities. In addition, the PDA called for preserving the integrity and inviolability of the borders of Bosnia-Herzegovina. The PDA, which by early 1991 claimed to have over 400,000 members, considered itself to be the representative of various strata in society. In fact, the party's initial calculations showed that during the pre-election period Bosnians were registering at a rate of 100,000 a month.

Throughout 1991, the PDA condemned Serbian steps toward autonomy. According to Muslim leaders, the newly formed Serbian authorities in self-declared autonomous municipalities were created without prior consultation with the republican government and contrary to the legislature's recommendations. PDA leaders asserted that the formation of such bodies completely negated and denied the rights of Muslims and other nations living in that territory; moreover, the declared unification of Croatian Krajina and Bosnian Krajina constituted a "violation of the territorial integrity, sovereignty, and constitutional order of Bosnia-Herzegovina." Sarajevo therefore declared it null and void. In mid-September 1991, in response to the creation of Serbian autonomous regions, the PDA warned that it would form an autonomous Muslim region in the Mostar area of Herzegovina. The PDA's suspicions were heightened when long-term Serbian designs became evident with the creation of a Serbian autonomous region of Mount Romanija between Sarajevo and the Serbian border.

The head of the Islamic Religious Community (IRC), Hadji Jakob Efendi Selimoski, claimed that the Muslims were undergoing a religious revival in Bosnia-Herzegovina. Apparently, an increasing number were observing the holy month of Ramadan, participating in Islamic rituals, and learning about their faith. As a result of this revival movement, during the summer of 1991, Belgrade claimed that Muslim extremists were calling for the transformation of Bosnia-Herzegovina into a separate Islamic state. The new entity, according to the Serb leadership, was slated to incorporate other areas of Yugoslavia with large Muslim populations. The PDA denied any such intentions. But despite this disclaimer, the Serbian media vilified Izetbegović for his alleged pan-Islamic and pan-Turkish sympathies.

In August 1991, the leader of the Muslim Bosnian Organization (MBO), Adil Zulfikarpašić, argued that Izetbegović should accept a proposal put forward by his party and endorsed by Karadžić calling for the "preservation of peace and life in the equality-based community of Yugoslavia." Zulfikarpašić believed that without Yugoslavia there would be no Bosnia-Herzegovina, and that the problem could not be solved without the participation of Serb leaders. Such statements were vehemently opposed by Izetbegović, who at that time did not want to enter into any agreement that would exclude a third party—in this case the Croats. He affirmed that the PDA would not take sides in the Serb-Croat dispute, as this would endanger Bosnia's political integrity and provoke an all-out war. While the MBO supported preserving an indivisible Bosnia-Herzegovina within a Yugoslav federation, regardless of whether Slovenia and Croatia seceded, the PDA favored a confederal Yugoslavia without the loss of Bosnian territory.

As tensions mounted within the republic, in October 1991 Muslim and Croat leaders in the Bosnian Assembly voted to declare the republic's sovereignty and neutrality. However, Serbian leaders boycotted the Assembly session and declared the vote illegal because it breached an agreement that called for consensus among all three major parties (PDA, SDP, and CDU) in passing legislation and undertaking constitutional changes. The PDA envisioned Yugoslavia as either a federation with various confederal elements or a confederation with federal elements. In March 1992, the party spoke out against the idea of dividing the state according to ethnic principles alone and claimed that it would support a unitary and civil Bosnia-Herzegovina, taking into account the multi-ethnic characteristics of the republic. This position was maintained by the party leadership throughout the war launched by Serb guerrillas in April 1992, despite some factionalization between pragmatic and more militant factions. Indeed, the war itself contributed to radicalizing a segment of the Muslim population and the PDA leadership, although Izetbegović, his deputy Ejup Ganić, and Foreign Minister Haris Silajdžić were able to preserve the party's unity.[16]

Muslim Bosnian Organization (MBO)
Muslimanska Bošnjačka Organizacija (MBO)

The MBO was formed after a split in the leadership of the PDA. It was founded in October 1990 by the former vice president of the PDA, Adil Zulfikarpašić, as well as by Muhamed Filipović and Hamza Mujagić, former members of the PDA who had been expelled from the party. The MBO called for a democratic Yugoslavia, contending that Yugoslavia as a union of republics was the best solution for its component nations. Zulfikarpašić asserted that the MBO would "give priority to Yugoslavia as a state community over an aggregate sovereignty of all constituent republics." The party claimed that it did not use Islam for political ends, although one of its main objectives was to ensure the rights of Bosnian Muslims to practice their faith freely. The leadership announced that the new party would have a liberal-democratic orientation and would not be ideological or nationalistic. The party also stood for the religious rights of all Bosnian citizens and explicitly distanced itself from the more Muslim-oriented PDA.

Adil Zulfikarpašić, a former *Partizan* major general, was once an ideologist of the Bosnian Brotherhood, an organization that had urged all Muslims to remain in the Yugoslav federation. He also founded the Institute of Bosnian Studies in Zurich, which propagated the theory that Bosnians were a separate ethnic group and that Orthodox, Catholics, and Muslims in the republic were actually Bosnians. In early 1990, Zulfikarpašić returned to Bosnia, where he founded the PDA together with Izetbegović. But differences soon emerged, and Izetbegović accused Zulfikarpašić of being a Yugoslav counterintelligence agent. When Zulfikarpašić proposed to Radovan Karadžić that a Serb-Muslim agreement be signed without the participation of the PDA, the largest Muslim party in the republic, Bosnian Muslim and Croat leaders declared him a traitor. Meanwhile, in 1991 leaders of the MBO accused Alija Izetbegović of sponsoring militant PDA groups who were said to be terrorizing members of the MBO. A letter was sent to Izetbegović from the leaders of the MBO stating that there was evidence of recent assaults on MBO members in Novi Pazar (Serbian Sandžak) and Zvornik. These incidents had allegedly occurred after the MBO and SDP agreed on a joint platform to form a federative order in Yugoslavia in August

1991. The draft agreement called for Muslims and Serbs to join together to "preserve Yugoslavia as a single state" and to maintain a "whole and indivisible" Bosnia-Herzegovina within the federation. Zulfikarpašić continued to criticize the Sarajevo leadership throughout the Bosnian war for its failure to reach an accord with the Serbs and for bearing responsibility for the collapse of the state and its descent into civil war.[17]

Muslim Democratic Party (MDP)
Muslimanska Demokratska Stranka (MDS)

The MDP was established during 1992 to challenge the policies of President Izetbegović and the PDA leadership. It was led by President Armin Pohara, who attacked the Sarajevo government for failing to prepare for the Serbian onslaught and keeping the Croatian side at arms length. Indeed, the MDP advocated "complete unity" between Bosnian Muslims and Croats and a confederation between Bosnia-Herzegovina and Croatia, possibly culminating in an integrated state to oppose Serbian aggression. It defended the CDU leadership and the self-styled president of "Herzeg-Bosnia," Mate Boban, and proposed a joint Croatian-Muslim command of Bosnia's armed forces. Pohara claimed that a Muslim member of the Bosnian presidency, Fikret Abdić, who controlled the Bihać-Cazinska Krajina pocket and was a long-time critic of Izetbegović, was planning to join the party. However, it remained unclear how much support the MDP actually had on the ground, especially as Muslim-Croat relations deteriorated throughout Bosnia in the wake of mutual "ethnic cleansing" campaigns during the spring and summer of 1993.[18]

SERBIAN SEPARATISTS

Serbian Democratic Party (SDP)
Srpska Demokratska Stranka (SDS)

The SDP was founded in July 1990 by Radovan Karadžić, a psychiatrist by profession, in the presence of 8,000 members. The party was a branch of the Croatian-based SDP, which led Serbian opposition to the independent Croatian state and was instrumental in establishing a parallel authority in the Krajina region. In Bosnia-Herzegovina, the SDP drew its support and ideological orientation from Serb intellectuals, professionals, military leaders, and the Milošević leadership in Belgrade. With regard to social programs, the SDP was considered a centrist party with some leftist leanings. The party's stated aim was to ensure the full and unconditional civil, national, cultural, religious, and economic equality of Serbs in Bosnia-Herzegovina. It called for the national, cultural, and spiritual unification of Serbs in Bosnia-Herzegovina and other Yugoslav territories. The SDP also advocated freedom of religion, the complete restructuring of the educational and social services administrations, the depolitization of government agencies, and the establishment of a modern army. The SDP initially encountered some competition from rival Serbian parties, including the Serbian Renewal Movement (SRM), but their political impact was curtailed by the support offered to Karadžić by the regime in Belgrade and by the extensive political apparatus inherited from the former Communist *nomenklatura.*

The prime objective of the SDP was to defend "Serbian interests" in the republic. In pursuit of this objective, during 1990 the SDP established a self-governing Serb National Council that was sharply criticized by both Muslim and Croat leaders for encouraging ethnic polarization and Bosnian disintegration. During the party's initiative committee meeting, Karadžiæ stressed that "there will not be revanchism or anti-communism, and the party does not dispute anyone's right to political life, elections, and participation in power." Following the elections, the SDP joined the PDA and the CDU to form a coalition government representing the republic's three major ethnic groups. Ethnic parity was maintained in the Chamber of Citizens, the Chamber of Municipalities, and the collective presidency; the results of the 1990 elections followed the republic's ethnic proportions, so that the SDP won a total of 72 seats in the 240-seat bicameral legislature.

Following the ballot, the SDP claimed that Serbs living in predominately Serbian areas of Bosnia-Herzegovina opposed Bosnian independence and were in favor of a union or close association with Serbia. Serb spokesmen affiliated with the SDP claimed that their rights would be endangered in an independent Bosnia. Karadžić and his followers asserted that an independent Bosnian state would be a unitary entity in which a combined Muslim and Croatian majority would disenfranchise and persecute the Serbian minority. The SDP claimed that all Serbs had the inalienable right to live in one state and contended that only nations and not republics had the right to separate from Yugoslavia. Insofar as other nationalities had endeavored to secede from Yugoslavia, the Serbs also possessed the right to secede from Croatia, Bosnia-Herzegovina, or any other Yugoslav republic. Since many Serbs resided in areas belonging to one of the secessionist states, the political and military strategies of the Serbian forces in Bosnia-Herzegovina and in Croatia focused on gaining control over territories inhabited predominately by Serbs. Karadžić denied that he and his supporters sought to separate Bosnian territory and annex it to a planned Greater Serbia. Instead, he proposed the division of Bosnia-Herzegovina into communal cantons that would function as autonomous entities under the control of the majority national group in each canton. Under such an arrangement, Karadžić and his followers believed that Serbian-controlled cantons would include about 70 percent of Bosnian territory, despite the fact that Serbs constitute only 31 percent of the republic's total population. The SDP leaders justified their claim on the fact that Serbs, who were mostly farmers and rural residents, purportedly owned 70 percent of the land.

In a referendum in March 1992, the Bosnian Assembly asked citizens if they supported a sovereign and independent Bosnia-Herzegovina. The SDP declared the act illegal and encouraged all Bosnian Serbs to boycott the plebiscite. The boycott was overwhelmingly successful among the Serbian electorate, and only 63.4 percent of eligible voters participated in the ballot. However, of those who did participate, mostly Muslims and Croats, the vast majority voted in favor of independence. Having met the requisite EC criteria, the republic was internationally recognized as an independent state in April 1992. Immediately after recognition, the SDP withdrew its representatives from the Bosnian presidency, the Bosnian Assembly, and all other governmental institutions and proclaimed the formation of the Serbian Republic of Bosnia-Herzegovina. As the civil war escalated during the spring and summer of 1992, it became evident that the governments of Yugoslavia and Serbia were providing economic, military, and political support to the Bosnian Serbs. It was widely believed that Karadžić was being directly sponsored by Serbia's President Milošević. Indeed, Belgrade both openly and clandestinely supported the SDP's military and political objectives. Despite the militant stance of the SDP, many Serbs in Bosnia-Herzegovina reportedly did not share its program of ethnic division, particularly those living in multi-ethnic cities such as Sarajevo. Similarly, Serb democrats in Serbia and some members of the academic community opposed the position of the SDP and its promulgation of conflict in Bosnia-Herzegovina.[19]

The SDP retained the majority of seats on the quasi-governmental Serb Assembly, based in the Bosnian town of Pale near Sarajevo. Its activists adopted the most militant positions, by pushing for the creation of a fully separate state, rejecting the EC-sponsored peace proposals, organizing a referendum on independence in May 1993, and calling for the political and military unification of the Serb Republic (in Bosnia-Herzegovina) and the Serb Republic of Krajina (in Croatia). Some rifts were visible both in the Assembly and in the party over strategic approaches toward Serbian unification and merger with Yugoslavia. Karadžić himself remained close to his patron Milošević, while balancing the uncompromising position of local activists and military commanders with those of more moderate politicians who preferred a longer-term approach and seemed willing to make short-term concessions. The militant line prevailed, especially when it became evident that the United Nations was not prepared to engage in military intervention. SDP ideologist Jovan Spremo and SDP activists from the radical stronghold of Banja Luka proposed early unification between the Serb Republic and the Krajina Republic. At a joint session between the two republican assemblies, SDP delegate Vojo Kuprešanin also proposed that the new state be declared a monarchy or a duchy under the constitutional rule of Prince Tomislav Karadjordjević. In this scenario, Tomislav's nephew Aleksander would be slated to inherit the throne as king of Yugoslavia. The two monarchies would then move toward royal and administrative unification in one Greater Serbian state. Although Prince Tomislav reportedly viewed the proposal favorably, Milošević seemed unlikely to be well disposed to an initiative that could challenge his own hold on power in Belgrade and his influence in Serb-held territories in Bosnia and Croatia. A potential power struggle among monarchist, neo-fascist, and socialist nationalists loomed on the horizon as Serbian unification neared.[20]

CROATIAN AUTONOMISTS

Croatian Democratic Union (CDU)
Hrvatska Demokratska Zajednica (HDZ)

The CDU was founded in October 1990 and was led by Stjepan Kljujić, a journalist, until March 1992, when Miljenko Brkić was elected acting president. The party propounded a liberal orientation, promoting all forms of private ownership, a free market economy, general Western-style capitalism, and the entry of Bosnia into the EC. The CDU described itself as the "only party that would guarantee the rights of Croats in Bosnia." The party sought a constitutional guarantee that Croats in the republic would have the right to "self-determination." As one of the three largest ethnically based parties, and with the additional support of its sister organizations in Zagreb, the CDU managed to gain 44 legislative seats, out of a total of 240, in the November 1990 republican elections. A number of other Croatian parties were initially formed, including the ultra-nationalist Zagreb-based Croatian Party of Rights (CPR), but their influence in Bosnia-Herzegovina proved marginal.

The programs of Croat activists in Bosnia and Croatia varied significantly, in particular with respect to the status of western Herzegovina and their cooperation with the Bosnian government. Liberal and moderate Croats supported an independent Bosnia-Herzegovina. This position was best exemplified by Kljujić, a member of the Bosnian presidency and supporter of an integral Bosnia, who was removed from the CDU leadership shortly after the outbreak of armed conflicts in March 1992. However, a nationalist wing of the CDU sought autonomy for the predominately Croatian areas of western Herzegovina presumably as a prelude to secession and union with neighboring Croatia. This position was represented by CDU's leader, Mate Boban, president of the Croatian Community of Herzeg-Bosnia, who was also regarded as a close collaborator of Croatian president Franjo Tudjman. Soon after the outbreak of hostilities, Boban established a separate military structure in the Herzegovina area, known as the Croatian Defense Council (CDC). Even though CDU members technically remained members of the Bosnian presidency, they barely participated in its deliberations. Croatian ultra-nationalists, including the militant CPR, also remained staunchly opposed to any partition of Bosnia-Herzegovina, contending that the entire republic should form a confederation with Croatia to counter Serbian pressures. The CPR established its own paramilitary units, styled as the Croatian Defense Forces (CDF), which were reportedly active in parts of Bosnia after the outbreak of war. As Boban moved to solidify his control, tensions between the CDC and CDF mounted, resulting in occasional firefights and culminating in the ouster or absorption of CDF units by the much more powerful CDC structure with the full backing of Zagreb.

The position of the Zagreb government with regard to the status and integrity of Bosnia has been contradictory. On one hand, Croatia recognized the republic's independence and territorial integrity in April 1992 and offered Sarajevo a formal military alliance. On the other hand, various incidents indicated that Tudjman and Boban had secretly planned to divide the republic. For instance, in March 1991, Tudjman and Serbian president Milošević met clandestinely in Karadjordje in Serbia to discuss the division of Bosnia-Herzegovina between the two republics. In May 1992, Boban met with Karadžić in Graz, Austria, to deliberate on Bosnia's future. Since both leaders were collaborating with Tudjman and Milošević, respectively, the meeting was believed to have been engineered by the Croatian and Serbian presidents. Such allegations, however, were disclaimed by the Croatian government and by Boban; they pointed out that the meeting in Graz was one in a series sponsored by the EC.

In July 1992, Boban proclaimed a quasi-independent Croatian state within Bosnia-Herzegovina, styled as Herzeg-Bosnia, with its capital in Mostar. The territory claimed by Boban comprised a region of 30 municipalities in which Croats formed clear majorities, with planned extensions toward central Bosnia and the Posavina region in northern Bosnia. According to both Boban and Tudjman, the crisis in Bosnia-Herzegovina could be solved only by organizing the republic as a community of three constituent nations on a cantonal basis. The CDU leadership and the quasi government in Mostar promptly accepted the Vance–Owen plan in early 1993, which envisaged decentralizing Bosnia into ten self-administered provinces including Sarajevo. Under the proposals, each ethnic group would have been allocated three provinces. Croat leaders supported the planned territorial delineations primarily because they allocated more territory to the Croatian side than they already controlled militarily. But the partition of Bosnia-Herzegovina remained a particularly divisive issue among Croats in Bosnia-Herzegovina and in Croatia. Moderate parliamentary deputies, Croat members of the Bosnian presidency, as well as opposition parties in Croatia generally opposed outright partition principally on the grounds that it could set a dangerous precedent for the future partition of Croatia. Nonetheless, as the military situation deteriorated during the summer of 1993 and Sarajevo's authority evaporated, CDU and CDC leaders increasingly favored a three-way division of the country.[21]

MINORITY ORGANIZATIONS

Democratic Alliance of Albanians (DAA)
Demokratski Savez Albanaca (DSA)

The DAA was formed during the post-1990 election period and was based in Mostar in Herzegovina. It issued warnings on several occasions that any agreement on a new Yugoslav or Bosnian structure of equal nations would not be acceptable without the participation of legitimate Albanian representatives. The party maintained that if Albanians were not allowed to express their political will on an equal basis with the other Yugoslav nations, this would have unforeseeable implications for the whole of Yugoslavia. Several other smaller parties and associations were formed in Bosnia-Herzegovina to represent minority populations, including Albanians, Slovenes, and Montenegrins. However, their role during the armed conflict and the disintegration of Bosnia remained negligible.[22]

CHRONOLOGY

February 1990: The Assembly of Bosnia-Herzegovina passes a law allowing for the free formation of political parties.

July 1990: The Bosnian Assembly seeks to assert greater autonomy for the republic, but without making any definitive moves toward secession from Yugoslavia, by declaring Bosnia-Herzegovina a "democratic and sovereign state with full and equal rights for all its citizens."

October 1990: Serb leaders establish a Serbian National Council in Banja Luka, allegedly to protect the Serb nation's interests from Muslim extremism.

November 1990: Multi-party republican elections are held in Bosnia-Herzegovina for the 240-seat bicameral legislature, consisting of a Chamber of Citizens and a Chamber of Municipalities, as well as for the republic's collective presidency. The elections are dominated by three main political parties (the PDA, CDU, and SDP), each representing one of the main ethnic groups. Guided by strict election laws, the ethnic make-up of the Assembly and the collective presidency closely mirror the republic's demographic proportions. Alija Izetbegović, head of the Muslim PDA, is chosen as president of the collective presidency on a rotational basis. A Croatian, Juro Pelivan, is chosen as prime minister, and a Serb, Momčilo Krajisnik, is selected as speaker of the Assembly. The PDA, CDU, and SDP agree to form a coalition government as no one party obtains a clear majority in the Assembly.

February 1991: The PDA and CDU agree on a proposal to assert the full sovereignty of the republic and to give Bosnian laws precedence over all Yugoslav laws. The SDP rejects the proposal, furthering the ethnic and political division in the republican government over the issue of Bosnian independence. Serb leaders claim that independence and secession from Yugoslavia would threaten the status of Serbs in Bosnia-Herzegovina, forcing them into "minority status."

April 1991: Serb leaders propose dividing the republic into economic regions, with each ethnic group controlling its own economic and political interests. Croatian and Muslim leaders reject the proposal on the grounds that it would facilitate Serbian separatism and annexation of Bosnian territory. A Serb Community of Krajina is declared in western Bosnia, comprised of 14 municipalities in which Serbs form a majority of the population; the area is later renamed an Autonomous Region.

September 1991: Serb leaders announce the creation of the Serb Autonomous Regions of Eastern and Old Herzegovina, comprised of eight Serbian municipalities in southeastern Bosnia. Three more autonomous regions are subsequently established. Armed "volunteer units" are formed by local Serb police forces and SDP radicals to "protect Serbian autonomy." Muslim and Croatian leaders condemn the moves as illegal and provocative.

October 1991: The PDA and the CDU sponsor a memorandum on sovereignty and neutrality for the republic, which is adopted by the Bosnian Assembly. SDP members walk out of parliament in protest and refuse to recognize the declaration, claiming that it is illegal because it violated a December 1990 agreement among the three parties on consensus in decision making.

November 1991: The SDP holds a retaliatory referendum asking Bosnian Serbs if they would prefer to remain in an integral Yugoslav state; this possibility is overwhelmingly affirmed by Bosnian Serb voters. Muslim and Croat leaders assert that the referendum is one in a series of acts, supported by the Milošević regime, paving the way toward a political crisis and armed warfare. A Croatian Community of Herzeg-Bosnia is established from 30 Croatian municipalities in western Herzegovina and central Bosnia, and a Croatian Community of the Bosnian Sava Valley is created from 8 Croatian municipalities in northern Bosnia. Croatian leaders claim the establishment of these areas is primarily a protective measure in the face of Serbian moves toward secession. They maintain that the new autonomous entities will recognize the government in Sarajevo only if Bosnia maintains its sovereignty from the Yugoslav federation.

January 1992: Four Croatian municipalities are joined to create a third Croatian Community of Central Bosnia. The self-declared Serb Assembly in Bosnia claims that it is entitled to control 60 percent of the republic's territory; it undertakes additional steps to create separate Serb security forces and governmental institutions within the republic's "autonomous areas." Slovenia and Croatia are recognized as independent sovereign nations by the international community. Despite meeting most of the EC requirements, Bosnia-Herzegovina does not receive recognition because the government has not elicited the opinion of its citizens. The Bosnian presidency makes preparations for a referendum, slated for February and March 1992. Serb deputies storm out of the Assembly in protest.

February 1992: The Serb Assembly adopts a constitution of the Serbian Republic of Bosnia-Herzegovina.

March 1992: In all, 63.4 percent of eligible voters participate in a referendum concerning the status of the republic, and 99.7 percent of those participating respond affirmatively to the question "Do you support a sovereign and independent Bosnia-Herzegovina?" The SDP and the Serbian Assembly, presided over by Radovan Karadžić, declare the process illegal and encourage all Serbian Bosnians to boycott the referendum.

April 1992: Bosnia-Herzegovina is recognized internationally as an independent state. The day after recognition, Serb leaders withdraw from the republican Assembly and all other governmental institutions, formally proclaim the existence of the Serbian Republic of Bosnia-Herzegovina, and underscore the legitimacy of separate administrative institutions.

May 1992: Outright war is launched by Bosnian Serb leaders in order to facilitate the division of the republic. The Bosnian government is glaringly unprepared for armed conflict and only after war breaks out does it formally establish the Army of Bosnia and Herzegovina.

June 1992: A state of war is officially declared by the Bosnian government in Sarajevo. Serbian forces seek to connect and expand the territories they control in western and eastern Bosnia. They conduct a campaign of "ethnic cleansing" to eradicate the non-Serb population in these areas. Based on overwhelming evidence, the Serb regime in Belgrade is accused of orchestrating the campaign. The United Nations mounts a humanitarian relief operation in Bosnia by dispatching approximately 7,000 troops to the republic.

July 1992: Mate Boban, newly selected president of the CDU, declares the establishment of Herzeg-Bosnia, an autonomous Croatian quasi state complete with separate administrative structures and its own capital in Mostar. The CDU's visible reversal in supporting an integral Bosnia fuels suspicions that Boban and Karadžić are forging a secret deal to divide Bosnia under the sponsorship of Zagreb and Belgrade. Croatian president Tudjman attempts to discredit the rumor by offering support for an independent Bosnia and makes overtures toward a possible Croatian-Bosnian military alliance.

August 1992: The Serb Assembly meets in Banja Luka and renames its own quasi state as the Serb Republic.

October 1992: In the United Nations, the Vance–Owen plan is presented as the most credible solution to achieve peace in Bosnia-Herzegovina. The plan advocates the creation of an extremely decentralized state, with most powers granted to nine ethnically dominated provinces. The nine provinces, three for each ethnic group, would control all political and economic questions save foreign affairs, international trade, taxation, and national defense; these would remain in the hands of a weak central government based in Sarajevo. The agreement is immediately accepted only by the Croats, who stand to gain territory according to the provincial divisions envisaged in the plan.

January 1993: In an attempt to gain broader acceptance for the Vance–Owen plan, the power of the proposed central government is diluted even further. Some observers charge that the plan could work only if the republic was transformed into a UN protectorate.

March 1993: Muslim leaders in Sarajevo, realizing that their military position is weakening, sign the Vance–Owen plan. Sarajevo believes that acceptance of the plan will facilitate increasing international pressure on the Serbs and will lead to some kind of UN military intervention. Serb leaders continue to negotiate, stalling the passage of the Vance–Owen plan, while simultaneously increasing their military offensives against Muslim-held towns.

April - May 1993: The Serbian Assembly organizes a referendum among Bosnian Serb voters on the Vance–Owen plan. The proposals are overwhelmingly rejected by the Serbian population, further delaying prospects for peace or a political settlement. The United States and its European allies fail to agree on an appropriate Western response to Serb defiance. They cannot reach consensus on bombing Serbian targets or lifting the arms embargo against the outgunned Bosnian forces. The republic descends into chaos as military forces on all three sides launch offensives to capture territory and drive out rival ethnic groups. The Vance–Owen plan becomes irrelevant. Over three million Bosnian residents are now dependent on the UNHCR relief mission.

June 1993: Serb and Croat leaders, with the connivance of Belgrade and Zagreb, finalize a new plan for the division of Bosnia-Herzegovina into three ethnic provinces. The plan is deemed unacceptable by the Bosnian presidency, which views it as tantamount to partition. The proposal receives the tacit support of the United Nations, whose representatives urge Sarajevo to accept an agreement, lest they face further bloodshed and loss of territory. The collective presidency becomes divided between the Muslim majority, which refuses to accept the plan, and some pragmatic Croat and moderate Serb delegates who believe the arrangement may be the last chance to salvage a peace settlement. The United Nations announces the establishment of six "safe havens" for entrapped Muslim civilians, including Sarajevo, Bihać, Tuzla, Srebrenica, Žepa, and Goražde. As the United

Nations is unwilling to defend these territories, Serb forces seek either their demilitarization or their surrender.

July 1993: Serbian troops, at times in collaboration with Croatian units, launch further offensives against government forces to open up new corridors connecting pockets of already controlled territory. Karadžić threatens an all-out offensive to defeat Muslim forces unless Sarajevo accepts the partition plan. The Bosnian government is on the verge of disintegrating, and the country is on the brink of a *de facto* partition. Presidents Milošević and Tudjman meet in Geneva to endorse the division of Bosnia-Herzegovina into three loosely confederated mini-states; Izetbegović is pressured by UN/EC negotiators to accept the new arrangement.

NOTES

1. Information on the Yugoslav census in Bosnia-Herzegovina in 1991 can be found in various official documents in Sarajevo, Belgrade, and Zagreb. See also G. Golubić, S.E. Campbell, and T.S. Golubić, "The Crisis in Bosnia-Hercegovina: Is an Ethnic Division of Bosnia-Hercegovina Desirable or Possible?" Center for the Study of Small States, Boston University, June 1992.

2. For useful background and history of Bosnia-Herzegovina, consult Richard F. Nyrop, ed., *Yugoslavia: A Country Study* (Washington DC: American University, 1982); Ivo Banac, *The National Question in Yugoslavia: Origins, History, Politics* (Ithaca: Cornell University Press, 1984); Dennison Rusinow, *The Yugoslav Experiment, 1948–1974* (Berkeley: University of California Press, 1977); Barbara Jelavich, *History of the Balkans* (2 Volumes) (Cambridge: Cambridge University Press, 1983); Paul Shoup, *Communism and the Yugoslav National Question* (New York: Columbia University Press, 1968); and Jozo Tomaševich, *The Chetniks: War and Revolution in Yugoslavia, 1941–1945* (Stanford: Stanford University Press, 1975).

3. Some details on the 1990 elections and the election campaign can be found in National Republican Institute for International Affairs, *The 1990 Elections in the Republics of Yugoslavia*, Washington, DC, 1991; D. Stanišić, "At Least One, At Most Seven," *Oslobodjenje*, Sarajevo, November 11, 1990, in Federal Broadcast Information Service, *Daily Report: East Europe*, FBIS-EEU–90–223, November 20, 1990; "Elections in Bosnia and Hercegovina," *Borba*, Belgrade, November 10, 1990; Milan Andrejevich, "Bosnia-Hercegovina: Yugoslavia's Linchpin," Radio Free Europe/Radio Liberty Research Institute (RFE/RL), *Report on Eastern Europe*, vol. 1, no. 49, December 7, 1990; and Milan Andrejevich, "Moslem Leader Elected President of Bosnia and Hercegovina," RFE/RL, *Report on Eastern Europe*, vol. 2, no. 3, January 18, 1991.

4. See Milan Andrejevich, "The Future of Bosnia and Hercegovina: A Sovereign Republic or Cantonization?" RFE/RL, *Report on Eastern Europe*, vol. 2, no. 27, July 5, 1991; and Milan Andrejevich, "Bosnia and Hercegovina Moves Toward Independence," RFE/RL, *Report on Eastern Europe*, vol. 2, no. 43, October 25, 1991.

5. Valuable discussions on ethnic questions and growing unrest in Bosnia can be found in Milan Jajcinović, "What Will Happen to Bosnia?" *Danas*, Zagreb, July 10, 1990, in Federal Broadcast Information Service/Joint Publications Research Service, *Daily Report: East Europe*, JPRS-EER–90–119, August 20, 1990; A. Kaurin, "Bosnia Too Has Gotten Its Kosovo," *Večernji List*, Zagreb, August 30, 1990, in *FBIS-EEU–90–172*, September 5, 1990; Nenad Kecmanović, "My Grave Is My Freedom," *Nin*, Belgrade, September 13, 1991; and Uroš Komnenović and Bogdan Ivanisević, "Noth-

ing Cheerful from the Drina," *Nin*, Belgrade, in *JPRS-EER–91–146*, September 30, 1991.

6. For Serbian moves toward autonomy, consult *Belgrade Domestic Service*, October 15, 1990, and October 16, 1990, in *FBIS-EEU–90–201*, October 17, 1990; *Tanjug*, Belgrade, April 29, 1991, in *FBIS-EEU–91–084*, May 1, 1991; *Tanjug*, Belgrade, June 27, 1991; Zoran Odić, "Constitutional Occupation of Bosnia-Hercegovina," *Oslobodjenje*, Sarajevo, October 2, 1991; *Tanjug*, Belgrade, September 13, 1991; *Tanjug*, Belgrade, October 22, 1991, in *FBIS-EEU–91–205*, October 23, 1991.

7. Discussions on the Croat position can be found in Goran Moravček, "The Opening of the Croatian Question," *Delo*, Ljubljana, March 9, 1991; *Radio Croatia Network*, Zagreb, November 18, 1991, in *FBIS-EEU–91–223*, November 19, 1991; K. Kozar, "Self-Organization of the Sava Valley and Herceg-Bosnia," *Oslobodjenje*, Sarajevo, November 20, 1991; Radovan Pavić, "Fantasy Becomes Reality," *Danas*, Zagreb, June 11, 1991, in *JPRS-EER–91–094*, June 28, 1991; and published material by Vlado Pogarčić, Foreign Affairs Advisor to the President of the Croatian Community of Herceg-Bosnia, Mate Boban, "Why the Croatian Community of Herceg-Bosnia Was Founded," July 1993.

8. See *Borba*, Belgrade, May 27, 1991; *Tanjug*, Belgrade, July 17, 1991; *Tanjug*, Belgrade, July 31, 1991; and Patrick Moore, "The Islamic Community's New Sense of Identity," RFE/RL, *Report on Eastern Europe*, vol. 2, no. 44, November 1, 1991.

9. Consult the Commission on Security and Cooperation in Europe, *The Referendum on Independence in Bosnia-Hercegovina, February 29–March 1, 1992*, Washington, DC, March 12, 1992.

10. See V. Janković and A. Borden, "National Parties and the Plans for Division," *Balkan War Report*, London, no. 16, November–December 1992.

11. For early reports on the war in Bosnia-Herzegovina see Milan Andrejevich, "Bosnia and Hercegovina: In Search of Peace," RFE/RL, *Research Report*, vol. 1, no. 23, June 5, 1992; and material from the Institute for Strategic Research, "Kapetan Hajro," Sarajevo, 1992 and 1993.

12. Military estimates of the contending forces are taken from Milan Vego, "The Army of Bosnia and Hercegovina," *Jane's Intelligence Review*, February 1993, and from private sources in Zagreb, Belgrade, and Ljubljana. See also D. Pusonjić, "New Detachments on Zelengora," *Borba*, Belgrade, September 13, 1991, in *JPRS-EER–91–145*, September 27, 1991.

13. See Janusz Bugajski, "Bosnian Blunders," *The World & I*, vol. 7, no. 11, November 1992. For reports on atrocities perpetuated primarily, but not exclusively, by Serb militias, check Helsinki Watch, *War Crimes in Bosnia-Hercegovina*, New York, August 1992; *Country Reports on Human Rights Practices for 1992*, Department of State, Washington, DC, February 1993; and "The Ethnic Cleansing of Bosnia-Hercegovina," Committee on Foreign Relations, U.S. Senate, Washington, DC, August 1992. See also Filip Svarm, "War Crime: Fighting to the Last Booty," *Vreme*, Belgrade, March 8, 1993, in *FBIS-EEU–93–065*, April 7, 1993; Kresimir Meler and Mirjana Glusac, "Rape as a Means of Battle," *Delo*, Ljubljana, February 23, 1993, in *FBIS-EEU–93–054*, March 23, 1993; Patrick Moore, "Ethnic Cleansing in Bosnia: Outrage But Little Action," RFE/RL, *Research Report*, vol. 1, no. 34, August 28, 1992.

14. A useful analysis of the Vance–Owen plan is contained in an article by Teodor Geršak originally published in the Slovene *Obrambo* in February 1993 and republished as "Paper Solutions Move Across the Ocean," *Ljiljan*, Zagreb, March 15, 1993, in *FBIS-EEU–93–077*, April 23, 1993. For a valuable overview of political fragmentation and Western involvement, see Robert M. Hayden, "The Partition of Bosnia and Hercegovina, 1990–1993," RFE/RL, *Report on Eastern Europe*, vol. 2, no. 22, May 28, 1993.

15. Discussions on the partition plan can be found in Duško Topalović, "Creation of a Corridor-State," *Danas*, Zagreb, June 28, 1993, in *FBIS-EEU–93–123*, June 29, 1993.

16. *Tanjug*, Belgrade, March 27, 1990, in *FBIS-EEU–90–060*, March 28, 1990; interview with Alija Izetbegović by Azra Kaurin, *Večernji List*, Zagreb, June 3, 1990, in *FBIS-EEU–90–113*, June 12, 1990; *Oslobodjenje*, Sarajevo, October 23, 1990, in *FBIS-EEU–90–210*, October 30, 1990; *The 1990 Elections in the Republics of Yugoslavia*, National Republican Institute, Washington DC, 1991; *Tanjug*, Belgrade, April 28, 1991, in *FBIS-EEU–91–082*, April 29, 1991; Fahrudin Radončić, "Goodbye, Bosnia," *Danas*, Zagreb, July 2, 1991, in *JPRS-EER–91–107*, July 19, 1991; *Tanjug*, Belgrade, August 16, 1991, in *FBIS-EEU–91–159*, August 16, 1991; "Can Bosnia Be an Islamic State, Asks the Sarajevo Weekly Ekspres 071: New Story on an Old Dilemma," *Borba*, Belgrade, May 27, 1991, in *JPRS-EER–91–089*, June 21, 1991; and interview with Bosnian presidency member Mirko Pejanović by Zdravko Latal, "On Conflicts in the Presidency," *Delo*, Ljubljana, June 17, 1993, in *FBIS-EEU–93–130*, July 9, 1993.

17. *Tanjug*, Belgrade, October 10, 1990, in *FBIS-EEU–90–198*, October 15, 1990; M. Lučić, "Without Islam for Political Purposes," *Borba*, Belgrade, September 27, 1990, in *FBIS-EEU–90–199*, October 15, 1990; *Tanjug*, Belgrade, July 31, 1991, in *FBIS-EEU–91–148*, August 1, 1991; *Tanjug*, Belgrade, August 16, 1991, in *FBIS-EEU–91–159*, August 16, 1991; *Tanjug*, Belgrade, August 19, 1991, in *FBIS-EEU–91–161*, August 20, 1991; interview with Adil Zulfikarpašić by Semra Saračević, "Izetbegović Is Worse Than the Muslims' Worst Enemy!" *Globus*, Zagreb, February 23, 1993, in *FBIS-EEU–93–059*, March 30, 1993.

18. See the interview with Armin Pohara by Andrej Rora, "We Offer Survival to the Muslim People," *Vjesnik*, Zagreb, May 25, 1993, in *FBIS-EEU–93–104*, June 2, 1993.

19. *Tanjug*, Belgrade, July 12, 1990, in *FBIS-EEU–90*; "Can Bosnia Be an Islamic State, Asks the Sarajevo Weekly Ekspres 071: New Story on an Old Dilemma," *Borba*, Belgrade, May 27, 1991, in *JPRS-EER–91–089*, June 21, 1991; *Tanjug*, Belgrade, July 31, 1991, in *FBIS-EEU–91–148*, August 1, 1991; *Radio Service Network*, Sarajevo, October 14, 1991, in *FBIS-EEU–91–200*, October 16, 1991; interview with Radovan Karadžić by Jovan Janjić, *Nin*, Belgrade, January 10, 1992, *FBIS-EEU–92–020*, January 30, 1992.

20. Milena Dražić, "Could Prince Tomislav Become Duke of Western Serbia: I Would Accept If It Would Not Divide the Serb Nation," *Borba*, Belgrade, May 19, 1993, in *JPRS-EER–93–055-S*, June 16, 1993.

21. Milan Andrejevich, "Bosnia-Hercegovina: Yugoslavia's Linchpin," RFE/RL, *Report on Eastern Europe*, December 7, 1990; *Radio Belgrade Network*, Belgrade, March 31, 1992, in *FBIS-EEU–92–063*, April 1, 1992; *Tanjug*, February 12, 1992, in *FBIS-EEU–92–031*, February 14, 1992; "War Crimes in Bosnia-Hercegovina," *Helsinki Watch Report*, prepared by Human Rights Watch, August 1992.

22. *Tanjug*, Belgrade, January 8, 1991, in *FBIS-EEU–91–006*, January 9, 1991.

2

Croatia

POPULATION

According to the April 1991 Croatian census, out of a population of 4,760,344, Croats formed 77.9 percent or 3,763,356, while Serbs constituted the largest minority numbering 581,663 or 12.16 percent of the total.[1] Prior to the outbreak of armed hostilities in the summer of 1991, the majority of Serbs lived in Zagreb and other larger towns. They constituted an absolute or relative majority in only 11 out of 115 Croatian municipalities along the border with Bosnia-Herzegovina, including Knin, Donji Lapac, Gračac, Obrovac, Benkovac, Titova Korenica, Vrginmost, Vojnić, Glina, Kostajnica, and Dvor, where they totaled a little under 150,000 inhabitants. These were the Krajina territories that became the center of the Serb-Croat war in 1991 after local Serb guerrillas declared their independence from the new Croatian state and expelled tens of thousands of resident Croats. According to official estimates, by early 1992, when the conflict subsided, over 10,000 people had perished or disappeared in the war and over a quarter of a million had been expelled or fled their homes. In addition, there was evidence that Serbs from other parts of the former Yugoslavia were resettled and moved into abandoned Croat homes. The demographic structure in the affected municipalities was thereby significantly altered as they became purely Serbian enclaves. Serb numbers outside the Krajina continued to shrink as numerous families left Croatia for fear of intimidation; by the close of 1992, only about 150,000 Serbs were believed to be left in areas under Croatian control.

The war in neighboring Bosnia-Herzegovina, which erupted in March 1992, also directly affected Croatia, as over half a million refugees, mostly Muslims and Croats, fled the republic to seek shelter and protection. This inflow overburdened the already strained Croatian economy, which lost billions of dollars as a result of the collapse of its tourist trade along the Dalmatian coast and the widespread destruction of towns, villages, and infrastructure. By the close of

Croatia: Population (1991)

Ethnic Groups	Number	% of Population
Croats	3,736,356	78.10
Serbs	581,663	12.16
Yugoslavs	106,041	2.22
Muslims	43,469	0.91
Slovenes	22,376	0.47
Hungarians	22,355	0.47
Italians	21,303	0.46
Czechs	13,086	0.27
Albanians	12,032	0.25
Montenegrins	9,724	0.20
Roma	6,695	0.14
Macedonians	6,628	0.14
Slovaks	5,606	0.12
Ruthenians	3,253	0.07
Germans	2,635	0.06
Ukrainians	2,494	0.05
Smaller Minorities	4,080	0.08
Regional Affiliation	45,593	0.95
No Affiliation	73,376	1.53
Unknown	62,926	1.32
Total Minorities	1,047,909	21.90
Total Population	4,784,265	100.00

1992, the total number of displaced persons and refugees from Bosnia-Herzegovina and various parts of Croatia reportedly numbered close to half a million and Zagreb continued to appeal to the international community for more substantial humanitarian assistance.

Croatia also contained smaller ethnic minorities scattered in various parts of the republic. The more substantial groups included 43,469 Muslims, 22,376 Slovenes, 22,355 Hungarians, 21,303 Italians, 13,086 Czechs, 12,032 Albanians, 9,724 Montenegrins, 6,695 registered Roma (Gypsies), 6,628 Macedonians, 5,606 Slovaks, 3,253 Ruthenians, 2,635 Germans, and 2,494 Ukrainians. In addition to several smaller minorities, numbering under 1,000 each (Romanians, Russians, Poles, Jews, Bulgarians, Turks, Greeks, Austrians, and Vlachs), 106,041 people declared themselves as Yugoslavs, 73,376 declined to declare their ethnic affiliation, 45,593 provided a regional affiliation (Dalmatian, Istrian), while the designation of 62,926 remained unknown. In seven Istrian municipalities, between 11 percent and 36 percent of the population declared themselves as Istrians.

HISTORICAL OVERVIEW

After losing their independent status in the twelfth century, the Croats fell under Hungarian and then Austrian Habsburg control for the next 800 years.[2] Turkish armies pushed into Croatian territories during the sixteenth century and captured most of the border regions. At the end of that century, the Habsburg emperor established a military frontier province along the Croatian-Bosnian borderlands where soldier-peasants were freed from feudal duties in exchange for military service. The province was extended southward and eastward after more Croatian territory was recovered from the Turks at the close of the seventeenth century. These regions were settled by large numbers of Serbs who migrated to the empire in order to escape Ottoman oppression. The descendants of these Serbs were later to become a source of conflict with the Croat government. Portions of the Croatian-inhabited lands also fell under French and Italian control for varying periods of time, particularly along the Dalmatian coast.

Croatian nationalists attempted to obtain greater regional autonomy under the Habsburgs but were thwarted by Hungarian and Austrian ambitions throughout the nineteenth century. Croatian activists were also at the forefront of the Yugoslav movement intent on uniting the south Slav peoples in one independent state. With the defeat of Austria and Germany during World War One and the disintegration of the Ottoman Empire in the Balkans, a new Kingdom of Serbs, Croats, and Slovenes emerged at the end of 1918. During the 1920s, Croatian leaders grew increasingly dissatisfied with Serbian domination and growing administrative centralization in the new state. In 1929, the Serbian King Alexander abolished the first constitution and introduced a monarchical dictatorship in which political parties were banned, freedom of speech and association were curtailed, and local councils were abolished. The country's name was changed to the Kingdom of Yugoslavia, and the historic provinces were reorganized into nine new regions. As a result of these reforms, Croatian opposition to Serbian policy accelerated. Although Belgrade restored some measure of pluralism during the 1930s, these moves failed to satisfy rising Croatian nationalism.

The Serbian king was assassinated by Macedonian nationalists in France in 1934; the gunmen were reportedly in the pay of exiled Croatian fascists. The new Serbian regent, Prince Paul, tried to appease the Croats by uniting several districts containing predominantly Croatian populations with central Croatia and Dalmatia. The new province was provided with a separate legislature and extensive administrative autonomy, but Croatian resentment against Belgrade continued to simmer. Yugoslavia's relations with Nazi Germany deteriorated at the opening of World War Two. Under pressure from Berlin, Yugoslavia was forced to join the Axis camp, but following a coup in Belgrade, King Peter's new government declared that Yugoslavia would not be drawn into the war. In April 1941, the Axis powers invaded and quickly overran Yugoslavia. The country was partitioned among several neighboring powers. Serbia was placed under German military occupation and a quisling government. Meanwhile, Croatia was proclaimed as an independent state by the *Ustaša* fascist regime; its leaders had returned to Zagreb from their exile in fascist Italy. The new government, headed by *poglavnik* (chief) Ante Pavelić, became a puppet of Nazi Germany.

Although most of Dalmatia was left outside its borders, Croatia did obtain virtually the whole of Bosnia-Herzegovina. The enlarged state contained a population of some 6.3 million, of whom about one-third were Serbs and a further one-third were Muslim Slavs. The *Ustaša* regime dealt brutally with the Serbian population; over 400,000 were slaughtered in their villages or in concentration camps, together with 20,000 Jews and several thousand Gypsies. The fascist authorities also engaged in forced Serbian conversions to Catholicism and in mass expulsions of Serb villagers. The mountainous territory of Bosnia-Herzegovina became the main battleground between Croatian *Ustaše, Serbian nationalist Četnik* forces, and Communist *partizan* guerrilla forces. Tito's *partizani* endeavored to appeal to all ethnic groups and obtained assistance from the Allies because of their more effective resistance to Nazi rule than the other Yugoslav factions. As the German and Italian armies retreated from Yugoslavia, the Croatian state collapsed and Communist leader Marshal Broz Tito seized power in Belgrade. The Communists dealt severely with the various nationalist forces and imposed a Stalinist one-party dictatorship at the close of the war.

The Communist regime abolished the monarchy and proclaimed the reconstituted state as the Federal Peoples Republic of Yugoslavia. Under the 1946 constitution, six republics were established, corresponding roughly to national-ethnic criteria. Croatia was largely restored to its pre-war areas, while Bosnia-Herzegovina was transformed into a separate republic. Although the state structure was nominally federal, the powers of each republic were subordinated to the central government in Belgrade and to the Communist Party leadership. During the 1950s, the command economy was decentralized and a system of industrial self-management was introduced. In the 1960s, the political system was also liberalized: the activities of the secret police were curtailed, direct Communist Party supervision of state institutions was decreased, and greater autonomy was given to the republican governments and parliaments as well as to the republican branches of the Communist Party.

During the late 1960s, there was a rise in inter-republican conflicts based around ethnic, national, and regional issues. In 1967, several Croatian cultural organizations issued a declaration demanding the reinstatement of the Croatian literary language; they were vehemently attacked by their Serbian counterparts. Meanwhile, republican control over federal decision making increased through the Chamber of Nationalities in the Federal Assembly. The richer northern republics of Croatia and Slovenia also demanded greater economic decentralization and direct control over their republican budgets. This culminated in Zagreb's open opposition to "unitarist" trends emanating from Belgrade, which were viewed as a smokescreen for rising Serbian nationalism. Nationalist unrest escalated in Croatia in the early 1970s among both the Croatian majority and the Serbian minority. On several occasions this led to confrontations and violent clashes. The federal government attempted to defuse the situation by reducing the powers of central institutions. But nationalist Croatian groups escalated their demands for the republic's autonomy amidst increasing factional struggles within the Croatian Communist leadership itself. The unrest resulted in a major crackdown by Belgrade: hundreds of nationalist activists were arrested, Croatian educational and cultural institutions were cleared of potential dissidents, the Communist Party was purged, and Tito attempted to reestablish tighter controls within the League of Communists and over all public institutions.

Croatian self-assertiveness mounted again following Tito's death in 1980 amidst growing resentment against alleged Serbian political domination and economic exploitation. As Communist controls began to unravel during the 1980s, each of the Yugoslav republics pushed toward sovereignty. Preparations were made for multi-party republican elections, while former Communist politicians adopted nationalist positions in order to garner public support. Croatian nationalism was also spurred by the rise of Slobodan Milošević in Serbia, with indications that Belgrade was seeking to recentralize the federation. Croatia's first multi-party elections in April 1990 were won comfortably by the Croatian Democratic Union (CDU), a broad-based political movement whose main plank was the achievement of national sovereignty. Franjo Tudjman, a former Titoist general and the CDU leader, was elected Croatian president. When talks stalled within the federal presidency on restructuring and further decentralizing the Yugoslav state, Croatia held a referendum on independence in late 1990. An overwhelming majority of voters cast their ballots in favor of separation from Yugoslavia. As the federal government began to fracture and Serbia assumed an increasingly obstructionist position, the authorities in Zagreb pushed toward political "disassociation" from Yugoslavia and declared Croatia's independence in June 1991.

With Croatia moving toward separation, leaders of the large Serbian minority grew restless and claimed growing discrimination and persecution in the new state. The restoration of Croatian national insignia and the reorganization of the republican bureaucracy and security forces alarmed many local Serbs. Hundreds of Serbs reportedly lost their jobs: Croat leaders claimed that this was because they held a preponderant number of positions under the Communist system, while Serbs charged deliberate ethnic discrimination by Zagreb. When Croatian authorities began to reorganize the republican security forces, Serb policemen refused to surrender their weapons. Leaders of Serb political groups also began to demand their own territorial autonomy, especially in areas where Serbs formed compact majority communities. Belgrade and local Serb spokesmen asserted that if Croatia gained its independence then it would stand to lose about a quarter of its territory where Serbs outnumbered Croats: this was primarily in the Krajina area—the old military frontier region. Zagreb was not opposed in principle to granting cultural autonomy to the Serbs but remained convinced that steps toward territorial self-determination were orchestrated by the Milošević regime in collusion with local radicals in order to undermine and fracture the Croatian republic.

Conflicts escalated throughout 1991 after local Serb policemen and guerrillas declared an autonomous region in the border region next to Bosnia and proceeded to eliminate representatives of the Croatian administration. Slovenia and Croatia declared their independence in June 1991, a move that provoked outright rebellion in the Krajina region. While federal government institutions remained paralyzed, the Yugoslav People's Army (YPA, the remaining intact federal institution) staged a partial crackdown in Slovenia and saturated Croatian territory with troops and weapons. Following its failure to subdue Slovenia, the army leadership, in line with the Serb government program, armed and supported Serbian guerrillas as they expanded and consolidated their control over approximately one-quarter of Croatian territory. Their long-term aim was to link these regions to a new Serb-dominated Yugoslavia.

Despite the war raging on its own territory, Croatia reaffirmed its declaration of independence in October 1991 and negated all Yugoslav federal jurisdiction in the republic. The armed conflict continued as Serb guerrillas and Yugoslav army troops linked up several autonomous enclaves to create a separately administered Serbian state encompassing eastern Dalmatia, Lika, Banija, Kordun, western and eastern Slavonia, western Syrmia (Srem), and the Baranja region. The new entity was declared as the Republic of Serbian Krajina. Although all sides eventually agreed to allow United Nations peacekeepers into Croatia, there was little indication that any of the captured areas would be surrendered by Serb guerrillas. The United Nations established a peace-keeping presence in four sectors of occupied Croatian territory and also patrolled the "pink zones" or neutral areas demarcated between the two protagonists. But it proved unable to complete its mandate, including the restoration of the prewar demographic structure, the disarming of Serb paramilitaries, and the reestablishment of a multi-ethnic police force in preparation for the return of Croatian authority. Even though Croatia obtained international recognition in early 1992, the government did not have the resources or opportunity to regain its lost territories forcefully.

In the general elections of August 1992, the Croatian Democratic Union retained its power but citizens in Serb-held areas could not participate in the balloting. The Tudjman government was charged with maintaining authoritarian controls over most aspects of public life. It responded by claiming that in conditions of war it was unrealistic to launch an extensive economic reform program and allow unfettered criticism of the government in the mass media. It also pointed out that political pluralism had been reestablished in the country as dozens of parties and associations were allowed to operate. Increasing political tensions, serious economic decline, and frustration over the inability of the United Nations to restore Croatia's occupied territories precipitated a new round of conflict in early 1993 when Croatian forces attempted to recapture a key bridge linking central Croatia with the Dalmatian coast. The prospects of another military confrontation accelerated in June 1993 when Serb leaders in Croatia abandoned peace talks with the Croat side and held a referendum on the unification of the Serb Krajina Republic with the Serb Republic in Bosnia.

OFFICIAL POLICIES

When Croatia held its first multi-party elections in April 1990, Yugoslavia's attention was once again focused upon the unresolved nature of the country's national question. More than 1,700 candidates vied for 356 seats in Croatia's tricameral legislature in a set of elections that would shape the future of Croatia's status within Yugoslavia. The elections were essentially a contest among three entities: the Croatian Democratic Union (CDU), the Party for Democratic Change (formerly the Communist Party), and the centrist National Coalition for Understanding, composed of the five major liberal parties—the Croatian Social Liberal Party, the Social Democratic Party, the Democratic Party, the Christian Democratic Party, and the Croatian Peasant Party—and a number of smaller groupings, including the Croatian Peace Party, the Democratic Alliance of Albanians in Croatia, and the Muslim Democratic Party. Additionally, several organizations stood outside these coalitions, including the Serbian Democratic Party and the Green Party. The voting was considered to be relatively fair by outside observers, and the final tabulations showed that the CDU took 206 seats and won a clear majority in the 356-seat legislature. CDU president, Franjo Tudjman was elected as Croatia's president.[3]

When the CDU and President Tudjman were swept into power, it occasioned considerable alarm among Serbs in both Croatia and Serbia proper. Although the CDU was formed as a national movement with a broad political spectrum and portrayed itself as the champion of democratic reform and political moderation, it was avowedly nationalist and made little effort during the election campaign to acquire the support of the country's Serbian population. During the election campaign, Tudjman and his associates sought to transform nationalist sentiments into electoral support and consequently ended up making many ill-chosen and inflammatory statements. Tudjman not only claimed that the CDU would achieve national sovereignty for Croatia, but he also promised a string of controversial changes. He implied that the republican borders would need to be revised in order to draw together elements of the Croatian nation resident outside Croatia. He stated that the Muslims of Bosnia-Herzegovina did not constitute a separate ethnic group but were in actuality an integral part of the Croatian nation. He also called for the overhaul of the bureaucratic structure, which, he claimed, had extended too many important positions of power to Serbs in Croatia in numbers that were grossly unfair in proportion to their share of the population.[4]

Tudjman's pronouncements rang alarm bells among Serb leaders in Croatia and Belgrade alike, and the situation was made more tense by the context in which they were issued. As Communist control of Yugoslavia began to unravel in the late 1980s, an ideological struggle erupted over the structure of the state, and the ammunition for this war became the historical record. In particular, during 1988 the Serbian press and the Belgrade government's propaganda machine began to refocus attention on the atrocities of the *Ustaša* regime.[5] When the CDU reintroduced Croatia's traditional national insignia, their display was depicted as the revival of the wartime Independent State of Croatia. The Zagreb authorities simultaneously declared the Latin alphabet to be the country's official script and proceeded to remove signs bearing the Cyrillic script, an action widely viewed as a gratuitous and unnecessary provocation. Serb leaders also charged that non-Croats were being pressured to abandon their home villages. Finally, the government's decision to reorganize the republican bureaucracy and security forces cost hundreds of Serbs their jobs and suggested deliberate ethnic discrimination by Zagreb. Many local Serbs, keenly sensitized to the bloody episode of *Ustaša* rule during World War Two, perceived these acts to be the first steps toward the reintroduction of a new fascist regime. As a result, when Croatian authorities began to build an "ethnically pure Croatian guard" to take over the functions of the republican police and territorial defense forces, Serb policemen, particularly in Serb-majority municipalities, refused to be disarmed and replaced.

Growing tensions in the Krajina region culminated in Serb calls for territorial autonomy. In June 1990, the self-appointed Assembly of Knin announced the establishment of a Community of Serb-administered Areas in northern Dalmatia and Lika, a move that was promptly overturned as illegitimate by the Croatian Constitutional Court. In July 1990, the Serbian National Council was created; this body, led by Milan Babić, formally declared Serb autonomy at the end of September 1990. Subsequent steps toward secession included the introduction of the Cyrillic alphabet to administrative institutions in Knin and the discontinuation of tax payments to the republican government. On the military side, local police chief Milan Martić began to distribute weapons to Knin residents and other volunteers and quickly built up an irregular force of several thousand combatants.[6]

The political and military insurrection of Serbs in the Krajina region appeared to be fully supported by the Serbian authorities in Belgrade. The Yugoslav People's Army, in which 70 percent of the officers were either Serbs or Montenegrins and which was increasingly becoming a tool of the Milošević regime, in October 1990 actively began to support rebel Serbs in the Knin district whose leaders were calling for autonomy. The army clandestinely dispatched arms to Serbian rebels. The intricate planning behind this operation, in which trains carrying weapons were unexpectedly rerouted to Knin where local Serbs waited to unload the cargo, strongly suggested that Belgrade had been planning the Knin rebellion for some time before the outbreak of hostilities and was simply waiting for the appropriate opportunity.[7] Serbia's intervention on behalf of the Knin insurgents caused the authorities in Zagreb to view the Krajina Serbs more as puppets of Milošević than as citizens with legitimate concerns about their future status. As a result, the Tudjman government was at first reluctant to negotiate seriously with the Serbs and was especially unwilling to discuss the question of territorial autonomy, a concession that Zagreb calculated would fuel "Greater Serbian" irredentist pressures and further destabilize the Croatian regime.[8]

While Tudjman proceeded cautiously over the question of Serbian autonomy, Serb demands visibly accelerated. In July 1990, the president of the Serbian Democratic Party, Jovan Rašković, met with Tudjman to discuss the ongoing problems in Krajina. At that time, Rašković stated that the Serbs were interested neither in independence nor in annexation by Serbia but in an "autonomy of a modern type, the kind that exists in hundreds of places in Europe."[9] However, he did reserve the right to hold a referendum that would decide on the status of Krajina in the event of the breakup of Yugoslavia. Indeed, in August 1990 the Serbs staged a referendum on cultural and territorial autonomy that the Croatian authorities attempted to ban. The Serbs voted in favor of a rather vaguely defined autonomous status and shortly afterward established roadblocks and took up arms, ostensibly to defend themselves against expected reprisals by Croatian security forces.

The crisis between Croatia and Serbia initially came to a head in January 1991 after the Yugoslav defense minister asserted that no republic would be allowed to create paramilitary units outside the federal military structure. The Croatian legislature had approved constitutional amendments giving republican governments jurisdiction over territorial defense and foreign relations. An armed confrontation was narrowly averted in early 1991, when Zagreb agreed to demobilize its reserve militia forces although not its main National Guard contingents. Despite this partial compromise, tensions remained high. Croatia stood accused by the Yugoslav and Serbian authorities of creating illegal armed formations, of importing weapons from abroad, and of allegedly planning to sabotage Yugoslav army operations. Despite the resistance of the Serb population in Krajina, Croatia held a referendum on independence in May 1991. According to Zagreb, 83.56 percent of voters cast their ballots; of these, 93.24 percent voted in favor of Croatian sovereignty and independence with the right to enter into alliances with other republics. The secession of Slovenia seemed acceptable to the Serbian government, as it would strengthen Serbia's ethnic demographics and political position vis-à-vis the remaining nationalities. But the separation of Croatia proved much more problematic for Belgrade. The Milošević regime asserted that Croatia could theoretically leave Yugoslavia, but it could not take with it the large Serbian minority. He thereby implied that Zagreb's secession would provoke claims to Serb-inhabited territories in Croatia and other Yugoslav republics. This in turn would lead to the establishment of either a smaller Serbian-dominated Yugoslavia or a larger Serbian state. An independent although much reduced Croatia would also remain subject to pronounced political and economic pressure from Belgrade, as Serbia would become the strongest regional power.

The draft of the new Croatian constitution was opposed by leaders of the Serbian Democratic Party (SDP), who were dissatisfied with its lack of provisions for minority rights. In December 1990, the SDP-dominated Serbian National Council in Krajina announced that it was adopting a statute to establish a fully autonomous Serbian region before Zagreb passed a new constitution. The region was to include all territories in which Serbs constituted a majority, as well as neighboring municipalities where no single group predominated. The new authorities in the autonomous region were to assume responsibilities for judicial and policing functions independently of the Croatian state. At the end of December 1990, the Serbian Autonomous Region of Krajina was proclaimed and it incorporated ten municipalities in the Knin region adjacent to northern Dalmatia. Zagreb immediately annulled the decision, contending that it was contrary to the republican constitution, which provided no legal basis for forming autonomous districts within Croatia.

Serbia promptly accused the Croatian government of imposing a state of siege in minority areas through the creation of its own National Guard. It also charged Zagreb with anti-Serbian discrimination and of creating an "ethnocracy" based along war-time *Ustaša* lines. In fact, purges in the old Communist apparatus in Croatia displaced many Serbs who held prominent positions in the defunct system. This policy was depicted by the Yugoslav media in Belgrade as a racist policy designed to turn Serbs into second-class Croatian citizens. The Croatian president himself came under severe criticism both within and outside the republic for allegedly concentrating too much power in his hands, for enacting various press restrictions, and for maintaining exclusive control over defense policies. Zagreb justified such measures as temporary but essential to preserve national unity during a national emergency, especially in the face of mounting threats and pressures from Belgrade.

In February 1991, as the Serb-Croat conflict escalated at the republican level, the Serbian National Council in Knin declared the independence of Krajina from Croatia. The city of Knin was named as the region's capital, but the legality of the move was not recognized by Zagreb. In April 1991, the Krajina Executive Council adopted a declaration on separation from Croatia and on federation with Serbia. A few weeks later the decision was reportedly endorsed in a public referendum among Serbs in the region. Serb leaders in western and eastern Slavonia, Baranja, and western Syrmia (Srem) also sought to link up with Krajina and in August 1991 proclaimed an autonomous region as an integral part of Serbian Krajina. The federal government, presumably in order to avoid international censure and not to be seen as breaking up the federation, did not formally acknowledge these decisions. It declared the creation of any new autonomous regions to be unconstitutional, particularly the secession of territory from one republic and its incorporation into another republic. The Serbian regime itself did not automatically approve the Krajina decision or accept the region as a constituent part of Serbia.[10]

At the end of June 1991, Croatia declared its independence and "disassociation" from Yugoslavia. Initially, the Yugoslav army focused its attention on crushing the Slovenian rebellion, but it also moved its troops and equipment to saturate Croatian territory. The bulk of the YPA forces that subsequently withdrew from Slovenia were also repositioned in various parts of Croatia. Having failed to subdue Slovenia, the army leadership put its weight behind the Serbian government program. This focused on one of two objectives: either to ensure that Zagreb remained in a centralized Yugoslavia controlled from Belgrade, or to carve away about a third of Croatia's territory and establish a "Greater Serbia" or a "Community of Serbian States" stretching to the Adriatic coast. Serb guerrillas in Krajina, with logistical and military assistance from the Yugoslav army, launched offensives across the republic to capture a contiguous tract of territory and to push out Croat residents from the contested zones. Reports also surfaced that Serbs were being resettled in some captured territories from other parts of the country in order to alter the demographic structure permanently.

During the summer and fall of 1991, Serb insurgents gained control over about a quarter of Croatian territory against the poorly armed Croatian National Guard. By December 1991, over 5,000 deaths were reported in the fighting, countless thousands were injured, and over a quarter of a million refugees had fled or been expelled from the conflict zones. With the expiration of the EC-brokered Brioni moratorium on independence in October 1991, the Croatian parliament restated the republic's independence and negated all federal laws and Yugoslav jurisdiction in Croatia. These moves neither forestalled the armed conflict nor ensured international recognition for the republic. Although the Serbian government expressed agreement for a UN peace-keeping force to enter Croatia, there was little indication that any of the captured territories would be surrendered by Serb guerrillas or by the Krajina government.

In order to obtain diplomatic recognition from the EC member states, the Croatian authorities moved to provide stronger guarantees of minority rights. Certain assurances were contained in Croatia's December 1990 Constitution, which declared all of Croatia's constituent nationalities as equal and their members were guaranteed freedom to express their nationality, language, and cultural autonomy (Articles 3 and 15); underscored that all citizens would enjoy all rights and freedoms regardless of race, color, language, sex, religion, political opinion, national or social origin (Article 14); and provided for the cultural autonomy of the members of all nations and minorities (Article 5). Nonetheless, serious concerns remained that the document was not explicit enough in institutionalizing minority rights and insuring against the domination of political life by ethnic Croats.[11] Serbian leaders charged that it was not forthright enough in recognizing and assuring the "collective rights" of the Serbian minority. While the human rights of all citizens were verbally guaranteed in the constitution, together with the cultural and educational rights of minorities, the issue of political or territorial self-determination was not clearly enunciated. Such omissions were condemned by Serbian leaders as a deliberate negation of specifically Serbian interests and an indication of growing Croatian repression.

As conflicts escalated, Croatian government officials came under mounting international pressure to make some clear concessions to the Serbian population and to underscore their commitment to minority rights. In July 1991, Zagreb offered an olive branch by agreeing to negotiate over the question of granting Serbs some form of limited political autonomy. Croatian officials proposed forming districts with a special status, in which the municipal Serbian authorities would have legislative powers and some control over the local police force, education, and culture. These were to include the areas of Knin, Krajina, Banja, Kordun, and parts of eastern Slavonia. But such proposals came too late to have any impact on the armed struggle, and the rebel government in Krajina rejected the status of an autonomous region within Croatia as a way of settling the crisis.

In December 1991, the Croatian parliament formulated, and eventually ratified in May 1992, a Constitutional Law of Human Rights and Freedoms and the Rights of National and Ethnic Communities or Minorities. This legislation (hereafter called the Constitutional Law) institutionalized within Croatian law the special position of minorities, with emphasis on the Croatian Serbs. The goal of the Constitutional Law was to amplify those provisions in the Croatian constitution and in Croatia's Charter on the Rights of the Serbs that dealt with the rights of minorities to cultural autonomy. The Constitutional Law guaranteed a special self-governing status for the Knin and Glina districts, proportional representation for all minority groups that comprised more than 8 percent of the population, the right to special education in one's own language upon request, and stipulations for international supervision of the implementation of the law.[12] The legislation would assign to Serbs almost complete internal governance of the two Krajina districts, including the authority to police and to raise taxes in the area, to run local courts, schools, and the media. The system of proportional representation required that Serbs be represented in parliament in numbers commensurate to their share of the population, thus ensuring that Serb deputies would have at least 12 percent of the *Sabor* seats. However, the law was largely irrelevant as long as the Serbian guerrillas refused to surrender their territories. Such legal initiatives and government pronouncements failed to reassure Serbian leaders, and in December 1991 a Republic of Serbian Krajina was officially proclaimed to include the autonomous regions of Krajina, Slavonia, Baranja, and Srem. The Krajina authorities were evidently prepared to weigh only three possible political options: unification with Bosnian Krajina as a separate federal unit within Yugoslavia, the creation of a Krajina republic in its own right within a federal Yugoslavia, or the transformation of Krajina into a component region of an expanded Serbia. All three options were unacceptable to Zagreb; the government refused to countenance any loss of territory, particularly as a result of armed aggression.

In January 1992, Croatia was officially recognized by the international community, after largely meeting a set of conditions laid down by the EC. In the same month, a UN-sponsored cease-fire came into effect. An agreement was reached between Zagreb, Belgrade, Yugoslav military commanders, and local

Serb authorities in Krajina to implant a UN peace-keeping force in the disputed territories; this was known as the Vance Plan, after the former U.S. secretary of state who helped to forge the agreement. The only persistent opposition to the UN proposals came from Milan Babić, the Serbian president of the Krajina region. He feared that Serbian militia forces would be disbanded and the local population subjected to Croatian control once the UN troops were withdrawn. Babić was accused by some of his colleagues in the Serbian Democratic Party (SDP) of creating an autocratic system in Krajina and abusing the rights of the Serbian community. In the internal power struggle that followed, Babić was replaced as president of Krajina by Goran Hadžić, an avowed moderate who benefited from the support of Belgrade. Although the Milošević government, facing mounting opposition to the war in Serbia, appeared to back away from a "Greater Serbia" policy, suspicions persisted that this was merely a tactical ploy to subdue domestic criticism and elicit international support for the beleaguered Yugoslav regime.

In January 1992, the UN Security Council adopted a resolution establishing the United Nations Protection Force (UNPROFOR) numbering 14,000 troops in four United Nations protected areas. UN troops were to act as a buffer between Croat and Serb forces in the Krajina area and the surrounding "pink zones." Under the UN plan, the Yugoslav army was to be withdrawn from Croatia and irregular Serbian and Croatian detachments were to be disarmed. Existing local authorities and police forces were to function on an interim basis under UN supervision, pending an overall political solution to the crisis. Croatian authorities and opposition parties expressed reservations about the UN mission, fearing that it could legitimize the separation of the Krajina region from Croatia and prevent Zagreb from retaking territory lost to the Serb militias.

Croatia's second multi-party elections took place in August 1992 at the presidential level and to the Croatian Chamber of Deputies. They were marred by instances of intimidation, an excessive degree of CDU influence over the mass media, irregularities in election procedures, inadequacies in civic education, incomplete voter registries, and the fact that elections could not be conducted in the Serb-held territories. Tudjman was reelected president for a five-year term with 56.73 percent of the vote; his nearest challenger, Dražen Budiša, leader of the Social Liberal Party, captured 21.87 percent. Opposition parties proved to be larger and better organized than in the first elections, but only six parties and one regional alliance received the minimum 3 percent of the vote necessary to capture a parliamentary seat. The CDU maintained its dominant position by gaining 85 out of 138 seats to the *Sabor*, aided as they were by the state bureaucracy, the media, and an electoral law that evidently favored the party in power.

Other pertinent results included a relatively reasonable showing by the regionalist party coalition, which gained 6 seats; the Social Liberal Party, which obtained 14 seats; and the Social Democratic Party (the successor to the Communists) capturing 11 seats; as well as serious setbacks for the ultra-nationalist

Croatian Party of Rights, which only managed five seats, as well as for smaller oppositionist parties including the Croatian People's Party and the Croatian Peasant Party. The Serbian National Party, which had been strongly supportive of Croatian independence, only gained 3 seats. The elections included voter and candidate lists for the occupied territories, although in several cases only a few hundred displaced people were able to elect deputies to constituencies in which Croatian authority did not function. The election law allocated 13 seats for Serbs in the lower house under the system of proportional representation for minorities: the individuals were designated by the Election Commission to officially represent the Serb population.[13] A government of "technocrats" was subsequently installed with the appointment of Nikica Valentić as prime minister in April 1993. Nonetheless, harder-line elements in the CDU and the army appeared to gain ascendancy during the summer of 1993, intent primarily on recapturing territory lost to the Serbs.

President Tudjman repeatedly made it clear that Croatia would not countenance any diminution of its territory. Ultimately, for the government and opposition alike, there could be no peace without the reintegration of the Krajina regions. Throughout 1992 and 1993, UNPROFOR stood as a buffer between Croatian and Serb forces, thus preventing Croatia from taking military action to regain these areas. Moreover, observers calculated that Zagreb's military position remained too weak to launch any major offensives even though it continued to stockpile weapons and established a more professional fighting force. The task assigned to UNPROFOR was to provide basic peacekeeping functions, to ensure the restoration of law and order, and to allow for the return of populations driven away by the fighting.[14] The UNPROFOR force, however, proved unable to complete its mandate of restoring the pre-war demographic structure, compelling the Serbs to lay down their arms, and permitting Croatian populations to return to their pre-war homes. As a result, there was a growing impatience among the Croatian leadership and even among the opposition parties over the presence of the UN force that appeared simply to freeze Serbian military gains in place. Tudjman stated that although Croatia's goal was to regain the Krajina region through peaceful means, Croatia could not tolerate the permanent occupation of its territory: "If it is necessary, Croatia can and will liberate every part of our territory."[15]

In order to regain lost regions, the Zagreb government needed to convince Serb leaders that their interests would be protected within the Croatian state, or it had to achieve victory on the battlefield. The former option called for a strategy of reconciliation that would limit the extent of post-war reprisals. In keeping with this concept, the Croatian parliament passed an Amnesty Act in October 1992 that guaranteed the safety of all citizens who were actively involved in the 1991 war, provided that they had not engaged in war crimes. This promise alone failed to encourage any Serb leaders to break ranks: a relatively moderate Serb faction in western Slavonia that appeared willing to negotiate with Zagreb was rapidly brought into line by hard-line leaders. Furthermore, the Serb authorities in Krajina employed a relatively effective self-policing mechanism based on fear and intimidation that tended to keep desertion rates low.

As Tudjman seemed unable to woo the Serbs from their barricades, he intended to reverse at least some of their military gains. This was evident in actions such as the liberation of the Maslenica bridge in January 1993, in which Croatian forces were able to recapture some territory and provisionally reopen traffic routes to the Dalmatian coast. While lacking the resources to launch a general offensive against Serbian Krajina, Zagreb may have calculated that it could successfully prosecute a more limited military campaign to regain some strategically key positions. Continuing Serb policies of "ethnic cleansing" in the occupied areas, coupled with frustration over the UN mission, were clearly contributing to building a momentum for intervention. As of early 1993, 800 Croats still lived in Knin itself and Serb paramilitary groups continued to intimidate locals to abandon their homes. The Zagreb government appeared to come under increasing domestic pressure to resolve the Krajina issue, while the failure of UN operations in both Croatia and Bosnia-Herzegovina to dislodge the Serb guerrillas from captured territories served to reinforce the war option in Croatia.[16] Negotiations between Zagreb and the Krajina authorities were stalled in the spring of 1993, and tensions again mounted when the local Serbian authorities organized a referendum in June 1993 in which over 98 percent of the electorate, of the 95.6 percent who voted, reportedly favored joining the area with Serbian Bosnia.

A power struggle seemed to be under way in Krajina between a more pragmatic faction supported by Milošević, which gave some indications that it would countenance trading full independence for far-reaching autonomy within Croatia, and more militant elements supported by radicals in Belgrade, who remained determined to move swiftly toward Serbian unification. Rumors also persisted that Tudjman and Milošević had discussed plans to exchange territory in Krajina and Bosnia. Following the Serb referendum, a commission was appointed to draw up a joint constitution of the Serbian territories west of the Drina River, but no announcement was made about imminent reunification. The perceptible moderation of the Serbian position led to another extension of the UN mandate in Croatia which had expired at the end of June 1993. The UN Security Council prolonged the mission for another three months, while Zagreb pledged that it would not agree to further extensions unless the Serbian side signed a binding agreement to implement fully the peace plan by disarming its militias, allowing for the return of refugees, and cooperating in setting a timetable for the restoration of Croatian authority. It appeared that the tug-of-war between Zagreb and Belgrade over Krajina would continue with no ultimate resolution in sight: neither side was prepared for a full-scale military conflict, but neither seemed serious in making meaningful concessions. The outcome in Krajina was also closely linked to the war in Bosnia, where Croatian-Serbian agreements on partition placed the Krajina issue temporarily on hold. The danger remained that with the consolidation of Croat and Serb control over Bosnia-Herzegovina, significant numbers of troops would be freed for combat duty in Croatia and Krajina.

It remained unclear as to what the CDU leadership believed the ultimate borders of Croatia should be. Although Tudjman opposed attempts by the Serbs to detach areas from Croatia and was putatively in favor of maintaining intact all internal frontiers of the former Yugoslavia, including the border with neighboring Bosnia, he has also asserted that the people of Bosnia must be given the right to decide by referendum in which state they preferred to live. In a February 1991 speech, Tudjman did not deny that a plan had been concocted to divide up Bosnia-Herzegovina between Croatia and Serbia, a rumor that has persistently circulated ever since. He noted at that time that Croatia maintained a special interest in the approximately 800,000 Croats who lived in Bosnia.[17] Such comments indicated that the CDU viewed portions of Bosnia-Herzegovina as properly belonging to Croatia. Furthermore, Croatian nationalists have claimed that the Bosnian Muslims did not constitute a separate nation with sovereign rights but were in reality an Islamicized branch of the Croatian nation. The Herzegovinian lobby in Zagreb has proved particularly tenacious in pressuring Zagreb to adopt a more combative stance in campaigning for the incorporation of western Herzegovina into Croatia. In addition, hard-line elements of the CDU were evidently intent on establishing a Croatian state in which Croat ethnicity would become a prerequisite for first-class citizenship and equal treatment in the country's political system. Such positions undermined the regime's commitment to a multi-ethnic society and laid the basis for ongoing tensions with Bosnian Muslims.

The Croatian-Bosnian relationship has also been complicated by the tremendous refugee burden that Zagreb has confronted. During 1992–93, more than half a million refugees fled Bosnia to find shelter in Croatia. This situation strained an already decimated Croatian economy that had lost billions of dollars as a result of the collapse of the Adriatic tourist trade. Without the resources to provide for these refugees adequately, Croatia attempted to manipulate citizenship and naturalization criteria in order to prevent Bosnians from permanently settling in Croatia. A relatively strict immigration policy came into effect: to obtain citizenship a person had to either be married to a Croatian citizen, be born in the territory of Croatia, or be a Croatian emigrant. Moreover, an individual needed to renounce his or her current citizenship, have at least five years of continuously recorded residence in Croatia, know the Croatian language and Latin alphabet, and through their behavior demonstrate "that they respected the legal order and customs in the Republic of Croatia and accepted Croatian culture."[18] The naturalization process remained lengthy and allowed for the possibility that individuals could be rejected on the basis of subjective judgments as to what constituted adherence to Croatian customs, language, and culture. The ambiguous criteria left open the possibility that officials could interpret the policy arbitrarily for members of different ethnic groups: ethnic Serbs or other minorities could be deliberately denied citizenship in order to further the state's ethnic homogenization. Furthermore, without citizenship individuals were not permitted to own property, obtain employment, or receive retirement pensions.

The process of effecting shifts in the demographic balance has been a recurrent theme in CDU ideology. For instance, Tudjman's 1990 inaugural address claimed that the policies of the last several decades had brought the Croatian national corpus into a state of demographic endangerment. These problems had to be combated by taking "urgent and purposeful steps with a view to both stemming the flow of our citizens leaving the country and increasing our birthrate."[19] Such assertions tapped into traditional Croatian nationalist ideas about reestablishing more extensive ties with the Croatian diaspora and reining in the number of Croatian guest workers. Tudjman's interest in such policies surfaced in proposals to negotiate with Romania over the resettlement of more than 20,000 Romanian Croats to the Istrian peninsula, a policy that could significantly alter the demographic balance in an ethnically mixed area.[20] Tudjman's emphasis on increasing the Croatian birthrate also signaled a desire to ensure the marginalization of certain minorities.

Some schisms have also appeared in Croatia on the basis of regional affiliation. In particular, there has been a growing tide of opposition to Zagreb's policies in several Istrian municipalities, including Rijeka and Pula. Istria, an ethnically mixed region that generated a large portion of Croatia's tourist trade, has been contested by Italy and Yugoslavia since World War One. Its mix of Italian, Croatian, and Slovenian cultures and its strong regionalist identity have contributed to stirring opposition to the CDU government. Opposition forces, including the Social Liberals and various regionalist movements, have polled successfully in the area, campaigning against Zagreb's political and economic over-centralization and Tudjman's penchant for power. The result of this has been a growing popular movement aiming at some form of regional autonomy, perhaps in a joint relationship between Slovenia, Croatia, and Italy.[21]

The war in Croatia has produced a legion of human rights abuses, including the summary execution of civilians and unarmed combatants; the torture and mistreatment of detainees; arbitrary arrests and disappearances; destruction of civilian property; and the killing of journalists covering the war. The most serious human rights abuses have been associated with the policy of "ethnic cleansing" undertaken primarily by Serb militants against non-Serb residents in the Krajina region. In its pursuit of ethnically homogeneous areas, Serb paramilitaries, with the complicity of local authorities, have conducted a campaign of intimidation, arrest, torture, and murder in order to force Croats to vacate their homes.[22] "Ethnic cleansing" has taken its toll in Croatia: by early 1992, about a quarter of a million people had been forced to flee their homes, whereupon Serbs from other parts of the former Yugoslavia were resettled and allowed to occupy abandoned Croatian houses. The demographic structure of several regions was thereby dramatically altered. For instance, about 20,000 Serb settlers were reportedly transferred to the Baranja region in eastern Croatia, thus dramatically altering the demographic structure: by mid-1992, Serbs constituted over 90 percent of the inhabitants as compared to about 25 percent before the war. The serbianization of these enclaves has not been reversed or even halted by the UN deployment, and Croatian patience with the UN forces has visibly diminished. As displaced Croats from Krajina have registered to vote in the Croatian elections, they have generated an increasing amount of support for the restoration of Serb-held houses to their original owners. Some of these voters helped to give the CDU its large margin of victory in 1992 and will predictably extend support to those parties that will guarantee to them the return of their homes.

Croatian paramilitaries have also engaged in atrocities against Serb civilians. It remained unclear whether the government in Zagreb has been unable or unwilling to control these violations. The forces most implicated in war-time offenses have been irregular formations such as the armed wing of the neo-fascist Croatian Party of Rights, styled as the Croatian Defense Force. Although the Croatian government prohibited the formation of paramilitary organizations and claimed by late 1991 that all former irregulars were under the command of the Croatian Ministry of Defense, the degree to which Zagreb actually exercised control over these units has remained highly ambiguous. Another disturbing development has been the harassment of critics of the Croatian government, whether Croats or Serbs, by individual extremists, policemen, and government officials. Members of the Serbian Democratic Party and veterans of the Yugoslav army have been especially targeted and accused of being spies. Some reports indicated that about 3,200 Serb homes were torched or bombed during 1992, evidently as reprisals for the "ethnic cleansing" of Croat residents in Krajina. The incidents evidently subsided during the course of 1993.

CROATIAN NATIONALISTS

Croatian Democratic Union (CDU)
Hrvatska Demokratska Zajednica (HDZ)

The Croatian Democratic Union has dominated the political life of independent Croatia. Billing itself as the "most Croatian of all parties," the CDU was established in Zagreb in February 1989, while Yugoslavia was still extant. It originally tried to present itself as the singular alternative to the old Yugoslav structure, and its program called for national sovereignty, free elections, and market reform. Led by the former Titoist army general and ideologist of the 1971 Croatian nationalist movement, Franjo Tudjman, the CDU drew support from across the political spectrum and was able to translate this endorsement into a sweeping victory during the April 1990 elections. Out of 356 seats in the Croatian Assembly, the CDU scored 206, the Communists and Socialist Alliance finished in second place with 90 seats, the Coalition for National Understanding gained 11, the Croatian Democratic Party 10, the Serbian Democratic Party 5, and the remaining seats went to independents. Tudjman was subsequently elected as president by the new legislature. At that time, the CDU claimed nearly half a million members with branches around the country; much of their political apparatus was simply appropriated from the former League of Communists.

In late 1990 and early 1991, Tudjman engaged in protracted negotiations within the federal presidency on restructuring relations among the six republics. Zagreb maintained that Croatia and Slovenia were paying the lion's share of the state budget and remained concerned over growing centralizing trends in Belgrade. However, even before the breakdown of negotiations over a new confederal arrangement, Croatia made important strides toward secession. The Tudjman administration began to purge Serb and Yugoslav loyalists from the bureaucracy and security forces, restored Croatia's historical state symbols, and held a plebiscite on independence in May 1991, in which the overwhelming majority of voters opted for full sovereignty. The outbreak of armed conflict with Serb guerrillas and the Yugoslav army in the summer of 1991 appeared to strengthen Tudjman's position and that of the CDU, which was depicted in the state-sponsored media as the prime defender of Croatian interests. However, Zagreb was not militarily prepared for the Serb-Yugoslav assault and lost over a quarter of its territory during the war. A cease-fire was put in place in January 1992 through the creation of a UN-protected zone, while the Tudjman government capitalized on the grievances of expelled Croats and the state of emergency to impose restrictions on media activities that were deemed unpatriotic. Observers also detected a growing personality cult around Tudjman, fostered by depictions of his critical role in regaining Croatian statehood. The CDU itself penetrated all the former Communist bureaucracies as a monolithic organization, controlling or supervising all major economic, cultural, educational, and media organs. The ruling party portrayed itself as the defender of Croatian statehood against the perennial Serbian threat, and prior to the August 1992 elections it endeavored to show that it had restored a marked degree of normality in the country.

The August 1992 parliamentary elections were marred by various irregularities, such as problems with voting lists, and by the impossibility of implementing voting procedures on Serb-held territory. Tudjman was returned to the presidency with 56.73 percent of the popular vote. The CDU maintained its dominant position in Croatia's lower house of parliament, the Chamber of Deputies, gaining 85 out of 136 seats with 43 percent of the popular vote. In elections held for the upper house in February 1993, the CDU also retained a nearly two-thirds majority, though defeats in certain opposition strongholds, such as Split, Rijeka, Pula, and Osijek, stripped the party of its aura of invincibility. Nonetheless, the CDU performed well in municipal elections, including in areas directly affected by the war.

The CDU leadership has viewed Croatia as a state of ethnic Croats, although it has recognized the need to deemphasize such assertions in its public proclamations. Furthermore, it maintained that the Croatian people extend beyond the current state borders, implying that Croatia's frontier with Bosnia-Herzegovina was not necessarily inviolable. Nevertheless, during 1992 Zagreb attempted to hold together a loose alliance with the Bosnian government against Serbian aggression, partly as a form of self-protection, partly to curry favor with the international community, and perhaps with a view to a future Croatian-Bosnian confederation. The CDU also actively promoted an expansion of the ethnic Croatian population, and some suspected that it was deliberately seeking to alter the demographic balance by attracting Croatian emigrants to return, placing tight stipulations on granting Croatian citizenship, and increasing the birthrate. While Croatia has provided shelter to a large number of Bosnian refugees, it has been slow in extending citizenship to Yugoslavs who are not of Croatian origin. The overall effect of these policies points to a long-term CDU interest in creating an ethnically homogeneous state.

Following the general elections, there were increasing signs of a rift in the CDU between a conservative nationalist faction led by Deputy Prime Minister Vladimir Seks and Defense Minister Gojko Šušak, and a more centrist-liberal wing. The latter, informally led by former Yugoslav president Stipe Mesić, called for greater press freedom and the curtailment of political party interference in the country's media. Observers believed that the liberal faction would probably attract three times the number of voters as the conservatives. Although there were no indications of an impending split, it was debatable whether the CDU could survive as a broad-based political movement until the next elections, particularly if stability were to return to the country and the Krajina question were to be resolved. Even though differences persisted in approaches to the Serbian issue, with some activists criticizing any prepared land swaps with Serbia, under essentially war conditions Tudjman was likely to prevail in keeping the Union together.[23]

Croatian Party of Rights (CPR)
Hrvatska Stranka Prava (HSP)

The Croatian Party of Rights was a modern revival of an organization founded in 1861 by Croatian nationalist Ante Starčević. The party was outlawed in the first Yugoslavia during the dictatorship of King Aleksander in 1929 and was revived in February 1990 under the leadership of Dobroslav Paraga, a former nationalist dissident. According to its general statutes, the CPR championed the "absolute sovereignty and national independence on the entire ethnic and natural territory of the Croatian people." According to its understanding, this "ethnic and natural territory" included the whole of Bosnia-Herzegovina and even parts of Serbian Vojvodina. The CPR therefore brooked no thought of compromise with Serb insurgents in Krajina and Bosnia. Instead, it openly advocated the creation of a Greater Croatia, which would extend the country's borders to include all of Bosnia-Herzegovina and parts of Serbia in line with its "historic frontiers" from the tenth century. Unlike the ruling CDU, the CPR rejected the idea of dividing Bosnia between Zagreb and Belgrade. Such proposals, it claimed, actually fueled "Greater Serbian" revanchism in Belgrade. Instead of allowing Serbia to expand, Paraga's group advocated reducing Serbia to its pre-1912 borders, and it claimed the Bosnian Muslims as an integral part of the Croatian nation who evidently converted to Islam during Turkish occupation.

The CPR remained strongly opposed to what it called the "cantonization" of Croatia that would be effected through the extension of autonomy to Serb-dominated regions, as specified in the Constitutional Law on the Rights of Minorities. Instead of unilaterally extending advantages to the Serbs, Paraga advocated defeating the insurgents in an outright war and bargaining from a position of strength. However, a war with the Serbs could not be conducted while the United Nations Protection Force stood as a buffer between the two sides. Since UNPROFOR had not succeeded in returning Serb-held territory to Croatian administration, the CDU demanded that UN contingents leave the country and permit Croatian forces to recapture the occupied lands. This policy was one of the chief CPR campaign planks during the August 1992 elections, when Paraga accused the Tudjman leadership of betraying Croatian interests by not engaging in an all-out war with Serb guerrillas. The party performed poorly in the ballot, capturing a mere five seats to the National Assembly: Paraga received only 5.4 percent of the vote in the presidential election.

The CPR has not limited itself merely to advocating victory in war and criticizing the CDU government for its lack of military preparation. Paraga's group also set up an armed wing, a paramilitary organization styled as the Croatian Defense Forces (CDF), *Hrvatske Oružane Snage* (*HOS*), which engaged in armed attacks against Serbian positions in Croatia and Bosnia. Officially, the Croatian government outlawed the formation of such paramilitary organizations and claimed that CDF forces (estimated to number between 300 and 2,000 troops) and other volunteer units came under the full control of the Croatian Ministry of Defense during late 1991. Paraga attacked the Tudjman regime for betraying both Croatia and Bosnia by arranging secret deals with Serbia to carve up Bosnia-Herzegovina. He claimed that the CPR supported Bosnian unitarism and independence; critics charged that Paraga envisaged this merely as a prelude to absorption by Croatia. In June 1993, Paraga and three of his associates were placed on trial in Zagreb, accused of forming a paramilitary organization to overthrow the elected government. The following month, the CPR was forcibly expelled from its Zagreb headquarters. Paraga had been previously acquitted in 1991 of armed rebellion against the state. It appeared that the Tudjman regime was intent on both reigning in opposition and displaying its determination to eliminate renegade armed units with contingents in Bosnia-Herzegovina.[24]

Several smaller Croatian nationalist parties were also formed before the republic's first multi-party elections and adopted a strong pro-independence stance. Moreover, after the collapse of talks on loosening the Yugoslav federation, most

Croatian parties came out in favor of secession from Yugoslavia. With the onset of independence and war in the summer of 1991, a number of parties adopted a critical stance toward the CDU government for its lack of preparedness in resisting the army-guerrilla assault and in some cases adopted a more forthright nationalist position. They included the Croatian Democratic Party (CDP), which held 10 seats after the first election but whose support base subsequently diminished when it failed to gain representation after the August 1992 balloting, the Croatian National Party (CNP), which scored 4 seats, and the Croatian Peasant Party (CPP), which captured 4 seats to the Chamber of Deputies in the August 1992 elections.

SERBIAN SECESSIONISTS

Serbian Democratic Party (SDP)
Srpska Demokratska Stranka (SDS)

The Serbian Democratic Party was formed in the town of Knin in late 1989. It was originally established to protect the interests of Serbs in Croatia during the breakup of Yugoslavia. Under the leadership of Jovan Rašković, the SDP sought to achieve an extensive guarantee of Serbian rights in Croatia. When the new Croatian government headed by Tudjman and the CDU came to power in April 1990 and began to display nationalist inclinations, Rašković and the SDP concluded that the Serbs in Croatia must secure some kind of institutionalized autonomy in order not to be summarily deprived of their rights. Although it was ostensibly committed to working within the parliamentary system to accomplish these goals, the SDP pulled its five elected representatives out of the Croatian Assembly shortly after the April 1990 elections and proceeded to rally support within the Serb community for more combative actions to assert Serbian autonomy. The SDP organized a mass rally in July 1990 in order to galvanize support for its calls for autonomy. Rašković pronounced that the demonstration constituted "a rebellion, an unarmed uprising," but underscored that the SDP would make every effort to avoid violent actions. The SDP leadership, however, with the evident support of Belgrade, was not interested in backing away from confrontation. Within several days, Rašković organized a referendum on political autonomy for the Serbs in the Krajina region. When Zagreb attempted to ban such a referendum, it touched off an armed confrontation between Serb gunmen and the Croatian authorities. The new SDP leader, Milan Babić, drew upon the party's close ties to Milošević and the Yugoslav People's Army in order to arm, equip, and train Serbian militias in Krajina. In June 1990, a self-proclaimed Serbian National Council was established, based in Knin and presided over by Babić; it functioned as an informal parliamentary body largely controlled by SDP activists.

According to the organizers of the August 1990 Serb referendum, nearly 100 percent of voters cast their ballots in favor of an extremely vague concept of Serbian autonomy. Bolstered by these results, the SDP announced that if Croatia separated from Yugoslavia then the Serbs in Croatia would secede to form their own independent state. The SDP was at the forefront of establishing the Serbian Autonomous Region of Krajina and later pushed for the region's annexation to Serbia proper. Babić and his associates centered their efforts on securing the independence of Serb-dominated regions and unilaterally declared the establishment of the Republic of Serb Krajina in December 1991. During this time, evidence also surfaced of a bitter power struggle among the Serb leadership in Krajina. Babić and his supporters in the SDP were seeking to consolidate their territorial gains and move rapidly toward unification with Serbia. By contrast, Milošević and his proxies in the Krajina calculated that such a move was premature and could both prolong the war in Croatia and precipitate international sanctions against the rump Yugoslavia. Milošević exerted intense pressure against the Krajina leadership and replaced Babić with loyalist Goran Hadžić as president of the Republic of Serbian Krajina. Hadžić displayed his willingness to reach an accord with Zagreb through UN mediation, and in January 1992 a UN-protected area was established in the occupied areas of Croatia. Babić asserted that a virtual coup d'état had taken place in which dissenters were excluded from decision making and only people benefiting from the full support of Belgrade remained in the Krajina administration.

The Assembly of the Republic of Serbian Krajina was composed of three parts: representatives of Knin Krajina, western Slavonija, and eastern Slavonija; Baranja; and western Srem. Although several parties were represented in the government, including the SDP and the Serbian Socialist Party (a branch of the SSP in Serbia proper), a normal parliamentary system did not function in the region but rather a civilian-military dictatorship. Although a relative peace was maintained in the area throughout 1993, tensions remained high as Zagreb was giving signals that it was intent on restoring its lost territories. In January 1993, Croatian forces launched an assault in the northern Dalmatian region and regained control over an airport and a key bridge linking central Croatia with the coast. Serb authorities used the occasion to remobilize their forces and initiate shelling of Croatian positions outside the occupied territories. In June 1993, the Krajina government held a referendum on linking the region with the newly carved Serb quasi state in neighboring Bosnia. Evidently, plans were being finalized to establish a joint assembly and a single government structure. The initiative was placed on hold during the summer of 1993 pending the outcome of negotiations between Zagreb and Belgrade on partitioning Bosnia-Herzegovina.[25]

REGIONALIST GROUPINGS

Dalmatian Action (DA)
Dalmatinska Akcija (DA)

This regionalist organization was formed in Split in December 1990 and therefore did not participate in the first Croatian elections. It remained a relatively small organization, claiming a membership of some 2,000 people by mid-1992 and led by President Mira Ljubić-Lorger and Secretary Radovan Kećkemet. The DA leaders asserted that Croatia consisted of several distinct regions including Dalmatia, Istria, Slavonia, and Lika that should be allowed to develop their specific economies, cultures, and regional self-governments. It claimed that the CDU and most of the opposition parties were Zagreb-centered and intent on maintaining a monolithic and centralized state. Ljubić-Lorger criticized Croatia's new administrative division into *županije*, describing them as offices of the central power that simply hierarchized the system of local administration. The *županije* evidently had little opportunity to take any significant economic decisions. Croatian nationalists have depicted the DA as anti-Croat separatists in league with militant Serbs intent on breaking up Croatia. DA leaders strenuously deny such charges and state that they simply wanted to restore greater regional decision making through, for example, budgetary control over culture and education. A regional assembly would also ensure closer Dalmatian links with the Alpine-Adria economic association, leaving Zagreb in control of defense, foreign policy, foreign trade, and the economic infrastructure.

According to DA spokesmen, a more autonomous Dalmatian region could purportedly also include much of the Serb-occupied areas of Knin Krajina, possibly offering an alternative to Serbian autonomy or separatism. The DA stressed that it was a multi-ethnic organization, considering regional issues more significant than questions of nationality. In the August 1992 general elections, the DA entered into an election coalition with Istrian, Rijekan, and Slavonian regionalists but was unable to gain any seats for Dalmatia in the National Assembly. DA spokesmen claimed that they were ignored by Croatian television during the election campaign and some of their candidates were harassed or threatened by the police. Moreover, they suffered from a debilitating shortage of funds, premises, and resources. They believed, however, that there was widespread latent sympathy for the DA's position; this would continue to grow if the Tudjman government became more authoritarian and if regionalists could offer an attractive and profitable alternative to central control. Tudjman's highly publicized opening of the Maslenica bridge in July 1993 was evidently designed not only to signal defiance of the Krajina Serbs but to indicate to Dalmatians that Zagreb was determined to reestablish normal communications with the region and to provide it with economic assistance.[26]

Istrian Democratic Assembly (IDA)
Istarski Demokratski Sabor (IDS)

The Istrian Democratic Assembly, established in February 1990, was headquartered in the city of Pula, with branches throughout the Istrian peninsula. Similarly to the DA, it believed that this region, one of the most developed in the former Yugoslavia, possessed a distinctive history, culture, and identity differentiating it from the rest of Croatia. IDA leaders claimed that Istrian identity was a symbiosis of Slavic, Latin, and Germanic cultures, and historically it had benefited from a large measure of autonomy. They contended that the region was unfairly deprived of its special status in post-war Yugoslavia, when Tito artificially divided the region between Slovenia and Croatia in order to assure the domination of Slavs over other ethnic groups. The IDA sought to restore Istria as an "inter-state region" and multi-ethnic unit without undermining the sovereignty of any neighboring state. In particular, it backed economic self-determination and the opportunity to deal directly with other "Euro-regions" in developing tourism and privatization. The authorities in Zagreb endeavored to discredit the IDA, claiming that its members were separatists in the service of Italian irredentists and Serbian agents. The IDA asserted that it had no radical or secessionist stream even though it encompassed a broad spectrum of political trends. Instead, it supported a form of "inter-governmental autonomy" or home rule with close contacts among Croatia, Slovenia, and Italy. The IDA remained troubled by what it considered to be excessive nationalism and ethnocentrism of the current Croatian regime; it felt that the regime's emphasis on nationality would serve to undermine the delicate multi-ethnic character of the Istrian region. It therefore tried to distance itself from decision making in Zagreb and avoided being drawn into the acrimonious debates over Croat-Serb relations.

In the August 1992 general elections for the House of Representatives, the IDA formed a loose coalition with Dalmatian Action, the Rijeka Democratic Alliance (RDA), and the List For Osijek (LFO), a small regionalist movement in eastern Slavonia that only had marginal influence in the region and was linked with the main opposition group, the Social Liberal Party. The IDA obtained 55 percent of the vote in three Istrian districts and elected four deputies to the Croatian parliament. In the second round of elections in February 1993, for the upper house, or Chamber of Municipalities, the IDA scored 72 percent of the vote and elected three more deputies. As a result, it established a parliamentary club consisting of eight members, including a representative from the Italian Union for Istria and Rijeka (IUIR). In addition, the IDA won all the local elections in Istria, scoring majorities in thirty-seven town councils as well as in five towns outside the Istrian *županja* (district). IDA leaders expressed anxiety about the depopulation of the peninsula and the resettlement of citizens from other parts of Croatia who had little knowledge of Istrian culture and could become loyal CDU supporters. Although legislation on regional administration had still to be passed by the Croatian parliament, during 1993 IDA spokesmen noted that Zagreb could become more receptive to their demands and thus boost the region's economy and directly assist the struggling Croatian economy. The CDU even gave indications that it would seek a coalition with the IDA. Indeed, the IDA representative for the city of Poreč, Ivan Herak, was offered a post as deputy prime minister and minister of tourism. IDA leaders have remained hesitant in accepting such overtures. The IDA also started to organize a branch in

Slovenian Istria, with exactly the same program, but its founding came too late for the December 1992 Slovenian elections. The IDA has not established a branch or affiliate in Italy, cognizant of Zagreb's political sensitivities.[27]

Rijeka Democratic Alliance (RDA)
Riječki Demokratski Savez (RDS)

The RDA was formed in early 1990 to press for a special status for the port city of Rijeka. Its leaders were concerned that protectionist policies and other forms of state interference were harming the economic well-being of the city. They wanted Rijeka to acquire the status of a free port that would be able to operate like a "Hong Kong of the Mediterranean" and profit economically from more intensive European integration. The RDA stood in an election coalition with three other regionalist organizations for the August 1993 ballot and performed reasonably well in the local city elections.

Dalmatian National Party (DNP)
Dalmatinska Narodna Stranka (DNS)

Launched in mid-December 1990, this more radical regionalist party rallied citizens who regarded Dalmatia as their homeland. Similarly to the DA, the party has urged that Dalmatia regain the status of a special region and has complained about the centralizing policies of the Tudjman administration. Its program lays stress on Dalmatia's legendary enterprising spirit, free market traditions, and ecological concerns that have been sorely neglected by Zagreb.[28]

Istrian Radical Organization (IRO)
Istarska Radikalna Organizacija (IRO)

The IRO was created in October 1991 as a reestablishment of the illegal TIGR (Trieste-Istria-Gorica-Rijeka) organization under a new name. In its previous incarnation it was a joint Slovene-Croatian organization that, in opposition to the war-time fascist regime, trained young people for an uprising and was involved in sabotage operations. The organization has avowedly supported the democratic opposition in Croatia, particularly those formations that want to restore a large measure of local autonomy for the Istrian peninsula.[29]

MINORITY ORGANIZATIONS

Serbian National Party (SNP)
Srpska Narodna Stranka (SNS)

The Serbian National Party was an entity reportedly set up by the CDU during 1992 to provide Croatian Serbs outside the Krajina region with organized representation and to counter the radical demands of Serbian nationalists. The SNP has been denounced by Serbian militants as well as by some Croatian opposition politicians of being stooges of the ruling party. Its program stipulated that the

SNP would work to reconstruct Croat-Serb relations and generally improve the position of Croatia's Serbian community. Its leaders officially distanced themselves from ex-Communists as well as the Serbian Democratic Party and sought in particular to appeal to urban Serbs living outside the Krajina region, who totaled nearly 200,000 inhabitants. SNP leaders contended that the preconditions for a lasting peace and healthy ethnic relations were already in place in the country. In general elections to the Chamber of Deputies in August 1992, the party obtained three seats. SNP spokesmen condemned the Krajina referendum in June 1993, asserting that Serbs had no right to secede from Croatia and that the Krajinas were dominated by a military junta. Several other Serbian organizations have been formed in Croatia over the past few years to try and pacify Serb-Croat relations and lend support to Croatia's independent status, including the Croatian Serb Alliance and the Alliance of Serbs of Istria, Rijeka, and Gorski Kotor. In many cases, suspicions persisted that these were front organizations for the ruling CDU and not properly representative of the Serb population, many of whose leaders have been hesitant in asserting minority rights for fear of retribution. However, the SNP also criticized the Zagreb authorities for failing to enforce minority-rights legislation or preventing discrimination against Serb residents.

Serbian Democratic Forum (SDF)
Srpski Demokratski Forum (SDF)

The SDF was established in early 1993 as a non-partisan umbrella body to represent the interests of Serbs in Croatia. It claimed a small membership, mostly consisting of Serb intellectuals and professionals resident in Zagreb and other major cities. Vice President Petar Ladjević underscored that the SDF would try to build contacts with Serbian intellectuals in the Krajina region, ties that had been severed since the start of the war. In addition, the SDF tried to establish communication with Serbian organizations in the rump Yugoslavia and has advocated the mutual recognition of both states: this would avowedly help to reconcile Croats and Serbs in Croatia itself. Forum leaders issued criticisms of the SNP, which they perceived as a puppet of the ruling CDU with little real influence among the Serb community. They criticized the government for generating perceptions of collective responsibility of the Serbian people for launching the war in the summer of 1991, as well as for failing to stem violations of human rights against the Serb community.[30]

National Community of Croatian Montenegrins (NCCM)
Nacionalna Zajednica Crnogorca Hrvatske (NZCH)

Under its chairman Drago Kastratović, the NCCM distanced itself from the policies of the Montenegrin government and its alliance with Milošević. It has striven to clear the names of all "honorable members" of the Montenegrin people following the Serb-Croat war in which Montenegrin volunteers had taken part and evidently besmirched the reputation of the Montenegrin nation.[31]

Romani Party of Croatia (RPC)
Stranka Roma Hrvatske (SRH)

The RPC was formed in July 1990; its stated goal was to seek recognition of the Romani (Gypsy) nationality and guarantee full minority rights. In this endeavor, it appealed to Croatia's National Assembly for primary- and secondary-level classes and textbooks in the Romani language.[32]

Hungarian People's Party (HPP)
Madjarska Narodna Stranka (MNS)

When the HPP was set up in June 1989, József Csorgics became party chairman. The party claimed to represent the political interests of the Hungarian minority, demanding equal rights for Hungarians, the opportunity to use the Hungarian language, and the provision of general schools with Hungarian-language instruction regardless of the number of students. Other aims of the HPP included the protection of human rights, religious freedom, and the environment.[33]

Croatian Muslim Democratic Party (CMDP)
Hrvatska Muslimanska Demokratska Stranka (HMDS)

The CMDP was established in Zagreb during 1991 under the presidency of Mirsad Baksić. It cast itself as a secular organization representing the interests of "Croats of Islamic faith," as well as Muslims who since 1968 had declared their nationality in Yugoslavia as Muslim. The CMDP has also tried to organize cells in Bosnia-Herzegovina, representing the Croatian nationalist position that Bosnian Muslims were in origin Croatian Catholics. It has vehemently attacked the Sarajevo-based Muslim Party of Democratic Action for claiming to represent all of Bosnia's Muslims. Baksić himself became a colonel in the Croatian Army, claiming that over 25,000 "Croat Muslims" participated in the defense of Croatia against "Serbian aggression."[34]

A number of other ethnically based minority organizations have been established in Croatia, in many cases since before Croatia achieved independence. They included the Democratic Alliance of Albanians in Croatia, the Democratic Union of Croatian Muslims, the Albanian Demo-Christian Party, the Alliance of Czechs and Slovaks, the Alliance of Germans and Austrians, the Slovak Association, the Alliance of Ruthenians and Ukrainians, the Alliance of Germans in Croatia, the Alliance of Slovenians in Croatia, the Italian Union of Istria and Rijeka, and the National Community of Macedonians.

CHRONOLOGY

April 1990: Croatia holds its first multi-party elections. Promoting an openly nationalistic platform, the Croatian Democratic Union (CDU) wins a clear majority in the legislature and its leader Franjo Tudjman becomes president. Tudjman makes inflammatory statements concerning Croatia's borders and the status of Muslims and Serbs in Croatia.

June 1990: The Serb-dominated Assembly of Knin *opština* decides to establish a "community of *opštine*" in northern Dalmatia and Lika. A Serbian National Council is formed; it adopts a Declaration on the Sovereignty and Autonomy of the Serbian Nation and schedules a plebiscite on autonomy.

August 1990: The Constitutional Court of the Republic of Croatia overturns Serbian moves toward the autonomy of Krajina as unconstitutional. A Serbian Council of National Resistance is formed in Krajina, with Milan Babić, Milan Martić, Jovan Rašković, and Dušan Orlović as members. Drnis, Knin, and Šibenik *opštine* adopt the Cyrillic alphabet as the official script of administrative institutions in these districts.

September 1990: The Serbian National Council, led by Milan Babić, declares the intention to create a fully autonomous Serbian region to include all territories in which Serbs constitute a majority. Rumors begin to circulate that the Croatian Democratic Union is attempting to smuggle in arms from Hungary and Germany.

October 1990: The Yugoslav People's Army begins covertly to arm and support rebel Serbs in the Knin area.

December 1990: Croatia adopts its new constitution. The document declares all nationalities to be equal, guarantees the freedom to express one's nationality, and provides for cultural autonomy. Serb leaders charge that it does not assure the "collective rights" of the Serbian minority and condemn the constitution as an example of Croatian chauvinism. The Serbian Autonomous Region of Krajina is established and the area is joined by the *opštine* of Benkovac, Vojnić, Obrovac, Gračać, Dvor, and Kostajnica. The new administrative entity claims the right to execute its own laws and ordinances, and those of the Yugoslav federation, and asserts the right to collect taxes in the region.

January 1991: An armed confrontation between Croatia and Serbia is narrowly averted after the Yugoslav defense minister states that no republic will be allowed to create paramilitary units outside the federal military structure. Zagreb accepts the demobilization of its reserve militia force but continues to maintain its main National Guard contingents. Serbs accuse the Croatian government of using the National Guard to impose a state of siege in Serb-dominated areas.

February 1991: The Serb-Croat conflict escalates when the Serbian National Council in Knin declares the independence of Krajina from Croatia. Zagreb declares the move as illegal and refuses to recognize the territory as sovereign. Tensions increase when President Tudjman implies that parts of Bosnia-Herzegovina belong to Croatia. He does not deny that a plan had been created to divide up Bosnia between Serbia and Croatia.

April 1991: The Krajina Executive Council adopts a declaration on secession from Croatia and federation with Serbia. The Serbs in Krajina reportedly endorse this declaration in a public referendum a few weeks later. Serb leaders in other parts of Croatia seek to join the Krajina entity. The federal Yugoslav government, Croatian leaders, and even some Serb community leaders do not approve the decision and proclaim it unconstitutional.

May 1991: Croatia holds a referendum on independence in which 93.24 percent of the 83.56 percent of the electorate casting ballots vote for Croatian sovereignty and independence. The Krajina Serbs comprehensively boycott the plebiscite.

June 1991: Croatia declares its independence and imminent secession from Yugoslavia. Yugoslav troops launch offensives across the republic and attempt to thwart progress toward independence. Serb guerrillas in Krajina attempt to connect areas already partially under Serb control. In the ensuing months, Serb forces capture about a quarter of Croatian territory along the border with Bosnia and Vojvodina.

July 1991: Croatian authorities court international recognition by addressing minority rights in the republic. Zagreb agrees to consider the possibility of granting Serbs some form of limited political autonomy, whereby municipal authorities in Serb areas would maintain power over the local police, education, and culture in certain designated areas.

October 1991: The Croatian parliament reasserts the republic's sovereignty and independence and officially negates all federal laws and Yugoslav jurisdiction in the republic. Zagreb announces its intention to offer broad autonomy to the Serbs. Serb representatives in the occupied territories of Slavonija, Baranja, and western Srem seek to become a federal state within Yugoslavia.

January 1992: Croatia is officially recognized by the international community. A UN-sponsored cease-fire takes effect. An agreement, known as the Vance

Plan, is reached between Zagreb, Belgrade, Yugoslav military commanders, and local Serb authorities in Krajina to implant a UN peace-keeping force in the disputed territories. Krajina president Milan Babić opposes UN involvement, fearing that the United Nations would disarm Serb forces and facilitate the region's return to Croatian control. Babić is replaced by Milošević loyalist Goran Hadžić who supports the ceasefire plan. The UN Security Council adopts a resolution establishing the UN Protection Force (UNPROFOR) to act as a buffer between Serb and Croat forces throughout the Krajina region; 14,000 troops are deployed to four sectors of the conflict zone.

May 1992: The Croatian parliament ratifies its Constitutional Law of Human Rights and Freedoms and the Rights of National and Ethnic Communities or Minorities. The legislation institutionalizes within Croatian law the special position of minorities, with special emphasis placed on Croatian Serbs.

August 1992: Croatia holds its second multi-party elections. There are questions about the CDU's control over the mass media, election procedures, and voter registries. The CDU maintains its dominant position in parliament. Citizens in Serb-held areas are not allowed to participate in the balloting by the local Serb authorities. The Tudjman government continues to be accused of maintaining authoritarian controls over most aspects of public life.

October 1992: In an effort to improve relations with minorities within the republic, the Croatian parliament passes the Amnesty Act; it guarantees the safety of all of those who may have been involved in the 1991 war, provided that they did not engage in war crimes.

January 1993: Croatian forces liberate the Maslenica bridge, a key link to the Dalmatian coast; the authorities hope to reopen important traffic routes despite Serb shelling.

June 1993: Serb leaders in Croatia abandon peace talks with the Croatian authorities and hold a referendum on the unification of the Serbian Republic of Krajina with the Serb Republic in neighboring Bosnia. The danger of full-scale war escalates in Croatia. Serb unification is placed temporarily on hold pending the outcome and speed of the partition of Bosnia-Herzegovina by Serb and Croat forces.

NOTES

1. For demographic statistics on Croatia, see the Yugoslav population census of 1991, "Refugees and Displaced Persons in the Republic of Croatia," Republic of Croatia, Ministry of Information, Zagreb, July 1992.

2. For useful histories of Croatia, see Fred Singleton, *A Short History of the Yugoslav Peoples* (Cambridge: Cambridge University Press, 1985); Ivo Banac, *The National Question in Yugoslavia: Origins, History, Politics* (Ithaca: Cornell University Press, 1984); Dennison Rusinow, *The Yugoslav Experiment, 1948–1974* (London, 1977); Richard Nyrop, ed., *Yugoslavia: A Country Study* (Washington: U.S. Government Printing Office, 1982); Aleksa Djilas, *The Contested Country: Yugoslav Unity and Communist Revolution, 1919–1953* (Cambridge, MA: Harvard University Press, 1991); Pedro Ramet, *Nationalism and Federalism in Yugoslavia, 1963–1983* (Bloomington: Indiana University Press, 1984).

3. See *The 1990 Elections in the Republics of Yugoslavia*, The National Republican Institute for International Affairs, Washington DC, 1991.

4. *Vjesnik*, Zagreb, February 25, 1990.

5. *Glas Koncila*, Zagreb, July 30, 1989, September 24, 1989, and October 8, 1989.

6. Olga Ramljak, "Dossier: Beginnings of Aggression: Anatomy of Serb Rebellion: Those Issuing Orders From Serbia Had Good Servants in War Criminals," *Danas*, Zagreb, February 26, 1993, in Federal Broadcast Information Service, *Daily Report: East Europe, FBIS-EEU–93–057*, March 26, 1993. For a valuable appraisal of the military situation, see James Gow, "Military-Political Affiliations in the Yugoslav Conflict," Radio Free Europe/Radio Liberty Research Institute (RFE/RL), *Research Report*, vol. 1, no. 20, May 15, 1992.

7. *Zagreb Domestic Service*, October 17, 1990, in *FBIS-EEU–90–202*, October 18, 1990.

8. Milan Andrejevich, "Croatia Between Stabilty and Civil War (Part II)," RFE/RL, *Report on Eastern Europe*, vol. 1, no. 39, September 28, 1990.

9. "Serbian People's Uprising," *Vjesnik*, Zagreb, July 25, 1990, in *FBIS-EEU–90–145*, July 27, 1990.

10. *Tanjug Domestic Service*, Belgrade, March 16 1991, in *FBIS-EEU–91–052*, March 18, 1991; *Tanjug Domestic Service*, Belgrade, April 1, 1991, in *FBIS-EEU–91–062*, April 1 1991; *Tanjug*, Belgrade, April 1, 1991; *Tanjug*, Belgrade, April 4, 1991; *Tanjug Domestic Service*, Belgrade, December 23, 1991, in *FBIS-EEU–91–247*, December 24, 1991. For the Charter of the Serbian Autonomous Region of Krajina, check *Borba*, Belgrade, January 4, 1991.

11. See *The Constitution of the Republic of Croatia*, Zagreb, 1991.

12. Republic of Croatia, *Constitutional Law of Human Rights and Freedoms and the Rights of National and Ethnic Communities or Minorities in the Republic of Croatia* (Articles 21, 18, 14, 58), Zagreb, December 1991.

13. Milan Andrejevich, "Croatia Between Stability and Civil War (Part I)," RFE/RL, *Report on Eastern Europe*, vol. 1, no. 37, September 18, 1990; Ivo Bicanić and Iva Dominis, "Tudjman Remains Dominant After Coalition Elections," RFE/RL, *Research Report*, vol. 1, no. 37, September 18, 1992.

14. Paul Shoup, "The UN Force: A New Actor in the Croatian-Serbian Crisis," RFE/RL, *Research Report*, vol. 1, no. 13, March 27, 1992.

15. Information Report, Ministry of Foreign Affairs, Republic of Croatia, Zagreb, February 8, 1993.

16. Kresimir Meler and Mirjana Glušac, "Both Sides Already Have Plans," *Delo*, Ljubljana, March 1, 1993, in *FBIS-EEU–93–060*, March 31, 1993.

17. Samo Kobenter report on news conference by Croatian president Franjo Tudjman, "Open Border Question on the Balkans," *Der Standard*, Vienna, February 22, 1991, in *FBIS-EEU–91–038*, February 26, 1991.

18. Svetlana Vasović-Mekina, "Slovenia and Croatia: How to Become a Citizen: State as Prison," *Vreme*, Belgrade, March 8, 1993, in *FBIS-EEU–93–065*, April 7, 1993.

19. Excerpts of inaugural address by Franjo Tudjman, "We Do Not Need Political 'Solidarity'," *Vjesnik*, Zagreb, May 31, 1990, in *FBIS-EEU–90–118*, June 19, 1990.

20. Milan Andrejevich, "Croatia Between Stability and Civil War (Part II)," RFE/RL, *Report on Eastern Europe*, vol. 1, no. 39, September 28, 1990.

21. Interview with Ivan Pauleto, president and founder of the Istrian Democratic Assembly, by Rajko Djurdević, "Istria: Why We Are Demanding Autonomy," *Nin*, Belgrade, January 11, 1991, in Federal Broadcast Information Service/Joint Publications Research Service, *Daily Report: East Europe, JPRS-EER–91–018*, February 11, 1991.

22. See the *Country Reports on Human Rights Practices for 1992*, Department of State, Washington, DC, February 1993; and Helsinki Watch, *Yugoslavia: Human Rights Abuses in the Croatian Conflict*, vol. 3, no. 14, September 1991.

23. Dejan Jović, "Who Is Preserving Yugoslavia?" *Danas*, Zagreb, March 6, 1990, in *JPRS-EEU–92–212*, May 21, 1990; Milan Andrejevich, "Nationalist Movements in Yugoslavia," RFE/RL, *Report on Eastern Europe,* February 23, 1990; RFE/RL Research Institute, *Daily Report*, no. 114, June 18, 1993.

24. Croatian Party of Rights, *Constitution of the Croatian Party of Rights*, Zagreb, February 24, 1991; Croatian Party of Rights, *Electoral Declaration of the Croatian Party of Rights*, Zagreb, 1992; *Die Presse*, Vienna, January 27, 1992, in *FBIS-EEU–92–018*, January 28, 1992. See also the Open Letter to Franjo Tudjman, Helsinki Watch, February 13, 1992; *ORF Television Network*, November 5, 1991, in *FBIS-EEU–91–215*, November 6, 1991; and *Die Presse*, Vienna, January 27, 1992, in *FBIS-EEU–92–018*, January 28, 1992.

25. Zoran Daskalović and Milan Čuruvija, "They Have Proclaimed Autonomy," *Vjesnik*, Zagreb, July 26, 1990, in *FBIS-EEU–90–149*, August 2, 1990; Milan Andrejevich, "Croatia Between Stabilty and Civil War (Part II)," RFE/RL, *Report on Eastern Europe*, vol. 1, no. 39, September 28, 1990; "The Right Is Gaining in Strength," *Borba*, Belgrade, October 29, 1990, in *FBIS-EEU–90–219*, November 13, 1990; Olga Ramljak, *Danas*, Zagreb, February 26, 1993, in *FBIS-EEU–93–057*, March 26, 1993; and interview with Milan Babić by Srdjan Radulović, "Milan Babić: The Krajina Administration Is a Puppet," *Borba*, Belgrade, April 2, 1993, in *FBIS-EEU–93–067*, April 9, 1993.

26. *Program Declaration of Dalmatian Action*, Split, May 30, 1992; and interview with Mira Ljubić-Lorger by Petar Grubisić, "Hostages to Zagreb and Knin," *Danas*, Zagreb, June 4 1993, in *JPRS-EER–93–060-S*, June 30, 1993.

27. Interview with Ivan Pauleto by Rajko Djurdjević, *Nin*, Belgrade, January 11, 1991, in *JPRS-EER–91–018*, February 11, 1991.

28. *Tanjug Domestic Service*, Belgrade, October 17, 1990, in *FBIS-EEU–90–204*, October 22, 1990.

29. *Tanjug Domestic Service*, Belgrade, October 5, 1991, in *FBIS-EEU–91–195*, October 8, 1991.

30. See the interview with Petar Ladjević, "Anything But War," *Monitor*, Podgorica, May 21, 1993, in *FBIS-EEU–93–116*, June 18, 1993.

31. *HTV*, Zagreb, December 21, 1991, in *FBIS-EEU–91–246*, December 23, 1991.

32. "Romany Party of Croatia Founded," July 22, 1990, in "Weekly Record of Events," RFE/RL, *Report on Eastern Europe*, vol. 1, no. 31, August 3, 1990.

33. *Budapest Domestic Service*, March 7, 1990, in *FBIS-EEU–90–047*, March 9, 1990; Patrick Moore, "The Question of All Questions: Internal Borders," RFE/RL, *Report on Eastern Europe*, vol. 2, no. 38, September 20, 1991.

34. See the interview with Mirsad Baksić, "Izetbegović Does Not Represent Us All," *Vjesnik*, Zagreb, April 5, 1993, in *FBIS-EEU–93–085*, May 5, 1993.

3

Slovenia

POPULATION

According to the results of the 1991 Slovenian census, out of a total population of 1,965,986, Slovenes accounted for 1,727,018 or 87.84 percent.[1] The largest minority were the Croats, totaling 54,212 or 2.76 percent of the population; they were mostly resident in mixed villages near the border with Croatia and in the capital city, Ljubljana. The number of Serbs amounted to 47,911 or 2.44 percent of the total, and Muslims 26,842 or 1.37 percent, with the biggest concentration in the capital. Of the smaller nationalities, there were 8,503 Hungarians, primarily inhabiting the "nationally mixed territory" in the northeastern municipalities of Murska Sobota and Lendava, known as the Prekmurje region, next to the Hungarian border. The Magyar population actually declined during the previous decade, from 9,497 in the 1981 census, mostly as a result of emigration. The Italian population, which numbered 3,064, inhabited the "nationally mixed territory" in the municipalities of Koper, Izola, and Piran close to the Italian border: their numbers increased from 2,187 in 1981. Slovenia also had 4,443 Macedonians, 4,396 Montenegrins, and 3,629 Albanians; the majority were either married to Slovenes or obtained employment in Slovenia's larger cities. Additionally, 2,293 Roma (Gypsies) were registered in the 1991 census; invariably, the true figure was believed to be higher, somewhere in the region of 6,000 to 10,000. Smaller nationalities, including Germans, Czechs, Ukrainians, Poles, Austrians, Russians, Slovaks, Romanians, Turks, Bulgarians, Greeks, Vlachs, and Jews, totaled 3,514 people. Of the remainder, 12,307 people declared themselves as Yugoslavs, 5,254 gave a regional affiliation, while unknowns totaled 53,589 and the "unspecified" 9,011. On the eve of Yugoslavia's disintegration, Slovenia was the most ethnically homogeneous republic and its larger minorities did not form compact regional communities. Since the outbreak of hostilities in Croatia and Bosnia-Herzegovina, an estimated 60,000 refugees, mostly Muslims, have also sought shelter in Slovenia. Fearful of an even larger influx and its effects on social and economic conditions, during 1992 and 1993 Ljubljana began to place restrictions on immigration from all other former Yugoslav republics.

Slovenia: Population (1991)

Ethnic Groups	Number	% of Population
Slovenes	1,727,018	87.84
Croats	54,212	2.76
Serbs	47,911	2.44
Muslims	26,842	1.37
Hungarians	8,503	0.43
Macedonians	4,443	0.23
Montenegrins	4,396	0.22
Albanians	3,629	0.18
Italians	3,064	0.16
Roma	2,293	0.12
Regional Affiliation	5,254	0.27
Yugoslavs	12,307	0.63
Others	3,514	0.18
Unspecified	9,011	0.46
Unknown	53,589	2.73
Total Minorities	238,968	12.16
Total Population	1,965,986	100.00

HISTORICAL OVERVIEW

The Slovene Slavs settled in the southeast Alpine area in the sixth century but soon fell under foreign rule. For nearly 1,200 years the Slovenes were subject to successive periods of outside domination.[2] Frankish rule gave way to pronounced Germanic influence, and the Slav peasants were enserfed by the German feudal nobility. Slovenian territories were divided into several Germanic borderlands governed by a number of petty princes. At the end of the thirteenth century, the region fell under the control of the Habsburg dynasty and remained under Austrian domination until the outbreak of World War One. The Protestant Reformation had a widespread impact among the Slovenes; to counter Protestant influence, Vienna launched a severe Counter-Reformation to restore the power of the Catholic Church and reinforce the feudal system. The Germanization process intensified during the seventeenth century. For instance, German was made the official language for all governmental affairs, business transactions, and educational programs in an attempt to extinguish a distinct Slovenian national consciousness. The Catholic Church was largely responsible for preserving Slovenian identity during this time. The Slovenian region temporarily fell under French control in the early nineteenth century, after Napoleon's victories over the Habsburgs led to the signing of the Treaty of Vienna. Slovenia was returned to Austrian control after the defeat of Napoleon's armies made possible the 1815 Congress of Vienna. The brief period of French rule saw a resurgence of Slovenian nationalism as Napoleon eased the restrictive Habsburg policies. The restoration of repressive Germanic rule bred widespread resentment and stimulated Slovenian support for sovereignty and south Slav unity as protection against Germanic influence. The Catholic clergy were instrumental in fostering Slovenian identity and maintaining the Slovenian language and culture intact throughout the Austrian occupation.

After the collapse of the Austro-Hungarian Empire, an independent south Slav state was created in 1918: the Kingdom of Serbs, Croats, and Slovenes. The new state was declared a constitutional and democratic monarchy, but it soon fell under Serbian domination. The Serb king Aleksander centralized the administration and limited the autonomy of other nationalities. Slovene politicians soon became disillusioned by these developments and campaigned for a looser federation without any success. They were also concerned that their economically developed republic would be exploited by Belgrade and its progress would be correspondingly slowed down. Following the Nazi invasion of Yugoslavia in 1941, Slovenia was divided into several parts: the western coastal area was annexed by Italy, a northern segment was occupied by Germany, a northeastern section was occupied by a pro-Nazi Hungarian state, and a southern sliver was assigned to the pro-Nazi Independent State of Croatia. Slovenia did spawn an anti-fascist resistance movement, although it was split between nationalist and Communist forces. But the region emerged relatively unscathed from World War Two in comparison to the other Yugoslav regions. After the war, Slovenia was incorporated into a re-created Yugoslav federation dominated by Marshal Tito's Communist Party.

Throughout the Communist era, Slovenia retained a relative degree of autonomy with a well-trained corps of local administrators. The ethnic and linguistic distinctiveness of Slovenia prevented the kind of mass inflow of Serbian Communist bureaucrats witnessed in neighboring Croatia. Slovenia also became the most industrially developed and productive republic, and its pronounced ethnic homogeneity precluded any rise in nationality conflicts. Slovenes also remained strongly Catholic despite the prevailing Communist ideology. A major point of contention in Slovenia throughout the post-war era was the issue of the federal government's financing of the development of the less-developed Yugoslav regions. Essentially this meant that tax revenues and investment capital were diverted away from the northern republics of Slovenia and Croatia, where funds would earn the best return on investment, and toward the southeastern republics of Montenegro, Macedonia, Bosnia-Herzegovina, and Serbia. The inefficient use of resources under the republican bureaucracies seemed to many in Slovenia to be evidence of Belgrade's efforts to exploit Slovenia and to promote its patronage networks in the underdeveloped republics. Although payments to Yugoslavia's Federal Fund for the Accelerated Development of the Underdeveloped Regions and Kosovo (FADURK) never amounted to huge contributions, they nevertheless provided additional fuel for the rise of nationalist resentments.

With the loosening of federal controls and the disintegration of the League of Communists throughout the 1980s, Slovenia moved swiftly to assert its sovereignty and eventual "disassociation" from Yugoslavia. The republican elections in April 1990 brought to power the pro-independence coalition *DEMOS* (Democratic Opposition of Slovenia), led primarily by the Slovene Democratic Alliance (SDA). In July 1990, the Slovenian National Assembly adopted a proclamation on the republic's sovereignty and began to draft a new independent constitution that would negate the validity of all Yugoslav federal laws in the republic. In December 1990, a plebiscite on independence was approved overwhelmingly by Slovenian voters; the results further aggravated Ljubljana's relations with the federal authorities. The new government sought a much looser confederal arrangement with the other Yugoslav republics. But agreements on a new confederation could not be reached with the Serbian and Montenegrin leadership. As a result, Ljubljana took a major step toward secession in February 1991, when the National Assembly annulled all federal laws and Slovenia's obligations to Belgrade.

Following Ljubljana's declaration of independence in June 1991, the Yugoslav People's Army mounted an armed intervention against Slovenia. The objective was to disarm the Slovenian territorial defense forces, destabilize the government, and reverse the decision on independence. The maneuver failed, and the Slovenian forces were able to resist the assault and inflict some damage on the Yugoslav military. In fact, the invasion force was too small and inflexible to operate in mountainous terrain that proved unsuitable for conventional warfare. The army withdrew within a few weeks to focus its attention on Croatia, and a cease-fire was arranged in Slovenia under EC sponsorship. Ljubljana agreed to place its independence on hold for three months pending a new series of inter-republican negotiations to restructure the federation. When the moratorium expired in October 1991 without any notable progress, Slovenia redeclared its independence and separation from Yugoslavia. In early 1992, the new state finally obtained comprehensive international recognition as an independent republic.

Since its achievement of independence, Slovenia has made steady progress toward a pluralistic democracy. It has not been beset by any significant territorial or minority problems, either domestically or with its neighbors. Tensions with Croatia increased somewhat during 1992 and 1993, particularly over such issues as fishing rights in the Adriatic and the restructuring of economic relations between the two republics. But there was little danger of any major confrontation between Ljubljana and Zagreb. Leaders of the Italian minority in Slovenian and Croatian Istria and the Hungarian minority in the eastern corner of the republic campaigned for greater protection and collective rights, but Ljubljana appeared to achieve some success in satisfying their demands and improving its relations with both Italy and Hungary.

OFFICIAL POLICIES

Slovenia's declaration of independence in June 1991 was the culmination of the republic's attempts to safeguard its status as a unique nation from the encroach-ments of the Yugoslav federal structure. Slovenian leaders had long expressed reservations about their position in the Yugoslav federation, fearing that their national and linguistic identity would melt away into the Serbian-Croatian mainstream, and resenting the fact that their tax revenues were being diverted to support Yugoslavia's less-developed southern regions. As the country became increasingly wary of Serbian president Slobodan Milošević's attempts to subvert the country's relatively decentralized federal structure, Slovenia's newly formed opposition forces found common cause with the reform-oriented League of Communists of Slovenia in seeking a more democratic polity and a greater measure of sovereignty.

The impulse toward reform was ignited in May 1988, when rumors began to circulate that the Yugoslav army was planning a coup in Slovenia to purge the republic of its liberal elements. When a sergeant-major in the Yugoslav army, Ivan Borštner, brought word of this plot to the weekly magazine *Mladina*, Borštner and three of the journalists he contacted were promptly arrested. The public outcry against the arrests was widespread and continued to accelerate throughout the summer of 1988 as crowds of ten to twenty thousand regularly gathered in Ljubljana to protest the army's actions and called for the prisoners' release.[3] Yugoslav military authorities sentenced the four men after a sham trial that only further antagonized the Slovenian public. The trial dominated the attention of citizens, created a sense of threat, and legitimized the embryonic opposition forces. A Committee for the Protection of Human Rights was established to monitor and oppose what it perceived as Yugoslavia's drift toward a police state, and the Slovenian League of Communists actually granted the organization its support.[4]

The Slovene Communist Party's willingness to recognize an alternative voice on policy matters paved the way in 1989 for the founding of several new democratic parties, including the Social Democratic Alliance of Slovenia (SDAS), the Slovenian Democratic Union (SDU), the Slovenian Christian Socialist Movement (SCSM), and a Slovenian Green Party (SGP).[5] An important step in these developments was the decision to delete from the Slovenian constitution the official vanguard role that had been accorded to the League of Communists since Tito's takeover. This allowed even freer political discourse and encouraged the non-Communist opposition to broach new ideas on the future of the republic. One of the most important instances of this was the so-called May Declaration of 1989, which envisioned a future in which the Slovene nation would enjoy total sovereignty.[6] It proved to be a vision more compelling to the public than anything that the reinvented socialist parties could offer. The position of opposition forces was also enhanced by the electoral law of December 1989, which enabled the non-Communist organizations to coalesce into a single movement, the Democratic Opposition of Slovenia (*DEMOS*). By the time of the April 1990 elections, the *DEMOS* alliance incorporated six parties: the Slovenian Democratic Alliance (SDA), the Social Democratic Alliance of Slovenia (SDAS), the Slovenian Green

Party (SGP), the Liberal Party (LP), the Slovenian Christian Democrats (SCD), and the Slovenian Farmers' Party (SFP).

Throughout 1989, Ljubljana felt increasingly threatened as events in Yugoslavia seemed to forebode the breakdown of the old federal structure. Of particular concern were Serbian actions toward the provinces of Kosovo and Vojvodina and amendments to the Serbian constitution that essentially eliminated the autonomous status of both regions and paved the way for a unitary Serbian state. In Slovenia, such measures were perceived as a direct challenge to other republics that could presage Belgrade's efforts to eliminate Slovenian autonomy. Throughout 1989, Slovenian political organizations and citizens' groups organized rallies to protest Serbian policies vis-à-vis Kosovo, and this earned the wrath of Serbian president Milošević, who dubbed the Slovene regime "fascist" and instituted an economic blockade of the republic. The embargo caused some hardships for the public and adversely affected the republic's productive capacity. However, it also proved beneficial in the long run, as Slovenia was forced to find new markets for its imports and exports, to liquidate some unproductive state-owned enterprises, and to seek a greater degree of foreign investment.[7] As a result, Slovenia became relatively better prepared for life after Yugoslavia than most of the other republics.

By early 1990, Slovenian leaders felt increasingly alienated from the Yugoslav state: they were struggling under an economic blockade and remained focused on their long-term autonomy. During the fourteenth emergency session of the League of Communists of Yugoslavia in January 1990, all Slovenian proposals for decentralization were blocked, and the Slovenian delegation stormed out of the session in frustration and protest. Shortly afterwards, the republican Assembly announced that new multi-party general elections were to be held. In March 1990, the Slovenian Assembly adopted proposals that dropped the word "socialist" from the constitution, defined Slovenia as a state founded on the sovereignty of its citizens, and began preparations for the republic's economic independence. The political climate for the first pluralistic elections in April 1990 was thus very restless, and there were great misgivings about the future of the Communist system and the Yugoslav federation in general.

Slovenian citizens participated in several simultaneous elections: for the republic's president, for members of the Slovenian state presidency, and for the three Chambers of the National Assembly: the Sociopolitical Chamber (101 seats), the Chamber of Municipalities (80 seats), and the Chamber of Associated Labor (59 seats). Fifteen parties and three "civil lists" were registered for the ballot, and a total of 2,103 candidates took part. However, the parties spanned a fairly narrow ideological and programmatic range, and there was little ethnicization of the political scene, primarily because of the small size of Slovenia's minorities. Moreover, none of the parties defined itself as "Yugoslav" and all expressed their goal of achieving sovereignty for the republic. The one significant difference was in the pace and method of achieving Slovenian sovereignty.

Two major forces competed in the polling: the *DEMOS* coalition, comprised of seven major registered parties, and the former League of Communists, which had changed its name to the Party of Democratic Renewal (PDR).

Milan Kučan, the former president of the League of Communists, was elected president. He benefited from a good measure of popularity as a result of his efforts to limit potential domination by Belgrade, although some anti-Communists charged that his late conversion to the cause of Slovenian independence was due more to personal motives than any strong patriotic sentiments. However, the *DEMOS* coalition displayed its soaring popularity by gaining 123 seats to the 240-member National Assembly; the Liberal Party gained 37; the PDR scored 25; the Alliance of Socialists 13; 2 candidates canvassed as independents; while the Italian and Hungarian communities obtained 1 parliamentary seat each. The two minority representatives gained seats in the 2 additional districts for election to the Sociopolitical Chamber. *DEMOS* representative France Bučar was selected president of the National Assembly, and another *DEMOS* leader, Lojze Peterle, became prime minister with the installation of the new government in May 1990.[8]

In its elections campaign, *DEMOS* promised its voters that Slovenian statehood would be achieved when the republic gained a distinct political, economic, military, and international legal status. Once in power, the new government pursued a policy consistent with these promises. President Kučan conferred closely with the newly elected president of Croatia, Franjo Tudjman, in crafting a design for a Yugoslav confederal arrangement that would replace the old federal structure. Belgrade charged that such a loose political structure would have been tantamount to the dissolution of Yugoslavia. In September 1990, Ljubljana offered proposals that would have converted Yugoslavia into an "alliance of sovereign states," purportedly on the model of the Benelux countries or the European Community. The Slovenian notion was to establish a "confederation" in order to maintain an economic community, a customs union, a common defense force, a very limited ministerial council, a confederal court (for interpreting the agreement of confederation), and various other organs for dealing with matters of common concern. According to this proposal, each state would retain the right to pursue an independent foreign policy and would receive a share of the property of the former Yugoslavia, in proportion to the republic's contribution to the national budget. This last element became especially problematic when it came to dividing and apportioning the value of the federal property.[9]

Nonetheless, there were stark differences between the European Community and any imagined future confederal Yugoslavia. The former was comprised of states with similar political and economic systems, which had voluntarily surrendered some elements of their national sovereignty, while the latter included both authoritarian socialist republics and nascent free-market democracies. This systemic disparity ensured that any project for creating an alliance on the EC model would prove extremely daunting.[10] In light of the very real differences among the Yugoslav republics, certain Slovenian leaders thought it wiser to create a smaller sphere of cooperation comprising Slovenia, Croatia, and Bosnia-Herzegovina. A smaller alliance would have benefited from more pronounced political and economic convergence and would have possessed an historical border: the old frontier of the former Habsburg Empire. Other leaders, including Prime Minister Lojze Peterle, also suggested the idea of a bilateral union or federation with Croatia; such calculations failed to materialize in the wake of Yugoslavia's dissolution.

In 1990, Slovenia's leaders still calculated that there would be some benefits from retaining an association with the other Yugoslav republics: for example, the establishment of an economic community, a tariff union, and perhaps even a joint monetary policy. The Slovenian leadership, however, was not determined to maintain this association at all costs. The Serbian economic blockade begun in 1989 demonstrated to Slovenia that its relations with Croatia and Bosnia were of far more importance economically than its relations with the southern Yugoslav republics. Even more important to Ljubljana was the country's eventual integration into the EC: such a step was considered to be a panacea for most of the country's problems. It would supposedly offer an unparalleled market for Slovenia's exports, long-term protection for its cultural distinctiveness, confirmation of its identity as a European rather than a Balkan civilization, and a workable system of regional security cooperation that would defuse any dangerous bilateral conflicts with its neighbors. Because this idea was so potent, Slovenia had little interest in being fettered to any confederation of states that might opt for a slower pace of entry into the EC. The government sought to confirm its national sovereignty so that it would not be consigned to the role of a subnational interest when European integration would finally embrace Yugoslavia.[11]

The precondition for Slovenia's entering into any kind of confederal arrangement was the achievement of full political and economic sovereignty. Pursuant to this goal, a plebiscite was held on the question of independence in December 1990, and 88.2 percent of the 95 percent of the electorate who cast their ballots opted in favor of sovereignty and independence. After several months of fruitless negotiation within the federal structures, Slovenia finally declared its independence from Yugoslavia in June 1991. This act of "disassociation" immediately provoked a Yugoslav Army intervention in an effort to coerce Ljubljana into rescinding its decision on independence. Instead of intimidating Slovenia, however, the attempted army crackdown had the reverse effect by stiffening Slovenian resistance and uniting virtually the entire political landscape behind the administration.

The Yugoslav incursion proved a disaster in that the cumbersome military units were outmaneuvered by highly mobile and motivated Slovenian defense forces who had managed to make significant operational and logistical preparations for such an encounter. Indeed, the Slovenian defense minister Janez Janša had skillfully and clandestinely organized special units within and outside the old territorial-defense-force structure; these units were at the forefront of resistance to the Yugoslav forces. Some observes speculated that the incursion itself was either half-hearted or prematurely aborted. It remained unclear, however, whether this was the result of political conflicts between the political and military leadership in Belgrade, or whether the whole episode had been designed to fail to disguise preparations for the forthcoming war in Croatia. Analysts believed that Milošević was prepared to allow Slovenia to secede and used the opportunity to discredit some high-ranking Yugoslav military commanders in preparation for a thorough overhaul of the military structure and its full subordination to the Serbian leadership. After ten days of hostilities, and only a dozen or so casualties, both sides agreed to an EC-sponsored ceasefire. The agreement stipulated that Slovenia and Croatia both consented to suspend their declarations of independence for three months. During this time Yugoslav forces, numbering about 20,000 troops, were withdrawn from Slovenia and repositioned inside Croatia and Bosnia-Herzegovina.

With the cause of independence having been confirmed by a referendum and the last remaining institution of the Yugoslav state, the Yugoslav People's Army, thoroughly discredited, independence still required a constitution that would provide a legal basis for Slovenia's new status. This requirement was fulfilled in December 1991, when Slovenia adopted a constitution that proclaimed the country to be a democratic republic governed by the rule of law. The document enacted a multi-party parliamentary system and provided a charter of human rights and fundamental freedoms that would establish the normative basis for the state. Article 3 defined Slovenia as "a state of all its citizens" that was "based on the permanent and inalienable right of the Slovene nation to self-determination." Article 5 addressed the question of the protection of ethnic minorities by affording special rights to autochthonous Hungarian and Italian minorities. Article 63 prohibited all incitements to discrimination, while Article 64 formally guaranteed the free expression of national allegiance, language, and script. For example, although Article 11 underscored that the official language was Slovenian, the Italian and Hungarian languages were also stipulated as official in those areas where the respective national communities resided. The constitution also affirmed that the state remained responsible for ethnic Slovenian minorities in neighboring states, including emigrants and migrant workers, and would promote their ties with the homeland.[12]

Some uncertainties remained about how extensive minority rights in Slovenia actually were. Slovenia institutionalized the rights of indigenous Hungarian and Italian minorities, who in 1991 together constituted less than 0.6 percent of the country's population. However, the rights of Yugoslav groups referred to as "immigrant communities," Croats, Serbs, Bosnians, and others who made up 11.7 percent of the population, did not benefit from constitutionally recognized cultural or group rights. The 1991 constitution, as well as various proposed outlines for the document dating back to 1989, seemed to indicate that Slovenia was establishing a three-tiered set of nationality definitions and privileges.[13] Seemingly, at the pinnacle were ethnic Slovenes. The language of the constitution remained unclear on whether the state fully guaranteed the "right of self-determination" to all citizens or specifically to ethnic "Slovene people."

Evidently, in second position were the "autochthonous minorities," or the Hungarian and Italian communities that possessed historical homelands on Slovenian territory. The two groups enjoyed some special rights, particularly within the designated "nationally mixed areas." These rights were guaranteed by the constitution and further elaborated in various legislation. The most important of these included the right to use their native language where Slovene and the minority language had equal status in nationally mixed territories, the free use of national symbols, the right to establish autonomous organizations and institutions, the right to foster the development of their own culture, the right to be educated in their own language, and the right to pursue cooperation with their homelands. The constitution placed an obligation on the republic to support, financially and morally, the implementation of the above rights. Both minorities were entitled to "self-governing national communities" that represented their interests through municipal assembly councils. Furthermore, both minorities had the right to direct representation in the National Assembly; each community obtained a permanent seat in parliament without having to contend with the system of proportional representation.[14]

A further noteworthy provision of the constitution was Article 65, which accorded special rights to the Romani-Gypsy communities in Slovenia. The constitution evidently anticipated threats to the cultural integrity of a population that possessed neither a home state to draw upon for support, nor any powerful existing minority organization to represent its interests. The authorities initiated preparations on a special law on the Roma to provide them with much-needed financial and education resources. Until 1993, the Roma have not obtained parliamentary representation largely because of their poor organizational efforts and lack of appropriate stipulations in the electoral laws. However, in the 1992 ballot they did manage to elect a number of local councilors in eastern Slovenia.[15]

The third tier of nationality rights apparently included those people who were classified as "immigrants," almost all of whom originated from other republics of the former Yugoslavia. The constitution did not offer guarantees of any collective rights to these communities. Perhaps this may have been the result of fears that well-organized Serbian or Croatian communities could have been manipulated by Belgrade or Zagreb to destabilize the republic. Hence, constitutional omissions or terminological vagueness may have been deliberately employed to defend Slovenia's national homogeneity from any ethnic communities large enough to present a potential threat. Whatever the reasons, members of "immigrant" communities received only those constitutional guarantees accorded to individual Slovene citizens, including the whole gamut of human rights, such as the right to form organizations, use the language and script of their choice, and freely develop their ethnic cultures. Although collective rights for distinct ethnic immigrant communities were not legally guaranteed, in practice several primary schools operated in the language of immigrants in larger cities. Such services, however, had to be organized privately and did not enjoy the benefits of state funding, unlike the school programs for the two autochthonous minorities.

The immigrant community in Slovenia numbered some 230,000 as of 1991, and this total increased significantly with the inflow of refugees from Bosnia. Of this number, some 178,000 immigrants from the former Yugoslav republics have received Slovene citizenship and can therefore enjoy all the benefits of the constitution. The ability of a large part of the immigrant community to acquire citizenship was a result of the liberal requirements for citizenship outlined in Article 40 of Slovenia's Law on Citizenship. That law stated that citizens of other former Yugoslav republics who held a permanent residence in Slovenia on the day of the independence plebiscite, and actually lived in the republic, could unconditionally acquire Slovenian citizenship. Some 160,000 immigrants, or 75 percent of all those from other Yugoslav republics, gained Slovenian citizenship through these provisions. Those who lacked a permanent residence in Slovenia, for instance, Bosnian and Croatian refugees, needed to undergo a process of naturalization. For those not married to Slovenian citizens, naturalization normally required ten-year residency in the republic, including the last five without interruption, a secure residence and livelihood, a command of the Slovenian language, and proof that they did not pose a threat to the order and security of the state.[16]

New restrictions on naturalization and citizenship appeared to be scheduled. In April 1993, the government moved to institute a supplemental requirement within Article 40 of the Citizenship Law. Henceforth, people applying for citizenship would have to furnish proof of the termination of any other citizenship that they might hold.[17] This stipulation was evidently aimed at people seeking to avert difficult conditions, whether economic, military, or political, in their home republic by assuming Slovenian citizenship as a temporary or permanent measure. Such moves barely masked the fact that Slovenes were fearful of the effects of continued mass immigration. Polls on ethnic relations in Slovenia revealed that a majority of respondents felt threatened by the influx of immigrant workers and many criticized the government's liberal legislation. There were resentments that foreigners were taking jobs away from Slovenes, especially at a time when Slovenia was experiencing high rates of unemployment. A lingering anxiety also existed that these workers could be exploited politically by Belgrade or Zagreb, possibly providing an excuse for intervention in Slovenia's internal affairs. As a result of these concerns, 23.9 percent of those polled argued that immigrants should not be allowed to establish their own organizations, and 45.8 percent felt that immigrants should only be permitted to form cultural associations and not political parties.[18]

Of all the former Yugoslav republics, Slovenia was clearly the most successful in disentangling itself from federal institutions, pressures, and conflicts. Significant success was also achieved in establishing a stable pluralistic democracy and the rudiments of a capitalist economy. Slovenia's second multi-party elections in December 1992 resembled Western elections and were generally free of any irregularities. The *DEMOS* coalition had fractured during 1991 and gave way to an intense competition for political office. The Liberal Democratic Party emerged as the strongest force, gaining 22 seats in the 90-seat Assembly: it seemed to have captured the public's support by championing privatization and more rapid movement toward a market economy. The Christian Democrats finished second and improved on their 1990 result with 15 seats. The third-best showing, with 14 seats, was achieved by the United List, a coalition of four left-of-center parties that included the former Communists renamed as the Social Democratic Party of Reformers (SDPR).

A surprisingly strong showing was achieved by the radical Slovenian National Party; it appealed in particular to impressionable young people and residents of the Italian and Austrian border regions. This ultra-nationalist party captured 12 seats in the legislature, while playing on popular fears over the effect of continuing to allow Bosnian refugees into the country. The Slovenian People's Party (SPP), a successor to the Slovenian Democratic Alliance, managed to elect 10 deputies, while the Democratic Party, the Green Party, and the Social Democratic Party shared the remaining seats. One seat each was also assigned for the Hungarian and Italian minorities. The presidential election was won comfortably by former president Milan Kučan, who ran as an independent candidate and obtained 63.5 percent of the vote. He evidently gained the support of some nationalists by backing Slovenia's drive for independence and maintained the support of the leftist United List, despite his formal break with the Communist Party.[19] Prime Minister Janez Drnovšek, the Liberal Democrat leader, assembled a fairly broad governing coalition and proceeded to implement various economic and social reforms without major controversies.

Slovenia's treatment of its ethnic minorities will also have an important bearing on its foreign relations. One case in point has been Slovenia's relationship with Croatia. With a reported surplus of refugees, during recent years Ljubljana has been disallowing Croatian and Bosnian refugees from remaining in the country, instead forcing many to choose between returning to Croatia or moving on to Germany. The nationalist government in Croatia has contended that it has been betrayed by Slovenia, which refused to carry more of the refugee burden, at a time when Croatia was flooded with refugees from the Bosnian war in addition to its simmering conflict with rebel Serbs. Zagreb has been angered by the fact that resident Croats in Slovenia have been denied a constitutional status accorded to tiny groups of Italians and Hungarians. As Croatian president Tudjman increasingly adopted a siege mentality, neighboring Slovenia was portrayed in collaborationist terms, as a treacherous former ally. Various disputes over fishing rights off the Istrian peninsula, land-border delineations, and foreign-policy objectives became symptomatic of the gulf between two erstwhile anti-federalist allies who proved unable to conclude a long-vaunted friendship treaty. Unless Ljubljana can reach a lasting accommodation with a state the Slovenian press regularly condemns as dictatorial, Croatia could become an unsettling force on Slovenia's southern borders.[20]

Italy could prove to be another thorny problem. Shortly after its international recognition, Ljubljana requested that Italy accept Slovenia as a legal successor to the Yugoslav federation in any Yugoslav-Italian agreements that affected the republic. In July 1992, Slovenia submitted a list of agreements that it wanted to inherit from Yugoslavia; the Italian Foreign Ministry accepted these proposals. When these documents were published in the official Italian gazette, strong opposition erupted in Italy from Communists and neo-fascists in the region around Trieste, demanding that the Italian government reexamine and renegotiate its treaties with the former Yugoslav republics. The most volatile issue may be the status of the Osimo Accords, which assigned to Yugoslavia the former zones of the free Trieste territories around Koper (today within Slovenia under the name of Slovensko Primorje) and Buje (in Croatia). Although few politicians in Italy cherished the hope that these areas might be placed under Italian suzerainty, considerable interest remained in obtaining a more favorable position for the Italian minority in both states, particularly if this did not require reciprocal concessions to Slovenian and Croatian minorities in Italy. Slovenia was fortunate in reaching a speedy agreement with Rome, but the future status of the transferred regions may again come into question if nationalist opposition forces gain in strength. Political forces in Italy could conceivably try to revise the Osimo Accords and other treaties that would directly affect both Croatia and Slovenia.[21]

Another area of foreign-policy concern was the status of Slovenian minorities resident in neighboring states. Some resentments were visible among nationalist groups over the inability to regain the Slovene-inhabited territories in Austria and Italy. Indeed, a part of Austrian Carinthia was considered by some to be the historical cradle of Slovenian culture. Although relations with Vienna have developed smoothly since the collapse of Yugoslavia, feelings persist that the Slovenian minority in Austria has been subjected to a deculturation process. For instance, children about to enter elementary school are given language tests, and if they do not speak Slovenian well, they are classified as German speakers and are thereafter limited in their opportunities to receive Slovene-language instruction.[22] Slovenian politicians have expressed similar fears for the Slovene minority in Italy, and the government has tried to ensure that the Slovenian language and culture would be preserved. In particular, Ljubljana has been demanding that Slovenian cultural institutions and media sources be guaranteed their independence and the minority be accorded a special status in the Friuli-Giulia province where it is concentrated.[23] The question of borders and minorities has been periodically raised by some small nationalist groups in Slovenia, some of whom have demanded an expansion of Slovenian territory. Although these are marginal political elements, suspicions also persist that they have been sponsored or manipulated by former Communists or Yugoslav-Serb security forces to keep Slovenia off balance by engineering conflicts with its western and southern neighbors.

SLOVENIAN NATIONALISTS

Democratic Opposition of Slovenia (DOS)
Demokratska Opozicija Slovenije (DEMOS)

Founded in December 1989, *DEMOS* was conceived of as a credible alternative to the ruling Communist Party. Its original members included the Slovenian Democratic Alliance, the Social Democratic Alliance of Slovenia, and the Slovenian Christian Democrats. In January 1990, two more parties, the Slovenian Farmers' Alliance and the Greens of Slovenia, joined the coalition, followed by the Liberal Party. In the elections of April 1990, the *DEMOS* coalition captured 47 of 80 seats in the Sociopolitical Chamber of the National Assembly. The *DEMOS* parties canvassed in favor of market reform, the abolition of social ownership, and Slovenia's rapid and deeper involvement in the political, economic, and cultural life of Western Europe. The main issue of the 1990 elections, however, was the achievement of national sovereignty, and *DEMOS* captured strong public support by promising that it would quickly achieve Slovenia's independence. Statehood itself was envisaged as an important starting point for full political freedom, economic prosperity, and European integration. The *DEMOS* platform was partially shaped by the more vehemently pro-independence members of the coalition. The Slovenian Democratic Alliance in particular argued for the primacy of Slovenia's national interests and strongly advocated the republic's withdrawal from all federal structures that were perceived as draining Slovenia's resources and subverting its national identity. The SDA found common cause with the Slovenian Farmers' Alliance, which campaigned for the imposition of tougher conditions for gaining Slovenian citizenship and a reduction in the privileges of immigrants from other republics. However, Slovenia's first elections were generally devoid of radical-nationalist competition or rhetoric. Following the April 1990 elections, the *DEMOS* coalition unraveled and several distinct parties emerged spanning a traditional political spectrum; the majority espoused a reasonably moderate agenda. They included Social Democrats, Socialists, Agrarians, Greens, Liberals, Liberal Democrats, and Christian Democrats.[24]

Slovenian National Party (SNP)
Slovenska Nacionalna Stranka (SNS)

The SNP was founded in Ljubljana in April 1991 as an offshoot of the former Slovenian Farmers' Alliance. Indeed its president, Zmago Jelinčič, was previously the head of the Farmers' Alliance. The SNP criticized the *DEMOS* government and most of its component parties for vacillating on the question of independence and sought to portray itself as the first genuinely Slovene party. It prohibited membership to non-Slovenes and former members of the Communist Party, because it allegedly did not want its national mission diluted by individuals whose loyalties to Slovenia were questionable. The party publicly stated that the League of Communists was an implacable enemy of the Slovenian nation; it thereby advocated that individuals in positions of authority who were formerly members of the League of Communists should be ferreted out and dismissed from public life. Indeed, in order to undermine their democratic opponents, SNP leaders argued that the *DEMOS* coalition became a hiding place for many Communists who endeavored to salvage their political careers.

Jelinčič's vision for his country was of a pure "Slovenia for the Slovenes": an essentially ultra-nationalist platform. According to him, the benefits of the state should first and foremost be made available to ethnic Slovenes. Jelinčič contended, for instance, that guest workers should not be allowed to take jobs away from Slovenian citizens; in fact, for as long as there was unemployment in Slovenia, guest workers should be sent home. The SNP was adamant about not accepting any more refugees into the country, especially as it claimed that there were many citizens who were underfed and ill-housed. The SNP asserted it would abolish Article 40 of the Law on Citizenship and make the naturalization process more restrictive. In Jelinčič's calculations, immigrants who wanted to acquire citizenship should reside in Slovenia for at least twenty years, with absolute mastery of the language and complete financial independence. The SNP has painted an apocalyptic vision of the country's future if migration is not halted. Claiming there were already 100,000 refugees in the country, Jelinčič asserted that the figure could quickly multiply unless Ljubljana took stringent measures to halt the influx. Refugees would also mushroom into a political problem, claiming minority rights and state funds for their cultural and religious pursuits. If unchecked these demands would rapidly escalate and provoke serious inter-communal hostilities and a growing crime wave. Both the SNP and the post-Communist parties have also criticized the West for failing to provide appropriate refugee assistance, using the issue in their sometimes less-than-subtle anti-Western attacks.

In the foreign policy arena, Jelinčič has sharply criticized the Ljubljana administration for accepting the current borders with Croatia and Italy, which the SNP considered to be unjust. He has contended that the border with Croatia should be on the Mirna River, not on the Dragonja, while claiming that Italy had stolen the border belt with Slovenia. The party has also voiced pretensions to the Carinthian region of Austria, inhabited by a sizable Slovenian minority. In addition, Jelinčič has complained about the status of Istria: in SNP estimations, the peninsula should be reunited and attain autonomy within the Slovenian state. The SNP has claimed that if a referendum were to be held in the area, the majority of

Istrians would evidently choose Slovenia over Croatia. Jelinčič's accusations against Zagreb and an alleged Vatican-Croatian conspiracy to absorb Slovenia led some observers to believe that the SNP may have been acting in the interests of Belgrade to deepen the Croat-Slovene rupture. The SNP seemed to emerge as a more important player on the Slovenian political scene during the 1992 elections when it entered parliament as the fourth-strongest party. Its main source of popularity was opposition to the influx of Bosnian refugees who were estimated to make up nearly 4 percent of Slovenia's population by the close of 1992. According to post-election assessments, the SNP gained considerable support among citizens aged under 25, as well as among people living along the Italian-Austrian border, a highly developed area with a strong tourism base. In February 1993, the SNP split into two factions, each retaining six seats in parliament. After a prolonged legal dispute for possession of the SNP name, the breakaway wing led by Marjan Stanić renamed itself the National Party of Slovenia (NPS) and entered into a coalition with the People's Party.[25]

Slovenian Alliance (SA)
Slovenska Zveza (SZ)

In early 1993, a new initiative was launched among Slovenia's marginal radical rightist groupings to forge a more effective union. Its initiator Aleš Žužek sought to capitalize on public trepidation over the refugee problem and over fears of growing unemployment. The SA's essentially anti-foreigner program was avowedly based on similar populist solutions espoused by radical right forces in Germany and France. Žužek underscored that the major goal of the Alliance was an "ethnically pure" Slovenia in which all immigrants and refugees would be returned to their original homelands. The Alliance issued a tentative Plan for Returning Immigrants and Refugees as a "final solution to the foreigner question." The planned return would encompass all residents who were not of Slovenian descent and who moved to Slovenia after 1945. To gain public support for its initiatives, the Alliance planned to hold a referendum, offering the country a clear choice between becoming an economically successful European state or a Balkan charitable institution. The SA also propounded the idea of a militarily strong Slovenia that would defend the "ethnic rights" of Slovene minorities in Italy, Austria, Hungary, and Croatia. The possibility of border adjustments with neighbors, in Slovenia's favor, has also been proposed by the SA leadership.[26]

MINORITY ORGANIZATIONS

Italian Union for Istria and Rijeka (IUIR)
Italijanska Zveza za Istro in Reko (IZIR)

The Union was established during 1989, before the breakup of Yugoslavia, to defend the interests of the Italian population in Slovenia and Croatia. Following the attainment of independence by these two states, the IUIR tried to maintain one organization despite the new frontier. After the 1992 elections, Roberto Battelli became the parliamentary representative of the Italian community. In addition, the IUIR had elected councilors in each local commune inhabited by the Italian minority. Although generally satisfied with the status of the minority in Slovenia, Battelli located several problem areas: emigration by young people, lack of Italian teachers in local schools, and insufficient legislation on minority rights. For instance, the IUIR sought more specific laws to regulate the status of minorities at local levels. Nonetheless, Italian activists expressed more concern about the minority's status in Croatia where they purportedly did not benefit from official bilingualism and other minority rights. Battelli believed that inter-state agreements between Rome and Ljubljana regulating the position of minorities in both countries would greatly help the Italian minority. Reportedly, some of the estimated 200,000 Italians who emigrated from Istria and Rijeka after World War Two were interested in buying back their property. Their organizations were believed to have some influence on Italian politics, but few activists other than neo-fascists were demanding outright border changes with Slovenia or Croatia.

Interest Community of the Hungarian Minority (ICHM)
Interesna Skupnost Madžarske Manjšine (ISMM)

Following the 1992 elections, ICHM activist Marija Pozsonec became the Hungarian deputy to the Slovenian parliament according to stipulations for automatic Magyar and Italian representation. The Community was not a specifically political organization, but simply a representative body inherited from the former Communist self-management structures that once included committees for local minorities. It published the weekly *Népújság*. Hungarian spokesmen contended that they encountered few problems in Slovenia and maintained good contacts with Hungary. In addition, they have tried to organize the delivery of aid to the Magyar minority in Serbian Vojvodina—ironically, economic and political assistance formerly flowed in the opposite direction.

CHRONOLOGY

January 1988: Sharp public debates take place in Slovenia over changes to the Serbian constitution that were perceived to threaten Yugoslavia's federal structure and the national autonomy of the constituent republics.

May 1988: Rumors abound that the Yugoslav People's Army (YPA) is planning a coup to displace Slovenia's republican leadership. A Yugoslav army sergeant-major, Ivan Borštner, brings some evidence of this plot to the editors of the journal *Mladina*. Although the government issues a firm denial of these rumors, it also arrests Borštner and the journalists he contacted.

July 1988: The trial of the four men begins, amid a storm of popular protest. The conduct of the trial further angers many Slovenes, and the whole episode turns into a campaign for the democratization of society.

February 1989: Various political organizations and associations organize rallies in support of striking Albanian workers in Kosovo. Serbia condemns the rallies as evidence of open support for Albanian separatists.

March 1989: Serbia imposes an economic blockade on Slovenia in retaliation for Slovenian support for the Kosovo Albanians.

May 1989: Large rallies take place in Ljubljana; more than 10,000 people assemble to protest the second arrest of Slovenian dissident Janez Janša. The May Declaration, which favors the full sovereignty of the Slovenian nation, is first read at this convocation.

June 1989: The Fundamental Document of Slovenia is published as an official Slovenian government reply to the May Declaration. It also envisions Slovenian sovereignty but within the framework of a Yugoslav state.

September 1989: The League of Communists of Slovenia convenes with other political organizations in Celje, an event that could be designated as the informal beginning of the election campaign. The Slovenian Assembly passes constitutional amendments that form the basis for Slovenia's sovereignty and widen the political arena.

November 1989: Rumors are circulated that Serb leaders from Kosovo Polje are planning to organize a million-strong march on Ljubljana. Slovenian authorities prohibit the rally, and Serbian leaders institute a full-scale economic embargo on Slovenia.

January 1990: Slovenian delegates storm out of the fourteenth emergency session of the League of Communists of Yugoslavia in Belgrade after all their proposals on decentralizing the Yugoslav federation are blocked or rejected.

March 1990: The Slovenian Assembly adopts supplements to the Slovene constitution eliminating the word "socialist" from the document and providing for the republic's economic independence.

April 1990: Slovenia's first multi-party elections are held. The *DEMOS* coalition, on the strength of its promises of national sovereignty, wins a comfortable victory. Respectable results are also achieved by the Party of Democratic Renewal (former Communists) and the Liberal Democrats, both of whom perform better than any individual *DEMOS* party. The office of president goes to the former head of the Slovenian League of Communists, Milan Kučan.

September 1990: Slovenia proposes a model of confederation for Yugoslavia that is rejected by Serb and Montenegrin leaders: there is no consensus in the federal presidency in altering or loosening the federal structure.

October 1990: The Slovenian Assembly initiates the process of nullifying federal laws on the republic's territory.

December 1990: Slovenia holds a plebiscite on independence from Yugoslavia: 93.2 percent of the electorate turn out to vote, and 88 percent of all votes are cast in favor of statehood.

April 1991: The *DEMOS* coalition begins to unravel, and several distinct parties emerge from the alliance; most are moderate political forces.

June 1991: Slovenia declares its independence after months of fruitless negotiations on confederalizing Yugoslavia. The Yugoslav army responds with a military intervention evidently seeking to cow the government into submission, to break armed resistance, and to capture strategic points in the republic, including its borders. Army commanders appear to miscalculate: the crackdown provokes stiff resistance and rallies all Slovenian political forces behind the drive for secession from Yugoslavia. Casualties are minimal, as the army does not engage in a full-scale assault and Belgrade decides to withdraw its forces. Ten days later both sides agree to a cease-fire.

October 1991: Following a three-month moratorium on independence sponsored by EC mediators and pending new negotiations on confederation, which fail to elicit any positive results, Ljubljana reasserts the country's independence and statehood. The remaining Yugoslav troops vacate the country.

December 1991: The new Slovenian constitution is ratified by parliament.

January 1992: Following the issuing of specific criteria for the international acceptance of all the Yugoslav republics, the EC officially recognizes Slovenia as an independent state.

December 1992: The second multi-party elections are held; the Liberal Democratic Party, which wins the ballot, proceeds to form a coalition government.

Milan Kučan gains reelection as president of Slovenia and Liberal Democratic Party leader Janez Drnovšek becomes prime minister and forms a coalition government in agreement with the Christian Democrats, the United List, and the Social Democrats.

July 1993: Slovenia is rocked by several scandals over illicit arms shipments to Croatia and Bosnia, financial misappropriations, and the continuing activities of Yugoslav security services. Some observers believe that government ministers and party leaders, including the SNP chairman Jelinčič, may be implicated in the scandals. The possibility of new general elections is raised.

NOTES

1. Slovenian population statistics taken from *Slovenski Almanah 93*, Delo Novice, Ljubljana, December 1992.

2. Background history on Slovenia can be found in Carole Rogel, *The Slovenes and Yugoslavia, 1890–1914* (Boulder, CO: East European Quarterly, 1977); Ivo Banac, *The National Question in Yugoslavia: Origins, History, Politics* (Ithaca: Cornell University Press, 1984); and Dennison Rusinow, *The Yugoslav Experiment, 1984–1974* (Berkeley: University of California Press, 1977).

3. Dušan Nečak, "A Chronology of the Decay of Tito's Yugoslavia 1980–1991," *Nationalities Papers*, vol. 21, no. 1, Spring 1993.

4. *Danas*, Zagreb, November 29, 1988; *Delo*, Ljubljana, July 26, 1988.

5. Sabrina P. Ramet, *Nationalism and Federalism in Yugoslavia 1962–1991*, 2nd. ed., (Bloomington: Indiana University Press, 1992), p. 211.

6. Nečak, "A Chronology of the Decay of Tito's Yugoslavia 1980–1991."

7. Speech by Dušan Šinigoj, president of the Slovenian Executive Council, to the Republican Assembly, February 7, 1990.

8. For information on the Slovenian elections, consult the National Republican Institute for International Affairs, *The 1990 Elections in the Republic of Yugoslavia*, Washington DC, 1991.

9. V. Zagorac, "Everything—Only Not a Federation," *Večernji List*, Zagreb, September 18, 1990, in Federal Broadcast Information Service/Joint Publications Research Service, *Daily Report: East Europe*, FBIS-EEU–90–185, September 24, 1990.

10. Jana Taskar, "Only an Independent Slovenia or a Confederate Union," *Delo*, Ljubljana, October 4, 1990, in *FBIS-EEU–90–197*, October 11, 1990; interview with Slovenian Democratic Alliance president Joze Pučnik by Hans-Henning Scharsach, "Slovenia Remains Sovereign Even if It Cooperates with Belgrade," *Kurier*, Vienna, October 7, 1990, in *FBIS-EEU–90–197*, October 11, 1990; and the interview with Slovenian prime minister Lojze Peterle by Rudolf Gruber, "Looking for Franz Ferdinand," *Profil*, Vienna, July 30, 1990, in *FBIS-EEU–90–148*, August 1, 1990.

11. Interview with Slovenian foreign affairs minister Dimitrij Rupel by B. Žukov and M. Gregorić, "We Will Not Enter Europe Through Belgrade," *Borba*, Belgrade, June 11, 1990, in *FBIS-EEU–90–121*, June 22, 1990; Valentin Hribar, "The Slovenes and European Transnationality," in *The Case of Slovenia*, (Ljubljana: Nova Revija, 1991).

12. *Constitution of the Republic of Slovenia*, Ljubljana, Uradni List Republike Slovenije, 1992.

13. Vojin Dimitrijević, "Ethnonationalism and the Constitutions: The Apotheosis of the Nation-State," paper presented at the conference on "Issues of Identity in Contempo-

rary Yugoslavia," University of Kent at Canterbury, England, August 20–23, 1992.

14. "Italian and Hungarian National Communities (Minorities) in the Republic of Slovenia," *Report on Nationalities from the Government of the Republic of Slovenia*, November 16, 1992.

15. Mitja Žagar, "Position and Protection of Ethnic Minorities in the Constitution of the Republic of Slovenia," *Treaties and Documents* (Ljubljana: Institute for Ethnic Studies, 1992).

16. Svetlana Vasović-Mekina, "Slovenia and Croatia: How to Become a Citizen, The State as Prison," *Vreme*, Belgrade, March 8, 1993, in *FBIS-EEU–93–065*, April 7, 1993.

17. Meta Roglič, "Fewer Slovene Citizens," *Dnevnik*, Ljubljana, May 3, 1993, in Federal Broadcast Information Service/Joint Publications Research Service, *Daily Report: East Europe JPRS-EER–93–047-S*, May 23, 193.

18. Zoran Medved, "That Is Slovenia," *Danas*, Zagreb, February 20, 1990, in *JPRS-EER–90–070*, May 18, 1990.

19. See *The Slovene Elections: A Report on the December 6, 1992, Presidential and Parliamentary Elections in Slovenia*, The Libra Institute, Ljubljana, January 1993.

20. "Analysis of Current Events," *Association for the Study of Nationalities*, New York, year 4, no. 7, May 1993.

21. Inoslav Besker, "Who Will Shout 'Trieste is Ours'?" *Novi Vjesnik*, Zagreb, October 29, 1992, in *FBIS-EEU–92–220*, November 13, 1992.

22. Karl W. Ryavec, "Observations: Slovenia," *Nationalities Papers*, New York, vol. 17, no. 2, Fall 1989.

23. Lojze Kante, "Slovenes Want Equal Rights for Everyone," *Delo*, Ljubljana, January 9, 1992.

24. Bojan Balkovec, "Political Parties in Slovenia," *Nationalities Papers*, vol. 21, no. 1, Spring 1993, pp.189–192.

25. For information on the Slovenian National Party, see the above-mentioned *The Slovene Elections* ... ; Miha Štamcar, "Pure Slovenia," *Mladina*, Ljubljana, April 2, 1991, in *JPRS-EER–91–071*, May 28, 1991; and *Tanjug*, Belgrade, March 22, 1993, in *FBIS-EEU–93–054*, March 23, 1993.

26. See Sveto Krašnik, "Union of the Slovene Radical Right," *Dnevnik*, Ljubljana, February 9, 1993, in *FBIS-EEU–93–041*, March 4, 1993.

4

Macedonia

POPULATION

According to the 1981 Yugoslav census, the population of the Macedonian republic stood at 1,909,136, of which 1,279,323 were Slav Macedonians (67 percent), 377,208 Albanians (19.8 percent), 86,591 Turks (4.5 percent), 44,469
Serbs (2.3 percent), 43,223 Roma or Gypsies (2.3 percent), and 39,513 Muslims
(2.1 percent). The republic also contained smaller groups of Vlachs, Greeks,
Bulgarians, and 14,225 self-declared Yugoslavs. According to a partial census
and official estimates based on statistical projections, in 1991 the total population of Macedonia had reached at 2,033,964, of whom 1,314,283 were Macedonians (64.62 percent) and 427,313 were Albanians (21.01 percent), with
97,416 Turks (4.79 percent), 55,575 registered Roma (2.73 percent), 44,159
Serbs (2.17 percent), 8,129 Vlachs or Arumunians (0.4 percent), and a mixture of
18 smaller nationalities and self-declared Yugoslavs amounting to 87,089 people
(4.28 percent).[1]

The Albanian community generally boycotted the April 1991 census, in protest against allegedly rising Macedonian nationalism and anti-minority stipulations in the new republican constitution. Albanian leaders vehemently contested
the census figures, claiming that the minority total exceeded some 800,000 people or approximately 40 percent of the population. The majority of Albanians
reportedly resided in seven western municipalities, in four of which they constituted a clear majority. Nearly 100,000 Albanians were found in the capital,
Skopje, whose total population reached 600,000. Over 90 percent of Albanians
had a Muslim religious background. The majority of Turks were resident in
several eastern municipalities, although 23,000 lived in Skopje. Over half the
Roma were found in the capital and in the nearby town of Šuto Orizari, a
settlement built specifically for Romani residents. Some Romani spokesmen
claimed their actual numbers reached over 100,000 people. Half of the Serbian
population also lived in the capital, although over 10,000 were found in the
northern municipality of Kumanovo next to the Serbian border. Preliminary

Macedonia: Population (1991)

Ethnic Groups	Number	% of Population
Macedonians	1,314,283	64.62
Albanians	427,313	21.01
Turks	97,416	4.79
Roma (Gypsies)	55,575	2.73
Serbs	44,159	2.17
Vlachs	8,129	0.40
Others	87,089	4.28
Total Minorities	719,681	35.38
Total Population	2,033,964	100.00

estimates indicated that the number of self-declared Bulgarians was in the region of 2,000 to 3,000, while the Greek population barely exceeded 1,000, despite claims by nationalists in Athens that Greek numbers were close to 300,000. Since the publication of the census and the ongoing statistical "psychological war" waged by Serbia and Greece, the Macedonian government has signaled its willingness to hold a full census under strict international supervision. Between the start of the Yugoslav wars in the summer of 1991 and the close of 1992, Macedonia also allowed in approximately 30,000 refugees, the majority being Muslims from Bosnia-Herzegovina. The number seriously strained Macedonia's limited capacities, and Skopje moved to restrict any further influx.

HISTORICAL OVERVIEW

The Slav Macedonian population in the south-central Balkans has been subject to outside domination since it first settled in the region by the seventh century. Bulgarian, Byzantine, and Serbian kingdoms controlled the area until the fourteenth century when it fell under the domination of the Ottoman Turks for the next 500 years.[2] As Turkish control in the Balkans weakened during the nineteenth century, Serb, Bulgarian, and Greek rivalry over the Macedonian region intensified. Bulgarian and Serbian nationalists claimed the Macedonian Slavs as ethnic kinsmen and refused to recognize a separate Macedonian national identity. Meanwhile, Greek leaders, fearing Slav claims to their own territory, also refused to consider the Macedonians as a separate ethnic category; Slavs residing on Greek territory were simply considered to be Slav speakers or Slavophone Greeks.

Following Russian intervention and the defeat of Turkish forces in 1878, Bulgaria attained its independence and obtained the entire Macedonian region in the treaty of San Stefano. But this decision was promptly reversed by the Congress of Berlin as the major European powers feared the expansion of Russian influence toward the Mediterranean. Macedonia was separated from Bulgaria, and Serbia was allocated some of its districts, while other regions were placed under Ottoman protection. During the 1890s, an independent underground Macedonian revolutionary movement was established and staged the abortive Ilinden uprising in 1903 against Turkish rule. It also became racked by internal divisions between pro-Bulgarian factions seeking to unite the region with an independent Bulgaria, and autonomists aiming for a wholly independent Macedonia in the context of a Balkan Slav federation. Macedonia enjoyed only a brief spell of independence during the two Balkan Wars in 1912–13. During the first war, Serbia, Greece, and Bulgaria joined forces in a successful campaign to drive out the Turks. Following the Turkish retreat, the victors proved unable to decide on the division of Macedonia. In the second war, Bulgaria attacked Serbian and Greek forces in Macedonia but sustained a major defeat when Romania, Montenegro, and Turkey joined forces with Serbia and Greece against Sofia. A peace treaty signed in Bucharest in 1913 ceded north and central Macedonia to Serbia, apportioned the southern regions to Greece, and allowed Bulgaria to retain a small portion of eastern Macedonia.

At the close of World War One, about a third of the territory of Ottoman Macedonia was placed under Serbian rule within the newly formed Kingdom of Serbs, Croats, and Slovenes. Bulgaria had sided with the defeated Central Powers during the war in the hope of recovering Macedonia but ended up relinquishing even more territory to Serbia. During the inter-war years, the Macedonian Slavs were not accorded the status of a national minority within Yugoslavia. The government in Belgrade simply considered them to be south Serbs and remained fearful of potential Bulgarian and Greek irredentism in the area. In fact, the name Macedonia was discarded under the centralized Yugoslav administration and thousands of Serbs were settled in the region to further the campaign of assimilation.

Throughout the inter-war period, Macedonian revolutionaries in Bulgaria applied intense pressure on the Sofia government not to neglect the Macedonian issue. Their paramilitary arm, the Internal Macedonian Revolutionary Organization, engaged in various acts of terrorism and sabotage in both Yugoslav and Greek Macedonia, as well as in Bulgaria itself. Their goal was either to incorporate Macedonia into Bulgaria or to create an independent Macedonian state. The revolutionaries were eventually combated by Sofia as the government arranged a rapprochement with Belgrade in the late 1930s. Bulgaria again allied with the Germans during World War Two, and following the Nazi dismemberment of Yugoslavia in 1941, Sofia obtained a large portion of Macedonia. Some of the western Macedonian areas in Yugoslavia also fell under Italian-Albanian occupation. All of these territories reverted back to Yugoslavia after the German defeat, and Bulgaria essentially failed to gain any permanent expansion of its Macedonian possessions.

Tito's Communist regime accorded Macedonia the status of a constituent Yugoslav republic. But the federal arrangement was initially more nominal than substantive. Central Communist controls were maintained until 1974 when the new Yugoslav constitution conceded more wide-ranging administrative powers to each of the six federal units. The creation of a distinct Macedonian republic was partially designed to undercut the dominant position of the Serbs and to maintain an inter-republican balance among the major Yugoslav nations. Tito originally planned to create a larger Balkan Communist federation to include an enlarged Macedonia together with Bulgaria and Albania. The project was capsized because of Stalin's opposition and the defeat of Communist insurgents in Greece in the late 1940s. Tito's policy goals raised tensions with Greece, and after Yugoslavia's expulsion from the Soviet bloc, hostilities with Bulgaria also increased. As Moscow's relations with Belgrade deteriorated, Sofia stepped to the forefront of the anti-Yugoslav campaign and revived its claims to Yugoslav Macedonia while eliminating the separate status of its own Macedonian population.

After the break with Bulgaria, Tito continued to promote a distinct Macedonian identity. For example, the Macedonian language was officially recognized and scripted and deliberately distinguished from Bulgarian. Macedonian cultural societies were established and Macedonian identity was promoted in the educational system. During the 1960s, an autocephalous Macedonian Orthodox Church was formally established in a government-engineered schism with the Serbian Orthodox Church. These moves were condemned by Serbian and Bulgarian Orthodox clergymen, but they contributed to satisfying some of the Macedonian aspirations for autonomy and self-determination. The Macedonian issue was played down somewhat by Belgrade on the foreign policy arena, while Moscow attempted to reestablish closer ties with Belgrade and held Sofia in check. But it was revived again during the Yugoslav-Bulgarian disputes in the 1970s and 1980s. The Yugoslav authorities periodically charged Sofia with violating the UN Charter and the Helsinki Agreements by refusing to recognize Macedonians as a distinct national minority and undermining the integrity of Yugoslavia by denying legitimacy to one of its constituent republics. Communist Bulgaria in turn claimed that it harbored no pretensions to Yugoslav territory but charged Belgrade with promoting annexationist ambitions toward Bulgarian territory.

After Tito's death in 1980, Yugoslavia's political crisis fueled nationalist demands in all six republics and energized demands for Macedonian sovereignty. As central controls weakened and the Communist stranglehold increasingly gave way to nationalist and autonomist forces, Macedonia prepared for its first multi-party elections. The balloting in November 1990 produced a fractured parliament in which no party or coalition benefited from a clear majority. However, a revived Internal Macedonian Revolutionary Organization scored remarkably well, as did a new party representing the large Albanian minority. A "government of experts" was formed, drawing on representatives from a spectrum of parties, while the former Communist activist Kiro Gligorov was elected president.

Gligorov at first moved cautiously on the question of secession and independence. He calculated that a renovated confederal Yugoslavia could be established with a much looser relationship between Belgrade and the republics. But following the disassociation of Slovenia and Croatia and the armed conflict in both republics during the summer of 1991, Macedonia affirmed that it would not remain in a Serb-dominated rump Yugoslavia. In a September 1991 referendum, the majority of voters voiced their support for Macedonian independence. The government in Skopje promptly declared Macedonia an independent state and appealed for international recognition. Although the republic evidently fulfilled all the European Community criteria for independent statehood, recognition was effectively blocked by Greece. Athens insisted that Macedonia change its name and desist from adopting any symbols linked with ancient Macedon, which Athens claimed as a purely Hellenic entity despite substantial historical evidence to the contrary. Moreover, the Greek authorities charged that the new republic harbored claims to Greek Macedonia; it was evidently anxious about international campaigns in defense of the suppressed minority rights of Greece's Slavic population. Skopje refused to abide by these demands, although it explicitly renounced all territorial pretensions in its new constitution and declared all of its borders as permanent.

As Macedonia moved toward sovereignty and separation from Yugoslavia, tensions perceptibly increased between the Slav majority and the large Albanian minority that formed its own political organizations. For example, amendments to the Macedonian constitution had redefined the republic as a "nation state of the Macedonian people" thus alienating both Albanian and Turkish activists fearful of anti-minority discrimination. Albanian leaders opposed the new constitution and organized a referendum on territorial autonomy in January 1992. The ballot resulted in an overwhelming pro-autonomy vote, but the outcome was dismissed as invalid by the Skopje government. Some local Albanian activists proceeded to declare an autonomous Albanian region in western Macedonia although the decision was not officially endorsed by minority leaders. Despite the pressures exerted by some Macedonian nationalist groupings to clamp down on Albanian activism, the authorities managed to keep inter-ethnic relations relatively calm by offering Albanian leaders several posts in the coalition government.

Skopje managed successfully to negotiate the withdrawal of Yugoslav troops in early 1992. However, suspicions remained pronounced that Serbia's Milošević leadership upheld expansionist ambitions toward Macedonia and could deliberately aggravate Macedonian-Albanian tensions to destabilize the republic or provoke a major conflict in neighboring Kosovo that would spill over into Macedonia. Such scenarios would provide an appropriate pretext for intervention in which Belgrade could pose as a defender of Macedonian sovereignty against alleged Albanian expansionism. The Albanians in turn could also seek closer links with both Kosovo and Albania if Macedonia experienced increasing internal turmoil. A conflict over Macedonia could quickly spread through the Balkans by embroiling Bulgaria, whose government recognized Macedonian independence but not the existence of a separate Macedonian nation; Greece, whose pro-Serb policies strengthened suppositions that it could be drawn into a partition of Macedonia; Albania, which could seek to defend its co-ethnics; and Turkey, which would find it difficult to sit on the sidelines in the event of Greek involvement, further Serbian expansionism, and a threat to its ally, Albania.

OFFICIAL POLICIES

The first multi-party Macedonian elections were held in November and December 1990, against a backdrop of ethnic tension, resurgent nationalism, growing ruptures among the Yugoslav republics, and accelerating economic deterioration. All of Yugoslavia's six republics were in the throes of the most serious constitutional crisis in the country's post-war history, particularly after the victory of pro-independence movements in Slovenia and Croatia earlier in the year. One hundred and twenty seats were contested for the unicameral Macedonian National Assembly (*sobranie*), and the ballot was widely considered to be a referendum on both Communism and Yugoslav federalism. To gain electoral support, the League of Communists of Macedonia emphasized its commitment to a multi-party system and a modern market economy, while most of the other parties blamed the Communists for Macedonia's economic and political problems. A process of political ethnification was also visible as the two major nationalities, Macedonian Slavs and Albanians, founded their own ethnically based parties. They were less concerned with specific economic prescriptions than with protecting their "national interests" and gaining a measure of self-determination.

Of the twenty registered parties, sixteen put forward candidates for the parliamentary elections. They included: the League of Communists of Macedonia—Party of Democratic Transformation (LCM-PDT); the Alliance of Reform Forces in Macedonia (ARFM), linked with Yugoslavia's reformist prime minister Ante Marković; the Party for Democratic Prosperity (PDP), the largest Albanian party; the Socialist Party—Socialist Alliance of Working People (SP-SAWP); the Movement for Pan-Macedonian Action (MPMA) and the Internal Macedonian Revolutionary Organization—Democratic Party of Macedonian National Unity (IMRO-DPMNU), two nationalist organizations seeking outright Macedonian independence; the Party of Yugoslavs (PY); the Democratic Alliance of Turks (DAT); and the Party for Complete Emancipation of Roma (PCER). After three rounds of balloting, no single party obtained a clear governing majority. A precarious balance was achieved in parliament among the three major political forces: the reform Communists, Macedonian nationalists, and Albanian nationalists.[3] The LCM-PDT, which later renamed itself the Social Democratic Union (SDU), won 31 seats, the Party for Democratic Prosperity and its coalition partner, the National Democratic Party (NDP), gained 23 seats, and IMRO-DPMNU captured 38 seats. The Alliance of Reform Forces obtained only 17 deputies, the Socialist Party of Macedonia 5, the Party of Yugoslavs 2, the PCER 1, while 3 seats went to independent representatives. Although IMRO-DPMNU performed poorly in the first round, the initial success of the PDP and IMRO's adroit use of nationalist issues helped the party to capture the largest bloc of seats after the runoffs. IMRO also took the steam out of the MPMA by advocating a broadly similar program. The Albanian parties lodged complaints over the election process, claiming that the Republican Electoral Commission had gerrymandered districts with large Albanian populations to restrict Albanian representation in parliament. Despite this, the majority of Albanian voters evidently cast ballots along ethnic lines and appeared to elect a total number of deputies commensurate with the estimated size of the Albanian community. With the impressive performance of the PDP in gaining 20 percent of seats to the National Assembly, charges of district gerrymandering were subsequently dropped.

In November and December 1990, the Macedonian electorate also cast ballots for local officials in the 34 county or commune administrations, including the capital, Skopje. As with the national elections, problems were noted in the incomplete and outdated registration lists and in the inability of guest workers from abroad to cast ballots until late on election day. Additional election shortcomings included the short campaign period and the small funds allocated by the state to competing parties. As a result of party complaints, results in 176 polling locations were annulled and the elections replayed. Albanian representatives scored well in the local elections. Out of 239 local officials in the city of Skopje, the ethnic mix included 181 Macedonians, 42 Albanians, 2 Turks, 7 Roma, and 2 Serbs. Out of 70 local representatives in the Skopje Assembly, 53 were Macedonians, 13 Albanians, 2 Roma, and 2 were members of other ethnic groups. In the 34 Macedonian communes, a total of 1,510 councilors were elected, including 1,911 Macedonians, 221 Albanians, 22 Turks, 16 Serbs, 15 Roma, 12 Vlachs, as well as 33 individuals from various smaller nationalities. Albanians obtained clear majorities in 3 western municipalities (Gostivar, Debar, Tetovo). The LCM-PDT gained the largest number of local seats, 512, followed by the ARFM with 313, the PDP with 226, IMRO-DPMNU with 199, the Socialists with 175, the MPMA with 34, the Social Democrats with 10, the Albanian NDP with seven, the PCER with seven, and the rest disbursed among smaller parties. Albanian leaders asserted that in the towns of Tetovo, Gostivar, and Debar, local councils were not properly constituted and remained under a "compulsory government." Local officials refused to transfer power to the victorious Albanian councilors. In fact, a parallel authority operated in these towns as two municipal assemblies—one dominated by Macedonians, the other by Albanians—continued to function.

A Macedonian government was finally installed in March 1991 following intense maneuvering by the major political parties. Neither IMRO-DPMNU nor the PDP were in a position to form an administration or to choose a president acceptable to all sides. The only serious candidate proved to be Kiro Gligorov, former president of the Federal Assembly, former Yugoslav deputy prime minister, and LCM-PDT leader, who was elected president by the republican legislature in January 1991. The new coalition "government of experts" was headed by Prime Minister Nikola Kljušev; the three deputy premiers included Blaže Ristovski, Bečir Zuta, and Jovan Andonov, and the ministries were distributed among the coalition partners. One deputy-premier and two government ministers were ethnic Albanians, but only two of the fifteen ministers had any party affiliation. The new administration seemed determined to avoid any escalation of tensions with the Albanian minority. In addition to gaining ministerial portfolios, the PDP obtained two presidencies and one vice-presidency in key parliamentary committees, as well as representation in the supreme, district, and communal judicial bodies and in Macedonia's Constitutional Court.

The question of the constitution remained a sore point in relations between Macedonian and Albanian leaders. Various proposals were tabled to amend the existing constitution and to design a new republican constitution that would underscore Macedonian statehood. In April 1989, the republic's National Assembly discussed 32 draft amendments to the constitution after several months of intense and sometimes acrimonious debate. The most controversial amendment redefined Macedonia as "the national state of the Macedonian nation," thereby significantly altering the 1974 constitution, in which Macedonia was defined as a state of the "Macedonian people and the Albanian and Turkish minorities." Albanian leaders expressed strong opposition to the amendments and viewed them as a negation of their national rights that could lead to severe discrimination. Despite Albanian protests, several constitutional revisions were formally adopted in October 1989 after the completion of a final round of debates in both private and public forums and after the nine-member state presidency issued a statement in support of the changes.[4]

In August 1990, the Macedonian government rejected an Albanian rights petition drafted by several Albanian organizations and civil leaders. Among other provisions, Albanians demanded the right to use the Albanian language in teaching and in the school administration, wide-ranging reform of the curriculum, and the reinstatement of Albanian teachers previously suspended on political pretexts. The Skopje government justified its decision by stating that the demands contained in the petition deviated from existing legal regulations and constitutional provisions. The National Assembly became more outspoken on the question of Macedonian identity and appeared to be less constrained by the position of the Yugoslav government or the Serbian republic. In June 1990, parliament adopted a declaration concerning Macedonia's relations with neighboring countries and expressed growing concern for the neglected status of Macedonian minorities. The document claimed that Greece, Albania, and Bulgaria continued to apply negative and discriminatory policies toward Macedonian Slavs, thus refusing to recognize their national distinctiveness. It denounced all such actions as essentially repressive and assimilationist.[5]

Cognizant of Macedonia's potentially precarious position in any direct conflict with Serbia in a smaller Yugoslavia, the republican Assembly adopted a declaration on sovereignty and statehood in September 1991. This was despite the concerns of Albanians and other minorities over growing ethnic discrimination in a sovereign Macedonia. Albanian deputies, in particular, charged that the authorities had failed to dispel persistent fears of minority persecution and manifestations of Macedonian chauvinism. Macedonian deputies responded by pointing to Albanian participation in the legislature and in the executive, while expressing fears of Serbian domination in a truncated Yugoslavia. Macedonia and Bosnia-Herzegovina had originally supported a looser federal arrangement with the other republics, but following the secession of Slovenia and Croatia and the outbreak of armed conflicts in the summer of 1991, Skopje moved to protect its integrity and sovereignty and organized a nationwide referendum on independence. In September 1991, 68.32 percent of registered voters cast their ballots in support of Macedonian sovereignty and independence.[6] The ballot also stipulated that a sovereign Macedonia would reserve the right to join a union of independent Yugoslav states at some future date.

Much of the Albanian population boycotted the independence referendum on the grounds that it would become a vulnerable minority in a sovereign Macedonia. The PDP did not discount the possibility of endorsing Macedonian statehood if the government was to guarantee Albanian rights in education, culture, language use, and local administration. To allay the fears of its neighbors, Prime Minister Nikola Kljušev declared that Skopje harbored no territorial claims on Bulgaria, Greece, or Albania. The Milošević regime responded by asserting that Macedonia would not be permitted to secede from Yugoslavia, while the Belgrade authorities were prepared to use force to prevent separation.[7] The Skopje government had initially adopted a more cautious approach than Slovenia and Croatia toward independence, fearing both a possible Yugoslav army assault and claims to its territories by hostile neighbors. The stridently pro-independence IMRO-DPMNU remained in a minority position in the republican parliament and could not push unilaterally for independence. Once the EC announced its conditions for recognizing the statehood of former Yugoslav republics, the Macedonian authorities reconfirmed the republic's independence in December 1991 and canvassed for comprehensive international recognition. Indeed, Macedonia met all the EC conditions for recognition as an independent state as laid out by the arbitration body, the Badinter Commission, including guarantees for rights of ethnic minorities, in accordance with Conference on Security and Cooperation in Europe (CSCE) commitments, and respect for the inviolability of all frontiers. Skopje also successfully negotiated the peaceful withdrawal of about 60,000 Yugoslav troops during early 1992. However, their departure left the nascent Macedonian army in possession of only light infantry weapons.

At the outset, only a handful of states, including Bulgaria, Turkey, and Russia, recognized the new state. The Greek government, not averse to employing hyper-nationalist rhetoric, successfully blocked comprehensive EC recognition on the grounds that Greece held exclusive rights to the name "Macedonia." It also charged Skopje with annexationist pretensions to northern Greek territory where a sizable Slavic population was resident. In order to reassure the international community that Macedonia harbored no expansionist ambitions, a constitutional amendment was promulgated in January 1992 explicitly prohibiting any territorial aspirations. President Gligorov noted that he was willing to enter into a bilateral agreement with Athens, guaranteeing the permanence of borders and establishing cooperative relations.[8] Greece rejected these overtures, and Macedonia was left in a precarious state of limbo. In April 1993, the republic was finally accorded UN membership under the provisional name the Former Yugoslav Republic of Macedonia, pending a final agreement between Skopje and Athens under international mediation.

The Macedonian Assembly adopted a new sovereign constitution in November 1991, despite the abstention of most Albanian deputies.[9] Its first chapter outlined some basic provisions pertaining to all Macedonian citizens including its national minorities. It defined Macedonia as the "national state of the Macedonian people, in which the integral civil equality and enduring coexistence of the Macedonian people with Albanians, Turks, Wallachians (Vlachs), Gypsies, and other nationalities are protected." According to Article 4, all nationals and residents of Macedonia were citizens and could not have their citizenship revoked. In Article 7, the constitution declared that the Macedonian language, written in the Cyrillic alphabet, was the official state language. However, in local self-governing entities in which the majority of inhabitants were members of non-Macedonian ethnic groups, their languages and alphabets would also have official status in accordance with the law and could be used in administrative transactions. Although the Macedonian Orthodox Church was singled out in the constitution, it was not provided with any special legal status or preeminence vis-à-vis other denominations.

Article 8 of the constitution discussed the fundamental values of Macedonia's constitutional system. It specifically underscored the free expression of national affiliation and declared that the Macedonian nation respected the universally accepted standards of international law. According to Article 9, "Citizens of the Republic of Macedonia have equal rights and freedoms regardless of sex, race, color of skin, national and social origin, political or religious beliefs, or property ownership and social status." Article 19 proclaimed that the freedom of religious belief was fully guaranteed and underscored the "free, public, single, or group expression of religious faith." Article 20 ensured freedom of assembly so that citizens could exercise and protect their political, economic, social, cultural, as well as other rights and beliefs. Citizens were able freely to establish associations and political parties and were at liberty to join or withdraw from these bodies. However, the programs and the activities of citizen associations and political parties could not be aimed at violating the constitutional order of the republic by force by "encouraging or calling for the commission of military aggression, or promoting national, racial, or religious hatred or intolerance."

Article 48 of the constitution proclaimed that members of ethnic groups possessed the right to express their ethnicity freely and to "promote and develop their identity and special ethnic character." The article affirmed that Macedonia guaranteed the protection of the "ethnic, cultural, linguistic, and religious identity of all ethnic groups." For instance, members of ethnic groups had the right to establish their own cultural and artistic institutions as well as scientific and other associations in order to express, promote, and develop their identities. In addition, members of all ethnic groups had the right to be taught in their own language at primary and secondary school level, through means approved by the law. The Macedonian language would also be taught in schools in which instruction was provided in the language of minority ethnic groups. Article 54 stated that any restriction on individual rights and freedoms may not be discriminatory in terms of sex, race, color of skin, language, religious faith, or social origin, as well as property ownership or social status.

Despite protestations by Albanian leaders that their educational, cultural, and publishing needs remained underfulfilled, the Macedonian government pointed out that the republic had an exemplary record in providing appropriate schooling and cultural and media outlets for the minorities. For instance, out of 1,087 elementary schools during the 1989–90 school year, 281 conducted instruction in the Albanian language and 56 schools offered classes in Turkish. At the secondary-school level, out of 91 schools, 10 provided Albanian classes, and 2 schools offered Turkish classes. Albanians contended that there was no Albanian-language university and minimal language instruction at the national university, while the number of Albanian-language schools at the secondary level remained insufficient. Out of 10 national theaters, Skopje had 1 "nationalities" theater with Albanian and Turkish performances, while 4 cultural centers provided facilities for Macedonians, Albanians, Turks, and Roma. Albanians benefited from 9 cultural-artistic and cultural-educational associations, while Turks possessed 4 cultural-artistic associations.

In the publishing field, Macedonia had 1 high-circulation Albanian-language newspaper and 3 smaller reviews, as well as 1 mass-circulation Turkish newspaper. In addition, books and school texts continued to be published in several minority languages. Although Albanian leaders were dissatisfied with media provisions, Skopje calculated that in a ten-month period during 1991 nearly 1,000 hours broadcast on Macedonian radio were in Albanian, 650 hours in Turkish, 18 hours in Romani, and 17 hours in Vlach. During the same period, Macedonian TV broadcast 111 hours in Albanian, 111 hours in Turkish, 12 hours in Romani, and 12 hours in Vlach. Albanian leaders demanded the operation of a minority television channel, even though the time allocated for Albanian-language news on existing channels doubled after the 1990 elections.

Article 78 of the constitution explained that the National Assembly was empowered to establish a Council on Inter-Ethnic Relations. This council was nominated in October 1992 and was comprised of the president of the Assembly, two Macedonians, and two representatives each from five minority groups: Serbs, Roma, Vlachs, Turks, and Albanians. The primary function of the council was to debate issues related to inter-ethnic relations in the republic and to submit ideas and suggestions for the resolution of impending problems. According to Article 84, the president of Macedonia was empowered to nominate the members of the council.[10] Albanian leaders complained that the council was only a consulting body whose decisions were not obligatory for state organs, while its composition did not proportionally represent the national minorities.

The PDP leadership lodged complaints that according to constitutional provisions, and despite numerous nominal guarantees, Albanians did not enjoy equal rights with the Slav Macedonians. Their principal claim was that Albanians should not figure in the constitution as a "national minority." They should either figure as a constituent "nation" with equal rights vis-à-vis other nations, or the document should not differentiate on the basis of ethnicity but simply focus on citizenship. The president of the PDP, Nevzat Halili, asserted that he would wait until after the new constitution was adopted by parliament to introduce changes in the definition and rights of Albanians. He warned that if constitutional stipulations proved unsatisfactory then the Albanians would organize a separate referendum, declare the Macedonian constitution as non-binding, and proceed to take measures toward "cultural and territorial independence."[11] This could culminate in the proclamation of an Autonomous Region of Western Macedonia that would have the right to enter into alliances with other states.

Indeed, in early January 1992, a referendum on "political and territorial autonomy" was held among the Albanian minority despite government protestations and charges of illegality. The turnout reportedly exceeded 90 percent, and over 95 percent of the ballots were cast in favor of political and cultural autonomy for Albanian areas in western Macedonia. Albanian activists claimed that organizers of the referendum had received threats and 260 polling stations were ransacked and voting material was confiscated. After the voting, in April 1992 activists in several predominantly Albanian municipalities in western Macedonia declared the region as the "Republic of Ilirida." The PDP leadership distanced itself from this decision, which was officially condemned by the government in Skopje. Despite its caution over partitioning Macedonia, the PDP was clearly in favor of wide-ranging autonomy. At its first congress in February 1992, the party passed a resolution asking the Macedonian authorities to recognize the independence of Kosovo and the autonomy of Albanian regions of western Macedonia.[12] Neither declaration was forthcoming from Skopje as it tried to avoid antagonizing Serbia or setting any precedents for the partition of Macedonian territory. Despite the referendum, PDP leaders did not push forward on the question of autonomy, calculating that this would further destabilize the state and give ammunition to Macedonian nationalists. Indeed, the autonomy question was manipulated more as a challenge to wrench various concessions from the government. Albanian spokesmen complained over a host of discriminatory measures against the minority in job opportunities, in media access, and in representation in the military and police forces. The government claimed that it was introducing limited measures to ameliorate the ethnic imbalance and to counter the pattern of discrimination.

Tensions with the Albanian minority mounted visibly on several occasions. For instance, in November 1992, thousands of Albanians demonstrated in central Skopje after the Macedonian police allegedly beat an Albanian cigarette vendor. The rallies turned into riots, and three Albanians and one Macedonian bystander were shot dead. Although the incident did not trigger an escalation of communal conflicts, it served as a warning that ethnic grievances and misperceptions could be exploited to destabilize the country. A government enquiry subsequently implied that foreign agents may have been responsible for the November events, while Albanian leaders claimed that the police simply used excessive force against protesters. Although Macedonia and Albania established reasonably cordial relations, several border incidents during 1992 and 1993 in which Macedonian guards shot dead Albanian citizens illegally crossing into the republic aggravated tensions within and between both states.

IMRO-DPMNU and other nationalist groupings adopted a militant stance toward both the Albanian leadership and the incumbent government. It accused the Albanians of planning to overrun the republic numerically, pointing to the high Albanian birthrate, and of calling for autonomy as a preliminary step toward outright secession and annexation by Albania. In addition, the PDP was charged with deliberately fanning ethnic tensions and of being an appendage of the pro-independence Albanian movement in Kosovo.[13] Conversely, IMRO-DPMNU accused the Skopje administration of being overindulgent with Albanian politicians, a policy that simply stimulated more extremist demands. Nationalists asserted that Albanians had no right to any special status. They opposed any extension of Albanian educational rights, any moves toward decentralization, federalism, or Albanian autonomy in western Macedonia, and demanded new republican elections to put the question of Albanian rights to all voters. The Gligorov leadership resisted calls for early elections, claiming that they could lead to intolerable ethnic polarization at a precarious juncture in Macedonia's quest for international recognition as an independent state. Throughout 1992, IMRO-DPMNU continued to attack the administration for failing to win outright international recognition, perversely accusing Gligorov and his associates of being Serb-Yugoslav agents while itself adopting a strong pro-Bulgarian position. Conflicts over international recognition, Skopje's foreign policy, and the position of the Albanian minority virtually paralyzed the legislative process. Meanwhile, the destructive impact of UN sanctions on Yugoslavia adversely affected the Macedonian economy (which was dependent on Belgrade for over 60 percent of its trade), thus raising social tensions in the republic.

After months of bitter dispute, the Kljušev government lost a vote of no-confidence in July 1992 and was replaced by a broad-based coalition in September

1992. IMRO-DPMNU was given the opportunity to form a government but proved unable to elicit sufficient parliamentary support. Branko Crvenkovski, a member of the Social Democratic Union, eventually assembled a coalition of SDU, ARF, and PDP representatives, together with several smaller parties. IMRO-DPMNU was once again left out of the equation. Albanian representatives received 5 out of the 21 ministries, including 1 deputy premiership, but they complained that this figure did not properly reflect their numbers and thereby diminished their influence in decision making. The SDU retained 11 ministries, including the key portfolios of defense, internal affairs, and justice. One minister was an ethnic Turk. This fairly moderate and broad coalition survived a no-confidence vote lodged by IMRO deputies in April 1993 over the unresolved issue of Macedonia's international recognition.

Relations among Macedonia's minorities have also not been trouble-free. Indeed, tensions have surfaced between Albanians and Turks, as some Turkish activists claimed that Albanian leaders were exaggerating their numbers by including other Islamic communities in their population estimates, including Turks, Roma, and Slavic Muslims. In January 1992, the Association of Macedonian Muslims issued a public statement opposing the Albanian referendum on autonomy. The party declared that the referendum was a deliberate anti-Macedonian act directed against the international recognition of the state and leading the Albanian population to further ghettoization.[14] Tensions have also been manifested between Slav Muslim and Turkish leaders, with the former evidently fearful of potential Turkification campaigns.

Serbian radicals have also been active in Macedonia, capitalizing on the country's precarious international position. During 1992, local followers of Serbian Radical Party leader Vojislav Šešelj reportedly made plans to set up a Serbian Autonomous Region of the Kumanovo Valley and Skopska Crna Gora in northern Macedonia. Leaders of Serbian parties explicitly objected to the omission of the "Serbian nation" in the republic's constitution and claimed that Serbs were denied elementary rights in education, employment, and in access to the mass media. Tensions have on occasion erupted in protest actions, and on New Year's Day 1993, Macedonian police clashed with Serbian youths in the village of Kučevište. The authorities suspected that the incidents were provoked by nationalists in Belgrade.

Conflicts have also persisted in relations between the Serbian and Macedonian Orthodox churches, particularly as the latter has never been officially recognized by the former, which sought to have the Church returned to its jurisdiction. In December 1992, the Serbian Orthodox Church created a Patriarchate in Niš (Serbia) to administer all former "Serbian" diocese until a new Metropolitan of Skopje was appointed. In May 1993, the Serbian Church appointed Archimandrite Jovan as its administrator of the diocese of the Macedonian Orthodox Church. The authorities in Skopje described this as a provocation confirming that Serbia was interfering in Macedonia's internal affairs. Skopje has also remained concerned over potential Serb-Greek collaboration in carving up the young Macedonian state. To counter such threats, it has demanded full diplomatic recognition by Western states and some credible security guarantees, in addition to economic assistance and financial credits to help stabilize the country. The small UN peacekeeping force, augmented by a unit of U.S. troops during the summer of 1993, was viewed as a positive step in this direction.[15]

In October 1992, the Macedonian government promulgated a new Citizenship Law with a fifteen-year residency requirement that placed many citizens of the former Yugoslav federation in an ambiguous position. In particular, Albanians charged that the measure would have a deleterious impact on the status of ethnic Albanians, Serbs, and Muslims. Under the law, non-Macedonians resident in the republic for less than fifteen years would only be eligible for citizenship if they could prove a permanent source of income and if they were above 18 years of age; those who did not meet these stipulations were likely to be deported.[16] Albanian leaders, who sought a maximum five-year residency requirement, asserted that the measure would in effect disenfranchise a large segment of the Albanian population that had evacuated from Kosovo in recent years. The passage of the Citizenship Law demonstrated that even a measure evidently designed to limit the potential for ethnic strife, by placating nationalist opposition and preserving the country's ethnic balance, could in itself foster conflict and polarization.

MACEDONIAN NATIONALISTS

Internal Macedonian Revolutionary Organization
—Democratic Party for Macedonian National Unity (IMRO-DPMNU)
Vnatrešna Makedonska Revolucionerna Organizacija
—Demokratska Partija za Makedonsko Nacionalno Edinstvo (VMRO-DPMNE)

Several nationalist parties were established during 1990 demanding complete Macedonian sovereignty and statehood in the face of mounting Yugoslav turmoil. The Internal Macedonian Revolutionary Organization—Democratic Party for Macedonian National Unity (IMRO-DPMNU) held its founding congress in June 1990 in Skopje. The party's platform called for a "spiritual, economic, and ethnic union of the divided Macedonian people and the creation of a Macedonian state in a future united Balkans and united Europe." IMRO-DPMNU was led by Ljupčo Georgievski, who had previously been a member of the Movement for Pan-Macedonian Action. He was elected chairman in April 1991, replacing Vladimir Golubovski, who left the party after bitter divisions over its leadership and program. IMRO-DPMNU advocated the creation of a parliamentary democracy respecting the equality of citizens. Georgievski specified, however, that "because of the aggression of Albanian nationalists and their parties, Macedonia can be the national state only of the Macedonian people."

In the first multi-party elections in November-December 1990, IMRO-DPMNU gained 37 seats to the 120-seat National Assembly, thereby surpassing all other parties but being insufficient to form a government. Georgievski became vice-president of Macedonia after the ballot but resigned during 1991 to indicate his dissatisfaction with both President Gligorov and the incumbent government. When the new administration was formed, IMRO-DPMNU went into parliamentary opposition. Although renouncing IMRO's pre-war terrorist heritage, it pledged to continue its political traditions and opposed any amendments to the republican constitution that would limit Macedonian sovereignty. IMRO leaders also called for the recognition of Macedonian minorities by neighboring states and appeared to depart from IMRO's traditional pro-Bulgarian orientation by calling for a sovereign Macedonia in a future Balkan confederation. Nevertheless, its critics asserted that the organization was "supremacist" and in the service of "Greater Bulgarianism." IMRO-DPMNU initially advocated a looser political arrangement in Yugoslavia but expressed apprehensions about Serbian domination in a smaller federation. Some IMRO factions also expressed more ambitious irredentist objectives by seeking the union of all former Macedonian territories in Yugoslavia, Bulgaria, and Greece. IMRO activists also claimed that the Albanians were a subversive element in Macedonian society. They accused Albanian leaders of turning the republic into a center for smuggling and black marketeering while hatching plans to tear away Macedonia's western regions.

In April 1991, IMRO-DPMNU held a congress in Prilep and passed a resolution emphasizing that the party would struggle for an independent Macedonian state that would embody the ideals of the Kruševo uprising and the revolutionary hero Goce Delčev. Party leaders insisted that the defense and security of the Macedonian state be ensured through the immediate creation of a Macedonian army. Spokesmen also advocated the demilitarization of the "Macedonian national space," clearly implying claims to parts of Bulgaria and Greece. By the close of 1992, IMRO-DPMNU boasted a membership of some 150,000 people, with branches in every region of the country as well as 10 sections abroad among Macedonian exiles. It also established a youth organization and published the newspaper *Glas* (Voice) at irregular intervals. However, because of factional disputes, the number of IMRO-DPMNU seats in parliament was reduced to 35 during the course of 1991–92. IMRO deputies continued to criticize the government on both national and socioeconomic grounds. They claimed that the governing coalition had failed in promptly ensuring Macedonia's international recognition and internal security while it allegedly pursued an essentially neo-Communist economic agenda. IMRO-DPMNU has also periodically staged nationalist rallies in Skopje and other large cities to mobilize its supporters. For instance, in February 1993, IMRO-DPMNU and MPMA organized a two-day anti-Muslim demonstration protesting against a government decision to construct a camp in Skopje's suburbs to house refugees from Bosnia. Nationalist leaders argued that the mass inflow of refugees would tilt the ethnic balance in Macedonia in favor of Albanians and other Muslims, thus undermining Macedonia's independence.[17]

Internal Macedonian Revolutionary Organization
—Democratic Party (IMRO-DP)
Vnatrešna Makedonska Revolucionerna Organizacija
—Demokratska Partija (VMRO-DP)

The new IMRO-Democratic Party was first constituted in Ohrid in January 1991 as an offshoot of IMRO-DPMNU. It was founded and directed by Vladimir Golubovski, who had previously led the IMRO-DPMNU but left the organization as a result of severe political and personality disputes. He claimed that IMRO-DPMNU had become dominated by outside forces and influenced by Serbs, and he refused to recognize the new leadership. Golubovski threatened to file charges against the leaders who had replaced him in IMRO-DPMNU, especially against the new president, Ljupčo Georgievski. Golubovski initially advocated a confederal status for Macedonia within the Yugoslav community, as well as a confederal army, and new legislative elections to "overcome the incompetence of the delegates in the Macedonian Assembly." With the collapse of Yugoslavia, IMRO-DP adopted a staunchly pro-independence program, while continuing to attack the ambitions of Albanian minority leaders. Golubovski repeatedly attacked the republican government for pursuing "an indulgent policy toward the Albanians." He denied that the party upheld an anti-minority position and claimed its willingness to recognize the rights of all minorities according to standards set by international conventions. However, IMRO-DP has been consistently critical of Albanian activists for their incessant demands for self-determination and autonomy that would in effect truncate Macedonian territory and leave the country exposed to renewed foreign domination. Golubovski stated that the national question would remain at the center of the party's program. Although the DP benefited from only limited public support, it claimed it would rapidly acquire a broader membership in an independent Macedonia. IMRO-DP has also been accused by its critics of adopting a militant pro-Bulgarian position and of favoring the eventual unification of Macedonia with Bulgaria. Party leaders stated that they simply wanted to reorient Macedonia away from its economic dependence on Serbia toward other regional powers.[18]

Movement for Pan-Macedonian Action (MPMA)
Dviženje za Semakedonska Akcija (MAAK)

The nationalist MPMA was established by Macedonian intellectuals in Skopje in February 1990. The party announced that it represented all Macedonian people no matter where they lived. Its leaders, Gane Todorovski and Ante Popovski, outlined the Movement's intentions in February 1990 when its founding assembly gathered. They stressed that the MPMA program advocated the immediate and accelerated development of the republic, the productive use of its human resources and natural wealth, as well as the free exchange of ideas, know-how, and experience. The Movement avowedly supported a law-governed, democratic state with a multi-party system and claimed to oppose any forms of discrimination. In August 1990, the organization reaffirmed its position when it issued a manifesto on a free, sovereign, and independent state of Macedonia in front of the tomb of Macedonian revolutionary hero Goce Delčev in the Holy Salvation church in Skopje. The declaration affirmed that Macedonia needed independent statehood in order to gain the attributes of a modern European nation and criticized the government for failing to attain this objective. Following national elections in November 1990, MPMA leaders demanded that a ban be placed on the Albanian parties because their activities were a threat to the constitutional order and allegedly incited national and religious intolerance. They claimed that Macedonian Slavs in the western part of the country were subjected to fear and uncertainty under an accelerated process of Albanianization.

Prior to the general elections in November 1990, MPMA, IMRO, the Peoples Party, and a number of smaller nationalist organizations formed a Front for Macedonian Unity in order to gain a sizable block of seats in the National Assembly and counter the electoral success of the reform Communists and Albanian parties. In its program, the Front called for a sovereign Macedonia in a confederal Yugoslavia and proposed forging a united platform against the Albanian political movement. Despite its nationalist agenda, the MPMA failed to gain seats in the November 1990 elections, claiming it was denied sufficient time to organize a proper election campaign; it barely reached 3.2 percent of the popular vote. Much of its nationalist appeal was captured by the better-organized IMRO-DPMNU. Following the ballot, the MPMA expanded its organization, and by early 1993 it claimed branches in 31 districts, with a membership of 20,000 people, and also established a youth wing and a newsletter. Critics of MPMA claimed that the organization was sponsored by Belgrade in an effort to disrupt the republic. Pro-Bulgarian nationalists also charged that MPMA leaders were providing clandestine assistance to the *Ilinden* organization in Bulgaria, an "illegal" grouping allegedly backed by Belgrade to wrest Pirin Macedonia from the Bulgarian state and to create conflictive rifts between Skopje and Sofia. In November 1991, the MPMA pushed for the immediate adoption of the Macedonian constitution, declaring statehood an urgent necessity for protection against encroaching extremist forces. It also displayed some moderation on the security arena by calling for the demilitarization of the republic under UN and CSCE guarantees of Macedonia's security.[19]

More radical nationalist splinter groups have also been formed during the last few years, unequivocally calling for a "united Macedonia" to embrace the Aegean (Greek), Pirin (Bulgarian), and Vardar (post-Yugoslav) regions, together with some border adjustments with Serbia in favor of Macedonia. They were banking on increasing their appeal among young people and workers experiencing economic deprivation in one of the poorest regions in the former Yugoslavia. They also seemed intent on garnering support among approximately 400,000 Macedonian Slavs living in Macedonia who traced their family origins to northern Greece. Several nationalist Macedonian groupings, including IMRO and MPMA, have supported the recognition and ethnic revival of the contested Macedonian Slav minority in northern Greece. Indeed, during 1990 an Assembly of Aegean Macedonians (AAM) reportedly established its headquarters in Skopje, as did the Dignity (*Dostoinstvo*) human rights organization focusing on violations of minority rights in Greece.

While these groups claimed that the Slav population in Greece totaled over 300,000 and was denied basic minority rights, Athens charged they were intent on provoking separatist tendencies in Greece. A group styling itself as the Central Committee for Macedonian Human Rights (CCMHR) was formed in Thessaloniki during 1989. Such organizations regularly condemned Greek policy, called for closer border ties between Macedonians in both states, and sponsored protest actions on frontier crossings. In early 1992, Macedonian activists in the Greek town of Sopotsko established a Macedonian Movement for Balkan Prosperity (MMBP); among its leadership was the former Orthodox cleric Archimandrite Nikodimos Carknjas, who was thrown out of the Greek Church on charges of being an "autonomist" and a "Skopje agent." The Movement was refused registration by the Greek authorities, who appeared determined to thwart any manifestations of a Slavic cultural or political revival in northern Greece. MMBP leaders called for the respect of human rights, schooling for Macedonian children in their native language, and permission for holding church services in the Macedonian language under the jurisdiction of the Macedonian Orthodox Church. The Movement also demanded that the Greek state grant rights of free communications and repatriation to all political and nonpolitical refugees and undertake measures to ensure them free information on clubs and societies "fostering genuine Macedonian culture." In January 1993, in Sopotsko, the first All-Macedonian Congress was held, with the participation of the MMBP's local committees. The congress adopted a declaration that cited the discriminatory policies that the Greek state was allegedly pursuing with respect to the Macedonian minority in *Belomorska* Makedonija (Aegean Macedonia). Congress participants called for closer cooperation between Macedonians in Greece and their compatriots in the diaspora, while affirming respect for the inviolability of borders.[20]

ALBANIAN AUTONOMISTS

Party for Democratic Prosperity (PDP)
Partija za Demokratski Prosperitet (PDP)

The Party for Democratic Prosperity was set up by Albanian minority leaders in April 1990. Its strongest base was in the western communes of Macedonia, where the majority of the Albanian population was concentrated, although it also claimed some Turkish, Romani, and Vlach members. The PDP's president, Nevzat Halili, and vice-president, Sami Ibrahimi, indicated early on that the PDP primarily represented Albanian interests, although it was also prepared to defend the rights of other minorities. The party called for constitutional changes to provide Albanians with a more equitable position in Macedonia, greater educational rights, the comprehensive use of the Albanian language, the release of all political prisoners, and an end to all forms of discrimination. The PDP quickly grew into the largest Albanian organization, claiming to have 18 local branches and several sections abroad. In coalition with the National Democratic Party, the PDP won 25 seats to the republican legislature in November–December 1990, as well as sizable majorities on local councils in 3 municipalities during the local elections. PDP claimed that it would have obtained a much larger parliamentary representation if a proportional election law had been in effect and if the election authorities had not gerrymandered several electoral districts. Party leaders asserted that approximately 40 percent of the country's population were Albanian, contrary to the official statistics of around 20 percent. In a display of protest against allegedly rising Macedonian nationalism, the party urged a boycott of the 1991 republican census asserting that the number of Albanians represented among census takers was not proportional to the size of the Albanian population, thereby opening up the possibility of statistical fraud. The PDP also abstained from voting on the new constitution, arguing that the document did not provide sufficient provision for the group rights of Albanians. Halili asserted that he would continue to press for amendments in the constitution to redefine the Albanians as a constituent nation and more solidly guarantee their "collective rights." If this proved impossible to achieve, then the PDP would consider the constitution invalid and undertake steps toward full minority autonomy.

PDP leaders have urged the holding of new elections once a fairer election law was passed by parliament and electoral districts were rearranged. They also supported some measure of territorial autonomy for regions containing Albanian majorities within an independent Macedonia. According to Halili, such regions could form an Assembly of Citizens that would be eligible to pass laws on education, the local economy, police, and local courts. A referendum on autonomy among the Albanian community in January 1992 was won overwhelmingly by a pro-autonomy vote, but the plebiscite was immediately dismissed as invalid by the Macedonian government. After the ballot, several local leaders in predominantly Albanian communes in western Macedonia declared the region as the Republic of Ilirida, stating their objective as the unification of all Albanians in the former Yugoslavia. In the interim, they favored the federalization of Macedonia in which Ilirida would cover approximately half of the republic's territory. The government vowed to combat any anti-constitutional attempts to create parallel authorities in Macedonia. PDP leaders criticized the Ilirida proclamation and denied that they intended to partition Macedonia and join the region with an independent Kosovo or with Albania. The state-controlled Belgrade media reported with some relish on the Ilirida declaration and the potential partition of Macedonia.

Despite their participation in the government and legislature, PDP leaders remained concerned about official discrimination, the provocation of ethnic conflicts in the republic, as well as potentially damaging spill-overs from the conflict in Kosovo. They attacked the IMRO organizations for their alleged anti-Albanian chauvinism and suggested that Serbian security forces were seeking to infiltrate these organizations in order to engineer ethnic unrest. The PDP held its first congress in February 1992 and passed a resolution recognizing the independence of Kosovo from Serbia and the principles of Albanian autonomy in western Macedonia. Some radical activists wanted eventually to unite the area with the Kosovo republic, a position that was at least publicly opposed by the party leadership.

The PDP held a mass rally in April 1992 in the main square in Skopje that was attended by thousands of ethnic Albanians. Chairman Halili presented the rally's purpose in thirteen points. He declared that Albanians considered Macedonia as their home and that Skopje itself held many of their graves. But he underscored that Albanians remained dissatisfied with their status as "second-class citizens" and condemned the EC for not providing sufficient support on behalf of the Albanian population in all the former Yugoslav republics. Among other demands, the PDP called for a petition drive to conduct a referendum on changing the constitution, proportional representation for nationalities in local government organs, a greater measure of local autonomy, and equal status for the Albanian and Macedonian languages. In September 1992, the PDP received five ministries in the Crvenkovski coalition government, including a deputy-premiership, but complained that they were excluded from the most important portfolios. Despite their criticisms of various government policies, PDP representatives realized that their withdrawal from the executive would further limit their influence and simply place them in long-term opposition.[21]

National Democratic Party (NDP)
Narodna Demokratska Partija (NDP)

The NDP was created in early 1990 and was chaired by Iljaz Halimi. It entered into an electoral coalition with the PDP for the first parliamentary elections in November 1990, and gained one deputy to the National Assembly. In parliament, the NDP maintained its coalition with the much larger PDP, while often adopting more radical positions in its criticisms of the government and in its approach toward Albanian political and territorial autonomy. The NDP was active in organizing the boycott of the Macedonian census as well as the referendum on Macedonian independence, and its leaders were outspoken critics of the new constitution. During 1992, the party promoted a "Draft Platform for National Equality in Macedonia," calling for the federalization of Macedonia with the creation of an autonomous Albanian region. It also proposed the formal redefinition of Macedonia as a binational state.[22]

Republican Party (RP)
Republikanska Partija (RP)

Founders of the Albanian-based Republican Party announced their program in July 1992. The RP was organized by an Initiative Committee that included its Chairman Miftar Ziberi, one of the founders of the PDP, and parliamentary deputy Muhamed Halili. The party aimed to establish a broad base among Albanian intellectuals, but it would remain open to all ethnic groups and would promulgate an essentially civic program. RP leaders believed that there were many uncommitted intellectuals in the country who would be willing to join the party and who sincerely supported the existence of an independent Macedonia. The RP appeared to distance itself from the more militant agendas of the larger PDP and the NDP.[23]

Albanian Democratic Union—Liberal Party (ADU-LP)
Albanski Demokratski Sojuz—Liberalna Partija (ADS-LP)

The Albanian Democratic Union-Liberal Party was legalized in 1992. Its chairman, Džemail Idrizi, stated that the party's fundamental goals for the Albanian nation in Macedonia included full civil liberties, equality, open borders, and the free flow of goods. Idrizi declared that Macedonia did not consist solely of one nation but was multi-national and multi-confessional and the constitution should acknowledge this state of affairs. The party condemned the forceful denationalization allegedly imposed on Albanian ethnics in the past and advocated the independent decision of every citizen, including Slavic Muslims, to choose their own national identity. The ADU-LP has placed emphasis on its civic orientation rather than any ethnically based platform. It has on occasion been critical of the PDP–NDP alliance for their more radical stance and has strongly supported Macedonian sovereignty and independence.[24]

MINORITY ORGANIZATIONS

Association of Macedonian Muslims (AMM)
Združenie na Makedonci Muslimani (ZMM)

The Association of Macedonian Muslims, led by Dževat Djulioski, who replaced Ljatif Pajkovski, aspired to work for the cultural and national renaissance of Slavic Muslims in Macedonia. According to the AMM, Muslim Macedonians encountered serious problems of awareness regarding their national identity. In addition, Muslim leaders claimed that both Albanian and Turkish activists were attempting to Turkify them. They resolutely opposed any attempts to denationalize segments of the Macedonian population on the basis of ethnicity, religion, or politics. Leaders of the AMM asserted that the PDP and other Albanian nationalist groups had used the Muslim religion for their own separatist goals and strenuously decried the manipulation of Islam for political purposes. The AMM urged all Macedonian Muslims to fight with "all available means" the alleged nationalism of some minority parties that were trying to recruit Slav Muslims for the separatist idea of a "Greater Albania," asserting that this would fan religious intolerance and cause a rift among Macedonian citizens. The AMM transformed itself into a political party during 1992 so that it could function more effectively among its Muslim constituency. Party leaders claimed that Muslims were exposed to serious restrictions and threats by elements of some Albanian parties, including the PDP and the NDP, and subjected to Turkification by leaders of the Turkish community. They protested against the Albanian referendum of January 1992, considering it a provocation directed against the recognition of Macedonia as an independent state, and urged all Slavic Muslims to boycott the ballot.[25]

Democratic Party of Turks (DPT)
Demokratska Partija na Turcite (DPT)

The DPT was converted from a union into a political party at its second extraordinary congress in June 1992 after the Macedonian parliament changed the legislation so that only parties could participate in national elections. Its chairman Avni Engülü emphasized the necessity for a more organized national orientation among Turks so that they would be viewed as an equal national community in an independent Macedonia. DPT leaders contended that Turks had not fully understood that in an embryonic pluralistic democracy it was necessary to form their own political party. The union pledged to support a free, sovereign, united, and independent Macedonia and called for the defense of its territorial integrity and the equality of all citizens before the constitution. It urged the full participation of Turks in Macedonia's political life and sought equitable representation for Turks in all government structures as this would help to stabilize the republic. But the DPT did not promote political or territorial autonomy, cognizant of the dispersal of the Turkish population and concerned about ethnic polarization in Macedonia. However, it demanded an expansion of educational programs for Turkish speakers and the inclusion of Turks in the country's security and police forces.

DPT leaders claimed discrimination in parts of the republic at the hands of local authorities; some charges were investigated and dismissed by the administration as grossly exaggerated. At one point, DPT president Erdoğan Saraç claimed that Turks in Macedonia were "threatened with extinction," and in April 1993 he declared a "state of emergency" for DPT members and threatened to urge all ethnic Turks to emigrate to Turkey unless "Macedonian authorities take seriously this final warning to stop the harassment of Turks." Saraç issued several specific demands, including the withdrawal of police forces from the Debar area in western Macedonia, the return of expelled Turkish teachers to their schools, and the appointment of ethnic Turks to ministry-level positions. Radical elements of the DPT have also openly demanded the conversion of Muslim Slavs into ethnic Turks leading to charges of "pan-Turkism" by Macedonian nationalists and Muslim leaders alike.[26]

Party for Complete Emancipation of Roma (PCER)
Partija za Celosna Emancipacjia na Romite (PCER)

The primary objectives of the PCER, as stated by Abdi Faik, the party's president, were to secure more substantive rights for the Romani population in Macedonia. Faik became a member of the Macedonian parliament for the Šuto Orizari township and displayed pride in citing the progress that the Roma had made in recent years in achieving recognition as a national minority. In September 1990, Romani leaders called on the population to stop identifying themselves as Albanians or Turks simply on the basis of their religious affiliation. In 1992, the PCER claimed to have 36,000 members in local branches throughout the country. The party held its third plenary meeting in Skopje in November 1992 and addressed several issues regarding the provision of education and information in the Gypsy language. It called for the standardization of the Romani language and its use in elementary and secondary schools, with daily newscasts on television and radio. Some progress was subsequently achieved and a Romani educational program was prepared by the Ministry of Education and scheduled for introduction in elementary schools beginning in September 1993. The PCER was also successful in securing the opening of a department of Romani studies at Skopje University, as well as the transmission of television and radio programs in Romani. Some Macedonian nationalists claimed that the PCER was being pressured to adopt more militant positions; its leaders have evidently suggested that a Gypsy state called "Romanistan" be founded in the Balkans, while claiming that nearly 220,000 Roma live in Macedonia. However, the PCER has condemned the more radical position of its rival, the DPPRM (see below), and has repeatedly expressed its support for the Skopje leadership. The "Romanistan" concept was not an outright separatist demand but appeared designed to underscore the existence of a Romani nation in the Balkans and to canvass for international protection.[27]

Democratic Progressive Party of Roma in Macedonia (DPPRM)
Demokratska Progresivna Partija na Romite vo Makedonija (DPPRM)

The DPPRM was formed in 1991 in opposition to what it considered the moderate stance of the PCER. Its general secretary, Djuneš Mustafa, complained that the Romani population was subject to social and political experimentation and assimilation; as proof, he cited an alleged agreement between Skopje and Bonn to return and reintegrate Gypsy refugees living in Germany. The DPPRM asked the government to take into consideration the possible consequences for Romani workers in the conversion of industry from public to private ownership, claiming Roma were often considered merely as surplus labor. Mustafa also made statements in support of establishing a separate state of "Romanistan" in the Balkan region that would encompass parts of Macedonia.

Egyptian Association of Citizens (EAC)
Združenie na Egipčanite (ZE)

The EAC was established in Ohrid in 1990, shortly before the first multi-party elections. Led by Nazim Arifi, it claimed a membership of 4,000 in the Ohrid and Struga areas of southwestern Macedonia; these people had renounced their Romani identity and asserted their purportedly Egyptian heritage. The EAC claimed that there were close to 30,000 people of Egyptian descent in Macedonia and petitioned to include this category in the 1991 census; the state complied with their demands, although the number of people declaring themselves as Egyptians fell below EAC expectations. The EAC also calculated that a further 100,000 Egyptians lived in Kosovo, a claim that was ridiculed by both Serbian and Albanian leaders. The basis of their identification revolved around the notion that thousands of Gypsies had migrated from Asia to Egypt during the Middle Ages and some of these people later crossed to the Balkans. Despite these assertions, the EAC has had only limited success in canvassing for a separate nation and in gaining public support among the Romani populace.[28]

Democratic Party of Serbs (DPS)
Demokratska Partija na Srbite (DPS)

Although a legally registered party, the DPS asserted that Serbs were the most discriminated-against population in Macedonia. The party protested the exclusion of Serbs and Montenegrins from mention in the Macedonian constitution, which explicitly guaranteed minority rights to Albanians, Turks, Roma, and Vlachs. It claimed that there were numerous problems regarding the status of Serbs in Macedonia: for example, in pursuing education in the Serbian language, maintaining cultural traditions, and observing religious practices in Serbian churches. The party was founded and based in the northern Macedonian town of Kumanovo, near the Serbian border. Kumanovo was seen as one of Macedonia's most volatile areas, as Albanians comprised 36 percent of the population and Serbs 15 percent. DPS president Borivoje Ristić outlined the party's intentions in an interview in January 1993. He discussed several future goals such as enshrining the legal status of Serbs and Montenegrins as distinct nations, the right to education in the mother tongue, full religious freedom, and Serb and Montene-grin broadcasts on state television. Ristić asserted that there was no reason for Serbs to be condemned for maintaining ties with their country of origin. How-ever, Macedonian nationalists countered that although Serbs comprised only 2 percent of the Macedonian population, they could be used as a pretext for Serbia to intervene in the republic and claim territory for a "Greater Serbian" state.

As Macedonia moved toward independence, some DPS leaders asserted that the aim of the Macedonian government was "the deliberate elimination of Serbs as a group." They underscored the necessity for Serbs to organize themselves, democratically struggle for their rights, and deter their "quiet assimilation." On the basis of the Albanian example, a motion was submitted by Serbian leaders to stage a referendum among Serbs and Montenegrins and to develop a Serbian autonomous region in northern Macedonia. During 1992, Serbs in the Kumanovo area began to organize themselves in associations and political parties and held demonstrations in support of the Serbian cause in Croatia and Bosnia-Herze-govina. Ristić intensified the party's demands for collective rights, improved economic conditions, and the possibility of dual citizenship (Yugoslav and Macedonian). DPS vice-president, Dobrivoje Tomić, stated that if the demands of Serbs were ignored, "the natural thing would be to demand and count on protection by the mother country, Serbia." Some Serb activists expressed support for Serbian Radical Party leader, Vojislav Šešelj, who has consistently called for the absorption or partition of Macedonia, claiming that Macedonians were in reality Serbs with no claims to independent statehood. Šešelj sympathizers have made efforts to establish a Serbian Autonomous Region of the Kumanovo Valley and Skopska Crna Gora. Macedonian nationalist organizations attacked the DPS for its intentions to destabilize Macedonia and claimed that accusations about anti-Serb discrimination were inaccurate and deliberately misleading. Mace-donian nationalists argued that Western failures to recognize the sovereignty of the republic fueled Serb resistance; despite official confirmations about the in-violability of existing frontiers, the Serbian regime seemingly viewed the borders as alterable administrative lines.

In January 1993, 500 Serb nationalists gathered in the town of Kučevište, north of Skopje, to protest police repression of a Serb rally on New Year's Eve. They claimed that the police attacked Serbian youths and injured thirteen people for hoisting a Yugoslav flag and displaying pictures of Šešelj. DPS leaders countered that the entire incident was incited by Macedonian nationalists in order to draw the UN Protection Force into the region. They also asserted that if Serbs continued to be mistreated by Macedonian authorities they would under-take measures for "self-protection." Conflicts between Serbs and Macedonians have also persisted over the status of the Prohor Pčinjski Monastery, which was technically on the Serbian side of the border but claimed as a major Macedonian shrine. Macedonian leaders have issued several protests over the treatment of Macedonian citizens who visited the monastery to celebrate their national holiday, while some nationalists have called for border adjustments to place the monastery within Macedonia.[29]

Association of Serbs and Montenegrins in Macedonia (ASMM)
Združenie na Srbi i Crnogorci vo Makedonija (ZSCM)

The ASM has cooperated closely with the DPS but on occasion has adopted even more militant positions toward the Macedonian authorities. For instance, in June 1993 the association rejected a draft agreement between Skopje and local Serb leaders concerning the regulation of the status of the Serb population proposed by the chairman of the Geneva Conference on the Former Yugoslavia. It insisted that Serbs and Montenegrins be explicitly mentioned in a new Macedonian constitution as a constituent nation and be afforded the full range of collective rights.[30]

League of Vlachs (LOV)
Liga na Vlasite (LV)

The League of Vlachs president, Mitko Kostov, stated that the goals of the organization were to resolve all problems revolving around Vlach (Arumunian) culture, education, and religion without any covert political aspirations. As in other Balkan states, the process of Vlach assimilation over the decades had seriously undermined the cultural and linguistic cohesiveness of this small and essentially rural population. In a League meeting in March 1993, steps were undertaken toward the completion of a Vlach-language grammar book, as well as the reintroduction of the Vlach publication *Feniks*, which had been taken out of publication for almost a year. The group united with other Vlach organizations to form an International Vlach League (IVL) in the town of Kruševo in August 1992. The IVL was created as the official representative body of the Vlach people in dealings with all external entities, including the EC nations, the CSCE, and the United Nations.[31]

CHRONOLOGY

February 1990: The Movement for Pan-Macedonian Action is created by Macedonian intellectuals in Skopje. Its leader, Gane Todorovski, outlines the party's nationalist agenda at its founding assembly.

April 1990: The Party of Democratic Prosperity is set up in 17 communes with a significant population of Albanians in western Macedonia and claims to include Macedonians, Roma, and other nationalities as members.

June 1990: The Macedonian Assembly adopts a declaration concerning relations with neighboring countries and expresses reservations about the position of the Macedonian ethnic minority in these states. The Internal Macedonian Revolutionary Organization—Democratic Party for Macedonian National Unity (IMRO-DPMNU) holds its founding congress.

August 1990: The Macedonian government rejects an ethnic Albanian Rights Petition from several Albanian political groups and civic leaders demanding equal status in the constitution and other special provisions.

November 1990: The Front of Macedonian Unity is formed by nationalist groupings primarily in order to gain a maximum number of seats in the National Assembly elections, to serve Macedonian national interests, and to counter the alleged political ambitions of Albanians parties. The first multi-party elections are held against a backdrop of ethnic tension, resurgent nationalism, and economic deterioration throughout Yugoslavia. The Macedonian electorate also casts ballots for local-level officials.

December 1990: Following run-off elections, a new parliament is constituted with no party obtaining a clear majority of seats. IMRO-DPMNU captures 38 seats, the former Communist LCM-PDT 31, the Albanian PDP-NDP coalition 23 seats; the remaining mandates go to several smaller parties.

January 1991:   Kiro Gligorov, a former president of the Yugoslav Federal Assembly, is elected president of Macedonia. IMRO-Democratic Party, a more radical offshoot of the IMRO-DPMNU, is organized in the town of Ohrid.

March 1991: A new Macedonian government is installed and styled as a "government of experts" headed by Prime Minister Nikola Kljušev. Only two of the ministers have any political party affiliation.

April 1991:   The IMRO-DPMNU Congress in Prilep passes several programmatic resolutions calling for swift moves toward Macedonian independence.

September 1991: A referendum on Macedonian independence is held: 68.32 percent of registered voters come out in support of Macedonian sovereignty and independence. The majority of the Albanian population boycotts the ballot. The National Assembly adopts a declaration on sovereignty and independence, despite the concerns of Albanian leaders over manifestations of ethnic discrimination and the content of the new constitution.

November 1991: The Macedonian parliament adopts of a new constitution despite the abstention of Albanian deputies who remain critical of several important provisions.

December 1991: The EC announces its willingness to recognize the independence of any Yugoslav republic that fulfills specific political and territorial criteria. The Macedonian authorities reiterate the republic's independence and request full international recognition.

January 1992: The government in Skopje adopts a draft law paving the way for the establishment of a national army to number between 25,000 and 30,000 troops. Yugoslav forces begin to withdraw form the republic after an agreement with Skopje in which they would keep all YPA weaponry deployed on Macedonian soil. Albanian leaders organize a referendum on "political and territorial autonomy" despite government opposition. Reportedly, over 90 percent of Albanians vote, out of which 95 percent cast their ballots in favor of Albanian autonomy in western Macedonia. Bulgaria becomes the first country to recognize Macedonian statehood.

February 1992: Turkey recognizes Macedonia's independence; other states adopt a more cautious position largely because of Greek intransigence over the country's name.

April 1992: The Albanian Democratic Union is legalized. In the Macedonian town of Struga, local leaders of ethnic Albanian parties declare an Albanian autonomous republic of Ilirida at a rally attended by members of several minorities, including Turks and Muslims. The move is criticized by PDP leaders and condemned by Skopje as illegitimate.

July 1992: The Kljušev government loses a vote of no-confidence largely due to criticism of its inability to secure international recognition. IMRO-DPMNU is unable to form a new government.

September 1992: Branko Crvenkovski finally assembles a new administration, consisting of a broad coalition between the SDU, the ARF, and the PDP and several smaller parties. IMRO-DPMNU excludes itself from the new government and continues to call for new elections.

November 1992: The Party for Complete Emancipation of Roma holds its third plenary meeting in Skopje in order to discuss such issues as the provision of education in the Gypsy language. Thousands of Albanians demonstrate in the capital after a confrontation between Macedonian police and Albanian traders. The rallies turn into a riot: three Albanians are killed and one Macedonian is shot dead. Skopje implies that Serbian agents could be behind the incident; Albanians condemn alleged police brutality.

January 1993: Five hundred Serb nationalists gather in Kučevište north of

Skopje to protest the dispersal of a Serbian rally by Macedonian police on New Year's Eve in the same village. Macedonian television conducts an interview with Borivoje Ristić, who outlines the goals of the Democratic Party of Serbs in Macedonia and the Association of Serbs and Montenegrins. The first All-Macedonian Congress is held in Sopotsko, Greece, with the participation of all the movements' local committees. The congress adopts a declaration citing the discriminatory policies pursued by Athens with respect to the Macedonian minority in northern Greece.

February 1993: IMRO-DPMNU, MPMA, and other nationalist organizations stage demonstrations in Skopje to protest the inflow of Muslim refugees from Bosnia-Herzegovina. The rallies turn violent when police use tear gas against several hundred rock-throwing protesters.

April 1993: The UN recognizes the Republic of Macedonia under the provisional designation of the Former Yugoslav Republic of Macedonia (FYROM), pending a final compromise regarding the republic's name. Greece continues to block a permanent settlement. The Skopje government narrowly survives a no-confidence vote sponsored by nationalist legislators dissatisfied with its acceptance of the UN-mediated temporary designation.

May 1993: Serb president Milošević visits Macedonia and meets with President Gligorov to discourage Skopje from allowing U.S. troop deployments in the republic. Reportedly, he also demands "self-determination" for Serbs in northern Macedonia and a transit corridor to Greece as preconditions for Belgrade's recognitions of Macedonian independence. Gligorov is not intimidated and preparations are made for stationing approximately 300 U.S. troops to supplement the UN contingent already present in the country.

July 1993: A contingent of U.S. troops is stationed in Macedonia, signaling Washington's concerns about the escalation of the Yugoslav wars. The small force is envisaged as a "trip wire" against potential aggression by Belgrade. As political pressures mount from Albanian and Macedonian nationalist parties, the authorities schedule new general elections and the holding of a national census in 1994.

NOTES

1. See *Basic Statistical Data*, Republic of Macedonia, Statistical Office, Skopje, December 1991; *Yugoslavia 1918–1988 Statistical Yearbook*, Federal Institution for Statistics, Belgrade 1989; and *Statistical Yearbook of the Socialist Republic of Macedonia 1990*, Republic Bureau of Statistics, Skopje, 1991.
2. For valuable histories of Macedonia, consult Stoyan Pribichevich, *Macedonia: Its People and History* (University Park: Pennsylvania State University Press, 1982); Stephen E. Palmer and Robert R. King, *Yugoslav Communism and the Macedonian Question*

(Hamden, CT: Shoestring Press, 1971); and Fred Singleton, *A Short History of the Yugoslav Peoples* (Cambridge: Cambridge University Press, 1985).

3. See The National Republican Institute for International Affairs, *The 1990 Elections in the Republics of Yugoslavia*, Washington, 1991; and Milan Andrejevich, "Macedonia's New Political Leadership," Radio Free Europe/Radio Liberty Research Institute (RFE/RL), *Report on Eastern Europe*, vol. 2, no. 20, May 17, 1991.

4. See "Macedonia Cracks Down on Legal Status on Minorities," RFE/RL, *Situation Report: Yugoslavia*, SR/7, May 26, 1989; and *Večernje Novosti*, Belgrade, May 13, 1989.

5. "Declaration on Respecting Rights of Minorities," *Borba*, Belgrade, June 8, 1990, in Federal Broadcast Information Service, *Daily Report: East Europe, FBIS-EEU–90–118*, June 19, 1990.

6. *Tanjug*, Belgrade, September 10, 1991.

7. Check *The Financial Times*, London, September 20, 1991.

8. See Duncan M. Perry, "The Republic of Macedonia and the Odds for Survival," RFE/RL, *Research Report*, vol. 1, no. 46, November 20, 1992.

9. For full text of the constitution, see *Nova Makedonija*, Skopje, November 25, 1991.

10. See "Constitution of the Republic of Macedonia," in Federal Broadcast Information Service/Joint Publications Research Service, *Daily Report: East Europe, JPRS-EER–92–016-S*, February 10, 1992; a letter from the Party of Democratic Prosperity, Tetovo, January 19, 1992; and *Country Reports on Human Rights for 1992*, U.S. Department of State, Washington, DC, February 1993.

11. See the interview with Halili in *Kossuth Radio Network*, Budapest, September 9, 1991, in *FBIS-EEU–91–178*, September 13, 1991.

12. RFE/RL, *Daily Report*, no. 28, February 11, 1992.

13. See *Tanjug*, Belgrade, March 8, 1991.

14. *Radio Macedonia Network*, Skopje, December 29, 1991, *FBIS-EEU–91–251*, December 31, 1991.

15. See Hugh Poulton, "The Republic of Macedonia After UN Recognition," RFE/RL, *Research Report*, vol. 2, no. 23, June 4, 1993; "War Games: Hell Bridge," *Puls*, Skopje, November 26, 1992, in *JPRS-EER–92–168*, December 14, 1992; Pance Zafirovski, "Political Irrationality," *Puls*, November 19, 1992, in *JPRS-EER–92–172*, December 22, 1992

16. *Tanjug*, Belgrade, August 20, 1992, *FBIS-EEU–92–163*, August 21, 1992.

17. Duncan Perry, "The Macedonian Question Revitalized," RFE/RL, *Report on Eastern Europe*, August 24, 1990; Nenad Batkoski, "The Victim of New and Alien Domination," *Borba*, Belgrade, August 17, 1990; *Oslobodjenje*, Sarajevo, December 23, 1990, in *FBIS-EEU–91–005*, January 8, 1991; *Borba*, Belgrade, March 6, 1991, in *FBIS-EEU–91–046*, March 8, 1991; *Borba*, Belgrade, May 31, 1991, in *JPRS-EER–91–084*, June 15, 1991; Velizar Enčev, "The International Macedonian Revolutionary Organization Prilep Congress—Between Realities and Illusions," *Zora*, Sofia, April 16, 1991, in *JPRS-EEU–91–091*, June 25, 1991; Julijana Kočovska, "Greeks Among Us," *Nova Makedonija*, Skopje, March 7, 1992, in *JPRS-EER–92–043*, April 8, 1992; interview with Ljupčo Georgievski, "Macedonia Will Not Sink to Its Knees," in *Zora*, Sofia, February 25, 1992, in *JPRS-EER–92–043*, April 8, 1992; RFE/RL, *Daily Report*, no. 35, February 22, 1993.

18. *Borba*, Belgrade, May 31, 1991, in *JPRS-EER–91–084*, June 15, 1991; *Borba*, Belgrade, January 29, 1991, in *FBIS-EEU–91–028*, February 11, 1991.

19. *Tanjug*, Belgrade, February 4, 1990; *Belgrade Radio Network*, November 12, 1991, in *FBIS-EEU–91–219*, November 13, 1991; RFE/RL, *Daily Report*, no. 136, July 19, 1990; interview with Emil Anastasov, *Borba*, Belgrade, April 10, 1990, in *FBIS-EEU–90–074*, April 17, 1990.

20. Check Milan Andrejevich, "Yugoslav Macedonians Demand Recognition of Aegean Macedonians," RFE/RL, *Report on Eastern Europe*, vol. 1, no. 22, June 1, 1990; Draško Antov, "Secret Document for a Pogrom Against Macedonians," *Nova Makedonija*, Skopje, May 15, 1992, in *FBIS-EEU–92–107*, June 3, 1992; "First Congress of the Macedonian Movement for Prosperity in the Balkans," *Nova Makedonija*, Skopje, February 5, 1993, in *JPRS-EER–93–026-S*, April 2, 1993; see the interview with Archimandrite Nikodimos Carknjas in *Nova Makedonija*, Skopje, March 28, 1993, in *JPRS-EEU–93–036-S*, April 29, 1993; and Vanjo Hadžiev, "The Aegeans and Macedonian-Greek Relations," *Puls*, Skopje, May 28, 1993, in *JPRS-EER–93–062-S*, July 1, 1993.

21. *Tanjug*, Belgrade, March 31, 1992, in *FBIS-EEU–92–063*, April 1, 1992; "Nevzat Halili Elected Chairman," *Flaka e Vëllazërimit*, Skopje, February 12, 1992, in *FBIS-EEU–92–035*, February 21, 1992; Daut Dauti report, "Macedonia—Europe's Common Homeland," *Flaka e Vëllazërimit*, Skopje, April 1, 1992, in *FBIS-EEU–92–069*, April 9, 1992; *Tanjug*, Belgrade, January 7, 1991, in *FBIS-EEU–91–005*, January 8, 1991; *Tanjug*, Belgrade, April 16, 1992, in *FBIS-EEU–92–074*, April 16, 1992; *Tanjug*, Belgrade, April 3, 1992, in *FBIS-EEU–92–067*, April 7, 1992; *Tanjug*, Belgrade, April 9, 1992, in *FBIS-EEU–92–070*, April 10, 1992.

22. See Iljaz Halimi, "The Constitution of the Republic of Macedonia and the Status of the Albanians," *Nova Makedonija*, Skopje, January 4, 1992, in *FBIS-EEU–92–019*, January 29, 1992; and Branko Geroski, "Losing Stance and Political Boss," *Večer*, Skopje, May 15–16,1993, in *JPRS-EER–93–057-S*, June 22, 1993.

23. Interview with Muhamed Halili in *Nova Makedonija*, Skopje, July 14, 1992, in *JPRS-EER–92–113*, August 21, 1992.

24. *Tanjug*, Belgrade, April 18, 1992, in *FBIS-EEU–92–076*, April 20, 1992; and interview with Džemail Idrizi, "Macedonia Is Pursuing a Peace-Loving Communicative Policy," *Nova Makedonija*, May 16, 1993, in *JPRS-EER–93–057-S*, June 22, 1993.

25. *Tanjug*, Belgrade, July 30, 1990, in *FBIS-EEU–90–147*, July 31, 1990; report by Panta Džambazovski, "Muslim Macedonians Will Form Party," *Nova Makedonija*, Skopje, February 13, 1992, in *JPRS-EER–92–028*, March 9, 1992; interview with Dževat Djulioski by Panta Džambazovski, "We Must Be Taken Into Account," *Nova Makedonija*, Skopje, December 5, 1992, in *JPRS-EER–93–006*, January 22, 1993; report by Panta Džambazovski, "Muslim Macedonians Will Form Party," *Nova Makedonija*, Skopje, February 13, 1992, in *JPRS-EER–92–028*, March 9, 1992; *Večer*, Skopje, March 4, 1993, in *JPRS-EER–93–029-S*, April 9, 1993.

26. J. Mirovski, "From an Association, a Political Party; Second Extraordinary Congress of the Association of the Democratic Union of Turks," *Nova Makedonija*, Skopje, June 28, 1992, in *JPRS-EER–92–104*, August 11, 1992; *Tanjug*, Belgrade, April 9, 1993, in *FBIS-EEU–93–068*, April 12, 1993.

27. Hugh Poulton, "The Roma in Macedonia: A Balkan Success Story?" RFE/RL, *Research Report*, vol. 2, no. 19, May 7, 1993; A. L., "The Gypsy Language in Education," *Nova Makedonija*, Skopje, November 16, 1992, in *JPRS-EER–93–001*, January 5, 1993; *Nova Makedonija*, Skopje, October 21, 1992, in *JPRS-EER–92–170*, December 17, 1992.

28. See Hugh Poulton, "The Roma in Macedonia: A Balkan Success Story?" RFE/RL, *Research Report*, vol. 2, no. 19, May 7, 1993.

29. *Tanjug*, Belgrade, January 10, 1993, in *FBIS-EEU–93–006*, January 11, 1993; *Tanjug*, Belgrade, November 1, 1992, in *FBIS-EEU–92–212*, November 2, 1992; *Tanjug*, Belgrade, August 2, 1990, in *FBIS-EEU–90–150*, August 3, 1990; *Nova Makedonija*, Skopje, September 10, 1992, in *JPRS-EER–92–139*, September 29, 1992; interview with Vojislav Šešelj, "The Serbs Will Not Surrender," *Otechestven Vestnik*, Sofia, April 27,

1993, in *FBIS-EEU–93–083*, May 3, 1993; Mirka Velinorska, "JNA Soldiers in Border Provocations," *War Report*, London, no. 15, October 1992; *Nova Makedonija*, Skopje, January 23, 1993, in *JPRS-EER–008-S*, February 17, 1993; *Puls*, Skopje, January 21, 1993, in *JPRS-EER–93–016-S*, March 3, 1993; *Belgrade Radio Network*, Belgrade, January 15, 1993, in *FBIS-EEU–93–011*, January 19, 1993.

30. *Tanjug*, Belgrade, June 17, 1993, in *FBIS-EEU–93–116*, June 18, 1993.

31. A.D., "International Vlach League Formed at Kruševo Congress," *Nova Makedonija*, Skopje, August 16, 1992, *JPRS-EER–92–133*, September 18, 1992; *Večer*, March 17, 1993, in *JPRS-EER–93–038-S*, May 6, 1993.

5

Serbia

POPULATION

According to the 1981 Yugoslav census, the last complete demographic survey, out of Serbia's population of 9,313,676, 6,182,155 were registered as Serbs; the rest consisted of various ethnic minorities or individuals who declared themselves as Yugoslavs. Albanians constituted the largest minority: approximately 1.3 million lived in the province of Kosovo, forming nearly 90 percent of the region's population where Serb numbers stood at 209,497, Montenegrin at 27,028, and Muslim at 58,562. Albanians also formed a relative majority in three neighboring municipalities of inner Serbia or Šumadija. Of the 2,034,772 inhabitants in the province of Vojvodina in 1981, Hungarians made up 18.9 percent of the total; the remainder included 54.4 percent Serbs, 5.4 percent Croats, 2.1 percent Montenegrins, 3.5 percent Slovaks, 2.3 percent Romanians, 8.1 percent Yugoslavs, and 5.3 percent "others." Other substantial minorities in Serbia as a whole included 215,166 Muslims, the majority of whom lived in Belgrade and in the Sandžak region of southern Serbia, 147,466 Montenegrins, 110,959 Romas, 33,455 Bulgarians, 48,989 Macedonians, and 25,596 Vlachs. The smaller minorities included Slovenes, Czechs, Germans, Poles, Russians, Ukrainians, and Ruthenians. In 1981, 441,941 people declared themselves as Yugoslavs; the figure has substantially decreased since then.

In the incomplete census of 1991, comprehensively boycotted by the Albanian population in Kosovo, the population of Serbia reached 10,345,464, of which 6,485,596 or 62.69 percent were ethnic Serbs.[1] Officials estimated the number of Albanians on the basis of projections and reached a total of some 1.7 million. Albanian spokesmen contended that the number was deliberately underestimated, claiming that the total exceeded two million despite an exodus of some 100,000 Albanians from Kosovo during the past few years; the percentage of Serbs and Montenegrins in the province fell under 9 percent from 14.9 percent in 1981. Albanians also formed majorities in three neighboring Serbian *opštine*:

Serbia: Population (1991)

Ethnic Groups	Number	% of Population
Serbs	6,485,596	62.69
Albanians	1,727,541	16.70
Montenegrins	520,508	5.03
Hungarians	345,376	3.34
Muslims	327,290	3.16
Roma (Gypsies)	137,265	1.33
Croats	115,463	1.12
Slovaks	67,234	0.65
Macedonians	48,437	0.47
Romanians	42,386	0.41
Bulgarians	25,214	0.24
Vlachs	17,557	0.17
Turks	11,501	0.11
Slovenes	8,747	0.08
Others	465,349	4.50
Total Minorities	3,859,868	37.31
Total Population	10,345,464	100.00

Preševo, Bujanovac, and Medvedja. Montenegrins constituted the second-largest nationality in Serbia, calculated at over 520,000, while Hungarians came in third at 345,376, concentrated primarily in the northern Baèka and northern Banat areas next to the Hungarian border. Magyars constituted 16.9 percent of the region's population of 2,012,517, a reduction of some 11.5 percent since the 1981 census; nonetheless, they still formed majorities in seven municipalities.

Since 1991, Magyar numbers have continued to decline, as tens of thousands left Vojvodina to avoid military conscription and intimidation by Serbian nationalists. Thousands of Serbs from Croatia and Bosnia-Herzegovina were resettled in various parts of Vojvodina, further altering the ethnic balance in favor of Serbs. According to the 1991 census, the Serbian percentage in the province grew from 54.4 percent in 1981 to 57.3 percent in 1991. Muslim numbers throughout Serbia reached 327,290, of which 156,115 resided in the six Serbian municipalities in the Sand<ak area (60.5 percent of the population in the region), although Muslim leaders believed the figure exceeded 165,000. They formed absolute majorities in the municipalities of Novi Pazar, Sjenica, and Tutin. Since 1990, about 70,000 Muslims have reportedly left the Serbian and Montenegrin Sand<ak, primarily as a result of persecution by Serbian militants and fears of a major crackdown.

Of the smaller nationalities, Roma (Gypsy) numbers in Serbia were calculated at 137,265. The Croat total in Vojvodina and Belgrade dipped to 115,463; since the beginning of the 1991 war, 35,000 had reportedly emigrated to Croatia, Hungary, or the West. Slovak numbers stood at 67,234, mostly resident in Vojvodina; Macedonians at 48,437, Romanians at 42,386, primarily in the Banat sector of Vojvodina, Bulgarians at 25,214, the majority inhabiting the Bulgarian border region; Vlachs at 17,557; Turks at 11,501; and Slovenes at 8,747. The remainder, making up 4.5 percent of the population, included Ruthenians, Ukrainians, Czechs, Greeks, Germans, Poles, and Russians. Between the outbreak of armed hostilities in June 1991 and the summer of 1993, Serbia also took in approximately 550,000 refugees from Croatia and Bosnia, of whom over 80 percent were ethnic Serbs. In July 1993, Belgrade announced measures to restrict the influx of more refugees, fearing a severe impact on Serbia's already strained economy.

HISTORICAL OVERVIEW

From the late fourteenth century onward, Serb-inhabited territories underwent over four centuries of Turkish rule.[2] Following several failed peasant uprisings during the seventeenth century, Ottoman reprisals resulted in mass migrations out of central Serbia northward to Habsburg-controlled Vojvodina. As Turkey came under increasing pressure from Russian and French forces, in 1804 a Serbian peasant, known as Karadjordjević, staged a revolt against foreign rule and established a short-lived administration in the capital Belgrade. A few years later, the Serbs were defeated and Karadjordjević fled to Austria. In 1817, a second major revolt led by Milo Obrenović forced the Turks to allow Serbia a significant degree of autonomy. In 1830, Russia pressured the Ottomans to turn Serbia into an autonomous principality. As a result of the Treaty of Berlin, in 1878 Serbia achieved full independence from Turkish domination, and a few years later Serbian rulers assumed the title of kings. Rivalries for the Serbian throne continued between the Karadjordjević and Obrenović dynasties, and outside powers exploited these divisions to keep the country relatively weak prior to World War One. Austria, in particular, maintained considerable influence over Serbia's trade, commerce, and foreign affairs.

At the turn of the twentieth century, Serbian rulers sought to expand their territories beyond the central Šumadija region in order to incorporate adjacent Serb-inhabited regions. In particular, the expansionist drive was directed southward toward Macedonia and westward through Bosnia-Herzegovina toward the Adriatic Sea. These moves brought Belgrade into direct conflict with Bulgaria and Austria-Hungary, respectively. In 1908, Vienna annexed Bosnia, causing intense opposition in Serbia and stirring Russian and British support for the Serb cause. During the First Balkan War of 1912, Ottoman power in the Balkans subsided as Serbia, Bulgaria, Greece, and Montenegro combined their forces to defeat the Turks. In the Second Balkan War of 1913, the Serbs and Greeks defeated Bulgarian troops and Belgrade acquired a large portion of Macedonia. But the creation of an independent Albania prevented Serbia from reaching the Adriatic. Serbian expansionism in turn served as an inspiration for other Slav peoples within the Habsburg Empire to press for independence and unification with Serbia. Growing Austrian-Serbian tensions provoked the First World War when the Austrian Archduke Franz-Ferdinand, the heir to the Habsburg throne, was assassinated in 1914 in Sarajevo, Bosnia, by a member of a pro-Serbian terrorist group. Austria declared war on Serbia, Germany rallied behind Vienna, while Britain, France, and Russia came to Serbia's defense.

World War One ended Austrian rule in the Balkans and culminated in the creation of a new state in 1918: the Kingdom of Serbs, Croats, and Slovenes. As the largest nation in the kingdom, forming 39 percent of the population, and a leader in the struggle for south Slav liberation, Serbia assumed a dominant position in the new political entity. In addition to the south Slav lands of Serbia, Croatia, Slovenia, Bosnia, Montenegro, and Macedonia, Belgrade also acquired the Vojvodina area of southern Hungary, as well as the Kosovo area inhabited by a sizable Albanian population. Belgrade became the capital, and Serbs occupied important positions in the armed forces and the civil bureaucracy. A centralist constitution was adopted in 1921 despite strong opposition from Croat politicians, and the administration was based on the concept of national unitarism expressed in the political union of the three major south Slav groups. The authorities did not recognize the multi-national character of the new state and were confident that the minority groups (Albanians, Germans, Hungarians, Macedonians, and Bosnian Muslims) could be easily assimilated or accommodated. In fact, the government refused to exchange reciprocal neighboring populations, as stipulated in the peace treaties with other Balkan states. These aggrieved nationalities became a source of instability encouraged by various revisionist powers. With growing internal political turmoil, the Serbian king Aleksander abolished the constitution in 1929 and imposed a personal dictatorship over the renamed Yugoslavia (land of the south Slavs).

The chief source of conflict in the inter-war years was between differing Serb and Croat approaches toward the state structure. Serbian leaders sought a unitary centralized state, while Croat representatives preferred a dualistic or federal system. But Belgrade remained suspicious that Croat demands were simply the first steps toward secession from the kingdom. Croatian politicians increasingly viewed the Serbian dynasty as a poor substitute for the Habsburg monarchs, and they obstructed the proper functioning of the Yugoslav parliament and protested against King Aleksander's authoritarianism. The 1931 constitution provided for a quasi-parliamentary system subordinate to the king, thus further alienating Croat representatives. King Aleksander was assassinated in Marseilles in 1934 by Croatian and Macedonian terrorists reportedly sponsored by Mussolini's Italy. A regency of the minor King Peter II was subsequently imposed, which lasted until the Nazi conquest.

Following the German-led invasion of 1941, Yugoslavia was completely dismembered. Serbia-Šumadija was placed under German military command, a large portion of Vojvodina was occupied by Hungary, Macedonia and a part of southeast Serbia was placed under Bulgarian administration, Kosovo was occupied by Albania under Italian control, while Montenegro was occupied by Italian forces.

Officers from the Yugoslav army, led by Colonel Draža Mihailović, organized *Četnik* detachments to resist Nazi rule in Serbia, Montenegro, and parts of Bosnia. The *Četnici* were also embroiled in a civil war with the Croatian *Ustaša* and the Communist *partizan* forces of Marshal Josef Broz Tito. Communist forces seized power in the country at the close of the war, having obtained Allied and Soviet support and proving themselves to be an effective multi-ethnic fighting force.

Post-war Communist Yugoslavia restored its pre-war borders and gained some additional territory from Italy in the northwest corner of the country. Tito established a federal Communist state and aimed to limit the powers and ambitions of any single national unit. Serbian influence was substantially reduced with the creation of the separate republics of Macedonia, Montenegro, and Bosnia-Herzegovina. The granting of autonomous provincial status to Kosovo and Vojvodina within the Serbian republic during the 1950s further undercut Serbian influence and bred resentment among Serb nationalists. However, the creation of two autonomous provinces as distinct federal units contributed to the partial satisfaction of the demands of Hungarian and Albanian leaders for decentralization. Vojvodina underwent a significant shift in ethnic composition after the expulsion of the large German population at the close of the war. Large numbers of Serbs were also settled in the region, and Magyar numbers fell to about 20 percent of the population. Nonetheless, the community benefited from a good measure of administrative and economic decentralization with extensive linguistic and educational rights. Stability in the province was also assured by the area's relative prosperity and the absence of any overt Hungarian territorial pretensions. The province held a complex ethnic mix: in addition to Serbs and Hungarians, sizable pockets of Croats, Slovaks, Ruthenians, and Romanians were also present. But there was no evident ethnic conflict and the region was renowned for its tolerance and diversity.

By contrast, in Kosovo-Metohija (the full name of this southern province of Serbia) pronounced ethnic and cultural divisions between Serbs and Albanians perpetuated ancient enmities. The Albanian population in the province had grown substantially since the seventeenth century, especially as Serbian families moved northward and westward to escape Turkish rule. This pattern continued into the twentieth century: for example, between 1953 and 1981, Serbian numbers dropped from 27.9 percent to 14.9 percent of the population. Although the majority evidently left for primarily economic reasons, some vacated the province due to pressure from the Albanian majority. Meanwhile, Kosovo's Albanian population underwent a dramatic growth, from 733,000 in 1948 to about 1.3 million by 1981. Serbian depopulation of this historically sensitive region raised popular resentment against Albanians. This was heightened during the 1960s and 1970s when Kosovo attained constitutional status within Yugoslavia virtually equal to that of the other republics. Moreover, Albanians attained a predominant position in the Communist apparatus, local administration, and the police forces, while able to expand their educational, cultural, and linguistic rights. Serb leaders remained perturbed by the high Albanian birthrate, estimated at about four times the national average. Tito's policy was one of measured appeasement and inter-ethnic balance, designed to give Albanians a stake in the Yugoslav federation without provoking a Serbian backlash. But Belgrade's policies generated resentment on both sides: among Serbs, over increasing Albanian domination in the province, and among Albanian leaders, over the lack of full self-government and republican status.

After Tito's death in 1980, Serbia's Communist leaders began to reassert the republic's position in the Yugoslav federation. With his ascent to the leadership of the Serbian League of Communists, Slobodan Milošević took up the Serbian nationalist cause. His initial successes focused on recentralizing the Serbian republic and limiting the autonomy of both Kosovo and Vojvodina. The Milošević regime strengthened direct controls over Kosovo on the pretext that the regional government dominated by Albanians was persecuting Serbs and seeking to detach the region from Yugoslavia. Various measures were taken to restrict Albanian political and social life. The powers of the regional government were undermined, states of emergency were imposed to limit protests, the public security organs were taken over by Belgrade, and the Serbian regime claimed the right to appoint or dismiss members of all legislative and judicial bodies.

In July 1990, Belgrade suspended the Kosovo Provincial Assembly days after the legislature had declared the independence of Kosovo as a sovereign Yugoslav republic. Albanian legislators from the dissolved parliament met secretly in September 1990 to pass a law on Kosovo's republican status; this became known as the "Kačanik Constitution." The Serbian authorities suspended the operations of much of the Albanian-language media, and under the new Serbian constitution Kosovo's autonomous statehood was eliminated. In March 1991, the Kosovo provincial presidency was officially abolished, thus sealing the province's full integration into Serbia. The curtailment of Albanian educational and cultural activities, together with discrimination in public employment, sparked protest actions and the growth of independent political activism as Albanian leaders increasingly demanded full independence and separation from Serbia. In May 1992, Albanians held their own illicit general elections and appealed for international recognition.

Milošević also reasserted Belgrade's control over Vojvodina. In October 1988, the Vojvodina provincial authorities were replaced in an orchestrated purge designed to eliminate "pro-autonomist forces" allegedly conspiring against Serbia. These moves intensified tensions in the region, increased protests against the centralist state apparatus, and stimulated the resurgence of ethnically based organizations. Although the crackdown against minority educational and cultural pursuits was not as comprehensive as in Kosovo, state policy clearly favored Serbs and Milošević loyalists in the administration and security forces. Moreover, the powers of the provincial government were curtailed and the province was increasingly governed directly from Belgrade.

The collapse of the Yugoslav federation since early 1991, with the secession of Slovenia and Croatia, and later Bosnia-Herzegovina and Macedonia, directly affected Serbia's national minorities. Albanians in Kosovo pushed toward separation from the rump Yugoslavia, fearful not only of Serbian domination but of the forcible expulsion of non-Serbs to alter Kosovo's demographic structure drastically. Hungarian and Croat minorities grew concerned about similar operations in Vojvodina as Belgrade began to exert pressure on minority inhabitants and resettled Serbs in the province from other parts of Yugoslavia. The large Muslim Slav population in the Sandžak area of southern Serbia was also subjected to intimidation by security forces and radical Serbian paramilitaries with the connivance of Belgrade. The Milošević regime maintained a tight grip over the Serbian government, economy, army, and the republic's security forces. The promulgation of the ethnically pure "Greater Serbia" doctrine and the support given to militant Serb formations alarmed minority leaders across the republic.

OFFICIAL POLICIES

Since his rise to the leadership of the League of Communists of Serbia in May 1986, Slobodan Milošević has set the political and national agenda in the republic. Recognizing that the Communist and Yugoslav causes had lost their potential for mass mobilization, Milošević fixed his attention on reviving Serb nationalism and manipulating Serb grievances to consolidate and expand his hold on power. Reiterating the position expressed in the famous 1986 memorandum issued by the Serbian Academy of Arts and Sciences, Milošević contended that Serbia had been deliberately weakened by the Tito regime.[3] The 1974 Yugoslav constitution had allegedly undermined Serbia's sovereignty over its two autonomous provinces, Vojvodina and Kosovo, which obtained equal representation in the federal administration and were even able to veto decisions in the Serbian National Assembly. Moreover, large numbers of Serbs resided in Croatia and Bosnia-Herzegovina without sufficient legislative or constitutional protection or appropriate political influence. Milošević focused his efforts on reversing this situation and restoring a centralized Serbian administration.

To achieve his aims, Milošević removed the most threatening political rivals and placed much of the Belgrade media under his strict supervision. He organized mass demonstrations to rally popular support behind Serbian unification in Belgrade, Montenegro, Vojvodina, and Kosovo.[4] In exploiting various political, ethnic, and economic grievances, Milošević orchestrated the ouster of the entire Montenegrin state and party leadership in January 1989, replacing them with pro-Belgrade loyalists. But his main attention was riveted on Kosovo where, according to Belgrade, Serbs had suffered harassment and discrimination since the mid-1970s at the hands of the Albanian-dominated provincial government. Serbian government propagandists claimed that Albanian leaders were planning to expel the remaining Serb and Montenegrin population, declare a separate republic, and eventually unify with Albania.

Starting in the summer of 1988, Milošević staged a number of Serbian rallies in Kosovo at which inflammatory speeches were delivered condemning the Albanianization of the province and pledging to protect the purportedly endangered Serb and Montenegrin population. A series of political steps were also taken to restrict and eliminate Kosovar autonomy, beginning with constitutional changes passed by the Serbian National Assembly in March 1989 that gave Serbia more direct control over security, justice, territorial defense, foreign policy, finance, and social planning in both Kosovo and Vojvodina. Large-scale Albanian demonstrations protesting these measures were violently suppressed by federal units and Serbian police: at least 24 people were killed in March 1989 and 6 more in October 1989.

In June 1990, the Serbian National Assembly passed a package of "special measures" further eroding the autonomy of both Kosovo and Vojvodina. The legislation bolstered the size and prerogatives of the security forces, enabled the republic's executive, legislative, and judicial branches to suspend the activities of any government authority in the provinces, and empowered the Serbian government to appoint new provincial officials. Albanian deputies stormed out of the Serbian National Assembly in protest, declaring the new measures unconstitutional. Belgrade also made preparations to adopt a new constitution in order to eradicate the sovereignty of its provinces. Fearing the imminent dissolution of the Kosovo Provincial Assembly, in July 1990, 114 Albanian deputies in the 183-seat Assembly issued a "constitutional declaration" announcing Kosovo as an "independent and equal entity in the framework of the Yugoslav federation."[5] The Serbian authorities condemned this move as illegitimate and a few days later formally dissolved the Kosovo Assembly and its Executive Council on the pretext that Albanian leaders were seeking to secede from Yugoslavia. The rights and duties of the provincial government were taken over by the Serbian Assembly for the first time since 1946 when Kosovo was constituted as a distinct region and transformed into an autonomous province in 1968. According to Belgrade, the Provincial Assembly would be unable to reconvene until after a new Serbian constitution was adopted and multi-party elections were held.

Albanian deputies sought several measures to reverse Serbian centralization. For instance, they demanded a new republican constitution that would enshrine Kosovo's status as an equal Yugoslav republic, that Albanians be declared a "nation" and not a "national minority" (as they outnumbered four of the six recognized Yugoslav "nations"), and that all Serbian constitutional amendments enacted since March 1989 be declared null and void. Serbian pressures against all semblance of Albanian independence continued unabated. For example, in August 1990 Belgrade closed down the Albanian language daily *Rilindja* after suspending the Albanian-language broadcasts of Priština Radio and Television. Freedom of movement and assembly were curtailed in the province, Albanian politicians became subjected to threat and intimidation, leading intellectuals and community leaders were fired from their posts, and a virtual state of siege was imposed in Kosovo by a large police and military presence. As repressive measures mounted, Albanian deputies from the disbanded Kosovo Assembly adopted a new "Kačanik Constitution" in September 1990 and proclaimed a new "Republic of Kosovo." The move was condemned by Belgrade as a direct attack on Yugoslav and Serbian territorial integrity. At the end of September 1990, the Serbian Assembly proclaimed a new Serbian constitution that formally terminated Kosovo's autonomy; Albanian leaders in turn condemned its passage as unconstitutional and non-binding.[6]

Serb government spokesmen claimed that the new constitution fully protected the rights of national minorities because, unlike in Croatia, Slovenia, and Macedonia, Serbia was not defined as a "national state" but a "democratic state of all citizens."[7] According to Article 49, citizens were "guaranteed the freedom to express their nationality and culture and the freedom to use their language and script." Albanians charged that such provisions failed to address the key issue of the status of the Albanian population and continued to relegate them to the position of a "nationality" or "minority." Moreover, Article 4 of the constitution underscored that the republic of Serbia was "unified and unalienable" thus formally restricting the autonomy of Kosovo and the will of the majority of its inhabitants for self-determination. The constitution was primarily a political document that buttressed the powers of the Serbian presidency, reaffirmed Serbia's "full sovereignty," and removed constitutional mechanisms for self-government by the largest national minorities.

Milošević consolidated his position in July 1990 when the League of Communists of Serbia and the Socialist Alliance, its front organization, united to create the Serbian Socialist Party (SSP) under Milošević's leadership. The new party adopted an openly nationalist platform, and its dominant position in the mass media contributed to limiting the appeal of newly formed Serbian opposition parties. The SSP maintained its unfair advantage in the first multi-party elections in December 1990 by benefiting from state resources, maintaining a nationwide political apparatus, and monopolizing the media. Milošević himself was elected president of Serbia with 65.34 percent of the vote; his nearest challenger Vuk Drašković, from the newly formed opposition group the Serbian Renewal Movement (SRM), barely reached 16.4 percent of the popular vote. In the republican assembly, the Socialists gained a clear majority by capturing 194 of 250 seats amid charges of various voting irregularities.[8] The overwhelming majority of Albanians in Kosovo boycotted the republican elections. Albanian leaders grouped in the newly formed Democratic League of Kosovo (DLK) asserted that Kosovars had already voiced their support for Kosovo's new constitution, proclaiming the province an equal and independent republic; the Serb elections were therefore considered irrelevant. Analysts also contended that the Serbian election law discriminated against potential Albanian voters by limiting the number of seats assigned to Kosovo in the Serbian parliament. The first round of balloting fell well under 50 percent, the minimum required to elect deputies, but despite a continuing boycott by Albanians, in the second round Serb representatives were elected in all Kosovo constituencies.

Following the 1990 elections in all six Yugoslav republics and the demise of both integral Communism and Yugoslavism, nationalist disputes accelerated both within and among the federal entities. A vicious spiral of conflict was set in motion as Slovene and Croat demands for a looser confederal system clashed with the Serbian resurgence and Milošević's opposition to permanently detaching from Yugoslavia the large Serbian minority resident in neighboring republics. Fears were also raised in Belgrade that the restless Albanian Kosovars would exploit the opportunity to pursue their secession from Serbia. The specter of Albanian separatism was in turn adroitly exploited by Milošević to invigorate Serbian nationalist passions, and Milošević himself was cast in the role of the principal defender of Serbian national and religious interests.

Throughout 1991 and 1992 state repression dramatically increased in Kosovo and assumed a multitude of forms.[9] Its most egregious examples included the shooting of protesters, kidnappings, beatings, tortures, arbitrary arrests, the jailing of political dissidents and human rights activists, summary legal procedures, widespread purges and dismissals from a variety of professions, strict censorship or elimination of the Albanian media, politically imposed mergers between Kosovar and Serbian enterprises, mass firings of Albanian workers, the closure of Albanian schools and cultural institutions, violent police raids on Albanian villages, the ransacking and closure of churches and mosques, and the eviction of residents from their homes. Paramilitary ultra-nationalist groups, under the direct sponsorship of Milošević, were also dispatched to Kosovo to intimidate and terrorize the Albanian population. The Albanian leadership adopted a non-violent approach to official provocations and proceeded to construct a parallel political structure, separate economic operations, and a virtually underground educational and cultural life. Following the declaration of independence by Slovenia and Croatia in June 1991, Ibrahim Rugova, the DLK leader, declared that Albanians would not remain in a truncated Serb-dominated Yugoslavia. However, he insisted that only peaceful means would be used to defend Kosovar interests.

During the summer of 1991, a Coordinating Council of Albanian Political Parties was established in Priština to prepare contingencies for creating a provisional "government of national salvation." When armed conflicts erupted in Slovenia and Croatia, the Assembly of the Republic of Kosovo in exile (some of whose members were resident outside Kosovo) endorsed a resolution that Kosovo would be transformed into a sovereign republic. It also announced the holding of a referendum on Kosovo's sovereignty and plans to form a newly elected government. Despite a heavy police presence, a reported 87 percent of the Albanian population voted in the referendum in September 1991, of which over 95 percent supported Kosovo's sovereignty and independence. Albanian majorities in three southern Serbian municipalities outside of Kosovo, making up over 60 percent of the population, also voted for autonomy, with the possibility of merging with Kosovo. In October 1991, the Kosovo Republican Assembly elected a new provisional coalition government, headed by Bujar Bukoshi, and the single-party Executive Council was replaced by a multi-party governing body.[10] Albanian leaders demanded a new agreement among the Yugoslav republics that would provide Kosovo with equal status in a confederal arrangement. They also raised the option of separating from Yugoslavia altogether if Slovenia, Croatia, and other republics proved successful in their bid for secession.

In the province of Vojvodina, Milošević also initiated several moves to undercut the region's autonomy and to preclude any calls for separation from Serbia. During October 1988, Vojvodina's party, state, and government leaders were replaced in a sweeping purge against alleged "pro-autonomist forces." The new leadership was made up largely of Milošević loyalists. In the new Serbian constitution, the autonomy of Vojvodina was practically abolished and most executive, administrative, and judicial functions were transferred directly to Belgrade. These measures led to protests not only by spokesmen of the large Hungarian population but also among several smaller independent groupings that quickly sprang up in defense of a multi-ethnic and autonomous Vojvodina. They argued that Belgrade's policy of centralization eliminated the unique status that the province had enjoyed since the collapse of the Austro-Hungarian Empire. Moreover, the rise of Serbian nationalism and its advocacy by the ruling party threatened to undermine the region's remarkably peaceful inter-ethnic relations. The ethnification of Yugoslav politics and growing Serbian nationalism also sparked ethnically based movements among Vojvodina's smaller minorities.

In late 1989, several Hungarian organizations were formed to defend minority interests and campaign against increasing pressures from Belgrade. The Democratic Community of Vojvodina Hungarians (DCVH) became the largest and most active body, and it published a program on redressing minority grievances and codifying minority rights. Unlike the Kosovar Albanians, the DCVH stood in the multi-party elections in December 1990 calculating that with parliamentary representation the Magyars would be in a better position to defend their interests. The authorities allowed for the participation of ethnically based parties and the DCVH won eight seats to the republican assembly. Magyar leaders contended that the Serbian authorities were whittling away minority rights in culture and education and were gerrymandering electoral districts to disperse Hungarian votes and limit their participation in the Serbian parliament. In January 1992, Vojvodina was divided into seven administrative districts, replacing the fifty previous ones, thereby placing Magyars in a minority in all districts.

The DCVH appeared to be less concerned about the suspension of the Vojvodinian Assembly, arguing that the institution had not adequately served minority interests in the first place.[11] At that time, the DCVH spoke out for the "cultural autonomy" of Hungarians not based on territorial principles. The idea was to establish a "self-government council" for all Magyar residents, with an advisory status in the Serbian parliament, that could represent their collective interests in relations with state institutions. It also envisaged a measure of political self-government at local commune level in areas where Hungarians constituted clear majorities, as in the northern portions of Vojvodina. During 1991, these concepts were overwhelmingly rejected by the Serbian Assembly, as were proposals to establish a republican ministry for national minorities and a law for minority rights.

Pressures on the Hungarian and other minorities in Vojvodina continued unabated throughout 1991. For instance, the number of Magyar schools and language classes suffered further decline, on the pretext that the state was reorganizing the school system. This was despite calls by the DCVH for constitutional guarantees for Hungarian education from kindergarten through university level. Belgrade intensified its supervision over the Hungarian-language media by appointing directors of all newspapers, journals, and radio and television stations. Moreover, anti-Hungarian sentiments were fanned by the state-controlled Serb media, which accused the DCVH of seeking separation from Serbia and Yugoslavia, despite the fact that the community had explicitly recognized the inviolability of existing borders. A further nail in the coffin of minority rights was delivered in July 1991 with the passage of a new language law by the Serbian Assembly that made Serbian the sole official language, thus ruling out the use of Hungarian in public life.

In April 1992, the DCVH issued a formal Memorandum on Hungarian Autonomy in Vojvodina as an important initiative to enshrine minority rights in the Serbian constitution.[12] It proposed the concept of tripartite autonomy: individual or cultural autonomy; a special status for communes in which Magyars formed clear majorities; and local self-government for dispersed minority towns and villages. The proposal went beyond the principles of cultural autonomy outlined the previous year, although it did not specify the content of self-government in the various branches of state administration. It amounted to a declaration of principle that a "measure of self-government should be granted to a defined territory" inhabited primarily by Hungarians, referring to eight municipalities in northern Bačka and Banat. The memorandum also called for the settlement of Vojvodina's constitutional status through a public referendum with a clear choice between autonomy and incorporation into an integral Serbia. In addition, DCVH leader Ándras Ágoston underscored that the community was not declaring territorial autonomy in northern Vojvodina. The DCVH proposals were rejected outright by the Serbian authorities, and some media outlets and parliamentary delegates charged the community with seeking secession. Several non-Hungarian oppositionist parties also criticized the DCVH program for its focus on exclusively Hungarian interests to the neglect of Vojvodinian autonomy as a whole or the democratization of the Serbian state. Vojvodinian groups also feared that the Hungarian program would serve Belgrade's interests by fostering division among the region's diverse ethnic groups.

The Croatian minority in Vojvodina formed the Democratic Alliance of Croats (DACV) to defend its interests against growing centralization and potential repression. The DACV also sought cultural autonomy and the control of its local affairs. It issued protests over increasing assimilationist pressures, Croat mobilization in the Yugoslav army, and the abandonment of the province by over 35,000 Croats as a consequence of intimidation by Serb nationalists and security forces. Both Croat and Magyar leaders claimed that a low-visibility policy of "ethnic cleansing" was being pursued by the Serbian authorities in Croatian villages to diminish minority numbers and resettle Vojvodina with loyalist Serbs transplanted from war zones in Croatia and Bosnia-Herzegovina.

The large Slavic Muslim minority in the Sandžak region that spanned southwestern Serbia and northeastern Montenegro also grew restless during the late 1980s. Although the Sandžak did not exist as a distinct political entity in either republic, Muslims formed absolute majorities in three *opštine* in the eastern part of the region and they quickly organized to protect their distinct interests as Yugoslavia began to disintegrate. The largest Muslim political organization, the Party for Democratic Action (PDA) was formed in August 1990 as an all-Yugoslav party for Muslims in Bosnia-Herzegovina, Sandžak, and Kosovo. The PDA initially sought cultural and educational autonomy for the Sandžak region, but its leaders declared that if Yugoslavia disintegrated and Serbia and Montenegro were to form a new state, then Muslims would demand territorial autonomy and a political link with a sovereign Bosnia. In the Serbian elections of December 1990, the PDA won in all the electoral units where Muslims constituted clear majorities. As inter-republican tensions increased throughout Yugoslavia, the PDA formed a Muslim National Council of the Sandžak (MNCS) in May 1991 as a parliamentary and quasi-governmental body. The council was to consist of representatives from all Sandžak municipalities under the chairmanship of PDA leader Sulejman Ugljanin. Its role was purportedly one of "self-defense" in case a state of emergency was declared by Belgrade. Council leaders underscored that they saw no credible future for Muslims in a revamped Greater Serbia. Serbian authorities did not recognize this body, declaring that it had no legal status in the republic.

After Croatia and Slovenia declared their independence in the summer of 1991, Muslim leaders proceeded to organize a referendum on the future status of the Sandžak. Several options were considered by council leaders: autonomous status, a new federal unit, merger with Bosnia-Herzegovina, or the creation of a new state to include all regions in Yugoslavia in which Muslims formed a majority of the population. Despite warnings from Belgrade that the vote was illegal, a referendum was held in the region in October 1991. Muslim residents in ten Sandžak municipalities balloted overwhelmingly in favor of political and territorial autonomy: according to the PDA, 70.19 percent of the population participated in the plebiscite, of which 98.92 percent voted for Sandžak autonomy. The referendum was reportedly less successful in the Montenegrin Sandžak where the position of local Muslims was less threatening. In the wake of the ballot, the Muslim National Council took on more explicitly governmental responsibilities in the region in preparation for Sandžak sovereignty. In January 1992, the MNCS voted to establish a "special status" for the Sandžak as an "optimal solution for the autochthonous Muslim nation in the remnants of Yugoslavia." Although the Sandžak was not declared an independent republic, the region's government would remain exclusively responsible for education, culture, media, privatization, agriculture, mining, social services, police, justice, banking, and taxation.[13]

Serbia's National Assembly maintained that the Sandžak did not constitute a "legal territorial entity" and could not be granted autonomy.[14] Belgrade also claimed that the Muslim referendum had been organized under the auspices of the PDA leadership in Bosnia whose objective was to annex Serbian and Montenegrin territory. Tensions sharply increased in the region after the outbreak of hostilities in neighboring Bosnia during the spring of 1992. As in Kosovo, Serbian government propaganda claimed that Serbian residents were being pushed out of the Sandžak by Islamic fundamentalists and Muslim nationalists intent on "ethnically cleansing" the area. Conversely, PDA leaders alleged that Muslim residents were increasingly subject to intimidation by Serbian security forces and paramilitary units sponsored by Belgrade. Due to fears of violence and military conscription, about 70,000 Muslims reportedly fled the region by early 1993. In particular, the western border area with Bosnia was purportedly being cleared of Muslim residents in order to break the connection between Muslims in both states. Serbian leaders also claimed that Muslims had established armed units in the Sandžak in preparation for an uprising and attacks on the Serbian population. The PDA dismissed such assertions as ludicrous, given the heavy army and police presence, and as a pretext to arm local Serbs, increase the number of Yugoslav troops, and allow ultra-nationalist irregulars to terrorize the local population.

When Yugoslavia began to divide after the summer of 1991, Milošević strengthened direct Serbian controls over the remaining federal institutions and conducted a sweeping purge of the armed forces. In Serbia itself, Milošević maintained a tight grip over the mass media, the legal system, major sectors of the economy, and the extensive security apparatus. An opposition movement was permitted to function to preserve an image of democratization and tolerance. Nonetheless, the development of a pluralist democracy was stymied as the Socialists manipulated the key media outlets, cracked down on public demonstrations, and exploited nationalist sentiments to question the patriotism of democratic opposition parties. Furthermore, Milošević cultivated the activities of the ultra-nationalist Serbian Radical Party (SRP) both to undermine the potential appeal of alternative national parties and to present the Socialists as a comparatively moderate political formation defending Serbian national interests. The

independent opposition itself remained deeply divided on programmatic questions and on their approach toward republican and federal elections; personal
rivalries also contributed to undermining any unified front vis-à-vis the Socialists.

When it was no longer feasible to hold the federation together, the Milošević
regime calculated that a Serb-dominated and smaller Yugoslavia could be crafted
from the remaining territories. The optimal goal was to keep Bosnia-Herzegovina and Macedonia in the federation in addition to the captured areas of
Croatia. When Muslim and Croat leaders declared the independence of Bosnia-
Herzegovina in February 1992 and the Macedonian government followed suit,
Milošević adopted a twin-track approach to preserve all Serb-inhabited territories
outside the new state entities. A war of partition was launched in Bosnia, similar
to the one in Croatia the previous year, with the direct assistance of Belgrade and
the Yugoslav Army. However, in order to depict the conflict as an internal civil
war among Serbs, Muslims, and Croats, the remaining members of the federal
presidency declared the founding of a new Federal Republic of Yugoslavia,
consisting of two republics, Serbia and Montenegro. A federal constitution was
rushed through in April 1992, explicitly leaving open the possibility that other
states could join the new state. According to Article 2 of the constitution, "the
Federal Republic of Yugoslavia may be joined by other member republics, in
accordance with the present constitution."[15] The objective was to allow for the
future accession of Serbian Krajina (captured from Croatia) and the Serbian
Republic (partitioned from Bosnia-Herzegovina).

Federal elections were staged at the end of May 1992 to provide a veneer of
legitimacy for the new state. They were easily won by the Socialists and their
allies in Montenegro. Opposition parties boycotted the ballot, claiming that the
elections were illegal and unconstitutional, that the election law was a sham
document, and that the campaign period was too short for proper multi-party
competition. Among the few parties that participated in the elections were the
Radicals, sponsored and encouraged by the regime, and the DCVH, whose leaders calculated that a boycott would leave them without any voice in federal
decisions pertaining to the position of the Magyar minority. Following the ballot,
emigré businessman Milan Panić was selected as prime minister as Belgrade
tried to court international favor.

During the fall of 1992, tensions visibly increased within Serbia, not only
between opposition parties and the ruling Socialists but also among various
governing institutions.[16] While Milošević had sponsored Panić's premiership as
a way of buying time and deflecting international criticism of Belgrade's policies, Panić himself became more outspoken and active, criticizing Milošević for
his support of the war in Bosnia and his thwarting of democracy in Serbia. Panić
made some overtures toward Albanian leaders in Kosovo and offered the prospect that Yugoslavia could recognize the independence of Slovenia and Croatia.
This approach led to vehement attacks by Socialist spokesmen and to bitter
denunciations by the Radicals who organized two votes of no-confidence in the

federal government on the grounds that Panić was betraying Serbian interests. Panić survived the vote and elicited the tacit support of Yugoslav president Dobrica Ćosić and the backing of the Montenegrin leadership and the oppositionist *DEPOS* coalition. However, despite Panić's growing popularity in Serbia, he neglected to form a credible and structured opposition alliance and delayed his entry for the Serbian presidential elections. Moreover, Ćosić hesitated in lending his support for Panić's candidacy, thus undermining the premier's popularity. Suspicions persisted that either Ćosić was trying to maintain a balance between Milošević and Panić to avoid allying with the losing side, or that he was working in tandem with Milošević while appearing as the moderate voice of Serbian nationalism. Indeed, observers pointed out that Milošević had faithfully applied the program laid out in the famous 1986 memorandum to unite all Serb-inherited territories. Ćosić had been one of the leading architects of this controversial document. Some critics even speculated that Panić was secretly collaborating with Milošević to ensure that the opposition would participate in the elections and lose, thereby sealing the credibility of the Socialists' election victory.

The opposition parties found themselves at an enormous disadvantage in the December 1992 federal, republican, and local elections, held to relegitimize the Milošević regime and to deflate oppositionist claims that they benefited from widespread popularity.[17] In addition to their privileged access to the chief media organs, election laws and procedures were skewered in favor of the ruling party and serious questions were raised over voter registries, the security of voting materials, the rights of refugees to vote, and the funding of different parties; the opposition also alleged large-scale fraud. The Albanian population boycotted the entire ballot and charged that Panić had failed to deliver on his promise to restore the Albanian educational system while intimidation and repression were intensifying in the province. Muslim parties in the Serbian Sandžak also boycotted the elections, although some Muslim voters did cast their ballots for the Serbian opposition parties. Milošević won the Serbian presidential election with 55.9 percent of the popular vote, while Panić scored 34.3 percent and was swept out of the political arena. The SSP gained 47 out of 138 seats in the federal Chamber of Citizens and 12 seats in the 40-member Chamber of Republics. The SRP gained 34 seats in the Chamber of Citizens and 8 in the Chamber of Republics. These results gave the pro-Milošević forces a working majority at the federal level in coalition with the Montenegrin DPS, even though Ćosić was maintained as Yugoslav president. In February 1993, a new Serbian government was installed and headed by Premier Nikola Sainović, an SSP loyalist.

The Socialists captured 101 seats in the 250-member Serbian parliament and the Radicals 73, thus combining an absolute majority at the republican level. The opposition Civic Alliance only scored 1 seat in the federal assembly and 5 in the republican assembly; 3 of the latter were gained by the Farmers' Party of Vojvodina, a non-ethnic regionalist grouping. The Vojvodinian bloc also obtained 2 seats in the federal assembly, while the DCVH gained 9 seats, in addition to 9 seats in the Serbian Assembly. The Serbian Renewal Movement obtained 20 seats at the federal level and 50 at the republican level, making it the largest democratic opposition party represented in both legislatures. The Group of Citizens from Kosovo and Metohija, led by the alleged war criminal "Arkan," obtained 5 seats in the Serbian legislature. The Socialists and the Radicals also performed well at the local level, as did the DCVH in the 8 Hungarian-majority districts. Hungarian and other Vojvodinian activists were concerned that the Radicals had captured the mayorship of Novi Sad, the Vojvodinian capital, as a prelude to further political restrictions. Elections to the regional Vojvodina Assembly were also staged: out of 120 deputies, 58 were from a loose coalition of democratic Serbian, non-ethnic, and minority parties, while 62 were Socialists and Radicals. The democratic bloc walked out of the first Assembly session in protest at its limited powers and its subordination to the Serbian republican assembly. Despite an evidently conciliatory gesture in May 1993, when the Novi Sad Assembly passed amendments giving the Hungarian language equal status with Serbian in official affairs, minority leaders continued to express fears of discrimination and persecution.

Pressures against Serbian moderates increased during the spring of 1993 and the opposition claimed that Serbia was gradually being transformed into a fascist state. Ćosić was ousted from the Yugoslav presidency in May 1993, after losing a vote of no-confidence sponsored by the Radicals, and he was replaced by Milošević loyalist Zoran Lilić. *DEPOS* leader Vuk Drašković was arrested and beaten up by the police before being placed on trial on charges of provoking riots in Belgrade. There were also indications of a brewing struggle for power between Milošević and Šešelj. The latter had created his own political power base and captured the support of sectors of the armed forces as well as militant Serb forces in Bosnia and Croatia. Speculations surfaced that Milošević was preparing to abandon Šešelj in order to consolidate his power and pose as the reasonable voice of Serbian nationalism vis-à-vis the international community. It remained unclear whether this could be accomplished without provoking bloodshed in Serbia itself.

At the end of May 1992, the Albanian community in Kosovo staged its own parliamentary and presidential elections despite police harassment. Competing in the parliamentary ballot were 22 parties and 490 candidates and 89.32 percent of registered voters participated, including representatives of several minority groups—Muslims, Turks, Romas, and Croats. The Democratic League of Kosovo gained 96 out of 125 direct election seats, while the Parliamentary Party of Kosovo obtained 13 deputies, the Peasant Party of Kosovo and the Albanian Christian Democratic Party 7 deputies each, and the remaining two seats were acquired by independent candidates. Election organizers also devised a system of proportional representation for Kosovo's nationalities: according to their percentage of the population, Muslims were allocated 4 seats, in addition to 1 Muslim who won in direct voting, and 2 Turks who were elected on the DLK ticket. Fourteen seats were left vacant for potential Serbian and Montenegrin candidates. Ibrahim Rugova was overwhelmingly elected as Kosovo's president. Although the imminent partition of Bosnia by Serbia and Croatia was condemned by Albanian leaders, Rugova also pointed out that it could set a precedent for the partition of Serbia and the separation of Kosovo. He dismissed speculations that Belgrade was seeking to solve the Kosovo problem by dividing the province between Albania and Serbia—neither the SSP nor the DLK would be willing to accept a truncated Kosovo.

In early 1993, an expert group for the Yugoslav federal government prepared a draft law on the "liberties and rights of minority communities and of their members."[18] The authorities were evidently seeking to counter growing international condemnation of their treatment of minority groups. Belgrade proposed to provide proportional representation for all minorities in federal, republican, and local assemblies on the basis of corresponding elections; to establish the office of ombudsman and a commission in the federal government to monitor the rights of minority communities; and to grant various forms of autonomy for minorities that did not undermine the integrity of the state. Despite these positive declarations, the draft document also contained stipulations that could further undermine the position of the Albanian minority in particular. For instance, the representative of any minority could only be someone who had been elected in a "democratic and free ballot" determined by the Yugoslav or Serbian authorities and who participated in the country's parliamentary life. If such rules were actually applied, not a single existing party in Kosovo would be authorized to represent the Albanian community in the province.

SERBIAN NATIONALISTS

Serbian Socialist Party (SSP)
Socialistička Partija Srbije (SPS)

The Serbian Socialist Party was created in July 1990 from the amalgamation of the League of Communists of Serbia and the front organization, the Serbian Socialist Alliance. The new party was forged and led by Slobodan Milošević, who since May 1986 had presided over the League of Communists. With its new "Socialist" guise, its increasingly nationalist agenda, and its firm control over the state bureaucracy, the security forces, and the mass media, the SSP gained 194 of 250 seats in Serbia's first multi-party elections in December 1990. Milošević himself was elected president of Serbia, gaining 65.3 percent of the popular vote. The party maintained enormous support among bureaucrats, military veterans, and factory managers, as well as large sections of the peasantry and working class dependent on the state. The Serbian Orthodox Church and the Serbian Academy of Sciences also lent their support to the SSP, largely because of its nationalist-oriented program at a time when Yugoslavia appeared to be on the verge of dissolution. As war erupted in Slovenia and Croatia in the summer of 1991, the Serbian regime was largely successful in depicting itself as the defender of Serbian interests throughout the country. The party easily won federal elections to the newly declared two-member Yugoslav government in May 1992 in a ballot that was boycotted by the majority of opposition parties in Serbia, which condemned the elections as illegal and unconstitutional. The Serb and Montenegrin authorities claimed that, despite the boycotts, 60 percent of eligible voters had participated.

Milošević and the SSP leadership deliberately undercut the popularity of the opposition by capitalizing on nationalist sentiments, sponsoring the ultra-nationalist Serbian Radical Party, and depicting democrats and moderate nationalist forces as traitors because they criticized the war in Croatia and Bosnia. Despite the imposition of international economic sanctions on Serbia and Montenegro as punishment for Belgrade's sponsorship of the conflict in Bosnia, the SSP preserved its hold on power. Economic decline, falling living standards, and increasing unemployment precipitated by a failed economic policy and the UN embargo were presented by the SSP as part of an international conspiracy against the Serbian nation. SSP leaders and bureaucrats also benefited from the thriving sanctions-busting black-market economy and assured much of the Communist *nomenklatura* that they could preserve their privileges. The SSP maintained enormous advantages in the run-up to the federal, republican, and local elections in December 1992, particularly in terms of funds and media access. The opposition remained weak, confused, disunited, and kept off balance by Milošević. In addition, various balloting and legal irregularities assured the Socialists and their Radical allies a victory at each administrative level. The SSP obtained 101 seats in the 250-member Serbian Assembly, 47 out of 138 deputies in the federal Chamber of Citizens, and 12 out of the 20 Serbian seats in the 40-member federal Chamber of Republics. In May 1993, Socialist deputies in the federal assembly voted with the Radicals in passing a vote of no-confidence against Yugoslav president Dobrica Ćosić. Milošević had evidently calculated that he needed to oust a potential rival source of power and placate Radical condemnations of his moderating policies and public criticisms of the Bosnian Serb leadership. The democratic opposition attacked the removal of Ćosić as an unconstitutional coup that heralded the consolidation of totalitarian or quasi-fascist rule.[19]

Serbian Radical Party (SRP)
Srpska Radikalna Stranka (SRS)

Founded originally during 1990 as the Serbian Freedom Movement and later renamed the Serbian *Četnik* Movement, the SRP became an ultra-nationalist party sponsored and bolstered by the Milošević regime. The SRP was established and led by Vojislav Šešelj, a former nationalist dissident who spent time in prison for his anti-Communist views. Šešelj originally joined the Serbian Renewal Movement with dissident Vuk Drašković but left the movement because he believed that Drašković had altered the nationalist purpose of the party. Šešelj disagreed with Drašković's emphasis on opposing the Socialist Party and promoting democracy, rather than primarily pursuing Serbian national interests throughout Yugoslavia. Milošević in turn used Šešelj against Drašković by releasing him from prison, engineering his election to parliament, and allowing him to promulgate his ultra-nationalist views on state television, thereby drawing support away from the SRM. Such a policy also helped Milošević to manipulate Serbian nationalism, deflect attention from deepening economic problems, and present the Socialist regime as a patriotic force. The Radicals were also provided with the funds, resources, and opportunities to establish paramilitary "volunteer" forces that engaged in attacks and atrocities during the Serbian offensives in Croatia and Bosnia. Radical leaders were also given a slice of the lucrative black market in Serbia. Campaigning in May 1992, Šešelj summarized the party's militant position: "Albanians should be driven from Kosovo to Albania, similar actions should be taken with the Muslims in Sandžak, Hungarians who were our brothers-in-arms may remain, but the Hungarians who follow Ágoston (the independent Hungarian leader) have no place in Serbia, (and) all Croats must be expelled from Serbia." Easy access to the media, especially to state television, helped the Radicals to win a sizable block of seats in the Yugoslav Federal Assembly in May 1992.

The Radicals maintained their positions as the second-largest force in the Serb Assembly by gaining 73 out of 250 seats during the December 1992 elections. They also captured 34 seats in the federal Chamber of Citizens and 8 seats in the Chamber of Republics. Radical deputies continued to be outspoken in support of the Bosnian Serb leadership and the creation of a Greater Serbian state. Their persistent criticisms of President Ćosić for his moderating influence culminated in a successful vote of no-confidence in May 1993. The ouster of Ćosić and the crackdown on the democratic opposition appeared to further expand SRP influence, leading to speculations that either Serbia was heading for full-scale fascism or that the hidden power struggle in Belgrade would culminate in a showdown between Milošević and Šešelj. In addition to his xenophobic stance toward Serbia's minorities and his condemnation of all democratic opponents, Šešelj took a combative stance against any UN intervention in Bosnia. In May 1993, he claimed that UN soldiers would be "the first to die" if the West took military action against the Bosnian Serbs.[20]

Serbian National Renewal (SNR)
Srpska Narodna Obnova (SNO)

Founded by the "cultural-historical" Sava Society, the Serbian National Renewal was launched in Nova Pazova (in Vojvodina) in January 1990. The Sava Society originally represented the nationalist demands of Serb activists in Vojvodina. It subsequently developed to represent nationalist goals throughout Serbia and the other republics. The SNR was founded in order to "preserve historical truth, the Serbian language, and the Cyrillic alphabet," as well as to "defend Kosovo." Mirko Jović was selected president of the Sava Society and the chairman of the Executive Committee of the Serbian National Renewal. After the SNR declared itself an independent political party in January 1990, Vuk Drašković, the party's chief ideologist at the time, proclaimed the goal of an enlarged Serbian state based on historical and ethnic borders that would include parts of Bosnia-Herzegovina and Croatia, the autonomous regions of Kosovo and Vojvodina, and all of Macedonia and Montenegro. Drašković abandoned the party during the summer of 1990 to lead the Serbian Renewal Movement after falling out with Jović and opposing his strongly pro-Milošević stance. During 1991, Jović established an irregular paramilitary formation, the White Eagles, which became active in anti-Muslim offensives in Bosnia and in terrorizing the Slav Muslim population in the Sandžak region of southern Serbia and northern Montenegro. The SNR itself did not become a significant political force in either republic.[21]

Serbian Renewal Movement (SRM)
Srpski Pokret Obnove (SPO)

Initially an offshoot of the Serbian National Renewal, the SRM was founded in August 1990 and continued to be directed by the charismatic orator and writer Vuk Drašković. The party maintained overall pan-Serbian goals but increasingly focused its attention on democratizing the Serbian political system. The SRM modified its extreme nationalist position in the wake of its poor showing in the December 1990 elections, particularly after Milošević and the Socialists successfully swayed many ultra-nationalist supporters over to their favored "opposition" party, the Radicals. Drašković finished second to Milošević in the Serbian presidential race, capturing 16.4 percent of the popular vote, while the movement only gained 19 parliamentary seats in the December 1990 republican elections. The SRM was obliged to try and broaden its political appeal by moving toward the center and promoting the establishment of a constitutional monarchy under the exiled king Aleksander Karadjordjević, avowedly in order to democratize the state.

The SRM, similarly to other nationalist groupings, initially sponsored its own paramilitary formation, the Serbian Guard, to participate in the Croatian war during the summer and fall of 1991. However, its numbers shrank due to competition with the SRP and the SNR and as Milošević's campaign against Drašković gathered momentum. With the adoption of a more moderate policy, the Serbian Guard lost its importance and Drašković was condemned by the state media for abandoning the goal of a Greater Serbia. In order to bolster its opposition to the Socialist regime, the Renewal Movement initiated a new anti-Milošević coalition, the Democratic Movement of Serbia (*DEPOS*), in late May

1992; it included the pro-monarchist Democratic Party of Serbia (DOS), the Serbian Liberal Party (SLP), the New-Democracy—Movement for Serbia (ND-MS), and the Peasant Party (PP). *DEPOS* leaders contended that Milošević and the Socialist government had to be replaced in order to reintegrate Serbia with the rest of the world. The SRM criticized the government for conducting a brutal war in Bosnia, although it was loath to abandon completely the goal of an enlarged Serbian state. In the elections of December 1992, the *DEPOS* bloc gained 20 seats to the federal Chamber of Citizens and 50 seats to the Serbian Assembly, thereby becoming the largest genuinely oppositionist party in both legislatures. In June 1993, protesting the ouster of Yugoslav president Dobrica Ćosić, the SRM staged a rally outside the federal parliament that was violently dispersed by the police. Drašković and his wife, Danica, were arrested and severely beaten by police, and the authorities began proceedings in the Constitutional Court to ban the SRM altogether. Drašković was released from prison in July 1993, pledging to unite the opposition movement and dislodge Milošević from power. However, observers questioned the extent of his popularity and his ability to mobilize the Serbian public.[22]

Homeland Non-Party Serbian Association (HNPSA)
Domovinsko Nepartije Srpske Udruženje (DNSU)

The HNPSA was formed in early 1991 as a Serbian ultra-nationalist organization based in Priština, Kosovo. It regularly called on citizens to defend the Serbian people and Serbian territories "with weapons in hand." In particular, it claimed to be concerned about the "genocidal threat" posed by the "Croatian *Ustaša*" and by "*Albanian separatists*" in Kosovo. *Reports indicated that the HNPSA had close ties with paramilitary units of the SRP and with the "Tigers," a unit led by the alleged war criminal "Arkan"* (Željko Raznjatović) and reportedly coordinated by Yugoslav army commanders. In December 1992, "Arkan" and four of his followers were elected to the Serbian Assembly in a body styled as the Group of Citizens from Kosovo and Metohija. The HNPSA also supported the arming of Serbian residents in Kosovo by the Yugoslav and Serbian security forces, a process that has proceeded apace during the last two years.[23]

Association of Serbs from Croatia (ASC)
Udruženje Srba Hrvatske (USH)

This Belgrade-based organization was created in January 1991 as a "non-partisan" organization committed to "helping Serbian compatriots in Croatia, whose cultural and social development" was avowedly endangered by the Croatian state. Under Milošević's sponsorship, the organization accused the Serbian Renewal Movement of "using the suffering and despair of the Serbian population under the threat of Croatian genocidal policies for its own gains." The SRM has in turn charged the ASC with having connections to the ex-Communist apparatus and the security forces and for distributing arms to radical forces in various parts of Serbia.[24]

KOSOVAR SEPARATISTS

Democratic League of Kosovo (DLK)
Demokratski Savez Kosova (DSK)

The DLK became the strongest and most active party campaigning for the rights of ethnic Albanians in the province of Kosovo. Founded in September 1990, the League was led by President Ibrahim Rugova and Vice-President Fehmi Agani. The DLK initially held valid the constitutional declaration adopted by ethnic Albanian deputies to the Kosovo Provincial Assembly in July 1990 that proclaimed the autonomy of Kosovo as an equal unit in the Yugoslav federation. Due to DLK opposition, the Albanian population overwhelmingly boycotted the December 1990 Serbian elections. In September 1991, the DLK helped to organize a referendum on the independence and sovereignty of Kosovo; the vote was supported by over 95 percent of Albanian voters. The plebiscite was followed in October 1991 by the declaration of Kosovo's independence from the crumbling Yugoslavia. In November 1991, Rugova asked the West to exempt ethnic Albanians from any sanctions imposed against Serbia for fomenting war in Croatia, and in February 1992, he requested that the EC and the United States recognize the independence of the state of Kosovo (Kosova in Albanian). Rugova contended that such recognition would prevent mass bloodshed in the region.

The Albanian population boycotted the rump-Yugoslav elections in May 1992 and held separate legislative and presidential elections in the "Republic of Kosovo" the same month. The ballot was intended to legitimize the Albanian political structures and win international recognition for Kosovo's drive for independence. Rugova was the only candidate for the presidency, while the DLK won the majority of seats to the Kosovo Assembly, gaining 96 out of 125 deputies in direct elections. Serbia's government immediately declared both the elections and the call for international recognition as illegal and provocative and accused Albanian leaders of irredentist demands by seeking to merge Kosovo with Albania. Rugova discounted these charges and declared that the Albanian population sought sovereignty, independence, and neutrality rather than outright unification with Albania.

Kosovo's new prime minister Bujar Bukoshi announced an eight-point peace plan in early 1993 that called for Kosovo to be placed under international UN protection; this was discounted by Western leaders as unrealistic. The creation of a UN protectorate was viewed by Albanians as an important step toward international recognition and as a means of defending the Albanian majority from further repression and possible mass expulsions. Linked with the DLK was the

Kosovo Women's Association, led by its president, Luleta Beqiri, as well as a youth wing. The DLK also sponsored and financed the independent Albanian educational system, publishing activities, cultural life, and economic ventures and continued to receive funding from Albanian exiles in the West. As state repression persisted throughout 1993 and the position of Albanians continued to deteriorate, Rugova came under criticism from some local activists for being too passive and patient in his approach. Kosovo's president contended that any combative moves by a largely unarmed community would result in a bloodbath. Nonetheless, he recognized that mass frustration was growing and young Albanians in particular were becoming increasingly radicalized.[25]

Coordinating Council of Albanian Political Parties (CCAPP)
Koordinirano Veće Albanske Političke Stranke (KVAPS)

The Coordinating Council was established in the summer of 1991 by leaders of several Albanian organizations in the former Yugoslavia: the DLK, the Party for Democratic Prosperity (in Macedonia), the Kosovo Peasant's Party, the Democratic Alliance of Montenegro, the Party of Democratic Action, the Albanian Democratic Christian Party, the Kosovo Social Democratic Party, the Party for the Unification of Albanians, the People's Democratic Party, and the Albanian Democratic Party. The Council was based in Priština and was created to enhance cooperative activities among parties aiming to maintain "the sovereignty of the Albanian people," and opposed to any threats from the Yugoslav regime. Rugova was elected chairman of the council, signaling his high prestige among Albanian activists in all former Yugoslav republics. In December 1991, the committee formally asked the EC to recognize the Republic of Kosovo as an independent political entity.[26]

Parliamentary Party of Kosovo (PPK)
Parlamentska Stranka Kosova (PSK)

The PPK was formed during 1990 to "help achieve a real parliamentary democracy and civil society in Kosovo." It declared its commitment to political pluralism and civil rights and initially insisted on the distinct political, legal, and cultural status of Kosovo within the framework of the Yugoslav federation. With the breakup of Yugoslavia, the PPK supported the DLK's position on Kosovo sovereignty. The party primarily relied on the work accomplished by the Kosovo Youth Parliament and was led by chairman Veton Surroi. In May 1991, Surroi created a coalition of opposition groups that included: the Albanian Christian Democratic Party, the Social Democratic Party, the Committee for Protection of Human Rights and Freedoms, the Party of Democratic Action, the Kosovo Women's Forum, and the Forum of Albanian Intellectuals. In the Kosovo elections of May 1992, the PPK gained 13 deputies to the "republic's" parliament.

The party recommended that Albanians in Kosovo make preparations for possible "ethnic cleansing" by Serb paramilitaries and criticized the DLK for adopting an overly pacifist position. Despite this, the PPK has not engaged in arming the Albanian population, contrary to charges by the Serbian media. Belgrade has tried to present Surroi and the PPK as violent armed secessionists in order to foster divisions among the Albanian opposition.[27]

Albanian Christian Democratic Party (ACDP)
Albanska Kršćanska Demokratska Stranka (AKDS)

Despite its name, this Priština-based party counted among its members both Christian and Muslim Albanians; indeed, about 80 percent were Muslim. The ACDP emphasized Albanian unity, both culturally and geographically. According to the secretary of the party, Ramush Tahiri, the ACDP did not believe in the existence of two Albanian nations and would create branches and organizations "in all parts of the world where Albanians live." He reiterated this position in May 1991, when he stated that if Yugoslavia disintegrated, the ACDP would promulgate full unification with Albania, respecting the "ethnic principle" in defining new state borders. The Serbian Federal Secretariat for Justice refused to register the party because it was avowedly demanding the right to secede from the federation. The ACDP won seven seats to the Kosovo Assembly in the "illegal" elections of May 1992. The same number of seats were gained by the Peasant Party of Kosovo (PPK), led by Hifzi Islami. Among other moderate Albanian parties, the Social Democratic Party of Kosovo (SDPK), led by Bajram Krasniqi, claimed to have significant support among intellectuals and one deputy in the underground Kosovo parliament. It criticized the DLK for its moderate position but avoided any overt conflicts that could play into Milošević's hands.[28]

Party of Democratic Action for Kosovo (PDAK)
Stranka Demokratske Akcije Kosova (SDAK)

Founded in 1989, and linked with the PDA in Bosnia and Sandžak, the party was composed of Albanians, Muslims, and Turks from Kosovo and neighboring areas of southern Serbia with a sizable non-Serb population. Under its chairman, Numan Baliç, the PDAK sought cultural and educational autonomy and local rule for the non-Albanian Muslim nationality in Kosovo. It demanded the right to use the Latin alphabet of the "Bosnian language" and for Muslim history and culture to be introduced into local textbooks. According to the PDAK, the best option for the status of the province was an independent and sovereign Kosovo republic. It underscored that an independent Kosovo could only be achieved through democratic and peaceful means. A PDAK member, Nasuf Behuli, was the only Albanian deputy in the Serbian Assembly, having been elected in December 1990.[29]

Council for the Protection of Human Rights and Freedoms (CPHRF)
Veće za Zastitu Ljudskih Prava i Sloboda (VZLPS)

The Council, under the leadership of Secretary Zenun Çelaj, has promoted pan-Albanian goals and sought ultimately to unite Kosovo with Albania. The council believed that the core of the Kosovo problem was that the Serbian authorities treated the Albanian majority as an ethnic minority. According to the Serbian media, the chairman of the council, Adem Demaçi, was also the leader of the military wing of the "Skipetar national-separatists" who has been advocating "secret mobilization." (The term "Skipetar" is a pejorative name for Albanians used by Serb nationalists.) The claim was denied as preposterous by CPHRF leaders who contended that the Albanian population was virtually unarmed while any violent provocations would be suicidal as they could precipitate a brutal Serbian crackdown.[30]

National Movement for the Liberation of Kosovo (NMLK)
Narodni Pokret za Oslobodjenje Kosova (NPOK)

The NMLK, an openly militant organization, entered Kosovo's political arena in March 1993 with a mass distribution of pamphlets calling for full mobilization and an uprising to liberate Kosovo. It aimed to organize and lead the armed struggle of the Albanian people for national liberation. Some military analysts calculated that Albanian militants had indeed mobilized diversionary and reconnaissance units in Kosovo in preparation for armed conflict. Other explicitly separatist organizations that did not discount the possibility of armed insurrection against the "Serbian occupation forces" included the Party of National Unity (PNU), which broke away from the DLK in May 1991 under the leadership of Ali Alidemaj, the Albanian Revolutionary Organization (ARO), formed by former Albanian Communists, and the Movement for the Republic of Kosovo (MRK), which has criticized Rugova for his alleged pacifism. There are strong suspicions that the NMLK and other small ultra-militant groups have been sponsored, funded, or penetrated by the Serbian security services to divide the Albanian political movement, to give credence to Belgrade's charges of Albanian extremism, and possibly to prepare for an armed provocation in Kosovo. Belgrade also helped to form a pro-Yugoslav movement in Kosovo, styled as the Association of Albanians, Serbs, and Montenegrins (AASM); it had virtually no support among the Albanian community.[31]

VOJVODINIAN AUTONOMISTS

Democratic Community of Vojvodina Hungarians (DCVH)
Demokratska Zajednica Madžara Vojvodine (DZMV)

Founded in April 1990, the DCVH became the largest and most active of the

Hungarian organizations in the former Yugoslavia. The DCVH defined itself as an "independent political organization that seeks to represent the collective rights of Hungarians and to participate in establishing a multi-party parliamentary democracy and a free democratic state based on the rule of law." Under the direction of President Ándras Ágoston, the DCVH demanded that the Hungarian national minority be provided with an array of cultural and political rights, including the opportunity to establish a local minority self-government. At the outset, Ágoston claimed that his organization viewed a united Yugoslavia as the most suitable state structure, whether this would be a federation or a confederation. But the DCVH increasingly blamed the Socialist Party for deteriorating relations between the Serbian government and the Hungarian minority. The DCVH dismissed all attempts to reform the Communist system and condemned the rise of ultra-nationalism sponsored by the Milošević regime.

The community described itself as right of center politically, supporting social and economic reform, constitutional changes, and a full-fledged market economy. Although the DCVH acknowledged Serbia's "historical right" to protect the territorial integrity of the state, it maintained that Hungarians in Vojvodina should be governed according to the principles of "cultural autonomy in the framework of minority self-government" but not based on territorial principles. In the DCVH's concept of self-government, all ethnic Hungarian citizens of Serbia, regardless of where they lived, would have the option of enrolling in a minority self-government, a provision that was evidently consistent with the 1974 constitution. For the most part, the DCVH stressed its loyalty to the state, despite Serb nationalist attempts to portray the organization as secessionist and a threat to Serbian national interests. The DCVH supported efforts to resolve the crisis between Serbia and Croatia through negotiations. However, in August 1991, Ágoston demanded that Hungarian soldiers be demobilized and withdrawn from the military conflict in Croatia because they did not wish to take part in inter-Slav conflicts. One of the twelve members of the DCVH's governing body, Béla Csorba, was arrested when he refused to comply with the draft papers he was issued.

In the elections of December 1990, the DCVH won 8 of the 250 seats to the Serbian parliament, but cooperation with Serbian opposition parties proved difficult, because most of them did not support the DCVH's position of codifying minority rights and promoting minority autonomy. Only the Democratic Community of Croats in Vojvodina backed the DCVH on minority questions. With the break-up of Yugoslavia from mid-1991 onward, the DCVH grew increasingly anxious over remaining in a truncated Serb-dominated state, particularly as anti-minority policies were accelerating and the media accused the DCVH leaders of being separatists. In addition, Serb refugees from Croatia and Bosnia were resettled in Vojvodina, and in some areas of the province minority communities were encouraged or pressured to leave the country; several thousand Hungarians left Vojvodina during 1991 and 1992. In April 1992, the DCVH issued a memorandum on autonomy proposing a tripartite system, including special status for municipalities in which Magyars formed clear majorities and the development of a Hungarian autonomous area. The memorandum was rejected by the Serb authorities and the DCVH was accused of separatism and irredentism. The DCVH participated in the federal and republican elections in December 1992, gaining 9 seats in the federal parliament and 9 seats in the Serbian Assembly. It performed well in the 8 Hungarian-majority districts and won the mayorship of Subotica. DCVH deputies were elected to the reconstituted Vojvodinian Provincial Assembly, forming a bloc of 58 out of 120 seats comprised of various democratic and minority parties. Together with other oppositionist parties, DCVH deputies stormed out in protest after the first parliamentary session describing the Assembly as a mere appendage of the Serb parliament with no authentic legislative powers.[32]

Association of Hungarians for Our Fatherland, Serbia and Yugoslavia (AHFSY)
Udruženje Madžara za Našu Domovinu, Srbiju i Jugoslaviju (UMDSJ)

The association was established in 1991 as a front organization for the Socialist regime to undermine the independent Hungarian movements and to draw distinctions between "loyal" and "disloyal" Hungarians. József Molnár became chairman of this Belgrade-sponsored organization, and he vehemently denounced the DCVH and its leader, Ágoston, for requesting that Hungarians be released from the Yugoslav army. Molnár claimed that such military separation would be "tragic for Hungarians" because it would pit them against Serbs and make Hungarians "enemies in our own republic." Parroting the official Serbian government position, Molnár claimed that Hungarians in Serbia "enjoyed civic and national rights greater than the rights enjoyed by any national minority in any country." The AHFSY made direct appeals to the Magyar minority to "resist the secessionists and the foes of Serbia and Yugoslavia," referring implicitly to the DCVH. The organization has regularly disagreed with other Hungarian parties over even the least-controversial issues; for instance, the association did not agree that the names of villages in Magyar areas should be written in both Serbo-Croatian and Hungarian. Despite the funds and resources it has received from Belgrade, the AHFSY has failed to gain any significant support from the Hungarian population and has been exposed as a Socialist proxy.[33]

Democratic Alliance of Croats in Vojvodina (DACV)
Demokratski Savez Hrvata u Vojvodini (DSHV)

The DACV was established in 1990 and Bela Tonković was elected president. The organization complained that Croats in Vojvodina had been prevented from nurturing their own national identity. Unlike most of the other ethnic opposition parties, the DACV took part in the May 1992 federal elections. Alliance leaders explained their participation as giving voters a "democratic option," and not as legitimizing the newly proclaimed Federal Republic of Yugoslavia. The DACV proposed a referendum for Vojvodina's citizens concerning the type of autonomy the province should be granted and what relations it should maintain with other components of the Serbian state. The alliance contended that Vojvodina should benefit, at the very least, from the autonomy specified under the 1974 Yugoslav constitution. The DACV won local seats in the December 1992 elections in Subotica after forming a coalition with the Democratic Community of Vojvodina Hungarians. Croat leaders regularly voiced concerns about Belgrade's policies that were evidently intended to push the majority of Croats out of Vojvodina and replace them with Serbs from Croatia and Bosnia. Between 1991 and 1993, Radical Party activists in cooperation with Serbian security forces reportedly forced over 35,000 Croats out of the province, particularly from the western Srem and Bačka areas, while Croatian activists have been sacked from work, beaten by police, or unjustifiably imprisoned. The DACV has found it difficult to cooperate with the Serbian opposition as the latter evidently feared that including Croats in their coalitions would diminish their popularity.[34]

Farmers' Party of Vojvodina (FPV)
Seljačka Stranka Vojvodine (SSV)

The FPV was founded in late 1991 by Dragan Veselinov, a democratic activist who supported a civic-oriented program and a multi-ethnic Vojvodina with a large measure of autonomy. By the close of 1992, the party claimed a membership of some 5,000, although most of its activists were intellectuals and students. The FPV voiced concern about the expulsion of minorities from Vojvodina and lodged protests against the "ethnic cleansing" of Croat communities. In June 1992, the FPV, together with the League of Social Democrats of Vojvodina, the Reformist Party, and the Republican Club, founded the Civic Alliance of Serbia as an alternative democratic coalition to the Socialist-Radical alliance and the monarchist *DEPOS* coalition. *DEPOS* in turn maintained links with the Democratic Reformists of Vojvodina, who were not strong autonomists but favored a decentralized state structure. The Civic Alliance claimed that "the nationalist regime of the Socialist Party of Serbia, alongside other nationalist regimes, bears the greatest political responsibility for the disintegration of the Yugoslav state." The alliance considered Milošević's rule to be autocratic and the formation of the Federal Republic of Yugoslavia as illegal, because it was created without public consent. Alliance leaders proposed the dissolution of the Serb Assembly, the resignation of Milošević, and the formation of a new transitional Serbian government. The coalition was supported by political independents, intellectuals, and other civic-oriented groups and peace organizations. The Civic Alliance scored poorly in the December 1992 elections, gaining only one seat in the

Federal Assembly and five in the Serbian Assembly; three of these were gained by the FPV. The alliance only registered 1.5 percent of the popular vote. In the aftermath of the ballot, the FPV and the LSDV founded an unofficial Vojvodinian coalition and the rest of the Civic Alliance transformed itself into a party under the leadership of Vesna Pesić and Radomir Tanić.[35]

League of Social Democrats of Vojvodina (LSDV)
Liga Socialdemokrata Vojvodine (LSV)

The league was established in July 1991 by activist Nenad Čanak who became its chairman. It cast itself as a multi-ethnic organization seeking autonomy for Vojvodina in a tripartite Serbian federation, consisting of Vojvodina, Kosovo, and Serbia-Šumadija. The LSDV claimed to have significant support across the ethnic spectrum among the old settlers in Vojvodina, but recognized that most of the Serb newcomers were Milošević supporters. The league cooperated with all parties that shared its views either on Vojvodinian autonomy or on the civic option in Serbian politics. It entered into an oppositionist coalition with the Civic Alliance for the December 1992 elections, but the coalition performed poorly, only gaining one seat in the Federal Assembly and five in the Serbian Assembly. The LSDV claimed that many of its members also belonged to the Farmers' Party of Vojvodina, with which it cooperated in an unofficial "Vojvodina bloc." The league has been critical of the DCVH for placing Hungarian ambitions above pan-Vojvodinian interests and suspected that Belgrade could be planning to split the province. By allocating the northern portion to Hungary, the position of the autonomist movement in the rest of Vojvodina would be seriously undermined. Hungarian and Socialist leaders dismissed such speculations as groundless.

MINORITY ORGANIZATIONS

Party of Democratic Action (PDA)
Stranka Demokratske Akcije (SDA)

The PDA was established in August 1990 as a pan-Yugoslav political formation. The Serbian-Montenegrin branch was presided over by President Sulejman Ugljanin. The party maintained close links with the PDA in Sarajevo even after the secession of Bosnia-Herzegovina from Yugoslavia in early 1992. It had to close its section in Belgrade but maintained branches in Serbian and Montenegrin Sandžak and in Kosovo. The PDA declared early on that if Yugoslavia disintegrated and the unification of Serbia and Montenegro intensified, the party would demand cultural and political autonomy for the Muslims in the Sandžak region. Sandžak Muslims claimed to speak the Bosnian language and to write in the Latin script, and their leaders declared that they would not accept the Serbo-

Croatian language and the Cyrillic alphabet. The party asserted that the ruling Socialist Party favored the Serbian nation and had attempted to convince the general public that the Sandžak was populated by a "savage people of criminals who are to be persecuted without the right to complain." In April 1991, Milošević sent police reinforcements to the Sandžak on the pretext that there was a possibility of widespread rioting sparked by Muslim unrest. Since that time, repression against the Muslim population has significantly increased and the PDA has initiated several steps toward forming an independent political structure in the Sandžak.

In October 1991, the Muslim National Council of Sandžak (MNCS), a quasi-governmental body established in May 1991, and whose authority purportedly extended to the Montenegrin Sandžak, organized a referendum on autonomy. Of Muslim voters in ten Sandžak municipalities, 98.92 percent out of the 70.19 percent that participated voted for political and territorial autonomy. The exercise was condemned by Belgrade as unconstitutional. After the plebiscite, the Muslim National Council selected a new Sandžak government: PDA Secretary General Rasim Ljajić was selected as prime minister and Ugljanin remained as president of the National Council. The PDA maintained a majority of seats in the new government; it also included members of the Liberal Bosnian Organization and the Party of National Equality. In January 1992, the MNCS declared the creation of a "special status" for the Sandžak that would give the region far-reaching autonomy. The initiative was not recognized by the Yugoslav or Serbian governments. As Serb ultra-nationalist paramilitaries became active in the region during 1992, the western regions of the Sandžak in the districts of Priboj (Serbia) and Pljevlja (Montenegro) were deliberately cleared of Muslim residents through bombings, assaults, intimidation, and economic discrimination. The PDA consistently protested against government policies and boycotted the federal, republican, and local elections in December 1992. However, divisions also appeared in the party over the question of participation and potential Muslim support for Yugoslav premier Milan Panić. The party has been unable to forge any meaningful cooperation with the Serbian opposition; the latter evidently perceived Muslim organizations as more of a liability than an advantage in election campaigns.[36]

Liberal Bosnian Organization (LBO)
Liberalna Bošnjačka Organizacija (LBO)

The LBO was established during 1990 as the Sandžak branch of the Bosnian-based Muslim Bosnian Organization but declared its independence once Yugoslavia began to disintegrate. The party emphasized a multi-ethnic "Bosniak" identity rather than a narrower Muslim religious-ethnic identification as defined by former Communists and nationalists. The LBO has focused on the democratization and decentralization of the Sandžak, and similarly to the PDA, claimed "special status" or autonomy for the region but opposed secession or any changes in existing republican borders. Led by Mehmed Slezović, the LBO claimed about 3,000 members with many more sympathizers; it also established an "initiative council" in the Montenegrin Sandžak. The LBO was open to all nationality groups, cooperated with the much larger PDA, and had members in the Muslim National Council and the National Assembly in Novi Pazar.

Democratic Political Party of Roma (DPPR)
Demokratska Politička Partija Roma (DPPR)

The DPPR was based in Kragujevac, in central Serbia. The party advocated the cultural, economic, and social emancipation of the Romani population so that they could emerge from their "state of backwardness." It wanted to see more Roma in schools and work organizations, to have representatives in all official bodies, and to obtain a "national status" for the Gypsy population in a democratic Yugoslavia.[37]

Democratic Union of Bulgarians in Yugoslavia (DUBY)
Demokratski Savez Bugarina Jugoslavije (DSBJ)

Created in October 1990 in Niš, southeastern Serbia, the DUBY was led by Kiril Georgiev, a journalist who worked for the Bulgarian language *Bratstvo* (Fraternity) paper issued in Niš. The founders established the union as a voluntary, independent, and democratic organization of Yugoslav citizens of Bulgarian origin, as well as representatives of other nationalities. It formed branches in the Bulgarian-populated towns of Dimitrovgrad and Bosilegrad. The union apparently excluded ethnic Bulgarians who displayed "nationalist, chauvinist, and separatist leanings." The DUBY aimed to enhance the national awareness of the Bulgarian minority, to safeguard the civil and national rights of Bulgarians, and to reach a rapprochement between Serbs and Bulgarians. Marin Mladenov, vice-president of DUBY, underscored that Bulgarians were in a very different position than either the Hungarian or to Albanian minorities. The latter had consistently defended their ethnicity and culture, while Bulgarians apparently allowed themselves to become much more assimilated. Union leaders asserted that their chief problem was not with the Serbian people but with the policies of the Serbian government, which endeavored to assimilate the shrinking Bulgarian population and constrict its cultural, educational, and political activities. DUBY was the only ethnic party to join the opposition coalition *DEPOS* for election-related activities. In May 1993, a Bulgarian organization with claims to eastern Serbia also declared its existence in Sofia. The Congress of the Western Bulgarian Outlands (CWBO), led by Stefan Rangelov, demanded the recognition of former Bulgarian territories and their placement under the jurisdiction of Slovenia and Croatia, which it viewed as the lawful successors to the first Yugoslavia (the Kingdom of Serbs, Croats, and Slovenes). It condemned Belgrade for pursuing assimilationist measures toward the Bulgarian population.[38]

Democratic Alliance of Vojvodina Romanians (DAVR)
Demokratski Savez Rumuna Vojvodine (DSRV)

The DAVR was established during 1990 because of growing fear over the status of minority ethnic groups if the Yugoslav federation collapsed. The organization was led by Ion Marković and was organized according to territorial principles. The DAVR did not claim to be a political party but a broad movement intent upon "preserving the collective identity of the Romanian nationality." In May 1993, the new president of the alliance, Pavel Gaetan, met with the Yugoslav president, apparently "for the first time in decades," and reported on the problems of schooling and publishing among the Romanian minority. Gaetan underscored that the Romanian community had no representative in the Vojvodina parliament. [39]

Alliance of Ruthenians and Ukrainians (ARU)
Savez Rutenca i Ukrajinca (SRU)

The ARU was founded in Novi Sad in May 1990 to defend the national identity of the Ruthenians and Ukrainians, of which there were an estimated 30,000 throughout the former Yugoslavia. The organization did not claim any party affiliation and was open to everyone, regardless of national identity or religious conviction. The organization sought to promote "positive ethnic relations" while stressing the importance of protecting the cultural and educational rights of Ukrainians and Ruthenians, as specified in the Serbian constitution.[40]

Slovak National Heritage Foundation (SNHF)
Osnivanje Slovačka Narodna Nasledstva (OSNN)

This organization officially renewed its activities in August 1990 in order to protect and represent the approximately 67,000 Slovaks living in Vojvodina. Chairman Mihal Spevak described the emphasis of the organization as the preservation of Slovak identity, particularly through the creation of a minority educational system. SNHF leaders protested the new Serbian education law because it allegedly "no longer provided for the specific needs of ethnic minorities and does not guarantee schools for minorities." In response to questions regarding the armed conflict among the Yugoslav nations, Spevak stated his support for everyone struggling for truth, sovereignty, the right to self-determination, and the preservation of his own identity. But the group has studiously avoided issuing statements of support for any one Yugoslav nation over another.[41]

CHRONOLOGY

March 1986: A controversial nationalist memorandum is issued by the Serbian Academy of Arts and Sciences claiming that Serbia had been deliberately weakened by the Tito regime and demanding complete equality for the Serbian state. The memorandum blamed the 1974 constitution for creating a "loose confederation" that required the consensus of all republics. The memorandum listed Serbian grievances against the state and against non-Serb leaders (including Tito) and ended by asserting the need for Serbs to create their own state. The memorandum served to fuel Serbian nationalism. Dobrica Ćosić (later Yugoslav federal president) was a central architect of the document.

May 1986: Milošević ascends to the leadership of the League of Communists of Serbia. Knowing that Communist and Yugoslav causes could no longer mobilize the masses, Milošević begins to resuscitate Serbian nationalism to strengthen and extend his power.

October 1988: Vojvodina's provincial authorities are replaced by a purge orchestrated by Communist leaders to eliminate pro-autonomy forces. The province becomes increasingly governed from Belgrade.

November 1988: Milošević proposes constitutional amendments that would effectively revoke the autonomous status of Vojvodina and Kosovo. Albanians participate in peaceful demonstrations calling for Kosovo's secession from Serbia. Serbian authorities respond by banning all public meetings in the province.

March 1989: The Serbian National Assembly passes constitutional amendments giving Serbia more direct control over Kosovo and Vojvodina. One hundred and fourteen Albanian deputies in the Kosovo Provincial Assembly issue a "constitutional declaration" announcing Kosovo as an independent and equal entity in the framework of the Yugoslav federation. Serbian authorities condemn the move as illegitimate and formally dissolve the Kosovo Assembly.

May 1990: The Yugoslav Federal Assembly elects Borislav Jović, a Serb, as Yugoslav president. The presidency is a rotating post heading a collective eight-member presidential council, designed to prevent power struggles among the republics after Tito's death. The eight members of the collective presidency were installed in 1989, and the leadership was to rotate every year. Late in the month, the collective presidency proclaims Yugoslavia to be in political crisis; Jović states that the government would take "urgent measures" to protect the integrity of the state.

June 1990: The Serbian legislature passes a law to extend "special measures" and direct control over the Kosovo and Vojvodina administrations.

July 1990: The League of Communists of Serbia and the Socialist Alliance merge to create the Serbian Socialist Party with Slobodan Milošević as the leader. The SSP adopts an openly nationalist platform.

July 1990: The Kosovo Assembly issues a proclamation declaring Kosovo an independent republic within the Yugoslav federation. Three days later Belgrade suspends the Kosovo Provincial Assembly.

September 1990: The dissolved Kosovo Assembly meets secretly in the town of Kačanik and adopts a new constitution, declaring Kosovo a sovereign republic within Yugoslavia. A clandestine government and legislature are elected.

December 1990: Serbia's first multi-party elections are held. The SSP, with its increasingly nationalist agenda and its firm control over the state bureaucracy, the security forces, and the mass media, wins a governing majority. Milošević is elected president of Serbia, capturing 65.34 percent of the vote.

March 1991: The Kosovo Provincial Assembly is officially abolished by Belgrade.

May 1991: The Party for Democratic Action forms the Muslim National Council of the Sandžak as a quasi-governmental body. Serbian authorities refuse to recognize this initiative.

June 1991: Slovenia and Croatia declare independence. Ibrahim Rugova of the Democratic League of Kosovo announces that Kosovo will not remain in a truncated Yugoslavia. He asserts, however, that only peaceful means will be used to achieve independence.

October 1991: Sandžak Muslims hold a referendum, organized by the Muslim National Council, on political and cultural autonomy. Of the 70.2 percent of eligible voters participating in the referendum, 98.9 percent cast ballots for autonomy. Serbian authorities declare the referendum "illegal, unnecessary, and senseless."

January 1992: Muslim leaders in Sandžak announce the creation of a "special status" for the region; the move is condemned by Belgrade.

April 1992: Following the secession of Slovenia, Croatia, Macedonia, and Bosnia-Herzegovina, the republics of Montenegro and Serbia (including the provinces of Kosovo and Vojvodina) declare the formation of a new Federal Republic of Yugoslavia. A new constitution is quickly adopted. The status of Vojvodina and Kosovo remains unchanged within the new state.

May 1992: Federal elections to the two-member Yugoslav federal government are held to provide a veneer of legitimacy for the new state; the Socialists and their Radical allies win an overwhelming majority of seats. Opposition parties boycott the ballot, claiming that the elections are illegal and unconstitutional, that the election law is a sham document, and that the campaign period was too short for proper multi-party competition. Later in the month, four democratic opposition parties establish the Democratic Movement of Serbia *(DEPOS)* in an attempt to coordinate their campaign against Milošević. Albanians in Kosovo hold their own general elections to their clandestine government. Ibrahim Rugova is elected president and 130 other activists are elected delegates to the legislature of the independent republic of Kosovo. The newly appointed government declares Kosovo an independent state and appeals for international recognition.

June 1992: Brutal "ethnic cleansing" policies perpetrated primarily by Serbian militias in Bosnia-Herzegovina increase apprehensions among minorities in Serbia, especially in Vojvodina, Kosovo, and the Sandžak.

July 1992: Milan Panić, a naturalized American citizen, is elected prime minister of the rump Yugoslavia by the SSD- and SRP-dominated Federal Assembly. Panić asserts the need to hold national elections and to bring peace to the former Yugoslavia.

December 1992: Serbia holds local, republican, and federal elections. Milošević wins the presidency against challenger Milan Panić, while the Socialists gain a plurality of seats in both republican and federal legislatures. The Radical Party, led by extremist Šešelj and backed by the Socialists, comes in second, ahead of the democratic opposition coalition, *DEPOS.*

February 1993: Serbia's National Assembly elects a new government headed by Socialist Prime Minister Nikola Sainović.

May-June 1993: The Yugoslav president, Dobrica Ćosić, is removed from office in a vote of no-confidence engineered by Milošević and Šešelj. The leader of the *DEPOS* coalition, Vuk Drašković, and his wife are arrested at a protest rally in Belgrade; they are badly beaten and imprisoned. The authorities indicate that they will ban Drašković's party, the Serbian Renewal Movement.

NOTES

1. Population statistics are based on the 1991 census in Serbia, presented in Prvoslav Ralić, *Minority Rights in Serbia: Facts, Figures, Orientation*, Belgrade, December 1992.

2. For valuable histories of Serbia, see Fred Singleton, *A Short History of the Yugoslav Peoples* (Cambridge: Cambridge University Press, 1985); Ivo Banac, *The National Question in Yugoslavia: Origins, History, Politics* (Ithaca: Cornell University Press, 1984); Michael Boro Petrovich, *A History of Modern Serbia 1804–1918* , 2 vols. (New York: Harcourt Brace Jovanovich, 1976); R.G.D. Laffan, *The Serbs: The Guardians of*

the Gate (New York: Dorset Press, 1989); Steven L. Burg, *Conflict and Cohesion in Socialist Yugoslavia* (Princeton: Princeton University Press, 1983); Dennison Rusinow, *The Yugoslav Experiment, 1948–1974* (London, 1988); Stevan K. Pavlowitch, *The Impossible Survivor: Yugoslavia and Its Problems, 1918–1988* (Columbus: Ohio State University Press, 1988); Pedro Ramet, *Nationalism and Federalism in Yugoslavia, 1963–1983* (Bloomington: Indiana University Press, 1984); and Sabrina Petra Ramet, *Balkan Babel: Politics, Culture, and Religion in Yugoslavia* (Boulder, CO: Westview, 1992).

3. For an analysis of the memorandum, see Slobodan Stenković, "The Serbian Academy's Memorandum," Radio Free Europe/Radio Liberty Research Institute (RFE/RL), *Yugoslav Situation Report*, no. 11, November 20, 1986.

4. Valuable background on the early Milošević years can be found in Milan Andrejevich, "Yugoslavia's Lingering Crisis," RFE/RL, *Report on Eastern Europe*, vol. 1, no. 1, January 5, 1990; Andrejevich, "Serbia Cracks Down on Kosovo."

5. See *Priština Domestic Service*, July 2, 1990, in Federal Broadcast Information Service, *Daily Report: East Europe, FBIS-EEU–90–128*, July 3, 1990.

6. For mutual criticisms of the two constitutions, check *Tanjug*, Belgrade, September 20, 1990, in *FBIS-EEU–90–184*, September 21, 1990, and Blerim Reka and Emin Azemi, "Life Under Two Constitutions," *Flaka e Vëllazërimit*, Skopje, September 30, 1990, in *FBIS-EEU–90–196*, October 10, 1990.

7. For the official Serbian position on constitutional and legal questions, see Prvoslav Ralić, *Minority Rights in Serbia: Facts, Figures, Orientation.*

8. For a report on the elections with full documentation, see *The 1990 Elections in the Republics of Yugoslavia*, National Republican Institute for International Affairs, Washington, DC, 1991.

9. For useful chronicles of human rights violations in Kosovo, see *The Crisis in Kosovo: Heading Towards an Open Conflict*, Priština Branch of the Yugoslav Helsinki Committee, Priština, February 1991; *Dismissals and Ethnic Cleansing in Kosovo*, International Confederation of Free Trade Unions, Brussels, October 1992.

10. See Milan Andrejevich, "Kosovo: A Precarious Balance Between Stability and Civil War," RFE/RL, *Report on Eastern Europe*, vol. 2, no. 42, October 18, 1991.

11. See Edith Oltay, "Hungarians in Yugoslavia Seek Guarantees for Minority Rights," RFE/RL, *Report on Eastern Europe*, vol. 2, no. 38, September 20, 1991.

12. *Memorandum on the Self-Government of Hungarians in the Republic of Serbia*, Working Document of the General Assembly of the Democratic Community of Hungarians in Vojvodina, April 25, 1992.

13. For some details, see M. Antić and F. Hamidović, "Muslim National Council of Sandžak Formed: Sandžak out of Serbia?" *Borba*, Belgrade, May 20, 1991; and the *Memorandum on the Establishment of a Special Status for Sandžak*, Muslim National Council of Sandžak, Novi Pazar, June 1993.

14. For details, see Milan Andrejevich, "The Sandžak: The Next Balkan Theater of War?" RFE/RL, *Research Report*, vol. 1, no. 47, November 27, 1992.

15. See the *Constitution of the Federal Republic of Yugoslavia*, Belgrade, 1992.

16. Useful analysis is contained in Milan Andrejevich, "What Future for Serbia?" RFE/RL, *Research Report*, vol. 1, no. 50, December 18, 1992.

17. See the *Commentary on the December 1992 Elections in Serbia and Montenegro*, International Republican Institute, Washington, DC, 1993.

18. See Branislav Radivojsa, "Law for Minority Communities Prepared: Anyone Can Be in a Minority," *Politika*, Belgrade, March 9, 1993.

19. *Tanjug*, Belgrade, June 13, 1990, in *FBIS-EEU–90–116*, June 15, 1990; Ljuba Stojić, "Pluralistic Ballot," *Nin*, Belgrade, September 28, 1990, in Federal Broadcast Information Service/Joint Publications Research Service, *Daily Report: East Europe,*

JPRS-EER–90–145, October 23, 1990; Milan Andrejevich, "Milošević and the Serbian Opposition," RFE/RL, *Report of Eastern Europe*, October 19, 1990; *Belgrade Domestic Service*, November 4, 1990, in *FBIS-EEU–90–214*, November 5, 1990; RFE/RL, *Daily Report*, no. 103, June 1, 1992; Milan Andrejevich, "What Future for Serbia?"

20. Interview with Vojislav Šešelj, *Heti Vilaggazdasag*, Budapest, May 18, 1991, in *FBIS-EEU–91–099*, May 22, 1991.

21. *Belgrade Domestic Service*, January 6, 1990, in *FBIS-EEU–90–009*, January 12, 1990; Milan Andrejevich, "The Yugoslav Army in Kosovo: Unrest Spreads to Macedonia," RFE/RL, *Report on Eastern Europe*, vol. 1, no. 8, February 23, 1990.

22. *Belgrade Domestic Service*, November 4, 1990, in *FBIS-EEU–90–214*, November 5, 1990; *Tanjug*, Belgrade, June 10, 1992, in *FBIS-EEU–92–113*, June 11, 1992; Andrejevich, "What Future For Serbia?"; Nešo Djurić, "Prosecutor Calls for Ban of Serb Opposition Party," *UPI*, Belgrade, June 6, 1993.

23. *Tanjug*, Belgrade, November 4, 1991, in *FBIS-EEU–91–214*, November 5, 1991.

24. *Tanjug*, Belgrade, January 12, 1991, in *FBIS-EEU–91–011*, January 16, 1991; *Tanjug*, Belgrade, July 15, 1991, in *FBIS-EEU–91–137*, July 17, 1991.

25. *Priština Domestic Service*, March 8, 1990, in *FBIS-EEU–90–047*, March 9, 1990; *Ljubljana Domestic Service*, July 13, 1990, in *FBIS-EEU–90–185*, September 24, 1990; *Tanjug*, Belgrade, November 8, 1991, in *FBIS-EEU–91–219*, November 13, 1991; *Radio Belgrade Network*, February 7, 1992, in *FBIS-EEU–92–027*, February 10, 1992; RFE/RL, *Daily Report*, no. 99, May 25, 1992; RFE/RL, *Daily Report*, no. 99, May 23, 1993.

26. *Tanjug*, Belgrade, August 28, 1991, in *FBIS-EEU–91–168*, August 29, 1991; Bexhet Halili, "The Albanians Must Also Be Included in Talks with Europe," *Bujku*, Priština, August 31, 1991, in *FBIS-EEU–91–176*, September 11, 1991; *ATA*, Tirana, December 20, 1991, in *FBIS-EEU–91–246*, December 23, 1991.

27. Emin and Blerim Reka, "When Will the Emigrants Return to Kosovo?" *Flaka e Vëllazërimit*, Skopje, November 18, 1990, in *FBIS-EEU–90–229*, November 28, 1990; Milovan Drečun, "Preparations of the Skipetars for an Armed Rebellion," *Politika*, Belgrade, July 14, 1991, in *JPRS-EER–91–111*, July 30, 1991.

28. *Vjesnik*, Zagreb, May 18, 1991; Emin Azemi and Blerim Reka, "Hunger Will Not Bring the Albanians to Their Knees," *Flaka e Vëllazërimit*, Skopje, November 16, 1990, in *FBIS-EEU–90–225*, November 21, 1990; and interview with Shkelzen Maliqi by Nadira Avdić-Vllasi, *Vjesnik*, Zagreb, September 1, 1991, in *JPRS-EER–91–143*, September 25, 1991.

29. *Flaka e Vëllazërimit*, Skopje, October 17, 1990, in *FBIS-EEU–90–205*, October 23, 1990; *Tanjug*, Belgrade, January 21, 1992, in *FBIS-EEU–92–015*, January 23, 1992; and interview with Riza Halimi, *Vjesnik*, Zagreb, March 16, 1992, in *FBIS-EEU–92–068*, April 8, 1992.

30. Milovan Drečun, "Preparations of the Skipetars for an Armed Rebellion," *Politika*, Belgrade, July 14, 1991, in *JPRS-EER–91–111*, July 30, 1991; *Tanjug*, Belgrade, February 5, 1992, in *FBIS-EEU–92–025*, February 6, 1992.

31. *Kosova Daily Report*, Priština, April 1, 1993, in *FBIS-EEU–93–063*, April 5, 1993; *Borba*, Belgrade, May 13, 1991, in *FBIS-EEU–91–099*, May 22, 1991; *Radio Croatia*, Zagreb, November 19, 1991, in *FBIS-EEU–91–225*, November 21, 1991; "Letters From the Illegal Movement for the Republic of Kosovo to Ibrahim Rugova," *Večer*, Skopje, June 7, 1993, in *JPRS-EER–93–057-S*, June 22, 1993.

32. *Borba*, Belgrade, May 19, 1990, in *FBIS-EEU–90–106*, June 1, 1990; *Magyar Nemzet*, Budapest, June 2, 1990, in *JPRS-EER–90–116*, August 14, 1990; Milan Andrejevich, "Vojvodina Hungarian Group to Seek Cultural Autonomy," RFE/RL, *Report on Eastern Europe* 1, no. 41 (October 12, 1990); *Tanjug*, Belgrade, February 4, 1991, in *FBIS-EEU–91–026*, February 7, 1991; *Budapest Domestic Service*, April 22, 1991, in

FBIS-EEU–91–079, April 24, 1991; Milos Antić, "Division of Serbs and Montenegrins Into 'Natives' and 'Newcomers' Increasingly Pronounced in Kosovo: Divide, Alienate, and Rule," *Borba*, Belgrade, April 19 1991, in *JPRS-EER–91–065*, May 14, 1991; *MTI*, Budapest, July 3, 1991, in *FBIS-EEU–91–129*, July 5, 1991; *Tanjug*, Belgrade, August 15, 1991, in *FBIS-EEU–91–159*, August 16, 1991; Oltay, "Hungarians in Yugoslavia Seek Guarantees for Minority Rights"; interview with Ándras Ágoston by Nandor Pilcz in Novi Sad, *Nepszabadsag*, Budapest, January 21, 1992, in *FBIS-EEU–92–016*, January 24, 1992; "Serbian Authorities Arrest Ethnic Hungarian Leader," Hungarian Human Rights Foundation, *HHRF Alert*, New York, February 9, 1992.

33. *Tanjug*, Belgrade, August 15, 1991, in *FBIS-EEU–91–159*, August 16, 1991; *Kossuth Radio Network*, Budapest, July 25, 1991, in *FBIS-EEU–91–144*, July 26, 1991.

34. *Danas*, Zagreb, April 30, 1991, in *JPRS-EER–91–071*, May 28, 1991; Bela Tonković, President, The Democratic League of Croats in Vojvodina, "Evaluation of the Political Situation and the Attitudes of the Democratic League of Croats in Vojvodina," Subotica, June 1992.

35. *Tanjug*, Belgrade, June 10, 1992, in *FBIS-EEU–92–113*, June 11, 1992.

36. *Vjesnik*, Belgrade, July 30, 1990, in *FBIS-EEU–90–150*, August 3, 1990; *Radio Sarajevo Network*, July 27, 1991, in *FBIS-EEU–91–145*, July 29, 1991; *Tanjug*, Belgrade, April 7, 1991, in *FBIS-EEU–91–067*, April 8, 1991.

37. *Belgrade Domestic Service*, October 13, 1990, in *FBIS-EEU–90–224*, November 20, 1990.

38. *BTA*, Sofia, October 21, 1990, in *FBIS-EEU–90–206*, October 24, 1990; *Tanjug*, Belgrade, October 20, 1990, in *FBIS-EEU–90–205*, October 23, 1990; Elena Urumova, "The Bulgarian Voice in Serbia Needs to Be Heard," *Demokratsiya*, Sofia, May 30, 1992, in *JPRS-EER–92–101*, August 4, 1992; *BTA*, Sofia, December 22, 1992, in *FBIS-EEU–92–247*, December 23, 1992; *BTA*, Sofia, May 28, 1993, in *FBIS-EEU–93–103*, June 1, 1993.

39. *Borba*, Belgrade, May 19, 1990, in *FBIS-EEU–90–106*, June 1, 1990; *Tanjug*, Belgrade, May 13, 1993, in *FBIS-EEU–93–092*, May 14, 1993.

40. *Tanjug*, Belgrade, May 12, 1990, in *FBIS-EEU–90–093*, May 14, 1990.

41. *Tanjug*, Belgrade, July 30, 1991, in *FBIS-EEU–91–147*, July 31, 1991.

6

Montenegro

POPULATION

According to the 1991 Montenegrin census, out of a total population of 615,267, 380,484 (61.84 percent) people were registered as ethnic Montenegrins.[1] Muslims formed the largest minority numbering 89,932, or 14.62 percent of the population, and mostly resident in the Sandžak area along the Serbian border. They formed an absolute majority in two Sandžak municipalities, Plav and Rožaje, and sizable minorities in Bijelo Polje, Ivangrad, and Pljevlja. Self-declared Serbs totaled 57,176, or 9.29 percent of the population. The figures continued to fuel disputes between those who considered Montenegrins a distinct ethnic group and those who viewed them simply as a sub-division of the Serbian nation. Indeed, Serb nationalists contended that the majority of those who declared themselves Montenegrins actually identified themselves as "Montenegrin Serbs." Montenegrin nationalists disputed such assertions. Albanians constituted the third largest minority in the republic, totaling 40,880 people, or 6.64 percent of the population. However, Albanian leaders claimed that the true number was somewhat larger as many citizens were unreported or declared themselves Yugoslavs. But they also admitted that thousands of Albanians had left Montenegro in recent years as a result of political pressure and shrinking economic opportunities. Albanian ethnics were particularly concentrated in the southern border zones with Albania, where they formed a clear majority in the municipality of Ulcinj and sizable minorities in Plav and Bar. A fairly viable 25,854 people, or 4.2 percent of the republic's citizens, continued to declare themselves Yugoslavs. Statisticians believed that these were invariably people from mixed marriages or Montenegrins who resisted the rise of ethnic nationalism in the shrinking Yugoslavia. Of the smaller minorities, Croats numbered 6,249, Macedonians 860, and Slovenes 407.

HISTORICAL OVERVIEW

The mountainous region of Montenegro (Crna Gora) was settled by Slavic tribes by the seventh century.[2] The central part of Montenegro fell under the control of

Montenegro: Population (1991)

Ethnic Groups	Number	% of Population
Montenegrins	380,484	61.84
Muslims	89,932	14.62
Serbs	57,176	9.29
Albanians	40,880	6.64
Yugoslavs	25,854	4.20
Croats	6,249	1.02
Macedonians	860	0.14
Slovenes	407	0.07
Others	13,425	2.18
Total Minorities	234,783	38.16
Total Population	615,267	100.00

the Serbian Kingdom in the twelfth century, but as Serbian power declined the region was governed by a succession of local rulers. Following the defeat of Serb armies by the Ottoman Turks at the end of the fourteenth century, thousands of Serbs fled to the mountains of Montenegro. This led to a further intermingling of two closely related Slav Orthodox Christian populations. Over the centuries, traditionalist Montenegrins claimed that they were subjected to a prolonged and often subtle process of Serbian assimilation. During the period of Turkish domination in the Balkans, close ties between Montenegrins and Serbs also provided a source of solidarity and mutual protection. Between the fifteenth and nineteenth centuries, Turkish forces repeatedly launched campaigns against Montenegrin defenders. But they were unable to fully subdue the kingdom, particularly the most mountainous regions where the Montenegrins gained a reputation for ferociousness and expertise in the tactics of guerrilla warfare. During the sixteenth century, Montenegro developed into a quasi theocracy in which Orthodox bishops (*vladike*) exercised political and religious control. Initially, the bishops were elected by national assemblies, but at the close of the seventeenth century succession was limited to the Njegoš dynasty, which ruled the country as bishop-princes for the next 150 years. During this time, Montenegrin territory more than doubled in size as various neighboring tribes were incorporated into the kingdom. The Treaty of Berlin in 1878 further increased the size of Montenegro, and the state was finally recognized internationally as an independent princedom.

The Montenegrin prince Nikola Petroviæ established a parliamentary constitution in 1905 and declared himself king five years later. At the outset of World War One, Nikola went into exile while a newly formed Montenegrin committee in exile called for the incorporation of Montenegro into a south Slav union; the committee was supported by Serbia. At the close of the war, Nikola's rule was terminated and the state became part of the new Kingdom of Serbs, Croats, and Slovenes. Belgrade was determined to prevent the return of the Montenegrin dynasty and the reemergence of an independent state. Serbian officials and local pro-Serb partisans moved to legalize Belgrade's rule over Montenegro and staged a pro-unification election. The list of candidates opposing unification was printed on green paper while the slate of pro-Serb proponents was issued on white paper. This led to the naming of the two main Montenegrin camps as Greens and Whites: the Greens favoring independence or equal status with Serbia, and the Whites pushing for full-scale unification with Serbia.

During the inter-war period, Montenegro remained under tight Serbian tutelage and the local administration was dominated by pro-Serb politicians and military leaders. But the seeds of opposition to Serbian annexation and assimilation remained intact in the heartland of Old Montenegro. A number of anti-Serb rebellions were staged in these areas, but the insurgents were not well organized or politically united and were defeated by Serbian forces. Belgrade subsequently imposed a reign of terror against Green supporters who were mostly mountain villagers. As a result, the pan-Serbian, pro-unification White forces predominated in the region. Following the German invasion and conquest of Yugoslavia in 1941, the bulk of Montenegrin territory was placed under Italian administration, the Montenegrin coastline was actually annexed by Italy, while areas with sizable Albanian populations were placed under the control of an Italian-dominated Albania. After the Communist takeover in 1945, Montenegro was awarded the status of a republic and the Montenegrins were declared a distinct south Slav nation. The Tito regime sought to preserve an inter-republican balance in the Communist federation and to undercut the preponderance and dominance of the Serbs by removing Montenegro from under direct Serbian jurisdiction. These measures heightened resentment among Serb leaders and nationalist politicians who emerged during the 1980s and used them as another pretext for reasserting Serbian authority throughout post-Titoist Yugoslavia.

In January 1989, the entire Communist Party and government leadership in the capital Titograd was replaced following large-scale worker demonstrations sponsored by Belgrade. This "anti-bureaucratic" coup ousted the older Yugoslav leaders and pro-sovereignty politicians and installed pro-Serb activists loyal to Serbian president Slobodan Milošević. The new leadership pledged to introduce political pluralism and prepared for republican elections as the Yugoslav federation came under increasing strain. Montenegro's first multi-party general elections in December 1990 were won convincingly by the League of Communists who continued to control the media and benefited from a preponderance of funds, assets, and an extensive political apparatus in comparison to the newly formed opposition parties. Following the elections, the Communists changed their name to the Democratic Party of Socialists (DPS) and proceeded to control closely the pace of political and economic reform.

Titograd openly sided with the Serbian authorities as the federation began to disintegrate during the course of 1991, and indeed the dominant position enjoyed by Montenegrin Socialists was largely the consequence of Belgrade's political, military, and economic support. The core of the DPS included a broad stratum of bureaucrats, security personnel, factory directors, and military veterans with a direct personal stake in preserving the Yugoslav federation and curtailing Montenegro's autonomy. President Momir Bulatović rushed through a republican referendum in March 1992 that approved Montenegro's continuing association with Serbia. The opposition Liberal Alliance, the strongest "Green" force in the republic, staged demonstrations in several cities claiming that the wording of the referendum did not inform voters on the alternatives to a close federation with Serbia. The Socialists also comfortably won the federal Yugoslav elections in May 1992, a ballot boycotted by virtually all opposition parties, which charged that the elections were unconstitutional. The election victory assured the DPS of continuing control over the key instruments of government, the mass media, and the economy.

Montenegro's Albanian and Muslim minorities also grew concerned about Serbian control over the republic and the spread of the Croatian and Bosnian conflict into Montenegro. Albanian and Muslim leaders were generally supportive of Montenegrin sovereignty and independence and campaigned for greater collective rights in education, culture, language, and local administration. But they asserted that they harbored no separatist ambitions and tacitly supported the democratic Montenegrin oppositionist parties. Belgrade and the Montenegrin regime charged that the minority leaders were extremists intent on dismembering the republic and creating a large Islamic or Albanian state. As the war in Croatia and Bosnia-Herzegovina escalated, radical Serbian guerrillas also become active in parts of Montenegro and Muslim communities in the Montenegrin Sandžak region became subject to harassment and intimidation.

The government in Podgorica (the restored name for Titograd) appeared not to condone the activities of militant Serb guerrilla formations sponsored or tolerated by Belgrade. In fact, following the appointment of Milan Panić as Yugoslav prime minister in the summer of 1992, the Bulatović regime appeared to distance itself from Milošević, calculating that his days in power could be numbered. The Montenegrin Socialists seemed to be repositioning themselves for a major crisis in Serbia in order to detach the republic and pose as pro-independence nationalists. Meanwhile, Serbian radicals continued to claim that Albanian and Muslim separatists were preparing to mount an uprising; such charges were either intended to rally Montenegrin citizens behind Belgrade or to undermine the "unpatriotic" Bulatović administration.

OFFICIAL POLICIES

The December 1990 elections marked the first multi-party elections in Montenegro since 1938. The bulk of the 125 contested seats in the National Assembly went to the League of Communists of Montenegro (LCM), which was subsequently renamed the Democratic Party of Socialists (DPS).[3] The LCM had utilized its monopoly over state funds and the media to assure itself of an electoral victory, winning 85 seats in parliament. The Alliance of Reform Forces of

Montenegro (ARFM), a pro-Yugoslav coalition of the Socialist Party, the Social Democratic Party, the Liberal Alliance, the Independent Communists of Bar, the Party of National Equality, and several smaller groupings, won a total of 17 seats. The Serb nationalist People's Party of Montenegro (PPM) benefited from its affinity with Belgrade and was able to garner 12 seats. The Democratic Coalition, a minority-centered alliance of Muslim and Albanian parties, won 13 seats to the Assembly.

By October 1992, the position of some of the political parties in the Montenegrin legislature had changed somewhat. The DPS had been reduced to 82 seats when 3 of its deputies resigned from the party in September 1992. The ARFM, now renamed the Reform Coalition, lost 4 seats as a result of the departure of the Party of National Equality; the PNE subsequently joined the Democratic Coalition minority bloc. The PPM was reduced to just 2 seats in the National Assembly in late 1992, when 8 deputies joined the ranks of the newly formed People's Democratic Party (PDP), a Serbian nationalist formation with close ties to the Serbian Radical Party in Belgrade.[4]

Although the loyalty of the Montenegrin government to Milošević was assured during the protracted and ultimately futile negotiations to confederate Yugoslavia during the early part of 1991, when war erupted in the summer of 1991 Podgorica began to show signs of distancing itself from Belgrade. There were several reasons for this change of track, although the opposition initially dismissed it as mere opportunism. First, President Momir Bulatović calculated that Milošević was purposively drawing Montenegro into a destructive and unpopular war with Croatia from which the republic was unlikely to benefit. Second, a long-drawn-out conflict and a deteriorating economy would broaden support for Montenegrin sovereignty and even independence from Yugoslavia; in such a scenario, the DPS could lose its respectable public backing. Third, the government wanted to avoid direct responsibility for the war and particularly for the atrocities committed by Serb-Yugoslav forces in the name of Serb unity. As a result, in September 1991 Prime Minister Milo Djukanović announced preparations for a declaration of Montenegrin sovereignty, although within a Yugoslav framework, while the following month President Bulatović called for the withdrawal of Montenegrin reservists from battle fronts in Croatia.

Podgorica's delicate balancing act between Yugoslav integralism and Montenegrin sovereignty was further displayed during 1992 after war erupted in Bosnia-Herzegovina. With reports of systematic war crimes against Muslim residents by Serb guerrillas and paramilitary formations operating from both Serbia and Montenegro, the Bulatović leadership increasingly adopted a pacifist stance. After the appointment of Milan Panić as Yugoslav prime minister in July 1992, the Montenegrin deputies consistently supported his overtures for a peaceful resolution to the Yugoslav wars and opposed Socialist and Radical criticisms. Indeed, Panić survived two votes of no-confidence largely because of Montenegrin support in the Federal Assembly. In addition, Bulatović publicly voiced his backing for the Vance–Owen plan for decentralizing Bosnia-Herzegovina despite persistent Bosnian Serb and Belgrade government opposition.

Nevertheless, to prevent outright condemnation by Milošević and forceful attempts to unseat the government, in March 1992 Podgorica moved ahead with a referendum on Montenegrin membership in the two-republic federation, despite the resistance of opposition parties. The DPS also participated in the federal elections rushed through in May 1992. Montenegrin leaders contended that through their involvement in Federal Assembly sessions the republic would maintain some degree of influence over Belgrade's policies, express its opposition to the war in Bosnia, and suggest proposals for solving the regional crisis. The Podgorica authorities were also apprehensive that Milošević and his Radical allies in Montenegro were planning to destabilize the republic by provoking conflicts with the Muslim and Albanian minorities and then using this as a pretext for replacing the regime and raising support for Belgrade's policies. With a large army and Serb paramilitary presence in Montenegro, Bulatović was clearly wary of a direct confrontation with his erstwhile sponsor.

After a hurried entrance into a rump Yugoslav federation with Serbia in March 1992 and the subsequent passage of a new federal constitution in April 1992, Montenegro adopted its own constitution in October 1992. The constitution asserted Montenegrin sovereignty in all realms not already explicitly claimed as the responsibility of federal institutions. The document changed the official state language from Serbo-Croatian to the Serbian Ijekavian dialect and addressed the rights of minorities in several articles. It asserted specifically the rights of national and ethnic groups to protect their national, ethnic, cultural, and linguistic identities in accordance with prevailing international standards. These included access to education and information in an individual's native language, the right to display national symbols, and the right to establish educational and cultural associations with material assistance from the state. The constitution also asserted that it was illegal for citizens to "provoke others" and "stir up trouble" on the basis of ethnic identity or racial animosity.

The Muslim population in the Sandžak was singled out for provocative assaults by Serb paramilitaries during the summer and fall of 1992. Serb Radicals were reportedly intent on clearing Muslim residents from the border areas with Bosnia through intimidation, harassment, and outright acts of violence. The Montenegrin authorities intervened belatedly to try and defuse rising tensions in the region, but they displayed great caution for fear of provoking Serb ultra-nationalist attacks elsewhere in the republic and outright condemnation by Belgrade. On the other hand, Podgorica also earned some credit by providing assistance to several thousand Muslim refugees from eastern Bosnia who had fled across the border from advancing Serbian forces or from brutal "ethnic cleansing" operations.

Although occasional incidents of violence were reported against the Albanian minority, criticisms of the Montenegrin government by Albanian leaders primarily focused on occupational discrimination and educational disadvantages. According to minority spokesmen, the powers of the local authorities have been curtailed, including in districts containing large Albanian populations. In addition, the key institutions, including police, finance, education, and culture, were directed by Montenegrins and the official language even in minority regions remained Serbian. All official documents, including private contracts and birth and teaching certificates, were drafted in Serbian, and it was obligatory to add a Serbian suffix to all family names of the Albanian minority. A salient point of the language dispute revolved around the media issue. Montenegrin state radio reserved only 30 minutes a day for Albanian-language programming, and there were no Albanian programs on Podgorica Television. No ready outlet existed in the print media, since there was no Albanian press agency and no state-funded minority news publications. Since 1982, the Montenegrin authorities have also prohibited the use of the Albanian flag, in violation of the federal law. Furthermore, Albanians were not authorized to celebrate their national holidays publicly.[5]

Albanian leaders also grew concerned over Montenegro's inclusion in the rump Yugoslavia in March 1992, the rapid passage of the new Montenegrin constitution, and the rushed federal elections in May 1992. Some minority activists planned to hold a referendum on Albanian autonomy in districts where Albanians formed a relative majority of the population. In September 1992, the largest Albanian party, the Democratic Alliance of Montenegro (DAM), issued a Memorandum on the Special Status of Albanians; the document was criticized by both the government and the opposition parties for encouraging separatism and playing into the hands of Serbian Radicals. Although some Albanian leaders voiced fears of potential Montenegrin nationalism, they remained more perturbed over the activities of Serb paramilitaries and purposely participated in the republican and local elections of December 1992 to undercut the Radical vote.

In the second multi-party elections, the DPS gained 45 seats to the Montenegrin National Assembly; the total had been constitutionally reduced from 125 to 85 seats. Despite complaints over the election law and the unfair advantage maintained by the DPS in terms of funds, resources, and access to the media, all major opposition parties participated in the republican and local elections. The People's Party finished second with 14 seats, the Liberals third with 13 seats, the Radicals fourth with 8 seats, and the Social Democrats fifth with 4 seats. The Democratic Alliance of Montenegro (DAM) failed to exceed the threshold for parliamentary representation, while the Muslim-based Party of Democratic Action (PDA) did not participate. In the 20-seat Montenegrin section of the federal Chamber of Republics, the DPS elected 25 deputies, the People's Party 3, and the Radicals 2. For the 138-seat federal Chamber of Citizens, the DPS elected 17 deputies, the Socialists 5, the People's Party 4, and the Radicals from both Montenegro and Serbia elected a total of 34 deputies. Momir Bulatović was reelected Montenegrin president: in a run-off with Radical candidate Branko Kostić, Bulatović obtained 63.3 percent of the popular vote after the opposition decided to support his ticket against the Radicals. The former Montenegrin prime minister and DPS member Radoje Kontić was nominated as the new Yugoslav prime minister to replace Milan Panić.

Following the ballot, the DPS seemed to display its wariness of Belgrade by moving to form a coalition government with several opposition parties. With the defeat of Panić in the Serbian presidential election, increasing pressure on Dobrica Ćosić to step down from the Yugoslav presidency, and the success of the Radicals in the Serbian ballot, Podgorica appeared to be more exposed to a potential crackdown by Belgrade. It proceeded to build a broader umbrella with the Montenegrin opposition. A new government was formed in April 1993: while the DPS retained the premiership and a number of key ministries, the Liberals and Social Democrats obtained two portfolios each, while the People's Party took one deputy premiership and two ministries without portfolio. The coalition government appeared to stabilize the republic by lessening political tensions while isolating the Radicals as the prime instigators of conflict.

Some analysts believed that out of political opportunism and sheer self-preservation, the Bulatović clique could adopt a more openly pro-sovereignty position, while closely watching for any hostile intervention by Milošević. After the ouster of Yugoslav president Ćosić, the evaporation of the threat of Western military intervention against the Serb militias, and the collapse of the Vance–Owen plan in Bosnia, for which Bulatović had declared his support, Podgorica appeared to soften its stance toward Milošević; a rapprochement with Belgrade could not be excluded. Indeed, in June 1993, Serbian Socialist Party secretary general Milomir Minić announced that talks were under way to merge with the Montenegrin DPS.[6] According to the Socialists, the objective was to ensure that the federal administration was streamlined and made more efficient. In reality, such a move appeared designed to undermine the independent stance of the DPS, to sow dissension within the Montenegrin political elite, and to prepare for the formation of a new pan-Serb federation that would undermine Montenegro's republican status.

MONTENEGRIN NATIONALISTS

Liberal Alliance of Montenegro (LAM)
Liberalni Savez Crne Gore (LSCG)

This strongest pro-independence organization was established in the traditional Montenegrin capital of Cetinje in January 1991. It sought to engage all political forces that believed in a sovereign Montenegro and the curtailment of central controls from Belgrade. Slavko Perović was elected executive president and Velimir Kudević president. Perović was previously active in the League of Communists in Montenegro and the Alliance of Reform Forces, led by Yugoslavia's former prime minister Ante Marković, which scored poorly in the December 1990 republican elections. The Liberals accused the ruling party in Podgorica of working closely with Milošević to establish a new federation of Serbian states from the ruins of Yugoslavia. They were vilified by the state-controlled media as agents in the pay of Croatia, the Vatican, and U.S. security services, intent on destroying the unity of the Serbian nation. Despite threats and police intimidation, the LAM managed to gather 13,000 members by mid-1992, mostly intellectuals, students, younger workers, and members of the "Old Montenegrin" families in the coastal and central regions of the country, the "Green" or pro-sovereignty heartland. The Liberals organized several rallies in March 1992 against the rushed referendum on Montenegro's membership in the rump Yugoslavia and backed a substantial boycott of the ballot. They demanded a new plebiscite, preceded by a proper debate in the media concerning the content and consequences of federalism. Its leaders maintained that they did not exclude belonging to a federation of equal republics but were opposed to Belgrade's centralism and the "ethnic assimilation" of Montenegro by Serbs.

The LAM protested against the activities of paramilitary ultra-nationalist Serbian formations on Montenegrin territory and the tolerance exhibited toward them by the Podgorica government. It claimed that Montenegro was a multi-ethnic and multi-religious state in which Montenegrin and Serb Orthodox, Croat Catholics, and Slav and Albanian Muslims could coexist. LAM spokesmen pointed out that Serbian Radicals were intent on stirring conflicts with the minorities in order to depict Albanians and Muslims as separatists. Liberals contended that the minorities would only demand autonomy or secession from an integral Serb-dominated state and not from an independent Montenegro. To strengthen Montenegrin identity, Perović suggested the return of the Montenegrin Autocephalous Orthodox Church and even a referendum on the establishment of a constitutional monarchy under the exiled Prince Nikola Petrović Njegoš. Although the alliance has tried to avoid being provoked by radical Serb forces that occasionally disrupted its election campaigns, Liberal leaders also contended that they could not remain passive if Montenegrin integrity was further undermined.

The Liberals boycotted the federal elections of May 1992 and December 1992, asserting that participation would simply give credence to the illegitimate federal structure. Instead, they demanded a public referendum on the question of sovereignty calculating that in a free ballot over 80 percent of the population would vote for independence. The LAM stood in the republican elections of December 1992 and was allowed some access to the media enabling it to mount a proper election campaign. It gained 13 seats in the 85-member Montenegrin Assembly, and a Liberal deputy, Džemal Perović, was nominated as one of the Assembly's three vice-presidents. Party leaders claimed that their support would have been much greater if the Yugoslav media had not painted them as armed radicals and if they had benefited from more funding and media exposure.

The LAM entered the coalition government in April 1993 led by the DPS, calculating that President Bulatović was adopting a more pronounced "Montenegrinist" position after supporting the failed candidacy of Milan Panić against Milošević. It obtained the ministries of environment and urban development but simultaneously reserved the right to withdraw from the government. Liberal leaders claimed that public respect for the alliance increased as it was seen as a responsible political force concerned with avoiding violent confrontations. In particular, the Liberals reported making inroads in gaining popular support in the northern regions of Montenegro. Following the crackdown on the Serbian opposition in Belgrade, the Liberals, together with the SDPR, the SPM, and the civil resistance movement "Public Against Fascism," organized a rally in Cetinje in June 1993 under the slogan "Democratic Montenegro for a Democratic Serbia."[7]

Social Democratic Party of Reformers (SDPR)
Socijaldemokratska Partija Reformatora (SDPR)

The SDPR was formed in late 1992, in the run-up to the general elections, from a coalition of the Social Democratic party, the Coastal Reformists, and the Independent Communists of Bar (the latter changed their name to the Social Democratic Party of Montenegro in November 1992). These organizations held 12 seats in the Montenegrin Assembly, following the December 1990 election, and were particularly active at the local level in opposition to the ruling DPS and the radical Serb forces. The Independent Communists of Bar (the major Montenegrin port) openly opposed the Milošević coup in 1988 and established their own separate organization in May 1990, which won the December 1990 local elections in Bar *opština*. President Mico Orlandić was also elected deputy to the republican assembly. These parties boycotted the Serbian referendum in March 1992 and the federal elections of May 1992 because they opposed the centralism and radicalization of Serbian policy.

As Yugoslavia disintegrated, the various reformist forces moved closer to the "Montenegrin option," although they initially criticized the Liberals for placing too much stress on national questions above social and economic programs. Because all the SDPR components welcomed members from all nationalities, they were condemned by Serbian nationalists as anti-Serb traitors. In the December 1992 election, the SDPR alliance gained four seats to the Montenegrin Assembly but did not compete for the federal ballot. The party's relatively poor performance was probably due to its unclear stance on the national question and its focus on social and economic reforms: under prevailing conditions these did not elicit wide popular resonance. After the ballot, SDPR president Zavko Rakčević declared that the ruling DPS was undertaking some positive steps away from Milošević's "Greater Serbia" program. However, he remained skeptical whether Bulatović's moves to form a coalition government were merely a tactical ploy. The SDPR itself appeared to adopt a more forthright pro-sovereignty position, claiming that about 75 percent of the population under "normal circumstances," in other words without fear of Serb intervention, would favor some model of Montenegrin independence. SDPR leaders also underscored that the Montenegrin political opposition, including the Liberals and Social Democrats, would fully cooperate with the international community in bringing to trial known war criminals operating in the republic who had engaged in atrocities against civilians in Bosnia-Herzegovina.

Socialist Party of Montenegro (SPM)
Socijalistička Partija Crne Gore (SPCG)

The SPM was founded in July 1990; its members were formerly active in the Alliance of Socialist Youth but grew increasingly restless after the "anti-bureaucratic revolution." SPM president Srdjan Darmanović criticized President Bulatović and the DPS leadership for their opportunism and neglect of Montenegrin interests. The party sought a sovereign and independent Montenegro and differed with the Liberals on methods rather than objectives, contending that the LAM engaged in too much demagogic rhetoric and neglected to address vital socioeconomic questions. The Socialists gained three seats in the December 1990 republican elections but boycotted the March 1992 referendum on federation with Serbia, demanding a new plebiscite and a prolonged period of open debate. SPM leaders understood Podgorica's difficult strategic position, in that any declaration of independence could provoke violent Serbian retribution. As a result, they urged a more pragmatic approach than the Liberals through the building of a broad pro-Montenegrin front in preparation for a more opportune occasion when Milošević was not in a position to intervene violently. The Socialists failed to gain seats in the December 1992 election to the Montenegrin Assembly for similar reasons to the SDPR. However, the SPM did manage to elect five deputies to the federal Assembly Chamber of Citizens. Unlike the other members of the "Montenegrin bloc," the SPM has urged close cooperation with the "national democratic bloc" in Serbia, including *DEPOS*, as well as the Civic Alliance. It calculated that support for Montenegrin statehood and independence was still not fully developed, as sentiments for the old Yugoslavia continued to predominate among broad sectors of the population.

Democratic Party of Socialists (DPS)
Demokratska Partija Socijalista (DPS)

The DPS changed its name in June 1991 from the League of Communists of Montenegro. It easily won the December 1990 republican elections obtaining 80 out of 125 seats. Its young leadership had been brought to the fore by Milošević during the "anti-bureaucratic" purge of potentially disloyal Montenegrin activists in January 1989. They were denounced by both the reformist and the pro-independence opposition as stooges, careerists, and opportunists. The DPS remained committed to preserving Yugoslavia, and its leader, Montenegrin president

Momir Bulatović, consistently voted with Milošević in the federal presidency against a looser confederal arrangement proposed by Slovenia and Croatia. After Yugoslavia began to disintegrate, the DPS staged a much-criticized referendum in March 1992 on Montenegro's continuing federation with Serbia: 63 percent of the electorate reportedly voted in favor of this option. The DPS participated in drafting the new federal constitution that was rushed through in April 1992 and heralded the proclamation of the Federal Republic of Yugoslavia (FRY). Montenegro's opposition parties boycotted the proceedings in protest. In May 1992, the DPS and the Radicals between them elected all the deputies to the 20-member Montenegrin section of the Federal Assembly's Chamber of Republics and the federal Chamber of Citizens. During the fall of 1992, a widening rift appeared between Bulatović and Milošević. The Montenegrin leader sided strongly with Yugoslav prime minister Milan Panić in his dispute with Milošević over ending the war in Bosnia. DPS deputies cast their ballots against the votes of no-confidence in Panić sponsored by the Serbian Radicals and Socialists.

The DPS gained 45 out of 85 seats to the Montenegrin Assembly elections in December 1992, 17 out of 138 seats to the federal Chamber of Citizens, and 15 out of 20 seats to the Montenegrin section in the federal Chamber of Republics. Bulatović was reelected as Montenegro's president in a second round run-off with the Serbian Radical candidate Branko Kostić. The opposition forces, including the Liberals, supported Bulatović in the second round, considering his candidacy as preferable to the militant pro-Milošević position of Kostić. With the failure of Panić to be elected as Serbian president and the weakening position of Ćosić in the federal presidency, Bulatović appeared to fall into disfavor with Milošević. After the elections, the DPS initiated the formation of a broad-based coalition government in Montenegro and appeared to move closer to a pro-sovereignty option for the republic. Opposition leaders remained undecided whether Bulatović had genuinely converted into a Montenegrist or was trying to protect himself against political pressure from Belgrade. Some even speculated that Bulatović continued to coordinate his policies closely with his mentor Milošević and was simply trying to defuse or absorb the appeal and impact of Montenegro's pro-sovereignty opposition.[8]

After the December 1992 elections, the DPS itself appeared to be increasingly divided between federalist and pro-sovereignty factions; its parliamentary delegates and middle echelons seemed to be moving closer to the Social Democrats and Liberals. The DPS leadership expressed concern over the growing influence of the Radicals in Serbian politics and feared that the relationship between Serbia and Montenegro could be further unbalanced to the disadvantage of the latter. This became evident when only Serbian Socialists and Radicals were nominated to the Serbian section of the Chamber of Republics, and their vote, together with that of the two Radical deputies from Montenegro, unseated Ćosić from the Yugoslav presidency in June 1993. DPS leaders also voiced fears about the radicalization of Montenegrin politics and remained apprehensive about the activities of the Radical Party and Serb paramilitary units sponsored by ultra-nationalists in Serbia. Svetozar Marović, secretary of the DPS Main Board, gave indications that the party would use the Montenegrin constitution to protect its republican status vis-à-vis potential Serbian domination. However, if it proved impossible to defend Montenegro's equal status through constitutional means, then the DPS appeared willing to conduct a new referendum on the republic's future.

SERBIAN NATIONALISTS

People's Party of Montenegro (PPM)
Narodna Stranka Crne Gore (NSCG)

Headed by Novak Kilibarda, a university professor, the PPM started out as a movement strongly favoring unification between Montenegro and Serbia and supportive of Serbian nationalism. The PPM declared that if the federal structure fell apart, Montenegro should join Serbia to form a separate integral state. It viewed the territories of Montenegro and Serbia as being populated by one essentially Serbian people, as evidenced by religious, ethnic, and linguistic affinities, and it thereby advocated the "spiritual unification and moral renaissance of Serbianism." The PPM won 6 out of 125 seats to the Montenegrin National Assembly in the December 1990 elections, and its leaders benefited from easy access to the media in which they advanced Belgrade's political line. In April 1991, the PPM called upon the republican authorities to arm the citizens of Montenegro in the event of a Yugoslav civil war. The statement warned of Croatian, Sandžak Muslim, and Albanian claims to Montenegrin territory and demanded armed preparations to defend the Montenegrin-Serb people. The party was reported to have organized its own paramilitary units with several hundred men under arms. In November 1991, People's party leaders criticized President Bulatović for accepting Lord Carrington's confederal proposal for Yugoslavia, which defined Montenegro as a nominally sovereign state. PPM deputies were among the 42 legislators who boycotted the National Assembly vote to uphold the government's decision.

The PPM initially supported Milošević's ambitions in Croatia and Bosnia-Herzegovina and backed the March 1992 Montenegrin referendum on federation with Serbia in the rump Yugoslavia. However, the party did not fully condone the new federal constitution, and it boycotted the May 1992 federal elections. During the course of 1992, the People's Party evidently moderated its position in a fashion parallel to that of the Serbian Renewal Movement and the *DEPOS* coalition in Serbia, with which it maintained close ties. It distanced itself from the ultra-nationalist Serbian parties and paramilitary formations engaged in war crimes in Bosnia, criticized Milošević and the DPS for being undemocratic, and tried to appeal to more moderate Serb voters, to Orthodox believers, and to monarchists in the republic. The Montenegrin opposition suspected that Kilibarda realized that Milošević's days could be numbered and that Montenegro could attain statehood; hence, to avoid marginalization or charges of supporting war criminals, he purposely distanced himself from his prior militant stance.

In the run-up to the December 1992 elections, the PPM claimed that it was defending Montenegrin interests in an equal federation with Serbia. It also criticized Montenegro's Albanian and Muslim minorities for allegedly seeking to separate from the republic. Kilibarda asserted that the party had successfully cleansed itself of "Communist and fascist elements" that wanted to provoke conflicts in Montenegro. He even asserted that if the majority of Montenegrin citizens voted in a referendum for an independent state, the party would accept their decision. In the December 1992 elections, the People's Party gained 14 seats in the Montenegrin Assembly, 4 seats in the federal Chamber of Citizens, and 3 seats in the federal Chamber of Republics.[9]

Serbian Radical Party (SRP)
Srpska Radikalna Stranka (SRS)

This extremist nationalist party was established during 1991 with close links to the SRP in Serbia headed by Vojislav Šešelj. The Radicals also established a paramilitary wing, based in Montenegro, that supplied weapons and manpower to Serb forces involved in the war in Bosnia-Herzegovina. When the People's Party moderated its stance, the SRP assumed the mantle of the most vehement pro-Serb formation. Under the direction of self-proclaimed *četnik* Major Čeko Dačević, SRP paramilitaries were allegedly behind the armed provocations and attacks on Muslims in Pljevljia and other cities in the Montenegrin Sandžak during the summer and fall of 1992. The Radicals obtained 8 seats in the Montenegrin Assembly during the December 1992 elections, as well as 2 seats in the federal Chamber of Nationalities; together with the Serbian-based SRP, they gained a total of 34 seats in the 138-seat federal Chamber of Citizens. In the Montenegrin presidential election, Radical candidate Branko Kostić lost in a run-off ballot with Bulatović but managed to gain 36 percent of the popular vote. Both the DPS and the pro-independence opposition believed that the SRP was being used by Milošević to destabilize Montenegro and undermine the new government. For example, the SRP organized rallies against the government's evident neglect of environmental problems (in 1992 Montenegro was declared an "ecological state" by the National Assembly); it established a "Serbian Council of Zeta" in an area of Montenegro where a twelfth-century Serbian state had been forged by tribal leaders; it proposed the creation of autonomous Serbian regions in Boka, Pljevlja, and Zeta; it engaged in anti-Muslim attacks in the Sandžak area and it attempted to stimulate conflicts with the Muslim and Albanian minorities by depicting these groups as anti-Montenegrin separatists. Radicals were also intent on capitalizing on social disquiet against deteriorating economic conditions; there were indications that its leaders were in favor of a second "anti-bureaucratic" revolution to unseat the Bulatović administration. Similarly to the SRP in Serbia, the Radicals' long-term objective was the creation of a new pan-Serb federation, incorporating Serb-held territories in Croatia and Bosnia together with Serbia proper and Montenegro.[10]

Democratic Party (DP)
Demokratska Stranka (DS)

Established in December 1989 as an opposition party to the declining Montenegrin League of Communists (LCM), the Democratic Party elected Slobodan Vujošević as president. It was granted observer status in the Montenegrin National Assembly, an ostensible first step toward the recognition of the party as a legal entity. In September 1990, due to irreconcilable conflicts among members concerning the issue of Montenegrin statehood, the DP split into two parties. The larger wing remained close to the Democratic Party in Serbia, with a strong pro-federalist and pro-Serbian stance, while the smaller offshoot took aboard a more Montenegrist position on the issue of republican sovereignty. Neither party performed well in the republican elections.[11]

People's Democratic Party (PDP)
Narodna Demokratska Stranka (NDS)

This party was created in late 1992 by militant pro-Serb elements in the People's Party of Montenegro. Eight PPM parliamentary deputies in the Montenegrin legislature, two-thirds of their total number of seats, defected to the PDP because of Kilibarda's support for federal president Dobrica Ćosić. PDP leaders established close contacts with the Radical Party, and to increase their numbers they endeavored to appeal to jobless people and other disaffected elements of society.

Movement for Montenegro's Autonomous Accession to Serbia (MMAAS)
Pokret za Autonomni Pristup Crne Gore u Srbiju (PAPCGS)

Established in May 1990, this Belgrade-based organization declared in its founding act that its chief purpose was to make Montenegro an autonomous province of Serbia. The MMAAS did not consider itself engaged in a struggle for political power, rather it depicted itself as a broad political movement open to all Montenegrin and Serbian citizens. It also proposed that a public referendum be held in Montenegro concerning the republic's autonomous status. A number of similar organizations have been set up in recent years to uphold a close Serb-Montenegrin relationship in the event of a Yugoslav break-up; they have included the Serbian-Montenegrin Unification Movement (SMUM).[12]

Serbian Democratic Party of Montenegro (SDPM)
Srpska Demokratska Stranka Crne Gore (SDSCG)

This pro-Serb party was created in January 1992 as a branch of the Serbian Democratic Party in Bosnia-Herzegovina, the separatist party led by Radovan Karadžić whose family origins were in Montenegro. Its initiative committee stressed that the formation of a Montenegrin branch would "influence the creation and strengthening of the new Yugoslavia that has been created by the two Serbian states, Montenegro and Serbia." The SDPM did not delineate between Serbs residing in Serbia proper and Serbs living in neighboring republics, thus it explicitly supported the gathering of all Serbs in one state. Moreover, the party did not recognize either Muslims or Montenegrins as separate nations or ethnic groups.[13]

MINORITY ORGANIZATIONS

Democratic Alliance of Montenegro (DAM)
Demokratski Savez Crne Gore (DSCG)

Mehmet Bardhi became the president and Ljeka Ljuljudjuray the vice president of this Albanian-based political organization founded during 1990. It was based in the southern town of Ulcinj, where 80 percent of the population was ethnic Albanian. By mid-1992, the DAM claimed about 3,000 members, with branches in all major Albanian communities, including Bar, Tuzi, and Ostrog. Following the December 1990 elections, the minority alliance, the Democratic Coalition, which included the DAM and the Muslim Party of Democratic Action (PAD), gained 13 seats in the Montenegrin National Assembly. The DAM performed well in local elections in Albanian-inhabited districts; for example, in Ulcinj it elected 35 out of 40 local councilors. The alliance favored a Yugoslavia consisting of equal federal units but opposed a truncated and recentralized Yugoslavia comprised only of Serbia and Montenegro. Moreover, the DAM platform stated that Montenegrin Albanians had the right to decide on the future of Montenegro and its relationship with Serbia. With the disintegration of the six-republic federation, Albanian and Muslim leaders grew concerned over both the status of Montenegro and the position of non-Serb minorities. The DAM boycotted the March 1992 referendum on Montenegro's membership of the new Yugoslavia and, together with other opposition parties, abstained from the federal elections in May 1992.

In response to the overwhelming approval in the plebiscite for Montenegro's continued association with Yugoslavia, there were rumors about a possible Albanian referendum to decide on autonomy for Albanian majority districts. President Bardhi reiterated that his party regarded unification with Serbia as "unfeasible" and condemned Milošević's anti-minority policies. In September

1992, the DAM leadership demanded the establishment of a special status for the Albanian minority, guaranteeing a large measure of local autonomy. In the Memorandum on the Special Status of Albanians in Montenegro, the DAM claimed that the Albanian minority in Montenegro was being excluded from decision making while the power of *opština* authorities was undercut, in that they did not control the police, education, and cultural life. Albanian leaders asserted that police units, often brought in from outside the district, engaged in provocative acts against the minority through harassment and tight surveillance. Such policies visibly increased tensions in the minority areas and seemed designed both to foster Albanian resentment against the Montenegrin authorities and to raise Montenegrin suspicions about the growth of Albanian separatism.

DAM leaders contended that their relations with "real Montenegrins" remained good and a certain level of cooperation was maintained with the Liberals, Social Democrats, and Socialists. By contrast, relations with the DPS and the People's Party remained strained, while the Radicals were rabidly anti-Albanian and intent on altering the demographic structure by pushing out ethnic minorities from their traditional areas. The DAM denied that they supported the creation of a "Greater Albania" but favored an independent Montenegro as such an entity could evidently better protect Albanian minority rights. Nonetheless, the DAM joined the Coordinating Council of Albanian Political Parties (CCAPP) under the leadership of Kosovo's Albanian leader Ibrahim Rugova to canvass for Albanian "national rights" throughout the former Yugoslavia.

The DAM objected to the election law for the December 1992 ballot because the system of proportional representation diminished the number of elected deputies. In addition, thousands of Albanians had reportedly left the republic during the previous year to escape military conscription, growing unemployment, and a potential Serb crackdown. The DAM boycotted the federal ballot and failed to win seats to the Montenegrin Assembly. The coalition with the Muslim PDA broke down a few days before the ballot as the PDA withdrew from all the elections, while the 4-percent threshold for gaining seats proved debilitating. DAM leaders calculated that with only a few hundred extra votes they would have obtained three parliamentary seats. They performed better in the local elections, particularly in Ulcinj and Bar: Bardhi was elected mayor of Ulcinj. After the elections and the formulation of a coalition government, from which the minorities were excluded, DAM leaders voiced some concern about rising Montenegrin nationalism in addition to pressures from radical Serbs. Some fears were expressed that a sovereign Montenegro could prove more restrictive of minority rights and cut the Albanian community off from Kosovo. Nonetheless, in a choice between Montenegrin independence and Serbian domination, Albanian leaders clearly favored the former. Some radical activists continued to harbor the goal of eventually separating Albanian-majority districts and unifying them with Albania.[14]

Party of Democratic Action—Montenegro (PDA-M)
Stranka Demokratske Akcije—Crna Gora (SDA-CG)

Harun Hadžić became the leader of this largest Montenegrin Muslim party. It was principally a branch of the PDA in the Serbian Sandžak and formerly of the PDA in Bosnia-Herzegovina. The PDA-M sought to articulate the demands of the Muslim population, situated primarily in the northern regions of Montenegro. It became a member of the Democratic Coalition, with the Albanian DAM, an alliance that gained 13 seats in the December 1990 republican elections. Following the outbreak of war in Bosnia-Herzegovina, the PDA came under increasing pressure on both sides of the Serb-Montenegrin border from Serb paramilitaries and local police forces evidently instructed by Belgrade to curtail Muslim political life. Its leaders were also subjected to constant vilification in the state-controlled media and were accused of preparing for armed confrontation and a rebellion against the Yugoslav federation. The PDA denied these charges and continued to participate in the political system. However, it boycotted the 1992 Montenegrin referendum and the federal elections, arguing that these were illegitimate acts orchestrated by Belgrade.

The PDA-M withdrew from the December 1992 minority election coalition shortly before the ballot, on the grounds that repression against the Muslim population was increasing and participation may have legitimized the Yugoslav authorities. Indeed, during the previous year, attacks on Muslim shopkeepers and families were reported from the northern parts of the Montenegrin Sandžak, close to the Bosnian border. Serbian paramilitaries also kidnapped and presumably murdered Muslim passengers from a train on route from Belgrade to Bar. The Montenegrin authorities made some attempts to pacify any potential escalation by sending in police units and restraining Serb militants. However, they were in no position to outlaw the irregular forces armed and sponsored by the Serbian government and the Yugoslav army. Although the PDA withdrew from the ballot, it did not discourage Muslims from casting their votes and indeed some activists encouraged them to vote for the "Montenegrin bloc," either Liberals, Socialists, or Social Democrats.[15]

Party of National Equality (PNE)
Stranka Narodne Jednakost (SNJ)

A predominantly Muslim party based in the Sandžak, the PNE came into conflict with the Party of Democratic Action over the political representation of Montenegrin Muslims. It viewed the PDA, and its parent organization in Bosnia-Herzegovina, as too extremist and militant in seeking special rights for Yugoslav Muslims. A statement issued by the PNE in September 1990 denied that the PDA in Bosnia-Herzegovina had the right to speak on behalf of Montenegrin Muslims. On the other hand, PNE leaders underscored that the Muslims in the republic were dissatisfied with their status and resented being referred to as "an invented nation" by Serbian nationalists. The PNE was a member of the Democratic Coalition, together with the Albanian DAM and the Montenegrin Muslim-based PDA, during the December 1990 republican election. The coalition won 13 out of 125 seats in the Montenegrin National Assembly. In February 1992, the party declared its opposition to a republican referendum concerning the future status of Montenegro on the grounds that the wording did not adequately delineate between the establishment of a new federal Yugoslav state and a "Greater Serbia" or "Serboslavia." In such a Serb-dominated state, the PNE believed that the position of the Muslims would inevitably deteriorate. Although the PNE participated in the minority coalition during the election campaign for the December 1992 ballot, it did not formally take part in the elections, although its members and sympathizers were not discouraged from voting against the "Serbian bloc."[16]

Boka Mariner's Association (BMA)
Bokaljska Mornarica (BM)

Tracing its origins to an organization founded in 1463, this Croat association was based in the Boka Kotorska region of southwestern Montenegro. It has sought to preserve the historical and cultural heritage of the republic's estimated 12,000 Catholics. Because of political pressure from the Montenegrin authorities and fear of persecution by the Yugoslav authorities after the outbreak of Serb-Croat hostilities, the BMA separated from its Zagreb branch during 1991.[17]

CHRONOLOGY

January 1989: The entire Communist and Yugoslav Party and government leadership in Montenegro is replaced following large-scale demonstrations organized by Milošević loyalists in the capital Titograd. This "anti-bureaucratic revolution" brings to power a younger cadre of Communists who remain dependent on Belgrade. The new administration pledges to introduce political pluralism and market reform while continuing to control all essential levers of government. Initially, Communist leaders claim they seek political pluralism within a "non-party system," but as pressures for change mount throughout Yugoslavia, the Party begins to advocate a full multi-party system calculating that its preponderant position and control of the media will assure it of an election victory.

January 1990: The Democratic Forum, of which the Liberal Alliance of Montenegro and the Democratic Party are members, is established to provide a political arena in which to establish a multi-party system.[18]

July 1990: The Montenegrin Assembly issues a statement expressing anxiety over the accelerating disintegration of Yugoslavia and criticizes Slovenian and Croatian moves toward independence following free elections in both republics.

October 1990: The Montenegrin Assembly passes a law legalizing the first multi-party election in the republic.

December 1990: Montenegro's first multi-party elections are held and easily won by the League of Communists, later renamed the Democratic Party of Socialists. The LCM gains 83 out of 125 seats to the Montenegrin Assembly. The Alliance of Reform Forces finishes second with 17 seats, the People's Party obtains 12 seats, while the minority bloc and independents reach a total of 13 seats.

March 1991: Montenegro's PEN Club vice-president, Jevrem Brković, issues an open letter in which he apologizes to Bosnians for the behavior of Montenegrin soldiers in Bosnia-Herzegovina. He is subsequently charged with "inciting ethnic and religious hatred" and is scheduled to be arrested and tried. To escape prosecution he reportedly seeks refuge in Croatia.[19]

April 1991: The People's Party issues warnings that Croats, Muslims, and Albanians are arming themselves throughout the republic, purportedly in preparation for seceding from Montenegro. The move is dismissed as a provocation engineered by pro-Serb forces intent on securing Montenegrin allegiance to Belgrade.

September 1991: Prime Minister Milo Djukanović states that the Montenegrin leadership is working on a declaration of sovereignty but within a limited federal framework while maintaining close links with Serbia. Thousands of Montenegrin residents are called up into the Yugoslav army; armed clashes are reported between Croatian and Montenegrin units in the coastal border regions. The Montenegrin government accuses Zagreb of trying to extend Croatian borders along the Adriatic at Montenegro's expense; Zagreb in turn charges Belgrade with orchestrating the conflicts in order to secure the strategic Prevlaka peninsula and to expel Croat residents.

October 1991: The National Assembly begins work on preparing a declaration on Montenegrin sovereignty. Bulatović explains that the affirmation of sovereignty does not equal a declaration of independence but simply a confirmation of Montenegro's internationally recognized position within the Yugoslav state. Nevertheless, the move appears to cause perturbations in Belgrade, particularly after Bulatović calls for the withdrawal of Montenegrin recruits from Croatian battle fronts.

February 1992: About 10,000 people rally in the town of Cetinje demanding Montenegrin independence. In response to the National Assembly's announcement about the March referendum on remaining in a federation with Serbia, another independence rally is held, this time in the capital Titograd, and draws about 10,000 supporters; a similar rally in Cetinje is attended by 5,000 people. The opposition condemns the wording of the referendum, which leaves little opportunity for citizens to opt for full sovereignty, as well as the short time frame in preparing the ballot that disabled any meaningful public discussion.

March 1992: In a republic-wide referendum, 96 percent of participants vote in favor of Montenegro remaining in Yugoslavia; the Albanian community and the pro-independence forces boycott the vote. Residents of Titograd vote 66 percent in favor of changing the city's name back to its original one, Podgorica.[20]

April 1992: The republics of Serbia and Montenegro form a rump Federal Republic of Yugoslavia after deputies of both parliaments adopt a new federal constitution over the objections of opposition forces in both republics.

May 1992: Federal elections are held and comprehensively boycotted by all opposition forces. Nationalist Serb paramilitaries linked with the Radical Party are accused of bombing several Muslim-owned businesses in the town of Pljevlja in the Montenegrin Sandžak.

June 1992: President Bulatović calls a special session of parliament to reconsider Montenegro's relation with Serbia and suggests another referendum to decide whether to remain in Yugoslavia. He states that "new, politically uncompromised figures should be found to represent the Yugoslav republic."[21]

August 1992: Self-proclaimed *Četnik* and Serbian Radical Party member Major Čeko Dačević is detained by Montenegrin police in Pljevlja in connection with radical Serb attacks on thirty Muslim-owned shops the previous May. In protest, several hundred armed Serb residents erect barricades on all roads leading to the town. Montenegrin authorities dismiss a number of Pljevlja's policemen, including the chief of police and the chief of criminal investigation, for tolerating the inflow of arms to Serb irregulars. Bulatović and Yugoslav president Dobrica Ćosić visit Pljevlja to assure local residents, especially Muslims, that republican authorities will guarantee their safety. Bulatović openly admits that paramilitary groups are operating in Montenegro but demands that local Muslim leaders desist from any demands for autonomy in the region. Pljevlja citizens take control of the post office, radio transmitter, gas station, and the security center building. Montenegrin Interior Ministry and federal Army troops arrive in Pljevlja to restore order and to disarm local paramilitary groups. After negotiations with the Montenegrin government, Dačević agrees to turn weapons over to the Montenegrin authorities. The Albanian Democratic Alliance of Montenegro plans a referendum on autonomy, although it is not stipulated whether the minority is seeking political, territorial, or cultural autonomy. The move is condemned by virtually all Montenegrin parties as it could assist Radical attempts to sow discord between Montenegro and its minorities.[22]

November 1992: Montenegrin delegates in the Federal Assembly help to block the attempts of Serb Radicals to oust Yugoslav prime minister Milan Panić during two votes of no-confidence in his leadership. DPS deputies indicate support for his efforts to reach a peace agreement in Bosnia-Herzegovina and implicitly back his criticisms of the Milošević leadership.

December 1992: Federal, republican, and local elections are held in the rump Yugoslavia. President Bulatović is reelected president of Montenegro after a second round run-off with the Serb Radical candidate Branko Kostić. In the Montenegrin National Assembly, the DPS gains 45 out of 85 seats, the People's Party 14, the Liberal Alliance 13, the Radicals 5, and the Social Democrats 4. The Montenegrin Liberals boycott the federal elections; in the Chamber of Citizens, the DPS elects 17 out of the 138 deputies, the Montenegrin Socialists 5, the People's Party 4, and the Radicals, from both Serbia and Montenegro, a total of 34. For the Chamber of Republics, the DPS elects 15 deputies, the People's Party 3, and the Radicals 2 to the 20-member Montenegrin section. The success of the Radicals in both republics enables them to have a majority vote with the Serbian Socialists in the Federal Assembly.

April 1993: Milo Djukanović, who is reelected as the Montenegrin prime minister, forms a multi-party government with the DPS, Liberals, Social Democrats, and People's Party representatives, thereby isolating the Radicals.

June 1993: A large demonstration of several thousand people, organized by the Liberals and other pro-independence forces, demands Montenegrin independence and opposes the rise of fascism in Yugoslavia following the ouster of Yugoslav president Ćosić by the Federal Assembly. Liberal leader Slavko Perović warns that pro-Milošević "mercenaries" threaten to spread Serbian "tyranny" to Montenegro. The leader of the newly formed Movement Against Fascism, Milika Pavlović, states that "the only way out for Montenegro is to separate from Serbia." A statement is issued condemning the expulsion of President Ćosić and the violent police actions against demonstrators, including opposition leader Vuk Drašković, in Belgrade.[23]

NOTES

1. Census figures can be found in *Stanovništvo SR Crne Gore Po Popisima Prema Nacionalnoj Pripadnosti*, Titograd (Podgorica), Republički Zavod Za Statistiku, Broj 42, June 25, 1991.

2. For some historical background on Montenegro, see Ivo Banac, *The National Ques-*

tion in Yugoslavia: Origins, History, Politics (Ithaca: Cornell University Press, 1984); Richard F. Nyrop, ed., *Yugoslavia: A Country Study*, Washington, DC: U.S. Government Printing Office, 1982; Christopher Boehm, *Montenegrin Social Organization and Values: Political Ethnography of a Refuge Area Tribal Adaptation* (New York: AMS Press, 1983); Dennison Rusinow, *The Yugoslav Experiment, 1948–1974* (Berkeley: University of California Press, 1977); and Paul Shoup, *Communism and the Yugoslav National Question* (New York: Columbia University Press, 1968).

3. For an election report, see the National Republican Institute for Independent Affairs, *The 1990 Elections in the Republic of Yugoslavia*, Washington, DC, 1991, pp. 26–34.

4. Milan Andrejevich, "The Elections in Montenegro," Radio Free Europe/Radio Liberty Research Institute (RFE/RL), *Report on Eastern Europe*, vol. 1, no. 51, December 21, 1990.

5. Dom Nike Ukguni, *Demand for the Defense of the Rights of Albanians in Montenegro*, paper presented by the Democratic Alliance of Montenegro to the Conference on Peace in Yugoslavia, Brussels, May 17, 1992.

6. See *Radio Belgrade Network*, June 30, 1993, in Federal Broadcast Information Service, *Daily Report: East Europe, FBIS-EEU–93–125*, July 1, 1993.

7. Janusz Bugajski, "Is Montenegro Next?" *Post-Soviet Prospects*, no. 15, The Center for Strategic and International Studies, Washington, DC, September 1992; M. Pavičević and S. Djukanović, "Fascism Must Be Stopped," *Pobjeda*, Podgorica, June 9, 1993, in *FBIS-EEU–93–114*, June 16, 1993.

8. For example, check Željko Ivanovic, "The Šešelj Enigma," *Monitor*, Podgorica, June 11, 1993, in *FBIS-EEU–93–115*, June 17, 1993.

9. *Tanjug*, Belgrade, June 30, 1990, in *FBIS-EEU–90–127*, July 2, 1990; *Tanjug*, Belgrade, April 8, 1991, in *FBIS-EEU–91–068*, April 9, 1991; Milan Andrejevich, "Montenegro Follows Its Own Course," RFE/RL, *Report on Eastern Europe*, vol. 2, no. 47, November 22, 1991.

10. *Vreme*, Belgrade, August 24, 1992, in Federal Broadcast Information Service/Joint Publications Research Service, *Daily Report: East Europe, JPRS-EER–92–127*, September 10, 1992; "Weekly Review," RFE/RL, *Research Report*, vol. 1, no. 33, August 21, 1992.

11. "To Power Legally," *Borba*, Belgrade, December 18, 1989, in *FBIS-EEU–90–008*, January 11, 1990; Milan Andrejevich, "Montenegro to Introduce Multiparty Elections," RFE/RL, *Report on Eastern Europe*, February 23, 1990; *Tanjug*, Belgrade, September 12, 1990, in *FBIS-EEU–90–178*, September 13, 1990.

12. "A Third Serbian Province," *Borba*, Belgrade, May 14, 1990, in *FBIS-EEU–90–097*, May 18, 1990; *Tanjug*, Belgrade, June 30, 1990, in *FBIS-EEU–90–127*, July 2, 1990.

13. *Tanjug*, Belgrade, January 3, 1992, in *FBIS-EEU–92–003*, January 6, 1992.

14. B. Milošević, "Announcement of Another Referendum of Albanians," *Politika*, Belgrade, March 25, 1992, in *FBIS-EEU–92–063*, April 1, 1992; Milan Andrejevich, "Montenegro Follows Its Own Course," RFE/RL, *Report on Eastern Europe*, vol. 2, no. 47, November 22, 1991.

15. Ž. Ivanović, "Conversation With the President and the Gentleman," *Borba*, Belgrade, July 30, 1992, in *JPRS-EER–92–109*, August 18, 1992; Velizor Brajović, "Montenegro: Pljevlja on a Powder Keg," *Vreme*, Belgrade, August 24, 1992, in *JPRS-EER–92–127*, September 10, 1992.

16. *Tanjug*, Belgrade, September 11, 1990, in *FBIS-EEU–90–178*, September 13, 1990; Milan Andrejevich, "Montenegro Follows Its Own Course," RFE/RL, *Report on Eastern Europe*, vol. 2, no. 47, November 22, 1991; *Tanjug*, Belgrade, February 21, 1992, in *FBIS-EEU–92–036*, February 24, 1992.

17. "Croatian Minorities in Vojvodina, Italy, Montenegro, and Bosnia and Herzegovina," *Newsletter 9: Current Affairs*, Croatian Ministry of Foreign Affairs, Zagreb, March 16, 1993.

18. "Weekly Record of Events," RFE/RL, *Report on Eastern Europe*, vol. 1, no. 5, February 2, 1990.

19. *Country Reports on Human Rights Practices for 1992*, U.S. Department of State, Washington, DC, February 1993.

20. *Tanjug*, Belgrade, March 3, 1992, and March 2, 1992, in *FBIS-EEU–92–042*, March 3, 1992.

21. "Weekly Review," RFE/RL, *Research Report*, vol. 1, no. 25, June 19, 1992.

22. Petar Nesić, "What Is Happening in Pljevlja? Tell Me, President ... ," *Nin*, Belgrade, August 21, 1992, in *JPRS-EER–92–127*, September 10, 1992.

23. RFE/RL, *Daily Report*, no. 107, June 8, 1993.

PART II

The Balkans

Nationalism Released

7

Romania

POPULATION

According to the preliminary results of the January 1992 Romanian census, the country's population stood at 22,760,449, of which about 10.6 percent were members of minority ethnic groups.[1] Hungarians formed the largest minority, totaling 1,620,199, or 7.12 percent of the population, with absolute majorities in two eastern Transylvanian counties, Harghita and Covasna. However, the Magyars comprised only 23.9 percent of the total population of the Transylvanian region, 21.2 percent of the population of the Crişana Maramureş region in northern Romania, and 6.6 percent of the population in the Banat region; an estimated 200,000 Hungarians resided in Bucharest. Hungarian activists disputed these figures and estimated the total Magyar population at nearer to 2 million. Gypsies or Roma accounted for 409,723 people, or 1.8 percent of the population, although their numbers were believed to be substantially underrecorded. Germans totaled 119,436, or 0.52 percent of the population. The remaining minorities included 66,833 Ukrainians, 38,688 Russians and Lipovans, 29,533 Turks, 29,080 Serbs, 24,649 Tatars, 20,672 Slovaks, 9,935 Bulgarians, 9,107 Jews, 5,880 Czechs, 4,247 Poles, 4,180 Croats, 3,897 Greeks, and 2,023 Armenians. People who were unregistered ("others") totaled 8,420, and 1,017 remained "undeclared." In comparison to the 1977 census, the total population grew by 5.6 percent of this, the ethnic Romanian component increased by 7.1 percent, while the Hungarian proportion declined by 5.5 percent. Gypsy numbers were recorded at 80.2 percent higher and German at 66.7 percent lower. The Ukrainian minority increased by 21 percent, the Russian by 18.4 percent, and the Turkish by 26.1 percent. All other minority groups experienced a decrease over the 15 years between the two censuses.

HISTORICAL OVERVIEW

Romania gained its independence from the Ottoman Turks in 1862, with the union of the principalities of Wallachia and Moldavia.[2] These provinces formed

Romania: Population (1992)

Ethnic Groups	Number	% of Population
Romanians	20,352,980	89.42
Hungarians	1,620,199	7.12
Roma (Gypsies)	409,723	1.80
Germans	119,436	0.52
Ukrainians	66,833	0.29
Russians and Lipovans	38,688	0.17
Turks	29,533	0.13
Serbs	29,080	0.13
Tatars	24,649	0.11
Slovaks	20,672	0.09
Bulgarians	9,935	0.04
Jews	9,107	0.04
Czechs	5,880	0.03
Poles	4,247	0.02
Croats	4,180	0.02
Greeks	3,897	0.02
Armenians	2,023	0.01
Others	8,420	0.04
Undeclared	1,017	--
Total Minorities	2,407,519	10.58
Total Population	22,760,499	100.00

the core of the Old Kingdom, but a substantial Romanian population was left outside the new borders in the regions of Transylvania, Banat, Bukovina, and Bessarabia. The Romanian population was numerically predominant in the Old Kingdom, which contained relatively small communities of Jews, Germans, Hungarians, and Bulgarians, and where few minority problems were evident at the time. During the 1860s, Hungary was given a significant measure of autonomy by the Habsburgs in administering the large Transylvanian region. The ethnic Romanian population was denied full legal status and deprived of equal educational and occupational opportunities. Budapest's policies in turn exacerbated ethnic frictions in Transylvania between Romanians and the privileged Hungarian and German elites. They also stimulated revisionist ambitions in Bucharest as various political groups sought to claim the Transylvanian territories and other lands containing large Romanian minorities. Romania obtained full international recognition in 1878, following the Russian-Turkish war. However, the Russians annexed Bessarabia, or eastern Moldavia, as payment for their defeat of the Ottoman armies. In addition, a large Romanian population was left in the Bukovina region, which became an autonomous province of the Austro-Hungarian monarchy after the 1840s. The denial of both territories also bred irredentist sentiments in Romania.

At the close of World War One, a Greater Romania was finally established. With the collapse of the Austrian Habsburg Empire, Hungary was obliged to surrender two-thirds of its pre-war dominions, including Transylvania and the

Banat, which were annexed by Bucharest. Romania also gained the province of Bukovina from Austria and the whole of Bessarabia following the revolutionary upheavals in Russia. As a result of its extensive territorial expansion, Romania acquired large minorities of Hungarians, Germans, Jews, and Gypsies (Roma) together with smaller communities of Ukrainians, Serbs, Turks, and Tatars. During the inter-war period, approximately one-third of the population of Transylvania, or about 1.5 million people, consisted of Magyar and Szekler Hungarians. Over one-half of the population were ethnic Romanians (about 2,850,000), with approximately 550,000 Germans (Swabians and Saxons). The loss of Transylvania spurred bitter resentment in Budapest, while the policies of the Bucharest government in the region inflamed already poor inter-ethnic relations. Shortly after unification, discriminatory policies were applied by the authorities, particularly against the Magyars, who lost many of their privileges and were largely excluded from the nation's political life. Ethnic, cultural, and linguistic differences between Hungarians and Romanians were aggravated by religious and class differences. The Magyars were predominantly Catholic or Protestant and constituted most of the noblemen, landholders, and professional classes, while the Romanians were largely Orthodox Christians and formed the bulk of the small or landless peasants. Bucharest's policies succeeded in destroying the political and economic power base of the Hungarian rural landlords and urban bourgeoisie, while the civil service and the professions were thoroughly Romanianized.

Tensions between Hungary and Romania mounted during the 1930s, as the defense of the Magyar community in Transylvania became a focal point of Hungarian foreign policy. Budapest gained the support of both Nazi Germany and fascist Italy in its revisionist campaigns and eventually joined in an alliance with the Axis powers. Ethnic relations further deteriorated in Transylvania as the government descended into a quasi dictatorship, but until the outbreak of World War Two there was no large-scale persecution or outright suppression of the Magyar minority. As an ally of Nazi Germany, Budapest regained northern Transylvania under the terms of the 1940 Vienna Award. Bucharest had little choice but to secede the territory or face serious repercussions from the Axis states. Following the establishment of the Fascist National Legionary State under the rule of General Ion Antonescu, Romania allied itself with Germany to forestall a further partition of Transylvania and in order to gain territorial spoils from the Nazi conquest of the Soviet Union. The Hungarian occupation of northern Transylvania resulted in a policy of systematic repression vis-à-vis the Romanian population. Similar anti-Magyar measures were pursued by the Antonescu regime in southern Transylvania. The war years left a painful legacy in both inter-communal and inter-state relations between Romania and Hungary.

During the early part of World War Two, Berlin also pressured Bucharest to cede Bessarabia and northern Bukovina to the Soviet Union to honor the Hitler–Stalin pact. Resentment mounted in Romania over Moscow's claims that the

Moldavians in Bessarabia were not ethnically Romanian but a separate nationality. Animosities were further spurred by a policy of russification in the province, as evident in the imposition of the Cyrillic alphabet. In return for Bucharest's alliance with the Axis powers, Hitler promised to restore Bessarabia to Romania after completing the conquest of the Soviet Union. The region was occupied by Romanian troops in 1941, and Bucharest contributed substantially to the German war effort against Moscow.

With the defeat of Nazi Germany, Soviet troops occupied Romania and helped to install a Communist regime in Bucharest. Under the post-war territorial settlements, Stalin incorporated northern Bukovina and parts of southern Bessarabia (the Herta district) into the Ukrainian Soviet Republic and annexed the rest of Bessarabia to create the Moldavian (or Moldovan) Soviet Republic. A policy of sovietization was accompanied by the transplanting of Russian and Ukrainian settlers, who formed a majority in some eastern districts of Moldavia along the Dniestr River. Romanian resentment over the loss of territories to the Soviet Union was somewhat muffled by overwhelming Soviet power and Moscow's acquiescence to a modicum of Romanian independence in return for the shelving of any land claims.

Romania was also compensated for the loss of Bukovina and Moldavia by regaining all of Transylvania from Hungary. Under Soviet overlordship, the Communist governments in both states were required to display international solidarity and minimize their minority problems. Under the 1952 Romanian constitution, a Hungarian Autonomous Region was established in the Szeklerland area of eastern Transylvania. About 1.5 million Hungarians inhabited Transylvania at this time, and they formed compact majorities in some central and eastern municipalities in the province. Extensive cultural rights were granted to the autonomous region: for instance, Hungarians were allowed to operate their own schools, publications, and places of worship, and benefited from unrestricted use of the Hungarian language in all official matters. Although the self-administration of the region was limited by the nature of Communist centralism, the Magyars were able to obtain political representation at all levels of the party and the state.

After Stalin's death in 1953, Bucharest secured greater independence from Moscow. Soviet troops were withdrawn from the country, and Romania stopped participating in Warsaw Pact military exercises. By the late 1950s, the regime of Gheorghe Gheorghiu-Dej increasingly manipulated Romanian nationalism as a popular legitimizing device and began to apply more repressive policies toward the Hungarians. This was especially evident after the unsuccessful anti-Communist revolution in Hungary in 1956, which gained some sympathy among Magyar intellectuals and students in Transylvania. The Magyar Autonomous Region was dissolved, and most of the key posts in the local administration were filled by loyal Romanians. The government began methodically to restrict the minority rights formerly enjoyed by the Hungarians. For example, in 1959 the Hungarian

Bolyai University was merged into the Romanian Babeş University. In fact, the position of all national minorities deteriorated as the process of Romanianizing culture, education, and socioeconomic life gathered pace.

Following the accession to power of Nicolae Ceauşescu in the mid-1960s, the assimilationist drive was pursued with new vigor. The remaining minority "privileges" were rescinded, and Hungarian representation in the local political and economic bureaucracies was limited to the proportion of Magyars in the total Romanian population. The number of minority members in party and state positions decreased. Romanianization was intensified through the mass resettlement of Moldavian and Wallachian Romanians into Transylvania. Many of these transplanted workers had little knowledge of Hungarian culture and proved a useful vehicle for diluting the Magyar identity of several parts of Transylvania. Some of these settlers were also at the forefront of various anti-Hungarian measures and proved loyal or malleable by the Ceauşescu regime. The coerced exodus of Hungarian intellectuals from Transylvania, who were compelled to take jobs in non-Hungarian areas, also contributed to the Romanianization and Communization process.

Bucharest remained concerned that the Soviet regime could exploit the Hungarian minority question. For example, it could encourage revisionist sentiments in Budapest as a way of applying pressure on Ceauşescu and curtailing his relatively independent stance. Although the Hungarian government occasionally denounced Bucharest's policies and its violation of minority rights, Budapest's generally low-key approach was criticized by embryonic opposition groups in Hungary itself. Nevertheless, threats of Hungarian revisionism and the protection of co-nationals in Transylvania had the effect of stiffening Bucharest's determination to Romanianize the province and forestall any external interference in the country's internal affairs.

The position of the Jewish and German minorities lost its importance in the post-war years. From about 800,000 Jews resident in Romania before World War Two, only a little over 380,000 were left as a result of deportation and extermination by the Nazis and their Hungarian, Romanian, and German collaborators. Thousands more emigrated to Israel, and the number shrank to some 175,000 by the mid-1950s, about 40,000 in the early 1980s, and under 20,000 by the early 1990s, with the majority resident in Bucharest. Although there was no systematic persecution of Jews, the Romanian Communist government did on occasion employ anti-Semitism, with some popular resonance, and removed Jews from important positions in the party and government. Once Ceauşescu established cordial relations with Israel and expanded his economic and political contacts with Western countries, the significance of the Jewish question was further eroded and emigration continued apace. The remaining Jews were entitled to operate their own religious and cultural organizations under government supervision and did not suffer from any distinctive forms of discrimination. By the late 1980s, the community had declined to some 9,000 people and continued to be led by Rabbi Moses Rosen, who justified his loyalty to Ceauşescu by claiming that he thereby managed to protect the Jews from official anti-Semitism.

Romania's German community numbered about 750,000 between the world wars. It benefited from its own schools and publications, as well as social, cultural, and political associations. Although some Germans collaborated with the Nazis during the war, the majority tried to maintain a separate identity and gain a measure of autonomy within Romania. After Romania joined the anti-German coalition in August 1944, the position of the German minority began to deteriorate. The post-war Communist government resettled German communities in Transylvania and the Banat, while tens of thousands fled the country. Although Bucharest officially granted Germans the same rights as other minorities, the government encouraged wide-scale emigration to West Germany, for which it obtained hard currency and trade agreements with Bonn. By the mid-1960s, the German population dropped to some 375,000 and continued to decline steadily during the next two decades.

Following Romania's post-war territorial losses of Bessarabia and northern Bukovina (to the USSR) and southern Dobrudja (to Bulgaria), much of the Ukrainian, Russian, Bulgarian, Turkish, Tatar, and Serbian minority ceased to be part of Romania's population. By the 1980s, these minorities constituted under 1.5 percent of the populace, or about 250,000 people, with their own circumscribed educational, cultural, and social organizations. Their relations with the Romanian majority did not result in any significant frictions. However, the position of the Gypsy, or Romani, population proved more problematic. According to official statistics, Gypsy numbers remained fairly constant after the war, in the region of 250,000 people. However, there were strong suspicions that the total was consistently underestimated, especially as a substantial proportion were not registered or simply declared themselves as Romanians. The Communist regime endeavored to settle the Roma in sedentary occupations and to integrate them in the Socialist structure. However, traditional anti-Gypsy sentiments surfaced periodically and resulted in inter-communal conflicts and acts of violence.

Ceauşescu manipulated Romanian nationalism and accelerated the program of Socialist construction. In the early 1980s, he launched an extensive program of "systematization" to hasten the development of large agro-industrial complexes. Over 6,000 villages were slated for demolition, many of these in Transylvania, in an evident attempt to speed up the process of Hungarian assimilation and homogenization into a "Socialist mass culture." Hundreds of traditional villages were destroyed and the inhabitants relocated to new housing estates that lacked the most basic facilities. The systematization program led to protests from Budapest, foreign governments, and from various international human rights organizations, but Ceauşescu appeared impervious to such criticisms. If anything, Bucharest intensified its repressive policies and Ceauşescu's personality cult assumed mammoth proportions. Ceauşescu's fall in December 1989 was sudden and bloody. As protests exploded on the streets of Bucharest and other large cities, the army switched sides to support the uprising. The Romanian dictator was executed after a summary trial, while the violent resistance of his loyalist *Securitate* forces proved futile. A provisional National Salvation Front, consisting of former Communists, dissidents, and army commanders, was formed to govern the country pending the first general elections.

OFFICIAL POLICIES

Immediately after the Romanian uprising in December 1989, the position of the Hungarian minority visibly improved. Both Hungarians and Romanians participated in the rallies and protest actions that contributed to toppling the Ceauşescu regime. Indeed, the spark of revolt was lit in the Banat city of Timişoara when police moved to arrest the popular Hungarian pastor László Tőkés. As large crowds gathered to protect the clergyman, Romanian security forces opened fire on protesters and the anti-Ceauşescu revolt rapidly spread to Bucharest and other parts of the country. The initial revolutionary phase was marked by cooperative efforts between Romanian and Hungarian activists. Various restrictive and repressive policies were abandoned by the new National Salvation Front (NSF) government, the Hungarian population was legally permitted to establish its own political organizations, and far-reaching concessions were granted in cultural and educational affairs.

Despite this auspicious beginning, relations between the new administration and the Magyar minority began to deteriorate in the first few months of 1990. Hungarian spokesmen charged that the anti-Ceauşescu revolution had been hijacked by reform Communists who thwarted the emergence of a democratic system and were willing to employ nationalism and exploit anti-Magyar sentiments to garner domestic support. The regime of President Ion Iliescu was also accused of tolerating and even sanctioning the exploits of extremist anti-Hungarian nationalist forces in Transylvania. Hungarian leaders insisted on the introduction of a new law on national minorities to regulate the unclear legal status of all minority groups. Although the position of minorities substantially improved after the revolution, many of the gains were considered reversible because they lacked firm legal safeguards. Hungarian leaders were also concerned over certain articles in Romania's new constitution that defined the country as a "unitary national state" with prohibitions on activities deemed to be "separatist." They feared that this could provide a constitutional underpinning for a possible future ban on ethnically based political parties. Their complaints were echoed by various political parties in Hungary. The Budapest government urged Bucharest to sign agreements on the mutual protection of minorities and to enshrine collective minority rights in the new constitution, which the Iliescu cabinet has consistently refused to do. It has also urged the Romanian administration to combat anti-Hungarian manifestations more actively and to outlaw radical groups that whipped up racist passions. As of mid-1993, a Romanian-

Hungarian treaty had still to be concluded; Bucharest held back from specifically guaranteeing the rights of the Magyar minority and insisted on a joint declaration that the two states harbored no territorial claims on each other.

Numerous other proposals have been put forward by both Budapest and Romania's Hungarian leaders to improve the position of the Magyar minority and enhance relations between the two capitals. These have included opening new consulates in Transylvanian cities with large Hungarian communities, promoting tourism and opening new border crossings, enlarging Hungarian cultural and educational facilities, and introducing the Hungarian language alongside Romanian in official transactions in regions with sizable minorities. Although some radical forces in Hungary have demanded territorial revisions, the majority of mainstream Hungarian organizations have primarily sought cultural self-determination and some form of local autonomy or administrative decentralization for the compact Magyar areas of Transylvania. Romanian spokesmen of various political orientations have strongly objected to any notion of Transylvanian or Magyar autonomy, whether cultural or territorial, pointing out that Romanians outnumbered Hungarians in the province by a proportion of three to one. Many Romanian politicians remained distrustful of the long-term objectives of Hungarian organizations and the policies of the Budapest administration. For example, Magyar demands for Hungarian schools, and the official use of the Hungarian language in minority areas, have been depicted as a first step toward regional autonomy and the eventual separation of Transylvania.

The activities of newly formed extremist Romanian organizations served to aggravate ethnic tensions in parts of Transylvania. Some have been directly assisted by the old Communist *nomenklatura* and the security forces, while factions in the National Salvation Front have courted and supported some of the radicals. Ultra-nationalist groups have opposed granting any "national privileges" to the Magyar minority, including language classes that were restored to some Transylvanian schools in 1990, and demanded a ban on all minority-based political organizations. They have preyed on popular fears among some sectors of the Romanian population that Hungarian aspirations will undermine their economic conditions and place them in a subordinate political position. Such accusations have carried some weight among the thousands of Romanians who were resettled in Transylvania by the Ceauşescu regime. Ethnic tensions have on occasion been exploited by ultra-nationalist Romanian groups to foster violence in Transylvania, as was evident in the city of Tîrgu Mureş in March 1990. Hungarian spokesmen contended that the Bucharest government failed to investigate the incidents properly and bring the culprits to trial. Romanian authorities have in turn accused Magyar activists of bearing much of the responsibility for inciting ethnic conflicts in Transylvania.

During the first few days of January 1990, a Commission on National Minorities was established in Bucharest and charged with clarifying inter-ethnic problems in order to present them to the Romanian parliament. Károly Király, a

Hungarian activist, was appointed president of the commission; he also served as vice-president of the Executive Bureau of the Provisional National Unity Council. The commission dealt with four issues: organizational and administrative problems, the development and organization of education in the mother tongue among local communities, the role of the mass media in covering the problems of national minorities, and the necessity of reaching a consensus on mutual relations. A colloquium on national minority questions was held in March 1990 and a long list of propositions was advanced, but little progress was subsequently registered in its work.

In May 1990, the Bucharest government issued Decision No. 521 concerning the organization and functioning of education in Romania. It included provisions on teaching in the mother tongue for persons belonging to ethnic minorities. The preamble stated that Romanian citizens "shall have the right to education, irrespective of nationality, race, sex, or religion, and with no other restriction that may infringe upon basic human rights." Although "all-grade education" was to be provided in the Romanian language, conditions were supposed to be ensured for the national minorities to be taught in their mother tongue. According to Article 42, children and pupils belonging to a national minority were guaranteed equal opportunities with Romanian nationals to receive instruction in their native language. Article 43 specified that in the towns and villages containing national minorities, "there may be kindergartens, primary and secondary schools, high schools, teaching schools, art colleges, with classes, groups, or sections in which the mother tongue is taught." However, Article 44 clarified that "in order to participate actively in the entire economic, social, political and cultural life of Romania, youths belonging to national minorities should know the Romanian language. Romanian language and literature are compulsory at the graduation examination." During the 1990–91 school year, there were 136 high-school sections using Hungarian as a teaching medium (as compared to 107 in 1989–90), out of which 27 were units teaching exclusively in Hungarian. There were also 7 pedagogical high schools. Some subjects were also taught in Hungarian at the Babeş-Bolyai University in Cluj, at the Medicine and Pharmacology Institute, and at the Theatrical Institute in Tîrgu Mureş. But the teaching of all courses in Hungarian at Babeş-Bolyai University was not authorized by the government, despite the demands of Hungarian leaders. Some courses were also taught in German, Serbian, Ukrainian, Slovak, Czech, and Bulgarian.[3]

During the general elections in May 1990, political parties and movements representing three of the country's ethnic minorities won a sufficient number of votes to be represented in the lower house of parliament, the Chamber of Deputies. The Democratic Union of Hungarians in Romania (DUHR) gained 991,601 votes, 7.23 percent of the total, and won 29 seats. The German Democratic Union (GDU) gained 38,768 votes, 0.28 percent of the total, and won 1 seat. The Democratic Union of Roma in Romania (DURR) gained 29,162 votes, 0.21 percent of the total, and also won 1 seat. Political groups representing various minorities that failed to gather the necessary number of votes acquired 1 seat each, according to the provisions of the electoral law. Article 4 of the law stipulated that the representation of all nationalities was guaranteed: "the organizations representing the national minorities registered at the date of adoption of the present law, which fail to gather the necessary number of votes in order to get a mandate to the Chamber of Deputies, are entitled to one deputy mandate." The following parties obtained 1 seat: the Armenian Union of Romania; the Bulgarian Union of Banat, and the Bulgarian Cultural Association of Bucharest (1 seat for the two); the Hellenic Union of Romania; the Lipovan Community of Romania; the Polish Union of Romania; the Democratic Union of Serbians; the Democratic Union of Slovaks and Czechs; the Muslim Turkish Democratic Union of Romania; and the Ukrainian Union of Romania.

In the Senate elections of May 1990, the DUHR won 1,004,353 votes, 7.20 percent of the total, and obtained 12 seats. The total number of Magyar representatives in parliament therefore reached 41. One of the four secretaries in the Chamber of Deputies was from the DUHR, in addition to the chairman of one of the fourteen parliamentary commissions and the vice-chairmen of two commissions. In the Senate, Hungarian senators included one of the four vice-chairmen, one of the four secretaries, and the chairmen in two commissions. One Magyar became a member of the Drafting Commission for the Draft Constitution of Romania. The DUHR established parliamentary groups in the Chamber of Deputies and in the Senate. A parliamentary group consisting of members of political parties belonging to other minorities represented in parliament was also formed.

According to the law on public administration, ratified in November 1991, "local government was to be based on the principles of local autonomy, and the decentralization of public services," while complying "with citizens' opinions on problems of particular local interest."[4] However, the institution of the prefect, who was appointed by the central government and represented the administration in the counties (judeţe), placed substantial limitations on local autonomy. Article 43 of the law also stated that mayors were responsible for insuring "public law and order and the inhabitants' peace with police support." Mayors could take measures to "prohibit or suspend performances or other public manifestations that contravene the order of the law or infringe upon good morals, public order, and peace." This article was subsequently used by the ultra-nationalist mayor of Cluj to forbid the holding of various Hungarian events in the spring of 1992, leading to numerous protest actions.

Article 54 of the public administration law specified that Romanian was to be the language employed in relations between citizens and the local public administration. Citizens belonging to national minorities could also use their mother tongue either in spoken or written form. If the representative of the public authority was not familiar with the language of the respective minority, the services of an interpreter were to be used. According to Article 126, judicial proceedings were to be conducted in the Romanian language. However, in the draft of the constitution, an article provided for citizens who belonged to national minorities to use their mother tongue in court. This stipulation subsequently disappeared as a result of pressure exerted by the National Salvation Front and by nationalist deputies. In Article 127 of the final draft, members of national minorities could only request the services of an interpreter. Representatives of the DUHR strongly protested against this amendment.

In December 1991, a new constitution was approved in a public referendum.[5] Article 1 declared Romania as a "national state, sovereign, unitary, and indivisible." Hungarian leaders raised no objection to the term "unitary" but contested the definition of the country as a "national state," pointing out that no state containing 14 recognized national minorities should describe itself as a "national" state. But their amendments were overruled by the majority of Romanian parliamentarians. According to Article 3 of the constitution: "The territory of Romania is inalienable. A foreign population may not be displaced or colonized on the territory of the Romanian state." This seemed to be an allusion to a *post factum* refusal to accept the loss of territory to the Soviet Union in 1940. Similar provisions were contained in the Romanian constitution of 1923: the term "colonized" was added in an amendment. Deputies supporting this amendment were apparently convinced that the unity of the state was endangered by the machinations of the Hungarian ethnic minority. Article 4 of the constitution declared the Romanian state as the "common and indivisible home for its citizens without any discrimination as to race, ethnic origin, language, or religion." Furthermore, according to Article 6, "the state recognizes and guarantees the rights to the conservation, development, and expression of the ethnic, cultural, linguistic, and religious identity of the national minorities." However, section two of the same article appeared to deny national minorities certain collective rights by focusing on individual rights: "The protective measures taken by the state to conserve, develop, and express the identity of the national minorities shall accord with the principles of equality and nondiscrimination which are applicable to other Romanian citizens."

Article 30 of the constitution, dealing with freedom of expression, prohibited the "slandering of the state and the nation, incitement to war, to aggression, and incitement to discrimination, and territorial separatism." This was evidently an allusion to the DUHR, which had been regularly accused of separatist intentions by Romanian nationalists. Article 32 focused on the right to education: "The legal teaching language in all schools, at all levels, is Romanian; schools may also teach in an international language. The rights of members of ethnic minorities to study in their mother tongue and to be educated in that language is guaranteed; the means of exercising those rights are established by the law." This meant that, while recognizing in theory the right of national minorities to be instructed in their mother tongues, in its application the ruling could prove more restrictive.

Article 118 of the constitution, on local and county public administration, declared that the basic principle on which local government was based was that of "local autonomy" and the "decentralization of public services." Local autonomy was to be exercised through the local councils of communes and cities, elected by the people resident in that area. But the office of prefect would continue to constrain local autonomy as these officials were appointed directly by Bucharest, and in addition to supervising the functions of central government organs in the *judeţe*, they could challenge before the solicitor's office acts approved by the local councils.

In November 1991, the new constitution was passed by a two-thirds parliamentary majority prior to its submission for public approval. Hungarian deputies voted against the proposed text of the constitution, as did several Romanian deputies, including the then minister of justice. Representatives of other minorities approved the constitution, indicating that they acquiesced to the policies of the ruling party. Hungarian deputy Király was excluded from the Senate for abstaining from the vote. In a subsequent interview, he declared that "from the point of view of crushing national minority rights, this basic law is even worse than the Communist constitution passed in 1965." According to Király, the constitution did not mention the rights of national minorities, but on the contrary it provided an exhaustive list of prohibitions. For example, at any administrative level, members of a national minority could not use their mother tongue, even if they formed an overwhelming majority in that area. The new constitution did not prohibit education in the mother tongue, neither did it determine the degree to which such education was allowed. It left such decisions to the law, and Hungarian leaders complained about the fickleness of laws. In Király's estimation, the constitution could be interpreted in several ways: "A democratic government could guarantee European-style national minority rights through this constitution. If the country is governed by an extremely nationalist leadership, however, the text could even lead to genocide." A referendum on the constitution was held in December 1991. The Hungarian population overwhelmingly rejected the proposed constitution, but the draft was passed by a majority of Romanian citizens.[6]

In the parliamentary elections of September 1992, the DUHR performance was consistent with its results in the previous national ballot. The Hungarian Union gained 7.45 percent of the national vote, obtaining 27 seats out of a total of 341 in the Chamber of Deputies and 12 seats in the Senate. The remaining national minorities garnered 0.94 percent of the vote and, according to electoral legislation, were allocated a total of 13 seats in the Chamber of Deputies having obtained at least 5 percent of the average number of valid votes required nationwide to elect a deputy outright. The parliamentary elections were narrowly won by President Iliescu's DNSF with 27.71 percent of the vote to the Chamber of Deputies (117 out of 341) and 28.29 percent of the vote to the Senate (49 out of 100 seats). The oppositionist Democratic Convention gained 82 seats in the lower house and 34 in the Senate. As a result of their slender plurality, the DNSF (subsequently renamed the Party of Social Democracy in Romania, PSDR) entered into a coalition with several smaller parties and non-party technocrats under Prime Minister Nicolae Văcăroiu. Iliescu was reelected president in a run off with Convention candidate Emil Constantinescu, gaining 61.43 percent of the vote after the ultra-nationalist parties had endorsed his candidacy. The three ultra-nationalist parties gained a total of 59 seats in the Chamber of Deputies and 25 seats in the Senate. Because of Văcăroiu's narrow margin, the new government also relied on the support of the nationalists to push through any significant legislation.[7]

Following the Iliescu victory, Hungarian leaders charged that the authorities began a systematic campaign to place DNSF loyalists in leading positions of various national institutions, including local government, education, and the legal system, and to eliminate ethnic Hungarians from influential positions.[8] Moreover, the authorities appeared willing to exploit ethnic tensions in parts of Transylvania, using the vehicle of the ultra-nationalist parties, to distract attention from economic hardships evident in rising unemployment, rising prices, and the curtailment of welfare-assistance subsidies. In what was viewed as a further provocation by Hungarian leaders, in March 1993 Bucharest announced the appointment of two new ethnic Romanian prefects in the Magyar-majority counties of Harghita and Covasna. Indeed, Vlad Adrian Căşuneanu, the Covasna prefect, admitted to being a member of the nationalist *Vatra Românească* organization, leading to vehement protests by local Hungarians. Observers believed that the government had acceded to the demands of nationalists in the appointment of Romanian prefects, in return for their continuing parliamentary support.

As ethnic tensions persisted in the country, a session of the Romanian government in March 1993 decided to establish a consultative Council for National Minorities to help pacify potential unrest. The Council was placed under the direction of government Secretary-General Victor Hrebenciuc. Following complaints from the DUHR that the Council would merely become another symbolic body, the authorities clarified and strengthened its mandate. The Council would reportedly be empowered to draft administrative decrees for the government on questions pertaining to the status of national minorities and would include 36 seats for the 17 legalized organizations representing the ethnic minorities, together with 14 seats reserved for the government. Each minority would possess veto power over decisions affecting its interests. The Consultative Council would supposedly aim to improve the implementation of ethnic minority rights in compliance with the provisions of the constitution. Its jurisdiction would extend to legislative, administrative, and financial questions revolving around the "perpetuation, development, and expression of ethnic, cultural, linguistic, and religious identity."[9] In June 1993, the Council drafted a decree to allow bilingual signs to be restored in Hungarian areas of Transylvania, where the minority represented 30 percent or more of the population. In July 1993, the Council sponsored an accord between senior government officials and Magyar minority leaders calling for an increase in elementary-school classes for minorities and for the training of 300 more Hungarian teachers at the Babeş-Bolyai University. The agreement was due to be approved by president Iliescu later in the summer.

Romania's Gypsy (Romani) population, estimated at somewhere between 400,000 and 1 million, has repeatedly suffered the most systematic discrimination since the ouster of Ceauşescu. Although Romani parties were allowed to register and stand in the elections and obtained a representative in the National Assembly under a provision of the electoral law that guarantees a deputy for each minority unable to win direct representation through elections to the Chamber of Deputies, the community has been subjected to repeated manifestations of prejudice. Human rights groups have reported that Romani houses have been burned down, their property vandalized, and individuals attacked by vigilante mobs in a number of Romanian villages. With the rise of ultra-nationalism and anti-minority xenophobia, Roma became easy targets for frustrated Romanian peasants and failed to receive sufficient protection from the police forces. Furthermore, Roma continued to experience discrimination in housing, employment, and education, and the negative Gypsy stereotype has been propagated by the state-run media. Various Romani organizations and media outlets have increasingly raised the issues of prejudice and discrimination that were taboo in Romania for decades and have campaigned to improve the position of Gypsy communities through a cultural, educational, and political revival. Romani leaders have complained that the government in Bucharest has done little to offer the community protection against vigilantism or to provide equal opportunities in public life. Roma have remained hamstrung by a shortage of resources, an inexperienced leadership, and deeply rooted tribal, occupational, and linguistic divisions. Some estimates indicated that there were at least 40 distinct groups of Gypsies in Romania, although the majority have become sedentary during the last few decades.[10]

As the Moldovan (Moldavian) Republic moved toward sovereignty and independence from the Soviet Union during 1991, the Romanian authorities and various political organizations became more outspoken on the issue. About 3.2 million Romanians lived in Moldova, constituting nearly three-quarters of the republic's population, and another 800,000 inhabited the northern Bukovina and southern Danubian districts of Ukraine. Approximately one-third of the Moldovan population consisted of Ukrainian, Russian, and Gagauz Turkish minorities. While the Moldovan government declared the country's independence, Russian and Ukrainian separatists proclaimed their own Trans-Dniestr Republic, carved out of the eastern sector of Moldova that was attached to the republic by Stalin. The Moldovan authorities charged Moscow and conservative Communist forces of encouraging and aiding these separatist forces. Meanwhile, local Russian and Ukrainian leaders accused Moldova of seeking reunification with Romania, even though the government had approached the question with some caution and underscored the republic's independence and self-determination. Paradoxically, pressures for the separation of Trans-Dniestr have actually encouraged calls for Romanian-Moldovan unification in both states, because of fears of renewed Russian domination. Concurrently, the Bucharest government has come under increasing domestic pressure to support the Moldovan authorities and adopt a more forthright anti-Russian position.

Moldovan-Romanian relations at the governmental level have continued to evolve steadily. Mircea Snegur, the president of Moldova, enunciated the doctrine of "one people, two states," or "two states cooperating with each other," a principle that became the cornerstone of Moldovan relations with Bucharest. In Moldova itself, organizations such as the Moldovan Popular Front called for speedy reunification with Romania and disagreed with Snegur's measured approach. Government leaders in Romania adopted a gradualist policy: they essentially supported Chişinău's stance on Moldovan independence and the "two-states" doctrine. They accepted Moldovan statehood, deferring reunification to a distant future. Romanian president Ion Iliescu envisaged a gradual evolution, beginning with the consolidation of Moldova's republican status and a Romanian-Moldovan rapprochement through "practical steps to develop direct relations in all fields, primarily economic and cultural, and building up a process that will advance faster or more slowly, depending on the international context." The Iliescu administration was attempting to find a middle ground between domestic expectations of rapid progress toward reunification and Moldova's insistence on its permanent independence. Nevertheless, the escalation of armed insurgency in the Trans-Dniestr, supported by Russia's Fourteenth Army, has consolidated security links between Romania and Moldova and injected nationalist and revanchist sentiments into the political debate in Romania itself.[11]

Most of Romania's political groups, including the democratic opposition, a part of the National Salvation Front, and the extra-parliamentary opposition, rejected Snegur's "two-states" doctrine and insisted on prompt reunification. The main opposition parties, as well as former premier Petre Roman, occasionally injected the Moldovan issue into domestic politics, seeking to use it as a weapon against the Iliescu administration. They accused Iliescu of sabotaging reunification and denounced Snegur's administration for promoting a separate Moldovan statehood. They envisaged resolving this issue through Moldovan self-determination within the framework of full Romanian control over its former provinces. Several Romanian nationalist organizations have campaigned for reunification with Moldova together with the return of Romanian provinces lost to Ukraine after World War Two. They organized rallies and other protest actions and demanded that the Romanian government and parliament take a more active role in defending Moldovan and Bukovinan interests. The Romanian Ecologist Movement and a number of nationalist parties tried to enlist Mircea Druc, a former Moldovan prime minister, to run on their party ticket for the Romanian presidential elections in September 1992. Although they were unsuccessful, the move indicated the importance attached to reunification by some sectors of the Romanian electorate. The Romanian population in Bukovina has also begun to organize, and activists have established contacts with pro-unification organizations in Romania and Moldova. Following Ukraine's declaration of independence in

January 1992, it remained unclear whether territorial controversies between Moldova, Ukraine, and Romania could be amicably resolved. The danger existed that Bucharest would be increasingly drawn into the fray as economic conditions deteriorated in all three states and separatist and pro-unification groups became more active. The government could even seek to capitalize on a foreign policy issue to garner domestic credibility. This could in turn aggravate conflicts with both Kyiv and Moscow.

ROMANIAN NATIONALISTS

Party of Romanian National Unity (PRNU)
Partidul Unităţii Naţionale Române (PUNR)

Since early 1990, a legion of ultra-radical Romanian nationalist organizations have mushroomed in the country. Some were viewed as a continuation in a new guise of the "national Communist" pro-Ceauşescu orientation; others constituted new incarnations of pre-war and wartime Romanian fascist movements seeking to draw support from sectors of the population disillusioned with the consequences of economic reform and seeking a strong authoritarian government. Future links between these two trends could not be discounted if the centrist and civic options failed to establish strong roots among Romanian voters. Of the more significant nationalist groupings, the PRNU was established shortly before the May 1990 elections with evident links to the old Communist *nomenklatura*. Its leadership included Chairman Radu Ceontea and First Deputy Chairman Petre Burcă. Both were elected at the PRNU's extraordinary national conference in May 1991. The PRNU platform bore similarity to that of the "sociocultural" nationalist organization *Vatra Românească*. Most members of PRNU were also reportedly members of *Vatra*. In particular, the PRNU claimed to represent the interests of the Romanian population in Transylvania. It opposed any claims for the establishment of administrative-territorial enclaves in the region and was decidedly anti-Hungarian in its orientation. PRNU leaders have persistently spoken out for strengthening Romanian unity, for reunification of the country in its historical boundaries, and for the renewal of the "spiritual unity" of Romanians all over the world. The PRNU has staged protests against the establishment of a Hungarian consulate in Cluj claiming that this was a dangerous step toward separatism. At its extraordinary national conference in May 1991, the organization issued a report on the DUHR, the major Hungarian organization in Romania. According to the report, the "DUHR is an anachronistic and extremist ethnic party that through its activities seriously endangers the unity and integrity of the Romanian state." The PRNU appealed without success to parliament to prohibit the holding of the DUHR's congress in 1991.

The PRNU gained 16 mayorships in the February 1992 local elections and captured 4.9 percent of the total votes cast, as compared to 2.12 percent in the general elections of May 1990. President Iliescu's Democratic National Salvation Front formed electoral coalitions with the PRNU in several Transylvanian counties. Most notably, the PRNU won the mayoral office in the large Transylvanian city of Cluj-Napoca, where Hungarians constituted about 25 percent of the population. The controversial new mayor, Gheorghe Funar, who obtained nearly 11 percent of the vote in the presidential race, proceeded to enact various anti-minority policies, including a ban on bilingual shop signs, street names, foreign banners, and anthems, and restrictions on freedom of assembly and Hungarian cultural and educational activities. These prohibitions sparked outrage among Magyar leaders and escalated ethnic tensions in the region. Although the central government declared several of Funar's actions illegal, he continued to use local statutes to harass Hungarian activists. In a gesture of defiance in October 1992, the PRNU appointed Funar as the party's interim president after the suspension of former president Radu Ceontea. In the general elections of September 1992, the PRNU captured 7.71 percent of the national vote and elected 30 parliamentary deputies and 14 senators, indicating a dangerous swing toward ultra-nationalism among a significant sector of the Romanian population.[12]

Romanian Cradle (RC)
Vatra Românească (VR)

Vatra Românească was established in February 1990; its leader, Radu Ceontea, was elected executive chairman at the RC's first national conference in May 1990. *Vatra*'s second national conference was held in Tîrgu Mureş in June 1991. Iosif Constantin Drăgan, a former Iron Guardist who financed numerous extremist activities, became honorary president, Zeno Opriş was subsequently elected president, and Ceontea founding president. The RC claimed to be a "social-cultural and civic organization whose program and activities serve no political party." According to its leaders, *Vatra* had no ambitions to become a political party; however, it did coordinate its efforts with the PRNU while boasting a membership of some 4 million people by early 1992. *Vatra* became an ultra-nationalist organization avowedly organized in response to the formation of the Democratic Union of Hungarians in Romania (DUHR). It considered the DUHR to be "a kind of Communist successor party" and a danger to Romanian unity. *Vatra* leaders asserted that Hungarians should have no special rights in Transylvania, while claiming that they currently enjoyed a privileged position. They viewed Romanian nationalism as the necessary response of a small country "under pressure from a united Europe, an internationalized world, and with the dilution of national culture."

Vatra considered proposals for separate Hungarian schools in Transylvania a threat to Romania's position in the region, and demanded overt Hungarian loyalty to Romania's territorial integrity. *Vatra* helped to organize the first anti-Magyar demonstration in March 1990 to protest against celebrations of the

Hungarian national holiday. *Vatra* was allegedly behind the Tîrgu Mureş distur-bances in March 1990, which involved violent clashes between Romanian and Hungarian residents. It was suspected of maintaining relations with the govern-ment and the ruling National Salvation Front. *Vatra* was also a harsh critic of the Romanian government's performance. It believed that the NSF had adopted an overly conciliatory approach toward minority groups. On the other hand, accord-ing to Ceontea, NSF members constituted a majority of RC members, and *Vatra* leaders encouraged their electorate to vote for the Front in the general elections of May 1990.

The RC supported Moldova's declaration of independence and pledged to bring all Romanians inside the same frontier. *Vatra* established two publishing houses, one named *Vatra Românească*, the other *Ţara Noastră*, in order to spread its propaganda. During 1991, its leaders demanded the passage of a new Romanian constitution, without special rights for minorities, and became increas-ingly aggressive in their anti-minority stance. In February 1992, the RC escalated its anti-Hungarian campaign, calling for the termination of Hungarian-language radio and television programs and the annulment of the cultural treaty signed between Bucharest and Budapest, because it was allegedly "anti-Romanian." The influence of *Vatra*'s nationalist ideas evidently grew in the judicial system in parts of Transylvania as well as in the Romanian army. The PRNU and the Romanian Cradle reportedly benefited from high-level military support, espe-cially in the Romanian Third Army based in Transylvania. The links between the army and nationalist forces were displayed during the local elections in Cluj in February 1992, when the commander of the Third Army, General Paul Cheler, appeared to infringe on Article 40 of the Romanian constitution, which pre-vented the army from involvement in politics. He accused the Democratic Con-vention of proposing to dismember the country, in line with similar nationalistic statements he had made in *Scutul Patriei*, the weekly newspaper of the Transyl-vanian Army. Soon afterward, the candidate of the PRNU, Gheorghe Funar, declared that the Romanian army should be ready to act as the "right arm of the PRNU." During the election campaign, RC representatives regularly visited mili-tary bases to talk to soldiers, and *Vatra*-produced films were shown to recruits. As a result, Romanian Cradle and PRNU candidates reportedly obtained the major share of votes on military bases throughout Transylvania.[13]

Greater Romania Party (GRP)
Partidul România Mare (PRM)

The GRP was established in May 1991 by a group of journalists writing for *România Mare*, a nationalist magazine created in June 1990. The founders were the chief editor of the magazine, Corneliu Vadim Tudor, and Eugen Barbu. Both were writers renowned for their conspicuous contribution to hagiography under Ceauşescu, as well as their links with the *Securitate* security police. The GRP became a strictly hierarchical organization, in many ways resembling the defunct Communist Party. By October 1990, the editors of *România Mare* claimed a circulation of some 600,000, making it one of the most widely read weeklies in the country. The GRP was widely viewed as the most extremist, nationalistic, chauvinistic, and anti-Semitic political group in Romania. GRP leaders believed that Romania's national unity and sovereignty were threatened from both within and outside the country, and they denounced the Romanian government for its inability to combat the danger. The GRP disseminated propaganda against the Hungarian minority, which it believed was taking steps to truncate Romania; it viewed the DUHR as an essentially "terrorist organization." According to its spokesmen, "Hungarian young people in Romania are guided by the Union of Hungarian Democratic Youth, which is led by the DUHR, and the DUHR receives orders from Hungary, a country that carries out the orders of the USA." *România Mare* demanded the elimination of the DUHR and the deportation of its members. It could conceivably form a future alliance with the PRNU, although it appears to be competing for essentially the same supporters.

In October 1991, the party issued a statement that "the Romanian Army will once and for all cool down the hotheaded Horthyites of Hungary, if it is forced to enter Budapest for a third time." *România Mare*'s articles against Jews and Hungarians were even condemned, albeit belatedly, by president Iliescu in August 1991 following intense Western criticism. In the September 1992 elections, the GRP gained 16 deputies to the lower house of parliament, capturing 3.8 percent of the vote, and 6 senators. At the party's first congress in March 1993, Tudor demanded a crackdown on the DUHR, accusing it of plotting to dismember Romania. Tudor also praised Ceauşescu for being a Romanian patriot and described the 1989 revolution as an "armed attack" against the country by Hungary and the former Soviet Union. The GRP unanimously reelected Tudor as party chairman while adopting new statutes and a revised program.[14]

Movement for Romania (MFR)
Mişcarea Pentru România (MPR)

This radical rightist grouping was established in December 1991 by Marian Munteanu, a former leader of the Bucharest University Students' League who gained renown for his oppositionist activities against the Iliescu government. The MFR has been criticized by both the pro- and anti-government forces for its ideological links to the pre-war fascist organization, the Romanian Legionary Movement (or Iron Guard). In its program, the MFR criticized liberalism and social democracy for contradicting the "cultural and spiritual nature" of the Romanian people and stressed Christian mysticism and collectivism above individualism. Its ideology has been defined as "national democratic" and "Romanianist," underscoring the linguistic, cultural, and religious unity of the Romanian nation and its avowed superiority among European peoples. Munteanu also cast himself as the champion of young people or the "new generation" who had been frustrated and betrayed by developments since the 1989 revolution. The MFR established its own publications, including the newspaper *Mişcarea* (The Movement), a "Veterans Corps," and reportedly received funds from Romanian neofascists in the West. It advocated close cooperation with other Orthodox Christian countries and with Romanian emigrés who were willing to defend the country's "national interests." The MFR's internal structure replicated the legionnaire cell organizations with no elected leadership but an enforced consensus based on discipline and obedience. Munteanu criticized other nationalist formations, including the GRP and the PRNU, for their links with former Communist structures and Ceauşescu appointees, even though their programs were in many respects similar. Although MFR statements have not appeared as blatantly racist or xenophobic, critics charged that the Movement sought to restrict severely the rights of Hungarians and other minority groups and establish a new dictatorship. Moreover, in May 1993 government officials condemned the revival of the "legionary phenomenon" in Romania and singled out the MFR as the prime culprit.[15]

New Christian Romania Party (NCRP)
Partidul Noua Românie Creştină (PNRC)

The NCRP was founded in May 1992 as an openly neo-fascist organization that visualized itself as the continuation of the Iron Guard movement. It was led by Serban Suru, claimed several hundred members, and revered Corneliu Codreanu, the former Iron Guard leader, as a national hero deserving of sainthood. The NCRP staged several public meetings in Bucharest, seeking to bridge the gap between fascist veterans and a younger generation of activists disillusioned with post-Ceauşescu developments. The Bucharest Municipal Court was sharply criticized by democratic parties for allowing the NCRP to organize, as it allegedly contradicted constitutional stipulations banning the formation of extremist parties. Several similar ultra-rightist groupings have also begun to operate during the past few years, including the Party of the National Right (PNR), formed in April 1992 and led by Radu Sorescu. In its publication, *Noua Dreaptă* (New Right), which berated the failures of democracy, the PNR attacked various ethnic minorities and called for the creation of an "ethnographic state." The National Legionary Party (NLP), established in September 1992 and led by Ionică Cătănescu, the Christian Democratic Union—Sibiu Convention (CDU-SC), and several other radical-right formations were believed to possess close ties with agents of the former *Securitate* and with Ceauşescu loyalists seeking to benefit from populist, nationalist, and xenophobic sentiments among segments of the Romanian population.[16]

Socialist Labor Party (SLP)
Partidul Socialist al Muncii (PSM)

The SLP, formed in November 1990 and led by Chairman Ilie Verdeţ and Deputy Tudor Mohora, drew its supporters from former Ceauşescu loyalists with

a strong nationalist orientation. Indeed, the party was viewed as the main successor to the defunct Romanian Communist Party. The SLP garnered 3.03 percent
of the vote in the September 1992 general elections and elected 13 deputies to
the Chamber of Deputies, along with 5 senators to the upper house of parliament.
The party has supported the government of prime minister Nicolae Văcăroiu on
various occasions, for example, during "motions of censure" sponsored by the
oppositionist Democratic Convention. Together with the PRNU and the GRP,
the SLP has assured the minority government of the Party of Social Democracy
in Romania (PSDR), the former Democratic National Salvation Front, of a parliamentary majority since the September 1992 elections.

HUNGARIAN TRANSYLVANIANS

Democratic Union of Hungarians in Romania (DUHR)
Uniunea Democratică a Maghiarilor din România (UDMR)

The DUHR was formed in December 1989; László Tőkés, one of the leading
figures of the 1989 revolution, became its honorary chairman. The first elected
president was Géza Domokos, a former member of the Romanian Communist
Party Central Committee and a member of the post-revolutionary provisional
government of the National Salvation Front. The DUHR became more of an
alliance than a political party, and although open to all Romanians citizens it was
principally a Hungarian movement. It included sixteen different parties and associations, including the Hungarian Christian Democratic Party of Romania, the
Party of Hungarian Farmers in Romania, the Independent Hungarian Party of
Romania, and the Union of Hungarian Democratic Youth. Each party was able to
preserve its independent status inside the Union. DUHR membership was organized in a loose structure of local chapters that were in turn grouped into autonomous county branches. The Union's statutes granted territorial organizations
wide latitude in local decision making. The Council of Delegates became the
main policy-making body, whose members were elected at the federation's congress. The DUHR's executive body consisted of a presidium with eleven members, elected by congress. Twelve groups of experts were also set up at the 1992
congress to deal with political, cultural, economic, and other issues.

The DUHR's objectives were two-fold: ethnic and national. The main ethnic
goals were to reverse persistent discrimination and longstanding anti-Hungarian
sentiments in Romania. The Union stressed increased cultural and social freedom: it promoted the right of Hungarians to run their own schools, operate
independent radio and television stations, publish an independent press, and
reopen the Hungarian Babeş-Bolyai University in Cluj. Each year on March 15,
the DUHR has celebrated Hungary's national day in commemoration of the 1848
revolution. The Union has both defended ethnic interests and participated in the
democratic opposition movement. It supported demands for "cultural and func-

tional" autonomy, including separate ethnic educational institutions and self-governing churches. It demanded local autonomy for Transylvania with Hungarian prefects and deputy prefects appointed in the counties of Covasna and Harghita. It envisaged such moves in the context of local government reform, rather than in terms of specifically minority issues. On the other hand, the Union did not pursue "territorial autonomy," despite the accusations of Romanian nationalists. Its hesitancy stemmed from the recognition that such autonomy would leave many ethnic Hungarians outside the autonomous regions without benefit of collective rights. It also calculated that any demands for "territorial autonomy" would trigger unpleasant associations with the former Hungarian Autonomous Region, set up during the Stalinist era.

The DUHR wanted Romania declared a multinational state and called for the creation of a Ministry of Minority Affairs. It also proposed that national minorities should use their own language in local government institutions. In June 1991, at its National Council of Representatives in Cluj, the Union recommended that the Romanian government, the governing party, and the opposition parties discuss the national minority issue at a national round-table conference. It also supported the creation of a Central European National Minority Forum or a joint association for Hungarians and other national minorities living in the Danube-Carpathian basin, based on a common identity of interests. It lodged protests against its inability to participate in the official Romanian delegation at the CSCE Conference on National Minorities held in July 1991. It called for "an internationally accepted, comprehensive system of national minority rights, and the formulation of a system of international norms that will both guarantee and supervise the implementation of these rights."

From the outset, the Union has also participated in domestic politics in opposition to the NSF. It insisted on "democratic values" and joined the National Alliance for the Proclamation of Timişoara, created in April 1990. In the presidential elections of May 1990, the DUHR called on people not to vote for Iliescu. The Union was close to the National Liberal Party but did not give the Liberals its official support because none of the Liberal candidates held a distinct position on minority issues. It opposed direct presidential elections, asserting that the president should be appointed by parliament. The DUHR finished second in the general election of May 1990, winning 29 seats in the Chamber of Deputies and 12 in the Senate, and received approximately 1 million votes. It participated in consultations on the settlement of the government crisis in September 1991 and supported the presidency of Theodor Stolojan. The Union declared its readiness to offer candidates, especially for the ministries of education, culture, and justice. It presented a Communique on Government Programs calling for the creation of a legal framework for national minority rights. It decided to participate in the new government and was offered three ministerial posts: economics and finance, industrial affairs, and trade. As a condition, the DUHR stated that the government should also have a Ministry for Nationalities. The government objected and the DUHR refused to participate in the new administration.

During the local elections of February 1992, the DUHR ran on joint lists with the Democratic Convention (DC) opposition coalition in most districts, but on separate ones in Transylvania. The Union finished third in the elections, winning 8.7 percent of the vote, gaining seats in 10 towns in Transylvania and 37 on common lists with the DC. It lost in many of the areas where it had run on separate lists, due to the strong showing of Romanian nationalists, who won 20 mayorships, including Cluj-Napoca. But the Union won the mayorship in Tîrgu Mureş after rescheduled elections in May. The Union announced that it would run on separate lists for the parliamentary elections of September 1992 while supporting the DC's presidential candidate. In the parliamentary ballot, the DUHR obtained a result similar to the one two years before. It captured 7.45 percent of the popular vote for the Chamber of Deputies, obtaining 27 seats, and 7.58 percent of the vote for the Senate, thus gaining 12 seats in the upper house.

The first DUHR congress was held in Oradea in April 1990. Participants discussed the problems facing Hungarians after the ethnic violence in Tîrgu Mureş the month before. The second congress was held in Tîrgu Mureş in May 1991, when 533,000 paid-up members were reported. A statement from the second congress read that the Hungarians of Romania considered themselves "a separate political subject, a constitutive state-forming element, and, consequently, an equal partner of the Romanian majority." The DUHR viewed itself as an important factor in the parliamentary elections, and although "the area of its political presence has remained a limited one, incipient forms of cooperation with the extra-parliamentary opposition are about to emerge, which opens new prospects for a civil society in a distant future, which might offer great chances for a settlement of the status of Hungarians in Romania." The DUHR adopted a new program and a resolution demanding that the Hungarians be recognized as a "co-nation" or a "state-building" nation.

Different trends were visible in the Union during 1992: a moderate tendency, led by president Géza Domokos and Király, and a more radical faction led by Géza Szőcs and Gábor Kolumbán, both vice-presidents. Bishop László Tőkés seemed increasingly sympathetic to the more radical wing. In an interview in April 1992, Domokos recognized the presence of different platforms within the DUHR: Liberal, Christian Democratic, and a movement favoring the involvement of young people in political life. In essence, all these trends respected Romania's independence and unity, but while one wing used the help of democratically minded Romanians to obtain minority rights gradually, the others considered it important to press for Magyar demands more forcefully. Domokos denied that any of these tendencies were extremist. It appeared that the younger wing, with some former dissidents, wanted to emphasize participatory democracy with spontaneous political activities at the grass-roots level, an outlook it shared with the Romanian extra-parliamentary opposition. By contrast, Domokos and like-minded leaders of his generation were accustomed to working within the institutions of the state to achieve what was possible with regard to minority interests. At the May 1991 congress, some fissures emerged, based mainly on generational and tactical differences among the participants. A more extreme fraction, styled the Magyar Initiative in Transylvania, led by Ádám Katona, wanted the DUHR to call for outright "territorial autonomy" in its program.

The DUHR held its third congress in January 1993 and avoided radicalizing the movement and thus playing into the hands of Romanian extremists. The DUHR's radical faction, which demanded a declaration of "self-determination" by the Hungarian population, failed to take over the executive leadership and to impose its demands on the DUHR program. The radicals had pressured the Union to adopt the Declaration of Cluj in October 1992 in response to the anti-Magyar measures adopted by Mayor Funar. The declaration had defined Hungarians as a "state-building nation" rather than a national minority, sought the redefinition of Romania as a multi-national not a unitary state, and demanded "communitarian autonomy" for Magyars in Transylvania. However, it failed to specify whether this would signify territorial autonomy or simply "ethnic and religious autonomy." The Cluj Declaration was condemned by virtually all Romanian parties, including the DUHR's partners in the Democratic Convention. Subsequently, the DUHR congress distanced itself from its propositions and criticized the radicals for leading the Union into isolation from the Romanian opposition. As a result, the new DUHR program did not propose "territorial autonomy" but the more ambiguous "local and regional self-administration," while avoiding mention of the Hungarians as either a "state-building nation" or a "national minority," opting instead for "national community." Domokos stepped down from the DUHR presidency and was replaced by Béla Markó, who adopted a moderate approach similar to that of his predecessor, while Tőkés was reelected honorary president. Although divisions within the Union were not resolved, workable compromises were reached among the different factions; the possibility of future radicalization also remained contingent upon the policies of the central and local governments.[17]

Union of Hungarian Democratic Youth (UHDY)
Uniunea Tineretului Democratic Maghiar (UTDM)

The UHDY was established in December 1989, and Chairman Tibor Toró from Timişoara became its principal leader. The Union defined itself as an independent organization without a political character as well as the youth affiliate of the DUHR. The Youth Union was dedicated to the realization of rights for young Magyars in Romania and equality for all nationalities, and it established an information center for young Hungarians. Eight of its members were elected to the DUHR presidium.[18] Other Hungarian organizations included: the Magyar Smallholders Party in Romania, chaired by Zoltán Éltes; the Hungarian Christian Democratic Party in Romania, based in Tîrgu Mureş and led by István Tőkés, the father of Bishop László Tőkés; the Independent Magyar Party, located in Tîrgu Mureş; the Association of Magyar Youth Organizations; and the Cultural Society of Hungarians in Transylvania. The Trianon Organizing Forum of the National Christian Union appeared in May 1990, calling for the condemnation of the Trianon Treaty. It was reportedly irredentist and considered by the DUHR as a provocation designed to instigate ethnic conflicts. The Pro-Transylvania Foundation was created in Budapest in August 1990, presided over by András Sütő. The Transylvanian emigré government was reported to be active in Budapest during the fall of 1991 but was also viewed as a provocation by the DUHR. It transpired that its president was an ethnic Romanian who claimed to have worked for the *Securitate*; a few days after its creation it announced that it was disbanding itself. The *Együtt* (Together) Association was established in mid-1991 by Győző Hajdú, a member of the Romanian Communist Party Central Committee under Ceauşescu. *Együtt* was critical of the DUHR's alleged extremism and irredentism and aimed to "fight chauvinism" and to achieve Romanian-Hungarian cofraternity. It advocated both the rights of the Hungarian minority and Romania's territorial integrity. Its creation was reportedly welcomed by *Vatra Românească*.[19]

MOLDOVAN MOVEMENTS

Pro-Bessarabia and Bukovina Association (PBBA)
Asociaţia Pro-Basarabia şi Bucovina (APBB)

The Association was formed in the spring of 1990 as an avowedly cultural association. Its leadership included President Nicolae Lupan and Vice President Vasile Tipordei, replaced in 1990 by Gheorghe Muntean. The PBBA cast itself as a broad movement seeking to develop cultural relations between Romania and Moldova, but it also engaged in more overt political activities. It established branches in several parts of the country; for instance, a Transylvanian branch was founded in Braşov in October 1990. The first large meeting of the Association was held in March 1990 in order to commemorate the historical union of Bessarabia with Romania. In May 1990, the Association organized the Bank of the Prut, a gathering on the Romanian–Moldovan border. In April 1991, it protested against the treaty of cooperation and friendship signed with the Soviet Union. It called on the Bucharest government to denounce the Ribbentrop-Molotov Pact and to recognize the sovereignty of the Moldovan Republic. The PBBA maintained direct contacts with Moldova and collected funds to help the natives of both Moldova and Bukovina deported to Siberia under Stalin's rule. The Association called for dual-citizenship status by supplying Romanian citizenship to all people of Moldovan origin, lineage, kinship, or spiritual affinity. The PBBA's political activities increased after the spring of 1992, as Moldova struggled to preserve its territorial integrity.[20]

League of Solidarity with the People's Front of Moldova (LSPFM)
Liga de Solidaritate cu Frontul Popular al Moldovei (LSFPM)

The League was established in March 1991 by a group of writers and engineers. It coordinated its initiatives in the cultural, social, economic, and political domains with those of the Moldovan People's Front in Moldova, headed by Iurie Rosca, an organization that supported reunification with Romania. It was an ardent critic of the Soviet Union's referendum in March 1991 on preserving the federation and believed that the Republic of Moldova had the full right to independence and self-determination.[21]

Romanian Popular Front (RPF)
Frontul Popular Român (FPR)

The RPF was established as a Romanian branch of the Popular Front of Moldova, which supported the reunification of Moldova and Romania. It was based in Iaşi, the capital of Romanian Moldova, where it published newspapers, including the first periodical in Romania dealing with Moldovan issues, *Flacara Basarabiei*; the publication first appeared in December 1990.[22]

MINORITY ORGANIZATIONS

League of Organizations of National and Ethnic Minorities in Romania (LONEMR)
Liga Organizaţülor Minoritaţilor Naţionale şi Etnice din România (LOMNER)

The League was established in July 1990, with leadership exercised by president Károly Király, a former member of the Romanian Communist Party Central Committee and vice-president of the Provisional Council of National Unity. LONEMR was designed as a consultative organization created to defend human rights and the individual and collective rights of national and ethnic minorities. It became an umbrella organization for several independent ethnic parties and alliances. In April 1991, Király announced somewhat prematurely that there was a decrease in the nationalistic and chauvinistic pressures exerted on the Hungarian minority. He declared that "extremist political forces were losing their support among the masses as a result of the maturity of the Romanian society and the sober-minded policy of the Hungarian Union."[23]

Democratic Union of Roma in Romania (DURR)
Uniunea Democratică Romilor din România (UDRR)

DURR was created in Bucharest in February 1990. It was led by Ion Onoriu, the provisional president. Lawyer Nicolae Bobu was elected president at the Roma

Special Congress in Deva in July 1990. At the Third Congress of Roma in September 1991, held under the auspices of the DURR, Ion Cioabă was elected "King of the Roma" and Nicolae Gheorghe was elected secretary-general of the DURR. A rival Gypsy chieftain, Iulian Rădulescu, proclaimed himself the "Emperor of all Gypsies" in September 1992. The DURR became an umbrella organization for several Romani associations and parties and was dedicated to ensuring social, cultural, and political freedom for the Romani people; six Gypsy parties were officially registered in Romania as of June 1990. It unanimously decided to support Iliescu's presidential candidacy, while protesting against continuing anti-Gypsy incidents in the Romanian countryside. The DURR has worked to set up an Ethnic Confederation of Roma that would promote Romani causes and publicize acts of discrimination, harassment, and violence. In addition, it has been effective in strengthening ties to the Romani community worldwide. Several other Romani organizations have been formed in recent years, including the Fiddlers and Wood Carvers of Romania, the Free Romani Democratic Party, the Gypsy Party of Romania, the Tinsmith Roma Progressive Party, the Free Democratic Union of Roma, and the Christian Democratic Party of Roma. Most of these are regionally based and in competition with each other. Such divisions have obstructed progress toward forging a united Romani platform.[24]

Democratic Forum of Germans in Romania (DFGR)
Forumul Democratic al Germanilor din România (FDGR)

The Forum was created in January 1990, in Sibiu, and was led by its President Naegler and Vice-President Nikolaus Kleininger. It was formed as a social-cultural organization and not a political party. The DFGR lobbied for enshrining the rights of minorities in the Romanian constitution. It advocated a German schooling system, cultural freedom, and the protection of Saxon and Swabian historical monuments. It assisted people who were deported to Russia after World War Two and aimed to stabilize the position of the approximately 120,000 Germans remaining in Romania in 1991; about 100,000 Germans reportedly emigrated during the early 1990s. The first meeting between DFGR and government representatives took place in September 1990. An Advisory Commission for Supporting Initiatives and Actions Aiming at Stabilizing the German Minority was established. DFGR leaders displayed great concern over the German exodus and organized a joint symposium with the authorities in Sibiu on the minority question.[25]

Muslim Turkish Democratic Union of Romania (MTDUR)
Uniunea Democratică a Musulmanilor Turci din România (UDMTR)

The Union called for increased cooperation between Romanians and the Turkish minority, for the organization of Turkish-language classes in Romanian schools, for the re-creation of an Islamic confessional school, and for the training of *imams* for the 62 remaining mosques in Romania; there were reportedly 82 mosques in 1963.[26]

Democratic Union of Slovaks and Czechs (DUSC)
Uniunea Democratică a Slovacilor și Cehilor (UDSC)

The Union was established in May 1990 as an avowedly political party representing and defending the interests of the small Slovak and Czech minorities in Romania.[27]

Democratic Union of Serbs (DUS)
Uniunea Democratică a Sîrbilor (UDS)

The DUS was formed in March 1990 in Timișoara to represent and defend the interests of Romanian citizens of Serbian and, initially, Croatian nationality in Timiș, Arad, Caraș-Severin, and Mehedinți counties. It sought to reinvigorate their spiritual life, preserve their cultural traditions, and develop their educational system. Following the outbreak of war in the former Yugoslavia, some Serb leaders adopted a vehemently nationalist position avowedly in defense of Eastern Orthodoxy against Romanian Catholicism and militant Islam.[28]

Union of Ukrainians in Romania (UUR)
Uniunea Ucrainienilor din România (UUR)

The Union was established at the close of 1992 as an apolitical organization seeking to mediate fruitful contacts between the government and the Ukrainian minority. Its president was Stefan Tcaciuk, who was also a parliamentary deputy. According to Union leaders, the Ukrainian population was dispersed throughout the country, with some compact concentrations in northern regions such as Maramureș next to the Ukrainian border. The minority benefited from a network of schools and language courses, and the UUR was planning to establish a Ukrainian-language newspaper and a radio station in Maramureș county.[29]

Arumunian Cultural Society (ACS)
Societatea Culturală Aromână (SCA)

This cultural society was established in Bucharest in March 1990 to represent the under-reported Arumanian or Vlach population in Romania. It traced its origins to the Macedonian-Romanian Cultural Society that was set up in 1880 but stopped functioning in 1949. It claimed to have no overt political character or aspirations.[30]

Armenian Union of Romania (AUR)
Uniunea Armenilor din România (UAR)

The Union was formed in Bucharest in August 1990 in order to cultivate and encourage contacts between Romania and Armenia. It has not engaged in openly political activities. Romania's smaller minorities also established their own independent social, cultural, and quasi-political organizations to protect their interests and campaign for an expansion of group rights.

CHRONOLOGY

December 1989: All ethnic groups combine their efforts to demonstrate against Ceauşescu. Ethnic Hungarians are joined by Romanians to defend Pastor László Tőkés. Both nationalities sustain casualties during the revolution. Humanitarian aid from Hungary is welcomed by both sides during the uprising. The Democratic Union of Hungarians in Romania (DUHR) is established.

January 1990: An agreement is reached between Hungary and Romania regarding inter-state travel. A Hungarian-Romanian Trade Agreement is signed, calling for the expansion of sales in Romania of books and newspapers published in Hungary. Hungarian broadcasts begin to appear on TV and radio. Tőkés and Király join the first National Salvation Front government, which promises to guarantee individual rights and freedom for ethnic minorities and to establish a Ministry for Ethnic Minorities. First tensions surface in Transylvania over the issue of education and the NSF's proposals to separate Hungarian and Romanian schools. The deputy minister of education, Hungarian Attila Pálfalvi, is removed from office and the DUHR threatens to leave the NSF. Local tensions increase because of the entrenchment of the old administration and traditional mistrust.

February 1990: Tensions become magnified in Transylvania over the reintroduction of Hungarian-language instruction in some high schools. Anti-Hungarian demonstrations are staged in Tîrgu Mureş, in which about 5,000 Romanians participate. Several people are injured during the clashes. On the same day, 10,000 Hungarians take part in a rally demanding independent Hungarian schools. A Hungarian demonstration is also staged in Tîrgu Mureş, with about 40,000 demonstrators calling for equal rights with Romanians.

March 1990: Commemorations by Magyars of Hungary's national day take place in a number of towns in Transylvania. Clashes are reported with Romanian nationalists. Sizable anti-Magyar demonstrations continue for several days in parts of Transylvania. On March 19, thousands of demonstrators in Tîrgu Mureş, mostly Romanians, led by *Vatra Românească*, protest against "acts of separatism and chauvinism displayed by Hungarians." Armed protesters attack the offices of DUHR; several people are injured, including DUHR county chairman, András Sütő. Police and army troops move to evacuate the offices while president Iliescu appeals for calm. On March 20, Hungarian workers stage a strike in protest against the previous day's "pogrom." Large Hungarian demonstration are held in Tîrgu Mureş calling for the dismantling of *Vatra*, followed by attacks on *Vatra* offices in the city. With reports of new injuries, a local state of emergency is declared and the army intervenes. A total of 8 people are reported killed and 300 injured during the Tîrgu Mureş clashes. Gatherings and demonstrations also take place in other Transylvanian towns. A special government commission is appointed to investigate the Tîrgu Mureş disturbances. The commission's report is finally presented in January 1992. According to its conclusions, the significance of the crisis for the post-totalitarian evolution of Romanian society is "a symptom of the difficult but firm path toward a democratic political regime."[31]

May 1990: In the national elections, the DUHR receives 7.2 percent of the vote, mostly from the predominantly Hungarian counties of Covasna and Harghita, where the DUHR won 77 percent and 85 percent of the vote, respectively. The Union obtains 29 seats in the Chamber of Deputies and 12 mandates in the Senate. The nationalist PRNU receives 2.1 percent of the vote, obtaining 9 seats in the Chamber of Deputies and 2 in the Senate. This is a relatively poor performance, but it registers a good showing in the counties of Cluj (3 deputies and 1 senator) and in Mureş (4 deputies and 1 senator).

June 1990: Roma are among the targets of the Jiul Valley miners who attack anti-government protesters in Bucharest evidently at the instigation of the Romanian government.

October 1990: Thirty-two houses belonging to Roma are burned down or demolished near Constanţa A similar incident takes place in December in the same district.

February 1991: Hungarian- and German-language programs on Romanian television are reduced by more than half and transferred to a channel that cannot be received in most parts of Transylvania. Moldovan president Mircea Snegur visits Bucharest and meets with president Iliescu. Bilateral economic and cultural agreement are finalized and discussions are held about the opening of consulates in Iaşi and Chişinău. Snegur advances the concept of a "cultural confederation" between the two states.

March 1991: Several parties, including the National Liberals, Social Democrats, and National Peasants, issue a declaration condemning the Soviet referendum in

Moldova as an aggressive act by an occupying power and at variance with the norms of international law.

April 1991: President Iliescu signs a treaty of cooperation and friendship with Moscow. The treaty is severely criticized by the opposition because it does not declare null and void the Molotov-Ribbentrop pact. Serious clashes occur between Romanians and Gypsies near Bucharest and 22 houses are incinerated. The government subsequently dismisses police and local officials in these areas. A spate of articles appears in the Romanian press, singling out Gypsy "bear trainers" as "inveterate black-marketeers, thieves, and criminals."

May 1991: Romani organizations issue an appeal to the "Romani musicians and dancers and all Roma in Romania," in which they condemn both individual criminal acts committed by Roma and collective violence against the ethnic minority. Romani leaders also denounce state-run television for contributing to the escalation of violence through biased coverage of the conflicts.

June 1991: Romani spokesmen ask for international mediation to protect the community from growing violence. Representatives of the Ethnic Confederation of Roma inform a conference in Washington that fifteen documented incidents of violence against Roma had taken place over the previous eighteen months; the attackers evidently included both ethnic Romanians and Hungarians.[32] The Romanian parliament condemns the Soviet annexation of Bessarabia and northern Bukovina and urges a strategy of "small steps" toward the integration of Romania and Moldova.

July 1991: In answer to the DUHR's proposition for a roundtable to find solutions to the minority problem, the NSF declares that it had "firmly engaged in promoting a policy aimed at achieving a democratic framework based on the rule of law." The endorsement of the new constitution apparently represents a decisive step in this direction. The rights and freedoms included in the draft allegedly offer guarantees for all minorities. As a result, discussions on the ethnic problem with the DUHR would "represent a groundless, inefficient, non-democratic, and unacceptable artificial formula."[33]

August 1991: A Polish newspaper publishes an article detailing plans for the economic integration of Central Europe that includes Transylvania, provoking a general outcry in Romania. Critics from across the political spectrum maintain that Hungary was taking advantage of its close relationship with Poland to push for Transylvania's secession. Warsaw denies any involvement in plans to redraw the map of the region. Bucharest blames the Hungarian news agency *MTI* for deliberately misinterpreting the text of the article.[34] Moldova declares its independence. Bucharest and Chişinău agree to exchange ambassadors. Romania recognizes the independence of Moldova and calls for international acceptance of the new state. Iliescu states that reunification is inevitable but underscores a cautious and gradualist approach toward this objective.

September 1991: The Romanian delegation to the CSCE conference includes three guest representatives from Moldova. The Romanian parliament issues a declaration on the Ukrainian referendum: it welcomes the plebiscite but asserts it should not supposedly take place on the former Romanian territories of northern Bukovina, the Herța district, and the counties of southern Bessarabia. The results of the referendum in these areas would be considered invalid.

October 1991: An alleged "political group" of the DUHR in the Szeklerland region of Transylvania announces that it will call a referendum for the establishment of an "autonomous territory." The instigators remain a mystery: it may have been extremist Hungarian emigrés critical of the DUHR's moderation, or Romanian nationalists who engineered the incident as a provocation. The DUHR promptly denies that the Szekler political group formed part of its organizational structure. A report by a special parliamentary committee describes the "anti-Romanian atrocities of the Szeklerland Hungarians since the revolution." It suggests that Hungarians would use any means to drive the Romanian population out of Transylvania, with the full support of local Magyar leaders. The alleged aim was to establish an autonomous region that would eventually separate from Romania. Hungarian activists call the report a deliberate attempt to divert public attention from everyday problems and to divide the opposition. The DUHR refuses to initial the report, which was signed by several parliamentary parties. The extra-parliamentary Civic Alliance also raises objections to the report. DUHR leaders announce that they were considering whether to remain in the legislature in view of its obvious anti-Hungarian bias.[35]

November 1991: A government declaration on ethnic minorities is issued. It concludes that the transition process toward democracy and a market economy will also create conditions for "correctly solving problems of interest to ethnic, linguistic, and religious minorities." The declaration seeks to ensure that the rights of ethnic, linguistic or religious minorities "will not lead to the separation or isolation of minorities from the rest of the population." The government declares that one of its objectives is to begin negotiations with Kyiv for the return of northern Bukovina and the Bessarabian counties to Romania.

December 1991: Romania's Foreign Ministry announces that it is ready to establish diplomatic relations with Ukraine but stresses that the Romanian territories remain "a highly sensitive issue" for Bucharest. The National Union Council, composed of parliamentarians from Moldova and Romania, is established in Iași. It is dedicated to enhancing contacts between Romanians on both sides of the River Prut and dispelling false views about Romanian history. The Council would seek to educate legislators on both sides of the border, create joint enterprises, make passports unnecessary for travel between the two countries, and promote the adoption of the Romanian currency in Moldova.

January 1992: DUHR leaders state that the Romanian census had been marked by a series of abuses, including the listing of Szekler as a separate language from Hungarian and the use of pencils to answer questions pertaining to nationality, mother tongue, and religion. Snegur and Iliescu meet on the Moldovan side of the border, and they express their intention to set up a free economic zone along the frontier region.

February 1992: In the Romanian local elections, support for the ultra-nationalist bloc reaches almost 9 percent of the total votes cast—more than double the percentage gained in the May 1990 elections. The nationalists win 20 mayorships, of which 16 are obtained by the PRNU, including the mayoral office in the large Transylvanian town of Cluj. The PRNU gains 4.9 percent of the total vote, compared to 2.1 percent in the May 1990 elections. *România Mare* wins less than 0.1 percent of the vote. The PRNU's major gains in mayoral and council elections are in the counties of Bihor, Buzău, Cluj, Maramureş, Mureş, Satu Mare, and Sălaj. The DUHR gains mayorships in 10 towns and several local council majorities in the counties of Bihor, Covasna, Harghita, Mureş, and Satu Mare. The Hungarian defense minister declares that "the defense of the entire Hungarian population in the Carpathian area is an inseparable part of the defense of the security of the Hungarian nation." The Romanian government issues a strong protest against the statement and the majority of Romanian parties follow suit.

March 1992: Problems arise shortly after the election of Romanian nationalist Gheorghe Funar in Cluj. Funar prohibits the use of the Hungarian language on posters in the town, arguing that the constitution stipulates that the country's official language is Romanian and that putting up Hungarian street signs and posters is an infringement of the law. Opponents charge that he is in fact infringing upon Article 54 of the Local Administration Law, according to which decisions by the City Council should not be made public only in Romanian. By mid-1992, only the State Posters Enterprise is allowed to post bills in the town. Soon afterward, Funar bans a Hungarian conference on local government. However, he allows another one to take place under condition that *Vatra* is invited. He protests against the privileges allegedly enjoyed by Hungarians and claims that they have more rights than Romanians. Funar seeks to close Hungarian high schools and refuses to reopen a Hungarian consulate that he describes as an intelligence agency. The DUHR appeals for Funar's removal and protests against the unconstitutional measures taken by the mayor as well as his incitement of violence, which threatens to heighten radicalism among the Hungarian minority.[36]

February-May 1992: In the local elections in Tîrgu Mureş, the DUHR candidate István László Pokorny wins 53 percent of the vote in the first round. The original candidate, István Káli Király is declared ineligible because of his supposed participation in the 1990 Tîrgu Mureş events. In elections to the town council, the DUHR wins 14 out of 24 seats, the PRNU wins 9, and the NSF 1. The electoral commission announces significant election irregularities and Pokorny has to resign. New elections take place in May; the DUHR's new candidate, Victor Nagy, is elected by 56.6 percent of the electorate, indicating that a substantial number of non-Hungarians voted for him. The Democratic Mureş Alliance, initially called the *Vatra Românească* Alliance, stands in the new elections, but the PRNU, the NSF, and other small parties obtain less than 40 percent of the vote.[37]

May 1992: The Democratic Convention comes out in favor of granting Romanian citizenship to residents of Moldova and to ethnic Romanians in Ukraine. Bilateral Hungarian-Romanian talks revolve around the expansion of cultural exchanges and the improvement of border-crossing facilities. No progress is made on an inter-state treaty because of continued disagreement over the question of minority rights. Hungary wants a statement on minority rights to be included in the treaty, while Romania seeks guarantees of the integrity of its current borders. Iliescu pays a two-day visit to Moldova and calls for the consolidation of Moldovan statehood. Snegur emphasizes the tenets of Moldovan independence and the principles of two Romanian states. The Romanian opposition attacks Iliescu for accommodating Chişinău's stance and for failing to promote unification.

June 1992: Mircea Druc, president of the Christian and Democratic Front of the Republic of Moldova, acquires Romanian citizenship. He is nominated by the Ecology Movement of Romania as a candidate in the September 1992 presidential elections. A summit meeting is held in Istanbul concerning the war in Moldova between Chişinău and Russian separatist forces. Iliescu, Snegur, Russia's president Boris Yeltsin, and Ukrainian president Leonid Kravchuk reach an understanding on preserving Moldova's integrity.

September 1992: Andor Horváth, state secretary for education and the only Romanian cabinet official of Hungarian nationality, is dismissed from his post without explanation. In the parliamentary elections, the ruling Democratic National Salvation Front wins 117 out of 341 seats in the Chamber of Deputies and 49 out of 143 Senate seats. Iliescu is reelected president with 61.43 percent of the vote in the run-off with Emil Constantinescu, the opposition candidate. The

Democratic Convention gains 82 seats in the Chamber of Deputies and 34 Senate seats. Nationalist parties increase their representation in parliament to a combined total of 59 seats in the lower house and 25 seats in the Senate. Their agreement with the DNSF gives the Front a governing majority. The DUHR obtains 27 seats in the Chamber of Deputies and 12 in the Senate, while other minorities capture a total of 13 seats in the lower house.

October 1992: The DUHR adopts the Declaration of Cluj following increasingly repressive moves by the nationalist mayor of Cluj. The declaration calls for "communitarian autonomy" for Magyars in Transylvania and is condemned by virtually all Romanian parties and criticized by Hungarian moderates.

January 1993: The DUHR holds its third national congress in Braşov and manages to assuage the demands of radical factions demanding some form of territorial or communitarian autonomy for the Hungarian population in Transylvania. The congress opts for continuing cooperation with Romanian democrats and elects Béla Markó as chairman to replace outgoing Géza Domokos.

February 1993: Iliescu criticizes a plan for establishing a "Carpathian Euro-region," after foreign ministers from Poland, Ukraine, and Hungary sign a declaration of intent for regional cooperation. The plan envisages the cooperation of local governments from three Hungarian provinces, two from Poland, and the Transcarpathian region of Ukraine. Bucharest charges that Hungary is seeking to promote the idea of Transylvanian separateness from the rest of Romania within the Carpathian association.

April 1993: Thousands of ethnic Hungarians demonstrate in several towns in eastern Transylvania protesting the government decision to appoint ethnic Romanian prefects to the counties of Covasna and Harghita, *judeţe* with sizable Szekler (Magyar) majorities. In particular, they protest against the appointment of Vlad Căşuneanu as prefect in Covasna because of his Communist past.

NOTES

1. See the Romanian census figures published in January 1992 and the *White Paper on The Rights of the Persons Belonging to Ethnic, Linguistic or Religious Minorities in Romania*, published by the Ministry of Foreign Affairs of Romania, June 1991. See also Michael Shafir, "Preliminary Results of the 1992 Romanian Census," Radio Free Europe/Radio Liberty (RFE/RL) Research Institute, *Report on Eastern Europe*, vol. 1, no. 30, July 24, 1992; and *Adevarul Economic*, Bucharest, no. 19, June 29–July 5, 1992.

2. For background histories of Romania, consult Andrei Oţetea,, ed., *A Concise History of Romania* (New York: St. Martin's Press, 1985); Michael Shafir, *Romania: Politics, Economics, and Society* (Boulder, CO: Lynne Rienner, 1985); S. Fischer-Galati, *Twentieth-Century Romania* (New York: Columbia University Press, 1970); Gerald Bo-

bango, *The Emergence of the Romanian National State* (Boulder, CO: East European Quarterly, 1979); and Stefan Pascu, *A History of Romania* (New York: Dorset Press, 1982).

3. For more details, see "How Are Protected The Rights and the Identity of Persons Belonging to Minorities in Romania," Embassy of Romania, Washington, DC, and *White Paper on The Rights of Persons*.

4. See the "Law and Local Public Administration," Parliament of Romania, Bucharest, 1992.

5. For an English translation of the Romanian constitution, check Federal Broadcast Information Service, *Daily Report: East Europe, FBIS-EEU–91–246-S*, December 23, 1991.

6. *Népszabadság*, November 21, 1991, in *FBIS-EEU–91–228*, November 26, 1991; Michael Shafir, "Romania's New Institutions: The Draft Constitution," RFE/RL, *Report on Eastern Europe*, vol. 2, no. 38, September 20, 1991; Michael Shafir, "Romania: Constitution Approved in Referendum," RFE/RL, *Research Report*, vol. 1, no. 2, January 10, 1992; Michael Shafir, "Romania: The Rule of Law," RFE/RL, *Research Report*, vol. 1, no. 27, July 3, 1992.

7. Michael Shafir, "Romania's Elections: Why the Democratic Convention Lost," RFE/RL, *Research Report*, vol. 1, no. 43, October 30, 1992.

8. See the interview with Béla Markó, president of DUHR, "Changes in the Administration or a Nationalist Diversionary Game," *22*, Bucharest, April 8–14, 1993, in Federal Broadcast Information Service/Joint Publications Research Service, *Daily Report: East Europe, JPRS-EER–93–047-S*, May 28, 1993.

9. See *Radio Romania Network*, Bucharest, March 30, 1993, and *Pesti Hírlap*, Budapest, March 26, 1993, in *FBIS-EEU–93–060*, March 31, 1993; Michael Shafir, "Minorities Council Raises Questions," RFE/RL, *Research Report*, vol. 2, no. 24, June 11, 1993.

10. For a useful report, see *Destroying Ethnic Identity: The Persecution of Gypsies in Romania* (New York: Helsinki Watch Report, September 1991).

11. Vladimir Socor, "Moldovan-Romanian Relations Are Slow to Develop," RFE/RL, *Research Report*, vol. 1, no. 26, June 26, 1992.

12. For details on the Party of Romanian National Unity, check Dennis Deletant, "The Role of *Vatra Românească* in Transylvania," RFE/RL *Report on Eastern Europe*, vol. 2, no. 5, February 1, 1991; *Budapest Domestic Service*, June 12, 1990, in *FBIS-EEU–90–114*, June 13, 1990; *Rompres*, Bucharest, March 19, 1990, in *FBIS-EEU–90–054*, March 20, 1990; *Rompres*, April 19, 1990, in *FBIS-EEU–90–077*, April 20, 1990; *Rompres*, May 20, 1991, in *FBIS-EEU–91–099*, May 22, 1991; *Country Reports on Human Rights Practices for 1992*, U.S. Department of State, Washington, DC, February 1993.

13. Details on *Vatra Românească* can be found in *Rompres*, Bucharest, March 19, 1990, in *FBIS-EEU–90–054*, March 20, 1990; *Rompres*, May 7, 1990, in *FBIS-EEU–90–090*, May 9, 1990; *Népszabadság*, Budapest, January 31, 1991, in *FBIS-EEU–91–024*, February 5, 1991; *News From Helsinki*, May 1991; Dennis Deletant "The Role of *Vatra Românească* in Transylvania," RFE/RL, *Report on Eastern Europe*, vol. 2, no. 5, February 1, 1991; *Budapest Domestic Service*, February 13, 1991, in *FBIS-EEU–91*-031, February 14, 1991; *22*, Bucharest, February 15, 1991, in *JPRS-EER–91–029*, March 8, 1991; *Beszélő*, Budapest, March 30, 1991, in *FBIS-EEU–91–006*, April 5, 1991; *Rompres*, Bucharest, May 24, 1991, in *FBIS-EEU–91–103*, May 29, 1991; *Rompres*, June 3, 1991, in *FBIS-EEU–91–106*, June 3, 1991, and *FBIS-EEU–91–168*, August 21, 1991; *Kossuth Radio Network*, Budapest, November 26, 1991, in *FBIS-EEU–91–229*, November 27, 1991.

14. Information on *România Mare* is contained in *România Mare*, Bucharest, May 17, 1991, and *Adevarul*, Bucharest, May 17, 1991, both in *FBIS-EEU–91–103*, May 29, 1991; *Kossuth Radio Network*, Budapest, October 15, 1991, in *FBIS-EEU–91–200*, May 16, 1991; *Magyar Hírlap*, Budapest, November 10, 1991.

15. See Michael Shafir, "The Movement for Romania: A Party of 'Radical Return,' " RFE/RL, *Research Report*, vol. 1, no. 29, July 17, 1992.

16. See Cornelius Antim, "After the Rampage of the Orthodox Communist Forces, an Iron Guard-Oriented Party Emerges," *România Libera*, Bucharest, December 1, 1992; *Tineretul Liber*, Bucharest, March 17, 1993, in *FBIS-EEU–93–055*, March 24, 1993; and Michael Shafir, "Growing Political Extremism in Romania," RFE/RL *Research Report*, vol. 2, no. 14, April 2, 1993.

17. For details on the Democratic Union of Hungarians in Romania, see *Magyar Nemzet*, Budapest, January 20, 1990, in *JPRS-EER–90–036*, March 21, 1990; *AFP*, January 5, 1990, in *FBIS-EEU–90–005*, January 8, 1990; *News From Helsinki Watch*, May 1990; *Rompres*, Bucharest, April 28, 1990, in *FBIS-EEU–90–083*, April 30, 1990; *Adevarul*, Bucharest, April 24, 1990, in *FBIS-EEU–90–088*, May 7, 1990; *Rompres*, Bucharest, May 11, 1990, in *FBIS-EEU–90–095*, May 16, 1990; *Budapest Domestic Service*, May 17, 1990, in *FBIS-EEU–90–099*, May 22, 1990; Judith Pataki, "Ethnic Hungarians Contest Romanian Elections," RFE/RL, *Report on Eastern Europe*, vol. 1, no. 22, June 1, 1990; *Rompres*, Bucharest, August 6, 1990, in *FBIS-EEU–90–152*, August 7, 1990; *Adevarul*, Bucharest, November 30, 1990, in *FBIS-EEU–91–005*, January 8, 1991; *Rompres*, Bucharest, May 16, 1991, in *FBIS-EEU–91–052*, March 18, 1991; *Rompres*, May 21, 1991, in *FBIS-EEU–91–099*, May 22, 1991; *Rompres*, May 29, 1991, in *FBIS-EEU–91–104*, May 30, 1991; *Romániai Magyar Szó*, Bucharest, July 10, 1991, in *FBIS-EEU–91–136*, July 16, 1991, and *FBIS-EEU–91–137*, July 17, 1991; *Romániai Magyar Szó*, Bucharest, September 6, 1991, in *FBIS-EEU–91–178*, September 13, 1991; *Romániai Magyar Szó*, Bucharest, October 1, 1991, in *FBIS-EEU–91–193*, October 4, 1991; *Kossuth Radio Network*, Budapest, October 10, 1991, in *FBIS-EEU–91–199*, October 15, 1991; Dan Ionescu, "Romania's First Postcommunist Census," RFE/RL, *Research Report*, vol. 1, no. 11, March 13, 1992; *Rompres*, Bucharest, April 3, 1992, in *FBIS-EEU–92–065*, April 3, 1992; *Curierul National*, Bucharest, April 8, 1992, in *FBIS-EEU–92–072*, April 14, 1992; Michael Shafir, "Transylvania Shadows, Transylvania Lights," in RFE/RL, *Research Report*, vol. 1, no. 26, June 26, 1992; Michael Shafir, "The HDFR Congress: Confrontations Postponed," RFE/RL *Research Report*, vol. 2, no. 9, February 26, 1993.

18. Background on the Union of Hungarian Democratic Youth can be found in *Rompres*, Bucharest, January 26, 1990, in *FBIS-EEU–89–022*, February 1, 1990; Edith Oltay, "The Hungarian Democratic Federation of Romania: Structure, Agenda, Alliances," RFE/RL, *Report on Eastern Europe*, vol. 2, no. 29, July 19, 1991.

19. Information on other Hungarian organizations is taken from *Budapest Domestic Service*, Budapest, February 22, 1990, in *FBIS-EEU–90–038*, February 27, 1990; Oltay, "The Hungarian Democratic Federation of Romania: Structure, Agenda, Alliances"; *Budapest Domestic Service*, May 31, 1990, in *FBIS-EEU–90–107*, June 4, 1990; *Rompres*, Bucharest, August 21, 1990, in *FBIS-EEU–90–163*, August 22, 1990; *Népszabadság*, Budapest, September 25, 1991, in *FBIS-EEU–91–187*, September 26, 1991; *România Libera*, September 28, 1991, in *FBIS-EEU–91–1–93*, October 4, 1991; *Libertatea*, May 28–29, 1991, in *FBIS-EEU–91–114*, June 13, 1991.

20. *Rompres*, Bucharest, March 28, 1990, in *FBIS-EEU–90–064*, April 3, 1990; *Rompres*, Bucharest, June 24, 1990, in *FBIS-EEU–90–122*, June 25, 1990; *Rompres*, Bucharest, October 26, 1990, in *FBIS-EEU–90–209*, October 29, 1990; *Rompres*, January 5, 1991, in *FBIS-EEU–91–004*; *Rompres*, April 22, 1991, in *FBIS-EEU–91–078*, April 23, 1991.

21. *Rompres*, Bucharest, March 14, 1991, in *FBIS-EEU–91–051*, March 15, 1991; *România Libera*, Bucharest, March 12, 1991, in *FBIS-EEU–91–052*, March 18, 1991; RFE/RL, *Daily Report*, no. 73, April 16, 1991; *România Libera*, Bucharest, April 26, 1991, in *FBIS-EEU–91–089*, May 8, 1991.

22. *Rompres*, Bucharest, November 12, 1990, in *FBIS-EEU–90–239*, November 12, 1990.

23. *Adevarul*, Bucharest, July 29, 1990, in *FBIS-EEU–90–151*, August 6, 1990; *MTI*, Budapest, April 23, 1991, in *FBIS-EEU–91–081*, April 26, 1991.

24. Dan Ionescu, "The Gypsies Organize," RFE/RL, *Report on Eastern Europe*, vol. 1, no. 26, June 29, 1990; *Budapest Domestic Service*, July 2, 1990, in *FBIS-EEU–90–128*, July 3, 1990; *Rompres*, Bucharest, July 15, 1990; Mihai Sturdza, "The National Salvation Front and the Workers," RFE/RL, *Report on Eastern Europe*, vol. 2, no. 25, June 21, 1991.

25. *Rompres*, Bucharest, March 12, 1990, in *FBIS-EEU–90–049*, March 13, 1990; *Neuer Weg*, Bucharest, May 16, 1990, in *FBIS-EEU–90–102*, May 25, 1990; *Rompres*, July 30, 1990, in *FBIS-EEU–90–146*, July 30, 1990.

26. *Rompres*, Bucharest, March 12, 1990, in *FBIS-EEU–90–049*, March 13, 1990; *Rompres*, March 17, 1990, in *FBIS-EEU–90–056*, March 22, 1990.

27. *Rompres*, Bucharest, May 17, 1990, in *FBIS-EEU–90–100*, May 23, 1990.

28. *Rompres*, Bucharest, February 22, 1990, in *FBIS-EEU–90–142*, March 2, 1990; and *Europa*, Bucharest, April 27–May 3, 1993, in *FBIS-EEU–93–086*, May 6, 1993.

29. *Rompres*, Bucharest, March 25, 1993, in *FBIS-EEU–93–057*, March 26, 1993.

30. *Rompres*, Bucharest, March 14, 1990, in *FBIS-EEU–90–053*, March 19, 1990.

31. *Rompres*, Bucharest, January 16, 1991, in *FBIS-EEU–90–012*, January 17, 1991.

32. For some details on the mistreatment of Gypsies in Romania, see Helsinki Watch, *Since the Revolution: Human Rights in Romania*, March 1991, New York, pp. 21–23.

33. *Rompres*, Bucharest, May 14, 1991, in *FBIS-EEU–91–094*, May 15, 1991; *AZI*, Bucharest, August 8, 1991, in *FBIS-EEU–91–159*, August 16, 1991.

34. Dan Ionescu, "Transylvania and Romanian-Polish Relations," RFE/RL, *Report on Eastern Europe*, vol. 2, no. 41, October 11, 1991.

35. For Hungarian responses to the allegations, see the statement by the Parliamentary Group of the DUHR issued on October 14, 1991, published in *Romániai Magyar Szó*, Bucharest, October 17, 1991, in *FBIS-EEU–91–204*, October 22, 1991; and interview with parliamentary deputies of the DUHR by Tibor Bogdan, "Hungarians in Romania on the Parliament Report—Every Part of It Is False," *Magyar Hírlap*, October 19, 1991, in *FBIS-EEU–91–205*, October 22, 1991; see also *Rompres*, Bucharest, October 24, 1991, in *FBIS-EEU–91–208*, October 28, 1991; *Romániai Magyar Szó*, Bucharest, November 10, 1991, in *FBIS-EEU–91–219*, November 13, 1991; "Weekly Record of Events," RFE/RL, *Report on Eastern Europe*, December 13, 1991.

36. *Új Magyarország*, Budapest, June 11, 1992, in *FBIS-EEU–92–121*, June 23, 1992; Tom Gallagher, "Ultranationalists Take Charge of Transylvania's Capital," RFE/RL, *Research Report*, vol. 1, no. 13, March 27, 1992.

37. Shafir, "Transylvanian Shadows, Transylvanian Lights."

8

Bulgaria

POPULATION

On the basis of the preliminary results of the 1992 census, the total population of Bulgaria reached 8,472,724. However, the statistics remained incomplete, as some internationally recognized minority groups such as Macedonians and Pomaks were either not distinguished, only partially recorded, or simply included in the category of "others."[1] Bulgaria's largest minority were ethnic Turks, who numbered 822,253, or nearly 10 percent of the population according to official statistics, and over a million according to unofficial Turkish estimates. They were concentrated in fairly compact communities in northeastern and southeastern Bulgaria, and in some towns they formed a relative majority of the population. Census figures disclosed the presence of 1,078,000 (12.72 percent) Muslims in Bulgaria, including Turks, Slav Muslims (Pomaks), and a large percentage of Gypsies, and 7,373,000 (87.02 percent) Christians. An estimated 350,000 Macedonians resided in Bulgaria, although they were not officially recognized as a separate ethnos. Some believed that a total of 1 million Bulgarian citizens could claim ancestors from the Macedonian region, although only a few thousand maintained some form of Macedonian identity. While most of the population was concentrated in the Pirin region of western Bulgaria, smaller communities reportedly flourished in the cities of Plovdiv, Burgas, Varna, Ruse, Dimitrov, and Kyustendil. The formerly derogatory term Pomak referred to Slav Bulgarians who were Muslim. Unofficially estimated at closer to 150,000, the Pomaks dwelt in tight-knit communities in the Rhodope Mountains in southwestern and southern Bulgaria.

The largest under-recorded minority were the Gypsy (Romani) population, which numbered in the region of 250,000 to 400,000; some unofficial estimates exceeded 1 million. Precise figures have proved difficult to assemble, partly because no census data on ethnic groups were published in Bulgaria after the mid-1970s, and partly because many Roma preferred to hide their ethnic identity for fear of discrimination. The Roma were divided between Muslims and Chris-

Bulgaria: Population (1992)

Ethnic Groups	Number	% of Population
Bulgarians (and Macedonians)	7,206,062	85.05
Turks	822,253	9.70
Roma (Gypsies)	287,732	3.40
Pomaks (Bulgarian Muslims)	65,546	0.77
Others	91,131	1.08
Total Minorities	1,266,662	14.95
Total Population	8,472,724	100.00

tians, with further sub-groups based on region, occupation, language, dialect, and residential longevity. The Vlachs, speakers of a language derived from Romanian, were traditionally a pastoral people living in scattered communities in several Balkan mountain ranges. Small Vlach settlements were found in Bulgaria, in the Stara Planina range, in the Struma Valley, and in the Dobrudzha region. In 1985, the Vlach population was unofficially reported at near 400,000, but experts believed this number was greatly inflated. There was a general lack of detailed information on the Vlachs; a similar situation prevailed with the small number of Sarakatsani or Karakachani, Greek-speaking pastoral people sharing many cultural traits with the Vlachs, surviving in a handful of communities in the Balkan and Rhodope Mountains. Among the smaller minorities not officially recognized as separate national groups, there were several thousand Gagauzi, or Turkic-speaking Orthodox Christians resident on the Black Sea coast, Lipovans, who speak a language akin to Russian, as well as small communities of Armenians, Russians, Greeks, Tatars, and Jews.

HISTORICAL OVERVIEW

Bulgaria achieved independence from Ottoman Turkish rule in 1878, although its territories were curtailed by subsequent peace conferences.[2] Border readjustments dictated by the major European powers and reversion to a semi-autonomous Ottoman principality created bitter resentments in Bulgaria. The country finally proclaimed its full independence from Turkey in 1908 after several popular uprisings. Bulgaria's territorial losses contributed to fueling two Balkan wars in 1912–13. In the first war, the new Balkan states combined their forces to drive the Turkish armies out of the region. In the second war, Bulgaria was unsuccessful in its military campaign against Serbia and Greece and once again lost territories in Macedonia and Thrace to its two neighbors. The result left a lasting sense of injustice in Sofia with regard to Bulgaria's rightful frontiers. During World War One, Bulgaria allied itself with Germany and Austria, but with the defeat of the Central Powers it was again forced to accept a harsh peace treaty and lost all access to the Aegean Sea.

In the inter-war period, approximately 86 percent of the country's population of 6 million were registered as ethnic Bulgarians. The largest minority were Muslim Turks who had settled in the country during 500 years of Ottoman occupation. In 1934, Turks formed about 10 percent of the population, or about 618,000 people. The size of the Turkish minority remained fairly constant despite a regular outflow of emigrants to Turkey. An equally large minority were the Pomaks, ethnic Bulgarians who had converted to Islam over the centuries but retained their Slavic Bulgarian culture and language. An estimated half-million Pomaks were concentrated in the Rhodope Mountains in southern Bulgaria and remained an important religious, although not a distinct ethnic minority according to Bulgarian authorities. The remaining minorities in inter-war Bulgaria were small and apart from the Gypsies (Roma) did not exceed 1 percent of the population. At the time, they included about 30,000 Jews, 23,000 Armenians, 16,000 Romanians, 11,000 Russians, 9,000 Greeks, 4,000 Germans, 4,000 Tatars, and small communities of Serbs, Czechs, and Slovaks. In 1934, 80,000 Gypsies were recorded, although the number was considered to be greatly under-estimated. Several other populations were absent or under-represented in the Bulgarian census; these included the Vlachs or Arumunians, claimed as co-ethnics by Romanians, Bulgarians, and Greeks.

The Macedonian region and its Slavic population presented an intractable problem for neighboring states who claimed the inhabitants as their fellow countrymen and not as a separate ethnic group. Macedonia itself achieved a very brief period of independence before it was partitioned among Serbia, Greece, and Bulgaria. After World War One, the Macedonian population itself was divided as to its ethnic identity although the most vocal political forces tended to consider themselves a subdivision of the Bulgarian nation and campaigned for the liberation of territories under Serb-Yugoslav and Greek control. However, some activists favored a separate Macedonian state that would incorporate the three traditional regions: Vardar (in Yugoslavia), Pirin (in Bulgaria), and Aegean Macedonia (in Greece). Macedonians were not registered as a distinct nationality in the inter-war Bulgarian censuses, even though many Macedonians were active in Bulgaria's political life. Their total numbers were therefore difficult to estimate.

While the inter-war Bulgarian regime was reasonably tolerant toward its minorities, it also pressed for territorial revisions with all of its neighbors. During World War Two, Sofia capitalized on the German occupation of Yugoslavia and Greece to forge an alliance with Berlin and regain parts of Macedonia and Thrace. Bulgaria's Jewish population survived largely intact during the war. Although the government deported Jews into German hands from the occupied areas of Macedonia and Thrace and placed onerous restrictions on its own Jewish population, it resisted Nazi pressures to ship this vulnerable minority to German death camps. The majority of the 48,000 Jews who survived in Bulgaria at the close of the war emigrated to Palestine and later to Israel, and by 1956 only about 5,000 remained in the country.

Bulgaria's territorial advances were again reversed at the close of World War Two. The Communist regime, under Soviet supervision, adopted a more conciliatory policy toward its Balkan neighbors, while at home it placed the customary Stalinist restrictions on the cultural and political autonomy of the minority populations. Although the majority of Bulgarians considered the Macedonians as ethnic compatriots, during the late 1940s the Communist regime accepted the existence of a distinct Macedonian republic in Yugoslavia and accorded its own Macedonians national minority status. At that time both Sofia and Belgrade appeared well disposed toward the creation of some kind of Balkan Communist federation, in which Macedonia would figure as one component political entity. In the 1956 census, nearly 188,000 Macedonians were registered, comprising 2.5 percent of the Bulgarian population. However, as tensions increased between Belgrade and Sofia after Tito's break with Stalin, the Bulgarian government stepped to the forefront of the anti-Yugoslav campaign and revived its claims to Yugoslav Macedonia while eliminating the separate ethnic status of its own Macedonian population. Henceforth, Bulgarian patriotism was strenuously propagated and Macedonia was described merely as a geographic region. Residents in Pirin were required to declare their nationality as Bulgarian. While some citizens complained that they had been forced to identify themselves as Macedonian during the 1940s and 1950s, others claimed they were coerced after 1964 into accepting new internal passports with a Bulgarian designation. Since the early 1960s, the identity of Macedonians continued to plague relations between the two Communist capitals, with both charging the other with unacceptable territorial pretensions.

Under the Communist regime, Sofia renounced its claims to Greek Macedonia and Turkish and Greek Thrace. But the large Turkish minority in Bulgaria, estimated at around 10 percent of the population, remained a serious bone of contention between Sofia and Ankara. Soon after the Communist takeover, collective privileges in education and cultural life were abolished and about 150,000 Turks were pressured to emigrate; these were primarily the least assimilable and most devout Muslims. Although Bulgarian Turks did not campaign for political or territorial autonomy, periodic campaigns were mounted by the authorities to eradicate their distinct ethnic and religious identity. Similar assaults were launched against the Pomak Muslims and the Muslim Gypsies, with activists claiming that these were ethnic Bulgarians who had converted to Islam due to pressure and persecution by the Ottoman administration.

The most intensive anti-Turkish campaign was launched in the mid-1980s. It was officially justified as a means for enlarging the Bulgarian population, which was allegedly threatened by an excessive Turkish demographic growth. The authorities forced Turks to Bulgarize their names and abandon their Islamic rituals and cultural traditions. The campaign provoked riots and clashes with police, and several dozen people were shot dead. About 350,000 Turks left the country; after the democratic changes in Bulgaria in 1989, between 120,000 and 180,000 subsequently returned from Turkey. Sofia's human rights violations were terminated, and most Turkish minority rights have since been restored. Turks were allowed to regain their original names, to restore their religious practices, and to establish their own political, social, and cultural organizations legally. The democratic changes also hastened a Turkish and Islamic revival in the country; moreover, the hostility of some ultra-nationalist Bulgarian groups has helped to buttress Turkish solidarity. The position of the Turkish community has remained the barometer of relations between Sofia and Ankara. Turkish activists were closely watchful for the impact of Bulgarian ultra-nationalist groups that have campaigned to limit the educational and linguistic rights gained by ethnic Turks. Some Bulgarian spokesmen also remained concerned about the potential growth of Turkish nationalism and of autonomist and separatist trends among minority organizations. Disagreement also continued to fester over the precise size of the Turkish community. According to official Bulgarian statistics, about 800,000 Turks lived in the country, while Turkish sources commonly doubled this figure.

In the early stages of democratization, some former Communists capitalized on widespread anti-Turkish feelings in order to gain public support. Party officials in provincial cities were fearful of losing their jobs and property, seized during the Turkish exodus, and of being held responsible for the anti-Turkish campaign. They helped to organize anti-Turkish demonstrations around the country and fanned ethnic tensions. Former Communists, in league with newly formed hyper-nationalist organizations, accused Turkish activists of seeking autonomy, secession, and annexation by Ankara, followed by the dispossession and expulsion of Bulgarian Christians. Such charges played on fears of demographic decline and economic turmoil among ordinary Bulgarians but seemed to bear little resemblance to reality.

The Macedonian question has also made an increasing imprint on Bulgarian politics, especially since the collapse of the Yugoslav federation. Bulgaria was one of the few countries to recognize Macedonia immediately when the republic declared its sovereignty and independence in early 1992. However, the Bulgarian authorities did not recognize the existence of a separate Macedonian nation and refused to countenance the recognition of a Macedonian ethnic minority within Bulgaria. Nationalist pro-Macedonian groupings have become more active in Bulgaria, calling for closer social, economic, and political links with the republic, which they hoped would culminate in re-absorption by Bulgaria. At the same time, some pro-independence Macedonian organizations became active in western Bulgaria, amid suspicions that they were funded by Belgrade and by some militant groups in Skopje, the capital of the Macedonian republic, to sow discord within Bulgaria and press for the separation of the Pirin region from the Bulgarian state.

OFFICIAL POLICIES

For the last fifty years, inconsistency has been the only constant in Bulgaria's minority policies. Although Communist ideology theoretically condemned ethnic conflicts as capitalist or nationalist deviations from the class struggle, in reality Bulgaria's Communist leaders dictated phases of extreme ethnic strife by either permitting, prohibiting, or revoking official minority status to key ethnic groups. Bulgaria's Socialist constitution of 1971 did not specifically acknowledge the existence of national minorities, even though the 1947 constitution did employ this term. Members of minorities were simply referred to as citizens of "non-Bulgarian origin," and they were no longer listed in the national census.

Ethnic Turks in particular were periodically subject to the most intensive assimilationist pressures. Under the rule of Todor Zhivkov, official anti-Turkish sentiments gave rise to a number of government-sponsored campaigns culminating in major persecution during the mid-1980s. It included the forcible changing of family names, limitations on language use, and restrictions on religious and cultural freedoms, pressuring hundreds of thousands of Turks to flee to Turkey. After Zhivkov's ouster in November 1989, officials made strenuous efforts to improve the country's minority policies and to repair much of the damage suffered by ethnic Turks. In December 1989, the ruling Socialists renounced forcible assimilation, allowing Muslims the freedom to choose their own names, practice Islam, observe traditional customs, and speak their native language on a daily basis. In January 1990, the National Assembly created a 30-member commission to research nationality issues; the commission recommended the adoption of a special statute for minority rights.

After the government's policy reversal, thousands of ethnic Turks returned to Bulgaria and faced new problems of adjustment. Most had lost their jobs, sold their houses and belongings for far less than their true value, and now demanded appropriate reparations. The government offered up to nine months of aid for these people, and legal measures were initiated to help retrieve their lost property. Ahmed Doğan, a political leader of the Bulgarian Turks, demanded a single legal resolution that would restore property to victims of the exodus, specifying that any compensatory payments should be of equal value to the goods or houses lost by emigrants. Turkish deputies in parliament eventually introduced a law that was adopted by the National Assembly in July 1992. It stipulated that all Turks be given back their property by the beginning of April 1993, particularly houses and apartments, for the low price at which they were originally sold. Those who proved unable to buy back their former homes would then be given low interest-rate credits toward the purchase of alternative housing. Bulgarians who legally and in good faith bought homes from the Turks during the exodus years would receive fair compensation from the government.[3]

The issue of the rights of minorities to use their mother tongue on a daily basis, to have regular access to the mass media, and to be educated in their native language continued to generate controversy in Bulgaria. According to Article 3 of the new 1991 constitution, Bulgarian was to be the sole official language in the republic. Under the Zhivkov regime, ethnic Turks were forbidden to use their mother tongue officially and children were even conditioned to inform the authorities if their parents did not speak Bulgarian at home. The legacy of language discrimination persisted and was evident in a variety of forms: shopkeepers reportedly still feared selling *Prava i Svobodi*, a magazine with a weekly Turkish-language edition, despite the lifting of any legal or distributive restrictions, while parliament hesitated in implementing Turkish-language programs in secondary schools for fear of ultra-nationalist reactions.[4]

In January 1991, a political consultative council that included the Bulgarian vice president, the prime minister, and the deputy chairman of the Council of Ministers met to discuss whether the teaching of Turkish as part of the public secondary-school curriculum was constitutional. It concluded that it was but failed to designate a schedule to implement an official program. Thus, in early February 1991 thousands of ethnic Turkish children in southeastern Bulgaria went on strike, demanding that Turkish be included in their second-term secondary-school classes. The Bulgarian parliament responded by promising to implement a state-controlled optional Turkish program in all public schools where there was significant Turkish enrollment. Programs were scheduled to commence in March 1991. The Bulgarian nationalist opposition claimed that these programs were unconstitutional. However, parliament issued assurances that they would not jeopardize the "unity of the Bulgarian nation"; they would be monitored by state agencies using "scientific studies" to determine the length and frequency of classes.[5]

The National Assembly decided in March 1991 to include Turkish in secondary schools on an optional basis, beginning with the 1991 fall semester. Prime Minister Dimitur Popov appealed to both Turkish and Slav Bulgarian parents to end their protests and to send their children back to school. Nevertheless, tensions persisted, and the government reversed its decision in October 1991, ruling that minority languages would not be allowed in state schools even on an optional basis. Turkish leaders in parliament were outraged and protests flared in several parts of the country. Consequently, another government ruling was passed in November 1991. Turkish was again permitted outside of regular school hours, for up to two hours per week. Nationalist forces reacted by staging various protest actions. Ethnic Turks in turn demanded that Turkish become part of the official obligatory curriculum for Turkish children. At the end of November, Sofia declared that secondary schools from grades 3 to 8 could teach up to four hours of Turkish per week, again on an optional basis. This latest decree became effective in January 1992. Article 36 of the Bulgarian constitution stated that: "1. The study and use of the Bulgarian language shall be a right and an obligation of every Bulgarian citizen. 2. Citizens whose mother tongue is not Bulgarian shall have the right to study and use their own language alongside the compulsory study of the Bulgarian language. 3. The situations in which only the official language shall be used shall be established by law."[6]

Along with housing and language battles, ethnic Turks have faced other obstacles in upholding their traditions. During Zhivkov's assimilation campaign,

Turkish names were subjected to a process of "Bulgarization." Typically, a Slavic suffix was added to a Muslim name, or an entirely new name could be chosen from a list of acceptable Bulgarian names and a new birth certificate was issued. Even the names of dead Muslims were changed and their gravestones painted over with Bulgarian versions. In March 1990, the country's major political forces agreed to pass a Bulgarian Citizens' Names Law that made the restoration of names possible for all victims of forcible assimilation. New birth certificates were issued, and the process of changing names was simplified from a judiciary process to a straightforward administrative measure. Nevertheless, for those Muslims who did not act before December 31, 1990, a more complicated procedure had to be endured, accompanied by the payment of an appropriate fee.[7]

Article 44 of the new Bulgarian constitution contended that: "No organization shall act to the detriment of the country's sovereignty and national integrity, or the unity of the nation, nor shall it incite racial, national, ethnic, or religious enmity, or encroach on the rights and freedoms of citizens; no organization shall establish clandestine or paramilitary structures or shall seek to attain its aims through violence." Article 11 asserted the prohibition of all political parties based on "ethnic, racial, or religious lines" and organizations "which seek the violent usurpation of power." While these articles avowedly served to protect the Bulgarian state, they were frequently cited in efforts by nationalists to undermine the rights of minorities. Nationalist organizations capitalized on Bulgarian fears of Turkish subversion and applied pressure on government organs to outlaw ethnically based associations on the grounds that they were politically motivated and therefore "anti-state."

The main Turkish organization, the Movement for Rights and Freedoms (MRF) was singled out in this regard. In August 1991, the Sofia City Court decided that a political party formed by the MRF was unconstitutional as it was ethnically based, and could not participate in upcoming elections. The MRF, however, claimed that it was not founded on an entirely ethnic basis and that it harbored no separatist or autonomist ambitions. Nevertheless, in September 1991, the Supreme Court banned the Rights and Freedoms Party (the political wing of the MRF) from participation in upcoming general elections on the grounds that it propounded an exclusivist ethnic and religious platform.[8] Nonetheless, the MRF itself and various Turkish cultural and social organizations were not prohibited from functioning, and the MRF legally competed in the second general elections in October 1991, gaining 24 parliamentary seats, with 7.55 percent of the popular vote, making it the third-strongest party in Bulgaria. The oppositionist coalition, Union of Democratic Forces (UDF), received 34.36 percent of the vote, with 110 of the 240 parliamentary mandates, and the ruling Bulgarian Socialist Party (BSP) 33.14 percent, with 106 seats.

During the summer of 1989, at the height of the Turkish exodus from Bulgaria to Turkey, the bulk of the Pomak population opposed Bulgarian efforts at forcible integration and some sought to emigrate. The authorities proved reluctant to allow these Slavs to leave the country and denied passports to persons residing in predominantly Pomak regions. These policies resulted in several substantial Pomak protests. Pomak regions have continued to suffer from steep economic decline in recent years with the closure of local industries; observers feared that material hardships could intensify social and political tensions in the Pomak regions. Indeed, Bulgarian officials have warned that unemployment and economic deprivations in regions of southern Bulgaria with ethnically and religiously mixed groups were alarmingly high, and minorities, including Pomaks, were increasingly complaining over discrimination in employment. Since 1989, many Pomaks adopted a Turkish identity or demanded Turkish-language education, viewing it as advantageous to associate with a stronger and more influential minority. There were also reports that some Pomaks were seeking to strengthen a distinct ethno-religious identity, neither Turkish nor Bulgarian, but may have been hampered by their political disunity and disorganization.

In some respects, Macedonian groups have incurred even more onerous treatment than both Turks and Pomaks. The Bulgarian government, together with a broad spectrum of Bulgarian political parties, refused to accept Macedonians as a legitimate minority, defining them as Slavic Bulgarians with the same language and a common history. For example, according to the Bulgarian Committee for Balkan Understanding and Cooperation, a Macedonian minority did not exist in the Pirin region of western Macedonia, and its residents have "repeatedly and unequivocally confirmed Bulgarian ethnic identity and Bulgarian national awareness."[9] Despite these inauspicious circumstances, an openly Macedonian organization styled as *Ilinden* was established and applied for official registration. In July 1990, the Blagoevgrad District Court denied them the right to legal recognition as a non-profit corporate body. The judges who refused to grant *Ilinden* legal status did so in accordance with the former Article 52 (current version, Article 44) of the constitution, which protected the "unity of the nation." Fifteen *Ilinden* supporters responded with a hunger strike. Authorities rounded them up, bussed them outside the city, and warned them of harsher consequences should such actions be repeated. The stubborn protesters, however, returned to their site in front of the courthouse. Later on, *Ilinden* representatives appealed the Blagoevgrad decision to Bulgaria's Supreme Court, which upheld the original verdict. In November 1990, the court concluded that *Ilinden* violated the unity of the Bulgarian nation. *Ilinden*'s statutes, which promoted the recognition of a sovereign Macedonian minority and the political development of Macedonia, evidently served as evidence that the organization intended to achieve "a united Macedonian state." *Ilinden* was ordered to disband, but it persisted in a covert fashion, claiming that the decisions of the Bulgarian courts were "in violation of international law and international standards."[10]

The position of the sizable Romani population has continued to preoccupy human rights observers in Bulgaria. Much of the persistent discrimination in housing, education, and job opportunities and the high mortality rates and health problems have been inherited from the Communist years. However, observers noted that the government had failed to address fully the plight of Roma by passing appropriate anti-discrimination legislation or ensuring equal treatment with ethnic Bulgarians at the hands of employers, educators, media directors, and local government officials. Unlike the Turks, whose leaders have seen the gravest threat coming from forcible assimilation, many Romani spokesmen have been particularly concerned about the segregation and marginalization of the Gypsy population. Many have opposed separate schooling for Romani children, a policy that has in effect resulted in inferior education and insufficient exposure to the Bulgarian language and stymied career advancement. Other Romani leaders supported a revival of Gypsy culture, education, and ethnic identity, fearing gradual assimilation by either the Bulgarian or the Turkish communities. In addition, the Law on Political Parties, adopted by parliament in April 1990, which prohibited the registration of political parties established on ethnic or religious criteria, worked to the detriment of Gypsy self-organization. Even though the Roma clearly did not represent a threat to Bulgaria's "territorial integrity" and the "unity of the nation," or "incite national, ethnic, and religious hostilities," under Article 3 of the law they were barred from forming electoral associations.[11]

While Bulgaria seemed to be addressing some of its most pervasive ethnic problems at an official level, observers noted that there remained much room for improvement. Prime Minister Dimitur Popov clarified Bulgaria's policy goals in December 1990 when he stated that "without exception all citizens, regardless of ethnicity, will be granted equal rights politically, economically, and legally." He claimed that Bulgarian policy on fair treatment was guided by the Human Rights Charter and the principles of the Bulgarian constitution: "Ethnic groups must be responsible, equally with Bulgarians, in overcoming the heat of ethnic dispute (not just the Turkish minority but Gypsies as well)." Perhaps inventive forums, such as the November 1991 roundtable discussions that were scheduled to ease ethnic conflicts through the participation of the country's main political and ethnic groups, would help bring Bulgaria closer to reducing its latent domestic tensions. In addition, international human rights organizations will undoubtedly contribute toward influencing the Bulgarian government to develop more coherent legislation that will balance genuine concerns over national security and state division with full respect for minority rights and ethnic aspirations.

BULGARIAN NATIONALISTS

Committee for the Defense of National Interests (CDNI)
Komitet za Zashtita na Natsionalnite Interesi (KZNI)

The Committee for the Defense of National Interests has been the most influential Bulgarian nationalist group since the onset of democratization. It served as an umbrella organization for several nationalist political parties. In November

1990, it claimed some 40,000 members nationwide. Under the chairmanship of Dimitŭr Arnaudov, a member of parliament, the main goals of the Committee were to protect the "territorial integrity" and "ethnic space" of Bulgaria by including all patriotic Bulgarians, regardless of their political or religious orientation. To achieve this objective, the Committee attacked the agendas of any organization that it felt threatened the integrity of the Bulgarian state. Its principal target was the Movement for Rights and Freedoms, the largest organization representing ethnic Turkish interests. The Committee challenged the legitimacy and participation of the MRF in the political system, claiming that the group harbored separatist intentions. When the MRF was allowed to participate legally for the first time in the June 1990 National Assembly elections, outraged CDNI supporters attempted to embarrass lawmakers who backed the MRF's right by publicly circulating a list of their names. The Committee also pressured the Bulgarian Ministry of Internal Affairs to publish statistics on crimes committed by members of various pro-Turkish groupings in order to promote public hostility toward minority activists.

The CDNI did not limit itself to rhetoric and publishing. In April 1990, members of the Committee rallied in the town of Haskovo, protesting against the sympathy allegedly shown by the Council of Ministers toward ethnic Turkish Bulgarians returning home from Turkey to reclaim their names and property. In July 1990, the organization planned several strikes in the city of Kŭrdzhali, in a region of southern Bulgaria where Turks formed over 70 percent of the population and where the CDNI claimed to have a strong base. It protested against the seats gained by the MRF to the National Assembly as well as against the introduction of schooling in Turkish. In early October 1991, a series of violent outbreaks occurred between nationalists and Turkish activists in Razgrad in northeastern Bulgaria, incited by the controversial issue of Turkish-language lessons in Bulgarian schools.

Bulgarian nationalist forces tried to benefit from difficult economic conditions and continuing political uncertainty in the country. In November 1990, as the Socialist government faced massive social unrest and mounting political opposition, nationalist groups in the Razgrad area, inhabited by large numbers of Turks, declared an "independent Bulgarian republic." They refused to recognize Sofia's authority in the region because the government had purportedly displayed too much leniency toward the Turks. Protests were staged against the restoration of Turkish family names, and nationalist leaders called for acts of civil disobedience to counter alleged Turkish radicalism. The CDNI and other groups opposed giving Turks the status of a national minority because this would have supposedly threatened Bulgaria's state integrity. In late November, the Razgrad Republic was renamed the Association of Free Bulgarian Cities, linking several towns containing large Turkish minorities. A civil parliament was to be formed to counterbalance the National Assembly, which the CDNI accused of favoring the Turkish minority and betraying Bulgaria's national interests. In recognition of mounting tensions fueled by the nationalist initiative, Bulgaria's president, Zhelyu Zhelev, appeared on national television to appeal for calm. Following his intervention, the free-cities campaign subsided.

The absence of a clear-cut official language policy left the question of teaching Turkish as an optional course in elementary schools open to various interpretations by nationalists as well as by ethnic Turks. Committee members held the view that Bulgarian, as the country's official language, should be the only language course offered to Bulgarian citizens. Many ethnic Turks felt that Turkish should become part of the Bulgarian school curriculum so that the children's mother tongue would continue to be used by future generations. When the National Assembly prepared to vote on the issue in February 1991, tensions soared, and the CDNI, in conjunction with other nationalist groups, formed a Bulgarian National Union (BNU) and organized protests in a dozen cities. They declared that Slav Bulgarian parents should keep their children away from school until Turkish was taken off the curriculum. The BNU specifically opposed the introduction of optional classes in Turkish to schools attended by large numbers of Muslims: this was depicted as the Turkification of Bulgarian education. The wave of protests subsided when the National Assembly voted to postpone the introduction of Turkish as an optional subject during the 1991 school year. The move was condemned by Turkish leaders as unconstitutional. The beginning of the school year in September 1991 was marred by boycotts in some Turkish areas, in protest against government failures to meet demands for Turkish-language instruction proposed by minority organizations. In October 1991, the National Assembly passed laws prohibiting the teaching of minority languages in state schools. This essentially anti-Turkish legislation was proposed by nationalist deputies and drew overwhelming support from the Socialist parliamentary majority. However, in November 1991, the new Bulgarian government decreed that ethnic-minority pupils in municipal schools could receive instruction in their native languages as an optional subject for a few hours a week.

Despite their evidently anti-Turkish agenda, the leaders of the Committee insisted that their frustrations with the MRF and other Turkish groups were based principally on legal stipulations. Arnaudov suggested that they did not "struggle against people who simply declare themselves to be Turks." Mincho Minchev, a parliamentary deputy and another leading figure in the organization, summarized its creed in the following words: "We are for the rights of the individual, but not for the rights of communities. We oppose any separation of a community on an ethnic basis. Anyone who does not like this should seek another country." In January 1990, the CDNI leadership announced a list of demands to prevent the spread of Turkification. The first issue of concern was the creation and implementation of an official minorities policy. The Committee suggested that any new program should be subject to public scrutiny and approval prior to its implementation. They called for a freeze on the procedure until appropriate public involvement could be arranged. The second issue concerned

Bulgarian names: they advocated a law that would enforce a unified national system of names in order to "preserve tradition" and Bulgaria's state identity. Suspicions persisted that the CDNI and other radical national associations were created, supported, and financed by local Socialist (Communist) activists whose leaders were implicated in assaults on Turkish spokesmen during the Zhivkov era. An indication of these close ties was the forging of a pre-election alliance in October 1991 between the Socialist Party and five nationalist groupings. Meanwhile, the UDF was accused of entering an "unholy alliance" with the MRF, which was allegedly financed by irredentist circles in Turkey.

CDNI delegates met in February 1992 and voted to dissolve the group as a "public supra-party political organization." They criticized the "unconstructive political approaches" of the Committee's leadership, which avowedly failed to "consolidate the interests" of Bulgarian citizens. Ultimately, these delegates transferred their allegiance and created a new party, the National Democracy Party (NDP). A more moderate agenda was adopted, focusing mostly on national and social issues. Dimitŭr Arnaudov, who also served as deputy chairman of the Fatherland Party of Labor, was appointed to chair the NDP.[12]

Fatherland Party of Labor (FPL)
Otechestvena Partiya na Truda (OPT)

Also known as the Patriotic Labor Party, the FPL served as the political wing of the CDNI. Rumen Popov was the FPL's chairman, while Dimitŭr Arnaudov, a parliamentary representative, became deputy chairman. Numbering approximately 5,600 by April 1991, the party's membership was composed mostly of middle-income shop owners, artisans, and farmers and, according to Turkish sources, sectors of the local Communist *nomenklatura*. FPL ideologists claimed that Bulgaria only contained one ethnic group and that the "so-called" Turks were in reality forcibly converted Bulgarians who were now being misled by radicals promoting pan-Turkic objectives. In this scenario, Bulgaria stood on the front line against Muslim penetration into Europe. The FPL purportedly emerged due to pressure from ordinary Bulgarian citizens who were outraged when the Turkish MRF was permitted to participate in the June 1990 parliamentary elections. Arnaudov argued that the party's complaints regarding MRF participation stemmed from a legal rather than an ethnic dispute, because the Bulgarian constitution explicitly prohibited political parties from organizing along ethnic, racial, or religious lines. The FPL leadership rejected a host of Turkish-oriented initiatives and accused ethnic Turks of intentionally flooding the Bulgarian cities of Kŭrdzhali, Haskovo, and Varna in order to register as residents and thereby vote in strategic blocks to boost MRF support in the local elections. According to FPL statistics, the massive influx of Turks into Kŭrdzhali had forced fifteen Slav Bulgarian families per month to relocate away from Turkish-populated areas.

The FPL held its first congress in Sofia in April 1991. Chairman Popov delivered a speech celebrating the party's first anniversary. He defined the role of the FPL as the "party of rebirth, development, and the defense of national virtues, ideals, and values" and characterized its membership as "free and economically independent." Popov announced that the party was not ashamed to be anti-Turkish and anti-Islamic. In fact, he claimed that he wished to "participate with all of Europe against Islam." Although the FPL and other ultra-nationalist groupings obtained less than 1.5 percent of the vote in the October 1991 general elections, they claimed to possess an extensive infrastructure and to benefit from substantial local sympathy in mixed-population areas. Although they were not a potent political force, with Socialist support they could create spots of tension and target parliamentary deputies to pay heed to their demands. During 1993, the FPL claimed to be building a "left-of-center alliance" in preparation for future elections; the coalition would evidently be open to all left-wing and patriotic Bulgarian parties. FPL leaders persistently warned that Turkey was intent on annexing parts of Bulgaria and was using the MRF as a vehicle in this long-range endeavor. The party claimed that while the MRF leadership appeared to be moderate, it contained ultra-nationalist elements with a secret agenda of radical proportions to dismember Bulgarian territory.[13]

Bulgarian National Radical Party (BNRP)
Bŭlgarska Natsionalna Radikalna Partiya (BNRP)

These nationalists, led by Chairman Ivan Georgiev, have also focused their political attacks on the Turkish MRF. So disturbed was the BNRP at the National Assembly's acceptance of the 23 victorious MRF representatives in June 1990, that it threatened to surround the parliament building on the day the new democratically elected parliament was scheduled to convene and to force away any "individuals with a foreign national self-awareness" who attempted to cross their human chain. Georgiev protested the participation of ethnic Turks in the National Assembly in a provocatively violent statement in June 1990. The National Radicals also strongly protested against the teaching of Turkish as part of a standard curriculum in secondary schools with large numbers of Turkish students. They claimed joint responsibility with other nationalist groups for protests against the Turkish-language issue in the predominantly Turkish city of Kŭrdzhali. The BNRP appealed to Slav Bulgarian parents to keep their children at home until the language issue was resolved to their liking. Party leaders claimed a membership of approximately 38,000 and asserted that the BNRP was a member of the European Nationalist Union since August 1991. It received moral and material support from this multi-national organization that struggled to "protect Christian values against the offensive of Islam in Europe." Georgiev has also spoken out for Bulgarian unification with Macedonia on the basis of a public referendum.[14]

Bulgarian Socialist Party (BSP)
Bŭlgarska Sotsialisticheska Partiya (BSP)

The BSP became the party of Communist reformers who renamed the former Bulgarian Communist Party in 1990. While its Socialist doctrine theoretically discouraged nationalism, the BSP tended subtly to condone it. Like the more outspoken nationalist groups, the BSP evidently felt threatened by Turkish participation in the Bulgarian National Assembly. BSP leaders asserted that ethnically oriented political parties stood in violation of the Bulgarian Constitution and formed a barrier in the transition to democracy. Elements of the BSP, particularly at the local level, were accused of helping to establish ultra-nationalist parties in order to tap potential anti-minority sentiments, to undercut the position of democratic forces, and to maintain *nomenklatura* privileges. The BSP was also accused of creating a special task force that deliberately staged acts of violence against Slav Bulgarians and then blamed them on ethnic Turks. BSP officials allegedly calculated that such simulated attacks would undermine the MRF's popularity prior to the elections. Most of the reported "victims" of these attacks were Bulgarian women. The Bulgarian newspaper *Demokratsiya* called this scheme a "mass psychosis" campaign and alleged that the BSP's prime motive was to procure an extra 5 percent to 10 percent of the popular vote in the fall 1991 parliamentary elections. The BSP has been more flexible than the right-wing nationalist groups regarding the issue of teaching Turkish in secondary schools. They believed that a language program should exist under state control and should be available to native Turkish-speaking children. The Socialists stood in an electoral alliance with five nationalist groups for the October 1991 national ballot and obtained 106 seats in the 240-seat National Assembly, capturing 33.14 percent of the popular vote, thereby losing nearly 14 percent of its electoral support since the June 1990 ballot. Since the elections, the BSP has focused most of its attention on socioeconomic issues and criticized the fast pace of market reform. Nonetheless, it was not averse to capitalizing on nationalist and anti-Turkish sentiments when it sensed that it would stand to benefit politically.[15]

TURKISH MOVEMENTS

Movement for Rights and Freedoms (MRF)
Dvizhenie za Prava i Svobodi (DPS)

Ahmed Doğan, a former Turkish activist during the Communist years, has chaired the MRF since its inception. Prior to this position, Doğan spent time in prison for organizing resistance to Zhivkov's anti-Turkish "rebirth" campaign of 1984–89. He was arrested in June 1986 and sentenced to ten years in prison for violating Bulgarian laws forbidding "anti-state" activities. The Zhivkov government considered Doğan politically dangerous, and he served nine months in solitary confinement. He subsequently stood trial, was found guilty, and was moved between prisons every few months. Despite his constant relocation, Doğan still managed to protest against the government's assimilationist measures by organizing strikes and sit-ins from his prison cell. His followers included fellow ethnic Turks, as well as members of other minority groups. Doğan was released under an amnesty following Zhivkov's ouster in November 1989. While in prison, Doğan formulated an agenda to serve the interests of Bulgarian Turks. His demands included freedom to use one's original name, freedom of language and religion, an amnesty for political prisoners, and the right to emigrate to Turkey. He later transferred this agenda to the MRF platform and broadened it by incorporating new goals such as the promotion of tolerance in all nationality issues; the opening of membership to all ethnic groups; the overcoming of economic problems among minorities; the creation of a moderating role for the MRF between the Bulgarian Socialist party and the Union of Democratic Forces (UDF), the party that won Bulgaria's first multi-party elections in June 1990; and above all, the struggle to overcome anti-Turkish sentiments prevailing in Bulgaria, a deep-rooted legacy of 500 years of Ottoman rule.

The MRF was established in January 1990 and promptly legalized. Prior to this, some members of the group, including Doğan, operated illegally under the name of the National Turkish Liberation Movement and staged anti-state protests before Zhivkov's ouster. The MRF initiated and organized campaigns for educational, religious, and linguistic rights and pressed for the political representation of all minority groups. By early 1991, the MRF claimed a membership of some 120,000, together with more than 1 million sympathizers. This made the MRF the fourth-largest political organization in the country. The movement won 23 seats in the Bulgarian parliament during the general elections of June 1990 and finished third in the ballot. However, it could not contest the elections as a distinct political organization representing only the Turkish community. The Socialist regime had arrived at an agreement with the UDF that parties organized along ethnic or religious lines would not be registered. To avoid accusations of being an exclusively Turkish party, the MRF decided to open the organization to all ethnic, religious, and cultural groups while openly renouncing any autonomist or separatist ambitions. Even so, over 90 percent of the MRF's membership remained Turkish.

The MRF also tried to appeal to the Bulgarian Muslim (Pomak) population. Opinion polls conducted in August 1990 showed that the majority of Pomaks (51 percent) were not politically active. About one-third were members of a national political organization, and of that number, approximately 20 percent were affiliated with the MRF. Three-quarters of the Pomaks polled approved the program and actions of the MRF, and only a tiny percentage disapproved. In general, Pomak approval ratings of the MRF were lower than similar ratings among ethnic Turks, even though Doğan remained a highly popular figure.[16] Nationalist

Bulgarians accused the MRF of launching a Turkification drive among the Pomaks by pressing them to declare themselves as Turks and campaigning for Islamic unity under the MRF umbrella. Movement leaders denied any ulterior motives in seeking to forge a multi-ethnic political movement, particularly as Pomaks had been unable to form an effective political organization to represent their interests. A parliamentary commission report issued in May 1993 accused local Turkish leaders of having pressured Pomaks to renounced their "Bulgarianness." It called on parliament to prosecute local authorities guilty of such practices, to declare invalid all statistics on ethnicity compiled in Pomak regions, and to cancel the opening of Turkish-language schools in these areas.

In August 1991, the MRF announced that it was establishing a separate political party, the Rights and Freedoms Party (RFP), to stand in the upcoming national elections. But the Sofia City Court refused to register the organization on the grounds that according to the Bulgarian constitution, parties could not be formed on the basis of ethnicity or religious conviction as this would threaten the "unity of the nation." However, the MRF was allowed to register by the Central Election Commission as a multi-ethnic movement despite the protests of Bulgarian nationalists. In the October 1991 general and local elections, the MRF gained 24 parliamentary seats, over 1,000 local councilors, 650 village mayors, and 20 district mayors. Its position in the Bulgarian parliament generated serious consternation among nationalist groups and even among more moderate forces fearful of growing Turkish influence and the possibility that the MRF could hold the balance of power in a parliament almost evenly divided between Socialists and Democrats. Concerns remained that the MRF's ability to operate as a political movement would be challenged again before the next general elections, under Article 11 of the constitution, which prohibited the formation of political parties along ethnic, religious, or racial lines.

The MRF has been one of the most highly structured ethnic-based organizations in Bulgaria. Spanning the country and targeting areas of Turkish density, the MRF possessed nearly 900 branches and 22 regional offices run by urban and rural local committees. A central administrative bureau, consisting of an executive committee and several regional coordinators, managed the organization's daily affairs. At the top of the hierarchy stood a central council that gathered every two months. Despite the influence of the Central Council, a national congress of MRF representatives held the principal authority. Every group of 500 MRF members was served by one representative, who participated in a congress that convened at least once every three years. MRF leaders denied that they were seeking either territorial autonomy or political self-determination for the Turkish community. Instead, they were pressing for an end to job discrimination against Turks, for greater cultural autonomy in education and language use, and for full political representation in the existing administrative structures. Doğan attributed currently poor relations between Muslim Turks and Christian Bulgarians not to a fundamental inability to co-exist, but rather to interference by the central authorities and to manipulation and provocation by ultra-nationalist forces. The position and treatment of the Turkish minority will continue to be one of the main barometers of relations between Sofia and Ankara; any deterioration or curtailment of Turkish political, religious, and cultural rights could seriously jeopardize relations between the Turkish and Bulgarian governments that have significantly improved since the fall of Communism.[17]

Turkish Democratic Party (TDP)
Turska Demokraticheska Partiya (TDP)

Leaders of this small Turkish political group, formed after the democratic turnaround, have accused Ahmed Doğan of appeasing former Communists with an overly compromising political platform. They have even labeled Doğan and the MRF an "assimilationist grouping." The main goals of the TDP were the achievement of "national self-determination" and "self-preservation" among the Turkish minority in Bulgaria. Doğan in turn has viewed the TDP as an essentially extremist clique, unrepresentative of the Turkish community and probably working in the service of Communist and nationalist forces intent on provoking ruptures between Turks and Bulgarians.[18]

MACEDONIAN GROUPINGS

Ilinden United Macedonian Organization (UMO)
Obedinena Makedonska Organizatsiya Ilinden (OMOI)

Founded in November 1989 by its national president Stoyan Georgiev and Pirin region president Yordan Kostadinov Ivanov, the *Ilinden* organization sought to foster the official recognition of a Macedonian minority in Bulgaria, the right to use the Macedonian language, and facilities to promote Macedonian culture. The name *Ilinden* held historical significance for both Macedonians and Bulgarians. On August 2, 1903, St. Elijah's Day, or *Ilinden*, an uprising against the Ottoman Empire was mounted by Macedonian rebels styled as the Internal Macedonian Revolutionary Organization (IMRO). They fought courageously against the larger and better-equipped Ottoman forces but were forced to retreat after several months and to postpone their vision of an independent Macedonia. IMRO persisted after World War One, with frequently violent tactics, to campaign for a united Macedonia. It was divided between a pro-Bulgarian orientation, seeking to re-create a Greater Bulgaria, and an autonomist wing that supported the creation of a large Macedonian state, incorporating the three traditional regions of Vardar, Pirin, and Aegean Macedonia.

According to its initiators, *Ilinden* UMO was founded in the town of Sandanski, in the Pirin region of Bulgaria. *Ilinden* was joined at its inception by the Independent Democratic Macedonian Front of Blagoevgrad (IDMFB). Several cultural and educational societies also became affiliated with *Ilinden*, among them groups named after Macedonian heroes Yane Sandanski, Nikola Vaptsarov, and Gotse Delchev. *Ilinden* has claimed at least 42 different regional cells or branches and estimated its membership at some 16,000. The UMO defined its purpose in the first three articles of its statutes. Article 1 explained that the organization wished to "unite every Macedonian and citizen of the republic of Bulgaria on a fraternal cultural basis," Article 2 demanded "the recognition of the Macedonian minority," while Article 3 claimed that *Ilinden* members would "fight to secure the right to present alternative opinions on problems in sociopolitical developments in Macedonia." *Ilinden* has been unsuccessful in implementing its statutes, and its fate was a prime example of Bulgarian reluctance to recognize the Macedonian minority. Dozens of other organizations have been legally approved since November 1989, because they represented the "official" minorities (Turks, Jews, Armenians, Roma), but not those whom the government defined as Slavic Bulgarians.

In July 1990, the Bulgarian press announced the date of an *Ilinden* congress scheduled to convene the following month. The press announcement triggered a warning from the Prosecutor's office in Blagoevgrad. The UMO was threatened with criminal prosecution on the grounds that its meeting would be deemed "anti-Bulgarian, separatist, and unconstitutional." While UMO Chairman Atanas Kiryakov did not officially acknowledge the warning, *Ilinden* appeared to comply with the law and canceled the congress. Krasimir Iliev, the UMO secretary and a Macedonian from Bulgaria who has been incarcerated for his illegal affiliation, relayed *Ilinden*'s goals in an interview in November 1990: "Our organization fights for the recognition of the national and civil rights of Macedonians in Pirin Macedonia." He advocated the affirmation of Macedonian culture and claimed not to have any territorial pretensions toward neighboring Balkan states. The UMO objective was primarily to unite all Macedonians in the cultural field and to organize symposiums, meetings, and discussion forums "at which documents and archival materials would be presented on the identity of the Macedonian nation."

To further its impact, *Ilinden* has held semi-clandestine meetings, disseminated leaflets, and gathered signatures for the formal recognition of a Macedonian minority. Secretary Iliev has blamed the structure of the Bulgarian economy for the generally low living standard shared by most Macedonians. He believed that the Bulgarian government intentionally avoided building industrial plants in the Pirin region so that Macedonians would be economically forced to relocate and assimilate. Other sources claimed that the Bulgarian authorities purposely built health spas and vacation resorts in the Pirin area so as to make any potential alliance between the Macedonian population and the Yugoslav Macedonian republic less attractive. According to its critics, the UMO benefited from more substantial support in the southern parts of the Pirin region and especially among younger people.

Ilinden members rallied in Sofia in March 1990 demanding "cultural and national autonomy" for Macedonians. Chanting slogans such as "We Are Macedonians and Nothing Else" and "United Macedonia: A Guarantee for Peace," they petitioned the National Assembly to recognize the existence and rights of a Macedonian minority. Hundreds of nationalist counter-demonstrators expressed strong opposition to such recognition. In April 1990, *Ilinden* organized a rally in Sandanski commemorating the seventy-fifth anniversary of the death of the revolutionary hero Yane Sandanski. Participants called for the promotion of freedom, peace, democracy, and unity among Balkan peoples. Several speeches openly endorsed "Macedonism" and criticized government policies toward the Macedonian issue. In April 1991, *Ilinden* issued sixteen demands to the Bulgarian government, including the restoration of the Macedonian language and culture in all educational institutions in the Pirin region, full access to the mass media, and the replacement of a Macedonian bishop in the Pirin area independent of the Bulgarian Orthodox Church but united with the Macedonian Autocephalous Church in the Republic of Macedonia. It also demanded the withdrawal of "Bulgarian occupation troops" from Pirin and full cultural, economic, and political self-determination for the region.

Throughout 1992 and 1993, *Ilinden* was prohibited from holding public meetings, although a Macedonian cultural group was legally recognized in June 1992 and allowed to operate freely. The UMO established its own Society for the Defense of Human Rights to promote its Macedonian agenda. *Ilinden* has been accused by both government spokesmen and nationalist Bulgarian organizations for being a front organization sponsored and funded by Serb Yugoslav authorities in Belgrade seeking to separate Pirin Macedonia in order to undermine the Bulgarian state and to counter Bulgarian claims to the former Yugoslav Macedonia. Other critics have claimed that *Ilinden* was an essentially pan-Macedonianist irredentist organization supported by the nationalist IMRO-DPMNU in Skopje and unwittingly playing into Serbian hands by seeking to enlarge the Macedonian republic at Bulgaria's expense.[19]

Internal Macedonian Revolutionary Organization—Independent (IMRO-I)
Vŭtreshna Makedonska Revolyutsionna Organizatsiya—Nezavisim (VMRO-N)

This Macedonian organization was founded in Sofia in November 1989 and claimed a membership of some 600 people. According to its president, Georgi Solunski, the organization had similar objectives as the UMO, and they have jointly organized campaigns for the official recognition of the Macedonian minority in Bulgaria. IMRO-I was also denied registration by Bulgarian courts as the authorities claimed they formed a separatist movement. The IMRO-I platform called for the "unification of all Macedonians living in Bulgaria on a cultural basis" and demanded the rights of citizens to "self-definition" as a distinct ethnic group. Organizers denied that the organization was terrorist, separatist, or chauvinistic, received support from outside the country, or violated

Bulgaria's territorial integrity. IMRO-I and the UMO have held joint meetings to coordinate their strategy but complained that they were harassed by the authorities and prevented from gathering signatures throughout the Pirin region for a petition in support of their aims. The group's leaders have sought closer ties with Macedonian compatriots in neighboring states; in the long term, they envisaged full "Macedonian autonomy" in both the cultural and the political sphere.[20]

Internal Macedonian Revolutionary Organization— Union of Macedonian Societies (IMRO-UMS)
Vŭtreshna Makedonska Revolyutsionna Organizatsiya—
Obedinenie na Makedonskite Druzhestva (VMRO-OMD)

Initially called the Union of Macedonian Cultural and Educational Societies (UMES), organizers changed its name to IMRO-UMS at the first national congress in December 1990. Pan-Bulgarian in nature, IMRO-UMS has opposed *Ilinden*, the IMRO-I, and similar Macedonian "separatist" organizations, claiming that they were "unconstitutional." The Union's first chairman was historian Dimitur Gotsev, a native of Vardar Macedonia. Gotsev believed that the Yugoslav authorities have endeavored to invent a "Macedonian self-identity" for Bulgarian residents in the former Yugoslavia through a system of "brain-washing, terror, and repression" that could undermine Bulgaria's territorial integrity. Instead, IMRO-UMS advocated the unification of all Macedonian lands within a larger Bulgarian state. Critics charged that IMPO-UMS and other pan-Bulgarian groupings were impregnated with former Communist functionaries who were deliberately manipulating the Macedonian issue in order to appear more patriotic than the UDF and other democratic forces. In March 1993, Stoyan Boyadzhiev was elected the new chairman. He insisted that the majority of members were not affiliated with other parties, although IMRO-UMS encompassed sympathizers of both the Socialists and the UDF. Boyadzhiev also underscored that his organization strongly supported the recognition of Macedonia under whatever name chosen by the population, with a view toward eventual unification with Bulgaria. The Union has not denied its links with the nationalist IMRO organizations in Skopje, particularly with leaders advocating closer links with Bulgaria.[21]

Macedonian Youth Society (MYS)
Makedonsko Mladezhko Druzhestvo (MMD)

A former affiliate of the Union of Macedonian Cultural and Educational Societies, the Youth Society was actually founded in April 1986 in the town of Gotse Delchev. The Society promoted the "spiritual unification" of all Bulgarian people. In order to fulfill its goals, the group was forced to address the Macedonian question, stating it was "convinced that two nations—a Bulgarian and a Macedonian—could not possibly exist considering their common language, common culture, and common history." The Society therefore denounced any versions of Macedonian history that ran contrary to its unitarist conceptions. In particular, it protested the interpretations propounded by *Ilinden* and by Macedonian politicians in the Republic of Macedonia.[22]

All-Bulgarian Union (ABU)
Obshto-Bŭlgarski Sŭyuz (OBS)

This nationalist organization was established in early 1990 to campaign for Bulgarian "cultural integrity." Its leaders pledged to lead a legal struggle against "pan-Serbian chauvinism" and "Macedonianism" and against Serbian attempts to assimilate the "Bulgarians" in Vardar Macedonia. The ABU contested the right of *Ilinden* to register as a legal political organization, concluding that it was too small to represent "Macedonian" interests and was aiming to detach the Pirin region from Bulgaria and place it under Serb domination. The Union emphasized the national unity and single identity of the Bulgarian and Macedonian peoples and their historic struggle for fraternity. The ABU has promoted the expansion of Bulgarian social, cultural, and economic links with the sovereign Macedonian Republic, with a view to drawing this state closer to Bulgaria and culminating in eventual absorption. ABU leaders have also asserted that they would defend the interests of "Macedonian Bulgarians" in Thrace (Greece) and northern Dobrudja (Romania). A small Society of Bulgarian Macedonians (SOBM) expelled from Aegean Macedonia was also operating in Bulgaria and cooperated with the ABU. The Association was believed to have developed close links with the nationalist IMRO organizations in Macedonia as well as with the Society of Bulgarians (SOB) in Skopje that has campaigned for the rebirth of Macedonia's "Bulgarian heritage."[23]

Fifth of October Society (FOS)
Obshtestvo Peti Oktomvri (OPO)

Chaired by Ivan Obetsanov and composed of representatives from various political organizations, the Fifth of October Society promoted a "non-distorted view" of Bulgarian and Macedonian history, emphasizing the community of the two groups in their liberation from Ottoman rule. The Society was formed in Bansko in May 1990, by the same group that founded the All-Bulgarian Union. October 5 represented the date Bansko had been freed from Ottoman occupation. Together with the ABU, the FOS appealed to the Bulgarian public to condemn the *Ilinden* organization and denounce its claims about the existence of a "Macedonian minority" in Bulgaria. It contended that *Ilinden* was responsible for the dangerous "rift in national consciousness" within the Bulgarian state.[24]

MINORITY ORGANIZATIONS

United Roma Organization (URO)
Obedinena Organizatsiya Roma (OOR)

Under the leadership of Chairman Manush Romanov, the Roma Democratic Union (RDU) was founded in Sofia in November 1989 and changed its name to the United Roma Organization (URO) in October 1992. It claimed to serve as a non-party union of all Bulgarian Gypsies and by early 1991 declared a membership of some 50,000. Delegates at the founding conference in March 1990 discussed the political, economic, social, and cultural disadvantages that Roma have historically endured. Their grievances included the forcible changing of Muslim Gypsy names under the Zhivkov regime and other forms of pressured assimilation, the absence of Romani-interest newspapers, the closure of Romani clubs, laws forbidding the use of the Romani language, and the disappearance of Gypsy customs. URO goals have included solving the severe housing and educational problems of Romani communities and the pursuit of political and social advancement for Gypsies to counter large-scale unemployment and a rising crime rate. The Union was denied registration as a political party for the June 1990 general elections because of its ethnic basis, but it could function as a social and cultural organization and was permitted to publish its own newspaper. Manush Romanov was elected to parliament in the first multi-party elections in June 1990 as a representative of the UDF. He became an energetic campaigner for social and economic improvements among the Romani population. Gypsy leaders, such as Romanov, complained that the UDF has avoided supporting Romani causes for fear that this could estrange a sizable number of Bulgarian voters. Christian Roma have also been wary of backing the Turkish-based MRF in case this hastened the Turkification of Gypsy communities. But despite its ambitions, the URO has suffered from a persistent lack of political cohesion among Romani leaders, even though it has not explicitly challenged the official prohibition on declaring itself a political party.[25]

Confederation of Roma in Bulgaria (CRB)
Konfederatsiya na Roma v Bŭlgariya (KRB)

This newest Romani pressure group was formed in Sofia in May 1993. Its mandate was reportedly non-political, but it intended to act as a pressure group to improve the social status and living conditions of Bulgarian Roma. The CRB has urged the government to prepare a development scheme for the Gypsy community, to formulate a special education plan, with optional teaching of Romani in schools, and to open a Romani cultural center.[26]

Movement for the Cultural, Educational, and Social Development of Gypsies (MCESDG)
Dvizhenie za Kulturno, Obrazovatelno i
Sotsialno Razvitie na Tsiganite (DKOSRTs)

This group of representatives of the Bulgarian Roma held its international conference in October 1990 in the town of Sliven. Their discussions focused on the difficulties encountered in changing prevailing popular attitudes toward Gypsies. They claimed that their "material, moral, and cultural backwardness" interfered with their ability to elevate their minority's image. MCESDG appealed to all Bulgarian Gypsies to improve themselves by taking more initiative and relying less on the state. Along with the call for amelioration, other pertinent issues covered included housing problems, literacy, theft, and gambling. Leaders of the movement suggested programs to eliminate Gypsy ghettos, to improve living standards and personal hygiene, and to promote community awareness and the promulgation of Romani literature, music, and the fine arts.[27]

Independent Democratic Socialist Association of Gypsies in Bulgaria (IDSAGB)
Nezavisima Demokraticheska Sotsialisticheska
Asotsiatsiya na Tsiganite v Bŭlgariya (NDSATsB)

The Romani population has probably been the most unorganized minority in Bulgaria, with about 80 percent having no affiliation with any ethnic, cultural, or political grouping. One of the first Gypsy organizations established during the collapse of Communist rule was the IDSAGB. This anti-nationalist and anti-separatist group, believed to include members of the former *nomenklatura* seeking to maintain their privileges, has sought full assimilation for Bulgarian Gypsies. It announced its agenda at a political rally in Sliven in January 1991; its main platform was "to define and improve the social and cultural standards for Gypsies in Bulgaria."[28]

Romani Christian Democratic Party (RCDP)
Roma Khristiyan Demokraticheska Partiya (RKhDP)

Founded in Popovo in December 1992, this controversial Romani organization has claimed to be an alternative to the Turkish-oriented Movement for Rights and Freedoms. The MRF had in fact invited other ethnic minorities to participate under its umbrella, and a Romani faction, mostly consisting of Muslims, subsequently developed under its auspices. Romanov, the leader of the Roma Democratic Union, dismissed the RCDP as "unserious," and other Gypsy clan leaders equally disapproved of the organization, claiming that it was created to provoke conflict among already established Romani organizations. In fact, several clan leaders stated that they would boycott and ostracize this organization. Several other, smaller Romani-based organizations have also been formed in Bulgaria, including the Indi-Roma Association.[29]

Peace
Shalom

The Jewish population in Bulgaria numbered between 3,000 and 5,000 and has been one of the few minorities, together with Armenians, that benefited from official recognition. Founded in Sofia in March 1990 as a renewed version of the former Communist-sponsored Social, Cultural, and Educational Association of Bulgarian Jews (SCEABJ), *Shalom* was a non-partisan organization that fostered the social, economic, and cultural development of the Jewish community. A branch of *B'nai B'rith*, the international Jewish society, was also reestablished in Bulgaria in March 1992, more than 50 years after it was banned in 1941. The rebuilding of the society was linked to Prime Minister Filip Dimitrov's visit to Israel. Members of *B'nai B'rith* asserted that they were devoted Bulgarian patriots, dedicated to solving their country's economic and ethnic problems.[30]

Party for Democratic Prosperity (PDP)
Partiya za Demokraticheski Vazkhod (PDV)

This ethnic Albanian political party became operative in the Pirin Macedonian region and supported Albanian political and cultural rights. The PDP was reportedly linked to its namesake in neighboring Macedonia. The Macedonian *Ilinden* organization has vociferously expressed its disapproval of the Albanian party, claiming it was unlawfully formed on an ethnic basis. Albanians numbered approximately 5,000 and were left stranded in Bulgaria after the Albanian government parted with the Soviet bloc in the 1960s. Evidence indicated that the Albanians were also subjected to a name-changing campaign under the Communist regime, but few details were readily available.[31] Bulgaria's other minorities, including Armenians, Gagauz, and Vlachs, have also established independent social, cultural, and quasi-political organizations since 1989.

CHRONOLOGY

November 1989: Todor Zhivkov is ousted and replaced by a reformist Communist leader, Petŭr Mladenov, who promises to reverse the existing ethnic assimilation policy "slowly and cautiously." The *Ilinden* United Macedonian Organization is founded.

December 1989: Petŭr Mladenov, Bulgaria's new president, promises that the government will carefully research the minority problem and prescribe appropriate solutions. Mladenov allows Bulgarian Turks to use their original Muslim names and language. The decision provokes two weeks of nationalist protests across the country.

January 1990: Local Communist authorities in the Bulgarian town of Kŭrdzhali defy government orders to restore full civil rights to Turkish minorities, indirectly jeopardizing official efforts to reassure the Muslim population. The rights in question include religious freedom and the use of Muslim names. Mladenov vows to end the Communist monopoly of power and holds talks with opposition groups. Mladenov calls for free, multi-party elections and initiates talks on forming a coalition government. Prime Minister Georgi Atanasov is shouted down by a crowd of 5,000 nationalists at the National Assembly Building as he tells them: "Bulgaria cannot become a democracy without guaranteeing equal rights to its national minorities." The National Assembly creates a 30-member task force to research nationality issues and make recommendations to the government. The Assembly also adopts an 11-point declaration clarifying minority rights. These include assertions that all citizens will be equal before the law, regardless of ethnicity, religion, or gender, that religion and names will be subject to free choice, and that Bulgarian is the official state language, although any language may be spoken in private conversation.

March 1990: The National Assembly unanimously passes a law allowing Turks to choose their names freely, but an elaborate judiciary process is established, requiring two witnesses, and the judge may deny the proposed change. After January 1, 1991, a fee is supposed to be charged for the service. *Ilinden* members rally in Sofia, demanding the recognition of Macedonian ethnicity. Bulgarian nationalists protest *Ilinden*'s actions.

April 1990: *Ilinden* rallies in Sandanski in the Pirin region to commemorate a local hero and to criticize Bulgarian policy toward Macedonian issues.

June 1990: Parliamentary elections are held. To the dismay of nationalists, the Turkish-based MRF is allowed to participate and secures 23 seats in the National Assembly. The Chairman of the Bulgarian National Radical party is outraged at the MRF's election success and issues a threatening statement calling for violent protests.

July 1990: The Blagoevgrad District Court in the Pirin region denies the *Ilinden* organization the right to legal recognition as a nonprofit body, thus maintaining the denial of minority status to Macedonians.

January 1991: A government political consultative council meets to discuss the legality of including the Turkish language in official secondary-school curricula.

They deem Turkish instruction legal but fail to specify a date by which to incorporate the classes into the current system.

February 1991: Thousands of Turkish children in the densely Turkish areas of southeast Bulgaria boycott schools to protest the lack of action to include Turkish language classes as part of their curricula.

March 1991: The National Assembly decides to include optional Turkish courses in secondary schools, starting in September 1991. In Sofia, the MRF is included in the call by the Union of Democratic Forces for mass anti-Communist demonstrations. This event signals the first significant inclusion of the MRF in large-scale political opposition.

April 1991: The Fatherland Party of Labor holds its first congress in Sofia. Chairman Rumen Popov defines the role of the party and confirms its anti-Turkish sentiments, claiming that Bulgarian patriots want "to participate with all of Europe against Islam."

July 1991: The new Bulgarian constitution is formally adopted.

August 1991: The election law is passed, prohibiting political parties from being formed on the basis of ethnic, religious, or racial criteria. The Sofia City Court decides that an MRF-based Turkish party cannot legally be registered as a political party because it violates the constitution.

September 1991: The Bulgarian Supreme Court upholds the Sofia City Court's decision of the previous month, ruling it unconstitutional for the Rights and Freedoms Party to register as a political party for the October 1991 elections, as it has a "religious and ethnic" platform. The MRF responds by threatening to boycott the elections and to persuade the CSCE not to recognize their legitimacy. The CSCE human rights conference in Moscow denounces Bulgaria for not permitting ethnically based parties to operate. It calls Bulgaria's policy "an infringement of the democratic rights" of ethnic Turks. The statement is backed by most EC members as well as Romania. Bulgaria's Supreme Court decides to allow the registration of the MRF in the October elections.

October 1991: The National Assembly passes a law prohibiting the teaching of minority languages in Bulgarian schools. Nationalist legislators put forward the proposal that receives overwhelming support from Socialist and nationalist deputies. Incidents of pre-election violence between nationalists and MRF members occur in Razgrad in northeastern Bulgaria. National Assembly elections and local elections are held on October 13. The UDF receives 35.5 percent of the vote, the BSP 32.91 percent, the MRF 7 percent, and the Bulgarian Agrarian

National Union (BANU)—United 3.83 percent. This election brings the issue of ethnic Turkish rights to the forefront of Bulgarian politics. The first Turkish mayor is elected in Kŭrdzhali.

November 1991: Turkish language lessons are again permitted outside regular school classes for two hours per week. Nationalists react by staging various protest actions. The government decrees that secondary-school grades 3 to 8 may study their native language as an optional subject in schools for four hours per week.

December 1991: Roundtable discussions on ethnic conflict are held. Representatives from ten parties that obtained over 1 percent of the votes in the National Assembly elections participate. After the first three speeches, the MRF abandons the roundtable, and the discussions are to be rescheduled for a later date.

January 1992: Presidential elections are held and Zhelyu Zhelev is reelected as head of state for a five-year term.

February 1992: Nationalists in Kŭrdzhali, which has a heavy ethnic Turkish population, call a protest boycott against the teaching of Turkish in schools. It is scheduled to last for a week. Schools remain open, but 17 percent of students do not attend. Delegates of the nationalist Committee for the Defense of National Interests meet and vote to dissolve the group. They adopt a more moderate agenda, calling their new organization the National Democracy Party.

March 1992: The Council of Europe plans to admit Bulgaria and sends an observation team to study the country's ethnic situation. The team is critical of the constitutional ban on parties based on religion and ethnicity. Bulgaria yields to the Council of Europe's opinion and offers to revise state policy toward the MRF and the national question.

July 1992: The National Assembly adopts an MRF-sponsored law stipulating that all Turks obtain the property they sold before their exodus between 1984 and 1989. Prices are to be comparable to the original sales price, while those unable to repurchase former homes may receive government-sponsored, low-interest credit rates.

October 1992: One of the largest Romani parties, the Roma Democratic Union, changes its name to the United Roma Organization in an attempt to unify the numerous Gypsy organizations and campaign more effectively for Romani rights.

June 1993: Representatives from several Romani organizations meet at a conference in Stara Zagora to discuss the problems of Bulgarian Gypsies. The meeting is attended by the vice president of the World Romani Union, who announces that the Union will shortly open up a Balkan Romani office in Sofia.

NOTES

1. Official population estimates on the basis of the 1992 census are from the National Statistical Institute, Sofia, released by *BTA*, Sofia, May 4, 1993, and *Vek 21*, Sofia, April 14, 1993, in Federal Broadcast Information Service/Joint Publications Research Service, *Daily Report: East Europe, JPRS-EER–93–049-S*, June 3, 1993.

2. For useful histories of Bulgaria, see R.J. Crampton, *A Short History of Modern Bulgaria* (Cambridge: Cambridge University Press, 1987); J.F. Brown, *Bulgaria Under Communist Rule* (New York: Praeger, 1970); Robert McIntyre, *Bulgaria: Politics, Economics and Society* (London: Pinter, 1988); John Bell, *The Bulgarian Communist Party from Blagoev to Zhivkov* (Stanford, CA: Hoover Institution Press, 1986); and Bilâl N. Şimşir, *The Turks of Bulgaria (1878–1985)* (London: Rustem & Brothers, 1988).

3. Stephen Ashley, "Migration from Bulgaria," Radio Free Europe/Radio Liberty Research Institute (RFE/RL), *Report on Eastern Europe*, December 1, 1989; Stephen Ashley, "Ethnic Unrest During January," RFE/RL, *Report on Eastern Europe*, vol. 1, no. 6, February 9, 1990; Kjell Engelbrekt, "The Movement for Rights and Freedoms," RFE/RL, *Report on Eastern Europe*, vol. 2, no. 22, May 31, 1991.

4. Goran Ahren, "Helsinki Committee on Turkish Bulgarians: Continued Political Oppression," *Dagens Nyheter*, Stockholm, December 24, 1989, in *JPRS-EER–90–009*, January 24, 1990; *Günaydin*, Istanbul, February 14, 1991, in Federal Broadcast Information Service, *Daily Report: East Europe, FBIS-EEU–91–036*, February 22, 1991.

5. Mitko Krumov, "New Deputies Yuriy Borisov and Vasil Kostov Replace Dobri Dzhurov and Georgi Velichkov Who Resigned," *Duma*, Sofia, January 10, 1991, in *FBIS-EEU–91–013*, January 18, 1991; *BTA* Sofia, February 5, 1991, in *FBIS-EEU–91–025*, February 6, 1991; *BTA*, Sofia, February 14, 1991, in *FBIS-EEU–91–032*, February 15, 1991; *BTA*, Sofia, February 15, 1991, in *FBIS-EEU–91–033*, February 19, 1991. For a discussion of the major strikes in Kŭrdzhali, see *BTA*, Sofia, February 26, 1991, in *FBIS-EEU–91–038*, February 26, 1991.

6. Dulinko Dulev, "The Banner Is Waving Again," *Vecherni Novini*, Sofia, March 22, 1991, in *FBIS-EEU–91–060*, March 28, 1991; *BTA*, Sofia, October 1, 1991, in *FBIS-EEU–91–191*, October 2, 1991; Kjell Engelbrekt, "Nationalism Reviving," RFE/RL, *Report on Eastern Europe*, vol. 2, no. 48, November 29, 1991; "Declaration of the Central Council of the Movement for Rights and Freedoms," *Prava i Svobodi*, Sofia, November 29, 1991, in *FBIS-EEU–91–235*, December 6, 1991.

7. *BTA*, Sofia, March 5, 1990, in *FBIS-EEU–90–044*, March 6, 1990; *BTA*, Sofia, March 12, 1990, in *FBIS-EEU–90–049*, March 13, 1990. For a discussion of cultural assimilation and the Name Change Law, see "Minority Problems Persist: Elections Set for June," in *News from Helsinki Watch*, News From Bulgaria, March 1990. For further discussion of assimilation and the New Law on Names, see "Deep Tensions Continue in Turkish Provinces, Despite Some Human Rights Improvements," in *News from Helsinki Watch*, News from Bulgaria, August 1990.

8. "Second Yilmaz Letter Is Unprecedented and Greatly Alarms Nationwide Committee of Defense of National Interests," *Duma*, Sofia, August 30, 1991, in *FBIS-EEU–91–172*, September 5, 1991; Kjell Engelbrekt, "The Movement for Rights and Freedoms to Compete in Elections," RFE/RL, *Report on Eastern Europe*, vol. 2, no. 91, October 4, 1991.

9. *BTA*, Sofia, March 2, 1990, in *FBIS-EEU–90–057*, March 23, 1990.

10. *BTA*, Sofia, March 2, 1990, in *FBIS-EEU–90–057*, March 23, 1990; *BTA*, Sofia, May 14, 1990, in *FBIS-EEU–90–094*, May 15, 1990; *BTA*, Sofia, May 14, 1990, in *FBIS-EEU–90–095*, May 16, 1990; *BTA*, Sofia, May 12, 1990, in *FBIS-EEU–90–095*, May 16, 1990; Duncan M. Perry, "The Macedonian Question Revitalized," RFE/RL,

Report on Eastern Europe, vol. 1, no. 24, August 24, 1990; Evgeni Gavrilov, *Duma*, Sofia, November 14, 1990, in *FBIS-EEU–90–223*, November 19, 1990; *BTA*, Sofia, September 23, 1991, in *FBIS-EEU–91–185*, September 24, 1991; *Khorizont Radio Network*, Sofia, October 15, 1991, in *FBIS-EEU–91–200*, October 16, 1991.

11. See Helsinki Watch Report, "Destroying Ethnic Identity: The Gypsies of Bulgaria," New York, June 1991.

12. *Sofia Domestic Service*, April 12, 1990, in *FBIS-EEU–90–072*, April 13, 1990; *Sofia Domestic Service*, July 18, 1990, in *FBIS-EEU–90–139*, July 19, 1990; *Sofia Domestic Service*, July 19, 1990, in *FBIS-EEU–90–140*, July 20, 1990; Kalina Bozheva and Purvan Stoyanov, *Demokratsiya*, July 3–5, 1990, in *JPRS-EER–90–124*, August 30, 1990; *Sofia Domestic Service*, February 18, 1991, in *FBIS-EEU–91–033*, February 19, 1991; also see Kjell Engelbrekt, "The Movement for Rights and Freedoms to Compete in Elections"; Kjell Engelbrekt, "Nationalism Reviving," RFE/RL *Report on Eastern Europe*, vol. 2, no. 48, November 29, 1991; and "Official Announcement on the Dissolution of the Nationwide Committee for Defense of National Interests and the Founding of a National Defense Party," *Presluzhba Kurier*, Sofia, February 19, 1992, in *FBIS-EEU–92–038*, February 26, 1992.

13. *Sofia Domestic Service*, July 19, 1990, in *FBIS-EEU–90–140*, July 20, 1990; *BTA*, Sofia, July 25, 1990, in *FBIS-EEU–90–143*, July 26, 1990; Kalina Bozheva and Purvan Stoyanov, *Demokratsiya*, Sofia, July 3–5, 1990, in *JPRS-EER–90–124*, August 30, 1990; *BTA*, Sofia, September 27, 1990, in *FBIS-EEU–90–189*, September 28, 1990; *BTA*, Sofia, January 15, 1991, in *FBIS-EEU–91–011*, January 16, 1990; Boris Kostadinov, "Bulgarian Social Democratic Party Invites SDS but Not BSP to Its Congress," *Duma*, Sofia, March 1, 1991, in *FBIS-EEU–91–043*, March 5, 1991; interview with Dimitur Arnaudov by Yana Mavrodieva, "I Am a Citizen of the World," *Mladezh*, Sofia, February 4, 1991, in *JPRS-EER–91–044*, April 5, 1991; *BTA*, Sofia, May 14, 1991, in *FBIS-EEU–91–094*, May 15, 1991; Elizabet Dafinova, "A Party of Pragmatic Nationalism," *Bŭlgariya*, Sofia, April 13, 1991, in *JPRS-EER–91–089*, June 21, 1991; Kjell Engelbrekt, "The Movement for Rights and Freedoms to Compete in Elections" and "Nationalism Reviving"; and interview with Rumen Popov, FPL Chairman, in *Duma*, Sofia, May 20, 1993, in *JPRS-EER–93–063-S*, July 2, 1993.

14. "Bulgarian Nationalists Plan Human Chain," *Frankfurter Allgemeine Zeitung*, Frankfurt, July 9, 1990, in *FBIS-EEU–90–132*, July 10, 1990; Kalina Bozheva and Purvan Stoyanov, *Demokratsiya*, Sofia, July 3–5, 1990, in *JPRS-EER–90–124*, August 30, 1990; *BTA*, Sofia, February 26, 1991, in *FBIS-EEU–91–038*, February 26, 1991; Dulev, "The Banner Is Waving Again"; Kjell Engelbrekt, "Nationalism Reviving"; interview with Ivan Georgiev, BNRP Chairman, by Nikolay Bozhev, "We Are Struggling for Christian Values Against the Offensives of Islam," *Otechestven Vestnik*, Sofia, February 4, 1993, in *FBIS-EEU–93–026*, February 10, 1993.

15. *BTA*, Sofia, February 5, 1991, in *FBIS-EEU–91–025*, February 6, 1991; RFE/RL, *Daily Report*, no. 180, September 20, 1991; Stefana Gergova and Evlogi Stoilov, "Bulgarian Socialist Party Prepares New Provocation Relating to the Ethnic Problems," *Demokratsiya*, Sofia, September 19, 1991, in *FBIS-EEU–91–186*, September 25, 1991; Kjell Engelbrekt, "Nationalism Reviving" and "The Movement for Rights and Freedoms to Compete in Elections"; RFE/RL, *Daily Report*, no. 193, October 10, 1991; Kjell Engelbrekt, "Opposition Narrowly Defeats Socialists in National Elections," RFE/RL, *Report on Eastern Europe*, vol. 2, no. 43, October 25, 1991.

16. Hugh Poulton, "Minorities in the Balkans," *The Minority Rights Group*, no. 82, Expedite Graphic Limited, London, October 1989; article by the Center for the Study of Democracy, "Where Are We Going After the Dark Little Room?" *Kultura*, Sofia, August 17, 1990, in *JPRS-EER–90–145*, October 23, 1990.

17. Interview with Medi Doganov by Angelina Petrova, "The Neighborhood Door Is Ajar," *Pogled*, Sofia, March 26, 1990, in *FBIS-EEU–90–066*, April 5, 1990; *BTA*, Sofia, May 9, 1990, *FBIS-EEU–90–091*, May 10, 1990; interview with Ahmed Doğan by Ivan Staevski, "Path of Unification and Prosperity," *Zemedelsko Zname*, Sofia, May 8, 1990, in *FBIS-EEU–90–093*, May 14, 1990; *Sofia Domestic Service*, May 22, 1990, in *FBIS-EEU–90–100*, May 23, 1990; *BTA*, Sofia, June 6, 1990, in *FBIS-EEU–90–110*, June 7, 1990; Volen Siderov, "The Parliament Must Be Bulgarian!" *Demokratsiya*, Sofia, July 17, 1990, in *FBIS-EEU–90–155*, August 10, 1990; *BTA*, Sofia, October 20, 1990, in *FBIS-EEU–90–205*, October 23, 1990; *BTA*, Sofia, November 5, 1990, in *FBIS-EEU–90–215*, November 6, 1990; *Günaydin*, Istanbul, February 14, 1991, in *FBIS-EEU–91–036*, February 22, 1991. For a detailed discussion of the MRF platform, see Kjell Engelbrekt, "The Movement for Rights and Freedoms"; RFE/RL, *Daily Report*, no. 164, August 29, 1991; "Second Yilmaz Letter Is Unprecedented and Greatly Alarms Nationwide Committee for Defense of National Interests," *Duma*, Sofia, August 30, 1991, in *FBIS-EEU–91–172*, September 5, 1991; *BTA*, Sofia, September 21, 1991, in *FBIS-EEU–91–185*, September 24, 1991; Kjell Engelbrekt, "The Movement for Rights and Freedoms to Compete in Elections" and "Nationalism Reviving"; and RFE/RL, *Daily Report,* no. 98, May 25, 1993.

18. *BTA*, Sofia, December 12, 1992, in *FBIS-EEU–92–240*, December 14, 1992; *BTA*, Sofia, December 13, 1992, in *FBIS-EEU–92–240*, December 14, 1992; *BTA*, Sofia, December 14, 1992, in *FBIS-EEU–92–240*, December 14, 1992.

19. *BTA*, Sofia, March 11, 1990, in *FBIS-EEU–90–049*, March 13, 1990; *BTA*, Sofia, February 28, 1990, in *FBIS-EEU–90–056*, March 22, 1990; *BTA*, Sofia, April 22, 1990, in *FBIS-EEU–90–078*, April 23, 1990; *Duma*, Sofia, April 23, 1990, in *FBIS-EEU–90–080*, April 25, 1990; Nikolay Zagorichanov, "What Is Macedonism, and Does It Have a Basis in Bulgaria?" *Duma*, Sofia, May 12, 1990, in *FBIS-EEU–90–095*, May 16, 1990; *BTA*, Sofia, May 23, 1990, in *FBIS-EEU–90–101*, May 24, 1990; *BTA*, Sofia, May 28, 1990, in *FBIS-EEU–90–105*, May 31, 1990; Pero Rakočević, "According to a Well-Known Recipe," *Borba*, Belgrade, June 8, 1990, in *FBIS-EEU–90–121*, June 22, 1990. For a discussion of Macedonian history, see *Demokratsiya*, Sofia, January 28, 1990, in *FBIS-EEU–90–120*, August 21, 1990; Perry, "The Macedonian Question Revitalized"; Evgeni Gavrilov, *Duma*, Sofia, November 14, 1990, in *FBIS-EEU–90–223*, November 19, 1990; interview with *Ilinden* Secretary Krasimir Iliev by Davor Ivanković and Želimir Zanko, "Sofia Continues to Negate Macedonians," *Večernji List*, Zagreb, November 24, 1990, in *FBIS-EEU–90–239*, December 12, 1990; *BTA*, Sofia, May 5, 1991, in *FBIS-EEU–91–087*, May 6, 1991; interview with Jordan Kostadinov by Mirche Tomovski, "It Is Not Easy to Be Human," *Puls*, Skopje, September 3, 1992, in *JPRS-EER–92–145*, October 14, 1992.

20. See Helsinki Watch, "Destroying Ethnic Identity: Selective Persecution of Macedonians in Bulgaria," New York, February 12, 1991.

21. *BTA*, Sofia, March 11, 1990, in *FBIS-EEU–90–049*, March 13, 1990; Miglena Veselinova, "Will We Read the *Makedoniya* Newspaper?" *Rabotnichesko Delo*, Sofia, March 1, 1990, in *FBIS-EEU–90–053*, March 19, 1990; and *Kontinent*, Sofia, March 26, 1993.

22. "Macedonian Youth Society Established," *Narodna Mladezh*, Sofia, March 8, 1990, in *FBIS-EEU–90–049*, March 13, 1990.

23. "Macedonian Youth Society Established"; *Vecherni Novini*, Sofia, May 3, 1990, in *FBIS-EEU–90–091*, May 10, 1990; also see Perry, "The Macedonian Question Revitalized."

24. *Vecherni Novini*, Sofia, May 3, 1990, in *FBIS-EEU–90–091*, May 10, 1990.

25. *BTA*, Sofia, March 18, 1990, in *FBIS-EEU–90–053*, March 19, 1990; Simon Simonov, "The Gypsies: A Re-emerging Minority," RFE/RL *Report on Eastern Europe*,

vol. 1, no. 21, May 25, 1990; Ivan Ilchev and Duncan Perry, "Bulgarian Ethnic Groups: Politics and Perceptions," RFE/RL, *Report on Eastern Europe*, vol. 2, no. 12, March 19, 1993.

26. RFE/RL, *Daily Report*, no. 88, May 10, 1993.

27. Petur Dobrev, *Otechestven Vestnik*, Sofia, October 30, 1990, in *FBIS-EEU–90–215*, November 6, 1990.

28. *Sofia Domestic Service*, January 7, 1990, in *FBIS-EEU–90–005*, January 8, 1990; Simonov, "The Gypsies: A Re-emerging Minority."

29. *BTA*, Sofia, December 19, 1992, in *FBIS-EEU–92–246*, December 22, 1992; *BTA*, Sofia, December 19, 1992, in *FBIS-EEU–92–246*, December 22, 1992.

30. *BTA*, Sofia, March 17, 1990, in *FBIS-EEU–90–053*, March 19, 1990; RFE/RL, *Daily Report*, no. 54, March 18, 1992.

31. For an in-depth discussion of Zhivkov's assimilationist policies, see Poulton, "Minorities in the Balkans"; and Ivanković and Zanko, "Sofia Continues to Negate Macedonians."

9

Albania

POPULATION

Similarly to several other East European states, Albania has lacked complete, precise, and up-to-date statistics on the size of its ethnic minorities. Aside from Greeks, Macedonians, Serbs, and Montenegrins, other minorities, such as Vlachs and Roma (Gypsies), were not officially listed in the national census or in government population estimates. Between 1960 and 1989, the Albanian ethnic population officially grew in percentage terms from 97.3 percent to nearly 98 percent, making Albania the most homogeneous country in the region.[1] According to official figures, the Greek population climbed during this time from 37,282 to 58,758. Greek sources have generally provided much higher estimates, ranging from 150,000, mostly resident in southern Albania and in the capital Tiranë. The Macedonian population grew slightly from 4,235 to 4,697, while the tiny number of officially reported Serbs and Montenegrins remained reasonably constant; all three Slavic groups claimed a much higher ratio that was unrecognized and unregistered by Tirana. Despite the obvious presence of Vlachs (Arumunians) and Gypsies (Roma), the category of "other nationality" officially declined from 3,053 in 1960 to only 1,261 in 1989. According to unofficial estimates from the respective minority communities, there are approximately 5,000 Arumunians in Albania, most of them rural residents in the southeastern area around Korçë, and anywhere up to 10,000 Roma distributed around the country. The post-Communist government that assumed power during 1992 has given indications that it intends to conduct a more thorough and accurate population census devoid of ideological or political manipulation.

HISTORICAL OVERVIEW

Albania declared its independence from the crumbling Ottoman Empire in 1912, on the eve of World War One.[2] The European powers recognized the country's sovereignty and territorial integrity, but extensive areas with large Albanian

Albania: Population (1989)

Ethnic Groups	Number	% of Population
Albanians	3,117,600	97.96
Greeks	58,758	1.85
Macedonians	4,697	0.15
Serbs and Montenegrins	100	—
Others	1,261	0.04
Total Minorities	64,816	2.04
Total Population	3,182,416	100.00

norities were assigned to the neighboring states of Yugoslavia and Greece. This arrangement left a lasting sense of grievance in Albania and bred irredentist movements for their eventual integration into a larger Albanian state. Conversely, Serbia remained frustrated that it had failed to gain access to the Adriatic Sea, Montenegro resented its inability to incorporate parts of northern Albania, while Greece was angered over the deprivation of what was considered northern Epirus (southern Albania). Albania was spared further partition after the Great War, despite the demands of its neighbors, who claimed that the country contained sizable Greek and Slavic minorities. During the Italian occupation in World War Two, Albania was assigned the Serbian area of Kosovo, together with parts of northern Greece, southern Montenegro, and western Macedonia containing large Albanian populations. With the defeat of Nazi Germany and fascist Italy, these territories reverted back to either Yugoslav or Greek control.

Albanians are traditionally divided into two sub-groupings, the Gegs and Tosks, based on significant territorial, linguistic, and cultural differences. The Gegs inhabit the northern mountainous regions, speak a distinct dialect of Albanian, and maintained their clan-based social system and tribal chieftainships during four centuries of Ottoman Turkish occupation. The Tosks reside in southern Albania and have been exposed to more pronounced Turkish political and economic influence. During the late-nineteenth and early-twentieth centuries, cooperation between the two populations increased and their leaders collaborated in the struggle for national independence. Although some regional and tribal differences persisted, the Geg-Tosk rivalry lessened in importance with the establishment of a central Albanian government. Religious affiliations played an even less divisive role in Albanian society, as the country was renowned for its religious tolerance and absence of messianic fanaticism. After the Communist takeover all religions were banned by the Hoxha regime and it became difficult to gauge the extent of religious affiliation. Approximately 60 percent of the population were Sunni or Bektashi Muslims, about 25 percent espoused Orthodox Christianity (mostly resident in the south), and the remainder were Roman Catholics (mostly resident in the north).

The new Albanian state contained substantial pockets of Greek and Slavic ethnics, whose presence and official treatment provoked disputes with Athens and Belgrade, respectively. Moreover, various influential circles in Greece continued to pursue their claims to southern Albania, asserting that all Orthodox inhabitants of this region were ethnically Greek, even though the majority identified themselves as Albanian Christians. The area was briefly declared an autonomous region in 1946, but any claim to special status was quickly overruled. The Stalinist regime of Enver Hoxha imposed a ruthless dictatorship in the country that lasted with little respite until Hoxha's death in 1985. Greek spokesmen charged that Tirana dealt brutally with its large Hellenic minority residing in compact areas in the southern part of the country. Their property and land were confiscated, churches and schools were closed down, and a number of independent-minded leaders were arrested or exterminated. Albanian observers pointed out that the policies applied by the Communists toward ethnic and religious minorities differed little from their treatment of all Albanian citizens. Regardless of their national origin and ethnic identity, they were equally deprived of all elementary human and civil rights.

The Hoxha regime did not allow any independent, ethnically based political organizations to operate, and it co-opted Greek activists in the service of the party-state. Severe restrictions were placed on cultural and religious expression, particularly after Tirana declared the country to be the world's first atheist state during the late 1960s. Although commentators maintained that all Albanian citizens were prevented from developing any institutions and associations separate from the state, a distinct sense of grievance persisted among the Greeks. Relations between Tirana and Athens also remained frozen, while some nationalist and irredentist organizations in Greece contributed to the prevailing sense of hostility. Some concessions to Greek sentiments were made in the mid-1970s, when the new Albanian constitution guaranteed ethnic Greeks in predominantly minority areas the right to develop their culture, use their language, and teach it in schools. But the concessions were deemed insufficient and a mere propagandistic ploy by a repressive Stalinist government.

As the Communist grip slackened during 1990, under the rule of Hoxha's successor, Ramiz Alia, thousands of people poured across the border to find refuge in Greece. Many of these were Greek ethnics seeking sanctuary and refusing to return to Albania for both political and economic reasons. Athens feared that the release of these refugees by Tirana was a deliberate attempt to denude the southern municipalities of a strong Greek presence and thereby dilute any demands for minority rights or ethnic self-determination. The Albanian-Greek dispute remained evident even over the question of population statistics. According to the 1981 Albanian census, the Greek community numbered some 55,000 out of a total population of over 3 million. By contrast, Greek sources on both sides of the border estimated the figure to be somewhere in the region of 200,000—a number that remained constant in Greek statements despite the large outflow of Greek refugees. Tirana claimed that Athens deliberately exaggerated the total by including various categories of people with little or no Hellenic background, including all Orthodox Christians in southern Albania regardless of their ethnic origins and cultural identity.

With the onset of political liberalization during 1990–91, Greek activists formed their own political party and won seats to the National Assembly in the first multi-party general elections. Increasing Greek activism inside Albania and growing suspicions about the influence of extremist revisionist circles in Greece spurred the new Albanian parliament to ban ethnic or regionally based parties from standing in future elections. The issue soured relations between Tirana and Athens, which had steadily improved under the Alia administration. Although a newly formed and predominantly Greek organization was allowed to function and participate in the multi-party elections of 1992, Albanian-Greek relations remained tense as the country began to undergo profound political and economic changes. Further controversies arose over the question of Greek maltreatment of Albanian refugees, over the activities and sponsorship of irredentist organizations in Greece with overt claims to Albanian territories, and over the influence of Greek organizations during and after the Albanian election campaigns.

A related issue that aggravated frictions between the two states revolved around the status of the Çam people. While Greek revanchists claimed southern Albania as northern Epirus, Albanian expansionists considered portions of northwestern Greece as part of the southern Albanian territories of Çamëria. Several thousand ethnic Albanians, or Çams, were estimated to live in the Greek border areas. However, Athens maintained that the local Çams were not a separate ethnic group and that the population in question was thoroughly Hellenized. In fact, under Greek rule in the years after World War One and World War Two, many Muslim Çams were expelled from the region to Turkey or Albania, while the Orthodox Christian Çams were assimilated and deprived of any distinct minority rights in education, culture, or language use. Since the democratic breakthrough in Albania, local Çams whose families were expelled from Greece promptly began to organize a pressure group on behalf of their co-ethnics in northern Greece. They lobbied the administration in Tirana to defend the rights of an estimated 200,000 Çam population in Greece and to press Athens to allow for the return of confiscated property and for lifting restrictions on travel and family contacts. But the Greek authorities have not displayed any indication of modifying their stance, while the government in Tirana has remained wary of taking aboard another potentially explosive foreign-policy issue and further jeopardizing relations with its southern neighbor.

Albania's Slavic populations have remained comparatively small since the war; according to the 1961 census, there were under 5,000 Macedonians and Montenegrins in the country and an undisclosed but limited number of Serbs, located mostly along the Albanian-Kosovo border. Unlike the Greeks, they demonstrated little sign of self-organization and did not appear to possess a dynamic and politically minded leadership. A similar situation prevailed among the unregistered Vlachs or Arumunians, numbering somewhere between 10,000 and

30,000, who inhabited some pockets of the rural hinterland, as well as the estimated 5,000 Gypsies (Roma). These minorities maintained little or no organizational structure and were prone to state-sponsored assimilationist pressures, especially in the wake of Hoxha's campaign against organized religion. Following Alia's liberalization, an unknown number of Macedonians, Serbs, and Montenegrins were reported to have sought refuge in their respective Yugoslav republics. Some attempts were also evident in organizing the remaining population to promote their ethnic interests.

The Kosovo question has increasingly preoccupied all Albanian parties, particularly since the break-up of the Yugoslav federation and the mounting repression against the Albanian majority in Serbia's Kosovo Province. The Tirana authorities have been supportive of Albanian demands for autonomy and sovereignty in Kosovo, although they have avoided provoking the Serbian government and causing a major international confrontation. A number of militant, although small, pro-Kosovar organizations were also formed in Albania following the democratic changes. They began to campaign for the rights of Kosovo Albanians and some even called for the creation of a "Greater Albania" to encompass Kosovo and parts of Macedonia and Montenegro containing large Albanian populations. To counter Albanian claims, Serbian leaders accused Tirana of interfering in Yugoslavia's internal affairs and of harboring territorial pretensions to Serbian lands. In this ongoing war of words, Belgrade also accused Tirana of persecuting its own Slavic minorities and denying them appropriate nationality status.

OFFICIAL POLICIES

For the Albanian state, only the Greeks and small populations of Slavs in the northeastern and southeastern parts of the country were officially recognized as distinct ethnic minorities. The government did not register the Arumun (Vlach) population, mostly inhabiting the rural areas around the southeastern town of Korçë, where they numbered about 5,000, although some sources have greatly inflated this number. In addition, the two distinct Gypsy (Romani) groups, the urban Jerg and the rural Arnxhi, numbering close to 10,000, have not been officially registered. Although popular attitudes toward Gypsies have generally been negative and prejudicial, they did not appear to suffer from any overt forms of discrimination.

"Minority rights" were officially acknowledged only for those villages deemed "minoritarian" by the government. Such was the case with 99 villages in the southern districts of Sarandë and Gjirokastër, where the Greek population was concentrated. Greek spokesmen claimed that 34 percent of the population of Gjirokastër and 42 percent of the population of Sarandë was Greek. If, however, even a few Albanian families settled in one of these villages, its minority inhabitants lost these distinct rights; for example, they were no longer provided with an education in their own language or the opportunity to publish their own newspaper. The same principles applied to other areas that were inhabited by ethnic minorities but that were not granted a special minority status.

As a result of these policies, Greek educational and linguistic rights were largely absent in several cities heavily populated by Greeks, such as Korçë, Himarë, Tepelenë, Fier, Vlorë, Shkodër, Berat, Përmet, and Elbasan. In the regions where Greek education was allowed, courses were designed to terminate at the fourth grade of elementary schooling, while Greek activists sought to extend optional classes through the secondary level. Even the cities of Sarandë and Gjirokastër were excluded from the minority-rights guarantees, although both were capitals of the two districts eligible for designation as minority areas. Despite the fact that a compact Greek population inhabited the area, in official legislation prior to the recent democratic changes the minority was technically considered as being of non-Greek origin.[3]

In 1991, a Draft Constitution of the Republic of Albania, proposed by the ruling Albanian Party of Labor (APL), was presented to parliament. Its first chapter outlined the basic rights of all Albanian people, including the national minorities. According to Article 7, "The legislation of the Republic of Albania takes into account, recognizes and respects the generally accepted principles and norms of international law, and recognizes the guarantees provided by international law to minorities." Article 8 of the draft constitution evinced strong criticism from the organized Greek minority, as well as from various international organizations and human rights groups. It declared that political parties and organizations could not be created on the basis of nationality or ethnicity; also barred were political organizations of a "fascist or racial character, or those that by their program and activities threaten to overthrow by force the constitutional order, against the independence and territorial integrity of the country." Greek leaders raised serious objections to stipulations prohibiting the formation of minority political organizations. They claimed that such provisions violated the right of minorities to express their political will and limited their participation in the country's political life.

The last paragraph of Article 12, dealing with foreign policy, stated that Albania would "defend the recognition and the respect for the national and democratic rights of the Albanian people residing in other countries." This provision explicitly recognized that after World War Two about 3 million ethnic Albanians were left outside the Albanian state, mainly in the Yugoslav republics of Serbia (in the province of Kosovo), Macedonia, and Montenegro. The term "national rights" evidently expressed the hopes of many Albanian deputies that Kosovo in particular would gain broader autonomy that would eventually lead the province toward sovereignty and close association with Albania.

Article 14 of the draft constitution focused on the right of minorities to use their own languages. The Albanian language was defined as the official language, but "in special localities, where the majority is made up of national minorities, the language of the minority may be used side by side with the

Albanian language according to conditions foreseen by law." According to leaders of the Greek minority, while in theory the right of ethnic minorities to use their mother tongue was recognized, the required conditions for applying this ruling were not specified in the legislation and in practice could prove extremely restrictive. In addition, the article did not mention any regulations concerning the right of education in languages other than Albanian.

The second section of the draft constitution dealt with the basic rights and freedoms of all citizens. Article 15, on freedom of thought, conscience, and belief, declared that freedom of thought, conscience, and religious and political beliefs were inviolable: "No restrictions apply to the practice of convictions and beliefs, provided that this right does not involve violence and does not conflict with the public order which is protected by law." Article 29 dealt specifically with the rights of ethnic minorities, whereby the state guaranteed to minorities "free preservation and development of their ethnic, cultural, religious, and linguistic identity." Moreover, individuals "belonging to certain ethnic minorities are free not to be assimilated against their will. They are free to establish and maintain contacts with people of the same ethnic origin inside the country and with foreign nationals of the same ethnic origin, cultural heritage, and religious belief outside the country." In June 1993, the draft constitution was finally published in *Gazeta Shqiptare* in preparation for scrutiny by parliament. During 1990, the government also legalized the private and public practice of all religions, and the Law on Major Constitutional Provisions declared Albania a "secular state," respecting freedom of religious faiths and obliged the government to create conditions enabling all denominations to exercise these liberties.

However, certain "collective rights" in the religious realm continued to be denied to the Greek minority, including the freedom to practice their religion in Greek. Albanian laws provided that in Albanian Orthodox churches masses were to be held only in the Albanian language, and that "Albanian religion is part of Albanian nationalism," which in effect contradicted provisions included in the draft constitution. Controversies also surfaced during 1992 in the appointment of bishops to the Albanian Autocephalous Orthodox Church. When the Ecumenical Patriarch in Istanbul named three bishops of Greek origin to the Dioceses of Korçë, Berat, and Gjirokastër, the government refused to agree to their installation. When an ethnic Greek was named the Orthodox Archbishop of Albania, a storm of protests erupted; although Anastas Junallatos was formally installed, Tirana only accepted him on a provisional basis until a suitable ethnic Albanian replacement could be found.[4]

The Law on Major Constitutional Provisions that has served as a substitute for a full constitution provided for the "human rights and fundamental freedoms of national minorities, as accepted by international documents." In practice, however, limitations were placed on the extent to which minorities could exercise their rights, especially for those groups that were not officially recognized by Tirana. Schooling in the mother tongue of different ethnic groups was not allowed in regions other than southern Albania, where the Greek minority was concentrated. However, Radio Tirana periodically broadcast Greek-language programs, and a Greek-language newspaper, *Liko Vima*, was published in the southern town of Gjirokastër.[5]

Although the Greek organization *Omonia* gained 5 seats in the March 1991 general elections, controversies over the participation of ethnically based parties culminated in the formulation of a new electoral and political-party law that prohibited political activities by parties based on ethnic or regional criteria. The draft of the election law submitted in January 1992 initially contained an article (number 13) allowing for the participation of ethnically based parties and was welcomed by the CSCE and by other multi-national bodies. This legislative amendment was partly a result of CSCE intervention, impressing on the Albanian authorities to abide by Helsinki principles when drafting the law. But after a serious dispute in the National Assembly over the role of ethnically based parties, there was a last-minute change in Article 13 that effectively disqualified *Omonia* from participating in the elections. The disqualification of *Omonia* enraged Greek activists and led to vehement protests by Athens. The election controversy was partially eased when the Albanian government agreed to register the Greek-based Unity Party for Human Rights and permitted it to stand in the March 1992 parliamentary elections. The new party succeeded in gaining 2 seats in the southern districts of Sarandë and Gjirokastër to the newly constituted National Assembly. But the election campaign itself was marred by conflicts, as some Albanian officials charged that irredentist Greek organizations were campaigning for the Unity Party and distributing campaign literature printed in Greece.

The National Assembly elections of March 1992 were held according to the electoral laws passed by the Albanian parliament in February 1992, together with Articles 16 and 17 of the Law on Major Constitutional Provisions. Certain provisions of that law affected the political rights of minorities in Albania. In order to qualify for the balloting, every candidate had to present a list of 400 signatures of voters from the same electoral district who supported his or her candidacy. Considering the fact that the country was divided into 100 voting districts, the number of signatures required proved relatively high compared to the number of eligible voters. Consequently, the collection of 400 signatures proved difficult for the smaller parties, especially those attempting to represent minority populations. Furthermore, Greek spokesmen contended that requirements for signatures in effect expressed voting preferences and thereby violated the secrecy of the electoral process.

Small parties that were formed to represent the interests of ethnic minorities were at a clear disadvantage during the elections. According to Article 15 of the election law, only parties presenting candidates in at least 33 electoral counties and 9 electoral districts could participate in the subsequent proportional distribution of additional parliamentary seats. These provisions virtually guaranteed that minority parties had little chance of gaining seats in the proportional second round. Furthermore, according to Article 21 of the law, voter registration lists had to be completed at least 25 days prior to election day. This requirement created a practical problem for Albanian citizens of Greek origin who were working in Greece and were unable to register on time.[6]

The local elections of July 1992 were held according to provisions barring the participation of ethnically based parties. As before, the Unity Party for Human Rights (UPHR) was permitted to field candidates for mayors and local council representatives. However, tensions were evident in the south of the country on election day, particularly in Gjirokastër and Sarandë. For example, some emigrants who worked in Greece or resided there as refugees and returned to Albania in order to vote discovered that they were not registered on the electoral lists. Albanian authorities accused political groups in Greece of pressuring people to return to Albania and vote for the UPHR, a party that clearly represented the interests of the Greek minority. This created a political crisis in the Sarandë district, where Albanian political parties protested against brazen Greek interference. But despite this localized storm and the grievances of some political leaders, the election results in Greek minority regions were accepted as legitimate. The UPHR received 5.69 percent of the district-council seats and 4.96 percent of the municipal-council seats, electing 53 district councilors, out of 932, and 32 municipality councilors, out of 645. It also managed to elect 1 of the 42 municipal mayors and 13 commune chairmen in the country's 314 communes.[7]

During the democratic changes, the overwhelming majority of the Albanian population experienced serious economic difficulties; thousands sought refuge and job opportunities in neighboring Greece. After the 1991 visit of Greek prime minister Constantine Mitsotakis to Albania, the two countries signed an agreement to halt the dramatic exodus of predominantly young Albanians. But despite these efforts, about 100,000 Albanian citizens reportedly crossed the Greek border during 1991, a large number of them claiming to be ethnic Greeks. Athens contended that the Albanian authorities were encouraging the exodus in an attempt to alter the demographic structure of the regions where ethnic Greeks were concentrated. Fearing an even bigger inflow of pauperized Albanians, Athens took harsh steps to tighten border controls and repatriate many of those already in the country.

The growing reports of ill-treatment of Albanian refugees in Greece during 1991 and 1992 were viewed by Tirana as a serious affront. The government publicly raised questions about the forcible return of some refugees as well as the increased presence of military forces along the Albanian-Greek border. Albanian officials accused Athens of violating the basic human rights of those seeking temporary employment in Greece and condemned what they claimed was a deliberate policy of persecution. The Albanian Foreign Ministry periodically sent notes protesting against the alleged attacks on Albanians and mounting "anti-Albanian" sentiments. It also claimed that Athens exploited the unstable situation to infiltrate radical *Omonia* activists into the south of the country, while the promised economic aid, under an agreement reached in 1991, was designated only for Albania's ethnic Greeks. Frictions over these questions mounted significantly on the eve of the parliamentary and local elections, particularly when some political leaders in Tirana used the issue of refugee mistreatment to try to discredit *Omonia* and the UPHR.[8] The Albanian authorities were also disturbed by the activities of Epirot irredentists in Greece, who had the backing of the Greek Orthodox Church and some senior Greek politicians. Indeed, the diocese of Metropolitan Sevastianos in the northern Greek town of Konitsa included most of Albania south of the Shkumbin River; Sevastianos himself was an ardent annexationist.

Persistent tensions erupted in violence in June 1993, after the Albanian authorities expelled a senior Greek Orthodox priest, Costa Stamos, on charges of fomenting separatism and Hellenization. Local police reported that a Greek referendum on autonomy was being secretly prepared in southern Albania, and after the expulsion, security forces clashed with Greek minority protesters near Gjirokastër, where they had attempted to rally in support of the evicted cleric. Evidently in retaliation for the priest's ouster, the Greek authorities proceeded to round up thousands of illegal Albanian residents and deport them back to Albania. Some distressed refugees claimed that they had been beaten by Greek police. Tirana withdrew its ambassador from Athens, and President Sali Berisha urged the UN Secretary General to intervene against the "grave violation of human rights." Meanwhile, the Greek government claimed that the expulsion of Stamos violated the "religious rights" of the Greek minority in Albania. Berisha countered that Tirana had accepted only the temporary appointment of an Orthodox archbishop, not the three archimandrites, including Stamos. The government also feared that the sudden inflow of tens of thousands of refugees could trigger further economic decline and seriously aggravate tensions with the Greek minority. In a conciliatory gesture in July 1993, the Albanian president met with Greek minority leaders and pledged to protect their rights. Indeed, plans had already been prepared to set up a university in Gjirokastër to train Greek teachers and to open up high schools for Greek students. Greek leaders lodged further demands for equal opportunities in the Albanian civil service and the opening of minority schools.

Relations between Albania and the Albanian leadership in Kosovo have been steadily developing following the democratic changes in Tirana. After the March 1992 elections, the Democratic Party government consistently expressed its concern about the Albanian majority in Kosovo and openly supported the "inalienable and legitimate rights" of Kosovar Albanians and their pursuit of closer political and economic links with Albania. Regular contacts were established between Tirana and Albanian leaders in Kosovo, Macedonia, and Montenegro. Officials in Tirana also pressed the international community to take more effective actions toward Kosovo, by demanding that Belgrade ease its repressive policies and restore autonomous status to the province. The authorities in Tirana closely monitored developments in Kosovo, and after the referendum for

Kosovar independence and the "illegitimate" elections in May 1992, they recognized the sovereignty and statehood of the republic despite Serbian protestations. Albania's serious economic difficulties notwithstanding, Albanian leaders promoted financial support for the Kosovar Albanians and fostered the creation of a joint economic commission planning to bring the economies of the two republics closer together despite Serbia's increasing isolation. Grave fears remained that in the event of a violent showdown in Kosovo, Tirana would find it difficult to remain detached and could be drawn into a war with Serbia to protect its co-ethnics. Indeed, a number of nationalist organizations were formed in Albania seeking to influence both the government and Albanian public opinion to support the Kosovars stridently and prepare for the creation of a "Greater Albania."[9]

ALBANIAN NATIONALISTS

Albanian National Unity Party (ANUP)
Partia e Unitetit Kombëtar (PUK)

The ANUP was registered in March 1991 under the chairmanship of Idajet Beqiri. The program of the ANUP has included calls for the creation of a pan-Albanian confederation encompassing all the territories inhabited by Albanian majorities in Yugoslavia, Macedonia, and Greece. ANUP leaders demanded that Tirana take a more forthright role in support of Albanian rights in Kosovo, and the party recognized the independent Kosovo constitution passed in September 1990 by the Kosovo Assembly and the subsequent declaration of independence in late September 1991. It voiced its readiness to work together with all political and non-political organizations whose goals were to "protect Albanian national interests," inside and outside the country. Observers believed that the ANUP included many former hard-line Communists who were seeking to capitalize on nationalist sentiments among the population. Although they openly sought to "recover" Albanian territories assigned to neighboring countries before World War One, ANUP leaders claimed they did not propose forceful reintegration. In ANUP estimations, the peaceful creation of a second Albanian republic, to include Kosovo and parts of Macedonia and Montenegro, would purportedly be followed by a formal union with Albania after a public referendum.

ANUP membership has remained small, although the party claimed latent support within other political parties and evidently received financial and material assistance from exiled Kosovo Albanians enabling it to publish a weekly newspaper. It failed to win seats in the general elections of March 1992, gathering under 1 percent of the total national vote. Although the major Albanian parties, including the Democrats and Socialists, also contained deputies, members, and sympathizers who have voiced militant nationalist sentiments, they have not managed to form significant political factions. In July 1993, Beqiri was sentenced to six months in prison for allegedly insulting and slandering President

Berisha. Beqiri had publicly claimed that Berisha was installing a "fascist dictator-ship" in Albania. Critics claimed that the government's measures were reminiscent of the former Communist system and signaled an unsettling trend toward autocracy.

Motherland Political Association (MPA)
Shoqata Politike Mëmëdheu (SPM)

The Association was founded in July 1991. Its leadership has worked in a close alliance with the ANUP, declaring their main goal as the creation of a pan-Al-banian confederation in the Balkans. The MPA, together with the ANUP and the Kosovo Patriotic and Political Association, demanded that Tirana take a more visible role in support of Albanian interests in Kosovo and unreservedly recog-nize the independent Kosovo constitution and the sovereignty and independence of the Kosovo Republic. Like the ANUP, the MPA has been critical of both the Albanian authorities and even the Albanian leadership in Kosovo for remaining too passive and conciliatory in the face of Serbian intransigence and constant provocations. In the event of armed confrontations in Kosovo, both the ANUP and the MPA appeared intent on mobilizing the Albanian population to defend their threatened kinsmen actively.[10]

Several other explicitly nationalist and expansionist organizations have sur-faced in Albania. These include a resuscitated *Balli Kombëtar* (National Front), the major anti-Communist resistance group during World War Two, which main-tained links with Albanian exiles and sought to revive its political impact. Al-though ultra-nationalist influence in Albania remains restricted, dire economic conditions coupled with regional instability could provide it with wider public reso-nance and give increasing prominence to nationalist sentiments within the main-stream Albanian parties: Democratic, Socialist, Republican, and Social Democratic.

GREEK ORGANIZATIONS

Democratic Union of the Greek Minority (DUGM)
Bashkimi Demokratik i Minoritetit Grek "Omonia" (BDMG)

The DUGM, otherwise known as the *Omonia* Sociopolitical Organization (OSO), was created in February 1991, in accordance with a decree dated Decem-ber 1990 on the creation of political organizations and associations. It was not originally a political party but a cultural association that subsequently engaged in political activities. *Omonia* (Harmony) placed strong emphasis on monitoring the alleged repression of the Greek population and received substantial support from the ethnic Greek minority concentrated in the southern districts of Sarandë and Gjirokastër. The leaders of *Omonia*, including President Thoma Sharra and Sec-retary General Vangjel Papakristo, called for an end to Albania's isolationism and the persecution of its minorities. They expressed concern over the mass exodus of refugees to Greece during 1990–91, and they appealed for a maximum commitment on the part of both the government and the local authorities to stabilize the situation in the minority areas affected by the exodus. *Omonia* openly opposed Tirana's official policies toward the Greek minority, and particularly the purported attempts to "assimilate it by force and deprive it of its ethnic and cultural identity." To express these concerns, *Omonia* sent a memorandum to the CSCE during the International Human Dimension Conference held in Moscow in September and October 1992.

The organization received permission to field candidates in the country's first multi-party general elections in March 1991, and it won 5 parliamentary seats. At that time, there were widespread suspicions that *Omonia* was principally a Labor Party front designed to subdue or dilute demands for minority rights and to divide the burgeoning opposition movement. In fact, *Omonia* proved itself to be an authentic and legitimate political body that occasionally cooperated with the Democratic Party against the Socialists in the Albanian legislature. However, the ban on all parties of ethnic, regional, or religious character, which was ratified by the Albanian parliament before the March 1992 ballot, changed *Omonia*'s political status, and it was unable to participate in the second general elections. As a result, Greek minority political leaders complained that the restrictions violated the principles of the CSCE and threatened to boycott the elections. They subsequently backed the candidates of the newly formed UPHR for the 1992 balloting; many of these were also *Omonia* members. Following an internal party shake-up in early 1992, some of the relatively moderate *Omonia* leadership was replaced by more militant elements who demanded a referendum to determine the future status of Greek-inhabited areas in southern Albania. In June 1993, *Omonia* presented a petition to the Albanian parliament calling for Greek children to be taught in their mother tongue at all school levels and for Greek to be used in Orthodox church services. In addition, Greek minority spokesmen wanted the freedom to play the Greek national anthem during major festivities and to hoist the Greek flag alongside the Albanian one. They also requested the restoration of property belonging to Greek families forced to leave Albania after the Communist takeover in 1944.[11]

Unity Party for Human Rights (UPHR)
Bashkimi i të Drejtave të Njëriut (BDN)

Due to the interdiction that prohibited the political activities of *Omonia*, the Greek minority was subsequently represented politically by the UPHR. It was founded in February 1992, just a few weeks prior to the second multi-party parliamentary elections. The late formation of the UPHR was attributed to expectations by Greek minority leaders that the Albanian government would finally give in to pressure exerted by CSCE and the EC and allow for the participation of *Omonia*. The lack of time resulted in a weak election campaign, and various election-law regulations limited the UPHR's impact in the balloting. Because *Omonia* had been declared illegal, no member of the Central Electoral Committee belonged to the UPHR: according to Article 35 of the electoral law, only parties that already had elected deputies could obtain representation on the committee. Thoma Xhai was elected chairman of the UPHR, which consisted of Greeks, *Omonia* activists, and a handful of Albanians. According to the initiating documents, the main objective of the party was to register electable candidates and represent the interests of all minorities in parliament. It did not openly seek political or territorial self-determination for the Greek minority and claimed to "oppose the policies of some chauvinistic circles in Greece." Although the UPHR depicted itself as a multi-ethnic organization, it was principally based among the Greek community and its platform stressed the individual and collective rights of the Greek minority. Despite the fact that it had only a few weeks to conduct an effective campaign, had little access to Albanian television or radio, and possessed insufficient funds to establish its own newspaper, the UPHR submitted 36 candidacies in as many electoral districts in order to assure its participation in the second round of the seat distributions.

The local supervisory committees initially barred 8 UPHR candidates from participating in the March 1992 elections, asserting that they did not meet all the necessary legal requirements. The Central Electoral Committee ratified these decisions and excluded 3 other candidates, making a total of 11. Such decisions were justified by claims that many of the required signatures were fraudulent. The UPHR took the issue to the Supreme Court, which ultimately ruled that only 4 of the 11 candidates were ineligible to participate. However, until the last days of the election campaign no one knew for certain how many UPHR candidates had actually been approved. As a result, the Union's pre-electoral preparations were rendered difficult, especially in districts where the participation of candidates was initially approved and later denied as a result of contradictory decisions by various official bodies. Finally, only 29 approved UPHR candidates were able to participate in the general elections. If the number of candidates had totalled 33, then the party would have been eligible for seats in the proportional allocation of mandates, provided that it had received more than the minimum 4 percent of total votes required on the national level.

Although it faced significant obstacles, the UPHR received strong support in the southern regions of the country and succeeded in gaining 2 seats in the newly constituted National Assembly with 2.92 percent of the popular vote. Sotil Qirjazati and Thomas Mico were elected deputies. The result fell short of what party leaders had expected, but nonetheless it ensured that the Greek minority would continue to have representation at the highest political levels and participate directly in the legislative process. The influence of the UPHR showed a slight increase in the following months, and in the elections for local representatives in July 1992, it received 4.34 percent of the popular vote and elected several Greek mayors and other local officials.[12]

ÇAM AND KOSOVAR MOVEMENTS

Kosovo Patriotic and Political Association (KPPA)
Shoqata Patriotike Atdhetare Kosova (SPAK)

This militant pro-Kosovar group was established in March 1991. It held its founding congress in Tirana in June 1991 and claimed a membership of about 12,700 people. A number of similar pro-Kosovar groups and cultural associations were created in both Tirana and the northern city of Shkodër. The association was headed by Murat Gjonbala and the Initiating Commission also included Husamadin Ferraj, Ibrahim Shatri, Agim Haxhia, and Shkelzen Berisha. The KPPA claimed to be an "all-national association." Although it did not participate in the parliamentary and local elections during 1992, it declared its backing for those political forces that supported the independence of the territories in the former Yugoslavia inhabited predominantly by Albanians. Its main goal was to achieve the "social, cultural, and political freedom of the Albanian majority in Serbian-ruled Kosovo" and eventually facilitate the national unification of all Albanians and the peaceful creation of a single Albanian state. The KPPA's platform encouraged pan-national unification in a "European context," claiming this to be in accordance with the basic documents of international justice (the UN Charter, the Helsinki Final Act, and CSCE documents). It considered the development of educational, cultural, and economic links with Kosovo not as final goals but rather as the fastest road toward Albanian unification.[13]

Çamëria Political and Patriotic Association (ÇPPA)
Shoqata Patriotike Atdhetare "Çamëria" (SPAC)

The Association was formed in January 1991 and was registered by the Ministry of Justice one month later. It was headed by Abaz Dojaka and claimed a membership of some 40,000 people by the end of the year. In March 1991, the first national conference of the CPPA was held in Tirana, with many of its activists drawn from the Albanian community expelled from Çamëria, an area of northwestern Greece occupied and then lost by Albania during World War Two. Delegates demanded the protection of the legitimate rights of the Albanian minority in Greece and called for the Greek authorities to recognize the persistence of the "Çam question." They urged the Albanian government to take up the issue with Athens at the highest bilateral levels and to be more assertive in defending the rights of Çam Albanians remaining in Greece. The CPPA intended to bring to international attention the neglected and suppressed linguistic, cultural, and educational rights of both Orthodox and Muslim Albanian Çams who were avowedly subjected to a policy of "Greek assimilation." The group also launched campaigns on behalf of dispossessed Çam exiles in Albania.

Although the CPPA did not participate in either of the two parliamentary elections, it claimed to represent the majority of an estimated 200,000 strong Çamëria population in Albania, which resided primarily in the southern parts of the country. Dojaka specified that his organization had three main demands on Athens: respect for international conventions on the treatment of minorities, including all relevant CSCE documents, such as the opening of Albanian schools (Çamërian exiles in Albania claimed that about 250,000 of their co-ethnics were still resident in Greece, although not all in Çamëria, and were deprived of all elementary collective rights); the return of property confiscated from expelled Çams or the payment of appropriate compensations by Athens; and permission for Albanian Çams to return to their ancestral lands and maintain contacts with family members and kinsmen. The CPPA asserted that the Greek government continued to prevent Çams form obtaining visas to visit Greece.

The Çamëria Association claimed a structure of some 23 local branches, primarily in southern Albania, and the support of a broad cross-section of Albania's political forces, as well as the Çam population in Greece. Çamërian leaders contended that they were expanding their influence across Albania's political spectrum and that several political parties had taken their cause aboard in their programs. It favored granting human and group rights to the Greek minority in Albania but opposed any steps toward political or territorial autonomy and demanded similar rights for the Çam population in Greece. The CPPA staunchly opposed any Greek territorial pretensions and believed that some elements of *Omonia* and the UPHR were radicals supported by chauvinistic and annexationist forces in Greece. Dojaka alleged that these elements sought to provoke ethnic conflicts in Albania in order to hasten Greek government intervention. CPPA denied that it was involved in attacks on Greek stores in Sarandë in February 1992, evidently in retaliation for the mistreatment of Albanian refugees in Greece, or that it sought to heighten ethnic tensions in Albania. It claimed to have some contact with Çams in Albania where Greek policy makes it difficult to organize pressure groups. Çamëria leaders confirmed that the Association supported the Democratic Party in the March 1992 elections, although some suspicions were initially voiced about the CPPA's links with the former Albanian Party of Labor (Communist Party). The CPPA clearly managed to raise public interest in the Çam issue, and the Democratic Party government has raised the question with Athens as a counterweight to Greek campaigns on behalf of the Greek minority in Albania.[14]

MINORITY ORGANIZATIONS

Association of Montenegrins (AM)
Shoqata e Malazezëve (SM)

The Association of Montenegrins was formed in Vraka, near the town of Shkodër in northern Albania, as a social-cultural organization and not as an avowedly political group. Although the Montenegrins were not recognized by the Albanian authorities as a distinct national minority, the Association claimed to have over 1,000 members while representing the interests of a 2,500-strong minority, residing mainly in the area around Shkodër. The AM challenged the official statistics issued by Tirana in the early 1990s, in which the number of Montenegrins and Serbs was placed at only 100. Some Albanian officials contended that several hundred Slavs had left the country since the onset of the democratic changes, including both Serbs and Montenegrins. Members of the Association advocated promoting the culture and customs of Montenegrins and urged the recognition of Montenegrin and Serbian minorities in Albania and the return of original Slavic names to members of these minorities. The AM planned to reopen elementary schools in the mother language and also formed a Montenegrin-Serbian cultural club.[15]

"Bratska" Political Association of Macedonians in Albania (BPAMA)
Shoqata "Bratska" e Maqedonave të Shqipërisë (SBMS)

This organization was established in September 1991 as an openly political group. It claimed to represent and defend the interests of the small Macedonian minority located primarily along Albania's Macedonian border region. In August 1992, Tirana and Skopje agreed that the Macedonian government would help to fund Macedonian-language education in several villages near the border.[16]

Association of Arumunians in Albania (AAA)
Shoqata e Arumunëve të Shqipërisë (SAS)

The AAA was established in October 1991 by activists in the town of Selenicë near Vlorë, which contained a large Arumunian population. Delegates at the first conference in April 1992 confirmed the existence, authenticity, and the legitimate rights of the Arumunian (or Vlach) population in Albania to its ethnic identity, language, customs, and culture. A council composed of 42 members was elected. Janko Ballamaçi became its chairman; Anastas Buneçi, Arqile Dhamaj, Anastas Kaporeni vice chairmen; and Nikolla Seferi secretary general. The conference specified the basic goals of the organization and issued a resolution demanding that the Arumunian community in Albania enjoy full ethnocultural rights similar to all other ethnic communities. The Association intended to conduct a census of the Arumunian population through its 15 local branches, although it recognized that many Vlachs were fully assimilated into Albanian culture and barely preserved their traditional language. The AAA assumed a cultural character, but although it did not involve itself directly in the political process, some of its demands could be classified as essentially political. Its members believed that the state had to create all necessary conditions to enable the Arumunians to maintain their language and to develop their religious and cultural heritage in their mother tongue. They demanded that the government guarantee Arumunians the right to have their own language classes in local schools, as well as radio and television programs, newspapers, magazines and other publications, and to restore several dilapidated churches and monasteries. Because of their chronic economic position, Vlach leaders sought financial aid from the state to support these endeavors. The AAA also tried to promote contacts and develop relations between Albanian Arumunians and Romania (a country to which they claimed to trace their historical links), as well as with Arumunian communities elsewhere in Eastern Europe and the West. The AAA invited Vlachs from Vojvodina, Macedonia, Romania, Greece, Bulgaria, and Ukraine to take part in their April 1992 conference. The Association proposed that the Romanian government allow the Arumunians to travel in and out of the country without visas in order to enhance the exchange of ethnocultural values and personal contacts.

The Romani (Gypsy) community has also become more active since the democratic changes in Albania. Reportedly, Jerg Romani activists formed an association during 1992 to press for various cultural liberties, but little solid information has been readily available about this and other Romani initiatives inside Albania.[17]

CHRONOLOGY

February 1990: The U.S. State Department reports significant limitations in Albania on the rights of minorities to exercise their cultural, educational and linguistic rights. Also mentioned are cases of prosecution and discrimination due to ethnic origin.[18]

September 1990: The Albanian Ministry of Foreign Affairs delivers a protest note to the Greek ambassador complaining about "chauvinist and anti-Albanian activities" in Greece. The reason for this was the holding of the second Pan-Greek Academic Congress on the Problem of Northern Epirus, held in the Greek town of Konitsa. The Albanian authorities accuse the organizers of employing anti-Albanian propaganda and embarking on a campaign of "threats and outright territorial claims." Greece's deputy prime minister and minister of justice takes part in the congress and calls for "a review of Europe's geographical map." The government in Tirana sends a protest letter to the EC, the United Nations, and CSCE accusing the Serbian authorities of genocide against the Albanian population in Kosovo. It does not rule out the possibility of military action if "violent hostilities increase."

Late 1990–Early 1991: The loosening of human rights restrictions by Tirana sparks a flow of refugees to Greece. Over 10,000 reportedly flee across the border and the majority claim to be ethnic Greeks. In January 1991, the Greek prime minister urges President Alia to encourage people to remain in Albania and to issue assurances that Albanian citizens who returned home would not be punished. The newly formed Albanian Democratic Party opposes the exodus, partly on the grounds that many of the refugees would have voted against the Communists.

March–April 1991: The first multi-party parliamentary elections are held with the participation of minority organizations. The Party of Labor (Communist) wins 169 seats, the Democratic Party 75 seats, and the predominantly Greek *Omonia* organization gains 5 seats to the National Assembly.

May 1991: *Omonia* issues a declaration demanding that the government stop the exodus of young people and intelligentsia from the southern regions of the country to Greece and endeavor to stabilize the situation in Greek minority areas.

July 1991: A ban on all parties of an ethnic, regional, or religious character is endorsed by parliament, with the support of both Socialist and Democratic deputies. The prohibition provokes a strong reaction from the international community, since it violates the basic principles of the Helsinki Final Act. The Albanian legislature passes a strongly worded resolution on Kosovo. Foreign Minister Muhamet Kapllani and President Alia demand that Serbian suppression of the Kosovo Albanians becomes an international issue.

September 1991: Albania's coalition government formally endorses the resolution of the exiled Kosovo Assembly that defines Kosovo as a sovereign republic within Yugoslavia. President Alia in a letter to Ilaz Ramajli, chairman of the Kosovo Assembly, also recognizes and accepts the decision on sovereignty as legitimate. The Ministry of Foreign Affairs publicly supports the decision of the Albanians in Macedonia not to take part in the referendum on the sovereignty and independence of this Yugoslav republic. The nationalist Motherland Political Association conducts talks in Tirana with a delegation of the National Unity Party in Yugoslavia (where the Unity Party claims to have a branch) and the Managing Committee of the Albanian National Unity Party. The creation of a pan-Albanian confederation is discussed. During its first national meeting, the Albanian Democratic Party (ADP) publishes a resolution on Kosovo. It declares that the decision of the Assembly of Kosovo to proclaim independence was based on the rights of the people to self-determination and was in accordance with the norms and precedents of international law. The meeting confirms that the ADP would work for the unity of all Albanians that "live in their own territories" but would desist from calling for imminent integration and discount the use of violent means.

October 1991: The Albanian National Assembly votes to recognize Kosovo as an independent republic, once the final results of the republican referendum are made public.

December 1991: The Greek newspaper *Kritianiki* reports that in an interview for the newspaper, the chairman of *Omonia* for Gjirokastër, Theodhori Bezhani, states that the organization will in future work for unification with Greece of all zones inhabited by the Greek minority in Albania. The article provokes a sharp reaction in Albania. The Albanian Democratic Party issues a statement in protest and demands that the government apply the law on preserving the integrity of the state.

Early 1992: Over 100,000 people find refuge in Greece, with about half of them claiming to be ethnic Greeks. Relations between Albania and Greece are again strained over the reported mistreatment and expulsion of Albanian refugees from Greece, and over alleged restrictions on the political activities of Greek minority organizations in Albania. Albania rejects a proposal by Athens for a UN delegation to visit the minority areas and for Greece to establish a consulate in the region. Albanian authorities reject Greek allegations about the mistreatment of minorities and begin to raise serious questions about the condition of the Albanian and Çam minority inside Greece.

January 1992: A student rally is held in Tirana to protest against the "aggressive nationalism of Slav and Greek chauvinists." Students criticize current policies and demand that the Yugoslav and Greek governments treat Albanians in their countries according to the principles of Helsinki. The rally condemns the entry of the Greek ferryboat *Kerkyra* with soldiers and military vehicles on board into the port of Sarandë and criticizes the statements of the chairman of the Gjirokastër branch of the *Omonia* organization.

February 1992: Heated speeches are made in the parliament after *Omonia* deputies offend some Albanians by stressing their Greek distinctiveness and asking for guaranteed seats in the parliament. Democratic Party deputy Abdi Baleta makes a speech attacking *Omonia*, which is interpreted as virulently anti-Greek. An election law is passed by parliament, barring ethnically based political parties from participating in the national elections. The Greek minority organization *Omonia* is not allowed to field candidates in any electoral zones. Ethnic clashes are reported on three consecutive days in the region of Sarandë. During these incidents, militant Albanians destroy and set fire to shops belonging to members of the Greek community and wreck the office of the *Omonia* organization. Shops that were not operated by Greeks remain untouched. *Omonia* accuses the police of having received word on an impeding attack and of failing to prevent it. After the incidents, the organization sends a protest letter to the EC mission in Tirana. Several other anti-Greek incidents are reported on the eve of the elections. For example, Thanasi Jorgji from the village of Bilisht, province of Korçë, withdraws his candidacy after local Albanians threatened to burn down his house.

March 1992: In the border station of Kakavia, Albanian police officers reportedly assault a member of the UPHR a few days before the parliamentary elections. A note of complaint by the UPHR president is sent to the Albanian president and the prime minister, to all political parties, the CSCE, and all foreign missions in Albania. The Albanian Foreign Ministry sends a protest note to the Greek ambassador, complaining that Greek leaflets were being distributed in some southern districts in an obvious attempt to influence the election outcome. The note also asserts that a radio station called Free Northern Epirus was daily broadcasting "anti-Albanian propaganda" from Corfu in both the Albanian and the Greek languages. In Tepelenë, southern Albania, a UPHR delegation is harassed, while near the village of Gramsh (Gjirokastër region), a local UPHR activist is shot; the seriously wounded man is transferred to a hospital in Ioannina, Greece. The attack is immediately reported by the UPHR leaders to the Albanian authorities, the CSCE, and foreign missions in Tirana. Nearly 7,000 members of the Greek minority assemble in Gjirokastër to protest the Gramsh incident. After being prohibited from participating in the parliamentary elections, *Omonia* sends a note to the CSCE Office of Democratic Institutions and Human Rights claiming that the Greek minority was prevented from freely expressing its political views. Police officers order Alekos Papadopoulos, a Greek parliamentary deputy and member of a delegation sent by the Greek parliament to monitor the Albanian elections, to halt his journey toward Gjirokastër, without explanation.

March 1992: The second multi-party parliamentary elections are held according to the new Electoral Law, which substantially limits the participation of minority organizations. In the first round, with a turnout of 90.35 percent, the Democratic Party wins 79 parliamentary seats, the Socialist Party (formerly Labor Party) 6 seats, the Unity Party for Human Rights (representing the Greek minority) 2 seats, and the Republican Party 1 seat. Seats are subsequently allocated on the principle of proportional representation, according to the percentage results in the first round. The UPHR does not receive the minimum 4 percent required on a national level and is not able to obtain any additional seats. In sum, the Democratic Party receives 62.29 percent of the popular vote, the Socialist Party 25.57 percent, the Social Democratic Party 4.33 percent, the Republican Party 3.15 percent, and the UPHR 2.92 percent. The 140 seats in the parliament are distributed as follows: Democratic Party 92, Socialist Party 38, Social Democratic Party 7, UPHR 2, and Republican Party 1 seat.

April 1992: President Sali Berisha and Prime Minister Aleksander Meksi meet in Tirana with Kosovo's prime minister Bujar Bukoshi and discuss future cooperation between the two governments.

May 1992: At a meeting of senior officials of the CSCE in Helsinki, Albanian deputy foreign minister Mehill Marku declares that the right of self-determination of the Albanians in Kosovo does not mean a forceful change of existing borders. He emphasizes that Albania does not demand a review of the map but would not accept an "inappropriate" solution to the problem. President Berisha issues a statement welcoming the coming multi-party elections in Kosovo. Berisha calls on all international organizations to recognize the human and "national rights" of Albanians in Kosovo. The Albanian People's Assembly invites CSCE and EC members to support and defend the elections in Kosovo.

July 1992: During the local election campaign, leaflets printed in Greece are distributed in the Greek minority areas and Greek flags are hoisted in Sarandë, Alikaj, and other southern towns. Albanian spokesmen criticize the "reactionary election campaign" of *Omonia* and the UPHR and accuse the Greeks of seeking to dominate all local governments. A regionalist group in southeastern Albania, calling itself the Labëria Association, issues a statement attacking *Omonia* and its election campaign methods. The Association condemns *Omonia* for allegedly employing "hostile propaganda against the Albanian nation and state" and demands that these acts be punished as a serious crime, applying Albania's main constitutional provisions and its Penal Code. Four ethnic Greeks returning from Greece for the Albanian local elections are arrested in Gjirokastër for distributing leaflets calling for areas inhabited by the Greek minority to be "reunited" with Greece. Local elections are held with a surprisingly low turnout of only 70.5 percent. Voting by party nationwide is as follows: Democratic Party 43.16 percent, Socialist Party 41.32 percent, Unity Party for Human Rights 4.34 percent, and Republican Party 3.43 percent.

September 1992: Prime Minister Aleksander Meksi meets with Kosovo President Ibrahim Rugova and Prime Minister Bujar Bukoshi of Kosovo and discusses expanding economic relations under the direction of a coordinating commission. Meksi further states that the struggle in Kosovo is a political conflict involving the "impossible coexistence" of Albanians in the republic with the "Serb occupiers."

November 1992: A working visit of the Kosovo prime minister Bukoshi to Tirana includes talks with Premier Meksi focusing on the extension of Albanian-Kosovar cooperation in all spheres.

January 1993: At a news conference Albanian foreign minister Alfred Serreqi states that the foreign policy of the government is concentrated on the national question: the priority of Albanian diplomacy is to avoid war and bloodshed in Kosovo. The foreign minister also discusses Albanian-Greek relations and the Çamëria question.

March 1993: The Çamëria Political and Patriotic Association, together with the Labëria Association, organizes a meeting in Tirana with leading Albanian intellectuals. They issue a statement condemning the alleged "Hellenization of south Albania" and appeal to the government and all political parties to "consolidate national identity" and protect the territorial integrity of Albania.[19]

June 1993: Clashes are reported between Greek protesters and Albanian police near Gjirokastër following the expulsion of a Greek Orthodox cleric from Albania on charges of encouraging separatism. Tensions between Tirana and Athens increase when the Greek authorities round up and expel thousands of Albanian refugees and illegal residents, claiming that they would expel tens of thousands more. Tirana dispatches a note calling on the Greek government to disassociate itself from nationalist and irredentist groups in Greece and to withdraw army reinforcements from the Albanian border.

July 1993: President Berisha seeks to defuse Albanian-Greek tensions by pledging to protect the rights of the Greek minority and meets with *Omonia* leaders. Socialist leaders attack Berisha and the Democratic Party leadership for their allegedly authoritarian tendencies. Legislative battles continue over the new constitution and Socialist deputies call for new general elections.

NOTES

1. The most recent population statistics are taken from the *Statistical Yearbook of Albania 1991*, Tirana, 1991.

2. For useful historical material on Albania, consult Anton Logoreci, *The Albanians: Europe's Forgotten Survivors* (Boulder, Co.: Westview, 1977); Stavro Skendi, *The Albanian National Awakening, 1878–1912* (Princeton, NJ: Princeton University Press, 1967); Stefanaq Pollo and Arben Puto, *The History of Albania* (Boston: Routledge and Vegan Paul, 1981); Peter Prifti, *Socialist Albania Since 1944: Domestic and Foreign Developments* (Cambridge, MA: MIT Press, 1978); Nicholas Pano, *The People's Republic of Albania* (Baltimore, MD: Johns Hopkins University Press, 1968); and Elez Biberaj, *Albania: A Socialist Maverick* (Boulder, Co.: Westview, 1990).

3. See *Human Rights Worldwide*, no. 5, November 1991; and Greek Helsinki Committee for Human Rights, *Report on the Parliamentary Elections of March 23, 1992, and the Political Rights of the Greek Minority*, Thessaloniki, May 1992.

4. The proposed constitutional provisions are cited from an unauthorized translation of the Draft Constitution of the Republic of Albania. Also see the statement by the Labëria Association, "Provocative and Insulting Acts by Greek Chauvinists," *Republika*, Tirana, July 16, 1992, in Foreign Broadcast Information Service/Joint Publications Research Service, *Daily Report: East Europe, JPRS-EER–92–106*, August 13, 1992. See also *Country Reports on Human Rights Practices for 1992*, U.S. Department of State, February 1993.

5. Refer to Section 5, "Discrimination Based on Race, Sex, Religion, Language, or Social Status" in *Country Reports on Human Rights Practices for 1991*, U.S. Department of State, February 1992.

6. Details about electoral procedures in 1991 and 1992 and provisions relating to the participation of ethnic minorities can be found in Greek Helsinki Committee for Human Rights, *Report on the Parliamentary Elections of 22 March 1991 and the Political Rights of the Greek Minority*, Thessaloniki, May 1992; National Democratic Institute for Interna-

tional Affairs, *Albania: 1991 Elections to the People's Assembly*, Washington, DC, April 30, 1991; Helsinki Watch, *Albania*, New York, April 19, 1991; and International Republican Institute, *Albania Election Information, Parliamentary Elections of 22 March 1992*, Washington, DC, April 1992.

7. For complete local election results, see *Tirana Radio Network*, August 13, 1992, in Foreign Broadcast Information Service, *Daily Report: East Europe, FBIS-EEU–92–157*, August 13, 1992. Also check *Tirana Radio Network*, July 26, 1992, in *FBIS-EEU–92–144*, July 27, 1992; *Tirana Radio Network*, July 31 1992, in *FBIS-EEU–92–149*, August 3, 1992; *Tirana Radio Network*, August 3, 1992, in *FBIS-EEU–92–150*, August 4, 1992; *Tirana Radio Network*, August 8, 1992, in *FBIS-EEU–92–151*, August 5, 1992; *Tirana Radio Network*, August 7, 1992, in *FBIS-EEU–92–154*, August 10, 1992.

8. Check Louis Zanga, "Albanian-Greek Relations Reach a Low Point," Radio Free Europe/Radio Liberty Research Institute (RFE/RL), *Research Report*, vol. 1, no. 15, April 10, 1992; and *AFP*, Paris, July 26, 1992, in *FBIS-EEU–92–144*, July 27, 1992.

9. See *Tirana Domestic Service*, Tirana, September 9, 1990, in *FBIS-EEU–90–175*, September 10, 1990; Shaban Murati, "Chauvinist Calls Which Damage Greek-Albanian Relations," *Zëri i Popullit*, Tirana, September 6, 1990, in *FBIS-EEU–90–178*, September 13, 1990; Louis Zanga, "Ramiz Alia Under Great Pressure," RFE/RL, *Report on Eastern Europe*, vol. 2, no. 8, February 22, 1991; *Tanjug*, Belgrade, July 31, 1991, in *FBIS-EEU–91–149*, August 2, 1991; *ATA*, Tirana, September 4, 1991, in *FBIS-EEU–91–172*, September 5, 1991; *ATA*, Tirana, September 26, 1991, in *FBIS-EEU–91–188*, September 27, 1991; *Tirana Radio Network*, May 22, 1992, in *FBIS-EEU–92–101*, May 26, 1992; *ATA*, August 16, 1992, *FBIS-EEU–92–160*, August 18, 1992; *Tirana Radio Network*, January 1, 1993, in *FBIS-EEU–93–005*, January 8, 1993.

10. Some information on the Albanian National Unity Party and the Motherland Political Association is contained in *Tirana Radio Network*, September 24, 1991, in *FBIS-EEU–91–188*, September 27, 1991.

11. For details about *Omonia*, see *Tirana Domestic Service* and *Tirana Radio Network*, May 18, 1991, in *FBIS-EEU–91–098*, May 21, 1991; *Tirana Domestic Service*, February 26, 1991, in *FBIS-EEU–91–039*, February 27, 1991; Zanga, "Albanian-Greek Relations Reach a Low Point;" Greek Helsinki Committee for Human Rights, *Report on the Parliamentary Elections*.

12. See *Elliniki Radiofonia Radio Network*, Athens, February 25, 1992, in *FBIS-EEU–92–038*, February 26, 1992; Greek Helsinki Committee for Human Rights, *Report on the Parliamentary Elections*; Zanga, "Albanian-Greek Relations Reach a Low Point."

13. Details on Kosovar movements in Albania can be found in *ATA*, Tirana, March 8, 1991, in *FBIS-EEU–91–046*, March 8, 1991; *ATA*, Tirana, February 3, 1992; and the "Program and Statute of the Kosovo Patriotic and Political Association," *Kosova*, Tirana, July 21, 1991, in *JPRS-EER–91–118*, August 7, 1991.

14. For more about the Çamëria question, check *Zëri i Popullit*, Tirana, March 19, 1991, in *FBIS-EEU–91–058*, March 26, 1991; and *ATA*, Tirana, September 17, 1991.

15. Check *Tanjug*, Belgrade, February 27, 1991, in *FBIS-EEU–91–040*, February 28, 1991.

16. See *Tirana Radio Network*, September 8, 1991, in *FBIS-EEU–91–174*, September 9, 1991.

17. Information about the Arumunian Association is taken from "Aremenil Din," The Albania "Cultural Association," Tirana, February 1993; and *ATA*, Tirana, February 12, 1993, in *FBIS-EEU–93–030*, February 17, 1993.

18. For more details, see *State Department Report on Human Rights in Albania*, U.S. Department of State, Washington, 1990.

19. *ATA*, Tirana, March 18, 1993, in *FBIS-EEU–93–053*, March 22, 1993.

PART III

Central Europe

Ethnicity Reborn

10

Czech Republic

POPULATION

According to the results of the 1991 Czechoslovak census, the total population of the Czech Republic reached 10,298,731.[1] Of this number, 8,372,868, or 81.3 percent, declared themselves ethnic Czechs, and 1,359,432, or 13.2 percent, were listed as Moravians for the first time in the state's post-war history. Aside from the Moravians, who were considered a regional rather than an ethnic category, Slovaks constituted the largest minority, totaling 308,962 people, or 3.0 percent of the total. However, according to some estimates the Slovak population actually exceeded 500,000 as many had become fully or partially assimilated and claimed Czech nationality in the census. The majority of Slovaks lived in Prague and other large cities, as well as in the German border areas. The overwhelming majority of the approximately 60,000 Germans and the 60,000 Poles in the federation lived in Bohemia and Moravia, while about 46,000 people declared themselves Czech Silesians. Estimates of Gypsy (Roma) numbers remained highly problematic. While official figures, based on the 1991 census, showed Roma totaling 114,116 of the Czechoslovak population, unofficial estimates ranged from 200,000 to half a million. According to government sources, approximately 50,000 Roma lived in the Czech Republic, while Romani leaders projected the figure at over 100,000. The remainder of the Czech population consisted of small numbers of Ukrainians, Ruthenians, Hungarians, Romanians, and Jews. With the achievement of independence in January 1993 and the registration of Czech citizens based on new citizenship regulations, a new population census will need to be conducted in the republic.

HISTORICAL OVERVIEW

The Czechoslovak state was created in 1918 following the collapse of the Austro-Hungarian Empire.[2] It was formed from the merger of the Czech territories of

Czech Republic: Population (1991)

Ethnic Groups	Number	% of Population
Czechs	8,372,868	81.30
Moravians	1,359,432	13.20
Slovaks	308,962	3.00
Poles	60,000	0.58
Germans	60,000	0.58
Roma (Gypsies)	50,000	0.49
Silesians	46,000	0.45
Hungarians	23,000	0.22
Jews	5,000	0.05
Others	13,000	0.13
Total Minorities	1,925,394	18.70
Total Population	10,298,731	100.00

Bohemia, Moravia, and Austrian Silesia, and the provinces of Slovakia and Ruthenia lost by Hungary at the end of World War One. Czech and Slovak leaders decided that an amalgamation of the two west Slavic nations would provide them with long-term security and protection against German and Hungarian expansionism. The new country was ethnically heterogeneous; in addition to a Czech majority and a Slovak minority, it incorporated large numbers of Germans, Hungarians, Ruthenians, Ukrainians, and Jews, and smaller populations of Gypsies, Poles, Romanians, and Russians. According to the 1921 national census, out of a total population of 13,613,172, "Czechoslovaks" constituted 8,760,937, Germans 3,123,568, Hungarians 745,431, Ruthenians and Ukrainians 461,849, and Jews 354,342. Poles numbered some 75,000, and a further 25,000 people included Gypsies and Romanians. About two-thirds of the population of Bohemia, numbering 6,670,582, were classified as Czechs, and nearly one-third were Germans. Four-fifths of the 2,662,884 inhabitants of Moravia were Czechs, and most of the rest Germans, while 47.6 percent of the 672,268 people in the Silesian area were Czechs, and 40.5 percent were Germans.

The large German minority in the Czech lands, located primarily in the Sudeten borderlands, presented the biggest headache for the new government in Prague. Many Germans, long accustomed to being the dominant nationality and now finding themselves in a minority position in a new Slavic state, were openly opposed to Czech rule. They feared their exposure as a vulnerable minority in the frontier areas that could result in various onerous restrictions. Some German organizations sought to detach German-inhabited territories and join them up with either Austria or Germany. Other parties demanded the right of territorial self-determination. In 1918, German deputies in Bohemia declared German-inhabited regions "an autonomous province of the German-Austrian state." But the rebellion was quickly subdued by the Czech government; troops were dispatched into the Sudetenland area to thwart German resistance.

The majority of German parties eventually accepted the legitimacy of the new administration, but criticisms persisted over the structure of the state and over alleged anti-minority discrimination. The Czechoslovak constitution of February 1920 defined the state as uni-national with a centralized administration. However, by East European standards the constitution was decidedly liberal, based on the principles of the civic equality of all citizens regardless of their ethnicity, religion, or language. German and other minority leaders objected to the composition of the National Assembly, which was dominated by the Czechs, and the privileged position of the Czech and Slovak languages in official transactions. A special language law specified that a minority language could be used in courts and in dealings with local authorities in administrative units where more than 20 percent of the inhabitants were German, Hungarian, or Polish. Germans felt aggrieved that the ruling did not apply to Czechs or Slovaks who could use their language regardless of their numbers in any community. Despite their protests, the major German parties entered Czechoslovakia's coalition government and received the bulk of the German vote in several national elections. However, the nationalist parties refused to accept the legitimacy of the new state and persistently agitated against it. The effects of the Great Depression in the 1930s on the industrial areas of Czechoslovakia were keenly felt among the German population. Growing unemployment and the rise of Nazism in Germany aggravated discontent among Germans and increased support for the autonomist and nationalist parties in the Sudetenland.

A second major point of conflict in the Czech lands was over the Tešín (Cieszyn, Teschen) area of the former Austrian Silesia. The region was highly prized by Prague because of its rich coal reserves and highly developed transportation network, but it was also claimed by Poland because of the large indigenous Polish population, making up about 11.2 percent of the total. Czech forces occupied the territory in 1919 but were repulsed by local Polish resistance. Prague successfully captured the region in 1920 when Warsaw was embroiled in a war with Soviet Russia. The incident left a lingering source of bitterness between the two states, and Warsaw reclaimed the Tešín area after the German occupation of the Czech lands on the eve of World War Two. In 1919, Czechoslovakia also gained Subcarpathian Ruthenia from Hungary. The region contained a large Ruthenian and Ukrainian population, estimated at about 62.3 percent of the 606,000 inhabitants. Initial promises of autonomy remained unfulfilled, while Budapest itself sought to regain the territory from Prague. Indeed, after the Nazi dismemberment of Czechoslovakia, Hungary reacquired large parts of Ruthenia for the duration of the war.

Czechoslovakia's Jewish population was highly differentiated. About one-third of the 356,830 Jews registered in 1931 lived in the Czech lands. In Bohemia and Moravia they were mostly urban residents and were highly integrated in Czech society. Jews gained considerable religious and cultural freedoms under the Czechoslovak constitution and many declared their nationality as Czech in the 1921 and 1930 censuses. By contrast, in Slovakia and Ruthenia the Jews maintained a separate communal existence and the majority following Orthodox Judaism lived in small towns and villages. In Bohemia, Moravia, and Silesia, Jews made an important contribution to Czech economic and cultural life, while in Slovakia and Ruthenia their role was less pronounced. Following Nazi Germany's occupation of Czechoslovakia, the majority of Jews were deported to extermination camps, particularly from the pro-Nazi Slovak satellite state. The puppet government in the Protectorate of Bohemia and Moravia also tacitly assisted in the deportation program. Only about 44,000 Czechoslovak Jews survived the Holocaust, many of whom were able to disguise their ethnic and religious identity. Thousands of Czechoslovak Gypsies also perished in Nazi death camps.

World War Two dramatically altered the ethnic composition of Czechoslovakia as the population became much more homogeneous. The Jewish population was decimated and the numbers continued to decline after the war as thousands emigrated to Israel or to the West; only 5,000 mostly assimilated Jews were left by the 1980s. The Germans fled or were deported *en masse* at the end of the war. According to the 1950 census, only 165,000 German ethnics were left out of a population of some 3,391,000. Their numbers continued to shrink: by 1970 only 85,000 remained, and 61,000 in 1980, with a majority resident in the Czech lands. The loss of Ruthenia to the Soviet Union eliminated a large Ukrainian and Ruthenian minority: only 54,000 were listed in 1964 and 47,000 in 1980. In addition, Prague launched a program of deportation vis-à-vis the Hungarian minority in Slovakia, but the expulsions were terminated due to opposition from both Budapest and Moscow. Less than 100,000 Magyars left the country in the late 1940s, out of a pre-war population of some 700,000. The size of other communities remained relatively stable, with about 67,000 Poles in 1961 and 65,000 in 1980, and approximately 9,000 Russians. Gypsy (Roma) numbers were extremely difficult to estimate, particularly as the Romani nationality was not recognized in post-war Czechoslovakia and many Gypsies declared themselves as Czechs, Slovaks, or Hungarians.

The Czech Republic became more compact ethnically than Slovakia. By 1980, out of a total population of 10,285,000 the Czechs (including Bohemians and Moravians) numbered over 94 percent, the Slovaks nearly 3.4 percent, and the minority total only reached 2 percent of inhabitants. Poles, Germans, and Hungarians continued to form the most substantial minorities. Although in theory all nationalities benefited from the same legal and political rights, the relatively small size of minorities tended to preclude any major pressures for protecting and developing collective rights in comparison to the two major nationalities (Czech and Slovak).

Since the 1989 "Velvet Revolution," which ended Communist Party rule, the federal government in Prague has adopted more conciliatory policies toward its minorities and toward neighboring states. Soon after his election, President

Václav Havel made an important speech apologizing for the forced expulsion of several million Germans in the years after World War Two. Some Czech critics were perturbed that such statements would raise the expectations of expelled Sudeten Germans and their offspring and increase demands for material compensation and some special privileges for the resident German minority. Indeed, the West German–based Sudeten German Association demanded that any treaty between Prague and Bonn include a clause for the creation of a commission to investigate all property claims and the right of Germans to resettle in Czechoslovakia. The issue did not interrupt the conclusion of a new treaty between the two states in October 1991. The treaty did not specifically deal with the question of property confiscations or war reparations. Moreover, territorial questions were not raised in either capital and the small size of the German minority mitigated against any major disputes over their future status.

Czechoslovakia's relations with Poland visibly warmed after 1989, as both states pursued market-oriented reforms and together with Hungary established the Central European or *Visegrád* "triangle" to help coordinate their foreign-policy initiatives. The small but compact Polish minority in the Zaolzie Silesian region of Moravia pressed for the restoration of property seized by the Communist regime at the close of World War Two. Polish groups were able to enhance their cultural and organizational endeavors with some state funding from Prague, and their position, as well as that of the small Czech community in Poland's Lower Silesian region, has not given cause for any disputes between Prague and Warsaw. Amicable relations were also maintained between Prague and Budapest, and unlike in Slovakia, the minuscule Magyar minority in the Czech Republic was not threatened with any curtailment of its collective rights.

With the disintegration of the Soviet Union, Czechoslovakia established cordial relations with Ukraine. Renewed interest was evident in Ukraine's Subcarpathian Ruthenian region that once formed part of the Czechoslovak state. Although the Czech and Slovak governments lodged no claims to the area and the federal authorities renounced any border revisions, newly formed ultra-nationalist parties took aboard the Ruthenian cause. In particular, some Prague-based nationalist parties sought a new status for Ruthenia, with eventual reunification on the basis of a regional referendum. But the question of Ruthenia became further complicated by a large Magyar-minority presence in the region, the opposition of the Ukrainian government to any separatist tendencies, and the ongoing collapse of the Czech-Slovak federation.

The Gypsy, or Romani, population in Communist Czechoslovakia was subjected to forced resettlement, dispersal, the persecution of linguistic and cultural traditions, attempts at mass sterilization, and discrimination in housing, employment, and education. The Communist authorities did not recognize Roma as members of a distinct nationality but, rather, as a backward ethnic minority that would be integrated and assimilated into the emerging Socialist society. During the 1968 "Prague Spring," the Roma enjoyed a fleeting period of cultural freedom, a Union of Gypsy-Roma was allowed to function, and Romani festivals were permitted. The Union was disbanded in 1973, and for the next sixteen years Gypsies were again unable to defend their interests, express their distinct traditions, or campaign for various minority rights. Following the 1989 revolution, the Czechoslovak Federal Assembly passed a Charter of Fundamental Rights and Liberties. It outlawed discrimination on the basis of national or ethnic identity and guaranteed the right to minority education in the native language, the right to use the mother tongue in contacts with officialdom, and the right of minority representatives to participate in all questions pertaining to ethnic status and development. Similar documents were ratified at the Czech and Slovak republican levels. Over 30 Romani organizations were registered, mostly in the cultural arena, and Gypsies were able to declare themselves as being of "Romani nationality" in the census and on their identity cards. But despite the progress achieved in lifting restrictions on Roma at the federal and republican level, discrimination and prejudice persisted at local levels in both republics.

The question of Moravian-Silesian autonomy within the Czech Republic has also surfaced in recent years. In the 1991 census, nearly one-half of the approximately 3 million inhabitants of the region openly declared their nationality as Moravian or Silesian for the first time in the country's recent history. Several new organizations were formed and placed demands for regional autonomy on the republic's political agenda. During 1991, representatives from an assortment of political groups gathered to discuss proposals for a new territorial set-up of the country. They suggested the drafting of a separate Moravian constitution for a tripartite federation of Czech-Bohemia, Moravia-Silesia, and Slovakia. The project was rejected by the Czechoslovak authorities. Despite Czech opposition, public opinion polls indicated growing popular support for Moravian self-determination and even republican status. Moravian autonomists also gained seats in the Czech National Council during two rounds of general elections. The emergence of two independent states from the Czechoslovak federation could further energize demands for sovereignty and self-determination in Moravia-Silesia.

OFFICIAL POLICIES

The ethnic-minority question was not paid much attention by Czechoslovak leaders until several years after World War Two; no complete statistics on the size of most minority populations were officially cited until 1965. In 1968, Constitutional Law No. 144 was introduced on the nationalities in the Czechoslovak Socialist Republic, establishing rules for the treatment of minorities. While this legislation included the right for minorities to receive education in their own language, the prevailing reaction was that the law was too vague and needed further specification. Throughout the years of Communist "normalization," from 1969 onward, the position of ethnically based associations was again diminished and they functioned mainly as folkloric diversions.

It has only been since the fall of Communism in 1989 that ethnic minorities have gained increasing recognition. Among the new important features of the first post-Communist census, held in March 1991, was the opportunity for citizens to declare themselves as members of the Gypsy (Romani) national minority and as Moravians or Silesians, categories not previously acknowledged by the state.

Another significant development was the Charter of Fundamental Rights and Liberties, adopted in January 1991 by the Czechoslovak Federal Assembly, which formed a new legal basis for the treatment of ethnic minorities. This document outlined the basic human, civil, and political rights of Czechoslovak citizens and was to serve as a foundation for the future federal and republican constitutions. Articles 24 and 25 directly addressed minority rights questions. The charter provided everyone with the right to decide his or her nationality, prohibited discrimination against all minorities, and provided minorities with the right to form their own ethnic associations. The charter also declared that under certain conditions, minorities would have the right to be educated in their own language and to use it in dealings with officialdom. No other laws were to supersede the charter's basic provisions, and all future federal and republican legislation was to be framed in accordance with its stipulations.

The election law, passed in February 1990, for the first pluralistic ballot in Czechoslovakia in 44 years, was an important step in framing the structure of the new parliaments and determining the degree of political stability. Restrictions were placed on parliamentary fragmentation: in order to participate a party had to obtain 10,000 signatures, and in order to qualify for parliamentary seats under the system of proportional representation, a party needed to gain at least 5 percent of the total vote. In sum, only 23 political parties, movements, and coalitions ran in the elections as several dozen groups failed to qualify for the balloting. The first multi-party general elections in June 1990 were primarily a plebiscite against Communism rather than an open competition between distinct parties. The maintenance of the Civic Forum (CF) and Public Against Violence (PAV) coalitions, which brought a negotiated end to Communist rule, guaranteed a sweeping election victory.[3] The alliance gained 170 out of 300 seats in the Federal Assembly, the Communists in both republics managed to score 47 seats, and the Christian Democratic Union obtained 40 seats. The remainder were divided among regionalist, nationalist, and ethnically based organizations: the Association for Moravia and Silesia, the Slovak National Party, and the Coexistence organization in Slovakia, respectively. In the Czech National Council, the CF gained 127 out of 200 seats, the Communists 32, the Association for Moravia and Silesia 22, and the Christian Democratic Union 19. The new Czech administration was dominated by the Civic Forum.

Following the national elections, progress was registered in decentralizing the government structure, not only by placing greater powers in the Slovak and Czech National Councils but in devolving various responsibilities to local governments. Under the old system, a structure of national committees at all administrative tiers executed orders from the next-highest level and ensured centralized decision making presided over by the Communist Party. Local government was in practice an arm of the central government. Following the June 1990 elections, the powers of the republican governments and the local administrations were strengthened. Several federal ministries were abolished and their responsibilities devolved to the republics. Local government was buttressed by limiting the size of district national committees and abolishing the regional tier altogether. Municipal and local-level committees were given greater autonomy. They were to become legal entities responsible for tax collection and budgeting under the regulation of the respective republican legislature and not the federal government.

Some regionalist activists demanded more far-ranging devolution and the creation of self-governing *länder* in Bohemia, Moravia, Silesia, and Prague; these proposals were not adopted by the Czech authorities. On several occasions, Czech government and parliamentary leaders met with representatives of Moravian and Silesian public organizations and civic initiatives to discuss the broad spectrum of views on the future arrangement of the three Czech regions. Although all participants agreed that some form of self-administration, with due regard to historical traditions, would prove indispensable, there were continuing disagreements on its precise structure between republican and local commune levels. Some Czech political leaders proposed dividing both Bohemia and Moravia-Silesia into several "autonomous land units." Moravian organizations favored either creating a single "Moravian-Silesian land," together with two or three such "lands" in Bohemia, or constructing a symmetrical relationship between Bohemia and Moravia. The latter proposal was criticized in Prague as threatening the integrity of the state.

A Moravian-Silesian political coalition was established on the platform of regional autonomy within the Czech Republic. It scored well in the 1990 national elections but then began to splinter on the basis of differing approaches toward federalism and administrative devolution. Some groups sought a German-type *länder* status for Moravia-Silesia within the Czech Republic, while others demanded a quasi-republican status within the Czechoslovak federation. Cleavages were also evident on whether to keep the association together as a civic movement or transform it into a political party. The association finally split into two groups in the spring of 1991, stressing two different approaches: radical republicanism within the Czechoslovak federation and regional autonomy within the Czech Republic.

The Moravian-Silesian phenomenon has been defined as "regional patriotism," rather than ethnic separatism, that was intensified by the ongoing decentralization of the Czechoslovak federation. Throughout 1991 and 1992, various public opinion polls disclosed pronounced popular support for Moravian autonomy and self-determination. Rallies were staged in the major Moravian towns of Brno, Ostrava, and Olomouc protesting against alleged political and economic discrimination by Prague. If regional issues were to be addressed fully by Prague through further decentralization and appropriate economic investment, public support for Moravian-Silesian autonomy would be likely to wane and regional autonomists would probably lose their popularity. However, if resentment were to mount in the region against Prague's heavy-handed policies or economic neglect, support for further decentralization and some measure of autonomy could actually increase.

The first multi-party local elections were held in November 1990 and were designed to democratize the administration at each tier.[4] They proved less constrained by coalition politics than the general elections. Fifty-five political parties and movements competed for seats in the Czech Republic. But the results were not fully representative of the influence of political forces at the central level, because many parties possessed only a skeletal local structure and did not compete in all electoral districts. Personal knowledge of the candidates proved a more compelling criterion for many voters than party affiliation or political platform. Interestingly, the nationalist, regionalist, and ethnic groupings performed poorly at the local level compared with the national elections. Citizens seemed to display more concern for practical local issues, while the newly formed groupings lacked a comprehensive organizational network. Although the CF remained the strongest force in the Czech Republic, its vote total decreased from 49.5 percent in June to 35.8 percent. The Communists finished second with 17.2 percent, up from 13.2 percent in June. The People's Party improved from 8.4 percent to 11.5 percent, while the autonomist Association for Moravia and Silesia gained only 4.2 percent of the Czech vote, down from 10 percent in June, although it only stood for elections in the Moravian counties. The Social Democrats slightly improved their total from 4.1 percent to 5 percent, as did the Socialists, up from 2.7 percent to 3.2 percent.

The Czech Republic's ethnic minorities began to organize after the "Velvet Revolution" and established various associations to protect their interests. However, because of their comparatively small size and the restrictive election law stipulations, they were unable to gain more than a handful of seats to the republican parliament. To improve their political position, Polish and German organizations entered the multi-ethnic Coexistence coalition based in Bratislava and coordinated by leaders of the large Hungarian population in Slovakia. Although Polish and German representatives welcomed the collapse of Communist rule and the process of democratization, they were concerned over the shortage of state funds for their publishing, cultural, and educational ventures and demanded the return of property confiscated either by the post–World War Two coalition government or by the Communist regime.

President Havel proved determined to place Czech-German relations on a sounder footing, and soon after his election he made a ground-breaking speech apologizing for the forced expulsion of several million Germans in the years after World War Two. Some Czech leaders and commentators grew concerned that such statements would raise the expectations of expelled Sudeten Germans and their offspring for the return of Czech property and real estate. Although expellee organizations in Germany demanded the creation of a commission to investigate all property claims, such pressures did not prevent the signing of a comprehensive new treaty between Prague and Bonn in October 1991. The Prague government endeavored to reassure its citizens that Czech property would not be confiscated and that large numbers of Germans were not about to settle in the republic. Although some disputes were evident on the status of the German minority, the Treaty on Good-Neighborliness and Friendly Cooperation contained provisions that appeared to settle the issue.[5] In June 1993, leaders of the four ruling coalition parties agreed to initiate unofficial talks with ethnic Germans on the delicate question of compensation for former expellees; a working group was to be established to examine the question further. The decision was condemned by the nationalist Republican Party, which opposed any dialogue with Sudeten Germans.[6]

While discrimination on the basis of race, religion, or ethnicity was forbidden under the Charter of Fundamental Rights and Liberties and under additional federal and republican legislation, it still permeated various facets of life, particularly against the most visible Romani minority.[7] Indeed, liberalization in Czechoslovakia may have given vent to previously stifled anti-Gypsy prejudices. According to some reports, with the decline of central government supervision, discrimination against Roma actually increased in housing, employment, and access to public and private services, particularly at local levels. In addition, anti-Gypsy violence mushroomed after 1989 as ultra-nationalist and racist groups were able to operate more freely. In conditions where Gypsies were widely scapegoated as criminals and where police displayed indifference or passivity to anti-Romani manifestations, skinhead gangs have targeted Gypsies for random violence. Romani leaders have in turn criticized the legal system and the security forces for failing to protect Romani communities and blamed much of the national media for perpetuating negative Gypsy stereotypes.

In December 1992, the prosecutor general of the Czech Republic submitted a bill to the parliament on extraordinary measures for the "preservation of public order" in view of racial problems in numerous cities and towns, especially in northern Bohemia. The bill was initiated in response to controversies surrounding a November decree on securing public order, passed by the North Bohemian town of Jiříkov. The decree had ordered fines of up to 100,000 crowns for actions endangering the morals, health, or security of others, immediate eviction without judicial approval, and other penalties. It was heavily criticized because of its evident anti-Romani bias, which apparently reinforced anti-Romani sentiments already prevalent in Bohemia. The prosecutor general asserted that such a decree was unacceptable as it violated the Charter of Fundamental Rights and Liberties.[8]

The 1992 general election law was designed to buttress the growth of stronger parties. The 5 percent vote minimum for obtaining parliamentary seats was supplemented by stipulations that coalitions of 2 or more parties had to gain 7 percent of the vote, and a 4-plus coalition needed 10 percent to qualify. The objective was both to counter unrestricted political fragmentation by excluding smaller parties and to build up distinct parties through durable mergers. In the second general elections of June 1992, a total of 36 parties, movements, and coalitions competed for the Federal Assembly and 19 for the Czech National Council. Right-of-center parties scored victories in the Czech Republic and left-of-center and pro-independence parties won in Slovakia; the biggest losses were sustained by centrist and federalist forces.[9] The Civic Democratic Party gained 29.73 percent of the total vote, obtaining 76 seats out of 200 in the Czech National Council; the Left Bloc (including the Communist Party) won 14.05 percent of the vote, with 35 seats. The Republican Party scored 5.98 percent and obtained 14 seats; the party performed particularly well in northern Bohemia (10.6 percent), southern Bohemia (7.2 percent), central Bohemia (6.8 percent) and southern Moravia (6.3 percent). The Association for Moravia and Silesia gained a total of 5.87 percent, obtaining 14 seats; in southern Moravia they registered 16.2 percent of the vote, and in northern Moravia 12.6 percent.

At the federal level, a transitional government was installed because there was no agreement among the most successful Czech and Slovak parties on preserving the federal arrangement. In the Czech chamber of the federal House of the People, the Civic Democratic Party won comfortably with 33.9 percent of the vote, followed by the Left Bloc (a coalition of reform Communists) with 14.27 percent. Social Democrats gained 7.67 percent, and the Republicans registered a modest 6.48 percent. The Civic Movement only managed a disappointing 4.39 percent of the vote for the Federal Assembly and the Civic Democratic Alliance 4.98 percent; both failed to gain seats in the parliament. The remaining centrist forces scored somewhat better: the Liberal and Social Union obtained 5.84 percent and the People's Party 5.98 percent.

Following the June 1992 elections, only a caretaker federal government was set up to administer the division of the country. The federal cabinet was reduced, and Havel himself failed to be reelected as Czechoslovak president due to opposition by Slovak deputies. In an agreement between Premiers Klaus and Mečiar, the republican governments were to decide on the federal split and establish the legal foundations for Czech and Slovak statehood. A timetable of separation was quickly agreed upon. In July 1992, the Slovak government declared sovereignty and in October 1992 ratified its own constitution. In September 1992, the federal cabinet approved a bill on methods of dissolving the federation: either by a declaration of the federal Assembly, by an agreement between the two republican parliaments, by a referendum in both republics, or by the withdrawal of one of the republics from the federation. Paradoxically, Slovak demands for sovereignty or independence and delays in signing binding constitutional agreements spurred calls for an independent Czech state. In particular, conservatives, free-marketeers, and some nationalists in Prague underscored the numerous advantages of a clean break, including a more streamlined administration, budget savings, and improved chances for the Czech Republic to join the EC. Preparations were undertaken to pass a separate Czech constitution and to reorganize the republic into several self-governing regions to pacify Moravian-Silesian demands for greater autonomy.

In October 1992, the federal government approved the draft of a constitutional act on terminating the federation. Two days later Mečiar and Klaus signed sixteen agreements defining relations between the two republics following the dissolution; these included stipulations on a customs union and a common currency. In November 1992, the Federal Assembly voted to disband the Czech and Slovak federation, phase out all federal institutions, and give the two republics equal successor status. More than 30 agreements were concluded regulating relations between the two republics and equally dividing federal assets. Nonetheless, some disputes were expected to materialize, particularly in valuing and apportioning federal property between Prague and Bratislava and in the acquisition of Czech and Slovak citizenship.[10]

The Czech Law on Citizenship passed in December 1992 laid down a range of stipulations for acquiring Czech citizenship.[11] Most of the articles appeared to be straightforward and non-controversial: in effect, persons who were simultaneously citizens of both Czechoslovakia and the Czech Republic prior to December 31, 1992, automatically became citizens of the new Czech Republic. However, on closer reading, some of the stipulations seemed more restrictive and could lend themselves to potential discrimination. In particular, the condition that Czech citizenship would be granted to those who "have not been convicted of a crime in the previous five years," if allowed to override the five-year residency stipulations, could be used to disqualify a substantial number of residents. A knowledge of the Czech language was also required: some observers noted that the clause could be used to disqualify a segment of the Romani population originally from Slovakia from gaining full citizenship.

Slovak citizens were given until December 31, 1993, to proclaim themselves as Czech citizens; they needed to prove permanent residence in the Czech Republic for two years, their release from Slovak citizenship, and the absence of a criminal conviction during the previous five years. According to the law, an individual had to renounce citizenship of all other states as dual citizenship was not permissible. Of the 309,000 Slovaks declared in the 1991 census, only 160,000 held Slovak citizenship; 46,000 applied for Czech citizenship in 1992 and another 63,000 in early 1993. In effect, the Slovaks constituted a new ethnic minority in the Czech Republic, whereas under the federal system they were defined as one of Czechoslovakia's two constituent nations. Although Slovaks did not suffer from any evident forms of discrimination and were well assimilated in the new Czech state, some local spokesmen argued that the minority should be provided with all the guarantees and group rights contained in international human rights agreements.

The Czech constitution was adopted in December 1992.[12] It proved to be a broadly liberal document defining the Czech Republic as "a sovereign, unified, and democratic, law observing state, based on the respect for the rights and freedoms of the individual and citizen." It reconfirmed that the Charter of Fundamental Rights and Liberties passed by the now-defunct Federal Assembly in January 1991 was an essential part of the country's constitutional order. The constitution provided few details about minority rights: Article 6 simply stated that "political decisions shall derive from the will of the majority expressed through free voting. Minorities shall be protected by the majority in decision making." Although the constitution placed no special emphasis on Czech ethnic identity and considered the individual and not the group as the basic subject, its lack of specificity on the position of minorities and their parliamentary representation will leave the question open to other legal documents and political interpretations.

CZECH NATIONALISTS

Republican Party—Association for the Republic (RP-AR)
Republikánska Strana—Sdružení pro Republiku (RS-SR)

Founded in December 1989, this extreme right-wing party was headed by Miroslav Sládek. The RP-AR has advocated the expulsion of Vietnamese and Cuban guest workers from the country and called for harsh measures against Gypsies, who were allegedly responsible for most of the crime plaguing Czechoslovakia. The party warned against allowing extensive foreign, especially German, investment into the country, arguing that it would make Czechs and Slovaks feel like guests in their own state. It has also demanded the return of Subcarpathian Ruthenia, a former Czechoslovak region that was annexed by the Soviets in 1945. The party claimed that the Soviet Union's annexation of Ruthenia was not in accordance with international law and that most Ruthenians wished to rejoin Czechoslovakia. Party leaders have demanded the reevaluation of all Communist laws and the removal of all former Communists from governmental positions and were vehement supporters of the far-reaching privatization of all state-owned property. The RP-AR has not issued comprehensive political and economic programs but instead relied upon public discontent with particular social issues. Delegates at the party's first congress in February 1990 claimed that they wanted to create an "American-style party" that would concentrate on concrete demands rather that broad ideologies.

Throughout 1990, the party remained on the fringes of the political system and failed to gain any parliamentary seats in the June 1990 elections. Most of its support appeared to come from Czechoslovak skinheads who were responsible for several racially motivated attacks on Gypsies and Vietnamese workers. However, during 1991, the party's popularity steadily grew. In fact, a June 1991 public-opinion poll showed the Republicans as the fifth most-popular party in the Czech Republic, benefiting from about 5 percent of public support. Pre-election evaluations for the June 1992 ballot indicated that public support for the Republicans might have been more widespread than its results at the polls. In the June 1992 general elections, the party won 14 out of 200 seats to the Czech National Council and registered 6.48 percent of the vote for the Czech Chamber of the federal House of the People. The party was particularly successful in regions suffering from high unemployment and social turbulence. While it won 10.6 percent of the vote in northern Bohemia, its popularity dipped to 3 percent in Prague. Post-election assessments indicated that 73 percent of its supporters were under thirty years of age.

The RP-AR made preparations for a world Ruthenian congress, purportedly enabling Ruthenian delegates to decide freely to which state they would prefer to belong. On several occasions, Sládek reportedly traveled to Mukachevo, in Ukrainian Ruthenia, where he publicly hoisted the Czechoslovak flag. In November 1990, on the first anniversary of the "Velvet Revolution," the RP-AR staged a nationalist demonstration near Wenceslas Square in central Prague where U.S. president George Bush and President Havel were addressing the crowds in celebration. The Republicans also continued to exploit the Romani issue to garner public sympathy, as did several other marginal nationalist groupings. For example, the chairman of the Club of Committed Nonparty Members from West Bohemia, Jiří Hájek, disclosed that plans were being made to establish home guards to protect citizens from alleged abuses perpetrated by Roma, since the citizens did not feel secure enough with current police protection. Moreover, links were believed to exist between the RP-AR and a number of unofficial neo-fascist groupings such as the White League (*Bílá Liga*) and various skinhead and vigilante gangs.[13]

Party of Businessmen and Tradesmen (PBT)
Strana Podnikatelů a Obchodníků (SPO)

Formerly known as the Popular Democratic Party, which ran on a coalition ticket with the Republican Party of Czechoslovakia in the first multi-party free elections of June 1990, this nationalist organization was led by Jaroslav Samek. At the end of June 1990, the PBT, under its former name, severed all relations with the RP-AR. Despite its attempts to appeal to the new Czech middle class, the PBT made little headway in capturing electoral support.[14]

MORAVIAN AND SILESIAN REGIONALISTS

Movement for the Self-Governing Democracy of Moravia and Silesia (MSDMS)
Hnutí za Samosprávnou Demokracii Moravy a Slezska (HSDMS)

Formerly known as the Movement for Self-Governing Democracy—Association for Moravia and Silesia (MSGD-AMS) and headed by Chairman Jan Krycer, this organization was not established as a political party but rather as an umbrella movement for a number of Moravian political groups. It advocated replacing the dual federation with a tripartite system in which Moravia and Silesia would figure as the third federal republic next to Czech Bohemia and Slovakia. The Movement demanded a large measure of autonomy for Moravia and Silesia, as a prerequisite for an efficient regional self-government and a fair distribution of state funds. In January 1990, the MSGD-AMS declared that it was leaving the Civic Forum coalition, at the time the most powerful political force in the Czech Republic. Movement leaders contended that CF representatives opposed the principal goal of "initiating genuine self-government in Moravia and Silesia." In addition, the group rejected draft resolutions regarding the Czech government's alleged budgetary discrimination against Moravian and Silesian districts; their protestations were largely ignored by the Czech parliament. The MSGD-AMS proved surprisingly successful in the June 1990 general elections, gaining about 6 percent of the popular vote nationwide and 10 percent in the Czech Republic. As a result, it acquired 16 seats in the Federal Assembly and 22 seats in the Czech National Council. The movement came third in the Czech National Council, fourth in the Czech Chamber of the Federal House of the People, and fifth in the Federal Assembly's Chamber of Nations. However, it fared poorly in the November 1990 local elections, winning only 4.2 percent of the popular vote. It based its election campaign entirely on the championing of "Moravian and Silesian identity." Bohumil Tichý, a member of the MSDMS Central Committee, believed that its relative success had been based on the movement's "civic structure" as well as on its specific programs. The key to Moravian conceptualizations of economic independence was the emphasis on "the formulation of principles for just distribution, especially in the state budget." MSDMS leaders did not believe that Moravia had been the recipient of preferential treatment in the past but that rather it was the victim of discrimination by "totalitarian centralism."

Four possible land-arrangement models were drafted by a Czech government commission during 1991, but they were received with some disappointment by Moravian leaders. Spokesmen claimed that if the federation was restructured into three components, tensions between Prague and Bratislava would be largely eliminated. Moravia would avowedly act as a buffer between Slovaks and Czechs. During 1991, Moravian leaders began to criticize the economic reforms instituted in Prague, claiming discrimination against the region. According to their estimations, a new regional division of the country, granting autonomy to Moravia and Silesia, was the essential ingredient for the success of economic reform. They asserted that the region's inhabitants accounted for 39.2 percent of the population of the Czech Republic, yet they received only 25.5 percent of industrial subsidies, 35 percent of contributions for the operation of non-profit establishments, and 34.8 percent of subsidies for housing, modernization, and heating. In sum Moravia's share of state subsidies for 1990 amounted to 31.6 percent, with only 16.2 percent of the allocations for health-care projects in the republic. As a result, Moravians felt discriminated against under the budget approved by the Czech National Council. Krycer, elected MSDMS chairman in July 1991, reiterated that the Movement was based on the idea of achieving autonomy for Moravia-Silesia vis-à-vis a "union-state" arrangement with Czechoslovakia. Support for some form of autonomy appeared to be broadening on the Czech side, although the CF and other major parties considered the issue to be more distant. Although Krycer considered Moravia-Silesia as an integral part of the Czech Republic, he has on occasion emphasized the "state-forming" goal of the Movement. While the MSDMS dismissed any cooperation with the Communists, since the Communist Party of Bohemia and Moravia gained more than 30 deputies in the Czech National Council, its opinions were to be elicited on fundamental issues pertaining to the status of Moravia.

The Land Council of the MSDMS met at a special session in August 1991 to discuss the actions of an independently formed "Executive Committee," which passed a vote of no-confidence in the current MSDMS leadership. The Land Council recommended to the MSDMS Assembly that it take vigorous action against "subversive elements and adopt measures in the interest of the movement's unity." Ivan Tuzinský, deputy chairman of MSDMS, claimed that the self-appointed "Executive Committee" set up in Brno acted in contravention of the movement's statutes, which had been operating in harmony with Czechoslovak legal stipulations. Krycer refuted charges of collaboration with the Petr Pithart government. He emphasized the need to utilize available legislative options for achieving autonomy, asserting that the idea of a union republic had not been discarded. A Moravian-Silesian Council (MSC) was formed in late 1991, encompassing a broad spectrum of 13 political parties and movements active in the region. It called for autonomous and equal status for the region in the Czechoslovak federation. A draft treaty presented by the MSC at a joint meeting of the Czech and Slovak National Council presidiums stressed that the question of autonomy and power sharing could be solved by entrusting authority to three regional entities. The unreliable dualist system would need to be replaced by a tripartite structure, in which three equal units, in terms of geographic size and population distribution, would act within confederative arrangements ratified by regional assemblies to coordinate economic and social policies. Krycer believed that Slovakia would endorse a union of "three constitutional, autonomous, and equal entities."

In late 1991, support for the Movement in Moravia-Silesia stabilized at about 5 percent. In the June 1992 elections, the MSDMS only won 14 seats out of 200 to the Czech National Council. Although the Czech government promised to reevaluate the republic's constitutional setup and address some of the Movement's concerns, no significant progress was registered. In an important and unusual move, in January 1993 three-quarters of the 242 delegates to the MSDMS's third congress rejected the nationalist and separatist tendencies of the Moravian National Party and distanced themselves from radical forces within the

Movement itself. Instead, they declared their allegiance to the principles of liberalism and the goals of a self-governing democracy, to be achieved only through parliamentary means. Although the decision on the self-administration of Moravia and Silesia was scheduled to be implemented by the Czech government during 1993, MSDMS leaders realized that they also needed to consider the movement's future. Most delegates concurred that the transformation of the Movement into a full-fledged political party was premature.[15]

Moravian National Party (MNP)
Moravská Národní Strana (MNS)

Founded in Brno, the Moravian capital, in the early part of 1990, the MNP became a political party under the chairmanship of Ivan Drimal. Unlike the Movement for Self-Governing Democracy, the MNP claimed that the Moravians were not a constituent part of the Czech nation and advocated an administrative arrangement for Czechoslovakia based on a tripartite "national" principle among Bohemia, Moravia, and Silesia. It consistently complained about Prague-centric policies that allegedly resulted in the economic and cultural exploitation of Moravia. In March 1991, the MNP protested against the national census, which allegedly discriminated against the Moravian and Silesian nationalities. The significance of this group remained restricted, but it had the potential for growth, especially in light of the MSDMS refusal to become a political party. In December 1992, Drimal attacked the new Czech constitution for aiming to break up Moravian integrity and suppressing its national identity. The MNP demanded the re-creation of the medieval Greater Moravia in its original borders and with its own executive and legislative bodies.[16]

Moravian-Silesian Citizens' Assembly (MSCA)
Občanské Shromáždění Moravy a Slezska (OSMS)

A preparatory committee of 24 members, chaired by author Jaromír Tomeček and including several federal and Czech parliamentary deputies, was formed in November 1990 in accordance with the "Moravian Declaration" and tracing its roots to the Moravian Margraviate as a state unit that was not always part of the Bohemian Crown. The committee endeavored to establish an assembly that would unite "representatives from the various streams of social, political, cultural, religious, economic, and administrative life." In March 1993, the MSCA formally approved the creation of a five-member Moravian-Silesian government headed by Václav Kobliha, a former militant leader of the Republican Party. The government was to be responsible for working out a program focusing on economic and social issues in Moravia-Silesia. It sought to preserve a single Moravian-Silesian Land either as an equal unit with Bohemia in a Czech federation or as a sovereign political entity. The creation of the unconstitutional

Moravian-Silesian government led to the initiation of criminal proceedings by the Czech prosecutor general in the spring of 1993.[17]

Radical Moravian Nationalist Party (RMNP)
Radikální Moravská Nacionální Strana (RMNS)

The RMNP was an illegal and unregistered militant group seeking full Moravian sovereignty and independence. Prague has accused the RMNP of being a front organization for unrepentant local Communists wishing to cling to their privileges and seeking to stage a political provocation to undermine the progress of democratic reforms.[18]

MINORITY ORGANIZATIONS

Union of Slovaks (UOS)
Sdružení Slováků (SS)

As the breakup of the federation approached, Slovak activists in the Czech Republic established a handful of independent organizations to represent what now became a minority population. The UOS was chaired by former dissident and Federal Assembly deputy Ján Mlynárik, who claimed that the Union was formed to eliminate the perception that Slovak leaders in Bratislava spoke for the Slovak population in the Czech Republic. The goal of the Union was to promote cultural and educational activities and to be active in the political arena either through citizens' initiatives or through independent candidates on the slates of various parties, including the Civic Democratic Party and various Christian Democratic organizations. In March 1993, Mlynárik made a point of disassociating the UOS from the recently formed Community of Slovaks (COS), which he claimed maintained links with the quasi-nationalist Slovak government. The COS considered itself an apolitical organization representing Slovaks who either permanently or temporarily resided in the Czech Republic.[19]

Community of Slovaks (COS)
Společnost Slováků (SS)

The COS held its first congress in Prague in February 1993; Jaroslav Skorik was elected president, and the Community declared itself a non-political organization open to all Slovaks and to "friends of Slovakia" resident in the Czech lands. Although it began with a small membership of under 200, it planned to open branches throughout the country and to expand its numbers quickly. Several other Slovak groupings sprang up in the first half of 1993, including the Democratic Alliance of Slovaks (DAS), which aspired to become a political party, and the avowedly apolitical Association of Slovaks (AOS), as well as the Club of

Slovak Culture (CSC), originally founded in 1969 as a Prague-based branch of the Slovak Heritage Foundation. In March 1993, leaders of most of these groups met, agreed to avoid unnecessary conflicts among themselves, and nominated several representatives to the Czech government's Council for Nationalities. They also put forward proposals for ensuring regular Slovak-language broadcasts on Czech radio and the creation of a Slovak magazine to be called *Džavot* (Babble), funded primarily by the COS.[20]

Romani Civic Initiative (RCI)
Romská Občanská Iniciativa (ROI)

Chairperson Emil Scuka headed this Romani association founded in Prague in November 1989, initially in coalition with the Civic Forum. It proclaimed no specific ideology but combined like-minded citizens on the basis of their convictions in the principles of "equality, freedom, and humanity." RCI leaders have disputed official population statistics, claiming that approximately 300,000 Roma lived in the Czech Republic, with a further 500,000 in Slovakia. The figures have been dismissed by most observers as vastly inflated. The RCI demanded that the Romani people be defined as a nationality in Czechoslovakia's new constitution and census. An RCI memorandum issued in November 1990 stated that, "Considering the number of people of Gypsy ethnicity, it is essential for Roma to be considered in the context of the multi-national Czechoslovak state as a *de facto* nationality." The party also wanted the Romani nationality to be named explicitly in the provisions of the Charter of Fundamental Rights and Liberties that prohibited ethnic discrimination. It has campaigned for full cultural and social freedoms for the Romani minority and the elevation of their language to the same position in schools as Hungarian in Slovakia and the languages of other minority nationalities, such as the German. By the close of 1992, over 30 Romani cultural organizations were registered with the Czech and Slovak ministries of culture, together with a Museum of Romani Culture in Brno and several cultural clubs for young Roma. The first Gypsy journal *Lacho Lar* (Good Word), was launched under the editorship of Vincent Danihel; its purpose was to help improve knowledge of the Romani language and prepare the ground for issuing Romani school textbooks. RCI leaders have supported the launching of a works program to induce Roma into building family houses in Gypsy settlements to replace all currently unsuitable residencies except one, which would be left as an open-air museum.

Representatives of the RCI have also lodged protests against the use of the word "Gypsy" when describing the perpetrator of a criminal act, since the same procedure was not followed in the case of criminals of other nationalities. The low level of education (only 1 percent of Roma were skilled workers or benefited from higher education) has been alluded to as the chief cause of criminality among Gypsies because of its link to high unemployment. Romani deputies have attacked data collecting on "Romani criminality" as a violation of the Charter of Fundamental Rights and Liberties. They have pointed out that the Gypsy population was highly differentiated and possessed its own cadre of qualified teachers, lawyers, and other professionals. The RCI was formally reconstituted as a political party in March 1990 at its founding congress in Prague. It participated in the elections at the federal level alongside the Democratic Union of Roma in Slovakia. Eight deputies subsequently represented the RCI in various legislative bodies in Czechoslovakia. In addition, several Roma were also elected as candidates on the Civic Forum and Communist Party tickets.[21]

Romani National Congress (RNC)
Romský Národní Kongres (RNK)

This small grouping, chaired by Vladimír Oláh, was created in February 1991 in opposition to the RCI, which it accused of being too "rightist." It claimed to be an amalgam of 15 social organizations and initiatives, including the Movement of Romani Activists, the Association of Romani Youth, the Romani Democratic Union, the Association of Slovak Roma, the Independent Organization of Roma, and the Christian Democratic Association, *Romani Matica*. The RNC considered itself to be a left-of-center organization; it demanded that the Romani nationality be anchored in the constitution and that Roma be represented in all offices and ministries.[22]

Polish Council (PC)
Rada Poláků (RP)

Led by Chairman Tadeusz Wantuła, the PC was founded in March 1990 to replace the Polish Cultural Union, which was considered a mouthpiece of the Communist regime rather than a representative of Polish interests in Czechoslovakia. It was composed of a nine-person council that oversaw and coordinated the activities of the six Polish minority organizations in Czechoslovakia. It has demanded an end to the alleged discrimination against Poles living in the Těšin Silesian region and called for the observance of human rights in accordance with the Helsinki Accords. Although Polish leaders have complained about Prague's patronizing and bureaucratic attitudes and the government's apparent failure to restore property seized by the Communist regime after the war, the Polish community has received some state funding for its cultural and organizational development. The PC unsuccessfully attempted to gain parliamentary representation in the June 1990 elections; however, one of its leaders was elected on the ticket of the Bratislava-based multi-ethnic Coexistence coalition. The existing voting system prevented it from running on its own in the June 1992 elections; hence, its only alternative was to run within Coexistence. As a result, it gained 1 seat in the Czech National Council and 2 seats in the Federal Assembly.[23]

Union of German Cultural Associations (UGCA)
Svaz Německých Kulturních Organizací (SNKO)

The UGCA was founded in October 1990 with the merger of two organizations to replace the formerly Communist-controlled Cultural Association of Czechoslovak Citizens of German Nationality and the Union of Germans in Czechoslovakia. Its leader was Walter Piverka, a Czech parliamentary deputy elected on the Civic Forum ticket. The UGCA called for the safeguarding of social and cultural rights for the German minority. Although it claimed over 8,000 members, it did not possess a large enough social base to have much of an impact on Czech politics. Although the German minority figured in Prague's disputes with German expellee organizations, its status did not upset the signing of a comprehensive treaty between the two states. As with the Polish Council, the voting system prevented the UGCA from running on a separate ticket in the national elections, thus persuading them to collaborate with Coexistence. As a result, the UGCA won 1 seat to the Czech National Council.[24]

German Landowners' Assembly (GLA)
Zemské Shromáždění Němců (ZSN)

This organization of Germans in Bohemia, Moravia, and Silesia, commonly known by its German name as *Deutsche Landsmannschaft*, was created in November 1992 as a non-party grouping that condemned any form of dictatorship or revanchism. Its 300 delegates approved new statutes and elected the GLA's first central bodies. The new president stated that the group was not intended to be a fifth column for German revisionists; instead, it wanted to build upon the amicable relations that used to exist among Germans, Moravians, Czechs, and Silesians. It disassociated itself from the more radical Society of Sudeten Germans (SSG), which demanded the return of all land and property to Germans expelled from Czechoslovakia at the close of World War Two.[25]

Council of Jewish Communities in the Czech Lands (CJCCL)
Rada Židovských Obcí Českých Zemí (RŽOČZ)

The Council was originally formed by the Communist authorities to help supervise the remnants of Jewish cultural and religious life in Bohemia and Moravia. Its leadership was directly appointed by the Ministry of Culture and was expected to apply all government policies toward the dwindling Jewish community. Following the "Velvet Revolution," several CJCCL leaders resigned, and in December 1989 an advisory group of young people was formed to help manage Jewish community affairs. Desider Galský, an older community leader, was appointed chairman until his death in late 1990. In addition, an Association of Friends of Jewish Culture (AFJC) was formed to preserve Czech Jewish heritage:

some non-Jews became members of this body under the chairmanship of Bedřich Nossek, the director of the State Jewish Museum.[26]

Union of Hungarians (UH)
Svaz Maďarů (SM)

Founded in February 1990, the UH claimed to represent the approximately 23,000 ethnic Hungarians living in the Czech Republic. Several other ethnically based associations also functioned in the Czech lands representing the smaller minority groups; they included the Society of Friends of Subcarpathian Ruthenia.[27]

CHRONOLOGY

February 1990: Deputies of the South Moravian Regional Committee in Brno declare that the present Czech state does not correspond with the rights of the citizens of Moravia-Silesia for territorial self-administration. To correct these distortions, they recommend that the Czechoslovak constitution be rewritten. Political and civic movements in Moravia seek an amendment of the draft election law to establish electoral districts according to the historical borders of the Moravian and Silesian lands.

March 1990: A seven-point agreement is reached between representatives of Moravian-Silesian civic initiatives and local Civic Forum cells in Olomouc. The result comes to be known as the Moravian Platform. Participants agree that autonomy and equal rights for Moravians and Silesians are the primary goals, and that they could not be achieved in the form of a federation but rather through a provincial system. The possibility of establishing a capital city in the Moravian-Silesian region is also discussed as one way to ease executive and legislative problems. Czech premier Petr Pithart asserts that the Czech Republic could act as a mediator in case of deteriorating relations between Hungary and Slovakia over the Hungarian minority issue.

May 1990: The RCI turns to President Havel for help because of threats and attacks on Gypsies by skinhead gangs. Havel promises that he will ensure order and security for all citizens. Havel states that the problem of racism is of general concern for society, while the safety of citizens is the responsibility of the Interior Ministry, which is not functioning properly. He believes that the paralysis within the security forces is the fault of commanders who should have resigned or been replaced.

June 1990: Although unable to run on their own due to the electoral law, seats are won by Poles (1 seat in the Czech National Council and 2 in the Federal

Assembly), Roma (3 seats in the Federal Assembly, including 1 from the Communist Party and 1 from the Public Against Violence in Slovakia), and a German (1 seat in the Czech National Council). The MSDMS performs well in Moravia-Silesia, winning over 10 percent of the popular vote and 22 seats in the Czech National Council. With increased political exposure, the MSDMS begins to place demands for regional autonomy more firmly on the political agenda.

June 1990: The newly established Civic Initiative in Silesia resolves to contribute new solutions for democratically administrating the territory of Silesia. It favors Czech national unity but also supports far-reaching self-government for towns and villages in the region to assists in successful economic development.

December 1990: Representatives from a broad spectrum of Moravian political parties and movements meet for the first time since the "Velvet Revolution" and agree that their final objective is the Union Republic of Czechoslovakia, in which both Moravia and Silesia would become independent legal entities.

January 1991: Several fledgling Moravian groups sign a Charter for Moravia and Silesia in Brno, the Moravian capital. The charter calls for a Moravian-Silesian government and parliament, the reevaluation of the region's historic boundaries and electoral districts, and increased distribution of Prague's resources so that the region could administer its own economic affairs.

February 1991: Deputies from various Moravian-Silesian political parties and movements gather to discuss proposals for territorial reorganization. They decide that the federal government must design a constitutional variant for a tripartite federation (Czech-Bohemia, Moravia-Silesia, and Slovakia) and propose a separate Moravian constitution. The country's prime minister, Marián Čalfa, disagrees with the tripartite proposal but agrees that the issue deserves further review. The Czech government comes under increasing attack from Moravian deputies over the slow pace of administrative restructuring.

March 1991: In the first post-Communist census, and the first in which citizens could declare themselves as part of a Moravian or Silesian national group, nearly 1.4 million do so out of the region's 3 million inhabitants. Representatives from 25 Moravian political organizations meet and reject a presidential resolution on the federal constitution because it does not give the region equal status as a constituent federal unit. The first census also recognizes Roma as a distinct national minority.

April 1991: The Society of Sudeten Germans spokesman Franz Neubauer insists that the proposed Czechoslovak-German Treaty include a clause asserting that both sides agree to set up a mixed Czechoslovak-German commission to deal with the question of mutual property claims.

August 1991: The Czech-Slovak ambassador to Germany criticizes the Kohl government for allegedly backing Sudeten German groups demanding compensation for their post–World War Two expulsions and the right to live and work in the Czech Republic. Bonn responds that the government cannot ignore the pleas of millions of expelled Sudetens and that Prague cannot deny Germans the right to settle in the country if it expects future EC membership.

October 1991: The Czechoslovak and German governments adopt the Treaty on Good-Neighborliness and Friendly Cooperation, in which they agree to grant full minority rights to Czechs and Slovaks living in Germany and to Germans living in Czechoslovakia. The treaty does not address the issue of expelled Sudeten German property claims or reparations for damages incurred by Czechoslovakia during the Nazi occupation. A Czechoslovak Foreign Ministry spokesman asserts that the government cannot initiate talks on incorporating Sub-Carpathian Ruthenia into Czechoslovakia as this would mean interfering in Ukraine's internal affairs. However, if "the region's inhabitants expressed interest in joining Czechoslovakia, with the consent of the Soviet and Ukrainian governments we would naturally not reject them." The two countries have no outstanding territorial claims on each other, since in June 1945 the Czechoslovak government signed an agreement ceding Subcarpathian Ruthenia to the Soviet Union.

November 1991: The Moravian-Silesian Council calls for equal and independent status for Moravia and Silesia. A delegation from the Movement for Self-Governing Democracy-Society for Moravia and Silesia writes a letter to President Havel summarizing the historical context of the emergence of an autonomous Moravia-Silesia. It claims to express the will of a majority of the people in both regions for the equal status of Moravia-Silesia with that of Slovakia and Bohemia.

February 1992: President Havel offers the possibility of restoring Czech citizenship to Sudeten German who lost it in May 1945, on condition that the German government desists from supporting the property claims of expelled Sudeten Germans and their families.

March 1992: The Ukraine-based Sub-Carpathian Republican Party holds its first congress and announces its main goal as the creation of a sovereign Republic of Sub-Carpathian Ruthenia. The guest of honor, the Czech Republican Party leader Miroslav Sládek, promises full support for the future state. His vision of the sovereign Sub-Carpathian state would include a return to pre-Munich borders. Sládek also criticizes Havel and the Czech leadership for their position toward Sub-Carpathian Ruthenia.

June 1992: The second multi-party parliamentary elections seal the division of Czechoslovakia into two separate states. The market-oriented Civic Democratic Party wins the elections in the Czech Republic, while the pro-independence Movement for a Democratic Slovakia scores a victory in Slovakia. A transitory government is assembled at the federal level while negotiations begin between Czech prime minister Václav Klaus and Slovak premier Vladimír Mečiar to arrange a peaceful dissolution of the federation.

January 1993: The Czech and Slovak Federal Republic is formally dissolved with the emergence of two new independent states: Slovakia and the Czech Republic. In response to right-wing attacks against Roma, a Gypsy gang, the Black Panthers operating in seven north Bohemian districts, declares war on all racists, fascists, skinheads, and followers of Miroslav Sládek. The Black Panthers appeal to Roma to "refrain from committing criminal acts" and threaten all those who "attack Roma without reason." Three-quarters of the 242 MSDMS delegates at the organization's third congress distance the Movement from the more radical Moravian nationalists. The delegates also refrain from transforming the organization into a political party and adopt its current name.

March 1993: Jiří Šetina, the Czech Republic's prosecutor general, orders criminal proceedings in connection with reports about the establishment of a Moravian-Silesian Land government. The initiators of the self-proclaimed Moravian-Silesian government were to be charged with the criminal offense of spreading false and alarmist reports. The Czech administration rejects a bill proposing the establishment of a Moravian-Silesian Land within the Czech Republic. Premier Václav Klaus objects to the fact that the territorial boundaries and administrative connections of the proposed entity were not clearly defined.

NOTES

1. For population figures in the Czech Republic, see *Basic Information on Population, Paramilitary and Government System and Historical Development of 1918–1992,* Czechoslovak News Agency, March 1992.

2. For useful histories of Czechoslovakia, check Jozef Korbel, *Twentieth-Century Czechoslovakia* (New York: Columbia University Press, 1977); Carol Skalník Leff, *National Conflict in Czechoslovakia: The Making and Remaking of a State, 1918–1987* (Princeton, NJ: Princeton University Press, 1988); Ihor Gawdiak, ed., *Czechoslovakia: A Country Study* (Washington, DC: U.S. Government Printing Office, 1989); John O. Crane, *Czechoslovakia: Anvil of the Cold War* (New York: Praeger, 1990); Zdenek Suda, *Zealots and Rebels: A History of the Ruling Communist Party of Czechoslovakia* (Stanford, CA: Hoover Institution, 1980); and Vladimír Kusin, *From Dubcek to Charter 77: A Study of "Normalization" in Czechoslovakia, 1968–1978* (New York: St. Martins Press, 1978)

3. See Jiří Pehe, "The Electoral Law," Radio Free Europe/Radio Liberty Research Institute (RFE/RL), *Report on Eastern Europe*, vol. 1, no. 11, March 16, 1990. For a full

list of participating parties, see *Pravda*, Bratislava, April 20, 1990; see also Ján Obrman, "The Main Contenders in the Election," RFE/RL, *Report on Eastern Europe*, vol. 1, no. 23, July 8, 1990; and Ján Obrman, "Civic Forum Surges to Impressive Victory in Elections," RFE/RL, *Report on Eastern Europe*, vol. 1, no. 25, June 22, 1990.

4. Check Jiří Pehe, "The Local Government Elections," RFE/RL, *Report on Eastern Europe*, vol. 1, no. 50, December 14, 1990.

5. See Ján Obrman, "Controversy Over Postwar Expulsion of Germans," RFE/RL, *Report on Eastern Europe*, vol. 1, no. 6, February 9, 1990; and Ján Obrman, "Relations with Germany," RFE/RL, *Report on Eastern Europe*, vol. 2, no. 46, November 15, 1991.

6. RFE/RL Research Institute, *Daily Report*, no. 103, June 2, 1993.

7. Consult *Struggling for Ethnic Identity: Czechoslovakia's Endangered Gypsies*, Helsinki Watch, New York, 1992.

8. *Mladá Fronta Dnes*, Prague, January 4, 1993, in Federal Broadcast Information Service, *Daily Report: East Europe*, *FBIS-EEU–93–005*, January 8, 1993.

9. See Ján Obrman, "The Czechoslovak Elections," RFE/RL, *Research Report*, vol. 1, no. 26, June 26, 1992.

10. For details on the federal split, see Jiří Pehe, "Czechs and Slovaks Prepare to Part," RFE/RL, *Research Report*, vol. 1, no. 37, September 18, 1992; Ján Obrman, "Czechoslovakia's New Government," RFE/RL, *Research Report*, vol. 1, no. 29, July 17, 1992; *Hospodárske Noviny*, Prague, September 10, 1992; Jiří Pehe, "Czechs and Slovaks Refine Postdivorce Relations," RFE/RL, *Report on Eastern Europe*, vol. 2, no. 45, November 13, 1992.

11. A useful summary of the Law on Citizenship can be obtained from the Czech Consulate in Washington, DC.

12. See the *Constitution of the Czech Republic*, December 16, 1992, adopted by the Czech National Council, Prague.

13. See Jiří Pehe, "The Emergence of Right-Wing Extremism," RFE/RL, *Report on Eastern Europe*, vol. 2, no. 26, June 28, 1991; Jiří Pehe, "Czechoslovakia's Changing Political Spectrum," RFE/RL, *Report on Eastern Europe*, vol. 1, no. 5, January 31, 1992; Obrman, "The Czechoslovak Elections."

14. *Lidové Noviny*, Prague, June 23, 1990, in *FBIS-EEU–90–124*, June 27, 1990; *ČTK*, Prague, June 27, 1990, in *FBIS-EEU–90–125*, June 28, 1990.

15. *ČTK*, Prague, January 14, 1990, in *FBIS-EEU–90–012*, January 17, 1990; interview with Bohumil Tichý, member of MSGD-SMS Central Committees, in *Rude Pravo*, Prague, June 23, 1990, in *FBIS-EEU–90–126*, June 29, 1990; interview with Boleslav Barta, MSDMS chairman, in *Zemědělské Noviny*, Prague, December 28, 1990, in *FBIS-EEU–91–002*, January 3, 1991; *ČTK*, Prague, January 2, 1991, in *FBIS-EEU–91–005*, January 8, 1991; interview with Jan Krycer, *Česke a Moravskoslezské Zemědělské Noviny*, Prague, July 1, 1991, in *FBIS-EEU–91–131*, July 9, 1991; interview with Jan Krycer, *Lidové Noviny*, Prague, July 23, 1991, in *FBIS-EEU–91–143*, July 25, 1991; *Hospodárske Noviny*, Prague, August 27, 1991, in *FBIS-EEU–91–170*, September 3, 1991; interview with Jan Krycer, *Rude Pravo*, October 14, 1991, in *FBIS-EEU–91–208*, October 28, 1991; interview with Jan Krycer, *Svobodné Slovo*, Prague, November 5, 1991, in *FBIS-EEU–91–217*, November 9, 1991; Ján Obrman, "The Issue of Autonomy for Moravia and Silesia," RFE/RL, *Report on Eastern Europe*, vol. 2, no. 15, April 12, 1991; Ján Obrman, "The Czechoslovak Elections: A Guide to the Parties," RFE/RL, *Report on Eastern Europe*, vol. 1, no. 22, May 29, 1992.

16. Ján Obrman, "Slovak Politician Accused of Secret Police Ties," RFE/RL, *Report on Eastern Europe*, vol. 1, no. 15, April 10, 1992; interview with Jan Krycer in *Lidové Noviny*, Prague, July 23, 1991, in *FBIS-EEU–91–143*, July 25, 1991; *ČTK*, Prague, De-

cember 18, 1992, in *FBIS-EEU–92–247*, December 23, 1992; interview with MNP member Alena Občačiková by Monika Voleková, "Moravian Disquiet, Discontent," *Slovenský Národ*, Bratislava, March 16, 1993.

17. "A New Parliament Is Being Established," *Rude Pravo*, Prague, November 14, 1990, in *FBIS-EEU–90–224*, November 20, 1990; *ČTK*, Prague, March 16, 1993, in *FBIS-EEU–93–052*, March 19, 1993; *ČTK*, Prague, March 17, 1993, in *FBIS-EEU–93–053*, March 22, 1993.

18. Ján Obrman, "Minorities Not a Major Issue Yet," RFE/RL, *Report on Eastern Europe*, vol. 2, no. 50, December 13, 1991.

19. See the interview with Ján Mlynárik, "We Are Not a Fifth Column," *Lidové Noviny*, Prague, March 9, 1993, and Vladimír Skalicky, "A Slovak Minority Exists," *Lidové Noviny*, Prague, March 23, 1993.

20. Jiří Pehe, "Slovaks in the Czech Republic: A New Minority," RFE/RL, *Research Report*, vol. 2, no. 23, June 4, 1993.

21. *ČTK*, Prague, February 21, 1990, in *FBIS-EEU–90–041*, March 1, 1990; *ČTK*, Prague, March 10, 1990, in *FBIS-EEU–90–048*, March 12, 1990; *Bratislava Domestic Service*, Bratislava, May 17, 1990, in *FBIS-EEU–90–097*, May 18, 1990; *ČTK*, Prague, November 15, 1990, in *FBIS-EEU–90–223*, November 19, 1990.

22. *Lidové Noviny*, Prague, August 7, 1991, in *FBIS-EEU–091–131*, September 4, 1991.

23. *PAP*, Warsaw, March 4, 1990, in *FBIS-EEU–90–046*, March 8, 1990; Vladimír V. Kusin, "Media in Transition," RFE/RL, *Report on Eastern Europe*, vol. 1, no. 18, May 3, 1991.

24. *Národná Obroda*, Bratislava, October 22, 1990, in *FBIS-EEU–90–207*, October 25, 1990; Obrman, "Minorities Not a Major Issue Yet"; Jiří Pehe, "Czechoslovakia: Parties Register For Elections," RFE/RL, *Report on Eastern Europe*, vol. 1, no. 18, May 1, 1992.

25. *ČTK*, Prague, April 25, 1991, in *FBIS-EEU–91–084*, May 1, 1991; *Stanice Československa Radio Network*, Prague, November 7, 1992, in *FBIS-EEU–92–217*, November 9, 1992.

26. See Charles Hoffman, *Grey Dawn: The Jews of Eastern Europe in the Post-Communist Era* (New York: Harper Collins, 1992), pp. 13–53.

27. *Práce*, Prague, February 26, 1990, in *FBIS-EEU–90–047*, March 9, 1990.

11

Slovakia

POPULATION

According to the results of the 1991 Czechoslovak census, the population of Slovakia totaled 5,268,935, of which 85.63 percent were ethnic Slovaks, only a slight drop from the 1980 total.[1] Hungarians (or Magyars) formed the largest minority, numbering 566,741 or 10.76 percent of the population, a drop of about 0.5 percent since the 1980 census. The majority of Magyars resided in compact communities along the southern border regions; according to official figures, Hungarians constituted over 50 percent of the residents in 434 towns and villages, with the highest concentrations in 11 *okresi* (districts) in the Danube Basin area. However, Slovak officials pointed out that Hungarian majority habitation did not create a continuous zone across this region as it was interspersed by sizable Slovak-inhabited areas. There were no reliable statistics on Romani (Gypsy) numbers. The former Communist regime refused to record them as an ethnic minority, and many Roma remained unregistered or were wary of disclosing their ethnic identity. An estimated 80,627 Slovak Roma were recorded in the 1991 census, although unofficial sources cited figures that fluctuated between 100,000 and 250,000; the highest numbers have been recorded in eastern Slovakia. Ethnic Czechs totaled 53,422, an increase of some 10,000 during the previous decade; the majority were resident in the Slovak capital Bratislava. A further 3,888 declared themselves Moravians for the first time in the republic's census. Disputes have continued over the precise ethnic identity of Slavic peoples in northeastern Slovakia: formerly considered Ukrainian, in the 1991 census a Ruthenian nationality was registered for the first time without parentheses; 16,937 people declared themselves Ruthenians and 13,847 Ukrainians. However, some unofficial estimates gave the combined Ruthenian-Ukrainian population at over 100,000. The remainder of Slovak residents included 5,629 Germans, nearly 3,000 Poles, and about 13,000 people of various smaller nationalities, including Croats, Bulgarians, Romanians, and Jews.

Slovakia: Population (1991)

Ethnic Groups	Number	% of Population
Slovaks	4,511,679	85.63
Hungarians	566,741	10.76
Roma (Gypsies)	80,627	1.53
Czechs	53,422	1.01
Ruthenians	16,937	0.32
Ukrainians	13,847	0.26
Germans	5,629	0.11
Moravians	3,888	0.07
Poles	2,969	0.06
Others	13,196	0.25
Total Minorities	757,256	14.37
Total Population	5,268,935	100.00

HISTORICAL OVERVIEW

After centuries of Hungarian domination, Slovakia became a constituent unit of the newly created Czechoslovak state at the close of World War One.[2] Although Czech and Slovak national leaders agreed on the union of the two Slav peoples as a means of protection from outside pressures, problems soon arose over the structure of the state and the position of both nationalities. Most Slovak leaders favored a loose federal system with a large measure of regional autonomy, while the more radical groups pushed for outright Slovak independence. Czech leaders generally supported a unitary government structure and a gradual blending of the two ethnic identities. Slovak activists increasingly complained that such an arrangement would extinguish their distinctiveness and leave Slovakia as a mere economic appendage of the Czech lands. Throughout the inter-war period, a persistent sense of grievance was therefore voiced by Slovak autonomist and nationalist groupings.

Territorial revisions following World War One left a substantial Hungarian minority in Slovakia. In 1920, Magyars numbered about 634,000 people, or 21 percent of the population. A majority of Hungarian politicians were unable to reconcile themselves to the loss of "Upper Hungary" (Slovakia) and together with Magyar minority leaders in Slovakia they pressed for the region's return to Budapest. Although the Czechoslovak state was comparatively liberal by standards prevailing elsewhere in Eastern Europe, Hungarian activists charged that discriminatory policies were applied against them, particularly as the constitution gave the Czech and Slovak languages a privileged position in public life. In addition to Magyars, inter-war Slovakia also contained about 140,000 Germans, 85,000 Ruthenians and Ukrainians, approximately 70,000 Jews, and a handful of smaller nationalities.

The Czechoslovak state was dismembered by Nazi Germany in 1938. The regions of Bohemia and Moravia were transformed into German protectorates,

Sub-Carpathian Ruthenia, the eastern-most province, was wholly annexed by Hungary in March 1939, while Slovakia became a quasi independent protectorate ruled by a pro-German fascist regime under the presidency of the Catholic cleric Monsignor Jozef Tiso. The government in Bratislava introduced various anti-Jewish measures, including the seizure of property and systematic exclusion from economic life. During 1942, the Slovak authorities assisted the Nazis in shipping the bulk of the Jewish population, over 50,000 people, to death camps in German-occupied Poland. The remaining Slovak Jews were either incarcerated in labor camps, escaped to Hungary, or perished after the Slovak uprising in August 1944 when the German authorities launched further deportations and exterminations.

Czechoslovakia was reestablished at the close of World War Two, initially under a multi-party coalition government. In 1948, the Communist Party under Soviet direction staged a *coup d'état* and began to centralize the political and economic systems along Stalinist lines. Despite earlier Communist promises, Slovakia did not attain autonomy in the revolutionary state. During the 1950s and 1960s, the country remained a staunchly pro-Soviet satellite, exhibiting little tolerance for regional autonomy or political dissent. At the close of the war, over 500,000 Magyars had been left in Slovakia. The new government in Prague initially planned to expel them or conduct large-scale population exchanges with Hungary, but it eventually desisted under Allied pressure and Soviet opposition and citizenship rights were restored to the Magyar minority. In the interim, between 1945 and 1948, about 90,000 Hungarians were transferred to Hungary in exchange for over 70,000 Slovaks.

The Communist authorities launched a program of Slovakization among Magyars believed to be of Slovak origin, and tens of thousands of Hungarians declared themselves to be Slovaks largely to avoid official recriminations. The Magyar population dipped to some 200,000 at the height of the campaign but rose again to over 530,000 in 1961 after the program was abandoned. The demographic strength and potential political influence of the Hungarian minority was also diminished through the reorganization and merger of Slovak counties; as a result, Magyars retained a majority in only two of the enlarged southern counties. Although under Communist rule Hungarians, Ukrainians, and Ruthenians were formally provided with legal rights to their own independent schools, newspapers, and cultural associations, many of these guarantees were not implemented or remained under strict party supervision. In addition, the Ukrainian Uniate Church and the Roman Catholic Church were subjected to vigorous government persecution.

During the short-lived Prague Spring liberalization in 1968, Slovakia attained some measure of political autonomy. The framework of this arrangement survived the Soviet-led invasion and the Communist "normalization" that extinguished democratic reform throughout the country. In January 1969, Czechoslovakia was declared a federal socialist state consisting of two republics

(Czech and Slovak) with nominally equal rights in the federation. In practice, the federal structure remained subordinated to the Communist Party's centralism and monopolistic control over the country's political, economic, and cultural life. The Prague Spring reforms also loosened restrictions on minority populations by improving their cultural and educational facilities and employment opportunities. The possibility of Ukrainian-Ruthenian and Hungarian autonomy within Slovakia was also discussed. However, following Moscow's intervention, the Slovak authorities reversed their policies toward the minorities in their pursuit of ethnic and republican homogenization. The campaign was opposed by local Hungarian leaders fearful of losing their hard-won linguistic and cultural liberties. Despite this resistance, they were subject to repression and persecution and had to operate under harsh political conditions throughout the 1970s and 1980s under the Gustáv Husák and Miloš Jakeš regimes.

Following the Czechoslovak "Velvet Revolution" of November 1989 and the rapid collapse of Communist Party rule, pressures began to increase in Slovakia demanding extensive political and economic autonomy. Several newly established Slovak parties placed demands for sovereignty on the national agenda even though they differed on the content and timetable for Slovak autonomy. Although the new federal government was supportive of administrative decentralization and the devolution of most ministerial powers to the republics, relations between Bratislava and Prague were strained by increasing demands from nationalist and separatist groups and disagreements over the content of newly framed republican and federal constitutions.

Several Slovak political parties became more outspoken on the issue of self-determination and capitalized on the painful effects of economic reform to accuse Prague of discrimination and of neglecting Slovak interests. Slovak deputies pressured the Federal Assembly into changing the country's name to the Czech and Slovak Federal Republic in early 1990, but the move simply revealed the deep-seated mistrust between representatives of the two nationalities and served to stimulate Slovak aspirations further. Public Against Violence (PAV), the democratic opposition movement that dislodged the Communists from power, split into a pro-federal and a pro-sovereignty wing, with the latter (styled as the Movement for a Democratic Slovakia) gaining broad public support and taking aboard an increasingly pro-separatist platform.

Prague and Bratislava also began to adopt divergent positions on the question of economic reform. Slovak leaders favored the retention of a sizable state sector, contending that the Slovak economy was more fragile than the Czech and the republic's population would suffer disproportionately from the closure of large factories. Bratislava also suspected that the Czechs would unfairly benefit from Western assistance and business investments and therefore sought greater self-determination in economic and foreign policy issues. Some Slovak deputies even proposed the formation of a separate Slovak home guard, a move that was depicted in Prague as designed to split the country's defense forces.

Slovak nationalists opposed President Václav Havel's calls for a referendum on the future of the federation. They feared that confronted with a simple choice, the majority of Slovaks would choose to remain in the federation. The pro-sovereignty forces scored well in the second multi-party general elections in June 1992, and a full separation between the two republics appeared more probable as talks on confederalism reached an impasse. There were signs that Czech leaders were also growing impatient with persistent Slovak demands that hindered legislative work, introduced vitriol into the political debate, and slowed down progress toward a market economy and European integration. Following the June 1992 election, in which pro-independence forces gained ground in Slovakia, Prague and Bratislava proved unable to agree on a restructured federal arrangement. The new Czech prime minister calculated that a formal separation was preferable to a long drawn-out dispute over constitutions, federal and ministerial powers, and intra-state treaties. By October 1992, the two sides agreed on a formal division, and on January 1, 1993, two new states, the Czech Republic and Slovakia, came into existence.

The position of the Hungarian minority has proved to be the most contentious nationality issue in Slovakia since the democratic changes. After the "Velvet Revolution," Hungarian activists began to organize openly and to campaign for their collective rights. Whereas some leaders calculated that demands for minority rights should not take precedence over the wider democratization process, other groups viewed the nationality problem as paramount and were accused of radicalism and separatism. The largest minority organization, Coexistence, styled itself as a multi-ethnic and not simply a Hungarian movement and denied that it was seeking secession from Slovakia. The organization gained seats in the Slovak National Council and campaigned for the expansion of minority educational, media, and publishing activities. Hungarian groups claimed that the position of minorities was under threat from rising Slovak nationalism and increasing disengagement by Prague. They claimed that Bratislava would apply various restrictions and discriminatory measures. Hungarian organizations also expressed concern over the incitement of ethnic conflict by ultra-nationalist Slovak forces, some of whom staged anti-Magyar demonstrations and even called for the wholesale expulsion of the Hungarian minority. Conversely, radical Slovak groups accused Budapest of assisting Hungarian organizations in search of territorial gains, a charge that was strenuously denied by the Hungarian government.

Hungarian leaders remained troubled that Slovak independence would have a negative impact on the position of the Magyar minority. They argued that Slovak self-assertiveness could be turned against Hungarians, who would be increasingly depicted as threatening national interests and challenging the republic's territorial integrity. Such conflicts could escalate during a period of severe economic dislocation, high unemployment, and popular susceptibility to nationalist and populist slogans. In fact, Slovak independence could prove to be a double-edged weapon for the Hungarian population. On the one hand, it could result in more repressive policies by Bratislava and undercut many of the rights gained since 1989, while Magyar leaders would have no recourse to protection from Prague. On the other hand, Slovak sovereignty could actually galvanize Hungarian activism and fuel demands for minority self-determination and even territorial autonomy under Budapest's patronage.

Since the democratic changes in Czechoslovakia, the Ruthenian and Ukrainian populations have also become more active. Indeed, questions have been raised over the precise size of these communities, as in previous censuses Ukrainians and Ruthenians reportedly disguised their ethnic identity for fear of official repercussions. An additional complication has arisen over the precise ethnic identity of this Slavic population that has been denominationally divided between Uniates (Greek-rite Catholics) and Orthodox. In the 1991 Czechoslovak census, a Ruthenian nationality was registered for the first time without parentheses and almost half of those who had previously declared themselves Ukrainian now defined themselves as Ruthenian. This rediscovered Ruthenian consciousness created rifts and conflicts within the community and even within villages and families at different stages of assimilation or reidentification. The free expression of Ruthenian and Ukrainian identity also began to have an impact on relations between Bratislava and Kyiv, particularly as Ruthenians in the Transcarpathian region rediscovered or strengthened their ethnic distinctiveness when Ukraine moved toward independence. Some Slovaks and Czechs grew concerned that with the break-up of Czechoslovakia, Ruthenia could become a magnet drawing Slovakia closer to Ukraine. Although revisionist sentiments in both states have not attained political significance, economic decline and fears of Slovak nationalism could stimulate Ruthenian and Ukrainian activists to press for autonomous status within Slovakia or closer association with Transcarpathian Ruthenia.

The Czechoslovak Communist regime refused to register the Romani (Gypsy) population as an ethnic minority. Unemployment rates remained high among Roma, but the authorities attempted to erase this problem by simply considering the unemployed as disabled and paying them pensions. Roma have maintained the highest birth rate of all nationalities in Czechoslovakia, and some sources predicted that they will compose almost 8 percent of the population within the next 10 to 15 years. The low number of Roma who openly declared their ethnic identity pointed to both a widespread fear of discrimination and a low level of national awareness. After the fall of communism, unemployment among Roma rose as high as 40 percent to 50 percent in some regions. While there were no official statistics, illiteracy rates were also believed to be overwhelming among this population. In addition, Roma were perceived to be the cause of a disproportionate percentage of crime, while prejudice, discrimination, and animosity against Gypsies remained commonplace among the general public.

OFFICIAL POLICIES

Czechoslovakia's transition toward a pluralist polity was accompanied by a structural and administrative division between the Czech and Slovak republics that affected political developments in both emerging states. Although the federal structure was one of the few reforms that survived the Soviet invasion and "normalization" in 1968 and 1969, in practice there was little decentralization of executive or legislative powers as envisaged in the 1969 constitution. Following the "Velvet Revolution" in November 1989, the federal authorities failed to regulate relations between the two republics and to satisfy growing Slovak aspirations for autonomy. The leaders of Public Against Violence (PAV) and the Civic Forum (the Czech counterpart), as well as President Havel, believed that democratization and decentralization would prove sufficient to keep the federation together. This neglect or lack of foresight allowed autonomist and separatist forces to gain ground in Slovakia.[3] Moreover, the lifting of centralist Communist controls and the national reawakening in Slovakia sparked a populist competition among the new Slovak parties primarily focused on the issue of sovereignty.

After prolonged dispute, in April 1990 the Federal Assembly adopted a new name for the state to provide equal recognition to both component nations: the Czech and Slovak Federal Republic. The first democratically elected central government set out to reorganize the federal structure. In June 1990, several federal ministries were merged, abolished, or had their powers transferred to republican ministries, and a series of meetings between Czech and Slovak leaders registered some progress in decentralizing the state. In October 1990, it was agreed to limit federal powers to defense, border controls, currency, taxes, prices, and foreign policy. This led to a constitutional amendment passed in December 1990.[4] However, by this time Slovak moves toward sovereignty were already far advanced. Slovak prime minister Vladimír Mečiar adopted an increasingly "anti-unitarian position," cognizant of the populist appeal of Slovak autonomy and the strident competition from other politicians.[5] Mečiar's outspoken position led to attacks on his motives from Slovak and Czech federalists, culminating in his ouster in April 1991 and appeals by the PAV to keep the federation together.[6]

Mečiar was accused by his former colleagues of pandering to nationalist feelings. But his removal from office served to exacerbate tensions and divisions in the PAV and raised Mečiar's popularity in Slovakia as a purported victim of a Prague-engineered coup. The new government of Christian Democratic Movement (CDM) leader Ján Čarnogurský, which pledged to work on a new federal constitution, rapidly lost support in the Slovak National Council, where anti-federalists gained a majority of votes. In September and November 1991, attempts were made to pass a Declaration of Slovak Sovereignty but the initiative narrowly failed in the National Council.[7] Meanwhile, Mečiar's MDS signed an Initiative for a Sovereign Slovakia, together with several pro-separatist parties, calling for the passage of a "full" Slovak constitution not derived from the

federal document and for Slovak laws to take precedence over federal legislation. Both the MDS and the CDM affirmed that the adoption of a new federal
constitution should be preceded by a state treaty between the two republics. This
was opposed by Czech politicians and pro-federalists in Slovakia who argued
that the republics did not have the sovereignty essential in international law to
sign such documents, while the forging of a state treaty would mean a prior
dissolution of the federation.[8] The content and timing of such a treaty also
became a source of dispute—for example, whether it should precede or follow
the adoption of new constitutions. Czech leaders wanted any constitutional
agreement to be preceded by a political declaration stating the intention of the
two nations to coexist in a common state.

A number of high-level meetings in late 1991 and early 1992 failed to determine the structure of relations between the two republics. Slovak leaders objected to the formulation that republics could only conclude international treaties
consented to by the "common state." A tentative compromise was reached specifying that a joint inter-republican document would take the form of an "intra-
state" and not an "inter-state" treaty. But a full agreement was again delayed by
Slovak insistence that the two National Councils ratify the new Federal constitution. Czech leaders argued that this would undermine the authority of the Federal
Assembly. Slovak politicians also continued to demand that the Slovak constitution should be adopted before the federal document. Although the Czech side
proved willing to make various compromises, for instance by agreeing that the
federal constitution could be ratified by the republican parliaments, Bratislava
gave conflicting signals on its willingness to reach a final agreement and sign a
constitutional treaty.

President Havel also became involved in the dispute, although his intervention may simply have added fuel to the flames. Havel was concerned that the
Czech-Slovak conflict was harmful to political and economic reform and dismissed
the notion of a "confederation" as a smokescreen for separation.[9] In November 1991,
Havel issued several proposals to break the constitutional deadlock, for example, by
proposing an amendment to the constitutional law giving the president powers to
declare a referendum on preserving the federation, and a constitutional bill defining
circumstances under which the Federal Assembly could be dissolved and new elections called, while in the interim the president would issue laws in the form of
decrees. The proposals were rejected by the Federal Assembly; they were blocked
by Slovak deputies who attacked Havel for seeking extraordinary powers and a
"presidential regime." Havel subsequently appealed directly to the public to support his initiatives and apply pressure on the parliament; his moves were opposed by
most Slovak and even some Czech politicians as populist and extra-constitutional,
and his political influence subsequently declined.[10]

Paradoxically, demands by the major Slovak parties for sovereignty and delays in signing binding constitutional agreements spurred calls for an independent Czech state. Right-wing conservatives and Czech nationalists in Prague

stressed the numerous advantages of a clean break, including a more streamlined administration, budget savings, and improved chances for the Czech republic to accelerate its integration into the EC.[11] At the same time, preparations were undertaken to pass a separate Czech constitution, specifying a weakened presidency and a stronger government, and to reorganize the republic into several self-governing lands to pacify Moravian-Silesian demands for greater autonomy.

The general elections of June 1992 propelled the process of federal dissolution. Parties advocating Slovak sovereignty or independence gained a comfortable majority in the Slovak National Council. Of the 150 available seats, the MDS captured 74, the ex-Communist Party of the Democratic Left (PDL) won 29 mandates, the Slovak National Party (SNP) 15, and the CDM 18, while a Hungarian-based ethnic coalition captured 14 mandates.[12] Ironically, even though public opinion polls in Slovakia indicated that the majority of citizens favored maintaining the federation, the most popular politician was the new premier, Vladimír Mečiar, who skillfully manipulated the issue of national independence during the election campaign.

Mečiar's talks with Czech prime minister Václav Klaus failed to resolve the federal question. Mečiar wanted the federation loosened to such a degree that it would no longer resemble a common state; this was unacceptable to Klaus, who declared that he preferred a complete split to an unworkable confederation. Mečiar proposed that two republican entities under international law agree to coordinate mutual defense, foreign policy, and the country's currency. Klaus considered such an arrangement to be worse than separation as it would prove constitutionally confusing. It appeared that Mečiar was banking on major political and economic concessions from Prague in return for preserving close ties between the two republics; when Klaus moved quickly to end the stalemate, the Slovak side was caught by surprise. For example, when Mečiar proposed the creation of a new Czech-Slovak Union, the notion was rejected by Prague, which suspected that Bratislava wanted to assure itself of continuing material support, fearing the economic impact of a full division.[13] Instead, the Czech side pushed strenuously for separation and the forging of international treaties between two new independent states.

Following the 1992 elections, only a caretaker federal government was set up to administer the division of the country. The federal cabinet was reduced, and Havel himself failed to be reelected Czechoslovak president due to opposition by Slovak deputies. In an agreement between Klaus and Mečiar, republican governments were to decide on the federal split and establish the legal foundations for Czech and Slovak statehood. A timetable of separation was quickly agreed upon. In July 1992, the Slovak government declared sovereignty and in October 1992 ratified its own constitution.[14] The federal government approved the draft of a constitutional act on terminating the federation, while Mečiar and Klaus signed various agreements defining relations between the two republics following the dissolution; these included stipulations on a customs union and a common currency.[15] In November 1992, the Federal Assembly finally voted to disband the Czech and Slovak Federation, phase out all federal institutions, and give the two republics equal successor status. More than 30 agreements were concluded regularizing relations between the two republics and equitably dividing federal assets. Nonetheless, some disputes were expected to materialize, particularly in valuing and apportioning federal property between Prague and Bratislava and in restructuring their trade relations. On January 1, 1993, Slovakia formally achieved its statehood, and a few weeks later Michal Kovac, the MDS candidate, was elected Slovakia's president by the National Council.

The division of Czechoslovakia raised serious questions about the future political stability of both political entities. While the Czech republic benefited from a comparatively healthy economy and its new government seemed committed to democracy, pluralism, and capitalism, Slovakia suffered from more debilitating economic decline and scant Western investment, while the new administration openly favored more pronounced state intervention in the economy. Some Czech officials and foreign observers issued warnings that an independent Slovakia would remain politically unstable and could veer toward some form of national authoritarianism and economic protectionism. These views were not shared by the major Slovak parties. Czech premier Václav Klaus also underscored that the division of the CSFR would mean a chance for Slovakia to develop a "normal political spectrum" and "create scope for right-wing and left-wing parties and for civic political parties."[16] But while there was general confidence that the Czech transition to democratic capitalism would prove successful, if not painless, significant concern remained that Slovakia's transition would take much longer to complete and could be diverted by nationalist and statist forces toward some new form of autocracy.

The ethnic-minority issue was not paid much attention by Czechoslovakia's Communist leadership until several years after World War Two; no authorized statistics were even cited until 1965. In 1968, Constitutional Law No. 144 was introduced on the nationality question in the Czechoslovak Socialist Republic, establishing rules for the treatment of minorities. While this law included the right for minorities to receive education in their own language, the prevailing view was that the law was too vague and needed further specification. While the short-lived Prague Spring in 1968 raised hopes for major constitutional and legislative enactments to codify minority rights, throughout the years of "normalization" the position of ethnic minorities deteriorated once again even while Constitutional Law No. 144 remained valid.

After the fall of communism, the status of ethnic minorities gained increasing importance in the country. Among the new features of the first post-Communist census, held in March 1991, was the opportunity to declare oneself part of an ethnic minority that had not been recognized by the previous regimes, for example, Romani, Moravian, or Ruthenian. Another key development was the Charter of Fundamental Rights and Liberties, adopted by the Federal Assembly in January 1991, that formed a new legal basis for the treatment of ethnic minorities. This document outlined the basic human, civil, and political rights of Czechoslovak citizens and was to serve as a foundation for the future federal and republican constitutions. In a special section that addressed minority rights, the charter provided everyone the opportunity to decide on his or her nationality, prohibited anti-minority discrimination, and permitted all minorities to form their own associations. It also stated that under certain conditions minorities would have the right to be educated in their own language and to use it in dealings with officialdom.

However, Hungarian spokesmen contended that the charter may have inadvertently reduced the existing rights of minorities by defining the state as the "national State of Czechs and Slovaks," and abrogating earlier constitutional laws relating to minorities. In protest, Hungarian deputies walked out of the Federal Assembly for the duration of the final vote on the charter. Hungarian leaders also objected to laws adopted by the Federal Assembly relating to compensation payments for property expropriated after World War Two. The Compensation Act and the Land Act passed in 1991 referred only to property confiscated after February 1948, the date of the Communist takeover. No compensation was offered for losses sustained by Hungarians between 1945 and 1948, a period when explicitly anti-Magyar decrees deprived the minority of their property and citizenship rights.

Article 12 of the Slovak constitution, ratified in September 1992 and effective the following month, guaranteed basic rights and liberties regardless of language, national or social origin, affiliation with a nation or ethnic group, as well as the right to choose nationality without pressure to assimilate. Articles 33 and 34 on the Rights of National Minorities and Ethnic Groups formally secured the right of minorities to develop their culture, to disseminate and receive information in the mother tongue, to establish educational and cultural institutions, and allowed for the functioning of national-minority associations. The language question was dealt with by reinforcing the need to master the "state language" while guaranteeing the right to education in the mother tongue and the right to use that language in dealings with officialdom. Minorities were assured the right to participate in solving problems pertaining to their status, but in doing so they needed to exercise their rights in a manner that would not jeopardize the sovereignty of the Slovak Republic.

Hungarian members of the Slovak National Council unanimously rejected the constitution, arguing that it failed to guarantee the identity and self-government of minorities or allow for the creation of territorial "self-administrative" entities that would satisfy Hungarian aspirations. Magyar deputies strongly objected to the constitutional definition of the new country as the "National State of Slovaks," claiming that there were no explicit guarantees for the preservation and safeguarding of minority identities. Specifically, they pointed out that only "national organizations" could be formed by ethnic minorities, thus opening up the possibility of dissolving Hungarian political parties at any time. Moreover, the constitution declared that the rights of minorities could not endanger Slovak sovereignty and territorial integrity, a provision that was allegedly open to abuse. Hungarian deputies proposed a constitutional amendment to guarantee the right to develop one's national, ethnic, linguistic, or cultural identity, while banning any activities that lead to assimilation.[17]

Magyar leaders claimed that the constitution failed to stipulate the rights of minorities to establish and maintain schools in their mother tongue. The constitution also replaced the concept of the "official language" with that of the "state language" and offered no legal guarantees for the use of minority languages in dealing with the authorities. The language issue was further defined by the controversial Language Law passed by the Slovak National Council in October 1990. The law declared Slovak the official language, allowing Czech to be used in official transactions, and stated that if members of an ethnic minority constituted 20 percent of the population in an administrative area they were entitled to use their language formally. There was, however, no stipulation requiring state officials either to be proficient in minority languages or to employ them if they were. The application of the law also resulted in Hungarian names no longer being registered in birth registers, invalidated any moves toward restoring Hungarian appellations for municipalities, and abolished bilingual street signs. It also permitted officials to refuse to conduct marriage and funeral services in Hungarian.[18] After Slovakia became a member of the Council of Europe in June 1993, Bratislava came under international pressure to alter some of its minority rights legislation. Indeed, in July 1993 the parliament passed a law again allowing minorities to register their names in their mother tongue. Further conciliatory measures to defuse domestic and international criticism appeared likely.

Although the version of the language law that was finally passed in 1990 was not as radical as some Slovak national parties had proposed, the legislation itself, as well as the Slovak constitution, were depicted by Hungarian leaders as impediments to minority rights. The Hungarian-dominated political movement Coexistence criticized the Language Law for not ensuring the rights of national communities to use their native language in official matters (prior to the adoption of the law, minorities not equaling 20 percent of the population were nevertheless able to use their mother language), for eliminating bilingual signs, and for disregarding the referendums that voted to replace the original township names. In late 1992, Magyar activists reported that during the past year, signs bearing Hungarian placenames had been forcibly removed by government agencies and replaced by Slovak signs.[19]

Hungarian activists also persistently complained that Slovakia's educational system had purportedly failed to reverse the assimilationist pressures evident since the 1950s. They argued that the steady reduction in the number of schools contributed to the fact that during the 1990–91 school year over 36 percent of school-age Hungarians were unable to attend Magyar-language schools. As a result, the educational level of Hungarians was purportedly lower than that of

Slovaks: 50 percent had only primary education, and a mere 2 percent managed to obtain a college or university diploma. Since 1989, the federal and republican governments have rejected the principle of educational autonomy, leaving no firm legal safeguards for developing education in the mother tongue for national minorities. Additionally, the Slovak government did not approve the creation of an independent Hungarian-language teacher's college. To counter Hungarian criticisms, Slovak officials asserted that Hungarian schools accounted for over 8 percent of all teaching facilities in the country, while 12 of the 135 senior high schools were Hungarian. In addition, the state evidently supported the publication of 25 Magyar magazines, as well as 2 theaters and several publishing houses.[20]

Since the onset of the democratic changes, several Slovak nationalist groups have not only campaigned for Slovak independence but have remonstrated against the republic's minorities, particularly against Hungarians, who were scapegoated for alleged subversion, and the Roma, the perennial stereotype of criminality and disorder. Although Jews barely numbered in the hundreds, mostly resident in Bratislava, anti-Semitism also resurfaced as ultra-nationalists sought to rehabilitate Jozef Tiso and other leaders of the wartime Nazi puppet regime, while various anti-Jewish tracts were published and disseminated in the country. In addition, the Slovak government has been criticized for failing to protect the Romani population from acts of violence perpetrated by racist radicals or from persistent discrimination in employment, education, and housing. Nonetheless, Roma have been able to establish their own political organizations and to participate in local and legislative elections. Because they remained embryonic and splintered, Romani parties proved unable to pass the threshold for parliamentary representation.

The Slovak citizenship law passed in January 1993 did not stir any significant controversy, although some of its stipulations for acquiring "state citizenship" could precipitate bureaucratic discrimination against some minority groups. For instance, in applying for citizenship by the end of December 1993, an individual needed to prove mastery of the Slovak language and the absence of a criminal record during the past five years. The former provision could theoretically be used to disenfranchise some older Hungarian residents whose knowledge of Slovak was often rudimentary, while the latter stipulation could discriminate against Romani residents, particularly if the onus was on the individual to prove his or her innocence.[21]

SLOVAK NATIONALISTS

Movement for a Democratic Slovakia (MDS)
Hnutie za Demokratické Slovensko (HDS)

The Movement splintered off from the pro-federalist Public Against Violence (PAV) coalition in March 1991. Led by former Slovak prime minister Vladimír

Mečiar, it depicted itself as a centrist political group with a measured approach toward market reform and the elimination of state economic control. The MDS program ranked Slovak national concerns above all other issues and adopted a much more pronounced nationalist stance than the PAV. It favored a loose confederal structure based on separate republican constitutions and a new inter-state agreement. The party asserted that a Slovak constitution had to be adopted before the conclusion of a state treaty with the Czech Republic. By March 1992, Mečiar's party became the strongest political force in Slovakia with an estimated 40 percent support in public-opinion polls. It increasingly spoke out against radical economic reforms, pointing to the growing unemployment rate in Slovakia. For the general elections of June 1992, the MDS program specified the following steps: the unconditional declaration of Slovak sovereignty without consultation with Prague; the adoption of a Slovak constitution; and a referendum in Slovakia on the form of co-existence with the Czech republic. It also called for a slower pace of privatization in Slovakia to guard against economic disruption and potential social unrest. In October 1991, the party chairman, Vladimír Mečiar, provocatively suggested a union between Slovakia and Moravia if the Slovak and Czech Republics failed to reach agreement on a state treaty.

In the June 1992 general elections, the MDS missed winning an absolute majority in the Slovak National Council by only 2 votes, gaining 74 out of 150 seats, and captured 37.26 percent of the popular vote. But opposition to Mečiar's party in the Council proved weak and splintered, especially as the PAV and the Christian Democratic Movement fared poorly in the balloting. Support for the MDS was highest in the industrialized ares of western and central Slovakia, where Mečiar's pledge, contrary to Prague's policies, to continue Slovak arms manufacturing boosted his popularity. His evident anti-Hungarian stance and his support for restrictions on Magyar autonomy also had some appeal among the electorate. Although public-opinion polls indicated that the majority of Slovaks favored preserving the federation, they also demonstrated that Mečiar was by far the most popular Slovak politician. The substantial MDS mandate in the 1992 elections thereby invigorated Mečiar's push toward Slovak independence, and following failed negotiations with Prague in the summer of 1992, a timetable for separation was mutually agreed upon in the fall. Slovakia formally attained its independence in January 1993, and Mečiar became the new Slovak prime minister. The MDS formed the core of the new government, capturing 11 of the 14 ministries; one minister was a member of the Slovak National Party and the other was unaffiliated. MDS member Michal Kovac was elected Slovak president by the National Council in February 1993.[22]

Christian Democratic Movement (CDM)
Kresťanskodemokratické Hnutie (KDH)

This political organization was founded in February 1990 and opted to keep the party's original name following a schism in the CDM in March 1992. Led by former Slovak prime minister Ján Čarnogurský, the majority of registered CDM members reportedly resided in the countryside. However, the party also included several urban organizations with a professional orientation. Many members in Čarnogurský's CDM welcomed the Movement's division, claiming that it would cleanse the movement of leftist and ultra-nationalist elements and enable it to become a traditional right-of-center Christian Democratic party. In its initial statements, the Movement supported the Czechoslovak federation although through a looser inter-republican relationship. However, some leaders proclaimed that its ultimate goal was the dissolution of Czechoslovakia. After its founding in early 1990, the CDM quickly developed into the strongest competitor of the Public Against Violence, emerging from the June 1990 elections as the second-most-popular party in Slovakia. It subsequently joined the Federal Assembly's ruling coalition with the Civic Forum and the PAV and supported the adoption of a constitutional amendment in December 1990 that ceded many of the federation's powers to the two republics.

During the summer of 1990, the Movement adopted a more nationalist orientation. In July 1990, the leadership issued a statement advocating a Czechoslovak confederation and a future "sovereign and equal" Slovakia. The movement's growing image as a defender of Slovak rights was reflected in its increasing popularity in the republic. After recasting its program in a more nationalist fashion, it became the strongest political force in the republic at the local level, gaining 27.5 percent of the vote during the local elections in November 1990. Following the PAV split in March 1991, the CDM became the strongest political force in the Slovak National Council by holding 31 parliamentary seats. However, due to pressure from its pro-federal coalition partners (PAV and the Democratic Party) the Movement diluted its pro-confederal stance and advocated a looser federation instead. This change in orientation was widely seen as a setback for Slovak sovereignty. It also appeared to diminish the CDM's popularity, which slipped to 12 percent in public-opinion polls, while the pro-sovereignty MDS increased its support to over 30 percent.

Internal factionalization became evident in the CDM by the summer of 1991. Despite its official support for preserving the federation, the Movement allied itself with Slovak nationalist parties in the Federal Assembly in vetoing propositions to hold a referendum on the country's future constitutional setup. On the other hand, the CDM blocked attempts by nationalist parties in the Slovak National Council to adopt a Declaration of Slovak Sovereignty. In February 1992, leaders of the Czech and Slovak National Councils tentatively agreed on the text of a state treaty for which Čarnogurský had vigorously campaigned. However, the Presidium of the Slovak National Council rejected the draft, and four members of the Christian Democratic Movement voted against the treaty. This was a clear signal that the CDM could no longer remain unified. Čarnogurský gave the nationalist wing an ultimatum either to follow the party line or to leave; the Klepáč faction responded by announcing its departure. In March

1992, František Mikloško, the chairman of the Slovak National Council and a member of the PAV, announced that he would join Čarnogurský's party. He suggested that the party should become a "modern conservative party," similar to other European Christian Democratic parties. The Movement continued to advocate the maintenance of the federal state on a temporary basis, with eventual independence for Slovakia. But it insisted that the adoption of the federal constitution, scheduled for the end of 1991, be preceded by a state treaty between the Czech and Slovak republics. The party platform advocated a degree of state intervention in the economy and gradual market transformation in order to reduce social tensions in Slovakia. The CDM fared poorly in the June 1992 general elections, scoring only 8.88 percent of the popular vote, winning only 18 out of 150 seats in the Slovak National Council, and losing more than half of its previous Slovak supporters. While Čarnogurský was effectively removed from power, he remained a member of the Slovak National Council.[23]

Slovak Christian Democratic Party (SCDP)
Slovenská Kresťanskodemokratická Strana (SKDS)

The SCDP emerged as an overtly nationalist wing of the Christian Democratic Movement. It formally seceded in March 1992, as its leaders were dissatisfied with the CDM's stance on Slovak independence. It was led by Ján Klepáč, the deputy chairman of the Slovak National Council. Of the 31 deputies representing the Christian Democratic Movement in the Slovak National Council, 11 decided to join Klepáč, together with 5 of the 25 deputies in the Federal Assembly. Four members of the Slovak government also defected to Klepáč's party. The SCDP's economic platform remained opposed to the methods and consequences of Prague-sponsored privatization and instead advocated a "social market economy" with pronounced state intervention. Most members of the former Economic Club of the CDM joined Klepáč's party, including the Club's most prominent member, Forestry Minister Vilém Oberhauser. But aside from a strong emphasis on Slovak sovereignty, the SCDP platform remained rather vague. Potentially an ally of Mečiar's MDS, it only attracted 3 percent of the popular vote during the June 1992 elections. Its failure to garner sufficient votes for parliamentary seats was blamed by party leaders on the large number of contenders who had adopted populist and nationalist orientations.[24]

Slovak National Party (SNP)
Slovenská Národná Strana (SNS)

Established in February 1990, the SNP was initially headed by the controversial leader Víťazoslav Móric. It finished third in the June 1990 Slovak National Council elections, winning 22 seats, and gained 15 seats in the Federal Assembly. During 1990, public support for the SNP climbed significantly: by late summer, sympathy for the SNP had reportedly grown to 14 percent, and at the time of the general elections to over 20 percent. However, its popularity dropped substantially during the local elections of November 1990 when it rallied only 3 percent of the vote. This appeared to be the result of internal party conflicts and competition with other nationalist groups and because the Christian Democrats and some PAV deputies had taken aboard nationalist issues and more actively campaigned for Slovak "national interests." An inner crisis became evident in the SNP, propelled by a power struggle in which prominent leaders were accused of programmatic inconsistency and an inability to increase the party's share of the popular vote. The party performed poorly in many villages where it had failed to build a viable network, and its pro-sovereignty position was skillfully espoused by several competing forces. Following a party shake-up, the former trade-union leader Jozef Prokeš became the SNP's new president.

The SNP displayed its willingness to capitalize on popular frustrations by organizing street rallies and other protest actions in support of outright independence and against alleged Czech domination and Hungarian subversion. For instance, it helped to organize some of the first anti-Magyar demonstrations in Bratislava and Nové Zámky in February 1990. It also sought to revitalize Slovak cultural traditions and contended that all nationalities in the republic had to respect Slovakia's national and state sovereignty in accordance with the rules of international law. The SNP underscored the primacy of "Slovak national interests" and the position of Slovaks as a "state forming nation." It fully supported the March 1991 Declaration of Slovak Sovereignty, formulated by several nationalist groups. This declaration demanded that Slovak laws take precedence over those of the federation. The party has often advocated short-term solutions to various pressing issues, rather than adhering to a consistent political philosophy, and has kept its attention fixed on the goal of complete Slovak independence. In the June 1992 general elections, the SNP performance was modest, obtaining 7.93 percent of the total vote and 15 Slovak National Council seats. Its center of support was in Bratislava, where it gained 17 percent of the ballots, and in some southern and western counties where anti-Hungarian sentiments remained pronounced. Despite its poor showing, the SNP gained one ministry in Slovakia's first independent government, in coalition with the MDS. In the summer of 1993, talks were initiated between the SNP and the MDS to form a new coalition government potentially giving the nationalists a bigger profile in the administration.[25]

Party of the Democratic Left (PDL)
Strana Demokratickej Lavice (SDL)

The PDL emerged from the Slovak Communist Party in October 1990, led by chairman Peter Weiss. After the 1989 revolution, the Slovak Communists became increasingly independent of the federal Communist Party of Czechoslovakia and introduced a number of internal political reforms. During its October

1990 congress, the party changed its name to the Party of the Democratic Left, and in November 1990 it agreed to form a provisional coalition with the Communist Party of Bohemia and Moravia. Regarding minority questions, the party initially favored the formation of political and cultural organizations and supported the right to use native languages in the press and in official contacts. In January 1991, PDL leaders decided to rid the party of conservative Communist elements by mandating a reregistration of all members. In March 1991, when Mečiar's pro-sovereignty MDS broke away from the PAV, PDL leaders increasingly sensed that the national issue combined with a social-democratic economic orientation could help to harness significant public support. As a result, the PDL underscored its support for Mečiar's program and became a quasi-nationalist party in its own right. By April 1991, the party reported 20,000 reregistered members, and while this represented a drop of some 100,000, public opinion polls at that time revealed that the PDL remained the second-strongest party in Slovakia, benefiting from about 16 percent of public support. Due to the party's social-democratic and pro-nationalist orientation, it moved away from traditional communism while new but marginal Communist parties emerged to fill the gap. During the June 1992 elections, the party scored particularly well in eastern Slovakia, where it obtained 21.5 percent of the popular vote. In sum, the PDL gained 14.7 percent of the vote, winning 29 seats in the Slovak National Council.[26]

Slovak Motherland (SM)
Matica Slovenská (MS)

This national-cultural association was originally established in 1863 during the period of Hungarian occupation to promote and defend Slovak identity. It was disbanded by the Hungarian authorities in 1875 but was resuscitated during the first Czechoslovak Republic. Throughout the most repressive Stalinist years (1948–68), the SM was suppressed but was once more reinstated during the 1968 Prague Spring and again in the wake of the 1989 "Velvet Revolution." Between the close of 1989 and the end of 1992, the SM held six national gatherings and significantly expanded its membership, program, activities, and influence. In August 1992, the SM General Assembly elected Jozef Markuš as its new president and issued a major national program calling for outright Slovak statehood and independence. By mid-1992, it claimed to have nearly 400 local branches, a membership of some 140,000, over 600,000 sympathizers, and cells in the Czech Republic, Poland, and in the West. The association was reported to have extensive influence among the nationalist-minded Slovak intelligentsia, placing enormous emphasis on strengthening Slovak culture and education; it has also established extensive publishing ventures. The SM program focused on alleged "deformations" in Slovak education caused by decades of Communist and Czech influence. It underscored that it would strive to rebuild the educational system and cultural life in a "national spirit" and cooperate closely with all relevant government organs.

Although the movement's program declared that it would protect the rights of all minorities in Slovakia, it claimed above all that the SM would work against the "denationalization" of Slovaks and other anti-Slovak phenomena, clearly alluding to demands by Hungarians for more extensive collective rights. SM leaders strongly supported a version of the Language Law that would make Slovak the exclusive language in the republic in all administrative affairs and public communications. In April 1993, the SM issued a strong statement on the position of Slovaks in southern Slovakia, claiming that the Slovak language, culture, religious services, and national identity were dying out in the region as a result of mounting Hungarian discrimination. It asserted that Hungarian political parties were creating an atmosphere of "national, cultural, and existential insecurity" for Slovaks in mixed population areas. The SM protested against all efforts at local autonomy that allegedly violated the "cultural and territorial integrity" of the Slovak republic. It proposed to the National Council that the law on local self-governments needed urgently to be amended to prevent domination by the Hungarian minority; ethnic Slovaks evidently had to be ensconced in all leading positions in public administration to eliminate opportunities for Hungarian discrimination. If tensions between Magyars and Slovaks continue to increase, the Slovak Motherland is likely to be at the forefront, providing the ideological and conceptual underpinnings for any anti-minority measures.[27]

Movement for an Independent Slovakia (MIS)
Hnutie za Nezávislé Slovensko (HNS)

Established in July 1990 by Vojtech Vitkovský, the MIS became a militant nationalist organization committed to full Slovak independence. It consistently voiced discontent with the proposed constitutional and political solutions to Slovak sovereignty and asserted that conditions were ripe for the assertion of Slovak statehood. The MIS considered that absolute Slovak independence was the only recipe for the country's development. The leadership also contended that coexistence with minority ethnic groups was guaranteed by "Slovak good will," and whenever this was violated it was primarily the consequence of minority activities and foreign subversion. The MIS remained in favor of close economic cooperation with the Czech Republic once Slovak-Czech relations were stabilized and equalized by the creation of two independent states. The party has remained fairly small since its inception, but its ultra-nationalist and anti-minority sentiments retained some appeal in society and could gain in popularity if economic and social conditions deteriorate in an independent Slovakia.[28]

Slovak National Democratic Movement (SNDM)
Slovenské Národné Demokratické Hnutie (SNDH)

The SNDM was founded in Bratislava in July 1990 on the initiative of members of the nationalist-cultural grouping, the Štúr Society and the Independent Party of Slovaks. The Movement was led by chairman Peter Brňák, elected in January 1991, and an independent deputy to the Slovak National Council. It stressed Slovak "national unity" as the most important step toward the creation of an independent Slovakia. The SNDM presupposed that the Slovak language would become the only official language of the future Slovak state. Its goal was to maintain the "well-being" of Slovaks during the transformation of the republic into an independent state; throughout 1991 and 1992 it called for full Slovak sovereignty and the speedy adoption of a Slovak constitution. Representatives of the SNDM have displayed a marked anti-Hungarian position; for example, during July 1991 they claimed that weapons were being smuggled to "Magyar extremists" in southern Slovakia and called on Slovaks to be vigilant and prepared for violent confrontations. Similarly to other ultra-nationalist groupings, the Movement viewed specific political and economic programs to be less important than the achievement of national independence.[29]

Party of Freedom—Party of National Unity (PF-PNU)
Strana Slobody—Strana Národnej Jednoty (SS-SNJ)

This party focused its program on Slovak independence, with a pronounced anti-Czech sentiment, gradual economic reform, continuing state intervention in the economy, and strong social programs. It also exhibited many anti-Hungarian elements and was instrumental in organizing the first of numerous anti-Magyar nationalist demonstrations in Bratislava and Nové Zámky in February 1990. It did not compete in the 1990 elections but participated in coalition with the Party of National Unification during the June 1992 elections, although failing to obtain any parliamentary seats.[30] Several other smaller Slovak nationalist and pro-independence organizations were formed in the aftermath of the "Velvet Revolution," including the Movement for a Free Slovakia, the Party for National Prosperity, the Party of Slovak Unity, the Slovak Heritage Foundation, the National Salvation Movement, the National Liberal Party, and the Slovak People's Party.[31]

HUNGARIAN AUTONOMISTS

Coexistence
Együttélés, Spolužitie, Wspólnota, Soužití

Coexistence, the former Forum of Hungarians in Czechoslovakia, was founded in February 1990 by the prominent dissident and national rights activist Miklós Duray. Its immediate forerunner was the Committee for the Protection of Hungarian Minority Rights (Legal Defense Community) in Czechoslovakia, an organization established in the late 1970s to campaign for Magyar causes under the Communist regime. Coexistence was the third Hungarian party to emerge after the "Velvet Revolution," following the Independent Hungarian Initiative (IHI) and the Hungarian Christian Democratic Movement (HCDM). Within a few months, it claimed a membership of some 40,000 people. It declared itself free of any particular ideology and pledged to represent the interests of all national minorities in Czechoslovakia. Its membership soon encompassed not only Hungarians but also Poles, Germans, Ukrainians, and Ruthenians. The movement aimed to deal with all problems faced by the country's minorities and called for firm legal safeguards that would protect their interests. For instance, it proposed the creation of a Ministry of Nationalities in the federal government and opposed high percentage thresholds for gaining seats in the Federal Assembly, as this effectively excluded minority parties from the parliament.

Coexistence differed from other Hungarian parties in its approach toward minority rights. Whereas the IHI believed that such campaigns should not take precedence over the broader process of democratization in the initial post-Communist phase, Coexistence viewed the nationality question to be resolvable alongside the democratization program. As a result, it was viewed as radical and nationalist, even by some pro-federalist Slovaks. With the rise of anti-Hungarian sentiment among several Slovak nationalist parties, Coexistence became a target for frequent political and media attacks and was accused of supporting revisionist territorial demands emanating from Budapest. Duray consistently rejected such interpretations of its policies, viewing them as a smokescreen for denying various rights to the Magyar community.

Coexistence consistently supported the federal system as the best environment for protecting minority rights, as opposed to outright Slovak independence. Its leaders felt that none of the Slovak parties had a clear minorities policy with which the Hungarians could remain comfortable. Coexistence claimed to understand Slovakia's national aspirations but voiced concern that an independent Slovak state would become intolerant of its minorities. Should Slovakia attain statehood, Coexistence envisioned the creation of regional self-governing bodies, while contending that external circumstances would play a critical role in determining the kind of guarantees Bratislava would provide for its minorities. Its program underscored "collective rights" for Czechoslovakia's minorities, including cultural autonomy for all ethnic groups and political autonomy in regions containing compact Magyar communities, particularly in southern Slovakia. Its economic goals stressed privatization, private ownership, and the transformation of collectives into private farms.

Coexistence formed a coalition with the Hungarian Christian Democratic Movement for the elections of June 1990. It won 12 seats in the Federal Assembly and 14 seats in the Slovak National Council, capturing 8.66 percent of the total vote and nearly 80 percent of the ethnic Magyar vote. However, during the November 1990 local elections, it only secured 6.25 percent of the ballot, although performing reasonably well in counties containing large Hungarian populations. For example, it managed to elect 105 mayors; since then the total has risen to 116. Other Hungarian parties elected 62 mayors in Slovakia. Coexistence objected to the package of language laws introduced by Bratislava in October 1990 that ensured Slovak as the sole official language even in minority areas, with the use of Hungarian limited to districts containing 20 percent or more Magyar inhabitants. Instead, it proposed legislation on the public use of minority languages in all areas with significant minority populations. However, Magyar leaders pointed out that at least the new law nullified the variant proposed by the Slovak National Party, which would have made Slovak the exclusive language in all districts regardless of minority proportions.

In mid-July 1991, Coexistence, together with the HCDM, objected to the newly introduced land law at a joint session of the Czechoslovak Federal Assembly. The law purportedly discriminated against some minorities: for example, Hungarians were only entitled to 50 hectares of private land, while members of other nationalities could receive as many as 250 hectares. Coexistence also protested against the Slovak-government decision in the summer of 1991 to cut subsidies to ethnic-minority cultural organizations. It also lodged complaints over the federal law on rehabilitation that set February 1948 (when the Communists seized power) as the retroactive limit for material compensation to unjustly dispossessed individuals. In fact, the Magyars lost much of their property between 1945 and 1948 under pressure from local Communists and the Soviet occupation forces.

Coexistence issued a series of legal and political proposals, including a draft supplement to the new federal constitution regarding minority rights, its own draft language law for Slovakia, and a comprehensive proposal on ways to improve the position of minorities, which was sent in October 1991 to the federal, Czech, and Slovak governments, as well as to various international organizations. It requested the creation of a constituent committee for representatives of all national minorities, a body that would draft a separate paragraph in the new constitution on the rights of national minorities. The party also called for the expansion of Hungarian language, educational, and media activities, including the establishment of a Hungarian university in the southern city of Komárno. By mid-1992, Coexistence increasingly feared that the achievement of Slovak statehood would prove unfavorable for minority groups. It also expressed strong apprehensions that economic deterioration could exacerbate social and ethnic unrest for which Magyars would invariably be blamed. For the June 1992 elections to the Slovak National Council, the party formed a coalition with the Hungarian Christian Democratic Movement; the Hungarian People's Party joined the coalition in the campaign for seats in the federal Assembly. In its election campaign, the coalition called for the right of all minorities to their own schools with instruction in the mother tongue from elementary to university level, for equitable political representation at the republican and federal levels, for the right to use the mother tongue at all tiers of public administration in districts where minorities formed a large proportion of the population, and for the right to have their own churches. The coalition won 14 out of 150 seats to the Slovak National Council, 9 of which represented Coexistence, garnering 7.42 percent of the popular vote. It also elected 12 deputies to the Federal Assembly, 8 of whom represented Coexistence.

Coexistence held its fourth congress in Komárno in February 1993, at which delegates condemned repressive Slovak government policies and called for "political and economic self-administration" for the Hungarian areas of southern Slovakia. Delegates drafted a document on the "Principles of Regional Self-Government and Personal Autonomy" in which the notion of "regional self-rule" was elaborated. Three kinds of areas were defined: "majority areas," in which Magyars formed over 50 percent of the population; "minority areas," where they formed between 10 percent and 50 percent; and "sporadic areas" where they totaled less than 10 percent. In the former, Hungarians should be able to establish local governments, linked together in a Hungarian "ethnoregion." Such proposals have been interpreted by Slovak politicians as the precursors of full-scale territorial autonomy based on ethnic principles that could lead to the separation of Hungarian-majority municipalities from southern Slovakia.[32]

Social and Democratic Union of Hungarians in Slovakia (SDUHS)
Sociálny a Demokratický Zväz Maďarov na Slovensku (SDZMS)

This organization, founded in April 1993 and formerly known as *Csemadok-Democratic Union of Hungarians in Czechoslovakia*, was led by Viktór (Győző) Bauer. Originally formed in November 1949 as the Cultural Association of Hungarian Working People in Czechoslovakia, *Csemadok* was the sole Hungarian organization in Slovakia approved by the Communist government and functioning in cooperation with the regime; the Communists did not allow ethnic minorities to form their own independent political groups. During its four decades of existence, the Association contained the largest membership of all Hungarian groups in Slovakia. However, when the organization attempted to move into the political arena after the 1968 Prague Spring, it was excluded from Czechoslovakia's "normalized" National Front in 1971. Since December 1989, it has attempted to transform itself into an umbrella political organization representing the interests of the Hungarian minority in Czechoslovakia's new political system. Reflecting this changing profile, *Csemadok*'s general assembly voted at its March 1990 extraordinary session to omit the designation "cultural" from its name and to add the appellation "democratic" instead.

The group gave its support to the Coexistence—Hungarian Christian Democratic Movement coalition in the June 1990 general elections and became an outspoken proponent of minority rights. It sought to prevent the political splintering of the Hungarian community, arguing that factionalization would disable the minority from being represented in public life to an extent commensurate with its strength. Its platform displayed similarities with that of Coexistence, and it unequivocally supported the Czechoslovak federal system as the best solution for guaranteeing minority rights. It called for the creation of a Ministry of Nationalities at the federal level and vehemently protested the 1990 Slovak Language Law that codified Slovak as the republic's exclusive official language. However, *Csemadok*'s reputation has remained tarnished because of its links with the previous regime. Since 1989, its membership dropped from some 100,000 to 80,000 persons, although it still claimed to possess the largest membership of all Hungarian groups in Slovakia. Following the 1992 elections and the moves toward Slovak independence, the Union contended that the most important task for ethnic Hungarian parties was to work with Slovak politicians who supported the safeguarding of minority rights. Its leaders believed that an independent Slovakia was unlikely to tolerate any form of political or territorial autonomy for the Magyar minority, and it severely criticized the Slovak state media for its belligerent anti-Hungarian tone.[33]

Hungarian Christian Democratic Movement (HCDM)
Maďarské Kresťansodemokratické Hnutie (MKDH)

Founded in March 1990 and headed by President Kálmán Jánics, the HCDM was the second Magyar political group to emerge in the wake of the democratic changes. The party grew out of the Hungarian Christian Democratic clubs in Slovakia, and its establishment was not especially welcomed by the Slovak Christian Democrats. The HCDM became the second most significant Magyar movement in the republic with regard to the number of its local chapters and local representatives. Shortly after its creation, the HCDM experienced internal ideological and personality disputes among its estimated 50,000 members. This resulted in the April 1991 expulsion of its four Federal Assembly deputies, who had accused the leadership (headed by Chairman Béla Bugár) of being undemocratic and of distancing itself from Coexistence. These four deputies subsequently joined the Hungarian People's Party. The HCDM stood as a coalition partner with Coexistence during the June 1992 election campaign for seats in the Slovak National Council; its representatives obtained 5 seats in Bratislava. The coalition was joined by the Hungarian People's Party in competing for seats in the Federal Assembly. Although it partially cooperated with the Slovak Christian Democratic Movement, the HCDM platform became almost identical to that of Coexistence, including its stance toward Slovak independence. After the general elections of June 1992, the party demanded educational, cultural, and partial territorial autonomy for its compatriots in southern Slovakia. It declared that if the rights of ethnic minorities were not guaranteed by the independent state, the party would consider intervening in the European Parliament against Slovak independence and would be compelled to ask the Hungarian government for assistance from international organizations.[34]

Hungarian Civic Party (HCP)
Maďarská Občianska Strana (MOS)

The HCP emerged from the Independent Hungarian Initiative (IHI) in January 1992. The original IHI was established in November 1989 and was chaired by László Nagy. Its most prominent leaders were long-time dissidents Lajos Grendel, Kálmán Balla, and Károly Tóth. Like Coexistence, the IHI regarded Duray's Committee for the Protection of Hungarian Minority Rights in Czechoslovakia as its forerunner. Various professionals gathered in the organization, including writers, artists, teachers, and technical intellectuals. The IHI was among the first groups to pledge support for the Civic Forum and was also represented in the national coordination plans of the Public Against Violence. It published its "declaration of principles" in November 1989, describing itself primarily as a "civic initiative." While Coexistence maintained that nationality problems should be solved simultaneously with political democratization, the IHI/HCP believed that a stable democracy must first be established before the minorities could fully gain their group rights. It contended that the fast pace at which Coexistence demanded the institutionalization of minority rights would unnecessarily antagonize Slovaks leaders. The HCP supported Slovak self-determination but feared that a break-up of the federation would have negative consequences for ethnic minorities. It rejected charges leveled by Coexistence activists that it had compromised too often with Slovak organizations. Its stated goal was minority rights within a democratic framework, but it did not support territorial autonomy for the Magyar community.

In December 1989, the IHI proposed that the new federal government should include a minister of nationality affairs and nominated Duray for the position. The proposal was vetoed by the newly appointed Czechoslovak prime minister Marián Čalfa, who argued that such a position was not envisioned in Constitutional Law No. 144, and that if a Magyar minister was appointed then every minority would demand a cabinet seat. In the June 1990 elections, the party ran on the PAV ticket and won a total of 6 seats in the republican assembly. In February 1991, the IHI became a member of the three-party Slovak coalition government, in which it had a parliamentary vice-chairman, László Nagy, and a deputy prime minister, Gábor Zászlós, after June 1991. In March 1991, the party held its seventh general assembly congregating 102 local groups; delegates elected a 30-member party leadership. László Nagy was elected party chairman, and Karóly Tóth, former chairperson of the Slovak National Council, became the secretary-general. While Coexistence accused the IHI/HCP of collaborating with Slovak parties, its leaders maintained that it was more effective to work inside the government and have the opportunity to influence policy rather than stand outside in permanent opposition. The party remained open to compromise with various Hungarian political and cultural organizations and established its own "minority council." In the minority coalition formed in early 1991, the HCP was denied a partnership in the Coexistence-HCDM coalition unless it withdrew from the Slovak government and reevaluated its participation in drafting legislation that was deemed harmful to Magyar interests. The HCP refused and subsequently failed to find another coalition partner. The PAV also denied them a coalition partnership as it had lost an estimated 20,000 Slovak votes in June 1990 by allowing the former IHI to run candidates on its election lists. Thus, the HCP was forced to run alone in the second multi-party elections in June 1992 and failed to obtain parliamentary seats.[35]

Hungarian People's Party (HPP)
Maďarská Ludová Strana (MLS)

The HPP was established in December 1991 and became the first Hungarian political party (as distinct from a political movement) to register with the Slovak Ministry of Internal Affairs. It was led by Chairman Gyula Popély, a historian and former member of Coexistence, and Vice-Chairman Ferenc Szőcs, one of the four Federal Assembly deputies expelled from the HCDM. The HPP advocated Christian moral values, national reconciliation, an "environmentally secure" social market economy, and universal human rights. The HPP was the only Hungarian party asserting that Slovak independence would have a positive impact on the Magyar minority. The party also maintained that a comprehensive law guaranteeing minority rights should become part of the new Slovak constitution. In July 1991, Popély criticized the poor organizational efforts among Magyar political movements as the main reason for their inability to defend minority interests in the Slovak parliament effectively. The HCDM subsequently accused the HPP of attempting to divide the Magyar community. The party joined a coalition with Coexistence and the HCDM during the June 1992 elections for seats in the Federal Assembly. But it could not enter this coalition for balloting to the Slovak National Council because it could not gather the 10,000 signatures required under the electoral law. It could, however, include its candidates on the Coexistence-HCDM candidate lists.[36] Other significant Hungarian organizations included the Association of Hungarian Students, the Federation of Hungarian Teachers, the Association of Hungarian Writers, and the Cultural Association of Magyars.[37]

MINORITY ORGANIZATIONS

Union of Ukrainians and Ruthenians in Czechoslovakia (UURCS)
Zväz Ukrajincov a Rusínov v Česko-Slovensku (ZURČS)

The UURS changed its name from the Cultural Association of Ukrainian Workers soon after the revolution of November 1989. It supported the preservation of a federal Czech and Slovak state and opposed efforts by various Slovak parties to establish an independent Slovak republic. It feared that in such an eventuality, the rights of various minorities would be denied while Prague would lack the leverage to protect their distinct interests. Three deputies representing the Ruthenian-Ukrainian nationality were elected to the Slovak National Council in the June 1992 balloting.

Ruthenian Revival (RR)
Rusínska Obroda (RO)

This social and cultural organization considered the Ukrainian-Ruthenian population in Slovakia to be a separate ethnolinguistic group. It set out to cultivate Ruthenian cultural and linguistic traditions and help develop a distinct self-identity among the population. Activists asserted that the process of Slovakization and Ukrainianization, visible since the close of World War Two, needed to be reversed. The Revival organized the First World Congress of Ruthenians, held in eastern Slovakia in March 1991, during which participants pressed for the full recognition and registration of Ruthenian cultural, social, and educational organizations. In May 1993, another Ruthenian grouping, the Ruthenian Association of Sub-Carpathia (RAS), based in neighboring Ukraine, set up a "provisional government" in preparation for a referendum on Ruthenian independence and eventual unification with Slovakia. Many of the Ruthenian Association officials reportedly resided in Slovakia.[38]

Democratic Union of Roma in Slovakia (DURS)
Demokratický Zväz Rómov na Slovensku (DZRS)

The DURS sought to ensure that Roma were recognized as members of a distinct ethnic group, with all the rights to which minorities were entitled, and that this recognition be enshrined in the Czechoslovak constitution. The DURS subsequently united with the Democratic Association of Roma (DAR) to prevent unnecessary fragmentation and to contest elections to the Federal Assembly, the Slovak National Council, and to local government organs. Romani organizations subsequently failed to gain legislative representation at the republican level. Leaders of various Romani bodies have appealed to Slovak leaders to promote the cultural and social development of Gypsy communities, claiming that the population was largely ignored by the government. Some Roma have also called for CSCE observers to be dispatched to Slovakia to investigate the observance of human rights.[39]

Party for Romani Integration (PRI)
Strana za Rómsku Integráciu (SRI)

Founded in Slovakia in February 1990, the PRI was headed by Chairman Koloman Gunar. The party's platform underscored the improvement of living

Koloman Gunar. The party's platform underscored the improvement of living conditions for the Romani people throughout Czechoslovakia. It differed from the DURS in that it did not seek the recognition of Roma as a distinct national minority. It regarded the Roma as an ethnic group that was part of the larger Slovak nation. It campaigned to increase the percentage of Romani children attending school and to solve the community's severe housing problems. The PRI formed the League of Romani Unity (LRU) in February 1991 in order to unite and coordinate the activities of all the divergent Romani organizations.[40] Representatives of various Romani organizations also formed a Romani National Congress (RNC) in preparation for the June 1992 general elections. Its leaders lodged a strong protest against the Prague-based Romani Civic Initiative Party and other Gypsy groups that they depicted as extreme right-wing organizations no longer representing the true interests of Roma. Since it considered that basic human rights and minority freedoms were abused in Slovakia, the Romani Congress intended to form a united opposition and build a "nationalities institution" enabling each minority to solve its specific problems. Other significant Romani organizations in Slovakia included the Party of Gypsies, the Romani Civic Initiative, the Movement of Involved Gypsies, the Democratic Association of Roma, and the Association of Romani Intelligentsia.[41]

Slovakia's smaller minorities also established their own cultural and social organizations, including the Croatian Cultural Union in Slovakia, the Independent Organizations of Romanians, and the Carpatho-German Association in Slovakia. In January 1993, the Slovak media reported that German activists had formed a political association, the German Party (*Deutsche Partei*); it was refused registration because its leaders allegedly contravened various laws in gathering signatures for its founding petition.

CHRONOLOGY

December 1989: Following the "Velvet Revolution," various Magyar political movements emerge. The Independent Hungarian Initiative (IHI) joins with the Public Against Violence (PAV) to counterbalance the impact of emerging nationalist groups. IHI proposes that the new federal government include a minister in charge of nationality affairs. The proposal is vetoed and Marián Čalfa, the federal prime minister, instead proposes the establishment of a governmental nationalities committee. This is vetoed by the Slovak authorities, who argue that nationality issues should be removed from the jurisdiction of the federal administration. A subsequent proposal that Magyar ethnics be named deputy ministers of education and culture is never addressed.

January 1990: Nationalist feelings intensify in Slovakia. A survey indicates that 80 percent of the ethnic Hungarians polled would prefer a united Hungarian political movement. A new electoral law is adopted placing smaller and newer political groups at a disadvantage. The law mandates that at least 10,000 signatures are needed for a party to register in the elections; 5 percent of the votes are required for any party to gain representation in the Federal Assembly and 3 percent in the Slovak National Council. Minority leaders contend that this contradicts Constitutional Law No. 144, which guaranteed minorities equitable proportional representation in parliament.

February 1990: Some officials in Prague propose the creation of a ministry for minority affairs in the federal government, but the decision is to be delayed until the drafting of a new constitution. Czechoslovakia's current constitution precludes the establishment of such a ministry. The Czechoslovak authorities also hold out the possibility of forming an extra-parliamentary institution to monitor government performance with regard to minority rights. The presidium of the Cultural Association of Hungarians asks for further TV programming in order to counteract misunderstanding and prejudice. The first of several anti-Hungarian demonstrations, organized by Slovak nationalists, is held in Bratislava and Nové Zámky. Protesters oppose the reopening of minority schools and the right to use minority languages in official transactions.

March 1990: With increasing displays of anti-Hungarian extremism, the Slovak government addresses the public on minority issues. Slovak prime minister Milan Čič urges understanding and toleration among all ethnic groups and rejects militant nationalism. Some Slovaks accuse the Hungarian press of exaggerating ethnic problems. Czech premier Petr Pithart comments on the possibility of the Czech government's acting as a mediator in case of deteriorating relations between Slovakia and Hungary.

June 1990: During the first multi-party general elections, the IHI runs its candidates on the PAV list, while the Hungarian Christian Democratic Movement and Coexistence run in a separate coalition. During the election, strong anti-Hungarian and anti-Gypsy sentiments are aired in Slovakia. Between 75 percent and 80 percent of ethnic Magyars vote for the Coexistence-HCDM coalition, giving them 270,000 out of 293,000 votes nationwide. In the Czech Republic, its 6,000 votes come primarily from Polish voters in northern Moravia. In Slovakia, the coalition finishes fifth, with 8.66 percent of the vote, and gains 14 seats in the Slovak National Council; much of its success is in predominantly Magyar regions, with additional success among Ukrainians and Ruthenians. Between 15 percent and 20 percent of ethnic Hungarians vote for the IHI, which gains a total of 6 seats through its association with PAV. The new 150-seat Slovak National Council includes 24 Magyar deputies: 14 from the Coexistence-HCDM coalition, 6 from the IHI, 3 from the Communist Party, and 1 from the Christian Democratic Movement. In the Federal Assembly, 16 Magyar deputies are elected, 12 from the coalition and 4 from the IHI. Slovak nationalist parties receive little more than 15 percent of the popular vote. The Christian Democratic Movement emerges as the second-strongest party in Slovakia, after the PAV. Following the election, the CDM, PAV, and the Democratic Party form a three-party coalition.

July 1990: The Hungarian government urges a quick solution to nationality disputes in Slovakia and the necessity of reaching bilateral agreements with Czechoslovakia.

August 1990: The results of a poll on minority relations, conducted by the Center for Research into Social Problems, reveal that only 33.5 percent of the Slovak population experiences no inter-ethnic tensions, while 21.4 percent feel such tensions with respect to all minority groups. Thirty-eight percent of respondents have a negative outlook on relations with Hungarians. Problems between Hungarians and Slovaks remain focused on one point, the delegalization of the Hungarian language.

September 1990: A Ministry for International Relations is established in Bratislava. The ministry lends legitimacy to Slovak demands for international recognition, even though it does not have the foreign-policy jurisdiction of the federal Foreign Ministry. Hungarian activists condemn nationalist propaganda and slanderous graffiti that promotes racial, religious, and national hatred.

October 1990: The controversial Slovak Language Law is passed; Coexistence deems it discriminatory against minorities. The Slovak government rejects a Hungarian proposal to negotiate a bilateral agreement governing the collective rights of minorities. It contends that the issue should be settled only on a multilateral international basis.

November 1990: In the local elections, Coexistence finishes fifth, with 6.23 percent of the vote, obtaining 110 mayoralties and nearly 2,500 posts in local government. The HCDM wins 3 percent of the vote, and the IHI 1.3 percent. The Christian Democratic Movement emerges as the strongest party with 27.5 percent of posts in Slovak municipalities. The new Hungarian ambassador in Prague, György Varga, denies any revisionist claims by his government toward existing state borders.

December 1990: Slovak leaders protest against draft amendments to the Czechoslovak constitution, seeking instead the passage of individual republican constitutions on the basis of which a federal one could be drawn up. The constitutional crisis is temporarily resolved by the passage of an amendment on power sharing between federal and republican jurisdictions. It gives broad economic powers to the Czech and Slovak republics, while the federal authorities maintain control over national defense, foreign affairs, and important macro-economic policies.

January 1991: Ten Magyar deputies, five from Coexistence and five from the HCDM, walk out on a parliamentary session when the Federal Assembly passes the Bill of Fundamental Rights and Liberties. They contend that the articles dealing with the legal status of national minorities are inadequate.

February 1991: The IHI becomes an independent member of the three-party Slovak coalition government. The state of education in the ethnically mixed regions of Slovakia becomes one of the main issues on the Slovak government's agenda. In the 11 regions concerned, there are 68 communities with only Slovak schools and 113 communities with only Hungarian schools. Prime Minister Mečiar comments that it is up to parents to decide their children's language of education freely. Slovak nationalists present a draft Declaration of Slovak Sovereignty. It stresses that legislation produced by the Slovak National Council should override federal laws; it also proposes that independent Slovak police and military forces be created. This last demand is especially ill-received in Prague, where officials view it as potentially disastrous for the country's security.

March 1991: Pro-federalist Czechs and Slovaks accuse Slovak nationalists and reform Communists of co-conspiring against the federation. Slovak nationalists mark the anniversary of the wartime Slovak state by organizing commemorative rallies. The Federation of Jewish Communities (FJC), based in Prague, condemns the rally for its fascist and anti-Semitic undertones. The PAV splits into pro-federal and pro-sovereignty wings. The latter moves closer to the CDM and SNP positions on autonomy, leading to additional Prague accusations of a leftist-nationalist conspiracy. The pro-federalist faction renames itself the Civic Democratic Union—Public Against Violence (CDU-PAV). Prime Minister Mečiar leads the breakaway PAV faction, Movement for a Democratic Slovakia, a pro-sovereignty splinter party. The CDM becomes the strongest political group in the Slovak National Council, holding 31 seats.

April 1991: Prime Minister Vladimír Mečiar is accused of demagoguery and populism by his opponents and is replaced by Christian Democratic leader Ján Čarnogurský. Pro-Mečiar demonstrators in Bratislava accuse Prague of staging his ouster to quell Slovakia's increasingly popular nationalist movement.

July 1991: The deputy chairman of the Slovak National Council proposes establishing an armed Slovak Home Guard. A third of the Council supports the proposal together with the Slovak interior minister Ladislav Pittner. The objective of the armed guard was to provide greater security for citizens in case of a natural disaster or major social upheaval. Nevertheless, the notion is defeated in the Slovak legislature. Pro-federalist Slovak and Czech leaders view the proposition as a move toward separation. The Czechoslovak Socialist Party expresses fears that the Yugoslav conflict could lead to attempts to revise international borders throughout Eastern Europe. The party refers to what it calls a "Hungarian suggestion" that if Yugoslavia breaks up, the territorial changes under the 1920 Trianon Treaty would be called into question.

September 1991: Having opposed President Havel's call for an early referendum, MDS leaders sign a document entitled the "Initiative for a Sovereign Slovakia" and press for the approval of a new Slovak constitution.

October 1991: Three Hungarian political groupings, the HCDM, IHI, and Coexistence, form a roundtable to seek cooperative models on minority policy issues. Ruthenian organizations demand the official recognition of their nationality, which has not been acknowledged for more than 40 years.

November 1991: President Havel publicly appeals to the population to support his calls for a referendum without the consent of the Federal Assembly.

January 1992: The IHI transforms itself into a political party called the Hungarian Civic Party. The Federal Assembly passes an amended version of the 1990 electoral law, retaining the 5 percent borderline for parties campaigning for parliamentary representation, but raising it to 7 percent for coalitions of two or three parties, and to 10 percent for coalitions of four or more. These new requirements place the Hungarian parties at a disadvantage and force them to consider building coalitions to improve their prospects.

February 1992: Coexistence and HCDM renew their former election coalition agreement. Although a breakthrough appears imminent during the negotiations over a "state treaty" between Prague and Bratislava, the Slovak Parliamentary Presidium narrowly rejects the draft treaty contending that the negotiators had offered too many concessions to the Czechs. The draft specifies that either republic has the right to secede from the federation on the basis of a referendum.

March 1992: Coalition talks between Coexistence, HCDM, and HCP collapse after more than a month of debate. The failure is mainly due to unsuccessful demands by Coexistence and HCDM that the HCP leave the Slovak government coalition. The Christian Democratic Movement (CDM) splits into two parties, one retaining the original name, the other, led by Ján Klepáč, becoming the Slovak Christian Democratic Party (SCDP).

April 1992: Coexistence and HCDM accept the Hungarian People's Party (HPP) into their coalition for elections to the Federal Assembly. In Slovakia, where the HPP has no deputies and could not gather the required 10,000 signatures, it is not named a coalition partner; the HPP can, however, run its candidates on the lists of the Coexistence-HCDM coalition.

June 1992: In the second general elections, the pro-independence parties (MDS, SNP, and the PDL) receive almost 50 percent of the popular vote, gaining 118 out of 150 seats to the Slovak National Council, and 90 out of 150 seats to the Federal Assembly. The MDS emerges as the clear victor, with 74 seats in the Slovak National Council. The CDM loses about half of its electoral support in the election, winning only 18 seats in the Slovak National Council. For the second time since 1989, a coalition of ethnic Hungarian parties (Coexistence, HCDM, and HPP) succeeds in electing deputies to both the Federal Assembly and the Slovak National Council. The victory of Mečiar's MDS undermines the existence of the federation and poses new problems for parties representing the Magyar minority.[42]

July 1992: The Slovak government declares the republic's sovereignty and enters into intensive talks with Prague concerning the abolishment of the Czech and Slovak Federation.

October 1992: The Slovak National Council ratifies a draft constitution while the federal government approves a constitutional act on terminating the federation.

November 1992: The Federal Assembly votes to disband the Czech and Slovak Federal Republic and to provide the two republics with equal successor status.

January 1993: Slovakia attains full national independence with the formal dissolution of Czechoslovakia.

February 1993: MDS member Michal Kovac is elected Slovak president by the country's National Council. The main Hungarian movement, Coexistence, holds its fourth congress, condemns Slovak government policies that are evidently intended to curtail minority rights, and calls for "political and economic self-administration" for the Hungarian-inhabited areas of southern Slovakia.

July 1993: Negotiations are under way for a new coalition government between the MDS and the Slovak National Party. Observers predict that if the talks break down, the country would hold early parliamentary elections, the first in an independent Slovakia.

NOTES

1. From Peter Prochazka, "Position of National Minorities in the Slovak Republic," and "The Hungarian Minority in Slovakia and the Autonomy Issue," in *International Issues: A Revue of Foreign Policy, Law, Economics, and Culture*, vol. 1, no. 3, November 1992, Bratislava, Ministry of Foreign Affairs.

2. For a background on Slovak history, see Carol Skalník Leff, *National Conflict in Czechoslovakia: The Making and Remaking of a State 1918–1987* (Princeton, NJ: Princeton University Press, 1988); Ihor Gawdiak, ed., *Czechoslovakia: A Country Study* (Washington, DC: U.S. Government Printing Office, 1989); Stephen Borsody, *Czechoslovak Policy and the Hungarian Minority, 1945–48* (New York: Columbia University Press, 1982); Eugen Steiner, *The Slovak Dilemma* (London: Cambridge University Press, 1973); and Peter Brock, *The Slovak National Awakening: An Essay in the Intellectual History of East Central Europe* (Toronto: University of Toronto Press, 1976).

3. Check Jiří Pehe, "The Inevitable Divorce," *Freedom Review*, vol. 23, no. 6, November-December 1992.

4. Ján Obrman and Jiří Pehe, "Difficult Power-Sharing Talks," Radio Free Europe/Radio Liberty Research Institute (RFE/RL), *Report on Eastern Europe*, vol. 1, no. 49, December 7, 1990.

5. See the statement by Vladimír Mečiar in *Národná Obroda*, Bratislava, July 26, 1990.

6. Consult "An Appeal to Slovak Citizens," *Verejnosť*, Bratislava, July 24, 1991.

7. For the text of the declaration check *Lidové Noviny*, Prague, November 9, 1991.

8. See Jiří Pehe, "The State Treaty Between the Czech and Slovak Republics," RFE/RL, *Report on Eastern Europe*, vol. 2, no. 23, June 7, 1991. For the text of the draft Czech-Slovak Constitutional Treaty, see *Hospodárske Noviny*, Prague, February 11, 1992.

9. See "Václav Havel: Separation Is Better Than Confederation," *Rude Pravo*, Prague, July 1, 1991, and the Speech at the Seventeenth Joint Session of the Federal Assembly, *Prague Radio Network*, September 24, 1991, in Federal Broadcast Information Service, *Daily Report: East Europe, FBIS-EEU–91–186*, September 25, 1991. See also Havel's "Address to the Nation," on *Prague Federal TV Network*, November 17, 1991, in *FBIS-EEU–91–222*, November 18, 1991.

10. Ján Obrman, "President Havel's Diminishing Political Influence," RFE/RL, *Research Report*, vol. 1, no. 11, March 13, 1992.

11. See Oskar Krejčí, "Czech Nationalism and Separatism," *Pravda*, Bratislava, June 14, 1991.

12. Jiří Pehe, "The New Slovak Government and Parliament," RFE/RL, *Research Report*, vol. 1, no. 28, July 10, 1992.

13. See Jiří Pehe, "Czechs and Slovaks Prepare to Part," RFE/RL, *Research Report*, vol. 1, no. 37, September 18, 1992, and Ján Obrman, "Czechoslovakia's New Governments," RFE/RL, *Research Report*, vol. 1, no. 29, July 17, 1992.

14. See *Hospodárske Noviny*, Prague, September 10, 1992.

15. Jiří Pehe, "Czechs and Slovaks Define Postdivorce Relations," RFE/RL *Report on Eastern Europe*, vol. 2, no. 45, November 13, 1991.

16. See the interview with Václav Klaus, "A Chance for Czechoslovakia," *Respekt*, Prague, no. 26, June 29–July 2, 1992.

17. Constitution of the Slovak Republic, published in *Hospodárske Noviny*, Prague, September 8, 1992, in *FBIS-EEU–92–179-S*, September 15, 1992; *Hungarians in Slovakia*, Information Bulletin, September 1992, compiled on behalf of Political Movement, Coexistence, Bratislava; *Memorandum on the Slovak Republic's Future Admission to the Council of Europe*, issued by the Coexistence Political Movement, Hungarian

Christian Democratic Movement, Hungarian People's Party, and Hungarian Civic Party, Bratislava, February 4, 1993; and "Excerpts from Speeches by Ethnic Hungarian Representatives in the Slovak Parliament," *Új Szó*, April 24, 1993, in Federal Broadcast Information Service/Joint Publications Research Service, *Daily Report: East Europe, JPRS-EER–93–046-S*, May 26, 1993.

18. See Ján Obrman, "Language Law Stirs Controversy in Slovakia," RFE/RL *Report on Eastern Europe*, vol. 1, no. 46, November 16, 1990; and Georg Brunner "Minority Problems and Policies in East-Central and South-East Europe," *International Issues*, vol. 1, no. 3, 1992.

19. From *Hungarians in Slovakia*, September 1992, compiled on behalf of the Political Movement Coexistence, Bratislava.

20. See the statement by Slovak Minister for Culture Dušan Slobodnik in *Národná Obroda*, Bratislava, May 25, 1993, in *FBIS-EEU–93–103*, June 1, 1993.

21. For the full text of the Law on State Citizenship of the Slovak Republic, see *Pravda*, Bratislava, January 21, 1993.

22. Michael J. Deis, "A Study of Nationalism in Czechoslovakia," in RFE/RL, *Research Report*, vol. 1, no. 5, January 31, 1992; Jiří Pehe, "Political Conflict in Slovakia," RFE/RL, *Report on Eastern Europe*, vol. 2, no. 19, May 10, 1991; *ČSTK*, Prague, October 30, 1991, in *FBIS-EEU–91–214*, November 5, 1991; *ČSTK*, Prague, March 18, 1992, in *FBIS-EEU–92–055*, March 20, 1992; *Rožlasová Stanica Slovensko Network*, Bratislava, March 22, 1992, in *FBIS-EEU–92–057*, March 24, 1992; Ján Obrman, "The Czechoslovak Elections," RFE/RL, *Research Report*, vol. 1, no. 26, June 26, 1992; and Jiří Pehe, "The New Slovak Government and Parliament," RFE/RL, *Research Report*, vol. 1, no. 28, July 10, 1992.

23. *ČTK*, Prague, May 28, 1990, in *FBIS-EEU–90–104*, May 30, 1990; Jiří Pehe, "The Local Government Elections," RFE/RL, *Report on Eastern Europe*, vol. 1, no. 50, December 14, 1990; Jiří Pehe, "Growing Slovak Demands Seen as Threat to Federation," RFE/RL, *Report on Eastern Europe*, vol. 2, no. 12, March 22, 1991; Jiří Pehe, "The Changing Configuration of Political Forces in the Federal Assembly," RFE/RL, *Report on Eastern Europe*, vol. 2, no. 16, April 19, 1991; Pehe, "Political Conflict in Slovakia"; Jiří Pehe, "Bid for Slovak Sovereignty Causes Political Upheaval," RFE/RL, *Report on Eastern Europe*, vol. 2, no. 41, October 11, 1991. See also Deis, "A Study of Nationalism in Czechoslovakia"; Jiří Pehe, "Slovak Nationalism Splits Christian Democratic Ranks," RFE/RL, *Research Report*, vol. 1, no. 13, March 27, 1992. See also Ján Obrman, "Atlanticists versus Eurasians in Russian Foreign Policy," RFE/RL, *Research Report*, vol. 1, no. 22, May 29, 1992; and Obrman, "The Czechoslovak Elections."

24. Pehe, "Slovak Nationalism Splits Christian Democratic Ranks"; Obrman, "Atlanticists Versus Eurasians in Russian Foreign Policy"; Obrman, "The Czechoslovak Elections."

25. "The Stand of the Slovak National Party," *Smena*, Bratislava, June 30, 1990, in *FBIS-EEU 90–130*, July 6, 1990; "Deputy Panis Is Leaving," *Pravda*, Bratislava, January 31, 1991, in *FBIS-EEU–91–025*, February 6, 1991; Pehe, "Growing Slovak Demands Seen as Threat to Federation"; Jiří Pehe "The State Treaty Between the Czech and the Slovak Republics," RFE/RL, *Report on Eastern Europe*, vol. 2, no. 23, June 7, 1991; Jiří Pehe, "Czechoslovakia's Changing Political Spectrum," RFE/RL, *Report on Eastern Europe*, vol. 1, no. 5, January 31, 1992; Obrman, "The Czechoslovak Elections."

26. *ČTK*, Prague, May 28, 1990, in *FBIS-EEU–90–104*, May 30, 1990; Jiří Pehe, "Divisions in The Communist Party of Czechoslovakia," RFE/RL, *Report on Eastern Europe*, vol. 2, no. 30, July 26, 1991; Pehe, "Czechoslovakia's Changing Political Spectrum"; Obrman, "The Czechoslovak Elections."

27. See the material on the *Valné Žromaždenie Matice Slovenskej, 1992*, Bratislava, 33/1992; and the *Second Memorandum of Slovaks from Southern Slovakia* adopted at the April 1993 *Matica Slovenská* meeting in Surany, Slovakia.

28. Interview with Vojtech Vitkovský by Renatá Havranová, "Breaking Up Czechoslovakia?" *Práce*, Prague, August 8, 1990, in *FBIS-EEU–90–157*, August 14, 1990.

29. *Bratislava Domestic Service*, July 27, 1990, in *FBIS-EEU–90–146*, July 30, 1990; interview with Peter Brňák by Ján Felix, "A New Boat in Slovak Politics," *Smena*, Bratislava, January 28, 1991, in *FBIS-EEU–91–022*, February 1, 1991; Editorial report on news conference held by representatives of the Slovak National Democratic Movement, in *Smena*, Bratislava, July 26, 1991, in Federal Broadcast Information Service/Joint Publications Research Service, *Daily Report: East Europe, JPRS-EER–91–113*, August 1, 1991; *Rožlasová Stanica Slovensko Network*, Bratislava, March 18, 1992, in *FBIS-EEU–92–055*, March 20, 1992.

30. Jiří Pehe, "Czechoslovakia: Parties Register for Elections," in RFE/RL, *Research Report*, vol. 1, no. 18, May 1, 1992; Ján Obrman, "The Czechoslovak Elections: A Guide to The Parties," RFE/RL, *Research Report*, vol. 1, no. 22, May 29, 1992.

31. *Bratislava Domestic Service*, January 28, 1991, in *FBIS-EEU–91–019*, January 29, 1991; Pehe, "Czechoslovakia: Parties Register for Elections"; Obrman, "The Czechoslovak Elections."

32. *Budapest Domestic Service*, March 2, 1990, in *FBIS-EEU–90–045*, March 7, 1990; *ČTK*, Prague, May 10, 1990, in *FBIS-EEU–90–092*, May 11, 1990; Edith Oltay, "Hungarians in Slovakia Organize to Press for Ethnic Rights," RFE/RL, *Report on Eastern Europe*, vol. 1, no. 22, June 1, 1990; Sándor Neszméri, "Harmful Discrimination Against Hungarians in the CSFR," *Magyar Nemzet*, Budapest, July 15, 1991, in *FBIS-EEU–91–141*, July 23, 1991; "In the Interest of Hungarians in Slovakia—Protection Against Hatred," *Új Magyarország*, Budapest, October 18, 1991, in *FBIS-EEU–91–205*, October 23, 1991; Pehe, "Czechoslovakia: Parties Register for Elections"; Obrman, "The Czechoslovak Elections"; Peter Miklósi, interview with Miklós Duray, President of The Coexistence Political Movement, "Time Trap: It Would Be Our Homeland That Would Give Us Strength in Facing Our Problems," *Vasárnap*, Bratislava, July 17, 1992, in *JPRS-EER–92–103*, August 10, 1992; Obrman, "Language Law Stirs Controversy in Slovakia"; Edith Oltay, "Hungarian Minority in Slovakia Sets Up Independent Organizations," RFE/RL, *Report on Eastern Europe*, vol. 1, no. 11, March 11, 1991.

33. Oltay, "Hungarian Minority in Slovakia Sets Up Independent Organizations," and "Hungarians in Slovakia Organize to Press for Ethnic Rights"; "Anxiety about the Incitements of Frictions," *Národná Obroda*, Bratislava, August 27, 1990, in *FBIS-EEU–90–174*, September 7, 1990; Alfred A. Reisch, "Hungarian Ethnic Parties Prepare for Czechoslovak Elections," in RFE/RL, *Report on Eastern Europe*, vol. 1, no. 18, May 1, 1992; "*Csemadok* with a New Name," *Republika*, Bratislava, April 5, 1993.

34. Editorial Report in *FBIS-EEU–90–092*, May 11, 1990; Edith Oltay "Hungarians in Slovakia Organize to Press for Ethnic Rights"; Reisch, "Hungarian Ethnic Parties Prepare For Czechoslovak Elections"; "We Want Educational, Cultural, and Partial Territorial Autonomy," *Národná Obroda*, Bratislava, July 23, 1992, in *JPRS-EER–92–103*, August 10, 1992.

35. Oltay, "Hungarian Minority in Slovakia Sets Up Independent Organizations"; *ČTK*, Prague, May 28 1990, in *FBIS-EEU–90–104*, May 30, 1990; Oltay, "Hungarians in Slovakia Organize to Press for Ethnic Rights"; *ČTK*, Prague, September 26, 1990, in *FBIS-EEU–90–189*, September 28, 1990; "Support for Parliamentary Democracy," *Národná Obroda*, Bratislava, March 4, 1991, in *FBIS-EEU–91–045*, March 7, 1991; Reisch, "Hungarian Ethnic Parties Prepare for the Czechoslovak Elections"; announcement by the Independent Hungarian Initiative, *ČTK*, Prague, August 1, 1991, in *JPRS-EER–91–115*, August 5, 1991; "Every Knife Would Flick Open," by István Lékó, *Respekt*, Prague, October 14–20, 1991, in *FBIS-EEU–91–202*, October 18, 1991.

36. Pehe, "Czechoslovakia: Parties Register for Elections."

37. Tibor Kis, "Democratic Cooperation Is More Important Today," *Népszabadság*, Budapest, November 30, 1989, in *FBIS-EEU–89–238*, December 13, 1989.

38. Interview with Paul Robert Magocsi, "Ruthenians Are No Longer in Parenthesis," *Smena*, Bratislava, March 29, 1991; Jaromír Horec, "Subject: Ruthenia," *Lidové Noviny*, Prague, September 21, 1990; Peter Juščák, "Ruthenian Renaissance," *Hlas Demokracie*, Košice, 1991, no. 7; RFE/RL, *Daily Report*, no. 98, May 25, 1993.

39. "Unification of Romanies in Slovakia," *ČTK*, Prague, in *FBIS-EEU–90–082*, April 27, 1990.

40. Editorial Report, *Pravda*, Bratislava, March 5, 1990, in *FBIS-EEU–90–046*, March 8, 1990; "Environmentally and Socially," *Pravda*, Bratislava, February 25, 1991, in *FBIS-EEU–91–039*, February 27, 1991.

41. Text of Romani National Congress, *Lidové Noviny*, Prague, August 7, 1991, in *JPRS-EER–91–131*, September 4, 1991; *Bratislava Rožlasová Stanica*, January 21, 1993, in *FBIS-EEU–93–013*, January 22, 1993.

42. Pehe, "Growing Slovak Demands Seen as Threat to Federation"; Alena Meličarková, "Will There Be a Slovak Home Guard?" *Národná Obroda*, Bratislava, vol. 2, no. 12, July 13, 1991; Pehe, "Bid for Slovak Sovereignty Causes Political Upheaval."

12

Poland

POPULATION

Although the Polish authorities have not officially identified national and ethnic minorities in previous demographic statistics and census figures, the approximate size of such groups can be gleaned from various official and unofficial estimates.[1] By the early 1990s, Ukrainians formed the largest minority, numbering some 300,000 people and widely dispersed in 22 voivodships, with some concentrations in southeastern Poland. Belarusians formed the second largest minority, estimated in excess of 300,000 and resident mainly in the Białystok voivodship of northeastern Poland. Germans were also believed to number 200,000, although exact figures were difficult to confirm because of widely disparate claims by Polish and German sources: numbers ranging from 7,000 to 500,000 have been offered. Most German communities were located in sections of Upper and Lower Silesia. A large number of ethnic Poles have also claimed German ancestry in recent years in the hope of obtaining German citizenship.

Of the smaller minorities, Gypsies (Roma) numbered at least 25,000 and were subdivided into four major tribal-clan groups; the majority lived a sedentary life and engaged in manual occupations or traditional crafts. About 15,000 Jews still lived in various Polish cities, although the majority were older people. However, some sources calculated that at least 50,000 Poles possessed Jewish ancestry. Ruthenians (Lemkos) constituted about 15,000 people. Originally from southeastern Poland, like the Ukrainians they were forcibly dispersed throughout the country after World War Two. Slovaks totaled some 12,500, primarily resident in the southern voivodships near the Slovak border. Lithuanians numbered some 15,000 and were concentrated in a few districts of Suwałki voivodship in northeastern Poland near the Lithuanian border. Approximately 10,000 Greeks and Macedonians, exiles from the Greek Civil War in the 1940s, lived in small pockets in Lower Silesia. About 7,500 Czechs inhabited several villages close to the Czech-Moravian border. Poland's remaining minorities included small numbers of Muslim Tatars, Karaims (or Judaic Tatars), Armenians, and Russians; an

Poland: Population (1992)

Ethnic Groups	Number	% of Population
Poles	37,605,108	97.88
Ukrainians	300,000	0.78
Belarusians	200,000	0.52
Germans	200,000	0.52
Roma (Gypsies)	25,000	0.07
Jews	15,000	0.04
Ruthenians	15,000	0.04
Lithuanians	15,000	0.04
Slovaks	12,500	0.03
Greeks and Macedonians	10,000	0.03
Czechs	7,500	0.02
Tatars	3,000	0.01
Others	10,000	0.03
Total Minorities	813,000	2.12
Total Population	38,418,108	100.00

unknown number of the latter, together with other aliens from the former Soviet republics, have settled in Poland since the collapse of the USSR. A persistent sense of ethnic distinctiveness was also visible among the 200,000 Kaszubians in northwestern Poland and a feeling of regional distinctiveness among several million Polish Silesians in both Upper and Lower Silesia. Some degree of regional identity was also found among Warmians and Mazurians in northeastern Poland, but without any notable autonomist trends.

HISTORICAL OVERVIEW

Poland regained its independence in 1918, at the close of World War One, after nearly 120 years of partition among its three imperialist neighbors, tsarist Russia, Prussia-Germany, and Habsburg Austria.[2] The boundaries of the new Polish republic were established in the wake of a full-scale war with Bolshevik Russia and protracted conflicts with the German and Lithuanian states. Smaller disputes also surfaced with the newly created Czechoslovak Republic. In the east, predominantly Ukrainian and Belarusian territories were divided between Warsaw and Moscow, while Poland captured the Vilnius province from Lithuania. Plebiscites were held in the German disputed areas of Upper Silesia and East Prussia, from which Warsaw managed to secure several territorial gains. Meanwhile, some small border areas remained a bone of contention with Prague. A substantial ethnic-minority population was left within the Polish state, comprising over 30 percent of the country's total. According to the 1921 census, these included Ukrainians (15.2 percent), Jews (8.0 percent), Belarusians (4.0 percent), and Germans (3.0 percent), together with smaller groups of Lithuanians, Russians, Czechs, and Tatars, and an indeterminate number of Gypsies, Ruthenians, Kaszubians, and Karaims. Sizable Polish minorities were also left in neighboring states, particularly numerous in Lithuania and the Ukrainian and Belarus.

The new Polish state was constructed along centralist rather than federalist lines. This led to sometimes-serious conflicts between the government and minority leaders aspiring to greater autonomy and self-determination, as well as inter-communal hostilities between Poles and non-Poles. Warsaw embarked on a program of assimilation and Polonization, and occasional local revolts led to repressive "pacification" campaigns. Under the League of Nations provisions, Poland was required to sign a minorities treaty guaranteeing all ethnic groups equal treatment and non-discrimination. Although its codes were periodically violated, Warsaw in turn charged that the treaty was manipulated by foreign governments, particularly by Germany, to undermine Polish stability, to stimulate revanchist and irredentist sentiments, and to discredit Warsaw in the eyes of the international community. As a result, demands for minority rights by ethnic leaders were often viewed with suspicion by Polish officials. Poland unilaterally abrogated the minorities treaty in the mid-1930s, further aggravating an already deteriorating inter-ethnic situation.

The Ukrainian population was the largest and in many respects the most problematic in inter-war Poland. Even its size has been disputed, although impartial observers estimated that it exceeded 5,600,000 by the early 1930s. Ukrainians were mainly concentrated in southeastern Poland, in the provinces of Galicia and Wołyń, and the overwhelming majority were farmers or peasants. The population was well organized into a spectrum of political parties, most of which demanded autonomy and eventual Ukrainian independence. The more moderate parties elected deputies to the Polish parliament, although there were periodic boycotts of its proceedings. The Ukrainians also established a network of rural cooperatives, publications, and schools that were periodically subject to government discrimination and repression. The Ukrainian rural population also experienced unfair treatment under the agrarian reform program, and over 300,000 Poles were resettled in primarily Ukrainian rural areas. Increasing radicalization among some sectors of the population and the creation of an openly separatist political and military Ukrainian organization in the late 1920s led to further ethnic polarization and government persecution through arrests, deportations, and military rule in some areas. Ukrainian aspirations for greater participation in the local administration and for bilingualism in official transactions in predominantly minority areas remained unfulfilled. Toward the end of the 1930s, more hard-line forces gained ascendance in the Polish government, and they opposed granting any concessions to the Ukrainians or other minorities. Moreover, Poland was facing increasing threats from both Nazi Germany and the Soviet Union and the government expected minority leaders to place loyalty to the republic above all other considerations.

Inter-war Poland contained the largest Jewish population in Europe, numbering about 2,850,000 in the early 1920s. The vast majority lived in urban areas, in cities, towns, and larger villages, and spanned a range of professions. The new Polish government sought to assimilate Jews into Polish society and applied restrictive policies on Jewish self-government, educational activities, and social welfare programs. Official policy also discriminated against Jewish businesses, civil servants, and professionals in favor of ethnic Poles. Quotas were placed on the number of Jewish teachers, bureaucrats, and university students, and Jewish economic and social life suffered correspondingly. Some extremist anti-Semitic organizations also became active, although Poland did not descend into a fascist-type dictatorship. A range of Jewish political parties continued to function and participated in the Polish parliament. But ideological and political divisions continued to plague Jewish politics and undermined effective collective action in defense of Jewish interests.

The Belarusian population numbered some 2,200,000 by the early 1930s, mostly concentrated in Poland's northeastern provinces. The majority were peasants and small farmers and among the poorest sectors of Polish society. Belarusians lacked the well-developed social, political, and economic self-help organizations found among Ukrainians, Jews, and Germans, and they too were exposed to campaigns of Polonization and assimilation. Polish pressures in turn spurred autonomist and separatist movements. Concessions offered by Warsaw failed to satisfy Belarusian leaders, many of whom looked toward union with Soviet Belorussia even though few were committed Communists. Poland's Ukrainians and Belarusians were generally unaware of Stalin's atrocities in the Soviet Union and saw both the Ukrainian and Belarusian republics as a progressive development toward statehood. Belarusian agitation and radicalism led to "pacification" drives accompanied by martial law, arrests, summary trials, and the banning of some political parties. Even the Belarusian Orthodox Church was not immune to restrictions following its demands for cultural autonomy. Government actions merely served to alienate the Belarusian population from the Polish state and ultimately aided Stalin's annexation of these territories under the pretext of restoring Belarusian sovereignty and unification.

Poland's German population declined to some 1,100,000 people following a large-scale emigration from the former German-inhabited regions. Germans were distributed around the country, although the majority resided in Upper Silesia, Poznania, and Pomerania. Most were engaged in industrial and commercial activities or were medium-sized farmers. Although the Warsaw government permitted German educational, cultural, social, and economic institutions to operate, various restrictions were imposed and a policy of assimilation was pursued in some regions. With Hitler's rise to power in Germany during the 1930s, the Polish authorities increasingly feared that the German minority sympathized with German irredentist designs and could be used as a fifth column to undermine Polish independence.

In the inter-war period, Poland's Lithuanian population reached some 83,000, according to official statistics, although many Lithuanians had been Polonized over the previous generations. Warsaw adopted a policy of rapid assimilation by thwarting Lithuanian educational and political life. The ongoing conflict between Poland and Lithuania contributed to souring inter-ethnic relations in Poland itself. The country's remaining minorities, numbering approximately 250,000, were not a major source of friction or controversy in inter-war Poland and were generally less exposed to repressive governmental pressures.

Poland was devastated by World War Two and sustained substantial population and territorial losses. Its total population dropped from 34,849,000 in 1939 to about 25,505,000 in 1951. It also became extremely homogenized, with over 95 percent registered as ethnic Poles. The Jewish population was systematically exterminated by the Nazis; an estimated 80,000 survived the war in Poland and another 150,000 returned from exile in the USSR. Jewish communal institutions were abolished; thousands more Jews emigrated from the country after the war, and less than 30,000 were left by the end of the 1950s. A further exodus during a Communist-sponsored anti-Semitic campaign in the late 1960s left less than 5,000 Jews in the country. The bulk of the German population fled at the close of the war or was deported by the Polish and Soviet authorities: about 6 million Germans left the Polish-occupied territories. In official estimates, less than 10,000 Germanized Poles or "autochthons" remained in the country by the early 1950s, although the figure was considered extremely conservative.

The loss of Poland's eastern territories to the Soviet Union eliminated large numbers of Ukrainians and Belarusians. Less than 200,000 Ukrainians and about 160,000 Belarusians were registered by the authorities in the early 1950s. Over 150,000 Ukrainians and Ruthenians were forcibly deported from southeastern Poland on charges of collaboration with anti-Communist guerrillas. They were settled in over a dozen voivodships and prohibited from returning to their ancestral lands. In addition, tens of thousands of Poles from the lost regions were resettled in the western territories that were reclaimed from a defeated Germany. The size of the remaining minorities remained fairly stable, and Poland also acquired approximately 10,000 Macedonians and Greeks following the exodus of families at the close of the Greek Civil War in the late 1940s.

The new Communist administration did not officially recognize nationality as a demographic category and deliberately under-counted or under-estimated the size of minority groups. Although the government formally declared its respect for minority rights, little was done to guarantee and develop their cultures, while their organizational activities were severely curtailed. Official policy became more conciliatory by the early 1960s: a limited degree of cultural autonomy was permitted, minority-based social and cultural associations were allowed to function under the supervision of the Interior Ministry, and some allowances were made for schooling in several native languages. But under the Communist system, there was little opportunity for independent political activities and assimilationist pressures continued unabated. Discriminatory pressures increased once more during the 1970s, as the ruling party pursued its thesis of a single Polish nation. Cultural activities were curtailed as state funding was scaled back and Interior Ministry controls were stiffened. Poland's minorities did not figure significantly in Warsaw's foreign relations, particularly as Moscow controlled all meaningful contacts between Poland and the Ukrainian, Belarusian, and Lithuanian republics. The German question remained the most sensitive, as Moscow and its Polish Communist surrogates played up the threat of German revisionism to muster popular legitimacy and prohibit any re-activization of German minority organizations.

During the initial Solidarity era in the early 1980s, there was some resurgence of minority activism as central controls were loosened and the party lost its grip over various aspects of public life. Several minorities sought to have their sociocultural associations transformed into politically representative bodies, demanded parliamentary seats, petitioned for greater access to the mass media, and claimed larger state funds for their publishing ventures. Moreover, religious life among Orthodox and Uniate Christians underwent a resurgence, as it did among Catholic Poles. This trend was reversed after the December 1981 martial-law crackdown, when attempts to form independent minority organizations were thwarted by the General Jaruzelski regime. But with the unraveling of Communist rule in 1989 and the election of the Solidarity coalition, restrictions on minority activities began to evaporate. Indeed, a representative of the Ukrainian minority was elected on the Solidarity ticket and a Belarusian also gained a seat in the parliament (*Sejm*) during the first multi-party elections in June 1989.

The Ukrainian and Belarusian populations began to organize their own independent associations in order to promote their distinct cultures and languages. Such activities were further spurred by the drive for independence in the neighboring Ukrainian and Belarusian republics. Although the new Polish government was well disposed toward a rejuvenation of religious, educational, and cultural activities, inter-communal enmities were also evident. For example, some Ukrainian activists called for the swift return of land and property seized by the state in the 1940s. Frictions also surfaced over the previous confiscation of Ukrainian Uniate and Belarusian Orthodox Church properties by Poland's Catholic Church. The Ukrainian question was compounded by two additional controversies. First, the ethnic identity of the Ruthenian Lemko population created disputes among minority activists, some of whom did not accept the "Ukrainian" appellation and pressed for the recognition of a separate Ruthenian nationality. Second, the position of the approximately 250,000-strong Polish community in Ukraine was also raised by activists in Poland who felt that Kyiv had not done enough to satisfy the minority's cultural and educational aspirations. Meanwhile, Ukrainian leaders expressed some anxiety over lingering Polish claims for special status for the city of Lvov, the capital of Polish Galicia before World War Two.

According to sociological investigations, the Belarusian minority could be divided into three broad clusters: residents who consider themselves "locals," Poles with "Belarusian heritage," and Belarusians "resident in Poland" who identify themselves as a component part of the Belarusian nation. The Belarusian minority question created some discord between Warsaw and Minsk. At one point, the sovereign Belarusian government demanded that a part of eastern Poland inhabited by large numbers of Belarusians be declared an "ethnic region." Warsaw opposed granting such a status, fearful that it would undermine the country's territorial cohesiveness. Polish spokesmen also spoke out for greater rights and recognition for the approximately 400,000 Poles resident in Belarus. Relations between Warsaw and the sovereign governments in Minsk and Kyiv visibly improved after the collapse of the USSR. Cordial relations among the three capitals were likely to rebound positively on the evolution of Poland's policies toward its sizable Slavic minorities. Moreover, Warsaw signed agreements with both Belarus and Ukraine underscoring that the current borders were permanent and there were no outstanding territorial claims with its two eastern neighbors.

Poland's relations with Lithuania became strained over the treatment of the approximately 350,000-strong Polish minority in the new independent state. While Vilnius accused some Polish minority leaders of undermining Lithuania's drive toward statehood and collaborating with the local Communist *nomenklatura*, Polish spokesmen voiced disquiet over the government's insensitivity to Polish demands for greater autonomy. Warsaw itself tried to prevent the dispute from escalating, and a wide-ranging declaration of friendship was finally signed between the two states. The position of the approximately 15,000 Lithuanians in Poland's northeastern regions has not figured prominently in inter-state discords. Although the minority has become more active in developing its educational and cultural life, it has not pushed toward political or territorial autonomy.

The position of the German minority in southwestern Poland has remained a contentious issue between Bonn and Warsaw. Successive Communist governments pursued a policy of assimilation and deliberately underestimated the size of the German minority. Meanwhile, some German politicians and militant German expellee associations claimed wide-scale discrimination by the Polish authorities and questioned the permanence of the Oder-Neisse border established at the close of World War Two. During the process of German reunification in 1990, the border question figured highly in disputes between Bonn and Warsaw, as Germany's chancellor Helmut Kohl procrastinated on concluding a treaty on the permanence of the frontier. The issue was eventually settled as the Western powers helped to bring the two sides together to sign a comprehensive treaty on inter-state relations. Further delays in ratifying the treaty also surfaced over the question of the rights of the German minority in Poland. Some Bonn politicians asked for national minority status for ethnic Germans; the proposal was rejected by Warsaw and condemned by some politicians as unwarranted interference in the country's internal affairs that would provide the German population with a special status under Bonn's supervision. Warsaw allowed German associations to operate in the country, especially in the cultural, educational, and economic domains. But the size and activities of the German population continued to generate disputes: Polish sources estimated about 200,000 ethnic Germans, while German calculations ranged from 400,000 to 500,000. Poles suspected that many non-Germans have claimed German heritage in order to benefit from Bonn's liberal immigration policies.

The status of the small Czech and Slovak populations in Poland has not resulted in any significant disputes between Warsaw, Prague, and Bratislava. Both minorities established independent associations and focused on their cultural, educational, and linguistic revival. Although the Polish minority in the Czech lands lodged various complaints against the Prague government, their position likewise improved and they were unlikely to figure in any inter-state animosities. Poland remained particularly concerned that a large-scale wave of refugees from the former Soviet republics could destabilize the country. Major unrest, warfare, economic breakdown, political chaos, or a military coup in Russia and in some neighboring republics could precipitate an exodus of desperate refugees. Poland would be hard pressed to accommodate large numbers of migrants and would fear that their presence could lead to economic crisis and social instability and even aggravate inter-ethnic relations and anti-foreigner sentiments. This in turn could undermine relations between Warsaw and some of its eastern neighbors.

OFFICIAL POLICIES

Poland's national-minority policies entered the post-Communist era with the appointment of Tadeusz Mazowiecki as prime minister in August 1989. Shortly after the accession of the new government, minority affairs were removed from the jurisdiction of the Interior Ministry and placed under the control of a new office in the Ministry of Culture, the Task Force for National Minorities. Other institutions were established to protect minority rights, including a Commission for National and Ethnic Minorities in the Polish parliament (*Sejm*) under the auspices of Solidarity deputies. The Commission included representatives of ten ethnic organizations, including Ukrainians, Belarusians, Germans, and Lithuanians, and deputies whose constituencies included sizable minority groups. Commission members pledged to provide a forum for cooperation and mutual aid and pressed for an increase in state funds for minority organizations and their cultural and educational activities. They also sought to amend the Polish constitution in order to strengthen the defense of minority rights and to create the office of an ombudsman for national minorities directly responsible to the prime minister.

While the need to protect minority rights was supported by all responsible Polish politicians, the legal framework for ensuring such protection was virtually non-existent. There was no agreement as to what sort of legal form minority protection should take and whether "group rights" should be enshrined in the law. In the fall of 1989, the *Sejm* Minorities Commission devised a draft law on national minorities that was subsequently held up in committee deliberations. Two distinct views on how to legislate these rights were expressed by minority organizations and by legal "purists." The former advocated clear constitutional guarantees of equal treatment and a "comprehensive minorities law upholding each minority's collective right to a distinct ethnic, cultural, linguistic, and religious identity." The latter proposed a "separate-but-equal" clause in the constitution, while leaving the precise areas of protection to be determined in individual statutes on education, local self-government, and church-state relations.[3]

During 1992, various legislation was passed seemingly in accordance with the "purist" viewpoint and in line with several bilateral agreements with neighboring states. Indeed, the establishment of diplomatic relations with the former Soviet republics strengthened the position of the eastern minorities in Poland. In March 1992, Poland and Belarus initialed agreements on diplomatic relations and on cooperation in culture and education. In June, a treaty was signed accepting the existing borders and vowing to protect minority rights. A declaration on good-neighborliness, friendly relations, and cooperation was signed with Ukraine in May 1992. An agreement of this kind with Lithuania was held up because of a dispute over the status of the Polish minority in Lithuania.

The question of minority education in native languages was carefully studied by Warsaw and various initiatives were undertaken. For instance, special plenipotentiaries for minority education were established in six voivodships with substantial minority concentrations. In March 1992, the minister of education introduced new directives whereby parents would in future decide whether their children would receive instruction in a minority language. Opportunities for language instruction at the primary and secondary levels increased significantly, and either distinct schools or special classes were established for all the larger minorities. Various cultural and media programs were also launched. For example, during 1990, daily radio broadcasts in the Belarusian language in the Białystok region were initiated, as well as programs in Lithuanian in the Suwałki voivodship. This practice expanded during 1991 to include broadcasts in Ukrainian and German. In July 1992, Polish TV and Belarusian TV agreed to exchange information and current-affairs programs and to broadcast one regional program in Belarusian and Polish, respectively. Similar agreements were expected with Russia and Ukraine.[4]

Legislation relating to the structure of the evolving Polish political system also encompassed the question of minority rights. In July 1991, the *Sejm* Commission for National and Ethnic Minorities recommended guarantees for minority representation in parliament, but its propositions were not ratified. In July 1992, the Extraordinary Commission for Electoral Affairs formulated an electoral law that lowered the number of signatures required by minority candidates for registration, eliminated the need for minority parties to acquire a minimum 5 percent of the vote, and established single-minority districts. This move specifically addressed the problems faced by minority populations such as the Ukrainians, who were spread throughout the country and not consolidated in easily demarcated electoral districts.[5]

The Charter of Rights and Liberties, a supplement to the Small Constitution signed by President Lech Wałęsa in November 1992, stated that all citizens were equal before the law, that no individual would be discriminated against because of his or her membership in an ethnic minority, that all detainees must be informed immediately and in an understandable language of the reasons for their detention, and that no one could be obliged to declare his or her beliefs, views, religion, or ethnic origin. Wałęsa presented the charter to the *Sejm* in January 1993, underscoring that it was intended to deal with relations between the state and citizens that were not addressed in the Small Constitution. The *Sejm*, however, voted 251 to 72 to refer the charter to a *Sejm* Extraordinary Commission for further examination. The charter was defended by Wałęsa's adviser as being beneficial for all Polish citizens; much of the criticism came from Catholic deputies, who were concerned that the law promulgated the separation of church and state.[6]

Poland has participated in several conferences dealing with practical methods for protecting ethnic minorities. The CSCE Copenhagen agreement of June 1990 declared it the right of minorities to use their mother tongue, to associate freely, to practice their religion, to engage in unrestricted contact across borders, to obtain access to the mass media, and to benefit from protection against discrimination and violence. In addition, in January 1993 Poland ratified the European Convention on the Protection of Human Rights and Fundamental Freedoms.[7] The Warsaw government also entered into various bilateral agreements with neighbors. In June 1991, Germany and Poland signed a comprehensive treaty of interstate friendship and cooperation.[8] It contained pledges to abstain from the use of force and guaranteed to respect the cultural rights of the German minority. However, not all issues were fully resolved. For example, Warsaw contended that Bonn's liberal policy, enabling Polish residents who claimed some German ancestry to obtain German citizenship, had produced split loyalties among a large number of people seeking to emigrate largely for economic reasons. The policy also purportedly undermined Polish sovereignty by inflating the number of German residents, heightening pressures for regional autonomy, and raising pretexts for outside interference in Silesia.

Under the Communist regime, the German minority was not officially recognized and many Germans disguised their identities, intermarried, assimilated, or emigrated to the West. The Communists also refused to register distinct German social, cultural, or political organizations and prohibited German-language classes in state schools. These repressive conditions eased substantially with the collapse of communism, and a marked growth in the number of schools offering German courses was registered, particularly in the Opole area in Silesia. However, problems persisted with the shortage of qualified language teachers. A chief feature of Bonn's diplomacy in Poland has been to assure linguistic, cultural, and religious rights for the German minority with a view to opening a consulate in Silesia. However, some more radical German activists in Poland criticized Bonn's accommodating stance on the border issue and complained that German minority leaders in Poland were not allowed to participate in Polish-German talks on the 1990 border treaty. In expressing support for the Federal Republic's Association of Expellees (*Bund der Vertriebenen*), they indicated that they did not consider the frontier agreement to be binding or final.

Warsaw permitted German associations to function, and indeed several social-cultural and quasi-political organizations have been registered during the past few years. They initiated publishing, educational, and artistic ventures in the German language, promoted regional business initiatives in Silesia, and campaigned for dual citizenship for ethnic Germans. During the May 1990 local elections, councilors representing the German minority obtained seats in 35 local councils in the Opole voivodship, while a German-based election coalition managed to elect 7 deputies to the lower house of parliament and 1 deputy to the Senate in the October 1991 general elections. Polish spokesmen expressed some uneasiness that the German population in Silesia could be vulnerable to expellee propaganda, including promises about eventual Silesian union with Germany. On this basis, a German fifth column could allegedly be created in the country whose activities would seriously jeopardize Polish-German cooperation.[9] Polish activists feared that strong German associations could increasingly collaborate with revisionist circles in Germany that did not accept the permanence of the current border and would press for German autonomy within Poland. German radicalism could in turn provoke the growth of ultra-nationalist Polish groups. Indeed, several such parties have become active, ranging from the nationalist "independence" organizations and national-Christians, who obtained parliamentary seats, to xenophobic nationalist and racist movements that, though marginal, promoted hostility toward their political opponents and violence against ethnic minorities.

Leaders of the West German Association of Expellees continued to raise questions about the future status of Silesia. Hartmut Koschyk, a Bundestag deputy and secretary-general of the association, reportedly visited Poland on a regular basis to meet with German minority leaders and assure them that Polish control over Silesia was only temporary. He claimed to have the support of leading Bonn politicians, including Chancellor Kohl himself. Koschyk proposed a "third way" to "Polish-German unification," consisting of the creation of a new territory along the Oder-Neisse rivers with a joint administration, parliament, and government. In this scenario, the city of Szczecin would become a "free port," while "free city" status would be provided to towns currently divided between the two countries, including Zgorzelec-Goerlitz. According to Polish critics, the Expellee Association intended to detach Silesia and link it with a united Germany through the transitional autonomous status, thus effectively terminating Warsaw's control over the region.[10]

The question of Silesian regionalism has also gained more prominence in Polish politics in recent years, and a Silesian movement elected two deputies to the lower house of parliament in the October 1991 elections. Some Polish Silesian organizations have pressed for administrative decentralization and greater autonomy in economic, cultural, and political affairs, claiming economic exploitation and discrimination by Warsaw. Some of these groupings calculated that Silesian autonomy would result in a substantial inflow of German capital into the region. By contrast, many local Polish activists feared that the autonomist movements could be courted and manipulated by radical German organizations in pursuit of their political ambitions. Members of Germany's Expellee Association have engaged in political agitation among the Silesian population. Some claimed that the Silesians were in reality a separate ethnic group and campaigned for a referendum among the region's current and former residents in order to determine Silesia's future status. In the interim, the association suggested creating a "Silesian land" in former East German territories that would act as a magnet for Polish Silesia before formal unification with Germany.

Radical expellee activists have provided material aid and disseminated political tracts among the German minority. They also advised people to claim German citizenship and to remain in their birthplaces in preparation for future reunification. Although the influence of the Expellee Association on German foreign policy was not substantial, its impact among radicalized young sectors of the population, especially those from the former German Democratic Republic who were experiencing profound economic dislocation, could not be underestimated. Periodic attacks by right-wing extremists and skinheads on Polish tourists and workers in Germany appeared to be symptomatic of deep-rooted anti-Polish and anti-foreigner prejudices. These could be reinforced by competition over jobs between German workers and East European migrants and exploited by revanchist groupings for their political objectives.

In Upper Silesia, extremist groups have been active among the German minority in an effort to establish regional associations of German right-wing parties. Relations between the German minority and the government in Warsaw were exacerbated in 1992 when German minority leaders demanded dual-language street and place names, some of which were used during the Nazi era, and erected war memorials honoring the German *Wehrmacht* (Armed Forces) of World War Two. For example, residents in the town of Dziewkowice proposed changing its name to Frauenfeld, the name it held during the Hitler era, instead of Schewkowitz, the town's name before 1936. Reports of increasing neo-Nazi activities provoked warnings from the Polish government. A statement in December 1992 by Andrzej Drzycimski, spokesman for President Wałęsa, underscored Poland's respect for the international standards of the CSCE process and demanded strict adherence to the law by all citizens, including its national minorities. Wałęsa himself indicated that any attempted separation of Silesia from Poland would result in outright war.

The January 1993 session of the *Sejm* Commission for National and Ethnic Minorities discussed the Polish-German conflicts in the Opole region. Both sides criticized the government's procrastinations in creating a central body to deal with national minority questions. In February 1993, a delegation from the German minority headed by *Sejm* deputy Henryk Kroll met with Prime Minister Hanna Suchocka, expressing the need for closer cooperation with the coalition government.[11] If amicable relations between Warsaw and Bonn were to be assured, the Polish government would be expected to offer full protection to the German minority and ensure that it benefited from comprehensive cultural, educational, and linguistic rights. However, any material benefits for German communities emanating either from Warsaw or Bonn-Berlin could aggravate inter-ethnic relations in Silesia by spurring indignation among the Polish majority. The Polish authorities have tried to avoid communal polarization and the ethnicization of politics in the Opole region and other areas with compact German minorities. They remained concerned about selective aid and investment for German districts, calculating that economic differentiation based on ethnicity at a time of general material hardship could provoke serious communal conflicts. Preferential treatment and growing economic influence could also raise public aspirations and encourage German minority leaders to press for various political concessions from Warsaw. This, in turn, could launch them on a collision course with the Polish government, particularly as the minority question had still to be fully regulated in bilateral inter-state accords.

Not burdened by a heavy historical load, relations between Poland and the Czech Republic and Slovakia were devoid of serious hostilities. For example, the border question has not been raised by any major political forces in either state, and even the question of "collective rights" for the small Polish, Czech, and Slovak minorities was likely to be settled amicably in future bilateral agreements. Nonetheless, the position of minority populations in the border regions needed to be watched closely, although their limited number would probably prevent the emergence of any serious disputes. The Czech minority in Poland was estimated at fewer than 8,000, resident in the Lower Silesian area near the Moravian border. The Slovak minority in the southern voivodship of Nowy Sącz near the Slovak border numbered approximately 12,500. Some apprehensions have been evident among local Poles about a resurgence of Slovak nationalism based on the occasional questioning of the border delineations around the towns of Spisz and Orawa. But Slovak minority leaders denied that any border readjustments were on their political agenda.

In May 1990, both the Ukrainian and the Polish governments confirmed the absence of any outstanding territorial claims. The July 1990 declaration of Ukrainian sovereignty was followed by expressions of support from the Warsaw government. In October 1990, Polish foreign minister Krzysztof Skubiszewski visited Ukraine and signed a declaration of friendship and cooperation with Kiev.[12] It fell short of a formal treaty but was part of Warsaw's effort to establish direct diplomatic and trading relations with several former Soviet republics. The declaration recognized the territorial integrity and existing borders of both states, thereby serving to reduce the possibility of frontier disputes. Following the Ukrainian parliament's declaration of independence in August 1991, in the wake of the failed Soviet coup, the Polish authorities established direct diplomatic relations with Kyiv. Indeed, Poland became the first country to recognize the Ukrainian state after the overwhelming vote for independence in the December 1991 referendum.

The Ukrainian minority in Poland, comprising about 300,000 people scattered in various regions of the country, could become an ingredient in future inter-state disputes. Newly established Ukrainian organizations have pressed for minority rights in culture, education, language, and religion. Some activists also demanded more controversial concessions, including the return of property seized during the Communist takeover, and demanded the passage of a national minorities law by the Polish parliament. Some Lemko Ruthenian leaders also established citizens' organizations to press for their rights as a distinct ethnic and cultural minority. They stressed that they did not want to become a bargaining chip in Polish-Ukrainian negotiations.[13] Conflicts arose over the ethnic identity of the Lemko Ruthenians and whether they formed a separate nationality or were actually part of the Ukrainian nation. Some younger Polish Lemkos adopted more militant, non-Ukrainian positions. But the Lemko organizations were not separatists and explicitly supported Poland's territorial integrity. Their objectives included the restoration of Lemko Ruthenian cultural and educational rights, with the possibility of returning some communities to their ancestral mountain areas in southeastern Poland.

In July 1990, the Belarusian declaration of sovereignty was recognized in a Polish Senate resolution, while the Warsaw government announced plans to develop inter-state cooperation in various spheres. The Belarusian legislature's declaration of independence in August 1991, after the Soviet coup fiasco, was welcomed by the Polish parliament. Even though no overt territorial demands were voiced by either side, Polish-Belarusian relations have not proved trouble free. This was evident during Foreign Minister Skubiszewski's visit to Belarus in October 1990, which failed to produce a joint declaration on cooperation. The Minsk government objected to any reference to the Polish-Soviet state border agreement of August 1945, at which Belarusian representatives were absent, although it evidently accepted the inviolability of the post-war boundaries. After months of negotiations, in October 1991 the Polish and Belarusian prime ministers signed a declaration on good-neighborly relations as a first step toward the conclusion of a full treaty and the restoration of diplomatic relations between the two states. The text of the agreement also included passages regarding the mutual respect of the ethnic, cultural, and linguistic identity of national minorities.[14] A growing ethnic consciousness has been visible among the Belarusian minority in Poland. Several new organizations were established to campaign for educational, linguistic, and cultural rights, although disputes surfaced periodically, particularly over alleged Polish religious, educational, and occupational discrimination.

Serious discords between Poland and Lithuania did not appear at the governmental level before Lithuania seceded from the USSR in August 1991. However, apprehensions were voiced in both capitals over the activities and aspirations of the Polish minority in Lithuania and the position of the small Lithuanian minority in Poland. In mid-September 1991, Foreign Minister Skubiszewski postponed his visit to Vilnius despite Poland's recognition of Lithuania's independence. During 1991, talks on bilateral relations were interrupted over the question of Polish minority rights. By mid-January 1992, however, a wide-ranging declaration of friendship and a consular convention was initialed by Vilnius and Warsaw, and the signing of a full bilateral treaty was expected by the end of August 1993. Vilnius itself has sought Polish government guarantees for the approximately 15,000 Lithuanians resident in northeastern Poland. Some Lithuanian activists claimed their actual number could be three times higher. Since Lithuania's declaration of independence, this minority has become more active by establishing separate cultural and educational associations. However, unlike their Polish counterparts in Lithuania, the leadership has not expressed any aspirations toward political or territorial autonomy.[15] In the early months of 1993, Warsaw and Vilnius indicated that they would work diligently on the issue of minority relations in both states, agreeing to allow names and surnames to be spelled in the mother tongue. Following a series of meetings conducted by Deputy Prime Minister Pawel Łączkowski with minority representatives, a list of postulates was presented to the Polish government by Lithuanian spokesmen, most of which concerned the promotion of Lithuanian language and culture. For example, Łączkowski announced that Lithuanians living in the Suwałki voivodship would henceforth be able to exchange marriage vows in Lithuanian.[16]

Both positive and negative trends were visible in the condition of Poland's ethnic minorities. On the plus side, the authorities recognized the right of all minorities to their distinct identity, culture, language, and social and political representation. Warsaw has taken several steps to improve opportunities for ethnic groups to establish independent organizations, gain education in their mother tongue, engage in cultural and artistic pursuits, and obtain some meaningful political representation at both local and national levels. Conversely, there has been a visible ethnic revival, particularly among members of the younger generation and among minorities emboldened by the achievement of national independence by Ukraine, Belarus, and Lithuania. On the minus side, state funding for minorities showed signs of stagnating or declining as a result of tight budgetary constraints. Financial restrictions could, in turn, curtail minority activities and even exacerbate political tensions. Minority rights have still to be legally codified, and wide differences remain among political leaders on whether these would necessitate a separate law or be included in the proposed constitution. Some manifestations of prejudice and conflict have also been evident at the local level, sometimes spurred by the activities of extremist groups. Skinhead and neo-fascist gangs periodically attacked Romani residents, and scattered anti-Semitic and anti-foreigner incidents have also been reported. Cooperative minority relations with local and voivodship authorities will remain a key component in assuring stability and limiting manifestations of inter-communal hostilities.

POLISH NATIONALISTS

Confederation for an Independent Poland (CIP)
Konfederacja Polski Niepodległej (KPN)

The CIP was established in September 1979 as a political party challenging the Communist monopoly of power and calling for an independent and non-Communist Poland. Its leader, Leszek Moczulski, served several prison sentences but was released shortly after the creation of the Solidarity free trade union in the summer of 1980. The CIP adopted a more militant position than the dissident movement linked with the Workers' Defense Committee and argued that Solidarity's agenda was too moderate in achieving independence and terminating Soviet domination. It obtained a following in several industrial centers, particularly in Szczecin, Łódź, and Upper Silesia, before the declaration of martial law by General Wojciech Jaruzelski in December 1981. The confederation continued to operate underground during martial law and throughout the 1980s, emerging as a distinct political formation in 1989 with the negotiated demise of Communist rule. The CIP traced its heritage to the "independence" political tradition of Marshal Józef Piłsudski, a military and political leader who was instrumental in the formation of an independent Polish state after World War One. It criticized the various Solidarity splinter groups for their compromising approach toward the former Communist apparatus. The CIP supported the creation of a market economy but expressed reservations about foreign investments and alien influence in Polish affairs. Although it considered its position to be both patriotic and pragmatic, it was criticized for its tendencies toward demagogy and populism and for calling for severe retribution against the deposed Communist leadership and its accomplices.

The confederation has undergone various splits and fractures, and several of Moczulski's associates have in recent years established their own parties and movements while continuing to draw upon the "independence" tradition. The CIP has maintained a respectable support base in several Polish cities. It competed separately from Solidarity for the June 1989 election, but failed to capture any parliamentary seats. Moczulski himself stood in the presidential elections in 1990 and gathered the required 100,000 signatures to be included on the ballot, but he finished in last place, garnering only 2.5 percent of the popular vote. In the May 1990 local elections, the CIP barely gained 0.1 percent of the available seats in local and municipal councils. For the next year, the confederation worked hard on expanding its national structures, and in the October 1991 general elections it gained 7.5 percent of the popular vote and obtained 51 *Sejm* seats, making it the third-largest party in parliament.

The CIP remained at odds with the governing coalition of Prime Minister Suchocka, and together with the former Communist Democratic Left, the Peasant Party, the Center Alliance, and the quasi-nationalist Movement for the Republic (MFR), it successfully pressed for a vote of no-confidence in May 1993 and brought down Poland's fifth post-Communist government. The CIP appeared to gain the support of citizens dissatisfied with the effects of economic reform and the failures to purge the old Communist structures. As with many nationalistically focused organizations, the CIP has been difficult to pigeonhole programmatically: it has adopted secular positions vis-à-vis the Catholic Church, has voiced some support for preserving the welfare state, and has not adopted any overt racist or xenophobic positions. On the other hand, its chief focus has been on increasing and preserving Poland's independence, guarding against unwelcome Russian influence, building an "Eastern Confederation" with Ukraine and Belarus, and defending the rights of Polish minorities in neighboring states.[17]

Christian National Union (CNU)
Zjednoczenie Chrześcijańsko-Narodowe (ZChN)

The CNU was founded in October 1989 by national-focused, right-of-center political activists from twenty regional centers. Led by Wiesław Chrzanowski and Antoni Macierewicz, the CNU cast itself as a Catholic-oriented, traditionalist party that sought to re-create a fully independent Poland on the principles of "Catholic ethics" and a "Christian state." The union sought to guarantee strong church influence in political and social life and declared a prolonged struggle against all left-wing formations, including the post-Communist and post-Solidarity Socialists. Its program stressed Polish national unity and opposed any political or legal measures that encouraged regionalist separatism. In the field of culture, the CNU sought to develop a strong "national culture" and educational system free of "Communist and materialist influences." In the general elections of October 1991, the CNU entered the Catholic Action Coalition with several smaller groupings, scoring 8.73 percent of the popular vote and thereby finishing third in an extremely fractured election. The union obtained 49 deputies to the 460-seat lower house, and 9 out of 100 senators. While several Christian Democratic groups disassociated themselves from the CNU because of its allegedly extremist orientation, the union was unofficially supported by many Catholic priests, some of whom reportedly instructed parishioners on how to cast their ballots on election day.

After the fall of the Jan Olszewski government in June 1992, a group loyal to the ousted prime minister established the MFR (Movement for the Republic), which retained 16 seats in the *Sejm* and adopted a quasi-nationalist, ultra-Catholic position. Macierewicz, a founder of the CNU, created a separate party, the Christian National Movement—Catholic Action, while another Olszewski supporter, Jan Parys, created a Third Republic Movement. The CNU subsequently entered the governing coalition under Premier Suchocka but continued to criticize its centrist and leftist partners for the evident failures to promote the desired Catholic renaissance. Leaders of various nationalist groupings purportedly hoped to build a larger "Christian coalition" in preparation for the September 1993 elections. The task was likely to prove difficult as Poland's Catholic and nationalist-oriented forces remained even more splintered than the center, the left, and the capitalist right.[18]

Polish Independence Party—Party of the New Right (PIP-PNR)
Polska Partia Niepodległościowa—Partia Nowej Prawicy (PPN-PNP)

This party, led by Romuald Szeremietiew, Tadeusz Stański, Ryszard Anders, and Marian Banaś, constituted part of the "independence" Piłsudskiite tradition. It claimed a membership of 2,000 and was formally registered in 1991. PIP-PNR advocated the regionalization of Poland according to historical borders, linking these regions through the institution of a strong national presidency. The party supported an activist foreign policy directed toward cooperation with the former Soviet states, Germany, the EC, and NATO. Its leaders believed that the Church and Christian social teachings should have lasting influences on social and political relations in Poland but declared that they were against discrimination on religious grounds. They supported a free-market economy as a means to guarantee human freedoms and would use education and cultural activities to improve the national consciousness. The PIP-PNR also cooperated with the Foundation of Polish Culture in Lithuania *(Fundacja Kultury Polskiej na Litwie)*, provided assistance to Polish communities in the former Soviet Union, and published several local and regional bulletins.

Universal Party of Slavs and Allied Nations (UPSAN)
Powszechna Partia Słowian i Narodów Sprzymierzonych (PPSiNS)

A self-described centrist and pan-national party led by Kazimierz Abramski, UPSAN stated its main goal to be the incorporation of Poland into a "Union of Free Nations" that would span an area stretching from the Black Sea to the Barents Sea. It supported the inviolability of all existing borders but appeared to have a pan-Slavic tendency by seeking close cooperation with neighboring Slavic states as protection against alleged German influence in the region. It also demanded reparations from Moscow for the illegal occupation of Polish territories after the 1939 invasion and payments from the Western allies for their betrayal of Poland at the Yalta peace conference, including the forgiveness of all Polish debts acquired by the Communist regime.

National Democratic Party (NDP)
Stronnictwo Narodowo-Demokratyczne (SND)

This party was founded in 1991 with the help of the National Party in exile that had its headquarters in London. It considered itself the only legitimate continuation of the National Democratic movement (*Endecja*), the ultra-nationalist trend established and led by the pre-war chauvinist leader Roman Dmowski and renowned for its extreme nationalist positions, consisting of anti-German, anti-Semitic, pro-church, and latent pan-Slavic tendencies. Despite this, the NDP in Poland was not viewed as a militant nationalist organization but closer to the Christian Democratic Union. The party leaders, Jan Zamoyski, Napoleon Siemiaszko, Jan Engelgard, Krzysztof Majek, Bogusław Kowalski, and Witold Staniszkis, considered the party's ideology to be similar to the right wing of the Conservative Party in Great Britain and the Gaullist movement in France. They supported a free-market economy and foreign investments, as long as this would be used to stimulate domestic capital. They also opposed the "Americanization" and commercialization of Polish culture and believed the state should play a "productive" role in the economy. The party goals also included propagating a strong national ideology and Christian values among Poland's young people. The NDP published the monthly *Nowe Horyzonty* (New Horizons).

National Party (NP)
Stronnictwo Narodowe (SN)

The National Party was originally founded in 1928 and reactivated in 1989. As an *Endecja* nationalist party, it used Dmowski's statement, "I am a Pole, therefore I have Polish duties," as its main platform slogan. Under the motto "God and Country," the NP emphasized the belief that Poles were able to improve the country by themselves, that the national interest of Poles should have a preferred position over that of foreigners, that the national economic system should be under government control, that privileges for foreign capital should be reduced, that Poland should receive war reparations from Germany, and that there should be a strong executive branch within a parliamentary democracy. NP leaders believed the state should be responsible for a cultural program that would promote moral values, require the media to be owned by Poles, and allow the Roman Catholic Church to participate fully in the social and cultural life of the Polish nation. NP leaders aimed to unify all nationalist movements. The leadership of this 4,000-member party included Leon Mirecki, Maciej Giertych, Józef Więcławek, Stefan Jarzębski, and Bogusław Jeznach. The NP published *Tygodnik Narodowy* (National Weekly) and the biweekly *Przegląd Narodowy* (National Review).

Polish National Front (PNF)
Narodowy Front Polski (NFP)

This party, led by Wojciech Podjacki, openly sought to build a "Great Poland," a reference to the fifteenth-century Poland that stretched from the Baltic Sea to the Black Sea. Its leaders advocated a large, modern army and believed only Polish capital should have a preferential position in the country. In this protectionist agenda, foreign capital would be limited to a necessary minimum and would remain under government supervision. The party believed the state had an obligation to protect Polish cultural traditions and to develop national culture above all other considerations. The PNF was believed to have ties with Poland's nascent skinhead movement, provoking attacks on Gypsy communities and calling on citizens to expel all of Poland's Roma.

National Rebirth of Poland (NRP)
Narodowe Odrodzenie Polski (NOP)

This ultra-nationalist organization was founded in Warsaw in 1981. It was reportedly co-sponsored by the Confederation for an Independent Poland and the Polish National Front. In 1989, it merged with the *Szczerbiec* political group in Katowice, Upper Silesia. The strongest branches functioned in Warsaw and Katowice. The NRP viewed itself as developing the traditions of Dmowski, although more in line with the coalitionist Great Polish Camp (founded in 1926) than the original National Party. The party advocated a "democratic national state," denied the existence of a German minority in Poland, and viewed the progressive unification of Europe and the creation of a joint European government as the greatest threat to individual nations and national movements.

National Movement (NM)
Ruch Narodowy (RN)

The National Movement, led by Mariusz Urban, purported to defend European civilization as a "Christian civilization" and promoted Catholic ethics as the priority in individual and social life. However, it has also expressed reservations about the direct participation by the Roman Catholic Church in formulating government policy. It demanded reparations from Germany and Russia for war damages and population losses, the defense of "Polish character," the recovery of the eastern territories lost to the Soviet Union during World War Two, and the acceptance of full Polish minority rights in the Zaolzie area of the Czech Republic. NM not only desired to prohibit the sale of land to foreigners but also to nationalize land previously sold to foreigners. It demanded official condemnation of the participation of Jews in the Communist regime as well as a concerted defense against alleged "Jewish demands." The party proposed to create a "classic" Polish model for culture that would serve as an alternative to the existing "commercial subculture." The NM published the yearly *Ruch Narodowy*.

Polish National Commonwealth—Polish National Party (PNC-PNP)
Polska Wspólnota Narodowa—Polskie Stronnictwo Narodowe (PWN-PSN)

An ultra-nationalist party originally founded in 1955, the PNC-PNP was reactivated in December 1990 by the eccentric, racist, and rabid anti-Semite Bolesław Tejkowski. Claiming 4,000 members, the party declared that it was neither a leftist nor a rightist organization but a nationalist movement and a centrist party encompassing "all Polish national forces" in the tradition of the pre-war National Democratic leader Roman Dmowski. The party's stated goal was to achieve full political and economic independence for Poland, as well as to facilitate the "moral rebirth" of the nation. It desired to build a state with a "national structure," rather than a Communist, Socialist, capitalist, or liberal system. It advocated that authority should only be held by Poles who understood the interests of the Polish nation, that property should only be owned by Poles without dual citizenship, that foreign investment should exclude property ownership and limit profit margins, and that foreign influence over Polish affairs should be eliminated. The PNC-PNP was against the concept of a "Europe without borders," preferring instead a model of cooperation among free, separate nations, in which collaboration among Slavic countries was a primary goal, thus displaying its pan-Slavic leanings. Its cultural program would attempt to keep Polish culture "clean" and separate from other nationalities. The party published the monthly *Myśl Narodowa Polska* (Polish National Thought). In March 1993, Tejkowski was brought to trail for defaming the government, the Catholic Church, and the country's Jewish community; the court ordered Tejkowski to be detained again in July 1993 after he refused to undergo psychiatric examination to determine his fitness to stand trial.[19] Several other small Polish nationalist organizations also operated in Poland, including the National Organization of the Republic, the Party of Working Legionnaires, and the Party of Loyalty to the Republic—Congress of National Solidarity.[20]

GERMAN MOVEMENTS

Social-Cultural Association of the
German Minority in Silesian Opole (SCAGMSO)
Towarzystwo Społeczno-Kulturalne
Mniejszości Niemieckiej na Śląsku Opolskim (TSKMNŚO)

This organization was officially registered in January 1990 in Opole, a region with a substantial German minority population. Like-minded bodies were established in two other German-inhabited areas: the Social-Cultural Association of

People of German Origin in Katowice voivodship (SCAPGOKV) and the Social-Cultural Association of People of German Origin in Częstochowa voivodship (SCAPGOCV). Other smaller organizations were established in Gdańsk, Toruń, and Olsztyn. The associations evidently maintained connections with the German Union of Expellees, a relationship that has provoked dispute within the German minority. Association membership in Opole reportedly reached 200,000 during 1991, 60,000 in Katowice, and 30,000 in Częstochowa, and its activities focused on developing German education, culture, and art. SCAGMSO leaders declared that they supported the political integration of Poles and Germans and the eradication of 45 years of distrust and isolation between the two sides. The SCAGMSO spokesman in Raciborz, Wilibald Jan Fabian, spoke out for the concept of a "Europe without borders" and this evidently superseded calls for Silesian autonomy. Because of the schisms within the Solidarity movement, SCAGMSO became the strongest political grouping in the Opole voivodship. In the local elections of May 1990, deputies representing the German minority gained 380 seats on local councils in 35 out of 61 townships or municipalities, with an absolute majority in 26. For the parliamentary elections of October 1991, 2 German election committees were established, 1 based in Opole and 1 in Katowice. From Opole, 7 German deputies were elected to the *Sejm*, receiving a total of 133,000 votes, and 1 deputy to the Senate (upper house), Gerhard Bartodziej, who obtained 82,000 votes. German deputies established a German minority parliamentary club under the leadership of Henryk Kroll.[21]

German Friendship Circles (GFCs)
Koła Przyjaźni Niemieckiej (KPN)

The circles were founded by Jan and Henryk Kroll at the end of 1988 as small support groups for Germans who faced discrimination in Communist Poland and as the basis of an influential minority organization. The GFCs were headed by five-member managing committees. Since January 1990, this organizational network has grown rapidly and established local circles throughout Upper Silesia, boasting a membership of over 300,000 people by early 1991. The circles championed the rights of Germans remaining in their Silesian homeland and supported the cultivation and development of German learning, culture, and art, the submission of recommendations to agencies and institutions to improve the living conditions of the German population, German-language instruction in all Silesian schools, regional business promotion in Silesia, and the recognition of rights to cultural autonomy. As a result of these objectives, they hoped to curb German emigration from Silesia. Furthermore, the circles have attempted to reestablish traditional relations with other ethnic groups and backed the German-Polish Treaty of 1990 without reservations, rejecting all attempts by either country to involve the minority in political disputes. In 1992, the group was accused of having connections to the neo-Nazi group *Nationale Offensive* (see below) because of the honorary membership granted to one of the group's members. Henryk Kroll called this a mistake, adding that the minorities should not be linked to any German nationalist groupings.[22]

Union of German Social-Cultural Associations in Poland (UGSCAP)
Związek Niemieckich Stowarzyszeń Społeczno-Kulturalnych w Polsce (ZNSSKP)

The union emerged from the Central Council of German Associations in September 1991 to coordinate the activities of German societies in various regions of Poland; the majority of voivodship-based associations subsequently entered the union. Estimated membership by the close of 1991 exceeded 220,000 people. As an umbrella organization, the UGSCAP attempted to combine the efforts of various German associations, societies, and groupings (including the German Friendship Circles) into a cohesive program. Its principal aim was to maintain German national identity and to develop the main regions inhabited by Germans (Silesia, Mazury, Warmia). The union has lobbied for such rights as dual citizenship for both Germans and Poles (Poland does not recognize dual citizenship), the free movement of people, and the easy transfer of capital. Its leaders rejected all attempts to involve the minority in political disputes and to misuse it in order to fan the flames of nationalism. Union leaders demanded constitutional stipulations guaranteeing minority rights and the use of German in all administrative affairs in regions with a substantial minority population. Overall, it encouraged increased Polish-German cooperation in all areas of social, political, and economic life, in the context of building a "common European home." For example, a closely linked organization, the Chief Council of Germans in Upper Silesia (CCGUS), sought to transform Upper Silesia into a "modern Euroregion."[23]

National Offensive (NO)
Nationale Offensive, Narodowa Ofensywa (NO)

A self-defined national-radical party that was founded in 1988 in Augsburg, Germany, National Offensive "struggled" for the rights of German workers, for the "national interests" of all Germans, and encouraged "German patriotism." It endeavored to create a pan-European nationalist movement, as well as to further German national identity in Silesia through publishing ventures, the teaching of German, and the preaching of its neo-Nazi ideology to young Silesians. As a means to this end, the NO has organized "patriotic discos" for young Germans in Silesia. Its platform was deliberately patterned after that of the National Socialist German Workers' Party (Nazis), particularly in attitudes toward Jews and other nationalities; its leaders believed that "the racial policies of Hitler's time were in general correct." According to party leader Michał Świerzek, NO membership stood at approximately 500, and it also maintained an outpost in the Kaliningrad region of Russia, on Poland's northern border. The party aimed to create a "socially just, nationally and patriotically directed Greater Germany" that would stretch from the Meuse to the Niemen. In the summer of 1992 it was reported to be operating out of the town of Dziewkowice, where it created an Opole branch in early 1992. However, the NO has not established a broad base of support and has been condemned by moderate German leaders. Gunter Boschuetz, head of National Offensive in North Rhine Westphalia who had been in Dziewkowice since November 1991 and organized a congress of the Silesian-based National Offensive attended by 30 Silesian representatives and 20 German representatives, was expelled from Poland in December 1992. When three leaders of the group left the region in December 1992, they were promptly replaced by three substitutes. The Polish senator from this region, Dorota Simonides, stated that all legal means would be used to rid the area of NO activists. But at a February 1993 briefing of the *Sejm* Committee on Ethnic Minorities, provincial governor of Opole Ryszard Zembaczyński admitted that the decision to deport groups of neo-Nazis had little practical effect.[24]

East Prussian Wolves (EPW)
Wilki Prus Wschodnich (WPW)

The goal of this small, youth-based German movement was to restore the northeastern corner of Poland to a Greater Germany encompassing the pre-war territories of East Prussia. It appeared to be a marginal association with little active support and an extremely slender potential social base in comparison to the Silesian German organizations.[25] Other smaller German groupings about which less information was readily available included the Union of the German Minority, the Social-Cultural Association of People of German Descent in Raciborz, the German Working Group "Reconciliation and Future," the Socio-Cultural Association of the German Minority in Warmia and Mazury, the Polish German Union, the Olsztyn Association of the German Minority, the "Elk" German Association, the Association of the German Minority in Ostroda "Fir Trees," the Socio-Cultural Association of the German Minority in Bartoszyce and Vicinity, the German Association "Nantagia," the Mrągowo Association of the German Minority "Bear Paw," the Cultural Association of Germans in Szczytno, and the Independent Association of Citizens of German Origin "Roots." By 1991, virtually every voivodship with a German population possessed its own sociopolitical organization.[26]

EASTERN MINORITIES

National Minorities Council (NMC)
Rada Mniejszości Narodowych (RMN)

Attempts were made during 1990 to integrate various minority groupings and create a nationwide political representation. In March 1991, leaders of ten organizations, including Belarusians, Lithuanians, and Ukrainians, established a

National Minorities Council (NMC). Its objectives revolved around speeding up legislation on minority rights in Poland, including the introduction of appropriate constitutional stipulations. Although the council was not registered and evidently ceased to function after a few months, the inter-minority contacts it established contributed to forging various electoral coalitions for the October 1991 ballot, including the Orthodox Electoral Committee and the Minority Electoral Bloc. The bloc put forward 60 candidates in 16 electoral districts and 10 candidates for the national list. However, the coalition only received 29,428 votes and failed to elect a *Sejm* deputy. Loose electoral coalitions and inter-minority lobbying groups were likely to continue operating in Poland to pursue the rights and interests of various ethnic and religious minorities.[27]

Union of Ukrainians in Poland (UUP)
Związek Ukraińców w Polsce (ZUP)

This organization, formerly known as the Ukrainian Social-Cultural Association, transformed itself into a union in February 1990. The UUP consisted of a network of local chapters chaired by Ukrainian professionals and presided over by a chief council and a general assembly. About 10,000 Ukrainians belonged to this organization, grouped in 180 local circles and 11 regional branches. The union dedicated itself to changing the poor image of Ukrainians in Polish society and strengthening their national identity. Its general goals included defending minority rights in culture, education, language, and religion. Within the Ukrainian community, the Union promoted the development of its own intelligentsia, increased research, and the production of accurate textbooks on the history of Ukraine and Polish-Ukrainian relations, the fostering of contacts with Ukraine and with the Ukrainian diaspora, and the formation of distinct economic institutions. More controversial demands included the official condemnation of the post-war deportations, "moral and material" compensation for property confiscated by Communist decrees in 1947, 1949, and 1958, the regulation of the legal and property status of the Uniate and the Polish Autocephalous Orthodox Churches, the passage of a minorities law, and guaranteed Ukrainian representation in the Polish parliament. The activities of the union won approval among officials in Warsaw, who argued that they would help in forging cooperative links with the Ukrainian republic. However, UUP leaders have expressed some concern over the activities of Polish nationalist groupings as well as some Eastern Territory societies consisting of former residents and offspring of the Polish Ukrainian territories.

By the beginning of 1992, an estimated 1,500 children and youth were enrolled in Ukrainian classes at 46 learning centers in Poland. Ukrainian elementary and secondary schools existed in the Suwałki, Koszalin, and Olsztyn voivodships; 30 cultural centers and 40 artistic associations were functioning; and three newspapers, *Nasze Słowo*, *Zustriczi*, and *Nad Buhom i Narwoju*, were being published in Ukrainian. But more contentious issues also materialized, including calls for the return of Ukrainians to the Bieszczady Mountains, from where many had been deported after World War Two on charges of collaboration with anti-Communist guerrillas, and the return of property seized by the state in the late 1940s. The latter included over 250 churches confiscated from the Greek-Catholic (Uniate) Church in 1947. The implementation of such proposals could aggravate frictions with the local Polish population, as was evident during the prolonged dispute over the Carmelite Cathedral of St. Theresa in Przemyśl during the spring and summer of 1991. The dispute was largely resolved by Pope John Paul II during his visit to the city in 1991 when the Ukrainian Uniates received an alternative place of worship. The pope had re-activated the Uniate diocese in western Ukraine and in the Przemyśl region. In sum, the Uniates had 60 parishes, 2 monasteries, and 3 nunneries in the country. A substantial portion of Ukrainians also belonged to the Autocephalous Orthodox Church, with dioceses in Przemyśl-Nowy Sącz and Chełm-Lublin.

At the August 1992 World Forum of Ukrainians, Jerzy Rejt, UUP chairman, stated that more financial aid from the Polish state was needed to promote Ukrainian culture but stressed that the most important priority for the Ukrainian minority was the creation by the Polish parliament of a national minorities law. Ukrainian leaders became politically active during the collapse of Communist rule, when Włodzimierz Mokry was elected to parliament in the June 1989 ballot on the Solidarity electoral list. In the May 1990 local elections, 70 Ukrainian representatives were elected to various local councils. Before the general elections of October 1991, Ukrainian leaders entered the Minority Electoral Bloc, which received 26,962 votes but failed to elect a parliamentary deputy; some entered alternative election coalitions, including Mokry, who was re-elected from the Solidarity list.[28]

Association of Lithuanians in Poland (ALP)
Stowarzyszenie Litwinów w Polsce (SLP)

Formerly the Lithuanian Social-Cultural Association, this 2,500-member organization, led by Eugeniusz Pietruszkiewicz, was established in March 1992. It supported the creation of an independent Lithuanian republic and called for guaranteed Lithuanian representation in the Polish parliament, for the nomination of a Lithuanian as deputy governor in the Suwałki voivodship and as governor in the Sejny district, for bilingualism in administrative work in the Sejny and Puńsk districts, for Lithuanian-language instruction in Polish schools, and for Lithuanian church services. The party financed the biweekly, Lithuanian-language *Ausra*, and the House of Lithuanian Culture in Puńsk. In the local elections of May 1990, Lithuanian representatives gained 16 seats to local councils in the Puńsk district. Ten candidates stood for the October 1991 parliamentary elections in the National Minorities Bloc but failed to gain any *Sejm* seats; the voting turnout among Lithuanians only reached 25 percent. As a result of ALP involvement, an increasing number of pupils enrolled in the six elementary schools and one lyceum that provided lessons in Lithuanian.[29]

Lithuanian Society of Saint Casimir (LSSC)
Litewskie Towarzystwo Św. Kazimierza (LTŚwK)

This organization, headed by Olgierd Skrzypka, was created in 1990, continuing the tradition of an identically named organization that existed prior to World War Two. Its key principle was the combination of religious work with the strengthening of Lithuanian identity among this compact ethnic minority. It endeavored to teach the Lithuanian language and propagate the nation's culture and customs, particularly through establishing libraries and aiding Lithuanian artistic groups. By creating a Center for Lithuanian Culture in the town of Sejny in the Suwałki region, the organization also endeavored to build better relations between Poles and Lithuanians.[30]

"Hospodar" Citizens' Circle of Lemkos (CCL)
Obywatelski Krąg Łemków "Hospodar" (OKŁ)

Paweł Stefanowski, Michał Kiec, and Zenobia Czerhoniak became the leaders of this Ruthenian political group, founded in 1990. The majority of Lemko Ruthenians lived in the western and northern areas of the country, to where many were deported by Communist authorities in the 1940s and where the movement claimed some 10,000 supporters. The Lemko Circle stressed Ruthenian civil rights rather than their ethnic or regional specificity while asserting their loyalty to the Polish Republic. They wanted to educate Poles about Lemko-Ruthenian history, including their forced deportations and colonization into deserted farms after World War Two. The group encouraged the formation of a Polish-Lemko roundtable that would stimulate the economic recovery of traditional Lemko territories in southeastern Poland. Lemko representatives endeavored to cooperate with the state and with various social organizations in order to boost the productivity and to improve the environment of the Lemko region so that the indigenous population could return to the area. The CCL believed in the necessity of protecting Ruthenian monuments and in the value of education in the mother tongue. One of their goals was to establish a Center of Lemko Culture, a Museum of Lemko Culture, and a Foundation of Lemko Culture.[31]

Lemko Association (LA)
Stowarzyszenie Łemków (SŁ)

The association was created in 1989 in Legnica voivodship in southwestern Poland. The chairman of the LA's chief council was Andrzej Kapoza, and it claimed nearly 400 members in 13 local circles. It financed the quarterly publication *Besida* and tried to promote Ruthenian cultural activities. LA spokesmen estimated the Ruthenian population in Poland to be somewhere between 60,000 and 80,000 on the basis of their native language and their place of residence before the deportations during the 1940s. They also claimed that the Lemkos formed part of the Carpatho-Ruthene nation and not a sub-division of the Ukrainian nation.[32]

Lemko Union (LU)
Zjednoczenie Łemków (ZŁ)

The union was formed in 1989 and registered in Nowy Sącz in southeastern Poland. Wacław Szlanta was elected chairman of the chief council, while the union claimed about 500 members in 27 local circles in 6 voivodships. As of early 1993, the LU did not have its own publication or cultural centers but did receive some funding from local authorities to organize Ruthenian cultural events. LU leaders estimated the Lemko population to be in the region of 100,000 people, including those who were deported to the Soviet Union after World War Two. The union supported the main Ukrainian organizations in Poland and evidently considered Lemko Ruthenians to be a branch of the Ukrainian nation.

Belarusian Democratic Union (BDU)
Białoruskie Zjednoczenie Demokratyczne (BZD)

This was the only official national minorities party in Poland as of January 1991. The union was co-founded in February 1990 by Sokrat Janowicz, a Belarusian poet, Eugeniusz Minorowicz, and Piotr Juszczuk and possessed a membership of some 1,500 people. The importance of this party did not extend far beyond Białystok voivodship and the nearby area inhabited by Belarusians. Its primary goals were to reinforce Belarusian ethnic identity in Poland, to prevent any further depopulation and acculturation of the minority, and to counteract the economic degradation of the region. This goal extended to the belief that foreign capital should be restricted in order to prevent the "colonization" of Poland. The party's other concerns have included the preservation of Belarusian culture and the full emancipation and independence of the Belarusian Republic. Together with the social committee *Hromada*, the BDU has campaigned for the official use of the Belarusian language in the local administration, the return of original Belarusian place names, the development of research on the history and culture of the Białystok region, and broader investment in resuscitating the area's economy, particularly its agriculture. The union complained about the shortage of Belarusian elementary and secondary schools and pressed for the introduction of bilingual schooling. In 1991, the Belarusian language was being taught in only 45 schools.

The BDA stood as a political party in Poland's local and national elections. seventy-three Belarusian deputies were elected to district councils in the May 1990 ballot, constituting 10.5 percent of all mandates in the Białystok voivodship. Clear majorities were obtained in four districts and a Belarusian inter-district union was subsequently formed to help coordinate economic development in the region. Two electoral blocs were formed for the October 1991 ballot: the Belarusian Electoral Committee and the Orthodox Electoral Committee. The latter elected Eugeniusz Czykwin as a deputy to the *Sejm* with the strong support of the Orthodox Church. The BDA backed the former bloc, which failed to elect any deputies principally because of a lack of campaign funds. They also pursued cross-border contacts with the Republic of Belarus, without advocating secession from Poland. One consistent source of tension has been over religious issues, as Poles were primarily Roman Catholic and Belarusians mostly Eastern Orthodox. Disputes have focused on such questions as the use of churches for Orthodox services, the language employed during masses, the allegedly anti-Belarusian and missionary attitude of the Polish clergy, as well as accusations about Polish discrimination in local education and employment.[33]

Belarusian Farmers' Society (BFS)
Białoruskie Stowarzyszenie Rolników (BSR)

The BFS was founded by Sergiusz Niczyporok, an Orthodox theologian and farmer residing in the village of Zaleszany in Białystok voivodship. The organization sought to promote reconciliation among all nationalities living in Poland and to create communal solidarity between Belarusian and Polish ethnics. Regarding agrarian topics, the group pledged to inform all citizens of the dire situation of the Belarusian countryside and to offer an alternate vision for the future development of the region's economy.[34] Other eastern minority organizations in Poland included the Ukrainian Christian Brotherhood of Saint Volodimir, the Union of Independent Ukrainian Youth, the Ukrainian Teachers' Society, the Belarusian Students' Association, the Association of Belarusian Journalists, the Belarusian Youth Association, the Brotherhood of Orthodox Youth, and the Belarusian Literary Society.[35]

REGIONALIST GROUPINGS

Kaszubian Pomeranian Union (KPU)
Kaszubski Związek Pomorski (KZP)

The union was founded by Lech Bądkowski, co-creator of the Gdańsk Agreement, which gave birth to Solidarity in August 1980. Józef Borzyszkowski became the union's president. Historically, the Kaszubian population in northwestern Poland was significantly more resistant to Germanization than its

Silesian counterparts. Few Kaszubians migrated to Germany, because they considered themselves to be a component part of the Polish nation. In addition, almost all of the Kaszubian intelligentsia remained in close cooperation with Roman Catholic priests. The KPU endeavored to introduce Kaszubian ethnicity into geography handbooks and history textbooks and worked to promote ethnic awareness in Polish schools. One such achievement has involved rescuing the Kaszubian People's University. Overall, the union supported the building of a Polish homeland that would respect all manner of ethnic diversity.[36]

Mazurian Association (MA)
Stowarzyszenie Mazurskie (SM)

This regionalist organization was set up in 1990 to cover three voivodships in northeastern Poland: Olsztyn, Elbląg, and Suwałki. It claimed to represent about 8,000 people who declared themselves to be Mazurian or Mazuro-Germans. The MA was composed of a chief council, whose chairman was Tadeusz Zygfryd Willan, and a membership of some 1,200 people. Among its activities, the MA financed the monthly *Mazurska Poczta Bociania* and supervised the *Chata Mazurska* Museum in the town of Sądry and small village libraries throughout the Mazury region. The MA has endeavored to cooperate with the local authorities, the Ministry of Culture, and the Polish mass media to promote Mazurian identity.

Movement for Silesian Autonomy (MSA)
Ruch na Rzecz Autonomii Śląska (RNRAŚ)

This organization was led by Paweł Andrzej Musioł, Rudolf Kołodziejczyk, and Ryszard Klinger. The MSA set out to develop and nurture a rising consciousness among Silesians favorably disposed toward autonomy and the "joint responsibility" of all residents in the region. In short, the movement advocated a division of authority between the central and regional administrations by creating an autonomous Silesian region with its own legislative and executive prerogatives, similar to the status of Silesia before World War Two. The plan would entail dividing Poland into the regions of Śląsk, Wielkopolska, Pomorze, and Małopolska and would include creating a separate state treasury similar to the pre-war republic's treasury, which received 55 percent of the income of the Silesian voivodship. Furthermore, the MSA wished to halt the increasingly devastating environmental degradation of Silesia's natural resources. Members also upheld the necessity of good economic and cultural contact among Silesians, the importance of integrating all Silesians into one political unit, regardless of their ethnic heritage, and the desire to prevent the Germanization of Silesia. In the October 1991 general elections, the MSA managed to gain 2 seats in the lower house of parliament, indicating that a potential base of social support existed for its program of devolution and autonomy.[37]

Upper Silesian Union (USU)
Związek Górnośląski (ZG)

The USU appeared to be the strongest regional movement in Upper Silesia, with many members holding key positions in the local administration. Leaders Jerzy Wuttke and Jan Rzymełka estimated its membership to be several-thousand strong. Party membership remained contingent upon supporting "Upper Silesian values" and considering the region a "small motherland." The union advocated that Poland become a state of self-governing regions, with Silesia expanding its current frontiers to assume its traditional historical borders, presumably including parts of Czech Moravia. The USU co-owned the *Trybuna Śląska*, the most widely sold newspaper in Silesia.[38]

Polish Western Union—Movement of Polish Silesia (PWU-MPS)
Polski Związek Zachodni—Ruch Polskiego Śląska (PZZ-RPŚ)

This group, re-activated in 1991, previously operated in the Prussian sector of nineteenth-century partitioned Poland. It became staunchly opposed to Silesian autonomy and separatism, fully respected Polish claims to these territories, and advocated strong public and minority allegiance to the Polish state. The union obtained 4 deputies to the lower house in the October 1991 parliamentary elections, gaining 0.23 percent of the popular vote.[39]

Alliance of Upper Silesian Societies and Associations (AUSSA)
Porozumienie Górnośląskich Stowarzyszeń i Towarzystw (PGST)

This alliance united seven Silesian organizations, including the Movement for Silesian Autonomy. It was formed in order to provide a defense of the region's "vital interests," and its spokesmen believed that Upper Silesia should eventually govern itself through the elected authorities of the Katowice, Opole, and Bielsko-Biała voivodships. Edward Połoczek was elected chairman of the alliance.[40] Other regionalist groups about which little detailed information is presently available included the Union of *Gminas* of Upper Silesia, the Union of the *Gmina* of Zagłębie, the Union of Wielkopolans in Poznań, the Association of Upper Silesians in Opole, the Union of the Upper Silesian Communes, and the Upper Silesian Christian Democracy.[41]

MINORITY ORGANIZATIONS

Social-Cultural Society of Czechs and Slovaks in Poland (SCSCSP)
Towarzystwo Społeczno-Kulturalne Czechów i Słowaków w Polsce (TSKLCZSwP)

The society's leaders included Eugeniusz Misiniec and Lubomir Molitoris. Although accused by Catholic priests of embracing Slovak nationalism, leaders of this 3,200-member organization stated that they harbored no intention to promote secessionist movements or border revisions. The society advocated the passage of a Polish law on ethnic minorities, increased Slovak-language instruction in schools, and Slovak church services. The monthly *Zivot* (Life) was financially supported by CSSCSP.[42]

Social-Cultural Society of Jews in Poland (SCSJP)
Towarzystwo Społeczno-Kulturalne Żydów w Polsce (TSKŻwP)

This organization was officially formed by the Communist authorities in 1956 to supervise and control the Jewish population. At the time of the democratic changes in 1989, its membership stood at approximately 2,000 and operated 15 local branches in Poland. The society produced the *Folks-Sztyme*, a publication in both the Polish and the Yiddish languages, and was connected with the biweekly *Słowo Żydowskie*. In 1991, the heads of the SCSJP, the Jewish Religious Union, and the Jewish Historical Institute established a Coordinating Commission for Polish Jewry (CCPJ), which officially represented the interests of the remaining Polish Jews.[43]

Podhale Social-Cultural Association of Gypsies in Nowy Targ (PSCAGNT)
Podhalańskie Stowarzyszenie Społeczno-Kulturalne
Cyganów w Nowym Targu (PSSKCwNT)

This Gypsy (Romani) organization was initially established in the Nowy Targ voivodship of southeastern Poland in 1970. Its membership remained small, but it claimed to represent the interests of about 3,000 local Gypsies. Similar organizations have been formed in a number of neighboring voivodships to cultivate Romani culture and defend Gypsy interests vis-à-vis the local administration. Other minority-based organizations included the Gypsy Cultural-Educational Society, the Association of Roms in Poland, the Association of "The Children of the Holocaust," the Greek Association in Poland, the Bulgarian Cultural Educational Society of Chrysto Bolew, and the Armenian Cultural Society.

CHRONOLOGY

June 1989: Poland holds is first pluralistic elections in which the Communists are resoundly defeated by the Solidarity movement, paving the way for the first coalition government formed in August 1989 and led by Prime Minister Tadeusz Mazowiecki.

September 1989: The *Sejm* formally decides to permit Lithuanian names of streets to be posted next to Polish names in Sejny, northeastern Poland.

January 1990: The first German Friendship Circles are registered in Katowice.

February 1990: The Social and Cultural Society of the German Minority is licensed. The Belarusian Democratic Union is founded in Białystok.

March 1990: Lithuanian broadcasts increase in Poland. Lithuanian residents in the Suwałki region acquire their own half-hour program. A local radio station in Białystok begins carrying a daily fifteen-minute program in Belarusian for Belarusians living in northeast Poland.

April 1990: The Polish and German newspaper, *News from Upper Silesia*, begins publication, signaling the implementation of one of the agreements between Chancellor Kohl and Premier Mazowiecki. A Voivodship Court rejects a petition to register the German Sociocultural Association under the rationale that statements by a certain group of people declaring their affiliation with the German nation is not sufficient for affirming the existence of a German ethnic minority. In view of this discrepancy, the registration would allegedly contravene Polish law.

May 1990: The Silesian Institute holds a symposium in Opole entitled "Upper Silesia as a Bridge Between Poles and Germans." Following the first multi-party local elections, German representatives obtain council majorities in 25 out of 63 communities in Opole voivodship.

June 1990: The first congress of the Upper Silesian Union is held; resolutions are passed, union officials are elected, and an operational program is devised.

August 1990: The Polish Senate adopts a resolution condemning "Operation Wisła," in which thousands of Ukrainians and Ruthenians were deported from their ancestral homelands in the late 1940s.

September 1990: The Polish episcopate authorizes Alfons Nosol, bishop of Opole, to conduct church liturgy in German on request in Silesian parishes.

October 1990: Representatives of the Lithuanian community in Poland voice their grievances to the Polish and Lithuanian ministers of culture. The Vilnius government promises that it will contribute to the project to build a Lithuanian cultural center in Puńsk, in Suwałki voivodship. The Lithuanian Ministry of Culture presently heavily finances the monthly journal *Ausra*.

November 1990: Prime Minister Mazowiecki and Chancellor Kohl sign a joint declaration expressing the view that people who identify themselves with the language and culture of either country have the right to nurture their cultural identity and establish their own associations. But Mazowiecki rejects demands for a special status for the German minority in Poland.

January 1991: Ukrainian and Belarusian political action committees are formed in the Bielsko-Biała area. The Belarusian Democratic Union charges the existence of a confidential report prepared by the Polish Foreign Ministry implying that Belarusians are an alien body in Poland and are a political instrument of Russian policy.

February 1991: Foreign Minister Skubiszewski postpones his visit to Vilnius charging that Lithuania had failed to call new local elections in two predominantly Polish areas and had redrawn district borders to the disadvantage of ethnic Poles.

March 1991: President Wałęsa appoints a presidential council to improve Polish-Jewish relations.

April 1991: In his visit to Upper Silesia, Prime Minister Krzysztof Bielecki calls on all Germans in Poland to participate actively and loyally in establishing self-administration and introducing a market economy in Poland. German minority leader Henryk Kroll reasserts the need to guarantee rights for Germans using the principles on minorities mandated at the CSCE Copenhagen conference. The German Council publicly estimates its membership in Opole voivodship at 150,000, in Katowice voivodship at 40,000, and in Częstochowa voivodship at 30,000. Foreign Minister Skubiszewski publicly opposes dual nationality for Germans in Poland.

June 1991: Germany and Poland sign a comprehensive treaty of inter-state friendship and cooperation containing guarantees to respect the cultural rights of the German minority. In the town of Mława, Polish hoodlums attack a community of Gypsies, beating them, destroying their homes, and eventually driving them out of the town. Several dozen Gypsies subsequently seek refuge in Sweden claiming racial persecution.

July 1991: Prime Minister Bielecki discusses regionalism with two representatives from the Movement for Silesian Autonomy from Rybnik and the Upper Silesian Union from Katowice. Officials decide that delegations from regional associations will inaugurate regular meetings to work out a joint declaration on the regionalization of Poland.

August 1991: The Union of Independent Ukrainian Youth, the Ukrainian Christian Brotherhood of Saint Volodimir, the Lemko Union, the Lithuanian Sociocultural Association, the Lithuanian Association of Saint Kazimierz, and the Sociocultural Association of Czechs and Slovaks in Poland establish an electoral bloc of minority parties in order to enable national groups to become an integral part of the body politic.

September 1991: "Our Homeland," a weekly radio program in Polish, German, and the Silesian dialect, begins broadcasting in the Silesian city of Opole. Bavaria's governing Christian Social Union calls for retired German-language teachers to provide lessons in Polish Silesia. A delegation of Lithuanian Poles arrives in Warsaw to discuss the problems of the Polish minority in the Vilnius region. One of the biggest problems of the Polish community is the question of Lithuanian citizenship. Lithuanian and Polish officials discuss the situation of minorities in both states and agree that compromises must be sought.

October 1991: The Movement for Silesian Autonomy wins 7 seats to the *Sejm* (lower house) and 1 seat to the Senate (upper house). The Polish-German Foundation is established with the specific goals of sponsoring youth exchanges, promoting cultural cooperation and knowledge of the German language in Poland and of Polish in Germany, and educating economic specialists. The foundation is chaired by the former German federal minister Heinrich Windelen and secretary-general of the Liberal-Democratic Congress and *Sejm* deputy Paweł Piskorski. Henryk Kroll and two other German Silesians win 3 of 10 mandates in the Opole region, receiving 5,000 more votes than all of the Democratic Union candidates, the largest party in the new parliament, and over three times more than the Solidarity representatives. A Polish-Lithuanian declaration, devised by the two foreign ministries, states that in dealing with issues related to ethnic minorities, the two countries will be guided by European norms. The Declaration on Good-Neighborly Relations, Mutual Understanding, and Cooperation Between Poland and Belarus is signed. The document mandates the mutual respect of the ethnic, cultural, and linguistic identity of national minorities in both countries, the preservation of buildings and monuments pertaining to each group's history, and the establishment of centers of culture and learning for minorities in both Minsk and Warsaw.

January 1992: Polish and Lithuanian foreign ministers sign a 10-point declaration of friendship and good-neighborly relations and a consular convention. The signing is delayed because of a dispute over the rights of the Polish minority in Lithuania. Lithuanian officials and Polish deputies to the *Sejm* negatively assess the Polish government's eastern policy in light of the recent Polish-Lithuanian declaration. Polish spokesmen continue to criticize the deteriorating position of the Polish minority in Lithuania. The problems cited include infringements of citizenship rights, colonization of the region around Vilnius traditionally populated by Poles, and the dismissal of ethnic Polish from local employment.

February 1992: Three hundred small ultra-nationalist organizations stage anti-Semitic and anti-German activities in the town of Zgorzelec, in western Poland.

In an open letter to *Gazeta Wyborcza*, the major Warsaw daily, Marek Edelman, the only surviving commander of the 1943 Warsaw Ghetto Uprising, condemns the lack of reaction by the Polish government and society at large to the incidents in Zgorzelec.

March 1992: After discussing topics with his Lithuanian counterpart, such as elections and titles to land properties inhabited by ethnic Poles, Polish foreign minister Skubiszewski tells a press conference that he is concerned about the future of Polish-Lithuanian relations. The Lithuanian Sociocultural Association adopts a resolution to change their name to the Association of Lithuanians in Poland.

April 1992: Belarus and Poland initial a Treaty on Good Neighborliness and Friendly Cooperation, including decrees pertaining to minority rights. This treaty replaces a declaration signed in the fall of 1991.

October 1992: A Warsaw court dispenses prison terms of between six months and two and a half years to seventeen of the several hundred young participants in the anti-Gypsy Mława riots of June 1991.

December 1992: A two-day congress of the nationalist *Sejm* of the National Movement is held in Warsaw. At the end of the congress a Council of the *Sejm* of the National Movement is formed. The council aims to unify all national groups, of which seven were represented at the congress.

May 1993: Poland's fifth post-Communist government, led by Prime Minister Hanna Suchocka, loses a no-confidence vote in the *Sejm*. The vote is engineered by various nationalist right and left-of-center parties. President Wałęsa dissolves parliament in preparation for new general elections scheduled for September 1993.

NOTES

1. Among the sources consulted: Sławomir Łodziński, *Poland's Nationality Structure and Nationality Politics 1989–1992*, Study and Expertise Bureau, Sejm Chancellery, no. 22, Warsaw, July 1992; Franciszek Kosma, "National Minorities in Poland," *Trybuna Opolska*, January 17, 1992; *GUS*, State Office of Statistics, Warsaw, 1992.

2. For valuable histories of Poland, see Norman Davies, *Heart of Europe: A Short History of Poland* (Oxford: Clarendon Press, 1984); Norman Davies, *God's Playground: A History of Poland*, Vols. 1 and 2 (Oxford, Clarendon Press, 1981); O. Halecki, *A History of Poland* (New York: David McKay Co., 1976); Anthony Polonsky, *Politics in Independent Poland, 1921–1929* (Oxford: Clarendon Press, 1972); Jakub Karpinski, *Countdown: The Polish Upheavals of 1956, 1968, 1970, 1976, 1980. . .* (New York: Katz-Cohl, 1982); and Lawrence Goodwyn, *Breaking the Barrier: The Rise of Solidarity in Poland* (New York: Oxford University Press, 1991).

3. See "Weekly Record of Events," Radio Free Europe/Radio Liberty Research Institute (RFE/RL), *Report on Eastern Europe*, vol. 2, no. 12, March 22, 1991; David McQuaid, "Poland: The Growing Assertiveness of Minorities," RFE/RL, *Report on Eastern Europe*, vol. 2, no. 50, December 13, 1991.

4. *PAP*, Warsaw, December 31, 1992, in Federal Broadcast Information Service, *Daily Report: East Europe, FBIS-EEU–92–252*, December 31, 1992; *Radio Warsaw*, May 18, 1992, in *FBIS-EEU–92–097*, May 19, 1992; *AP*, May 23, 1992; *PAP*, Warsaw, June 23, 1992, in *FBIS-EEU–92–112*, June 24, 1992; *Warsaw Television*, July 9, 1992, in FBIS EEU–92–133, July 10, 1992.

5. *Rzeczpospolita*, Warsaw, July 8, 1992, in Federal Broadcast Information Service/Joint Publications Research Service, *Daily Report: East Europe, JPRS-EER–92–115*, August 25, 1992.

6. On the Small Constitution, see *Radio Warsaw*, November 17, 1992, in *FBIS-EEU–92–223*, November 18, 1992; On the Charter, see *Rzeczpospolita*, Warsaw, November 14–15, 1992, in *JPRS-EER–92–169*, December 15, 1992; *PAP*, Warsaw, January 22, 1993, in *FBIS-EEU–93–014*, January 25, 1993; and *Radio Warsaw*, January 21, 1993, in *FBIS-EEU–93–013*, January 22, 1993.

7. McQuaid, "Poland: The Growing Assertiveness of Minorities"; *PAP*, Warsaw, October 30, 1992, in *FBIS-EEU–92–212*, November 2, 1992.

8. Consult Jan B. de Weydenthal, "The Polish-German Reconciliation," RFE/RL, *Report on Eastern Report*, vol. 2, no. 27, July 5, 1991.

9. Check the interview with Polish Senator Dorota Simonides in *Rzeczpospolita*, Warsaw, December 10, 1990; and articles by Tadeusz Lubiejewski, "Poles, Germans, Silesia," *Trybuna Opolska*, August 2, 1990; Jerzy Tomaszewski, "The Tail of the Ostrich, a Few Words on Ethnic Minorities: The Germans," *Polityka*, Warsaw, April 28, 1990.

10. Mirosław Machnacki, "League of Expellees Proposes Szczecin, Zgorzelec, and Other Free Cities," *Gazeta Wyborcza*, Warsaw, July 10, 1990; Janina Hajduk-Nijakowska, "Manipulation of the German Minority in Upper Silesia," *Trybuna Opolska*, Opole, November 3–4, 1990.

11. *Warsaw Information Service*, December 3, 1992, in *FBIS-EEU–92–236*, December 8, 1992; *Warsaw Information Service*, December 7, 1992, in *FBIS-EEU–92–239*, December 11, 1992. Regarding neo-Nazi groups, see *Berliner Zeitung*, November 26, 1992, in *FBIS-EEU–92–231*, December 1, 1992, and *PAP*, December 8, 1992, in *FBIS-EEU–92–237*, December 9, 1992; *Trybuna Opolska*, January 21, 1993, in *FBIS-EEU–93–020*, February 2, 1993; and *PAP*, Warsaw, February 5, 1993, in *FBIS-EEU–93–024*, February 8, 1993.

12. See Anna Sabbat-Świdlicka, "Friendship Declarations Signed with Ukraine and Russia," RFE/RL, *Report on Eastern Report*, vol. 1, no. 44, November 2, 1990.

13. From interview with Paweł Stefanowski, head of the Lemko Citizens Circle, by Zaneta Semprich, "We Don't Want to Be a Bargaining Card," *Rzeczpospolita*, Warsaw, October 30, 1990.

14. For an abridged form of the Good Neighbor Declaration, see *Rzeczpospolita*, Warsaw, October 11, 1991, in *FBIS-EEU–91–201*, October 17, 1991.

15. See "Lithuanians and Poles," in *Kontrasty*, Warsaw, July 1990.

16. See Ewa K. Czaczkowska, "Concern for Culture and Language," in *Rzeczpospolita*, Warsaw, January 12, 1993, in *FBIS-EEU–93–010*, January 15, 1993; *Warsaw TV Network*, January 7, 1993, in *FBIS-EEU–93*, January 8, 1993.

17. See Louisa Vinton, "From the Margins to the Mainstream: The Confederation for an Independent Poland," RFE/RL, *Report on Eastern Report*, vol. 2, no. 46, November 15, 1991.

18. *Partie Polityczne w Polsce* (Warsaw: Polish Information Agency, October 1991); David McQuaid, "The Parliamentary Elections: A Postmortem," RFE/RL, *Report on Eastern Europe*, vol. 2, no. 45, November 8, 1991; and Marcin Dominik Zdort, "The Competitive Ticket of Death," *Rzeczpospolita*, Warsaw, June 6, 1993, in *FBIS-EEU–93–129*, July 8, 1993.

19. See *Country Reports on Human Rights Practices for 1992*, U.S. Department of State, February 1993.

20. Information on Polish nationalist parties is taken from *Partie Polityczne w Polsce*.

21. For information on the German minority, see Thomas Kleine-Brockhoff, "The Creeping Anschluss," *Die Zeit*, October 5, 1990; *Frankfurter Allgemeine Zeitung*, April 26, 1991; Daniel Tresenberg, "Who Wants Autonomy?" *Panorama*, Warsaw, April 14, 1991; Włodzimierz Kalicki, "The Closet Germans: A Holiday Issue Report on the German Minority in Poland," *Gazeta Wyborcza*, Warsaw, September 21, 1991; and Bolesław Wierzbiański, "On Polish and German Minorities," in *The Polish Review*, vol. 37, no. 4, 1992.

22. *Frankfurter Allgemeine Zeitung*, October 12, 1989, in *JPRS-EER–89–134*, December 4, 1989; *Rzeczpospolita*, Warsaw, December 11, 1992, in *JPRS-EER–93–004*, January 14, 1993.

23. *Dziennik Bałtycki*, Gdańsk, October 12, 1990, in *JPRS-EER–0–157*, November 26, 1990; *Trybuna*, Warsaw, October 16, 1990, in *FBIS-EEU–90–203*, October 19, 1990; *Frankfurter Allgemeine Zeitung*, April 26, 1991, in *JPRS-EER–91–081*, June 12, 1991; Halina Kowalik, "Short Cut," *Prawo i Życie*, Warsaw, May 4, 1991; and Barbara Cieszewska, "Upper Silesia Together or Separately," *Rzeczpospolita*, Warsaw, September 5, 1991,

24. See Mirosław Pęczak, "At the Unity Tavern: The Platform of Nationale Offensive Is Modeled on the Program of the NSDAP," *Polityka*, Warsaw, October 31, 1992, in *JPRS-EER–92–161*, November 20, 1992; Eva Wilk and Jerzy Ziołkowski, "Strong Men from a Woman's Field," *Spotkania*, Warsaw, no. 45, November 5–11, 1992, in *JPRS-EER–93–002*, January 7, 1993; *PAP*, Warsaw, February 24, 1993, in *FBIS EEU–93–037*, February 26, 1993.

25. "Poland and the German National Minority," *Tygodnik Gdański*, Gdansk, August 18, 1991.

26. Refer to interview with Dietar Brehmer in *Trybuna Opolska*, November 24, 1992, in *FBIS-EEU–92–237*, December 9, 1992; and Adam Jerzy Socha, "The German Minority in the Olsztyn Region," *Rzeczpospolita*, Warsaw, July 6, 1992, in *JPRS-EER–92–110*, August 19, 1992.

27. Sławomir Łódziński, "Social Political Activism and Cultural-Educational Activities Among National Minorities in Poland in the Period 1989–1992," Sejm Chancellery, International Affairs Section, Report no. 29, Warsaw, November 1992.

28. See *Gazeta i Nowoczesność*, Warsaw, June 7, 1990, in *JPRS-EER–90–119*, August 20, 1990; McQuaid, "The Growing Assertiveness of Minorities"; Grzegorz Polak, "Dispute Over the Cathedral," *Gazeta Wyborcza*, Warsaw, March 6, 1991; *Radio Warsaw*, August 24, 1992, in *FBIS-EEU–92–164*, August 24, 1992; and Hanna Maksim, *Glob*, Warsaw, January 3–5, 1992, in *JPRS-EER–92–017*, February 12, 1992.

29. *Warsaw Domestic Service*, March 1, 1990, in *FBIS-EEU–90–042*, March 2, 1990; see Ryszard Walicki, "National Minorities in Poland in 1992 in Light of Empirical Studies," Bureau of Studies and Expertise, Sejm Chancellery, no. 12, Warsaw, March 1993.

30. *Warsaw Domestic Service*, March 1, 1990; Walicki, "National Minorities in Poland in 1992 in Light of Empirical Studies," Bureau of Studies and Expertise, Sejm Chancellery, no. 12, Warsaw, March 1993.

31. *Rzeczpospolita*, Warsaw, October 30, 1990, in *JPRS-EER–91–001*, January 2, 1991.

32. Information on the Lemko organizations can be found in Walicki, "National Minorities in Poland in 1992 in Light of Empirical Studies."

33. *Trybuna*, Warsaw, October 25, 1990, in *JPRS-EER–91–001*, January 2, 1991; also see *Partie Polityczne w Polsce*; Agnieszka Magdziak-Miszewska, "Understanding Belarus," *Życie Warszawy*, Warsaw, October 16, 1990; and Stanislaw Brzeg-Wieluński, "The Belarusian Democratic Union," *Ład*, Warsaw, October 7, 1990; information on language issues can be found in *Rzeczpospolita*, Warsaw, March 12, 1991, in *JPRS-EER–91–055*, April 29, 1991.

34. *Tygodnik Solidarność*, Warsaw, May 4, 1990.

35. *Warsaw Domestic Service*, March 1, 1990; Walicki, "National Minorities in Poland in 1992 in Light of Empirical Studies."

36. Information on Polish regional organizations is taken from *Prawo i Życie*, Warsaw, June 23, 1990, in *JPRS-EEU–90–124*, September 30, 1990; and *Prawo i Życie*, May 4, 1991.

37. For more information, see *Radio Warsaw*, July 22, 1991, in *FBIS-EEU–91–141*, July 23, 1991; *Trybuna Robotnicza*, Warsaw, June 18, 1990, in *JPRS-EER–90–109*, July 24, 1990; *Wspólnota*, Warsaw, June 6, 1992; *Prawo i Życie*, May 4, 1991; "Weekly Review," RFE/RL *Research Report*, vol. 1, no. 7, February 14, 1992; and *Partie Polityczne w Polsce*.

38. Ciszewska, "Upper Silesia Together or Separately"; Kowalik, "Short Cut"; see also Andrzej Bęben, "Will There Be a Silesia?" *Sztandar Młodych*, Warsaw, September 5, 1991.

39. Bęben, "Will There Be A Silesia?" and Ciszewska, "Upper Silesia, Together or Separately."

40. *Prawo i Życie*, Warsaw, October 31, 1992, in *JPRS-EER–92–61*, November 20, 1992.

41. See Stanisław Bubin, *Prawo i Życie*, October 31, 1992; Kowalik, "Short Cut."

42. *Smena*, Bratislava, July 23, 1990, in *FBIS-EEU–90–143*, July 25, 1990; also see "A Panorama of Nationalities," *Rzeczpospolita*, Warsaw, March 12, 1991, in *JPRS-EER–91–055*, April 29, 1991; Walicki, "National Minorities in Poland in 1992 in Light of Empirical Studies."

43. From "A Panorama of Nationalities"; Walicki, "National Minorities in Poland in 1992 in Light of Empirical Studies"; and Charles Hoffman, *Gray Dawn: The Jews of Eastern Europe in the Post-Communist Era* (New York: Harper Collins, 1992), pp. 243–314.

13

Hungary

POPULATION

By East European standards, Hungary's population was relatively ethnically homogeneous. According to official Hungarian statistical estimates made available
in 1991, out of a population of 10,375,323, approximately 8.65 percent was
comprised of national, ethnic, and religious minorities.[1] The Gypsies (Roma)
were estimated at around 400,000, or nearly 3.9 percent, of the national population and almost half of the total minority numbers. Romani leaders believed that
their actual figure surpassed 500,000. Gypsies were officially considered an
ethnic minority rather than a national minority because of the absence of a
Romani homeland and a unified or standardized language. In 1991, German
numbers stood at about 175,000, or 1.69 percent of the population, although the
figure has since declined due to emigration. The Slovaks constituted the third-
largest minority, in the vicinity of 110,000 or 1.06 percent of the population.
Jews, considered members of a religious confession rather than an ethnic group,
numbered around 80,000; Croats were also estimated at approximately 80,000;
and the Romanian minority close to 25,000. The remaining minorities included
smaller groups of Greeks, Serbs, Slovenes, Armenians, Bulgarians, and Poles.

HISTORICAL OVERVIEW

During the nineteenth century, Hungary maintained a measure of autonomy
within the Habsburg Empire as Vienna authorized the government in Budapest
to help administer its large multi-national state.[2] Periodic Hungarian nationalist
revolts to gain full independence were subdued, and the Habsburgs pursued a
policy of divide-and-rule, playing off one nationality against another by providing selective political and economic benefits. After the empire was transformed
into a "dual monarchy" in 1867, Budapest obtained greater control over territories that included substantial Hungarian populations in Transylvania, Slovakia,
and Ruthenia. This new arrangement served to intensify hostilities between Hun-

Hungary: Population (1991)

Ethnic Groups	Number	% of Population
Magyars	9,477,362	91.35
Roma (Gypsies)	404,461	3.90
Germans	175,000	1.69
Slovaks	110,000	1.06
Jews	80,000	0.77
Croats	80,000	0.77
Romanians	25,000	0.24
Greeks	6,000	0.06
Serbs	5,000	0.05
Slovenes	5,000	0.05
Armenians	3,000	0.03
Bulgarians	2,500	0.02
Poles	2,000	0.02
Total Minorities	897,961	8.65
Total Population	10,375,323	100.00

garians and the subordinate Romanian, Slovak, Ruthenian, Ukrainian, and Croatian populations. Moreover, Hungarian activists continued to press for full independence from Austria and for extensive social and economic reforms.

At the close of World War One, the Habsburg Empire disintegrated and Budapest relinquished large tracts of territory in central and southeast Europe under the 1920 Treaty of Trianon. In fact, Hungary lost about two-thirds of its lands as punishment for its alliance with the Central Powers of Austria and Germany. Nearly 3 million ethnic Hungarians were left outside of Hungary, in the Slovak and Ruthenian regions of Czechoslovakia, in Transylvania and Banat (Romania), and in the Vojvodina region of Serbia (Yugoslavia). These drastic border changes left a lingering sense of resentment in Hungary and stimulated the activities of revisionist and irredentist forces inside and outside the country. They also eliminated sizable ethnic minorities from the Hungarian state and diluted a potential source of internal friction. The minority population in interwar Hungary did not exceed 10 percent of the total number of inhabitants. In general, it was not a major point of contention, either domestically or internationally. The Budapest government adopted a nationality decree providing for the equality of all Hungarian citizens regardless of their language, religion, or ethnicity. Native tongues were also permitted as the language of instruction in schools with minority students, and a high degree of tolerance was shown for the cultural development of minority groups.

During the late 1930s, Budapest increasingly allied itself with Nazi Germany and Fascist Italy, as both powers appeared to be the most promising patrons for regaining former Hungarian territories. At the onset of World War Two, Hungary regained parts of Slovakia and Ruthenia as the Germans carved up the Czechoslovak republic, as well as portions of Transylvania and Yugoslavia following the German invasion. But these lands were lost again at the close of

World War Two as the price of the Axis defeat by the Allied powers. The minority population in Hungary shrank further after the war. The number of Germans decreased by half to about 220,000 following mass expulsions by the post-war administration. The remaining Germans were initially subject to repression and virtual second-class status. Their situation improved during the 1950s when they obtained equal status with other Hungarian citizens. Nevertheless, restrictions were maintained on their collective activities, and thousands of Germans continued to leave the country; by the 1980s, under 200,000 were left.

Jewish figures decreased dramatically during World War Two, from about 825,000 to 250,000; the majority perished in the Holocaust following mass deportations to Nazi death camps after the German occupation of Hungary in March 1944. Thousands more emigrated to Israel and the West after the war; by the late 1960s, about 80,000 Jews were left in Hungary, and the number has remained stable ever since. Jewish political and cultural life was stifled by the Communist regime, but after Stalin's death Jews were able to restore many of their cultural, religious, and educational activities. In fact, Jewish life in Hungary, particularly in Budapest where the vast majority resided, proved to be the most vibrant in Communist-controlled Eastern Europe.

The Gypsy, or Romani, population also sustained serious losses during the war as a result of deportations and Nazi extermination, although precise numbers have proved difficult to ascertain. They maintained a high birthrate, although their numbers remained under-reported in the national census. For example, the official count in 1960 was about 25,000, but the unofficial estimate exceeded 200,000. Many continued to resist integration into Hungarian society and experienced persistent public prejudice. Gypsies did not benefit from an organized political, religious, or cultural life, but various governmental economic programs were launched to improve their material conditions and employment opportunities.

Hungary's south Slav population dropped after the two world wars as a result of territorial changes and demographic movements. From approximately a quarter of a million people in 1941, the total barely reached 100,000 after the war. The Croats along the Drava River formed the largest group, followed by Serbs and Slovenes settled in a few territorial pockets. They did not present a significant source of dispute between Hungary and Yugoslavia and were permitted to create their own cultural and social associations. The Romanian population in the eastern counties of Hungary also declined from about 1 million in 1940 to a little over 12,000 in the 1970 census. Despite some claims of discrimination and persecution by Romanian nationalists, Budapest's policies proved reasonably tolerant and congruent with its treatment of other minorities. Hence, the Romanians were able to establish their own schools, clubs, libraries, and cultural associations, although many remained at various stages of cultural assimilation.

The Slovak population in Hungary has been relatively dispersed in several northern and western counties. Their numbers decreased from approximately

200,000 at the close of World War Two to under 22,000 in the 1970 census. Much of the loss was the consequence of a major population exchange with Czechoslovakia after World War Two, when about 73,000 Slovaks were more or less forcibly transferred to Slovakia and a commensurate number of Magyars was dispatched to Hungary. At various times, Slovak nationalists claimed that the Slovak minority bore the brunt of human rights violations and sustained assimilationist pressures. Some also asserted that the Slovak population was larger than Budapest admitted because a proper census had not been conducted, while many Slovaks avoided revealing their identity for fear of repercussions. Figures in excess of 150,000 have been floated by some Slovak activists. Despite claims of persecution and enforced Magyarization under the post-Stalinist governments, the Slovaks were able to establish their own national organizations, schools, and cultural groups. Nonetheless, the departure of a large intellectual stratum after the war had a negative impact on ethnic coherence and cultural development among the remaining Slovaks.

In general, under the reformist Communist government of János Kádár, the Nationalities Department in the Ministry of Culture was reasonably active in furthering schooling, publishing, and cultural activities. Nevertheless, as in other Communist states, the various nationality associations were supervised by state bodies and scrutinized for their ideological and political content. Furthermore, there was no distinct law to assist in the preservation of minority cultures and there was an absence of authentic political representation. During the 1980s, the government increasingly stressed the close relationship between the treatment of minorities in Hungary and the position of Hungarian minorities in neighboring states. It emphasized its own record as a policy to be emulated by other Communist governments, stressing bilingualism and biculturalism rather than autonomy or self-determination.

OFFICIAL POLICIES

In the Hungarian constitution of 1949, Article 61 stated that all Hungarian citizens were equal before the law and enjoyed equal rights; any discrimination based on sex, religious denomination, or nationality would be severely punished by the law. The Hungarian People's Republic guaranteed for all resident nationalities the right to use their mother tongue and to cultivate their own cultures. Despite these lofty guarantees, the Communist regime adhered to Leninist principles regarding its nationalities policies. Any minority aspirations were subsumed under the process of "socialist construction" and the leading role of the party. Moreover, since there was no law that delineated the rights of minorities, they had no means of seeking redress for instances of discrimination. The government permitted "democratic associations" of minority groups to function, but these were primarily official organs of the Communist regime. In effect, nationality problems and ethnic aspirations in Communist Hungary were largely ignored.

Since the democratic turnaround in 1989, the Hungarian government has deemed the arrest and reversal of state-sponsored assimilation as the main priority of its minorities program. This policy was divided into three main tenets, the first of which involved active protection to preserve the identities of ethnic and religious minorities, such as the right to uphold their culture, education, and language. Second was a provision for the special treatment of minorities, or "positive discrimination," to ensure equal opportunities for all citizens regardless of their ethnic identity. Third was the assurance of cultural autonomy, to be exercised on the local governmental level. The post-Communist government granted minorities the right to self-organization, lending more credibility to existing and newly founded minority associations, and began a more comprehensive codification of minority rights.

In October 1989, the Hungarian National Assembly adopted a series of constitutional amendments that created a legal framework for multi-party elections and augmented the recognized human and civil rights. The amended constitution stated that "the Hungarian Republic recognizes the inalienable and inviolable basic rights of man" and that the state was responsible for ensuring those rights. Nonetheless, some of those rights could be suspended in situations where the "security of the state" or the "internal social order" was endangered; however, any elaboration on conditions that would warrant such a suspension was absent from the document. Most importantly, the amended constitution enfranchised minorities, stating that they retained the right to their own culture, religion, and the use of their mother tongue. Providing redress for human rights violations, the constitution allowed for the establishment of the office of Commissioner of Human Rights in the National Assembly (or Parliamentary Commissioner) to act as an ombudsman.[3]

Hungary's minister of justice Kálman Kulcsár put forward a proposal to allow each national minority to be represented by 1 deputy elected by the parliament, thus exceeding the 386 mandated deputies. Meanwhile, minority participation in local council self-governments was legally guaranteed. Churches and religious groups were unable to receive similar representation because, as Minister Kulcsár stated, "the National Assembly would become a parliament of churches rather than parties." However, this proposal would present problems for Jewish representation since the official definition of a Jew was a member of a religious group rather than an ethnic minority. An August 1992 government proposal on parliamentary representation for national minorities called for a minimum of 3,000 votes in order to garner a seat in the National Assembly. The National Minority Roundtable declared the proposal unrealistic and rejected it on the grounds that if it was implemented, some minority candidates would require 100 percent of the minority's vote to win representation. Thus, for some groups, such as the Poles and the Bulgarians, whose numbers fell short of the 3,000 mark, there would be no representation at all.[4]

In the constitutional amendments adopted in June and August 1990, Article

32 defined the role of the Parliamentary Commissioner for Human Rights, who was to be nominated by the state president and elected by parliament. The commissioner's activities were overseen by a body appointed by representatives of all national and ethnic minority groups. Article 68 was a revision of Article 61 of the 1949 constitution and stated that Hungary's national minorities shared in "the power of the people and are a constituent element." The article guaranteed their collective participation in public life, protected the cultivation of their own culture, allowed for the use of and instruction in their mother tongue, permitted the adoption of original ethnic names, and provided the right to establish local and national self-governing bodies. The use of the mother tongue in court proceedings was also guaranteed by additional legislation.[5]

The Draft Law on Local Government allowed the local administration, within the limits of the law, to "join a regional or national association to promote and safeguard its interests; cooperate with a foreign local government, within the scope of its functions and authority; and join international organizations of local governments." In effect, this permitted local municipalities numerically dominated by a national minority to participate in the activities of national-minority organizations. As to the functions of local governments, Section 8 of the law stated that they must "ensure the exercise of the national and ethnic minorities' rights." In mayoral and local council elections, the national or ethnic minority's candidate who received the most votes automatically became that minority's local spokesman. If the minority candidate was not elected as a councilor, he or she could still attend the meetings of the municipal council as an *ex-officio* member.

In further amendments to the Hungarian constitution, Law 63 passed in early 1990 stipulated that "national and ethnic minorities may establish local and national autonomous governments." Autonomous governance was defined in chapter 9 as the administration of local public affairs and the exercise of local public authority in the interest of the populace.[6] Law 27 adopted in 1990 allowed for the parliamentary representation of Hungary's seven main minorities (Germans, Gypsies, Romanians, Slovaks, Serbs, Croats, and Slovenes), in addition to the Jewish community. They were to be elected by parliament through a secret ballot, but this provision was subsequently revoked by a constitutional amendment in June 1990.

Although many of the aforementioned legal stipulations conferred certain rights upon minorities, a comprehensive law on minority rights, the Draft Law on the Rights of National and Ethnic Minorities in Hungary (the Minority Codex) had still not been approved, ratified, or implemented by the close of 1992. The Hungarian government, under the auspices of the Office of National and Ethnic Minorities (ONEM), the Justice Department, which replaced the Secretariat for National and Ethnic Minorities, the parliament, and the umbrella minority organization, the National Minority Roundtable (NMR), collaborated on drafting the project for a new minority law. The ONEM was established in

September 1990 as an organ of state administration, and not a body of interest representation, to coordinate the implementation of the official minority policy. Its chairman, János Wolfart, sought to establish an active government minority-protection policy in order to halt assimilationist trends, to grant minority groups a large measure of cultural autonomy, and to enhance minority education by introducing a network of schools using minority languages from kindergarten to middle level. He also underscored that the minorities needed educational assistance from their mother countries and that the print and broadcast media in minority languages had to be expanded.

In June 1992, the Constitutional Court ruled that parliament was in "default" for failing to draft the comprehensive law on national minorities by the original May 1992 deadline. It specified that the error should be rectified by December 1992. In addition, in July 1992 the ONEM promised to submit to parliament draft legislation granting parliamentary representation to ethnic minorities. If adopted, the measure would take effect in 1994, providing 13 more seats for the national minorities. In September 1990, Hungarian Radio announced its intention to broadcast Slovene-, German-, Romanian-, Serbian-, and Slovak-language programs six days a week rather than two. It also promised to increase the power of the broadcasts so that they could be received nationwide.

The purpose of the Minority Codex was to protect minority communities and individuals from discriminatory policies and assimilationist measures practiced by individuals or enacted by organs of the state, especially executive authority. It would also seek to protect minorities from "the paternalistic or even dictatorial aspirations of their own organizations or institutes." Its basic premise was that the right to national, ethnic, and linguistic identity constituted "a fundamental human right." The Minority Codex would regulate the appointment of parliamentary ombudsmen for minority rights, allow minorities to appoint their own representatives at the local level, and stipulate the legal framework in which minority organizations could be created. The inclusion of provisions for minority organizations created by the "mother country," such as the Secretariat for Hungarians Abroad, was also planned for inclusion in the draft law.[7]

In March 1993, the six parliamentary parties finally reached agreement on the passage of the minority law that required a two-thirds majority vote. The administration was authorized to supply 500 million *forint* per year to local governments in support of minority education, culture, media, and language use. Starting in July 1993, Hungarian Radio's Szeged station would broadcast daily programs in Romanian and Slovak and also expand local German-, Croatian-, and Serbian-language programming. The draft bill recognized thirteen "authentic ethnic minorities" (Bulgarian, Romani, Gypsy, Greek, Croat, Polish, German, Armenian, Romanian, Ruthenian, Serb, Slovak, Slovene, and Ukrainian) and confirmed that any group of 1,000 persons could apply for recognition as a minority. Hungarian deputies also emphasized that the census laws would need to be modified to enable all citizens to declare their minority affiliation anonymously.[8] In July 1993, the Hungarian parliament finally passed a bill on the rights of national and ethnic minorities. Under the law, a minority was defined as any group with at least 100 years of residence in Hungary and with its own language and culture. The choice of identity was voluntary, and minorities had the right to set up their own institutions, including "local and national self-governments" to ensure their "cultural autonomy."

In June 1993, the National Assembly also passed a nationality or citizenship law. According to its provisions, Hungarian citizenship was largely based on descent. Children of Hungarian citizens and of foreign citizens married to Hungarians automatically became Hungarian citizens. Non-Hungarian citizens could apply for naturalization after eight years of continuous residence; applicants had to pass a constitutional examination in Hungarian. Preferential treatment in naturalization was to be given to foreigners married to Hungarians for at least three years, to widows and widowers of Hungarian citizens, and to persons given refugee status by Budapest. In addition, former Hungarian citizens and their descendants could now be renaturalized: those deprived of citizenship were entitled to have it restored.[9]

Budapest also initialed several bilateral treaties in which the position of minorities was clarified. For example, Article 19 of the February 1992 German-Hungarian Treaty called for the protection of national minorities and specifically discussed the situation of German Hungarians in light of the agreement. It underscored that Hungary would not countenance the forced assimilation of the German minority, which could maintain the right to develop its ethnic, cultural, and religious identity freely, including the use of the German language. Budapest would protect the identity of the German minority through legislative measures.[10]

In recent years, there has been an increase in Hungarian radical-right activity directed against some minorities, specifically Roma. This has included political protests staged by ultra-nationalist parties and violent attacks by skinhead youth. The Hungarian authorities have had to confront the serious problem of hate crimes. Section 1 of the Criminal Code stated that "incitement to hatred against, respectively, the Hungarian nation, a nationality, people, denomination or race, and individual groups of the populace" was a felony. Section 2 stated that the use of expressions that were insulting or demeaning to the Hungarian nation, or to a minority nationality, people, denomination, or race, was a misdemeanor. However, laws enacted against hate crimes could be interpreted as conflicting with certain civil liberties. The Constitutional Court Decision No. 30 of May 1992 stated that the "Criminal Code of Laws unnecessarily and disproportionately restricts the freedom of expression and the freedom of the press guaranteed in the constitution . . . and is therefore unconstitutional." Paragraph 8 of the court decision underscored that the Hungarian Republic recognized the inviolable and inalienable basic rights of people and that it was the state's duty to respect and to protect these rights. The state could restrict a fundamental right only if the protection or enforcement of another fundamental right or liberty, or the protection of some other constitutional value, could not be otherwise achieved. The court still upheld the principle that the incitement of hatred was a criminal offense as defined in the Criminal Code but deemed that the criminality of "abuse" was unconstitutional.[11]

The Hungarian government under Prime Minister József Antall placed substantial emphasis on the well-being of some 3.5 million Magyars residing in neighboring states—a number equivalent to one-third of Hungary's population. Shortly after the April 1990 elections, which brought Antall's Hungarian Democratic Forum (HDF) to power, both the parliament and the government embarked on active policies to address the concerns of Magyar minorities. Parliament discussed a draft resolution calling upon the Hungarian government to initiate talks with neighboring states to obtain bilateral agreements mutually protecting the rights of minorities. In the words of parliamentary deputy Gáspár Miklós Tamás, "Hungary is ready to give its minorities all those rights which it claims for the Magyars beyond her borders. [Hungary] would like to establish the cultural autonomy of national minorities in Central and Eastern Europe by means of a series of bilateral contacts."[12] President Árpád Göncz declared that the primary goal of Hungarian foreign policy was the "enforcement of collective and personal human rights for Magyars living in the Carpathian basin."[13] Göncz went further in stating that "the Magyar minorities in neighboring countries are subject to the laws of the countries in which they live, but the president of Hungary has a duty to take notice of their situation and ensure the observance of their human and civil rights."[14]

In 1990, the post-Communist government established the Secretariat for Hungarians Abroad to rectify the absence of a viable Magyar minorities policy under the Kádár regime. The secretariat was responsible for maintaining links with Magyar organizations outside Hungary and for representing these minorities in international diplomacy. Most of its financial backing came from the Foreign Ministry's budget; its director, Political State Secretary Géza Entz, has pursued numerous consultations with minority organizations in Slovakia, Romania, Ukraine, and Serbia to ensure the rights of approximately 3.5 million Magyars. The secretariat was an official department of the Hungarian government that monitored the situation of Magyar minorities and endeavored to protect them by eliciting guarantees from neighboring states on civil rights and cultural autonomy.[15]

Hungary's activist policy of advocating the rights of Magyar minorities has caused some trepidation in the capitals of Slovakia, Romania, and Serbia. Charges of resurgent nationalism and irredentism have been leveled at Hungary, despite the fact that Budapest reiterated publicly that it abided by the post–World War Two territorial and border settlements, as well as the 1975 Helsinki Final Act, which rejected the use of force as a means to alter international borders. The strategy of the Hungarian government was either to internationalize the minority issue by adopting European norms on minority policy or to establish bilateral agreements with neighboring countries to ensure Magyar rights. In particular, the government has endeavored to generate international concern for the situation of the 1.5 million Magyars in Romania. Its efforts were due in part to the perceived intransigence of the Romanian authorities in settling the issue and were intended to demonstrate Budapest's determination to abide by the norms established by the Helsinki process. Hungary was better able to deny accusations of irredentism by consistently vowing to adhere to the principles outlined in the Helsinki Final Act. Budapest underscored that tensions involving minorities could lead to interstate conflicts and thus threaten the security of the region. It therefore tried to enlist the assistance of the Council of Europe, the EC, and the CSCE to help resolve its disputes with Bucharest.

For the past two years, Hungary has been seeking international support for the creation of an institutional framework for the protection of minority rights. It has promoted the codification of rights embodying the free use of the mother tongue in the administrative and judicial systems in minority areas, education in the mother tongue from kindergarten through university level, and proportional minority representation at all administrative levels, including the national parliament. These rights fall under the aegis of collective rights, which, in the government's view, provided a more adequate bulwark against discrimination and assimilation than simply individual rights. The governments of Romania, Serbia, and Slovakia have rejected the Hungarian concept of "collective rights" on the grounds that these had no legal basis. They asserted that previously established international agreements conferred civil and political rights on all citizens and not on groups or collectivities. Officials also feared that most of the funding for such minority entitlements would be earmarked from state budgets, even though the Hungarian government has also elicited financial assistance for its own minorities from neighboring "mother countries."[16]

In agreements with Ukraine in June 1991, the Hungarian government succeeded in obtaining guarantees for collective and individual rights for the Transcarpathian Magyars. Budapest hoped to use the agreement as a model for further negotiations with neighboring states containing large Magyar communities. Indeed, Croatia subscribed to this arrangement, and a similar agreement was concluded with Germany in the 1992 treaty. In the Hungarian-Ukrainian bilateral agreement, both countries were to respect their citizens' right to decide to which nationality they belonged. Both governments were also required to ensure that the ethnic, cultural, linguistic, and religious identities of minorities were preserved. The minorities were to be involved in the establishment of regional state bodies dealing with minority affairs. The agreement also provided for the creation of a joint Hungarian-Ukrainian committee to coordinate educational activities in the mother tongues of minority groups. As stipulated in the agreement, certain rights were ensured for members of minorities on both an individual and a collective basis. The Hungarian government calculated that collective rights for minorities would eventually be widely recognized internationally. In addition, Budapest and Kyiv prepared to open a Ukrainian consulate in Hungary and a Hungarian consulate in Transcarpathia. Budapest hoped that these bilateral agreements would serve as a model for expanding cooperation with neighboring states encompassing sizable Magyar communities. The only domestic criticisms came from ultra-nationalist groupings that harbored latent claims to the Ruthenian region and questioned Ukraine's territorial integrity; they included the former deputy president of the ruling HDF, István Csurka.[17]

Whether through international forums or through bilateral treaties, Budapest's minorities policy became a major foreign-policy objective, not only as a means to promote cooperative relations with its neighbors, but also to demonstrate to the West, specifically to the EC and the Council of Europe, that Hungary abided by international agreements on human rights and was striving toward the Western model of a civil society that guaranteed minority rights. Official and public concern for Magyar minorities abroad also served to defuse the criticisms and rationale of small but vocal nationalist and irredentist groups. By advocating rights for all minorities, while adhering to international security accords, the Hungarian government assumed the mantle of protector of the Magyars within the parameters of established diplomatic norms.

Aside from the obvious benefits they provided in terms of economic, cultural, and military cooperation, bilateral agreements served Budapest's interests by guaranteeing the rights of Magyar minorities. Instead of relying on an umbrella doctrine that would apply to the entire region, the government maintained a measure of flexibility in negotiations with its neighbors, modulating between individual and collective rights. This flexibility was also designed to regulate the extent of reciprocity between states regarding their respective minority groups. For example, the position of over 1.5 million Magyars in Romania appeared to be of greater practical importance than that of the approximately 25,000 Romanians in Hungary. However, the signing of a bilateral agreement between Hungary and Romania was inhibited by continuing disagreements over minority issues. Budapest wanted guarantees for minority rights to be stipulated in any state agreements, while Bucharest insisted that a bilateral treaty should include phraseology that renounced any territorial aspirations or border revisions. Both countries refused to yield on their respective positions and contended that issues raised by the other party were already dealt with in international documents, including the Helsinki Final Act.

The democratically elected Hungarian government has explicitly assumed responsibility for all Magyar populations, indicating a more activist policy than that of the previous regime. This responsibility often extended to the political as well as the cultural sphere, and the treatment of Magyars in neighboring countries has served as a litmus test for bilateral relations. According to Prime Minister József Antall, although minority questions were not the only factor in inter-state relations, "we find it impossible to have good relations with a country that mistreats its Hungarian minority."[18] The Budapest government, dominated by the self-proclaimed "national party," the Hungarian Democratic Forum (HDF), has avoided making compromises on the minority issue, despite or because of the fact that they were dealing with authoritarian or quasi-nationalist governments in Serbia, Romania, and Slovakia. According to Gyula Kiss Csaba, a member of the HDF presidium, the situation of minorities in Hungary was different from the position of Magyars in neighboring countries because of the demographic ratio, geographical situation, and relations with the mother country. Absolute reciprocity in minority rights was therefore impractical and unnecessary. In addition, the government avoided making the Magyar minority issue into a factor in domestic politics, while seeking a "cooperative regional framework" whereby all forms of nationalism and ethnocentrism could be resisted.[19]

The regional instability caused by the Yugoslav wars, by manifestations of anti-Magyar violence in Romania, and by the break-up of Czechoslovakia has prompted some officials in Budapest to call for the redefinition of Hungary's citizenship law as a means of offering protection to Magyar communities. Interior Minister Péter Boross declared that preparations were under way for a law that would "make it easier for everyone born to a Hungarian mother to obtain Hungarian citizenship, while making it harder for those who were not." The Hungarian media suggested applying the broad-based German legal model for repatriation. Boross stated that if the government failed to espouse a redefined citizenship law, either adopted from the German model or from the "option rights" provision in Article 63 of the Trianon Peace Treaty, it could not "claim moral legitimacy, and would directly violate its own principles."[20]

Once Budapest strengthens its political and economic bonds with Western Europe, it may be able to use its newly acquired European ties as leverage to ensure Magyar rights in neighboring states. On the other hand, if the situation worsens to the point of widespread inter-ethnic violence involving Magyar minorities in Vojvodina or Transylvania, nationalist fervor might also increase in Hungary. Such a development may at best result in the ossification of the government's position and preclude any agreements with neighbors. At worst, the political climate would give rise to a radically nationalist government more inclined toward militant measures to settle simmering minority problems.

The war in the former Yugoslavia raised serious concerns in Budapest. Thousands of Yugoslav Magyars sought refuge in Hungary not only to escape the war in Croatia but also because of fears emanating from the increasingly chauvinistic and xenophobic policies of the Serbian regime in Vojvodina. Prime Minister Antall's government understood its own limitations in influencing Serbia's minority policies, particularly in light of Serbia's persistent accusations about Hungarian irredentism and partisanship. In fact, Antall has been one of the stronger advocates of an international settlement of the conflict. Secretary Entz has alluded to potential security problems for the West stemming from ethnic conflicts in the former Yugoslavia, stating that "Western voters do not yet fully understand the real problems in this region, and they are not yet aware of the fact that chaos in Eastern Europe will also directly affect their long-term security."[21] As a result, Budapest's policy has focused on making the West more attuned to ethnic struggles in the region and on enticing the EC to draw upon its economic and political resources to formulate viable solutions.

HUNGARIAN NATIONALISTS

Hungarian Democratic Forum (HDF)
Magyar Demokrata Fórum (MDF)

The HDF was established in September 1987 in Lakitelek as an opposition group to the ruling Communists. It defined itself as a center-right "national party" and won the first multi-party parliamentary elections in March and April 1990, gaining 164 out of 386 seats, or 42.26 percent of the total. The HDF was composed of three broad political-ideological trends: Christian democrat, populist-nationalist, and national liberal; all were recognized as integral components of the Forum. Its chairman, József Antall, who was considered to belong to the centrist Christian democratic stream, became prime minister of the first post-Communist government. He consistently tried to balance the three HDF wings and prevent the growth of extremism. The HDF endeavored to have a national-and ethnic-minorities law passed by the Hungarian National Assembly and advocated the drafting of a regional charter providing for the rights of all European minorities. The government has provided financial assistance for all minorities, including Gypsies, to help support their political and cultural organizations and to fund their election campaigns.[22] The HDF was referred to as a "national party" because one of its primary activities since taking control of the government was the protection of Magyar minorities abroad. Through organizations such as the Secretariat for Hungarians Abroad, the government has made the position of Magyar minorities one of its core foreign-policy objectives.

Critics have accused the HDF of anti-Semitism and other extreme nationalistic tendencies, although such trends were visible only in one section of the forum. In August 1992, *Magyar Fórum* published an article by István Csurka, a writer and deputy president of the HDF, that was peppered with anti-Semitic and other racist remarks. It suggested that Hungary was the victim of the ubiquitous Jewish "conspiracy" that obstructed the country's democratic transformation. Csurka attributed the apparent deterioration of Hungary to "genetic causes" and discussed the need for Hungarian *lebensraum* (living space). The virulent nationalism that underlay the tract caused a political uproar in Hungary and spawned a pro-Csurka ideological movement called *Magyar Út* (The Hungarian Way). In October 1992, Csurka's supporters started to establish their own network of "circles" or "workshops" within the HDF, financed by the Hungarian Way Foundation. Their objective was to educate a new class of politicians concerned with "national and patriotic" questions and to gain broad support among rank-and-file HDF members. Because of Csurka's high position in the party, there was a pronounced fear that the HDF would swing toward the radical right, elevating a xenophobic ideology to the forefront of Hungarian politics. Alternatively, there were fears that the HDF could split into separate parties prior to the next general elections.

A number of parliamentary deputies from the HDF and the Independent Smallholders' Party (ISP) displayed some sympathy toward Csurka's views, although HDF leaders claimed Csurka's supporters were clearly in the minority in the National Assembly. HDF leaders met on two occasions in late August 1992 to discuss Csurka's tract, but no official condemnation was issued as they calculated that the storm would soon subside. But Csurka's activities continued to fuel controversy by tacitly lending support to the burgeoning neo-Nazi skinhead movement and clearly hurting Hungary's reputation as a model post-Communist state. Csurka's policies were eventually condemned by Prime Minister Antall, who asserted that Csurka wanted to seize political power in the country through a takeover in the HDF. Meanwhile, the HDF presidium ruled that the "Hungarian Way" circles were not permitted to operate within the HDF basic party organization. In response, at its first national congress in February 1993, *Magyar Út* was launched as a "national movement" that would operate alongside the HDF. Csurka evidently estimated that the time was not yet ripe to establish a distinct political party, while *Magyar Út* could attract support from a broad range of citizens dissatisfied with the adverse effects of economic reform.

Csurka claimed *Magyar Út* had some 60,000 followers, organized in about 400 local groups. It cooperated closely with the "Imre Mikó Circle" within the HDF parliamentary caucus, which sought to "strengthen Hungarian consciousness," and the Society for the Protection of the Hungarian Spirit. In May 1993, a handful of HDF deputies established a "Hungarian Truth National Policy" inside the party's parliamentary faction. One of the group's leaders, Lajos Horváth, declared that it would support Csurka if he were ousted from the HDF. Some sources estimated that about 10 percent of HDF's membership backed Csurka's extremist positions. In June 1993, the HDF's national steering committee voted to expel Csurka from the party. Csurka announced the creation of a new Hungarian Justice Party (HJP) that would include the *Magyar Út* network and about 10 parliamentary deputies. The party intended to promote a more "nationally oriented policy" and keep a close eye on "Hungarian national interests."[23]

Independent Smallholders' Party—Torgyán Faction (ISP)
Független Kisgazda Párt—Torgyán Frakció (FKGP)

The ISP was a mainstream party and one of the HDF's coalition partners, but the self-styled Torgyán faction, named after the ISP legal-affairs expert József Torgyán, has displayed various ultra-rightist sympathies. The faction split from the governing coalition in February 1992 and held the support of 9 out of 46 ISP parliamentary deputies. Torgyán, a virulent anti-Communist, stated that fascist rule in war-time Hungary paled in comparison to the activities of the Communist regime. After the arrest of László Romhányi and the subsequent disarray within the radical rightist Hungarian National Alliance (see below), it was reported that the HNA would be allowed to reestablish its headquarters at the main office of the ISP at Belgrad Quay, a street in Budapest. The ISP also allegedly set up a club for Budapest skinheads in the basement of their headquarters. In January 1993, Torgyán announced the creation of a new nationalist bloc, styled as the Christian National Union, that would build solidarity to "save the Hungarian people." During April 1993, Torgyán instructed all ISP organizations to support the "Hungarian Way" circles in order to help build a right-wing electoral alliance.[24]

Christian National Union (CNU)
Keresztény Nemzeti Unió (KNU)

The CNU was one of several right-wing organizations that appealed for a "renewal" of the Hungarian nation after decades of imposed Communist "internationalism." Like other extreme-right groups, it not only regarded the stipulations of the 1920 Trianon Treaty to be unjust but also called for a redefinition of Hungary's borders to include the Magyar minorities in neighboring states. On the seventieth anniversary of the treaty, the CNU staged a protest rally in Budapest. Despite its revisionist pronouncements, the CNU appeared to be less militant than other rightist groups. It advocated a "peaceful" way of redrawing borders and did not seem to espouse an explicitly racist philosophy. It was unclear whether the organization was supported by any other political groups or religious bodies despite its vehemently Christian pronouncements.

Holy Crown Society (HCS)
Szentkorona Társulat (SzT)

The Holy Crown Society was a purportedly neo-fascist grouping that claimed to exert substantial influence over the activities and organization of Hungary's nascent skinhead movement. Its leadership and goals were not widely known, but there was a suspected connection with László Romhányi, the editor of the neo-fascist political journal *Szent Korona* (Holy Crown). The skinhead groups were loosely structured, although there appeared to be some direction from extreme rightist groups such as the '56 Anti-Fascist and Anti-Bolshevik Association; indeed, skinhead youths have acted as security guards for these organizations. Most skinhead spokesmen espoused a Nazi-like philosophy regarding the superiority of the Magyar race. There were strong parallels with other skinhead groups in Europe and North America in their appearance, the youthful age of members, their political inclinations, and their avid use of violence. Skinhead groups have not formed any distinct political parties, but they were associated with various right-wing youth groups. By the end of 1992, at least four such groups had been legally registered. According to the police unit investigating race-related crimes in Hungary, during 1992 there were approximately 450 active skinheads and about 1,000 sympathizers in Budapest alone.

Independent National Youth Front (INYF)
Független Nemzeti Ifjúsági Front (FNIF)

This neo-Fascist organization was established in October 1992, claiming nearly 2,000 members nationwide, most of whom were active or former skinheads. The INYF possessed several branches in the towns of Eger, Veszprém, Szeged, Miskolc, and Debrecen. According to István Szőke, the self-proclaimed "patron of the Hungarian skinheads," the INYF aimed to "organize the military and patriotic education of young people" and provide physical education, sports training, and camping programs for nationalist youth. Its political goals included the removal of Jews and former Communist activists from positions of power, alleging that this small "elite" still controlled national life. If skinheads could be considered to have a unifying goal, it was the creation of an ethnically pure Hungary. Most skinhead activities have involved violent acts, such as the beating and the stabbing of non-Magyars, usually Gypsies; Hungarian police recorded 51 assaults on Roma and foreigners during 1992. Often these juveniles have shouted Fascist slogans and displayed Nazi relics, such as swastikas, pictures of Adolf Hitler, and symbols of the Arrow Cross movement, Hungary's war-time Fascist organization. Skinhead groups in Hungary were also believed to maintain contacts with neo-Fascist Hungarian organizations in the West. In one notorious incident, Hungarian skinheads, along with skinheads from Austria and Germany, attempted to disrupt a 1991 May Day festival in Szépasszonyvölgy, assaulting Romani participants and engaging in verbal abuse. On October 23, 1992, skinheads sporting Nazi symbols disrupted a rally commemorating the anniversary of the 1956 uprising and the 1989 proclamation of a post-Communist Hungary, forcing President Göncz to leave without speaking. The Interior Ministry was criticized for allegedly ignoring the growing danger of neo-Nazi violence in Hungary.[25]

Hungarian National Alliance (HNA)
Magyar Nemzeti Szövetség (MNSz)

Until his arrest in July 1992, László Romhányi was the chairman of this pronouncedly nationalist party. The subsequent alliance leader was reputed to be Romhányi's deputy, Imre Bosnyák. The HNA had its origins in the initial burgeoning of opposition to the Communist regime. In April 1987, Romhányi was appointed director of the Jurta Theater, which later became the center for opposition parties, including the HDF, the Alliance of Free Democrats, and the Federation of Young Democrats. After the parliamentary elections in 1990, the Jurta Theater became a center catering to extreme right-wing political entities. The HNA, the CNU, the Hungarian Legitimist Party (HLP), chaired by László Pálos, and other rightist groups congregated at Jurta to formulate an ultra-rightist ideology later referred to as the "Spirit of Jurta." In May 1992, Romhányi delivered a speech at the "national ceremonies" at the Jurta Theater in which he urged cooperation among all right-wing forces, called for the disbanding of parliament, and demanded the resignation of the government. In July 1992, Romhányi and four associates were arrested and accused of torturing and then murdering a homeless man whom they had employed as a courier. Romhányi's arrest appeared to thwart his political ambitions.

Hungarian National Front (HNF)
Magyar Nemzeti Front (MNF)

Formerly known as the Hungarian National Socialist Action Group, the HNF became an openly neo-Nazi organization, led by the radical Fascist István Györkös. The HMF intended to transform itself into a mass-based political party based on the heritage of the war-time Arrow Cross movement, which engaged in atrocities against Hungary's Jewish population. Györkös claimed to have contacts with several skinhead gangs, other ultra-right-wing groupings in Hungary, and with neo-Fascist emigré organizations and neo-Nazi movements in Germany, Austria, and Spain. In February 1993, Györkös was arrested and charged with inciting hatred against minorities and aliens and for the illegal possession of firearms; he received a one-year suspended sentence.[26]

1956 Anti-Fascist and Anti-Bolshevik Association (AAA)
1956-os Antifasiszta és Antibolseviszta Szövetség (AASz)

A rightist organization led by Sándor Hajós and István Porubsky, the AAA was allied with extreme nationalist political groups such as the Hungarian National Alliance. Providing what Hajós described as history lessons and physical training, the association became a youth group for skinhead gangs in Budapest, referred to by the AAA as "national conservative-thinking youth." It claimed to have the support of elements of the Independent Smallholders' Party, such as the József Torgyán faction, as well as István Csurka and Interior Minister Péter Boross. Its objective was to counter the government's "lukewarm centrist politics" strongly criticized in Csurka's anti-Semitic document.[27]

World Federation of Hungarians (WFH)
Magyarok Világszövetsége (MVSz)

The WFH was initially established in 1929 and re-created in Budapest in December 1991 to preserve the bonds of dispersed Magyar communities around the world. It was headed by the writer Sándor Csoóri, president, and Előd Kincses, first secretary. After the post-war Communist takeover, WFH leaders served to express the interests of Magyars exiled in the West and were instrumental in aiding refugees from the 1956 revolution. Although not an overtly nationalist grouping, the federation has focused on assisting Magyar communities in politically unstable neighboring regions in Serbia, Romania, and Slovakia. It has striven to safeguard the native culture of Magyars abroad, to improve the economy of these communities, and to protect their group rights. It also sought to commemorate Hungarian "martyrs" by advocating the creation of a national memorial museum. President Csoóri was hoping to make the federation independent from all governments and political parties. In July 1991, the WFH asked the Hungarian government to ensure the safety of Yugoslav Magyars and issued a condemnation of the repression of the Hungarian minority "by extremist southern Slavic groups and political tendencies." However, at a meeting with British Magyars in London, Csoóri stated that any revision of Hungary's borders was a "pipe dream." The WFH held its second post-Communist convention in Budapest in August 1992 and announced the official rehabilitation of former political refugees, specifically those involved in the 1956 anti-Communist uprising.[28]

World Federation of Transylvania (WFT)
Erdélyi Világszövetség (EVSz)

This Hungarian emigré organization has sought to draw international attention to the situation of the Magyar minority in Romania. It has also provided material and educational support to Transylvanian Magyars. The WFT planned a march in June 1992 through Hungary to Timişoara (in Romania) "under the sign of Hungarian-Romanian friendship and common Europeanness." The march was subsequently canceled due to opposition from various Hungarian groups that feared the possibility of official Romanian reprisals.

MINORITY ORGANIZATIONS

National Minority Roundtable (NMR)
Kisebbségi Kerekasztal (KK)

Toso Doncsev became the executive chairman of this umbrella lobbying group created in January 1991. It was composed of representatives from minority organizations and was directly involved in the creation of the law on ethnic and national minorities. Groups comprising the roundtable included; the Phralipe Independent Gypsy Association, the Roma Parliament, the Association of Germans in Hungary, the Democratic Union of Slovaks in Hungary, the Croatian Democratic Alliance, the Federation of Romanians in Hungary, the Federation of Slovenes in Hungary, and the Democratic Federation of Serbs. The NMR has garnered support from the liberal opposition parties such as the AFD and the FYD. It was created to coalesce minority support in negotiations with the government and sought to play an active role in the formulation of a minority law. Another of its primary goals was to ensure cooperation and promote understanding among the various minorities. A first draft of the minorities bill, drawn up by the Justice Ministry at the end of 1990, was rejected by several minority organizations, which then decided to establish the NMR. Two subsequent drafts were drawn up independently by the NMR and the government's Office of National and Ethnic Minorities (ONEM), from which a common version was finalized. This draft, accepted by the Hungarian government in December 1991, was rejected by the NMR because of unacceptable modifications. According to the roundtable, the bill resubmitted by relevant government ministries applied rules that allegedly discriminated against certain minorities. However, it remained unclear which stipulations were being questioned or which minorities would be affected. The revised bill also purportedly limited cultural autonomy through the self-governing bodies established for minorities and did not solve the problem of parliamentary representation. The final version of the Minority Code passed in July 1993 was evidently approved by NMR representatives.[29]

Nationality Council of Gypsies in Hungary (NCGH)
Magyarországi Cigányok Nemzetiségi Uniója (MCNU)

The council was created in June 1990 and regarded itself as the highest organ of the Romani community. It became an umbrella organization for seven Gypsy parties and groups, the most important of which were Phralipe, the Democratic Alliance of Hungarian Gypsies (DAHG), and the Hungarian Gypsy Party (HGP). Other organizations forming the council included the Social Democratic Party of Gypsies in Hungary, the Budapest Gypsy Band Union, the Gypsy Workers' Federation, the Baranya County Cultural and Educational Union, and the Justice Party of Hungarian Gypsies. The main goal of the NCGH was to promote cooperation among the often-quarrelsome Romani organizations and to try to end the fragmentation that has plagued Gypsy politics since 1989.[30]

Democratic Alliance of Hungarian Gypsies (DAHG)
Magyarországi Cigányok Demokratikus Szövetsége (MCDSz)

Gyula Náday became the chairman of this leftist Gypsy political party formed in January 1989. It tried to gain representation in the National Assembly in order to pursue its program of Romani "societal renewal." One of its prime objectives was to ensure economic progress and self-sufficiency by patterning Gypsy village settlements along the lines of the Israeli *kibbutz* system. The DAHG has been one of the major players in the ongoing conflict among Gypsy organizations. Náday has orchestrated demonstrations at the Roma Parliament (RP) headquarters (see below) to protest alleged moral misconduct of the three main RP leaders. He also sought to persuade Péter Tölgyessy, the chairman of the Association of Free Democrats (AFD), to review and revoke the membership of Aladár Horváth, the RP chairman. Charges of corruption against alliance leaders, stemming from a substantial infusion of government money, led to a factional split in the DAHG in December 1989.[31]

Roma Parliament (RP)
Magyarországi Romaparlament (MRP)

The Roma Parliament became the governing body for different Romani political factions, chaired by Aladár Horváth. Although not a political party, the Roma Parliament played an important role in articulating Gypsy demands to the Hungarian authorities. It wanted the government and the National Assembly to specifically ensure human, constitutional, and national minority rights for the Gypsy population. In the summer of 1991, the RP presented a petition to the government demanding parliamentary representation for all national and ethnic minorities. It also requested that a national minorities bill be presented to parliament by the end of September 1991 and asked the National Assembly for 2 billion forints to be used for Gypsy vocational retraining and employment programs. The Roma Parliament has had an adversarial relationship with the Antall government; for instance, there have been disputes with ONEM over what the RP viewed as government antipathy toward Gypsies. In November 1991, the RP asked the prime minister to remove János Báthory, the deputy director of ONEM, because of his alleged anti-Gypsy remarks. The Roma Parliament also accused the DAHG of complicity in the April 1991 theft of 1 million forints from the office of Deputy Chairman Béla Osztojkán. The ensuing polemical dispute between the Roma Parliament leadership and DAHG chairman Gyula Náday resulted in demands to dismiss Horváth from the major opposition party, the AFD. The RP, together with other Gypsy groupings, undertook various initiatives to coordinate Romani interests. For instance, it helped to establish a National Coordinating Center of Roma Communities in January 1993, which was designed to prepare individuals for local and national elections. In July 1993, the RP helped to organized a Romani rally in the town of Eger, labeled as Hungary's "skinhead capital," protesting against skinhead attacks on Romani communities. Náday later complained that rally organizers had failed to inform other Romani organizations about the event.[32]

"Phralipe" (Brotherhood) Independent Gypsy Association (PIGA)
"Phralipe" (Testvériség) Független Cigány Szervezet (PFCSz)

Established in April 1989, *Phralipe*, which means brotherhood in Romani, became an organization dominated primarily by Romani intellectuals and was openly critical of government policies toward the Gypsies during the 1980s. Its aim was to consolidate an awareness of Romani identity and to strengthen Gypsy community solidarity. It has endeavored to ensure Romani rights in the workplace and in their dealings with the authorities. It reported on racist violence against Gypsy communities by skinhead gangs and abuses perpetrated by policemen. A similar organization, the Amalipe Union for the Promotion of Gypsy Culture and Tradition (AUPGCT), was created to represent one of the many traditional trade-oriented Gypsy clans, such as the tinkers and the bear trainers.[33]

Anti-Fascist Organization of Hungarian Gypsies (AFOHG)
Magyar Cigányok Antifasiszta Szervezete (MCASz)

Ostensibly, the AFOHG sought to protect Gypsies against racially motivated attacks. During German hancellor Helmut Kohl's visit to Hungary for the signing of the German-Hungarian Treaty, the organization (along with the Roma Parliament's presidium) sent the German leader a letter requesting compensation for the relatives of the estimated 70,000 Hungarian Gypsies deported and killed by the Nazis during World War Two. According to the letter, in 1970 the West German government gave the Hungarian Communist government DM 100 million as compensation for war crimes, none of which was channeled to the Roma.[34]

Hungarian Gypsy Party (HGP)
Magyar Cigány Párt (MCP)

Established in June 1989, the HGP became the largest Gypsy political party in Hungary. But despite its size, the HGP only garnered 1 percent support among respondents in a survey conducted prior to the March 1990 general elections.[35]

Hungarian Gypsy Social Democratic Party (HGSDP)
Magyar Cigány Szociáldemokrata Párt (MCSzP)

The HGSDP was created as a political party in October 1989 as an ally of the Hungarian Social-Democratic Party (HSDP). By February 1990, it included more than 15,000 members. Although the HGSDP and the HSDP provided each other with mutual assistance prior to the 1990 elections, by the end of March 1990 the alliance collapsed. The HGSDP accused the HSDP of failing to abide by its promise to field Romani candidates on the Social Democratic ticket, while the HSDP proved unable to win any seats in parliament.

Association of Germans in Hungary (AGH)
Magyarországi Németek Szövetsége (MNSz)

Géza Hambuch became the executive secretary and Karl Manhertz (Károly Manherz) the vice president of the AGH. It did not style itself as a political party but as an umbrella organization articulating the demands of the German minority. Its primary goal was to promote German educational and cultural needs, such as expanding the German-language school system and providing for more German radio and television programs. The AGH opposed the restoration of land to the pre-Communist, pre-1947 owners, regarding this as an injustice against the German minority. It demanded an accurate count of ethnic Germans in the country in order to establish native-language schools corresponding to the size of the population. German-language education evidently needed to be instituted from kindergarten through high school in order to help preserve the language. According to Hambuch, the German language in Hungary had become a "grandmother language, spoken only by elderly people." During a meeting of the AGH national board in January 1990, a call was issued for the direct election of three German representatives to the national parliament. At the completion of the February 1992 German-Hungarian Treaty, Secretary Hambuch met with Chancellor Kohl to request assistance for teaching the German language in schools. In fact, the German government has spent about DM 2 million per annum since 1987 on cultural and educational aid to Hungary's German minority. The AGH published a weekly, *Neue Zeitung*, which received assistance from the German Danubian Swabian Cultural Foundation. German activists established the Association of German Writers and Artists in Hungary (AGWAH) in February 1992 to revive and promote German artistic traditions in Hungary. A conference scheduled for September 1992 in Pécs was attended by representatives of German-minority communities from various parts of Europe.[36]

Democratic Union of Slovaks in Hungary (DUSH)
Magyarországi Szlovákok Szövetsége (MSzSz)

Although approximately forty years old, the DUSH was finally allowed to create a membership base in 1989. Mária Jakab, its chairwoman, was also the parliamentary representative-at-large for national minorities. She was transferred from the post of general secretary at the November 1990 party congress. The union became a political-interest bloc representing different Slovak organizations dispersed among 104 Slovak communities in Hungary. Other Slovak organizations included the Association of Slovak Writers in Hungary, whose chairman was Gregor Papucsek, and the Organization of Slovak Youth in Hungary, led by Anton Pavlik. The DUSH's main goals were to halt the assimilation of Hungarian Slovaks. The Slovak population declined steadily during the 1960s and 1970s; 32,000 people claimed to be Slovaks in 1960, 16,000 in 1970, and 9,000 in 1980. It wanted to strengthen Slovak national consciousness and to preserve the community's mother tongue. It intended to create a self-governing body that would represent the interests of Slovaks in Hungary on the national level and to coordinate the activities of local organizations. The DUSH supported the passage of a nationality law that could economically empower ethnic minorities. Jakab also voiced opposition to proposals issued by the Slovak Heritage Foundation and the Institute for Slovaks Living Abroad to allow international forums to settle the status of Slovaks in Hungary. At the beginning of January 1991, Jakab attempted to secure funds in the national education budget for several Slovak communities, but her motion was rejected by the National Assembly. The DUSH's deputy chairwoman, Anna István, cited a government discrepancy in how the affairs of Magyars residing outside Hungary's borders measured against government assistance to ethnic minorities in Hungary. According to her, there was too much official emphasis on the well-being of Magyars abroad.[37]

Hungarian Jewish Cultural Federation (HJCF)
Magyar Zsidók Kulturális Egyesülete (MZsKE)

The JCF was formed in 1988, shortly before the democratic changes, under the chairmanship of Endre Rózsa, a radio journalist. It was the first major Jewish organization created independently of the Communist-supervised communal structures, and its leaders were critical of the subservient role played by various Jewish religious and cultural bodies. The JCF organized lectures on Jewish topics and published the magazine *Szombat* (Sabbath). Several of its leaders became active in the liberal opposition grouping, the Alliance of Free Democrats, and were elected to parliament.

Alliance of Hungarian Jewish Religious Communities (AHJRC)
Magyarországi Zsidó Hitközségek Szövetsége (MAZsIHISz)

In 1991, the former Communist-sponsored National Representation of Hungarian Israelites (NRHI) was renamed and revamped, and a democratic constitution was adopted. At the same time, a Council of Jewish Organizations (CJO) was created to reorganize various aspects of Jewish communal affairs. The first elections to the AHJRC presidency were won by Gusztáv Zoltai, a former director of the Central Board of Hungarian Jews (CBHJ). These organizations were instrumental in preserving and reviving the Jewish religious, cultural, and educational heritage. In March 1990, a Hungarian Zionist Organization (HZO) was reestablished and headed by Tibor Englander as an affiliate of the World Zionist Organization based in Jerusalem, and an office of B'nai B'rith was also opened in Budapest.[38]

Croatian Democratic Alliance in Hungary (CDAH)
Magyarországi Horvátok Szövetsége (MHSz)

The CDA was created in January 1990 in Baja and Pécs as a result of the schism within the Democratic Alliance of South Slavs (DASS); independent Serb and

Slovene groups were also formed at this time. Its president, Djuro Franković (György Frankovics), was the former secretary of the DASS. The CDA wanted to have an input into the policies of Hungarian political parties concerning minority rights. It has also striven for the rejuvenation of Croat culture by reestablishing Croatian elementary schools and training Croatian clergy to serve churches in the 70 to 80 Croat settlements in western Hungary.[39]

Democratic Association of Romanians in Hungary (DARH)
Magyarországi Románok Demokratikus Szövetsége (MRDSz)

The DARH was originally founded in 1949 to promote cultural traditions and the Romanian mother tongue. It was formerly known as the Democratic Federation of Romanians in Hungary (DFRH), one of the numerous minority organizations created under the auspices of the Communist regime. Because of mistrust among the Romanian minority, the DARH decided to dissolve and restructure itself in June 1990. National Assembly deputy György (Gheorghe) Márk became the association's executive secretary, while Gheorghe Mihaiescu became chairman of the board and the national council. Headquartered in Gyula, the DARH endeavored to play a part in the creation of a law governing the rights of all minorities in Hungary. The DARH has promoted Romanian-language instruction in schools and has taken part in negotiations with the government in developing a nationalities law. Like all minority organizations in Hungary, the DARH was an advocate of the 1990 law awarding direct parliamentary representation to all minorities, over and above the 386 MPs elected under the rules of the electoral law. The association wanted to maintain close relationships with Romania but condemned the human rights abuses committed in Romania against resident minority groups, specifically against Magyars in Transylvania. DARH members aided Romanian refugees fleeing to Hungary in the last months of the Ceauşescu regime by distributing Romanian-Hungarian dictionaries and by finding temporary shelters for them in the homes of Hungarian Romanians.[40]

Federation of Romanians in Hungary (FRH)
Magyarországi Románok Szövetsége (MRSz)

The FRH was established in December 1990 in Gyula as an avowedly more democratic and grass-roots oriented alternative to DARH. Its president, Gheorghe Petrusan (György Petrusan), claimed it represented the interests of all ethnic Romanians living in Hungary as a mass movement rather than as a partisan political organization. The FRH's primary concern was the preservation of Romanian culture, manifested in the use of the Romanian language. It supported the passage of the national minorities bill in order to obtain government resources for the establishment of ethnic schools. The federation also concerned itself with the cultural reawakening of the Romanian people based around its intellectual heritage.

Federation of Slovenes in Hungary (FSH)
Magyarországi Szlovének Szövetsége (MSzSz)

Established in 1990, this umbrella organization was led by President József Hírnök. In June 1992, the FSH signed a five-year cooperation agreement with the local administration of Murska Sobota district in Slovenia. The agreement dealt with economic, transportational, cultural, and sports-related cooperation between Murska Sobota and the FSH-represented districts in western Hungary.[41]

Democratic Federation of Serbs (DFS)
Szerb Demokratikus Szövetség (SzDSz)

A Serbian Action Committee was created in January 1990 in the wake of the dissolution of the Democratic Alliance of South Slavs. During a gathering of the DFS assembly in November 1992, its leaders underscored that the Serb minority was entitled to parliamentary representation following the general elections scheduled for 1994. The DFS also announced that it would allocate a larger share of its budget to the cultural and educational activities of local branches, and it pressed for the return of property previously confiscated from the Serbian Orthodox church. Complaints have been raised that Budapest only had one Yugoslav school, which was in the process of splitting into Serb and Croat factions. Serbs sought assurances that they would receive financial support from the state to open a purely Serbian school by September 1993.[42]

"Mladost" Youth Association (MYA)
Ifjúság Szervezet—"Mladost" (ISzM)

This youth organization, representing young Croats, Serbs, and Slovenes, was established in January 1990. Ivica Djurok became its first leader. *Mladost* wanted institutional guarantees for the political representation of national minorities. It also demanded that minority members elected to parliament achieve their posts through mainstream political organizations already represented in the legislature, rather than through the direct election of minority parties. *Mladost* called for an infusion of minority professionals into ethnic organizations to "enable national minorities to have a serious and genuine influence on the issues that concerned them in the areas of politics, economics, legislation, as well as state administration."[43]

Federation of Bulgarians in Hungary (FBH)
Magyarországi Bolgárok Szövetsége (MBSz)

The Federation of Bulgarians in Hungary reportedly represented about 2,500 Bulgarian residents. Its executive chairman, Toso Doncsev, was also the executive chairman of the National Minorities Roundtable.[44]

CHRONOLOGY

February 1990: The Democratic Association of South Slavs dissolves into autonomous Croat, Serb, Slovene, and Yugoslav youth groups. The government submits a proposal on nationality representation in parliament to the National Assembly. The proposal calls for a single representative for each minority group (Roma, Germans, Slovaks, Jews, Croats, Romanians, Slovenes, and Serbs), in addition to elected representatives.

March 1990: Hungary holds its first multi-party elections, sweeping the Communists from power. The Hungarian Democratic Forum (HDF) scores an overwhelming victory, gaining 164 out of 377 seats in the National Assembly, with 42.29 percent of the popular vote. The Alliance of Free Democrats (AFD) captures 92 seats (23.83 percent of the vote); the Independent Smallholders' Party 44 seats (11.4 percent); the Hungarian Socialist Party (HSP) 33 seats (8.55 percent); the Alliance of Young Democrats (AYD), or *Fidesz*, 21 seats (5.44 percent); the Christian Democratic Party (CDP) 21 seats (5.44 percent); and the Agrarian Alliance 1 seat (0.26 percent). HDF leader József Antall becomes prime minister and forms the first post-Communist government. Hungarian National Assembly chairman Mátyas Szűrős calls on the Romanian government to allow the Hungarian minority free access to Hungary's print media. Foreign Minister Horn states that "some leaders of the fallen [Romanian] dictatorship are still in office and seeking to preserve the [old regime's] anti-Hungarian policy."[45] Foreign Minister Gyula Horn protests against the inter-ethnic violence in Tîrgu Mureş, Transylvania, to the Romanian ambassador and appeals to the UN Secretary General to intercede to protect the Hungarian minority. About 20,000 people attend a rally in Budapest's Heroes' Square to protest anti-Magyar violence in Tîrgu Mureş. All major Hungarian political parties, with the exception of the Hungarian Socialist Workers' Party (Communists), issue a joint statement condemning anti-Hungarian attacks in Romania.

May 1990: "Phralipe" Gypsy supporters stage a demonstration at the Romanian Embassy to protest the arrest and conviction of fifteen Gypsies in Tîrgu Mureş. The Gypsies had sided with Magyars during the outbreak of ethnic violence in mid-March and were subsequently charged with non-political crimes. The Raoul Wallenberg Society organizes a rally in Budapest to protest anti-Semitic acts, including the desecration of Jewish cemeteries and the painting of anti-Semitic graffiti on the Wallenberg statue. Prime Minister József Antall, President Árpád Göncz, and National Assembly Speaker György Szabad participate in the rally. The six major parties represented in parliament issue a joint statement declaring that they regard Hungary's present borders "as determinants of Europe's current stability."

June 1990: The seventieth anniversary of the Treaty of Trianon is commemorated publicly, for the first time in over forty years. The Christian National Union holds a rally attended by about 500 people calling for the rectification of Hungary's borders by "peaceful means." The Board and National Council of the Democratic Association of Romanians in Hungary dissolves the organization in order to dissociate itself from its Communist origins. It seeks to garner support from the Romanian Orthodox constituency in Hungary who, for the most part, support the Federation of Romanians in Hungary.

July 1990: The president of the World Jewish Congress, Edgar Bronfman, and Prime Minister Antall unveil a memorial to the 600,000 Hungarian Jews killed during World War Two. Hungary promises to rescind its endorsement of a UN resolution equating Zionism with racism.

September 1990: President Göncz visits Kyiv and Uzhgorod in Ukraine and meets with representatives of the Magyar minority. Steps are taken to establish diplomatic ties and to guarantee full cultural rights for the Magyar population. Ukrainian president Leonid Kravchuk agrees to grant "cultural autonomy" to the Magyars and to draft a joint "national minority charter" with Hungary.[46]

October 1990: A Jewish kindergarten and a 1–12 grade school are officially inaugurated in Budapest. The schools were jointly established in September by the Jewish community and American businessman Ronald S. Lauder to educate a class of 160 students. A Jewish Holocaust memorial is unveiled in Budapest in memory of the 85,000 Hungarian Jews killed by pro-Nazi Hungarian groups.

November 1990: The Croatian Democratic Alliance (CDA) holds its first nationwide congress and speaks up for cultural autonomy for Croats in Szombathely, Pécs, Zala, Somogy, and Bácska.[47] The Democratic Union of Slovaks in Hungary (DUSH) holds an extraordinary congress and articulates a plan to halt the assimilation of Slovaks. The congress focuses on Slovak education and the problem of administering the Slovak-language school system.

December 1990: An initial minority bill drafted by the Justice Ministry is judged unsatisfactory by minority organizations; they charge the government with failing to consult them on the draft law.

January 1991: The National Minority Roundtable (NMR) is established by various minority organizations to augment their negotiating position vis-à-vis the Hungarian government.

April 1991: An ethnic German youth symposium is held in Budapest attended by German youths from Poland, Hungary, Romania, and Germany. Hungarian

Germans stress the difficulty in maintaining ethnic identity in the wake of decades-long assimilationist pressures. Representatives of the Hungarian government as well as Hungarian political parties attend a meeting of the Democratic Community of Hungarians in Vojvodina to express solidarity with the Serbian Magyars.[48] At a meeting between Prime Minister Antall and Croatia's president Franjo Tudjman in Budapest, Antall praises Croatia's treatment of its Magyar minority. A joint statement describes relations between the two countries as "historically good," and both sides pledge cooperation in economic, cultural, and minority affairs.

May 1991: The National Minority Roundtable begins consultative talks with the Office of National and Ethnic Minorities (ONEM).

June 1991: CDA president Djuro Franković sends a letter to Prime Minister Antall, President Göncz, and the chairman of the National Assembly calling for an official condemnation of the "Yugoslav military aggression" in Slovenia and Croatia. Inhabitants of four Magyar villages in the Slavonia region of Croatia press their case for protection to the Hungarian National Assembly.

September 1991: Because of disclosures about an illegal arms sale to Croatia, Serbia accuses Hungary of irredentism. Antall responds that Hungary was opposed to any forcible border changes. He also meets Magyar minority representatives in the Serbian province of Vojvodina. The CDA organizes a rally in Pécs to call on the Hungarian government to recognize Croatian independence. The organization becomes involved in assisting Croatian refugees fleeing the war in Yugoslavia.

December 1991: Hungary signs a bilateral agreement with Croatia guaranteeing minority rights. This document is similar to the June 1991 Hungarian-Ukrainian agreement.

January 1992: The Hungarian news agency MTI reports on the exodus of hundreds of Magyars from Transcarpathia since 1979, due to economic problems and the rise of nationalism in Ukraine. The issue is slated to be discussed at the first meeting of the Hungarian-Ukrainian Joint Minority Committee. A Hungarian-Austrian police academy is inaugurated, which will conduct joint training in tracking neo-Nazis in both countries.

February 1992: The Hungarian government produces a revised version of the draft law on minorities. The NMR calls the draft unacceptable and in violation of the consensus reached earlier with the government. The NMR claims that the bill contains "discriminatory regulations," excludes most minorities from exercising the right to local self-government, and does not provide for proper parliamentary representation. Defense Minister Lajos Für says that the preservation of the entire Magyar "linguistic nation" is an "essential element" of Hungary's national security; the government is to use "every legal and diplomatic means" to safeguard the position of Magyar minorities.

March 1992: Géza Hambuch, a German minority leader, attacks the February 1992 draft law on minorities approved by the government on the grounds that it fails to fulfill the demands of minorities for cultural autonomy and parliamentary representation.

April 1992: The Hungarian government and the NMR fail to achieve a consensus on the draft bill submitted by the government. The NMR objects to the exclusion of the principle of "positive discrimination," granting special rights to Hungary's minorities.

May 1992: Prime Minister Antall proposes to Ukrainian prime minister Vitold Fokin that a form of autonomy be granted to the Transcarpathian Magyars.

June 1992: Foreign Minister Géza Jeszenszky stresses that granting autonomy to Magyars in Slovakia would curb any separatist tendencies among them.

July 1992: Gheorghe Petrusan, president of the Federation of Romanians in Hungary, reports that the Romanian minority is served by thirteen elementary schools, one secondary school, and four teachers' colleges and that he approves of bilingual instruction for Romanians. The Hungarian-Ukrainian Joint Minority Committee opens its first meeting in Budapest.

August 1992: The Hungarian government issues a statement supporting Magyar minority efforts to preserve their ethnic identity through various degrees of autonomy in neighboring states. The statement urges the international community to thwart attempts to incite minority conflict. At the opening of the Third World Congress of Hungarians in Budapest, Antall states that "it is the constitutional duty of the Hungarian government to take responsibility for Hungarians living abroad." The conference, organized by the WFH, is attended by 7,000 participants. István Csurka, a founder and vice-president of the HDF, publishes an inflammatory anti-Semitic article in *Magyar Fórum*. Eurom, the European Romani Parliament, is established in Budapest by 22 Gypsy organizations from ten European countries.

September 1992: Foreign Minister Jeszenszky meets with Slovak officials in Bratislava stressing that Hungary wants to conclude a bilateral agreement on the treatment of ethnic minorities. Antall and Slovak prime minister Mečiar hold their first meeting in Budapest to discuss the situation of their respective minorities. They agree to establish a joint parliamentary commission for minorities. Mečiar also meets with representatives of the Hungarian Slovaks, who ask for Slovak-government support for their publishing ventures. A demonstration in Budapest is attended by 50,000 people to protest the resurgence of right-wing nationalism. Speakers call upon Antall to distance himself from the extreme nationalist wing of the HDF. Antall meets with leaders of Coexistence, the coalition of minority parties in Slovakia, to discuss political developments in Czechoslovakia. Coexistence delegates voice support for Hungary's minority bill.

October 1992: The Hungarian government announces the creation of the Hungaria Television Foundation to finance satellite transmissions of Hungarian programs to Magyar communities abroad. President Göncz is prevented by skinheads from delivering a speech on the anniversary of the 1956 revolution.

April 1993: The Hungarian parliament votes to amend the penal code banning the display of Nazi and Communist symbols, including the Arrow Cross, the Hungarian wartime Fascist symbol. The dissemination or display of such symbols will be punishable by a fine or up to one year's imprisonment.

June 1993: About 1,000 extreme-right supporters gather in Budapest to commemorate the anniversary of the 1920 Trianon Treaty. The rally is organized by the 1956 Anti-Bolshevik and Anti-Fascist Association. Speakers call for the Hungarian government to recover the territories lost to neighbors at the close of World War One.

July 1993: The Hungarian parliament passes a comprehensive law on the rights of ethnic and national minorities. Minorities gain the right to establish their own institutions, including "local and national self-governments" to guarantee their cultural autonomy.

NOTES

1. Population figures are conservative estimates provided by minority organizations, official or semiofficial sources, and media reports. In some cases the highest credible figures are provided. See also Andre Leibich, "Minorities in Eastern Europe: Obstacles to a Reliable Count," Radio Free Europe/Radio Liberty Research Institute (RFE/RL), *Report on Eastern Europe*, vol. 1, no. 20, May 15, 1992; and Alfred A. Reisch, "First Law on Minorities Drafted," RFE/RL, *Report on Eastern Europe*, vol. 2, no. 50, December 13, 1991. For other census data, see "National and Ethnic Minorities in Hungary," *Fact Sheets on Hungary*, Budapest: Hungarian Ministry of Foreign Affairs, no. 9, 1991.

2. For background histories of Hungary, see Stephen Borsody, ed., *The Hungarians: A Divided Nation* (New Haven: Yale University Press, 1988); Jorg K. Hoensch, *A History of Modern Hungary, 1867–1986* (London: Longman, 1988); Bennett Kovrig, *Communism in Hungary: From Kun to Kádár* (Stanford, CA: Hoover Institution Press, 1979); Hans-

Georg Heinrich, *Hungary: Politics, Economics and Society* (Boulder, CO: Lynne Rienner, 1986); and Charles Gati, *Hungary and the Soviet Bloc* (Durham, NC: Duke University Press, 1986).

3. For background on the constitutional changes, see Edith Oltay, "Constitutional Amendments Strengthen Civil Rights, Pave Way for Multiparty System," RFE/RL, *Situation Report: Hungary*, SR/17, November 30, 1989; Reisch, "First Law on Minorities Drafted"; "National and Ethnic Minorities in Hungary."

4. *MTI*, Budapest, February 27, 1990, in Federal Broadcast Information Service, *Daily Report: East Europe, FBIS-EEU–90–040*, February 28, 1990; see also the interview with Toso Doncsev and Pero Lasztity by Andrea M. Rimas, "Bill on National Minorities: Dissatisfaction," *Népszabadság*, Budapest, August 1, 1992, in *FBIS-EEU–92–154*, August 10, 1992.

5. "The Constitution of the Republic of Hungary," *Hungarian Rules of Law in Force*, I/no. 26, December 1990, p. 1656.

6. For the text of the Draft Law on Local Government, see *Magyar Közlöny*, Budapest, no. 78, August 9, 1990, in Federal Broadcast Information Service/Joint Publications Research Service, *Daily Report: East Europe, JPRS-EER–90–143-S*, October 19, 1990.

7. See also *Budapest Domestic Service*, August 24, 1990, in *FBIS-EEU–90–167*, August 9, 1990; *Magyar Hírlap*, Budapest, August 28, 1990, in *JPRS-EER–90–136*, October 1, 1990. For details on radio broadcasts, see "Weekly Record of Events," RFE/RL, *Report on Eastern Europe*, vol. 1 no. 37, September 14, 1990. *MTI*, Budapest, June 2, 1992, in *FBIS-EEU–92–109*, June 5, 1992.

8. Géza Entz, Political State Secretary, Office of the Prime Minister of Hungary, "States and Nations in the New Europe, Central and Eastern Europe at the Crossroad," speech given on November 14, 1991; "The Minority Bill Is Exemplary," *Népszabadság*, Budapest, April 6, 1993; and RFE/RL, *Daily Report*, no. 128, July 8, 1993.

9. *MTI*, Budapest, June 1, 1993, in *FBIS-EEU–93–104*, June 2, 1993.

10. Bulletin, "Vertrag zwischen der Bundesrepublik Deutschland und der Republik Ungarn über Freundschaftliche Zusammenarbeit und Partnerschaft in Europa [Treaty Between the Federal Republic of Germany and the Republic of Hungary on Friendly Cooperation and Partnership in Europe]," Presse und Informationsamt der Bundesregierung, no. 15/S 106, February 11, 1992.

11. The text of this law can be found in *Magyar Közlöny*, Budapest, no. 53, May 26, 1992, in *JPRS-EER–92–108-S*, August 15, 1992.

12. *Budapest Domestic Service*, May 9, 1990, in *FBIS-EEU–90–091*, May 10, 1990.

13. Interview with Árpád Göncz by Tibor Ferk, "The Roads to a National Identity," *Národná Obroda*, Bratislava, July 12, 1990.

14. "Weekly Record of Events," RFE/RL, *Report on Eastern Europe*, vol. 2, no. 40, October 4, 1991.

15. Interview with Géza Entz by János A. Szilagyi, "We Do Not Want Political Window-Dressing," *Magyar Hírlap*, Budapest, February 19, 1992, in *FBIS-EEU–92–046*, March 4, 1992; *MTI*, Budapest, June 28, 1992, in *FBIS-EEU–92–126*, June 30, 1992.

16. In February 1991, the National Assembly approved a $2,700,000 state subsidy for minorities, nearly one-third of which went to Romani organizations. For details, see Reisch, "First Law on Minorities Drafted."

17. Alfred A. Reisch, "Agreements Signed with Ukraine to Upgrade Bilateral Relations," RFE/RL, *Report on Eastern Europe*, vol. 2, no. 25, June 21, 1991; István Csurka, "The New Grand Coalition or the '93 Ukrainian Front," *Magyar Fórum*, Budapest, May 20, 1993, *JPRS-EER–93–050–5*, June 4, 1993.

18. See Edith Oltay, "Minority Rights Still an Issue in Hungarian-Romanian Relations," RFE/RL, *Research Report*, vol. 1, no. 12, March 20, 1992.

19. Interview with Gyula Kiss Csaba by László Györffy, "Csaba Gy. Kiss [as published] on Public Opinion on Politics, Development of Bourgeois Society, and Minorities— The Issue of Hungarians Living Beyond Our Borders Should Not Be Used for Domestic Political Feuding," *Magyar Nemzet*, Budapest, September 12, 1991, in *FBIS-EEU–91– 179*, September 16, 1991.

20. Article 63 of the Trianon Treaty states that persons 18 years of age or older who lost their Hungarian citizenship after World War One and became citizens of neighboring states could "request citizenship of the state where they had claimed domicile prior to acquiring domicile in the annexed territories." *Magyar Hírlap*, Budapest, January 17, 1992, in *JPRS-EER–92–018*, February 19, 1992.

21. Interview with Géza Entz by Desző Pinter, "Will Democracy Replace the Right of Fist?" *Magyar Hírlap*, Budapest, October 3, 1992, in *FBIS-EEU–92–196*, October 8, 1992.

22. For election results, see Zoltán D. Bárány, "The Hungarian Democratic Forum Wins National Elections Decisively," RFE/RL, *Report on Eastern Europe*, vol. 1, no. 17, April 27, 1990. Background information on the Hungarian Democratic Forum is taken from Alfred A. Reisch, "The Democratic Forum at the Finish Line," RFE/RL, *Report on Eastern Europe*, vol. 1, no. 14, April 6, 1990; *Magyar Hírlap*, Budapest, December 17, 1991, in *JPRS-EER–92–011*, January 28, 1992; Zoltán D. Bárány, "Democratic Changes Bring Mixed Blessings for Gypsies," RFE/RL, *Research Report*, vol. 1, no. 20, May 15, 1992.

23. See Reisch, "The Democratic Forum at the Finish Line." For a summary of the Csurka article, see *Népszabadság*, Budapest, August 27, 1992, in *FBIS-EEU–92–172*, September 3, 1992; and Judith Pataki, "István Csurka's Tract: Summary and Reactions," RFE/RL, *Research Report*, Vol 1, no. 40, October 9, 1992 . The complete text of the tract plus official responses can be found in *JPRS-EER–92–132-S*, September 17, 1992. Further analysis of the consequences of the article is found in J.F. Brown, "A Challenge to Political Values," RFE/RL, *Research Report*, vol. 1, no. 40, October 9, 1992. See also Edith Oltay, "A Profile of István Csurka," RFE/RL, *Research Report*, vol. 1, no. 40, October 9, 1992; Edith Oltay, "Hungarian Democratic Forum Rent by Dispute Over Extremism," RFE/RL, *Research Report*, vol. 1, no. 47, November 27, 1992; Teddie Weyr, "Trouble in Hungary," *AP*, December 14, 1992; Edith Oltay, "Hungary: Csurka Launches 'National Movement,'" RFE/RL, *Report on Eastern Europe*, vol. 2, no. 13, March 26, 1993; and Csurka's speech on the "Hungarian Way," in *Magyar Fórum*, Budapest, April 29, 1993, in *JPRS-EER–93–052-S*, June 9, 1993.

24. For background information on the Independent Smallholders' Party, see Judith Pataki, "Smallholders' Party Could Decide the Outcome of the Elections," RFE/RL, *Report on Eastern Europe*, vol. 1, no. 11, March 16, 1990. See also: "ISP: A Home for the Hungarian Way," *Népszabadság*, Budapest, April 3, 1993, in *FBIS-EEU–93–065*, April 7, 1993.

25. Interview with István Szoke by László Bartus, "The Police Provided Protection to the Skinheads," *Magyar Hírlap*, Budapest, November 2, 1992, in *FBIS-EEU–92–216*, November 6, 1992.

26. *MTI*, Budapest, December 7, 1992, in *FBIS-EEU–92–237*, December 9, 1992; and *Country Reports on Human Rights Practices for 1992*, Department of State, Washington, DC, February 1993.

27. Information on Hungarian right-wing organizations is taken from a series of articles reprinted in *Tallózó*, Budapest, July 30, 1992, in *JPRS-EER–92–126*, September 9, 1992; *Magyar Hírlap*, June 5, 1990, in *JPRS-EER–90–129*, September 17, 1990; Elemer Magyar, "Neofascists in Eger," *Beszelo*, Budapest, November 9, 1991, in *JPRS-EER–91– 175*, December 3, 1991; *Kossuth Radio Network*, Budapest, August 8, 1992, in *FBIS-*

EEU–92–154, August 10, 1992; Judith Pataki, "Increasing Intolerance of Foreigners," RFE/RL, *Research Report*, vol. 1, no. 19, May 8, 1992; interview with Mihály Hansély, "Not Skinheads But National Youth—Are Fascism and Anti-Fascism Only Political Terms for Right Wing?" *Magyar Hírlap*, October 5, 1992, in *FBIS-EEU–92–198*, October 13, 1992. For more information on skinhead groups see Teddie Weyr, "Trouble in Hungary."

28. Information on international Magyar organizations is taken from Alfred A. Reisch, "Hungary's Policy on the Yugoslav Conflict: A Delicate Balance," RFE/RL, *Report on Eastern Europe*, vol. 2, no. 32, August 9, 1991; interview with Elod Kincses by Marton Matuska, "Two Great Absentees: The Democratic Union of Hungarians in Romania and the Democratic Association of Hungarians in Vojvodina," *Magyar Szó*, Budapest, June 18, 1992, in *JPRS-EER–92–099*, August 1, 1992; Veronika R. Hahn, "The Revision of Trianon Borders Is a Pipe Dream," *Népszabadság*, Budapest, June 26, 1992, in *JPRS-EER–92–102*, August 7, 1992; Alfred A. Reisch, "Hungarian Parties Seek to Reassure Romania on Border Issue," Radio Free Europe/ Radio Liberty, *Report on Eastern Europe*, vol. 1, no. 24, June 15, 1990; "Weekly Review," RFE/RL *Research Report*, vol. 1, no. 35, September 4, 1992.

29. *MTI*, Budapest, January , 1991, in *FBIS-EEU–91–022*, February 1, 1991; Reisch, "First Law on Minorities Drafted"; Rimas, "Bill on National Minorities: Dissatisfaction"; "Hungary's National Minorities Reject the Bill," *Népszabadság*, February 21, 1992, in *FBIS-EEU–92–037*, February 25, 1992.

30. *MTI*, Budapest, June 28, 1990, in *FBIS-EEU–90–126*, June 29, 1990; Zoltán D. Bárány, "Hungary's Gypsies," RFE/RL, *Report on Eastern Europe*, vol. 1, no. 29, July 20, 1990.

31. Bárány, "Hungary's Gypsies"; P.Sz. [as published], "Gypsies Demonstrated Against Gypsies," *Magyar Hírlap*, Budapest, December 19, 1991, in *JPRS-EER–92–011*, January 28, 1992; and RFE/RL, *Daily Report*, no. 138, July 22, 1993.

32. Z.O., "Roma Parliament: Báthory Should Resign," *Magyar Hírlap*, Budapest, November 26, 1991, in *JPRS-EER–92–001*, January 2, 1992; P. Sz., "Gypsies Demonstrated Against Gypsies"; RFE/RL, *Daily Report*, no. 21, February 2, 1993.

33. "Representation in Parliament!" *Magyar Hírlap*, Budapest, July 29, 1991, in *JPRS-EER 91–113*, August 1, 1991. See also *Helsinki Watch Report*, vol. VII, no. 39, August 1, 1990.

34. Alfred A. Reisch, "Hungarian-German Treaty Cements Close Relations," RFE/RL, *Research Report*, vol. 1, no. 10, March 6, 1992.

35. For more information on the Hungarian Gypsy Party and the Hungarian Gypsy Social-Democratic Party, see Bárány, "Hungary's Gypsies."

36. For information on the German minority, see "Germans in Hungary Expect More Assistance form the State and from Society," *Népszava*, January 8, 1990, in *JPRS-EER–90–016*, February 7, 1990; *MTI*, Budapest, June 8, 1990, *FBIS-EEU–90–112*, June 11, 1990; Reisch, "Hungarian-German Treaty Cements Close Relations"; RFE/RL, *Daily Report*, no. 46, March 6, 1992.

37. "Short of Priests," *Zemědělské Noviny*, Prague, February 20, 1991, in *FBIS-EEU–91–038*, February 26, 1991. See also Ján Babak, "Slovaks in Present-Day Hungary," *Literarný Tyzednik*, Bratislava, July 7, 1989, in *JPRS-EER–89–129*, November 22, 1989; interview with Mária Jakab by Péter Matyuc, "The Cry for Help of a Diminishing National Group," *Népszabadság*, Budapest, November 12, 1990, in *FBIS-EEU–90–223*, November 19, 1990; interview with Mária Jakab and György Popović by Katalin Decsi, "If Circumstances Do Not Change, National Minorities in Hungary Will Be Threatened by Assimilation—Rights on Paper, Sad Reality," *Népszabadság*, Budapest, May 23, 1990, in *FBIS-EEU–90–109*, June 6, 1990; series of articles by Frigyes Varju, "To Be a Slovak in

Hungary," *Nepszava*, Budapest, April 4–6, 1991, in *FBIS-EEU–91–069*, April 10, 1991; *ČSTK*, Prague, October 1, 1992, in *FBIS-EEU–92–194*, October 6, 1992.

38. See Charles Hoffman, *Gray Dawn: The Jews of Eastern Europe in the Post-Communist Era* (New York: Harper Collins, 1992), pp. 55–112; and *MTI*, Budapest, February 27, 1990, in *FBIS-EEU–90–040*, February 28, 1990.

39. Jovo Paripović, "Three Alliances Instead of One," *Vjesnik*, Zagreb, January 28, 1990, in *JPRS-EER–90–029*, March 8, 1990; *MTI*, Budapest, November 4, 1990, in *FBIS-EEU–90–214*, November 5, 1990. See also *Kossuth Radio Network*, Budapest, July 31, 1991, in *FBIS-EEU–91–149*, August 2, 1991.

40. Interview with György Márk by Imre Szenes, "The Way the Leader of Romanians in Hungary Sees It," *Népszava*, Budapest, November 14, 1989, in *JPRS-EER–90–003*, January 4, 1990. Information on Romanian organizations is taken from *Budapest Domestic Service*, June 15, 1990, in *FBIS-EEU–90–118*, June 19, 1990; interview with Gheorghe Petrusan by Livmos Ágoston, "We Need a Law on National Minorities," *Magyar Nemzet*, December 18, 1991, in *FBIS-EEU–91–245*, December 20, 1991; *MTI*, Budapest, December 18, 1990, in *FBIS-EEU–90–244*, December 19, 1990.

41. *MTI*, Budapest, June 9, 1992, in *FBIS-EEU–92–112*, June 10, 1992.

42. Paripović, "Three Alliances."

43. János Gyurok, "Why Are There No National Minority Representatives in Parliament?" *Népszabadság*, Budapest, October 15, 1990, in *FBIS-EEU–90–202*, October 18, 1990; Paripović, "Three Alliances."

44. Rimas, "Bill on National Minorities: Dissatisfaction."

45. For more information on the Tîrgu Mureş violence, see "Weekly Record of Events," RFE/RL, *Report on Eastern Europe*, vol. 1, no. 13, March 30, 1990.

46. For background, see Alfred A. Reisch, "Hungary and Ukraine Agree to Upgrade Bilateral Relations," RFE/RL, *Report on Eastern Europe*, vol. 1, no. 44, November 2, 1990; RFE/RL, *Daily Report*, no. 8, January 14, 1992, and no. 98, May 22, 1992.

47. See RFE/RL *Daily Report*, no. 77, April 22, 1991, no. 176, September 16, 1991, and no. 237, December 16, 1991; *MTI*, Budapest, November 4, 1990, in *FBIS-EEU–90–214*, November 5, 1990. For more information on Hungarian-Croatian relations, see Reisch, "Hungary's Policy on the Yugoslav Conflict: A Delicate Balance."

48. For background information on Hungarian relations with the former Yugoslav republics, see RFE/RL, *Daily Report*, no. 77, April 22, 1991, and Reisch, "Hungary's Policy on the Yugoslav Conflict: A Delicate Balance"; RFE/RL, *Daily Report*, no. 168, September 4, 1991. See also Edith Oltay, "Hungarians in Yugoslavia Seek Guarantees for Minority Rights," RFE/RL, *Report on Eastern Europe*, vol. 2, no. 38, September 20, 1991.

CONCLUSION

Minority Rights and Ethnic Ethics

Most international human rights conventions and agreements define "minority rights" fairly narrowly.[1] In general, they include the rights of individuals to non-discrimination, cultural development, and religious freedom, in addition to the freedom of speech, assembly, and organization. Such universal principles of liberty and equality do not provide any specific rights to minorities as collective entities. As Patrick Thornberry argues, since the UN Universal Declaration of Human Rights, the protection of minorities has been absorbed into the broader concept of human rights, with some minor provisions for group protection.[2] This omission has been partly deliberate and evasive, as few governments have been willing to tackle the complex question of group rights and enshrine stipulations into international law that could, in theory and in practice, be used to challenge the integrity of existing state units. Such fears are compounded by the real and potential territorial claims of some neighboring states.

At the "Eurasian" level, the resolutions and agreements of the Conference on Security and Cooperation in Europe (CSCE) have only contained general provisions for protecting the "collective rights" of minorities. Indeed, these are generally understood and defined as the rights of individuals to engage in group activities. CSCE officials and member states remain concerned over the difficulties inherent in defining minorities, in delineating clear-cut distinctions between individual and group rights, in determining the parameters of minority autonomy or self-determination, and in reaching an international consensus on the extent of minority rights and the precise obligations of governments.

For instance, the CSCE Copenhagen Document of June 1990 included several passages confirming the rights of individuals belonging to recognized minorities to participate in collective activities, including using their "mother tongue," forming religious, cultural, and other associations, engaging in unimpeded cross-border contacts, and participating in public affairs and in the local administration. Although the document appeared to move somewhat beyond the traditional focus on individual human and civil rights, it did not signal any concrete multilateral agreements on the protection of minority groups. In addition, the signatories were at pains to underscore that none of the commitments to group-based rights could be interpreted as implying any right to engage in activities that contravened the principles of the United Nations Charter or the provisions of the Helsinki Final Act, "including the principle of the territorial integrity of States."[3]

The CSCE meeting in Geneva in July 1991 dealt more specifically with minority issues as a consequence of growing inter-ethnic tensions in Eastern Europe. Although the Geneva report stated that questions regarding minority rights did not constitute an exclusively internal affair of the respective states, the meeting produced little broad consensus and few new initiatives.[4] Controversy continued to surround such issues as the definition of a national minority, the distinctions between individual and group rights, and the extent to which governments should actively protect their minorities. The concluding document simply stressed the importance of non-governmental organizations in resolving ethnic conflicts and promoting tolerance among ethnic, religious, and cultural groupings. However, acknowledging the gravity of minority questions in Eastern Europe, in December 1992 the CSCE Helsinki follow-up meeting established the office of High Commissioner for National Minorities; former Dutch foreign minister Max van der Stoel became the first appointee.[5] The high commissioner was empowered to investigate problems relating to national minorities confidentially before they reach crisis proportions. If the commissioner was unsatisfied with the results of consultations with disputing parties, he or she could issue an "early warning" that would be placed on the agenda of the CSCE Committee of Senior Officials (CSO).

In future CSCE deliberations, the delicate issue of minority rights may require more solid definitional underpinnings if it is to acquire a sense of urgency in dealing with pending intra-state and inter-state disputes. Agreements on this question will need to focus on three complimentary components: state obligations toward minorities; minority obligations toward the state; and international involvement in resolving disputes over minority rights.

With regard to state obligations, a broader definition of "minority rights" will need to be ratified by each government on the basis of international conventions to cover a spectrum of provisions. Specifically, such definitions would need to be explicit on the questions of non-discrimination, the promotion of tolerance, bilingualism, minority education and culture, affirmative-action programs, and appropriate political representation.

At the outset, and as a base minimum, each citizen must have the undisputed right to determine and express his or her ethnic identity and religious conviction and to associate with like-minded individuals for the purpose of maintaining his or her cultural, ethnic, religious, or cultural self-definition. Minority groups throughout Eastern Europe contend that the rights they possess as individual citizens are simply insufficient to guarantee the maintenance of their cultural and ethnic identity, particularly during an unsteady process of political and legal transition.

Domestically, each state has to ensure the full array of internationally sanctioned minority rights in national constitutions and other legal documents, beginning with non-discrimination on ethnic, religious, or cultural grounds. International laws explicitly protect the right of individuals to belong to an ethnic minority and to preserve and develop their languages, cultural traditions, religious beliefs, and ethnic identities.[6] Article 14 of the 1950 European Convention on Human Rights and Fundamental Freedoms asserts that all rights and freedoms should be ensured without discrimination on grounds of "sex, race, color, language, religion, political or other opinion, national or social origin, association with a national minority, property, birth, or other status." Article 27 of the 1966 UN Covenant on Civil and Political Rights declares that persons belonging to ethnic, religious, or linguistic minorities will not be denied the right, "in community with the other members of their group, to enjoy their own culture, to profess and practice their own religion, or to use their own language."

These and other stipulations not only underscore the necessity of protection from all forms of discrimination, but they also imply that states should take active measures to offer such protection by amending or nullifying any laws that perpetuate racial or other forms of discrimination and by issuing guarantees against expulsion, segregation, or forcible assimilation. According to international conventions, all states are obligated to promote racial and ethnic tolerance through the educational system, by teaching the history and culture of national and religious minorities, and by dispelling or combating racial prejudice and animosity toward different cultures and religions. Under Article 26 of the 1984 Universal Declaration of Human Rights, state-funded education is supposed to enhance "understanding, tolerance, and friendship among all nations, and racial or religious groups." This was reiterated by CSCE statements affirming that each state should encourage a "climate of mutual respect, understanding, cooperation, and solidarity among all persons living on its territory, without distinction as to ethnic or national origin or religion."[7] Other existing international conventions require states to promote "integrationist multi-racial organizations and movements" and to eliminate barriers between races while "discouraging anything that strengthens racial divisions."[8]

Beyond fostering non-discrimination and promoting inter-group tolerance, minorities invariably seek positive recognition together with the rights and conditions to facilitate their distinctive group life. Several arenas can help advance this process, and the basis has already been laid in a number of international agreements. States need to provide full legal guarantees to enable ethnic groups to benefit from their own associations, organizations, schools, media, churches, libraries, economic bodies, and self-help institutions. In addition, minorities should have the freedom to uphold cultural, social, informational, and other contacts with different states, including their "mother countries," without diminishing their responsibilities as citizens.

An important starting point is the assurance of bilingualism for minorities. Indeed, international law obliges states to ensure that minority groups have proper opportunities for instruction in their mother tongue in order to fully express their identities. According to CSCE provisions, persons belonging to national minorities must receive adequate opportunities for instruction in their mother tongue and wherever possible for the use of this language in any dealings with officialdom.[9] The latter principle should particularly apply in towns or regions where a minority forms a relative majority, even though state institutions also have a duty to propagate the universal use of the country's major language or languages. Native-language use should not hinder communications with the majority population or obstruct minority participation in the nation's political and economic life. International conventions cannot of course lay down precise domestic arrangements for language use. Full or partial bilingualism at local, regional, or even at national levels, as evident in several Western states, must be left to the discretion of democratically elected parliaments. However, Western bilingual models can be presented more effectively to East European governments to help reduce fears that multi-language use will inevitably increase pressures for autonomy or secession.

Discrimination in education on the basis of race, religion, or ethnicity has been deemed contrary to international law. Moreover, some provisions specifically underscore the right of members of national minorities to pursue their own educational activities by maintaining their own schools and furnishing lessons in their own language, provided that this does not prevent the minority in question from understanding and participating in the culture and language of the wider community and does not undermine national sovereignty.[10] Even if governments cannot supply separate or supplemental schooling for minorities, they should give all ethnic groups maximum leeway to establish, fund, and control their own private educational and cultural facilities without official hindrance. In the words of one analyst, a government that both protects individual freedom of choice and seeks to preserve cultural diversity and encourages a pluralistic society, rather than a uni-cultural, monolithic society, is in essence an authentic, democratic, and liberal government.[11]

In instances where severely under-privileged or pauperized minorities possess precious few resources to resuscitate their cultural, educational, and religious life, some "affirmative action" or "reverse discrimination" programs initiated by the state may prove necessary to remedy existing disadvantages, to improve economic conditions, and to enable individuals both to engage in group activities and to contribute to national development. Indeed, some international accords allow or encourage governments to undertake "special measures" for an indeterminate period of time in order to advance the position of certain ethnic minorities, especially those that have suffered from severe neglect or pervasive discrimination in the past. Not only would such measures enable them to benefit from equal citizenship rights, but they would provide minorities with boosted economic and employment opportunities. For example, temporary preferential treatment may be initiated by allocating state investments in deprived minority neighborhoods; by encouraging private and cooperative enterprises through loan opportunities, technical-assistance programs, and job-creation schemes for minority-group members; and by pursuing some form of ethnic proportionality in government and civil-service employment. According to international conventions, such measures are not intended to result in permanent "special rights" for different racial or ethnic groups. However, they are designed to enable underprivileged groups to "catch up" materially with the majority population and give them a direct stake in the nation's development.[12]

In the political realm, minorities need to be included in the administrative and legislative processes, and in the case of small or widely dispersed groups some flexibility may need to be introduced in the application of straightforward democratic majority rule. In an ideal civic-oriented polity, ethnic identity should not figure as a determinant of political preference. However, in the transitional states of Eastern Europe, where ethnic or regionally-based political organizations among both majority and minority populations provide representation and compete for office at various administrative levels, some provision must be made to balance their influence in order to avoid charges of estrangement, alienation, and exclusion. On the other hand, the impact of minority organizations should not be allowed to exceed their population size grossly as this could lead to opposition and outright hostility among the majority or among other minorities.

As a basic starting point, minorities must be allowed to participate fully in the country's political system through involvement in local, regional, and national elections. Although some governments explicitly prohibit ethnic or regionalist parties from standing in elections, some flexibility in these rulings, with allowances for openly multi-ethnic associations to compete, could reduce minority resentment, encourage cooperation across ethnic boundaries, and increase opportunities for parliamentary representation. Of course, it would be difficult for international organizations to dictate the precise forms of minority representation in state institutions or determine whether this is based on ethnic proportionalities, the provision of bicameral legislatures with a regionally composed upper house, or some kind of regulated parliamentary quotas at local, regional, and national levels.[13] However, domestic agreements must be reached that, on the one hand, contribute to satisfying minority aspirations and, on the other hand, reassure the majority ethnicity that its rights, access, and influence will not suffer as a consequence. Indeed, an absence of such provisions, and the exclusion of minorities from administrative and legislative work, could actually heighten calls for political or territorial self-determination and even separatism among aggrieved minorities.

Although it may not be feasible in the short term to eliminate ethnicity as an organizing principle in the formation of political parties, the discriminatory effects of majority rule in ethnically divided societies can be diminished. In the estimation of some analysts, policies should aim to provide both gains and concessions for all ethnic groups. For example, various electoral devices can be applied, including constituency delimitation and parliamentary-seat allocations on the basis of variable quotas adjusted for changing demographic proportions. In addition, electoral laws may provide incentives for inter-ethnic cooperation and coalition building, or alternatively they could encourage party fragmentation to counter ethnic polarization.[14] Power and policy decision making can also be dispersed among various government bodies at central, regional, and local levels. In such cases, inter-ethnic competition and conflict can be compartmentalized and managed within sub-state units, rather than allowing them to threaten the stability of the state.

In some instances, where minorities reside in reasonably compact territorial units, whether in towns, municipalities, communes, or distinct regions, they may be provided with a measure of local administrative autonomy without undermining the government's key economic, political, and security functions. Of course, exact arrangements depend largely on historical and administrative precedents in the country in question. Some states have a tradition of local or regional autonomy; in others political and economic decentralization combined with cultural autonomy and local bilingualism can mitigate against possible majority–minority conflicts. Governments of course may fear that regionalization and autonomy may encourage secession. Such apprehensions could be reduced if the state can be assured of retaining ultimate control over regional governments or if the principle of autonomy is equally applied to all regions, thus countering the development of ethnic particularism.

While each government needs to ensure a wide array of minority rights, minority leaders must also abide by specific obligations to the state. Some of these have already been outlined in considering the parameters of collective rights. As a general principle, minority leaders need to recognize the state's constitutionality and territorial integrity where human rights are respected and minority interests are represented, regardless of the precise administrative or territorial structure. Ethnic, cultural, and religious pluralism should be allowed to flourish, but it cannot be allowed to fracture and undermine a democratic polity. In this regard, neighboring states must be careful in the kind of support they lend to co-ethnics across their borders and must remain sensitive to the apprehensions of potentially vulnerable governments. Democratization and decentralization should not provide easy opportunities for secession and annexation. Indeed, such moves could actually threaten the democratic transition and stimulate an authoritarian turnaround. Minority leaders must contribute to the emergence of a liberal democratic system that is tolerant of minority rights and not automatically oppose the government on the grounds that collective rights remain incomplete. International monitoring groups can play a direct role here, not only in tracking government compliance with multilateral accords, but also in assessing minority compliance with their obligations to the state.

Minorities will of course have sounder justification for opposition and even separation in an autocratic system that abuses both individual and collective rights. In such cases, they would also have recourse to international intervention or mediation as a means to pressure the government legally to enshrine and guarantee minority rights. International agreements could actually underscore the right to autonomy and self-government in cases where the central government is unprepared to grant fundamental minority rights as specified in various international documents. The option of autonomy or even secession could thereby be applied as a weapon of last resort against repressive states in order to elicit governmental concessions. Autonomy leading to independent statehood could then be presented as a viable and internationally sanctioned alternative where human and group rights are persistently violated.[15]

This approach could also be reversed. One writer has proposed that the international community should withhold political support for an autonomist or separatist movement unless the self-determination of a particular province or region will enhance democracy rather than retard it.[16] Beyond this, he argues that "excessive self-determination" may actually work against the process of democratization and can even threaten democracy in countries that have already attained it. This argument can, of course, easily be reversed for non-democratic states.

The international arena is critically important for helping to ensure that states and minorities interact productively and peacefully. Each government needs to conclude binding bilateral agreements with neighboring states, mutually guaranteeing the rights of the relevant minorities and renouncing any latent territorial pretensions. Simultaneously, binational or multi-national monitoring teams could be established to observe and report on the position of minorities in both states. Such arrangements would deflect charges that specific states were being singled out for special and unfair treatment or were being pressured to grant more rights to resident minorities than their neighbors. Some moves in this direction have in fact already been taken. In April 1993, Budapest and Bratislava agreed to create a panel of independent experts to examine the situation of minorities in both states. According to the tentative agreement, the panel was to serve for at least two years, gathering information and issuing recommendations to the CSCE High Commissioner for Minorities, who in turn would pass these on to the governments involved.[17] Such independent panels exploring bilateral relations and monitoring the treatment of minorities could serve as a pattern for other pairs of states.

International bodies must be involved early on to prevent the escalation of ethnic conflicts. Such engagement can be pursued through diplomacy, institution building, human- and minority-rights monitoring, and the settlement of disputes. In October 1992, CSCE ministers meeting in Geneva adopted a "comprehensive set of measures" on the "peaceful settlement of disputes." The package included a draft convention on conciliation and arbitration and a process of "directed conciliation," whereby the CSCE Committee of Senior Officials or the Council of Ministers could direct two disputants, even without their consensus, to a conciliation procedure. The non-treaty elements of this package were accepted as mandatory by all participating states, while the treaty or convention would only become binding on those states that formally ratified it; the majority of participants indicated their intention to do so.[18]

Alongside this dispute-resolving initiative, some progress needs to be made in respect of standardizing minority rights across the region. Bearing in mind that the situation in different multi-ethnic states varies enormously, a regional or sub-regional focus could prove more effective in outlining at least the minimum requirements of minority protection. Furthermore, CSCE and other multi-national fora could take steps toward forging something resembling a "minority-rights charter." Such an international agreement would help clarify and codify the obligations of participating states and the responsibilities of their constituent minorities. Within its ambit a "minorities forum" could be initiated to enable minority leaders from diverse states to share their experiences and even devise common strategies. These initiatives can be reinforced through the creation of a commission of international legal experts and minority-rights observers who can be promptly dispatched to monitor and develop the charter's provisions. Such a "minority-rights committee" would provide early warning of any impending conflict, issue recommendations for appropriate counter-measures, and contribute to the creation of an arbitration body between adversarial parties. Supervision over the application of the charter could be assigned to an existing CSCE body such as the Conflict Resolution Center or the High Commissioner for National Minorities; it could also be linked to the European Court of Justice at the Council of Europe.

Continuing calls for neutrality on the question of minority or group rights, however well-motivated, and an exclusive focus on individual human rights simply avoid confronting a problem that will bedevil Eastern Europe and the former Soviet republics for at least the next decade.[19] The road to hell has often been paved with good intentions. Indeed, neglecting the issue of group rights may have the reverse effect, by unwittingly giving certain governments a green light to pursue assimilationist policies in order to eliminate minority groups politically and undermine or even eradicate distinctive minority identities. The consequences could be grave: repressive regimes may provoke direct conflict with neighboring states seeking to defend specific minorities from persecution, discrimination, or assimilation. This in turn could precipitate international involvement by way of conflict prevention and peacekeeping, or in a worst-case scenario trying to cope with a low-intensity war. One way or another, international institutions could find themselves embroiled in a local or even a regional conflict.

Contrary to the anti–group-rights position, some observers have noted that even though the United Nations has not adopted a system of minority-rights protection, it is already involved in the issue of minority rights in at least three areas: the Genocide Convention, the work of the Sub-Commission for Prevention of Discrimination and Protection of Minorities, and the question of the right of national self-determination.[20] In the absence of more concerted and early involvement in minority-rights issues across the post-Communist world, the United Nations may find itself drawn into a plethora of inter-ethnic trouble spots in a variety of humanitarian or peace-keeping roles. Indeed, proposals are already on the table to create a standing peace-keeping force consisting of troops recruited from member nations on a rotational basis, as well as a UN mediation center to train diplomatic and military peacemakers. Instead of allowing a dangerous spiral of escalation to unfold, preemptive measures can help reduce the need for costly and unpredictable military entanglements at a future date.

Although the steps outlined above will not rapidly eliminate all the sources and manifestations of conflict in Eastern Europe, they can provide some basis for dialogue, compromise, and conflict reduction. The early and persistent involvement of international institutions in evolving ethnic relations could directly assist the democratization process, help propel each country toward accepted international standards, and mitigate against the kind of destructive ethnic polarization that invariably leads to conflict, mayhem, and even outright war. It is certainly easier to prevent swimmers from entering dangerous waters than to pull them out in one piece from the jaws of a crocodile.

NOTES

1. For various definitions of "minority rights" currently in use, see Edward Lawson, *Encyclopedia of Human Rights* (New York: Taylor and Francis, 1991).

2. See Patrick Thornberry, *Minorities and Human Rights Law*, Minority Rights Group, Report no. 73, London, 1987.

3. See the *Document of the Copenhagen Meeting of the Conference on the Human Dimension of the CSCE*, published by the U.S. Commission on Security and Cooperation in Europe, Washington, DC, June 1990.

4. Check the Report of the *CSCE Meeting of Experts on National Minorities*, Geneva, July 1991; and Bob Hand, "Minority Questions Prove Difficult in Geneva," *CSCE Digest*, Summer 1991, Washington, DC.

5. See *Beyond Process: The CSCE's Institutional Development, 1990–1992*, prepared by the staff of the Commission on Security and Cooperation in Europe, Washington, DC, December 1992.

6. See the *Document* of the Copenhagen Meeting of the Conference on the Human Dimension of the CSCE, 1990, Paragraph 32.

7. *Document* of the Copenhagen Meeting Conference on the Human Dimension of the CSCE, 1990, Paragraph 36.

8. For example, see the International Convention on the Elimination of All Forms of Racial Discrimination, 1966, Article 2.

9. See the *Document* of the Copenhagen Meeting of the Conference on the Human Dimension of the CSCE, 1990, Paragraph 34.

10. See the UNESCO Convention Against Discrimination in Education, 1960, Article 5.

11. J.A. Laponce, *The Protection of Minorities* (Berkeley, CA: University of California Press, 1960), p. 181.

12. See the International Convention on the Elimination of All Forms of Racial Discrimination, 1966, Article 1.

13. For a useful discussion of election issues, see Claire Palley, *Constitutional Law and Minorities*, Minority Rights Group, Report no. 36, London, April 1978.

14. For an invaluable analysis of policy prescriptions, see Donald L. Horowitz, *Ethnic Groups in Conflict* (Berkeley, CA: University of California Press, 1985), pp. 563–680.

15. For a useful analysis of international involvement with regard to secessionist movements, see Alexis Heraclides, *The Self-Determination of Minorities in International Politics* (London: Frank Cass, 1991).

16. See Amitai Etzioni, "The Evils of Self-Determination," *Foreign Policy*, no. 89, Winter 1992–93, pp. 21–35.

17. Radio Free Europe/Radio Liberty Research Institute, *Daily Report*, no. 80, April 28, 1993.

18. See *CSCE Digest*, vol. 16, no. 1, Washington, DC, January 1993.

19. For an anti–collective-rights position, see Robert Cullen, "Human Rights Quandary," *Foreign Affairs*, vol. 71, no. 5, Winter 1992–93.

20. See Stephen Ryan, "Ethnic Conflict and the United Nations," *Ethnic and Racial Studies*, vol. 13, no. 1, January 1990, pp. 25–49.

POSTSCRIPT

Since this manuscript was finalized in 1993, developments in Eastern Europe have continued to outpace all attempts to chronicle and interpret them. Ethnic politics remains a fast-moving target in which domestic and international factors propel hitherto unimportant or underreported issues while discarding or postponing formerly pressing ones. It would serve little purpose to try to update the condition of each ethnic group in the region or the position of each ethnic or regionalist organization included in this guidebook. Instead, a brief synopsis of major developments in each East European state between August 1993 and February 1994 will help shed some light on the direction of events.

Bosnia-Herzegovina continued to be wracked by a three-sided irregular war in which the civilian populations of all three major ethnic groups remained the prime target. The republic's ethnic separation gathered pace, encouraged by the Geneva process and UN mediation that evidently sanctioned the creation of three ethnically based mini-states from the ruins of multi-ethnic Bosnia. While Serb guerrillas consolidated their positions primarily in territories already under their control, Muslim forces scored some successes in central Bosnia against weaker Croatian targets. Zagreb and its political and military allies in Herzegovina appeared willing to surrender territory in central Bosnia in order to concentrate on forging a Croat para-state in western Herzegovina. The Bosnian government led by Alija Izetbegović and the Bosnian Assembly assumed a more exclusively Muslim profile, particularly after several Croat members abandoned the presidency and threw their support behind the partition plan.

Despite continuing peace talks and a tentative federal agreement between Croat and Bosnian Muslim representatives under U.S. sponsorship, the war seemed likely to continue through 1994. All three sides were seeking territorial and strategic advantage, seemingly undeterred by the limited UN/NATO military mandate. Indeed, the proposed Muslim-Croat federation and a confederal link between Croatia and Croat-Muslim Bosnia could encourage Serbian Bosnia to confederate with Serbia proper, thus effectively partitioning the republic. Moreover, the Bosnian example of ethnic division and religious exclusivity, promulgated by force and coercion, could set a potentially dangerous precedent elsewhere in the Balkans.

The situation in both Croatia and Serbia remained tense. Zagreb was confronted with an intractable problem in Serb-controlled Krajina. Local Serb authorities would not contemplate rejoining the Croatian state and held their own legislative and presidential elections, preparing the ground for a future merger with the "Serbian Republic" in Bosnia and Serbia-Yugoslavia. The Tudjman government was militarily unprepared to launch major offensives against Serb positions, while negotiations over a land swap between Zagreb and Belgrade failed to produce any viable agreements. Tudjman also faced increasing resistance from regionalist movements in Dalmatia and Istria: government pressures failed to stem growing demands for far-reaching decentralization.

Despite increasingly onerous international sanctions and the collapse of the Serbian economy, President Milošević retained a large measure of public support, as was evident in the results of the Serbian parliamentary elections. Belgrade continued to pursue its nationalist agenda in Bosnia, Croatia, and Kosovo, and even the oppositionist parties appealed to nationalist sentiments in order to garner some measure of public support. If sanctions persisted, Serbia faced the possibility of growing social pauperization, atomization, criminalization, and even civil unrest while Milošević continued to play the nationalist card vis-à-vis neighboring states.

The Kosovo Albanians again boycotted the Serb elections and no progress was made in addressing their grievances or restoring Kosovar autonomy. While Milošević was unlikely to launch a major "ethnic cleansing" operation in Kosovo, the possibility of active Albanian resistance continued to grow, fueled by widespread frustration and dissatisfaction with the pacifist policies of the Kosovo Albanian leadership in Priština.

Montenegro remained trapped in the Serbian vice. The government of President Bulatović made some gestures toward the "Montenegrin option" by allowing for the restoration of the Montenegrin Autocephalous Orthodox Church and by forming a broader coalition government. However, Podgorica was cognizant that any steps toward outright independence would be met by a forceful response form Belgrade. Opposition influence continued to grow, buttressed by the political ripple effects of the restored Montenegrin Church and its conflicts with the Serb Orthodox patriarchate. Podgorica feared that any attempts by Belgrade to restructure the Yugoslav federation would lead to a major conflict with Montenegrin nationalists.

Macedonia remained in a precarious position, buffeted by pressures from neighbors and volatile internal ethnic relations. A process of radicalization was demonstrated among the Albanian parties and some evidence of plans for armed resistance surfaced when Skopje conducted a purge in the Defense Ministry, claiming that armed Albanian formations had been established. Macedonia faced a national census and parliamentary elections during 1994; the results would undoubtedly set the tone for either stability or unrest in the republic.

In Albania, the Greek minority question continued to give rise to grave concern in government circles. Although tensions subsided somewhat after the summer of 1993, Tirana feared that a confrontation over Kosovo would encourage

Athens to renew pressures for some kind of autonomy status for Greek-inhabited southern Albania; this position could in turn radicalize the Albanian political debate and provoke a resurgence of expansionist ultra-nationalism.

Of all the Balkan states, Bulgaria appeared to be the most ethnically stable, although of a conflict in Macedonia would undoubtedly precipitate a nationalist response in Sofia and raise the specter of Bulgarian militancy and claims to Macedonian territory.

Romania continued to face three ethnically impregnated problems: dissatisfaction among segments of the Hungarian minority over local government policy and the activities of Romanian ultra-nationalist groupings; tense and sometimes violent confrontation between Romanians and Romas in the countryside; and the future status of Moldova. Regarding the first question, a great deal hinged on the signing of comprehensive agreements with Hungary regulating the position of minorities in both states and discounting any possible border claims.

While the Czech Republic made a smooth transition to independence, Slovakia was beset by rising ethnic tensions involving the Hungarian minority. Magyar leaders protested Bratislava's plans for an administrative reorganization that would divide ethnic Hungarians among five territorial units. Instead, they proposed establishing a semi-autonomous "Hungarian province" in southern Slovakia, in which Magyars would acquire more extensive cultural and political prerogatives. The move provoked condemnation by the Slovak government and was viewed as a step toward territorial secession supported by ultra-nationalist circles in Hungary. Upcoming parliamentary elections in Hungary would help to determine Budapest's position on all of its volatile external minority questions and either moderate or worsen relations with its neighbors.

One additional factor contributed to the ethno-nationalist brew throughout Eastern Europe. The success of ultra-nationalist and imperialist forces in the Russian parliamentary elections, led by the fascist politician Vladimir Zhirinovsky, raised tensions around the region. If imperialist pressures continue to swell in Russia, they could stimulate either pro- or anti-Russian nationalist responses in Eastern Europe and embolden xenophobic forces exploiting popular dissatisfaction with economic reform and preying on popular prejudices against minority groups. This scenario could also seriously aggravate relations between some states, particularly where ethnic identity became a prime determinant for political influence, economic advancement, and citizenship rights. It seems clear that at least until the end of this decade, ethnicity will remain a central ingredient in political life. Its role in framing popular perceptions and public policies could determine progress in all other endeavors. This critical factor can simply no longer be underestimated by Western governments and international institutions.

APPENDIX 1A

List of East European Acronyms

AASz	1956-os Antifasiszta és Antibolseviszta Szözvetség
ADS-LP	Albanski Demokratski Sojuz—Liberalna Partija
AKDS	Albanska Kršćanska Demokratska Stranka
APBB	Asociaţia Pro-Basarabia şi Bucovina
BDMG	Bashkimi Demokratik i Minoritetit Grek "Omonia"
BDN	Bashkimi i të Drejtave të Njëriut
BNRP	Bŭlgarska Natsionalna Radikalna Partiya
BSP	Bŭlgarska Sotsialisticheska Partiya
BM	Bokaljska Mornarica
BSR	Białoruskie Stowarzyszenie Rolników
BZD	Białoruskie Zjednoczenie Demokratyczne
DA	Dalmatinska Akcija
DEMOS	Demokratska Opozicija Slovenije
DKOSRTs	Dvizhenie za Kulturno, Obrazovatelno i Sotsialno Razvitie na Tsiganite
DNS	Dalmatinska Narodna Stranka
DNSU	Domovinsko Nepartije Srpske Udruženje
DPPR	Demokratska Politička Partija Roma
DPPRM	Demokratska Progresivna Partija na Romite vo Makedonija
DPS	Demokratska Partija na Srbite
DPS	Demokratska Partija Socijalista
DPS	Dvizhenie za Prava i Svobodi
DPT	Demokratska Partija na Turcite
DS	Demokratska Stranka
DSA	Demokratski Savez Albanaca
DSBJ	Demokratski Savez Bugarina Jugoslavije
DSCG	Demokratski Savez Crne Gore
DSHV	Demokratski Savez Hrvata u Vojvodini
DSK	Demokratski Savez Kosova
DSRV	Demokratski Savez Rumuna Vojvodin

DZMV	Demokratska Zajednica Madžara Vojvodine
DZRS	Demokratický Zväz Rómov na Slovensku
EVSz	Erdélyi Világszövetség
FDGR	Forumul Democratic al Germanilor din România
FKGP	Független Kisgazda Párt—Torgyán Frakció
FNIF	Független Nemzeti Ifjúsági Front
FPR	Frontul Popular Român
HDS	Hnutie za Demokratické Slovensko
HDZ	Hrvatska Demokratska Zajednica
HMDS	Hrvatska Muslimanska Demokratska Stranka
HNS	Hnutie za Nezávislé Slovensko
HSDMS	Hnutíza Samosprávnou Demokracii Moravy a Slezska
HSP	Hrvatska Stranka Prava
IDS	Istarski Demokratski Sabor
IRO	Istarska Radikalna Organizacija
ISMM	Interesna Skupnost Madžarske Manjšine
ISzM	Ifjúság Szervezet—"Mladost"
IZIR	Italijanska Zveza za Istro in Reko
KDH	Kresťanskodemokratické Hnutie
KK	Kisebbségi Kerekasztal
KNU	Keresztény Nemzeti Unió
KPN	Koła Przyjaźni Niemieckiej
KPN	Konfederacja Polski Niepodległej
KRB	Konfederatsiya na Roma v Bŭlgaria
KVAPS	Koordinirano Veće Albanske Političke Stranke
KZNI	Komitetza Zashtita na Natsionalnite Interesi
KZP	Kaszubski Związek Pomorski
LBO	Liberalna Bošnjačka Organizacija
LOMNER	Liga Organizaţülor Minoritaţilor Naţionale şi Etnice din România
LSCG	Liberalni Savez Crne Gore
LSFPM	Liga de Solidaritate cu Frontul Popular al Moldovei
LSV	Liga Socialdemokrata Vojvodine
LTŚwK	Litewskie Towarzystwo Św. Kazimierza
LV	Liga na Vlasite
MAAK	Dviženje za Semakedonska Akcija
MAZsiHiSz	Magyarországi Zsidó Hitközségek Szövetsége
MBO	Muslimanska Bošnjačka Organizacija

MBSz	Magyarországi Bolgárok Szövetsége
MCASz	Magyar Cigányok Antifasiszta Szervezete
MCDSz	Magyarországi Cigányok Demokratikus Szövetsége
MCNU	Magyarországi Cigányok Nemzetiségi Uniója
MCP	Magyar Cigány Párt
MCSzP	Magyar Cigány Szociáldemokrata Párt
MDF	Magyar Demokrata Fórum
MDS	Muslimanska Demokratska Stranka
MHSz	Magyarországi Horvátok Szövetsége
MKDH	Maďarské Kresťansodemokratické Hnutie
MLS	Maďarská Ludová Strana
MMD	Makedonsko Mladezhko Druzhestvo
MNF	Magyar Nemzeti Front
MNSz	Magyar Nemzeti Szövetség
MNS	Madjarska Narodna Stranka
MNS	Moravská Národní Strana
MOS	Maďarská Občianska Strana
MPR	Mişcarea Pentru România
MRDSz	Magyarországi Románok Demokratikus Szövetsége
MRP	Magyarországi Romaparlament
MNSz	Magyarországi Németek Szövetsége
MRSz	Magyarországi Románok Szövetsége
MS	Matica Slovenská
MSzSz	Magyarországi Szlovákok Szövetsége
MSzSz	Magyarországi Szlovének Szövetsége
MVSz	Magyarok Világszövetsége
MZsKE	Magyar Zsidók Kulturális Egyesülete
NDP	Narodna Demokratska Partija
NDS	Narodna Demokratska Stranka
NDSATsB	Nezavisima Demokraticheska Sotsialisticheska Asotsiatsiya na Tsiganite v Bŭlgariya
NFP	Narodowy Front Polski
NO	Narodowa Ofensywa
NOP	Narodowe Odrodzenie Polski
NPOK	Narodni Pokret za Oslobodjenje Kosova
NSCG	Narodna Stranka Crne Gore
NZCH	Nacionalna Zajednica Crnogorca Hrvatske
OBS	Obshto-Bŭlgarski Sŭyuz
OKŁ	Obywatelski Krąg Łemków "Hospodar"
OMOI	Obedinena Makedonska Organizatsiya Ilinden
OOR	Obedinena Organizatsiya Roma

OPO	Obshtestvo Peti Oktomvri
OPT	Otechestvena Partiya na Truda
OSMS	Občanské Shromáždění Moravy a Slezska
OSNN	Osnivanje Slovačka Narodna Nasledstva
PAPCGS	Pokret za Autonomni Pristup Crne Gore u Srbiju
PCER	Partija za Celosna Emancipacjia na Romite
PDP	Partija za Demokratski Prosperitet
PDV	Partiya za Demokraticheski Vazkhod
PFCSz	Phralipe" (Testvériség) Független Cigány Szervezet
PGST	Porozumienie Górnosląskich Stowarzyszeń i Towarzystw
PNRC	Partidul Noua Românie Creştină
PPN-PNP	Polska Partia Niepodległościowa—Partia Nowej Prawicy
PPSiNS	Powszechna Partia Słowian i Narodów Sprzymierzonych
PRM	Partidul România Mare
PSK	Parlamentska Stranka Kosova
PSM	Partidul Socialist al Muncü
PSSKCwNT	Podhalańskie Stowarzyszenie Społeczno-Kulturalne Cyganów w Nowym Targu
PUK	Partia e Unitetit Kombëtar
PUNR	Partidul Unităţ ii Naţ ionale Române
PWN-PSN	Polska Wspólnota Narodowa—Polskie Stronnictwo Narodowe
PZZ-RPŚ	Polski Związek Zachodni—Ruch Polskiego Śląska
RDS	Riječki Demokratski Savez
RKhDP	Roma Khristiyan Demokraticheska Partiya
RMN	Rada Mniejszości Narodowych
RMNS	Radikální Moravská Nacionální Strana
RN	Ruch Narodowy
RNK	Romský Národní Kongres
RNRAŚ	Ruch na Rzecz Autonomii Śląska
RO	Rusínska Obroda
ROI	Romská Občanská Iniciativa
RP	Rada Poláků
RP	Republikanska Partija
RS-SR	Republikánska Strana—Sdružení pro Republiku
RŽOČZ	Rada Židovských Obcí Českých Zemí
SAS	Shoqata e Arumunëve të Shqipërisë
SBMS	Shoqata "Bratska" e Maqedonave të Shqipërisë
SCA	Societatea Culturală Aromână
SDA	Stranka Demokratske Akcije
SDA-CG	Stranka Demokratske Akcije—Crna Gora

SDAK	Stranka Demokratske Akcije Kosova
SDF	Srpski Demokratski Forum
SDL	Strana Demokratickej Lavice
SDP	Srpski Demokratski Forum
SDPR	Socijaldemokratska Partija Reformatora
SDS	Srpska Demokratska Stranka
SDSCG	Srpska Demokratska Stranka Crne Gore
SDZMS	Sociálny a Demokratický Zväz Maďarov na Slovensku
SKDS	Slovenská Kresťanskodemokratická Strana
SŁ	Stowarzyszenie Łemków
SLP	Stowarzyszenie Litwinów w Polsce
SM	Shoqata e Malazezëve
SM	Stowarzyszenie Mazurskie
SM	Svaz Maďarů
SN	Stronnictwo Narodowe
SND	Stronnictwo Narodowo-Demokratyczne
SNDH	Slovenské Národné Demokratické Hnutie
SNJ	Stranka Narodne Jednakost
SNKO	Svaz Německých Kulturních Organizací
SNO	Srpska Narodna Obnova
SNS	Slovenska Nacionalna Stranka
SNS	Slovenská Národná Strana
SNS	Srpska Narodna Stranka
SPAC	Shoqata Patriotike Atdhetare "Çamëria"
SPAK	Shoqata Patriotike Atdhetare Kosova
SPCG	Socijalistička Partija Crne Gore
SPM	Shoqata Politike Mëmëdheu
SPO	Srpski Pokret Obnove
SPO	Strana Podnikatelů a Obchodníků
SPS	Socialistička Partija Srbije
SRH	Stranka Roma Hrvatske
SRI	Strana za Rómsku Integráciu
SRS	Srpska Radikalna Stranka
SRU	Savez Rutenca i Ukrajinca
SS	Sdružení Slováků
SS	Společnost Slováků
SS-SNJ	Strana Slobody—Strana Národnej Jednoty
SSV	Seljačka Stranka Vojvodine
SZ	Slovenska Zveza
SzDSz	Szerb Demokratikus Szövetség
SzT	Szentkorona Társulat
TDP	Turska Demokraticheska Partiya

TSKLCZSwP	Towarzystwo Społeczno-Kulturalne Czechów i Słowaków w Polsce
TSKMNŚO	Towarzystwo Społeczno-Kulturalne Mniejszości Niemíeckiej na Śląsku Opolskim
TSKŻwP	Towarzystwo Społeczno-Kulturalne Żydów w Polsce
UAR	Uniunea Armenilor din România
UDMR	Uniunea Democratică a Maghiarilor din România
UDMTR	Uniunea Democratică a Musulmanilor Turci din România
UDRR	Uniunea Democratică Romilor din România
UDS	Uniunea Democratică a Sîrbilor
UDSC	Uniunea Democratică a Slovacilor şi Cehilor
UMDSJ	Udruženje Madžara za Našu Domovinu, Srbiju i Jugoslaviju
USH	Udruženje Srba Hrvatske
UTDM	Uniunea Tineretului Democratic Maghiar
UUR	Uniunea Ucrainienilor din România
VMRO-DP	Vnatrešna Makedonska Revolucionerna Organizacija—Demokratska Partija
VMRO-DPMNE	Vnatrešna Makedonska Revolucionerna Organizacija—Demokratska Partija za Makedonsko Nacionalno Edinstvo
VMRO-N	Vŭtreshna Makedonska Revolyutsionna Organizatsiya—Nezavisim
VMRO-OMD	Vŭtreshna Makedonska Revolyutsionna Organizatsiya—Obedinenie na Makedonskite Druzhestva
VR	Vatra Românească
VZLPS	Veće za Zastitu Ljudskih Prava i Sloboda
WPW	Wilki Prus Wschodnich
ZChN	Zjednoczenie Chrześcijańsko-Narodowe
ZE	Združenie na Egipčanite
ZG	Związek Górnośląski
ZŁ	Zjednoczenie Łemków
ZMM	Združenie na Makedonci Muslimani
ZNSSKP	Związek Niemieckich Stowarzyszeń Społeczno-Kulturalnych w Polsce
ZSCM	Združenie na Srbi i Crnogorci vo Makedonija
ZSN	Zemské Shromáždění Němců
ZUP	Związek Ukraińców w Polsce
ZURČS	Zväz Ukrajincov a Rusínov v Česko-Slovensku

APPENDIX 1B

List of English Acronyms

AAA	Association of Arumunians in Albania
AAA	1956 Anti-Fascist and Anti-Bolshevik Association
ABU	All-Bulgarian Union
ACDP	Albanian Christian Democratic Party
ACS	Arumunian Cultural Society
ADU-LP	Albanian Democratic Union—Liberal Party
AFOHG	Anti-Fascist Organization of Hungarian Gypsies
AGH	Association of Germans in Hungary
AHFSY	Association of Hungarians for Our Fatherland, Serbia and Yugoslavia
AHJRC	Alliance of Hungarian Jewish Religious Communities
ALP	Association of Lithuanians in Poland
AM	Association of Montenegrins
AMM	Association of Macedonian Muslims
ANUP	Albanian National Unity Party
ARU	Alliance of Ruthenians and Ukrainians
ASC	Association of Serbs from Croatia
ASMM	Association of Serbs and Montenegrins in Macedonia
AUR	Armenian Union of Romania
AUSSA	Alliance of Upper Silesian Societies and Associations
BDU	Belarusian Democratic Union
BFS	Belarusian Farmers' Society
BMA	Boka Mariner's Association
BNRP	Bulgarian National Radical Party
BPAMA	"Bratska" Political Association of Macedonians in Albania
BSP	Bulgarian Socialist Party

CCAPP   Coordinating Council of Albanian Political Parties
CCL   *"Hospodar"* Citizens' Circle of Lemkos
CDAH   Croatian Democratic Alliance in Hungary
CDM   Christian Democratic Movement
CDNI   Committee for the Defense of National Interests
CDU   Croatian Democratic Union
CIP   Confederation for an Independent Poland
CJCCL   Council of Jewish Communities in the Czech Lands
CMDP   Croatian Muslim Democratic Party
CNU   Christian National Union
COS   Community of Slovaks
CPHRF   Council for the Protection of Human Rights and Freedoms
ÇPPA   Çamëria Political and Patriotic Association
CPR   Croatian Party of Rights
CRB   Confederation of Roma in Bulgaria

DA   Dalmatian Action
DAA   Democratic Alliance of Albanians
DACV   Democratic Alliance of Croats in Vojvodina
DAHG   Democratic Alliance of Hungarian Gypsies
DAM   Democratic Alliance of Montenegro
DARH   Democratic Association of Romanians in Hungary
DAVR   Democratic Alliance of Vojvodina Romanians
DCVH   Democratic Community of Vojvodina Hungarians
DFGR   Democratic Forum of Germans in Romania
DFS   Democratic Federation of Serbs
DLK   Democratic League of Kosovo
DNP   Dalmatian National Party
DOS   Democratic Opposition of Slovenia
DP   Democratic Party
DPPR   Democratic Political Party of Roma
DPPRM   Democratic Progressive Party of Roma in Macedonia
DPS   Democratic Party of Serbs
DPS   Democratic Party of Socialists
DPT   Democratic Party of Turks
DUBY   Democratic Union of Bulgarians in Yugoslavia
DUGM   Democratic Union of the Greek Minority
DUHR   Democratic Union of Hungarians in Romania
DURR   Democratic Union of Roma in Romania
DURS   Democratic Union of Roma in Slovakia
DUS   Democratic Union of Serbs
DUSC   Democratic Union of Slovaks and Czechs
DUSH   Democratic Union of Slovaks in Hungary

EAC	Egyptian Association of Citizens
EPW	East Prussian Wolves
FBH	Federation of Bulgarians in Hungary
FOS	Fifth of October Society
FPL	Fatherland Party of Labor
FPV	Farmers' Party of Vojvodina
FRH	Federation of Romanians in Hungary
FSH	Federation of Slovenes in Hungary
GLA	German Landowners' Assembly
GFCs	German Friendship Circles
GRP	Greater Romania Party
HCDM	Hungarian Christian Democratic Movement
HCP	Hungarian Civic Party
HCS	Holy Crown Society
HDF	Hungarian Democratic Forum
HGP	Hungarian Gypsy Party
HGSDP	Hungarian Gypsy Social Democratic Party
HJCF	Hungarian Jewish Cultural Federation
HNA	Hungarian National Alliance
HNF	Hungarian National Front
HNPSA	Homeland Non-Party Serbian Association
HPP	Hungarian People's Party
ICHM	Interest Community of the Hungarian Minority
IDA	Istrian Democratic Assembly
IDSAGB	Independent Democratic Socialist Association of Gypsies in Bulgaria
IMRO-DP	Internal Macedonian Revolutionary Organization—Democratic Party
IMRO-DPMNU	Internal Macedonian Revolutionary Organization—Democratic Party for Macedonian National Unity
IMRO-I	Internal Macedonian Revolutionary Organization—Independent
IMRO-UMS	Internal Macedonian Revolutionary Organization—Union of Macedonian Societies
INYF	Independent National Youth Front
IRO	Istrian Radical Organization
ISP	Independent Smallholders' Party—Torgyán Faction

IUIR	Italian Union for Istria and Rijeka
KPPA	Kosovo Patriotic and Political Association
KPU	Kaszubian Pomeranian Union
LA	Lemko Association
LAM	Liberal Alliance of Montenegro
LBO	Liberal Bosnian Organization
LONEMR	League of Organizations of National and Ethnic Minorities in Romania
LOV	League of Vlachs
LSDV	League of Social Democrats of Vojvodina
LSPFM	League of Solidarity with the People's Front of Moldova
LSSC	Lithuanian Society of Saint Casimir
LU	Lemko Union
MA	Mazurian Association
MBO	Muslim Bosnian Organization
MCESDG	Movement for the Cultural, Educational, and Social Development of Gypsies
MDP	Muslim Democratic Party
MDS	Movement for a Democratic Slovakia
MFR	Movement for Romania
MIS	Movement for an Independent Slovakia
MMAAS	Movement for Montenegro's Autonomous Accession to Serbia
MNP	Moravian National Party
MPA	Motherland Political Association
MPMA	Movement for Pan-Macedonian Action
MRF	Movement for Rights and Freedoms
MSA	Movement for Silesian Autonomy
MSCA	Moravian-Silesian Citizens' Assembly
MSDMS	Movement for the Self-Governing Democracy of Moravia and Silesia
MTDUR	Muslim Turkish Democratic Union of Romania
MYA	*"Mladost"* Youth Association
MYS	Macedonian Youth Society
NCCM	National Community of Croatian Montenegrins
NCGH	Nationality Council of Gypsies in Hungary
NCRP	New Christian Romania Party
NDP	National Democratic Party
NM	National Movement
NMC	National Minorities Council
NMLK	National Movement for the Liberation of Kosovo

NMR	National Minority Roundtable
NO	National Offensive
NP	National Party
NRP	National Rebirth of Poland
OSO	"Omonia" Sociopolitical Organization
PBBA	Pro-Bessarabia and Bukovina Association
PBT	Party of Businessmen and Tradesmen
PC	Polish Council
PCER	Party for Complete Emancipation of Roma
PDA	Party of Democratic Action
PDAK	Party of Democratic Action for Kosovo
PDA-M	Party of Democratic Action—Montenegro
PDL	Party of the Democratic Left
PDP	Party for Democratic Prosperity
PDP	People's Democratic Party
PF-PNU	Party of Freedom—Party of National Unity
PIGA	*"Phralipe"* (Brotherhood) Independent Gypsy Association
PIP-PNR	Polish Independence Party—Party of the New Right
PNC-PNP	Polish National Commonwealth—Polish National Party
PNE	Party of National Equality
PNF	Polish National Front
PPK	Parliamentary Party of Kosovo
PPM	People's Party of Montenegro
PRI	Party for Romani Integration
PRNU	Party of Romanian National Unity
PSCAGNT	Podhale Social-Cultural Association of Gypsies in Nowy Targ
PWU-MPS	Polish Western Union—Movement of Polish Silesia
RC	Romanian Cradle
RCI	Romani Civic Initiative
RCDP	Romani Christian Democratic Party
RDA	Rijeka Democratic Alliance
RMNP	Radical Moravian Nationalist Party
RNC	Romani National Congress
RP	Republican Party
RP	Roma Parliament
RP-AR	Republican Party—Association for the Republic
RPC	Romani Party of Croatia
RPF	Romanian Popular Front
RR	Ruthenian Revival

SA	Slovenian Alliance
SCAGMSO	Social-Cultural Association of the German Minority in Silesian Opole
SCDP	Slovak Christian Democratic Party
SCSCSP	Social-Cultural Society of Czechs and Slovaks in Poland
SCSJP	Social-Cultural Society of Jews in Poland
SDF	Serbian Democratic Forum
SDP	Serbian Democratic Party
SDPM	Serbian Democratic Party of Montenegro
SDPR	Social Democratic Party of Reformers
SDUHS	Social and Democratic Union of Hungarians in Slovakia
SLP	Socialist Labor Party
SM	Slovak Motherland
SNDM	Slovak National Democratic Movement
SNHF	Slovak National Heritage Foundation
SNP	Serbian National Party
SNP	Slovak National Party
SNP	Slovenian National Party
SNR	Serbian National Renewal
SPM	Socialist Party of Montenegro
SRM	Serbian Renewal Movement
SRP	Serbian Radical Party
SSP	Serbian Socialist Party
TDP	Turkish Democratic Party
UGCA	Union of German Cultural Associations
UGSCAP	Union of German Social-Cultural Associations in Poland
UH	Union of Hungarians
UHDY	Union of Hungarian Democratic Youth
UMO	*Ilinden* United Macedonian Organization
UOS	Union of Slovaks
UPHR	Unity Party for Human Rights
UPSAN	Universal Party of Slavs and Allied Nations
URO	United Roma Organization
USU	Upper Silesian Union
UUCRS	Union of Ukrainians and Ruthenians in Czechoslovakia
UUP	Union of Ukrainians in Poland
UUR	Union of Ukrainians in Romania
WFH	World Federation of Hungarians
WFT	World Federation of Transylvania

APPENDIX 2

List of Major Nationalist and Ethnic Organizations (by Country)

ALBANIA

Albanian Nationalists
Albanian National Unity Party (*Partia e Unitetit Kombëtar*)
Motherland Political Association (*Shoqata Politike Mëmëdheu*)

Greek Organizations
Democratic Union of the Greek Minority (*Omonia* Sociopolitical Organization) (*Bashkimi Demokratik i Minoritetit Grek "Omonia"*)
Unity Party for Human Rights (*Bashkimi i të Drejtave të Njëriut*)

Çam and Kosovar Movements
Kosovo Patriotic and Political Association (*Shoqata Patriotike Atdhetare Kosova*)
Çamëria Political and Patriotic Association (*Shoqata Patriotike Atdhetare "Çamëria"*)

Minority Organizations
Association of Montenegrins (*Shoqata e Malazezëve*)
"Bratska" Political Association of Macedonians in Albania (*Shoqata "Bratska" e Maqedonave të Shqipërisë*)
Association of Arumunians in Albania (*Shoqata e Arumunëve të Shqipërisë*)

BOSNIA-HERZEGOVINA

Muslim Organizations
Party of Democratic Action (*Stranka Demokratske Akcije*)

Muslim Bosnian Organization (*Muslimanska Bošnjačka Organizacija*)
Muslim Democratic Party (*Muslimanska Demokratska Stranka*)

Serbian Separatists
Serbian Democratic Party (*Srpska Demokratska Stranka*)

Croatian Autonomists
Croatian Democratic Union (*Hrvatska Demokratska Zajednica*)

Minority Organizations
Democratic Alliance of Albanians (*Demokratski Savez Albanaca*)

BULGARIA

Bulgarian Nationalists
Committee for the Defense of National Interests (*Komitet za Zashtita na Natsionalnite Interesi*)
Fatherland Party of Labor (*Otechestvena Partiya na Truda*)
Bulgarian National Radical Party (*Bŭlgarska Natsionalna Radikalna Partiya*)
Bulgarian Socialist Party (*Bŭlgarska Sotsialisticheska Partiya*)

Turkish Movements
Movement for Rights and Freedoms (*Dvizhenie za Prava i Svobodi*)
Turkish Democratic Party (*Turska Demokraticheska Partiya*)

Macedonian Groupings
Ilinden United Macedonian Organization (*Obedinena Makedonska Organizatsia Ilinden*)
Internal Macedonian Revolutionary Organization—Independent (*Vŭtreshna Makedonska Revolyutsionna Organizatsiya—Nezavisim*)
Internal Macedonian Revolutionary Organization—Union of Macedonian Societies (*Vŭtreshna Makedonska Revolyutsionna Organizatsiya—Obedinenie na Makedonskite Druzhestva*)
Macedonian Youth Society (*Makedonsko Mladezhko Druzhestvo*)
All-Bulgarian Union (*Obshto-Bŭlgarski Sŭyuz*)
Fifth of October Society (*Obshtestvo Peti Oktomvri*)

Minority Organizations
United Roma Organization (*Obedinena Organizatsiya Roma*)
Confederation of Roma in Bulgaria (*Konfederatsiya na Roma v Bŭlgariya*)
Movement for the Cultural, Educational, and Social Development of Gypsies (*Dvizhenie za Kulturno, Obrazovatelno i Sotsialno Razvitie na Tsiganite*)
Independent Democratic Socialist Association of Gypsies in Bulgaria (*Nezavisima*

Demokraticheska Sotsialisticheska Asotsiatsiya na Tsiganite v Bŭlgariya)
Romani Christian Democratic Party (*Roma Khristiyan Demokraticheska Partiya*)
Peace (*Shalom*)
Party for Democratic Prosperity (*Partiya za Demokraticheski Vazkhod*)

CROATIA

Croatian Nationalists
Croatian Democratic Union (*Hrvatska Demokratska Zajednica*)
Croatian Party of Rights (*Hrvatska Stranka Prava*)

Serbian Secessionists
Serbian Democratic Party (*Srpska Demokratska Stranka*)

Regionalist Groupings
Dalmatian Action (*Dalmatinska Akcija*)
Istrian Democratic Assembly (*Istarski Demokratski Sabor*)
Rijeka Democratic Alliance (*Riječki Demokratski Savez*)
Dalmatian National Party (*Dalmatinska Narodna Stranka*)
Istrian Radical Organization (*Istarska Radikalna Organizacija*)

Minority Organizations
Serbian National Party (*Srpska Narodna Stranka*)
Serbian Democratic Forum (*Srpski Demokratski Forum*)
National Community of Croatian Montenegrins (*Nacionalna Zajednica Crnogorca Hrvatske*)
Romani Party of Croatia (*Stranka Roma Hrvatske*)
Hungarian People's Party (*Madjarska Narodna Stranka*)
Croatian Muslim Democratic Party (*Hrvatska Muslimanska Demokratska Stranka*)

CZECH REPUBLIC

Czech Nationalists
Republican Party—Association for the Republic (*Republikánska Strana—Sdružení pro Republiku*)
Party of Businessmen and Tradesmen (*Strana Podnikatelů a Obchodníků*)

Moravian and Silesian Regionalists
Movement for the Self-Governing Democracy of Moravia and Silesia (*Hnutí za Samosprávnou Demokracii Moravy a Slezska*)
Moravian National Party (*Moravská Národní Strana*)

Moravian-Silesian Citizens' Assembly (*Občanské Shromáždění Moravy a Slezska*)

Radical Moravian Nationalist Party (*Radikální Moravská Nacionální Strana*)

Minority Organizations
Union of Slovaks (*Sdružení Slováků*)
Community of Slovaks (*Společnost Slováků*)
Romani Civic Initiative (*Romská Občanská Iniciativa*)
Romani National Congress (*Romský Národní Kongres*)
Polish Council (*Rada Poláků*)
Union of German Cultural Associations (*Svaz Německých Kulturních Organizací*)
German Landowners' Assembly (*Zemské Shromáždění Němců*)
Council of Jewish Communities in the Czech Lands (*Rada Židovských Obcí Českých Zemí*)
Union of Hungarians (*Svaz Maďarů*)

HUNGARY

Hungarian Nationalists
Hungarian Democratic Forum (*Magyar Demokrata Fórum*)
Independent Smallholders' Party—Torgyán Faction (*Független Kisgazda Párt—Torgyán Frakció*)
Christian National Union (*Keresztény Nemzeti Unió*)
Holy Crown Society (*Szentkorona Társulat*)
Independent National Youth Front (*Független Nemzeti Ifjúsági Front*)
Hungarian National Alliance (*Magyar Nemzeti Szövetség*)
Hungarian National Front (*Magyar Nemzeti Front*)
1956 Anti-Fascist and Anti-Bolshevik Association (*1956-os Antifasiszta és Antibolseviszta Szövetség*)
World Federation of Hungarians (*Magyarok Világszövetsége*)
World Federation of Transylvania (*Erdélyi Világszövetség*)

Minority Organizations
National Minority Roundtable (*Kisebbségi Kerekasztal*)
Nationality Council of Gypsies in Hungary (*Magyarországi Cigányok Nemzetiségi Uniója*)
Democratic Alliance of Hungarian Gypsies (*Magyarországi Cigányok Demokratikus Szövetsége*)
Roma Parliament (*Magyarországi Romaparlament*)
"Phralipe" (Brotherhood) Independent Gypsy Association (*"Phralipe" [Testvériség] Független Cigány Szervezet*)

Anti-Fascist Organization of Hungarian Gypsies (*Magyar Cigányok Antifasiszta Szervezete*)

Hungarian Gypsy Party (*Magyar Cigány Párt*)

Hungarian Gypsy Social Democratic Party (Magyar Cigány Szociáldemokrata Párt)

Association of Germans in Hungary (*Magyarországi Németek Szövetsége*)

Democratic Union of Slovaks in Hungary (*Magyarországi Szlovákok Szövetsége*)

Hungarian Jewish Cultural Federation (*Magyar Zsidók Kulturális Egyesülete*)

Alliance of Hungarian Jewish Religious Communities (*Magyarországi Zsidó Hitközségek Szövetsége*)

Croatian Democratic Alliance in Hungary (*Magyarországi Horvátok Szövetsége*)

Democratic Association of Romanians in Hungary (*Magyarországi Románok Demokratikus Szövetsége*)

Federation of Romanians in Hungary (*Magyarországi Románok Szövetsége*)

Federation of Slovenes in Hungary (*Magyarországi Szlovének Szövetsége*)

Democratic Federation of Serbs (*Szerb Demokratikus Szövetség*)

"*Mladost*" Youth Association (*Ifjúság Szervezet—"Mladost"*)

Federation of Bulgarians in Hungary (*Magyarországi Bolgárok Szövetsége*)

MACEDONIA

Macedonian Nationalists

Internal Macedonian Revolutionary Organization—Democratic Party for Macedonian National Unity (*Vnatrešna Makedonska Revolucionerna Organizacija—Demokratska Partija za Makedonsko Nacionalno Edinstvo*)

Internal Macedonian Revolutionary Organization—Democratic Party (*Vnatrešna Makedonska Revolucionerna Organizacija—Demokratska Partija*)

Movement for Pan-Macedonian Action (*Dviženje za Semakedonska Akcija*)

Albanian Autonomists

Party for Democratic Prosperity (*Partija za Demokratski Prosperitet*)

National Democratic Party (*Narodna Demokratska Partija*)

Republican Party (*Republikanska Partija*)

Albanian Democratic Union—Liberal Party (*Albanski Demokratski Sojuz—Liberalna Partija*)

Minority Organizations

Association of Macedonian Muslims (*Združenie na Makedonci Muslimani*)

Democratic Party of Turks (*Demokratska Partija na Turcite*)

Party for Complete Emancipation of Roma (*Partija za Celosna Emiancipacija na Romite*)

Democratic Progressive Party of Roma in Macedonia (*Demokratska Progresivna Partija na Romite vo Makedonija*)

Egyptian Association of Citizens (*Združenie na Egipčtanite*)
Democratic Party of Serbs (*Demokratska Partija na Srbite*)
Association of Serbs and Montenegrins in Macedonia (*Združenie na Srbi i Crnogorci vo Makedonija*)
League of Vlachs (*Liga na Vlasite*)

MONTENEGRO

Montenegrin Nationalists

Liberal Alliance of Montenegro (*Liberalni Savez Crne Gore*)
Social Democratic Party of Reformers (*Socijaldemokratska Partija Reformatora*)
Socialist Party of Montenegro (*Socijalistička Partija Crne Gore*)
Democratic Party of Socialists (*Demokratska Partija Socijalista*)

Serbian Nationalists

People's Party of Montenegro (*Narodna Stranka Crne Gore*)
Serbian Radical Party (*Srpska Radikalna Stranka*)
Democratic Party (*Demokratska Stranka*)
People's Democratic Party (*Narodna Demokratska Stranka*)
Movement for Montenegro's Autonomous Accession to Serbia (*Pokret za Autonomni Pristup Crne Gore u Srbiju*)
Serbian Democratic Party of Montenegro (*Srpska Demokratska Stranka Crne Gore*)

Minority Organizations

Democratic Alliance of Montenegro (*Demokratski Savez Crne Gore*)
Party of Democratic Action—Montenegro (*Stranka Demokratske Akcije—Crna Gora*)
Party of National Equality (*Stranka Narodne Jednakost*)
Boka Mariner's Association (*Bokaljska Mornarica*)

POLAND

Polish Nationalists

Confederation for an Independent Poland (*Konfederacja Polski Niepodległej*)
Christian National Union (*Zjednoczenie Chrześcijańsko-Narodowe*)
Polish Independence Party—Party of the New Right (*Polska Partia Niepodległościowa—Partia Nowej Prawicy*)
Universal Party of Slavs and Allied Nations (*Powszechna Partia Słowian i Narodów Sprzymierzonych*)
National Democratic Party (*Stronnictwo Narodowo-Demokratyczne*)
National Party (*Stronnictwo Narodowe*)
Polish National Front (*Narodowy Front Polski*)

National Rebirth of Poland (*Narodowe Odrodzenie Polski*)
National Movement (*Ruch Narodowy*)
Polish National Commonwealth—Polish National Party (*Polska Wspólnota Narodowa—Polskie Stronnictwo Narodowe*)

German Movements

Social-Cultural Association of the German Minority in Silesian Opole (*Towarzystwo Społeczno-Kulturalne Mniejszości Niemieckiej na Śląsku Opolskim*)
German Friendship Circles (*Koła Przyjaźni Niemieckiej*)
Union of German Social-Cultural Associations in Poland (*Związek Niemieckich Stowarzyszeń Społeczno-Kulturalnych w Polsce*)
National Offensive (*Nationale Offensive, Narodowa Ofensywa*)
East Prussian Wolves (*Wilki Prus Wschodnich*)

Eastern Minorities

National Minorities Council (*Rada Mniejszości Narodowych*)
Union of Ukrainians in Poland (*Związek Ukraińców w Polsce*)
Association of Lithuanians in Poland (*Stowarzyszenie Litwinów w Polsce*)
Lithuanian Society of Saint Casimir (*Litewskie Towarzystwo Św. Kazimierza*)
"Hospodar" Citizens' Circle of Lemkos (*Obywatelski Krąg Łemków "Hospodar"*)
Lemko Association (*Stowarzyszenie Łemków*)
Lemko Union (*Zjednoczenie Łemków*)
Belarusian Democratic Union (*Białoruskie Zjednoczenie Demokratyczne*)
Belarusian Farmers' Society (*Białoruskie Stowarzyszenie Rolników*)

Regionalist Groupings

Kaszubian Pomeranian Union (*Kaszubski Związek Pomorski*)
Mazurian Association (*Stowarzyszenie Mazurskie*)
Movement for Silesian Autonomy (*Ruch na Rzecz Autonomii Śląska*)
Upper Silesian Union (*Związek Górnośląski*)
Polish Western Union—Movement of Polish Silesia (*Polski Związek Zachodni—Ruch Polskiego Śląska*)
Alliance of Upper Silesian Societies and Associations (*Porozumienie Górnośląskich Stowarzyszeń i Towarzystw*)

Minority Organizations

Social-Cultural Society of Czechs and Slovaks in Poland (*Towarzystwo Społeczno-Kulturalne Czechów i Słowaków w Polsce*)
Social-Cultural Society of Jews in Poland (*Towarzystwo Społeczno-Kulturalne Żydów w Polsce*)
Podhale Social-Cultural Association of Gypsies in Nowy Targ (*Podhalańskie Stowarzyszenie Społeczno-Kulturalne Cyganów w Nowym Targu*)

ROMANIA

Romanian Nationalists
Party of Romanian National Unity (*Partidul Unității Naționale Române*)
Romanian Cradle (*Vatra Românească*)
Greater Romania Party (*Partidul România Mare*)
Movement for Romania (*Mişcarea Pentru România*)
New Christian Romania Party (*Partidul Noua Românie Creştină*)
Socialist Labor Party (*Partidul Socialist al Muncü*)

Hungarian Transylvanians
Democratic Union of Hungarians in Romania (*Uniunea Democratică a Maghiarilor din România*)
Union of Hungarian Democratic Youth (*Uniunea Tineretului Democratic Maghiar*)

Moldovan Movements
Pro-Bessarabia and Bukovina Association (*Asociaţia Pro-Basarabia şi Bucovina*)
League of Solidarity with the People's Front of Moldova (*Liga de Solidaritate cu Frontul Popular al Moldovei*)
Romanian Popular Front (*Frontul Popular Român*)

Minority Organizations
League of Organizations of National and Ethnic Minorities in Romania (*Liga Organizaţülor Minoritaţilor Naţionale şi Etnice din România*)
Democratic Union of Roma in Romania (*Uniunea Democratică Romilor din România*)
Democratic Forum of Germans in Romania (*Forumul Democratic al Germanilor din România*)
Muslim Turkish Democratic Union of Romania (*Uniunea Democratică a Musulmanilor Turci din România*)
Democratic Union of Slovaks and Czechs (*Uniunea Democratică a Slovacilor şi Cehilor*)
Democratic Union of Serbs (*Uniunea Democratică a Sîrbilor*)
Union of Ukrainians in Romania (*Uniunea Ucrainienilor din România*)
Arumunian Cultural Society (*Societatea Culturală Aromână*)
Armenian Union of Romania (*Uniunea Armenilor din România*)

SERBIA

Serbian Nationalists
Serbian Socialist Party (*Socialistička Partija Srbije*)
Serbian Radical Party (*Srpska Radikalna Stranka*)

Serbian National Renewal (*Srpska Narodna Obnova*)
Serbian Renewal Movement (*Srpski Pokret Obnove*)
Homeland Non-Party Serbian Association (*Domovinsko Nepartije Srpske Udruženje*)
Association of Serbs from Croatia (*Udruženje Srba Hrvatske*)

Kosovar Separatists

Democratic League of Kosovo (*Demokratski Savez Kosova*)
Coordinating Council of Albanian Political Parties (*Koordinirano Veće Albanske Političke Stranke*)
Parliamentary Party of Kosovo (*Parlamentska Stranka Kosova*)
Albanian Christian Democratic Party (*Albanska Kršćanska Demokratska Stranka*)
Party of Democratic Action for Kosovo (*Stranka Demokratske Akcije Kosova*)
Council for the Protection of Human Rights and Freedoms (*Veće za Zastitu Ljudskih Prava i Sloboda*)
National Movement for the Liberation of Kosovo (*Narodni Pokret za Oslobodjenje Kosova*)

Vojvodinian Autonomists

Democratic Community of Vojvodina Hungarians (*Demokratska Zajednica Madžara Vojvodine*)
Association of Hungarians for Our Fatherland, Serbia and Yugoslavia (*Udruženje Madžara za Našu Domovinu, Srbiju i Jugoslaviju*)
Democratic Alliance of Croats in Vojvodina (*Demokratski Savez Hrvata u Vojvodini*)
Farmers' Party of Vojvodina (*Seljačka Stranka Vojvodine*)
League of Social Democrats of Vojvodina (*Liga Socialdemokrata Vojvodine*)

Minority Organizations

Party of Democratic Action (*Stranka Demokratske Akcije*)
Liberal Bosnian Organization (*Liberalna Bošnjačka Organizacija*)
Democratic Political Party of Roma (*Demokratska Politička Partija Roma*)
Democratic Union of Bulgarians in Yugoslavia (*Demokratski Savez Bugarina Jugoslavije*)
Democratic Alliance of Vojvodina Romanians (*Demokratski Savez Rumuna Vojvodine*)
Alliance of Ruthenians and Ukrainians (*Savez Rutenca i Ukrajinca*)
Slovak National Heritage Foundation (*Osnivanje Slovačka Narodna Nasledstva*)

SLOVAKIA

Slovak Nationalists

Movement for a Democratic Slovakia (*Hnutie za Demokratické Slovensko*)

Christian Democratic Movement (*Kresťanskodemokratické Hnutie*)
Slovak Christian Democratic Party (*Slovenská Kresťanskodemokratick Strana*)
Slovak National Party (*Slovenská Národná Strana*)
Party of the Democratic Left (*Strana Demokratickej Lavice*)
Slovak Motherland (*Matica Slovenská*)
Movement for an Independent Slovakia (*Hnutie za Nezávislé Slovensko*)
Slovak National Democratic Movement (*Slovenské Národné Demokratické Hnutie*)
Party of Freedom—Party of National Unity (*Strana Slobody—Strana Národnej Jednoty*)

Hungarian Autonomists

Coexistence (*Együttélés, Spolužitie, Wspólnota, Soužití*)
Social and Democratic Union of Hungarians in Slovakia (*Sociálny a Demokratický Zväz Maďarov na Slovensku*)
Hungarian Christian Democratic Movement (*Maďarsk Kresťansodemokratické Hnutie*)
Hungarian Civic Party (*Maďarská Občianska Strana*)
Hungarian People's Party (*Maďarská Ludová Strana*)

Minority Organizations

Union of Ukrainians and Ruthenians in Czechoslovakia (*Zväz Ukrajincov a Rusínov v Česko-Slovensku*)
Ruthenian Revival (*Rusínska Obroda*)
Democratic Union of Roma in Slovakia (*Demokratický Zväz Rómov na Slovensku*)
Party for Romani Integration (*Strana za Rómsku Integráciu*)

SLOVENIA

Slovenian Nationalists

Democratic Opposition of Slovenia (*Demokratska Opozicija Slovenije*)
Slovenian National Party (*Slovenska Nacionalna Stranka*)
Slovenian Alliance (*Slovenska Zveza*)

Minority Organizations

Italian Union for Istria and Rijeka (*Italijanska Zveza za Istro in Reko*)
Interest Community of the Hungarian Minority (*Interesna Skupnost Madžarske Manjšine*)

APPENDIX 3

National Minority Parties and Organizations (by Ethnic Group)

ALBANIAN
Democratic Alliance of Albanians (Bosnia-Herzegovina)
Party for Democratic Prosperity (Bulgaria)
Albanian Democratic Union—Liberal Party (Macedonia)
National Democratic Party (Macedonia)
Party for Democratic Prosperity (Macedonia)
Republican Party (Macedonia)
Democratic Alliance of Montenegro (Montenegro)
Albanian Christian Democratic Party (Serbia)
Coordinating Council of Albanian Political Parties (Serbia)
Council for the Protection of Human Rights and Freedoms (Serbia)
Democratic League of Kosovo (Serbia)
National Movement for the Liberation of Kosovo (Serbia)
Parliamentary Party of Kosovo (Serbia)
Party of Democratic Action for Kosovo (Serbia)

ARMENIAN
Armenian Union of Romania (Romania)

ARUMUNIAN
Association of Arumunians in Albania (Albania)
League of Vlachs (Macedonia)
Arumunian Cultural Society (Romania)

BELARUSIAN
Belarusian Democratic Union (Poland)
Belarusian Farmers' Society (Poland)

BULGARIAN
Federation of Bulgarians in Hungary (Hungary)
Democratic Union of Bulgarians in Yugoslavia (Serbia)

CROATIAN
Croatian Democratic Union (Bosnia-Herzegovina)
Croatian Democratic Alliance in Hungary (Hungary)
Boka Mariner's Association (Montenegro)
Democratic Alliance of Croats in Vojvodina (Serbia)

CZECH
Social-Cultural Society of Czechs and Slovaks in Poland (Poland)
Democratic Union of Slovaks and Czechs (Romania)

GERMAN
German Landowners' Assembly (Czech Republic)
Union of German Cultural Associations (Czech Republic)
Association of Germans in Hungary (Hungary)
East Prussian Wolves (Poland)
German Friendship Circles (Poland)
National Offensive (Poland)
Social-Cultural Association of the German Minority in Silesian Opole
    (Poland)
Union of German Social-Cultural Associations in Poland (Poland)
Democratic Forum of Germans in Romania (Romania)

GREEK
Democratic Union of the Greek Minority (Albania)
Unity Party for Human Rights (Albania)

HUNGARIAN
Hungarian People's Party (Croatia)
Union of Hungarians (Czech Republic)
Democratic Union of Hungarians in Romania (Romania)
Union of Hungarian Democratic Youth (Romania)
Association of Hungarians for Our Fatherland, Serbia and Yugoslavia (Serbia)
Democratic Community of Vojvodina Hungarians (Serbia)
Coexistence (Slovakia)
Hungarian Christian Democratic Movement (Slovakia)
Hungarian Civic Party (Slovakia)
Hungarian People's Party (Slovakia)
Social and Democratic Union of Hungarians in Slovakia (Slovakia)
Interest Community of the Hungarian Minority (Slovenia)

ITALIAN
Italian Union for Istria and Rijeka (Slovenia)

JEWISH
Peace (*Shalom*) (Bulgaria)
Council of Jewish Communities in the Czech Lands (Czech Republic)
Alliance of Hungarian Jewish Religious Communities (Hungary)
Hungarian Jewish Cultural Federation (Hungary)
Social-Cultural Society of Jews in Poland (Poland)

LITHUANIAN
Association of Lithuanians in Poland (Poland)
Lithuanian Society of Saint Casimir (Poland)

MACEDONIAN
"Bratska" Political Association of Macedonians in Albania (Albania)
All-Bulgarian Union (Bulgaria)
Fifth of October Society (Bulgaria)
Ilinden United Macedonian Organization (Bulgaria)
Internal Macedonian Revolutionary Organization—Independent (Bulgaria)
Internal Macedonian Revolutionary Organization—Union of Macedonian Societies (Bulgaria)
Macedonian Youth Society (Bulgaria)

MONTENEGRIN
Association of Montenegrins (Albania)
National Community of Croatian Montenegrins (Croatia)
Association of Serbs and Montenegrins in Macedonia (Macedonia)

MUSLIM
Muslim Bosnian Organization (Bosnia-Herzegovina)
Muslim Democratic Party (Bosnia-Herzegovina)
Party of Democratic Action (Bosnia-Herzegovina)
Croatian Muslim Democratic Party (Croatia)
Association of Macedonian Muslims (Macedonia)
Party of Democratic Action—Montenegro (Montenegro)
Party of National Equality (Montenegro)
Muslim Turkish Democratic Union of Romania (Romania)
Party of Democratic Action (Serbia)
Liberal Bosnian Organization (Serbia)

POLISH
Polish Council (Czech Republic)

ROMANI (GYPSY)

Confederation of Roma in Bulgaria (Bulgaria)

Independent Democratic Socialist Association of Gypsies in Bulgaria (Bulgaria)

Movement for the Cultural, Educational, and Social Development of Gypsies (Bulgaria)

Romani Christian Democratic Party (Bulgaria)

United Roma Organization (Bulgaria)

Romani Party of Croatia (Croatia)

Romani Civic Initiative (Czech Republic)

Romani National Congress (Czech Republic)

Anti-Fascist Organization of Hungarian Gypsies (Hungary)

Democratic Alliance of Hungarian Gypsies (Hungary)

Hungarian Gypsy Party (Hungary)

Hungarian Gypsy Social Democratic Party (Hungary)

Nationality Council of Gypsies in Hungary (Hungary)

"Phralipe" (Brotherhood) Independent Gypsy Association (Hungary)

Roma Parliament (Hungary)

Democratic Progressive Party of Roma in Macedonia (Macedonia)

Egyptian Association of Citizens (Macedonia)

Party for Complete Emancipation of Roma (Macedonia)

Podhale Social-Cultural Association of Gypsies in Nowy Targ (Poland)

Democratic Union of Roma in Romania (Romania)

Democratic Political Party of Roma (Serbia)

Democratic Union of Roma in Slovakia (Slovakia)

Party for Romani Integration (Slovakia)

ROMANIAN

Democratic Association of Romanians in Hungary (Hungary)

Federation of Romanians in Hungary (Hungary)

Democratic Alliance of Vojvodina Romanians (Serbia)

SERBIAN

Serbian Democratic Party (Bosnia-Herzegovina)

Serbian Democratic Forum (Croatia)

Serbian Democratic Party (Croatia)

Serbian National Party (Croatia)

Democratic Federation of Serbs (Hungary)

"Mladost" Youth Association (Hungary)

Association of Serbs and Montenegrinsin Macedonis (Macedonia)

Democratic Party of Serbs (Macedonia)

Democratic Party (Montenegro)

Movement for Montenegro's Autonomous Accession to Serbia (Montenegro)

People's Democratic Party (Montenegro)
People's Party of Montenegro (Montenegro)
Serbian Radical Party (Montenegro)
Serbian Democratic Party of Montenegro (Montenegro)
Serbian Radical Party (Montenegro)
Democratic Union of Serbs (Romania)

SLOVENIAN

Federation of Slovenes in Hungary (Hungary)

SLOVAK

Community of Slovaks (Czech Republic)
Union of Slovaks (Czech Republic)
Democratic Union of Slovaks in Hungary (Hungary)
Social-Cultural Society of Czechs and Slovaks in Poland (Poland)
Democratic Union of Slovaks and Czechs (Romania)
Slovak National Heritage Foundation (Serbia)

TURKISH

Movement for Rights and Freedoms (Bulgaria)
Turkish Democratic Party (Bulgaria)
Democratic Party of Turks (Macedonia)
Muslim Turkish Democratic Union of Romania (Romania)

UKRAINIAN AND RUTHENIAN

"Hospodar" Citizens' Circle of Lemkos (Poland)
Lemko Association (Poland)
Lemko Union (Poland)
Union of Ukrainians in Poland (Poland)
Union of Ukrainians in Romania (Romania)
Alliance of Ruthenians and Ukrainians (Serbia)
Ruthenian Revival (Slovakia)
Union of Ukrainians and Ruthenians in Czechoslovakia (Slovakia)

REGIONALIST

Çamëria Political and Patriotic Association (Albania)
Kosovo Patriotic and Political Association (Albania)
Dalmatian Action (Croatia)
Dalmatian National Party (Croatia)
Istrian Democratic Assembly (Croatia)
Istrian Radical Organization (Croatia)
Rijeka Democratic Alliance (Croatia)
Moravian National Party (Czech Republic)

Moravian-Silesian Citizens' Assembly (Czech Republic)
Movement for the Self-Governing Democracy of Moravia and Silesia (Czech Republic)
Radical Moravian Nationalist Party (Czech Republic)
Alliance of Upper Silesian Societies and Associations (Poland)
Kaszubian Pomeranian Union (Poland)
Mazurian Association (Poland)
Movement for Silesian Autonomy (Poland)
Polish Western Union—Movement of Polish Silesia (Poland)
Upper Silesian Union (Poland)
League of Solidarity with the People's Front of Moldova (Romania)
Pro-Bessarabia and Bukovina Association (Romania)
Romanian Popular Front (Romania)
Farmers Party of Vojvodina (Serbia)
League of Social Democrats of Vojvodina (Serbia)

INDEX OF NAMES

INDEX OF PARTIES
AND ORGANIZATIONS

Janusz Bugajski is Director of East European Studies at the Center for Strategic and International Studies in Washington, D.C. He holds an M.Phil. from the London School of Economics and previously served as a Senior Research Analyst at Radio Free Europe in Munich. Bugajski has published several books on the region, including *East European Fault Lines: Dissent, Opposition, and Social Activism* (1989) and *Nations in Turmoil: Conflict and Cooperation in Eastern Europe* (1993).